CRIMINAL LAW

Eighth Edition

CRIMINAL LAW

Sue Titus Reid, J.D., Ph.D.

FLORIDA STATE UNIVERSITY

Oxford · New York

OXFORD UNIVERSITY PRESS

2010

Oxford University Press, Inc., publishes works that further Oxford University's
objective of excellence in research, scholarship, and education.

Oxford New York
Auckland   Cape Town   Dar es Salaam   Hong Kong   Karachi
Kuala Lumpur   Madrid   Melbourne   Mexico City   Nairobi
New Delhi   Shanghai   Taipei   Toronto

With offices in
Argentina   Austria   Brazil   Chile   Czech Republic   France   Greece
Guatemala   Hungary   Italy   Japan   Poland   Portugal   Singapore
South Korea   Switzerland   Thailand   Turkey   Ukraine   Vietnam

Copyright © 2007, 2010 by Oxford University Press, Inc.

Published by Oxford University Press, Inc.
198 Madison Avenue, New York, New York 10016
http://www.oup.com

Oxford is a registered trademark of Oxford University Press

Library of Congress Cataloging-in-Publication Data
Reid, Sue Titus.
Criminal law / Sue Titus Reid.—8th ed.
       p. cm.
Includes bibliographical references and index.
ISBN 978-0-19-538903-6 (alk. paper)
1. Criminal law—United States—Cases.   I. Title.
  KF9219.R448 2010
  345.73—dc22
2009002618

9 8 7 6 5 4 3 2 1
Printed in the United States of America
on acid-free paper

About the Author

Sue Titus Reid, a professor and director of the undergraduate program of the Reubin O'D. Askew School of Public Administration and Policy at Florida State University, Tallahassee, has taught law students, graduate students, and undergraduate students in many states. She has served on the board of the Midwest Sociological Society and the executive staff of the American Sociological Association. She has served as chairperson, associate dean, and dean. In 1985 she held the prestigious George Beto Chair in criminal justice at the Criminal Justice Center, Sam Houston State University, Huntsville, Texas.

Dr. Reid's formal training in criminology began in graduate school, but her interest in the field dates back to her early childhood. She was strongly influenced in her career by her father, who was born in the jail where his father, the under sheriff of a small east Texas county, lived with his family. As a child, she helped her father in his grocery store and was quite disturbed when, on three separate occasions, he was victimized by criminals, one an armed robber. In each instance the offender took all the cash and checks; no one was ever apprehended.

Dr. Reid graduated with honors from Texas Woman's University in 1960 and received graduate degrees in sociology (M.A. in 1962 and Ph.D. in 1965) from the University of Missouri–Columbia. In 1972 she graduated with distinction from the University of Iowa College of Law. She was admitted to the Iowa Bar that year and later to the District of Columbia Court of Appeals. She has also been admitted to practice before the U.S. Supreme Court.

Dr. Reid is unique among authors in the criminal justice field because of her distinguished qualifications in both law and the social sciences. She launched her text publishing career with *Crime and Criminology* in 1976, and that text, now in its twelfth edition, has been widely adopted throughout the United States and in foreign countries. Dr. Reid's other titles include *Criminal Justice*, eighth edition; *The Correctional System: An Introduction;* and *Criminal Law: The Essentials*. She has contributed articles to the *Encyclopedia of Crime and Justice* and the *Encyclopedia of American Prisons*, as well as to other books, in addition to publishing scholarly articles in both law and sociology.

Dr. Reid's contributions to her profession have been widely recognized nationally and abroad. In 1982 the American Society of Criminology elected her a fellow "for outstanding contributions to the field of Criminology." Other national honors include the following: Who's Who Among Women; Who's Who in America; Who's Who in American Education; Who's Who in Criminal Law; 2,000 Notable Women (Hall of Fame for Outstanding Contributions to Criminal Law, 1990); Personalities of America; and Most Admired Woman of the Decade, 1992.

Her international honors include numerous recognitions from the International Biographical Centre (IBC), Cambridge, England, including the prestigious International Order of Merit. The IBC most recently named Dr. Reid an inaugural member as one of the Top 100 Educators–2008, an honor limited by the IBC "to those individuals who, in our belief, have made a significant enough contribution in their field to engender influence on a local, national or international basis." Among the other international honors received by Dr. Reid are the following: International Woman of the Year, 1991–1992; International Who's Who of Intellectuals; International Who's Who of Professionals; International Who's Who of Professional and Business

Women; International Order of Merit, 1993; Who's Who in the World; International Biographical Centre, England, Marquis Who's Who in the World; and the Manchester Who's Who Among Executive and Professional Women.

In 1979 Dr. Reid received the Distinguished Alumna Award from Texas Woman's University, and in 2000 she received a university teaching award from Florida State University.

Dr. Reid has traveled extensively to widen her knowledge of criminal justice systems in the United States and in other countries. In 1982 she was a member of the Eisenhower Foundation–sponsored People-to-People Crime Prevention delegation to the People's Republic of China. Her several trips to Europe included a three-month study and lecture tour of 10 countries in 1985. She lives in New Hampshire.

Brief Contents

Contents

CHAPTER 9 Crimes Against Public Order and Public Decency

CHAPTER 10 Crimes Against the Government and Terrorism

Preface

In the study of criminal law, it is important to analyze the actual facts of cases and the judicial interpretations of those facts, along with legal terms and statutes and the various reasons for court decisions. I believe that these purposes are best accomplished by including carefully excerpted appellate court opinions to illustrate the text's discussion of relevant topics. In my many years of teaching and writing texts, I have been challenged and intrigued by students' excitement with this approach, and thus it is continued in this edition. Excerpted cases within the text give readers a sample of the traditional case method utilized in law schools without burdening them with the massive amounts of material covered in that setting.

It is also important for students to understand that principles of criminal law vary from state to state and between states and the federal system. Although it is not reasonable to survey all jurisdictions, this text includes a broad sampling of federal and state statutes and cases to illustrate the agreements and divergences within criminal law. The emphasis, however, is on state statutes because most crimes are tried in state rather than federal courts.

The text also includes a discussion of current cases and events to assist the reader in understanding the principles of criminal law. These events bring criminal law to life as they demonstrate its relevance. Though current events change rapidly, every effort has been made to give the most up-to-date information possible; but like some of the legal cases, they may change after publication. The challenge to faculty and students is to keep researching these events until they are resolved.

This text focuses on *substantive* rather than procedural criminal law. Case excerpts have been edited to exclude complicated procedural issues that are not necessary for an understanding of criminal law per se. Despite this focus on substantive criminal law, it is necessary to discuss some constitutional principles that relate directly to criminal law, and that is done where applicable.

FEATURES

Statutes and case excerpts are included within individual chapters rather than at the end of the text to facilitate their integration into the discussion of principles. Focus boxes, which also highlight recent examples of crimes and criminals as well as some statutes or appellate opinions, are included to illustrate points discussed in the text. Figures, graphs, and charts, including recent data when available, are used to enhance the reader's interest while relating general principles and laws to current events.

To help students master the text material and prepare for exams, chapters contain several study aids. Each chapter begins with an outline, followed by a summary overview of the chapter's contents. Chapters conclude with study questions to facilitate the combined purposes of mastering and analyzing the chapters' contents, as well as a debate issue or issues to provoke lively discussions on relevant topics. Throughout the text key terms are boldfaced and defined. A list of key terms, along with the pages on which they are located, is featured at the end of each chapter, and key terms are defined at the end of the text in the Glossary.

Each chapter closes with a detailed *case analysis,* which includes a *case preview* and followed by discussion issues and questions, all designed to stimulate class discussions.

Each chapter also features an *Internet activity*, which students can use to explore topics on the World Wide

Web. Appendix A reprints relevant portions of the U.S. Constitution to provide easy reference to the sections mentioned throughout the text. Appendix B features a legal case citation, along with an explanation of how to read and interpret it. Case, name, and general indexes enable readers to find information quickly.

THE EIGHTH EDITION

Significant changes have been made in this edition, which features the most recent relevant court decisions, especially those of the U.S. Supreme Court, along with recent current events. All reasonable efforts have been made to keep the text current to the time of publication, but because many of the cases are recent, some will be reversed or altered on appeal after this text is published. Likewise, some of the current events will have had major developments or resolutions since the last opportunity to update the text. Many areas of criminal law have been changing rapidly, and it is reasonable to expect this trend to continue. This edition contains numerous updates of subjects discussed in the seventh edition, along with new topics, cases, and other material. It follows the previous edition's chapter outline for the most part; the few changes are noted in the appropriate chapters.

Chapter 1, "An Introduction to Criminal Law," contains an overview of criminal law, which is contrasted with civil law. It encompasses the nature and purposes of punishment and raises the issue of which acts should be covered by the criminal law. The nature and purpose of U.S. court systems is explored, followed by an introduction to the Model Penal Code, a brief look at criminal law reform in general, and a discussion of the impact of the English common law on U.S. criminal justice systems.

Chapter 1 explains the sources of criminal law and considers the impact of discretion in criminal justice systems. The ways in which crimes are classified, along with the constitutional limitations on criminal law, are noted, including such concepts as cruel and unusual punishment, illustrated by the 2008 U.S. Supreme Court decision in *Baze v. Rees*, upholding lethal injection as a form of execution, and the Court's 2007 decision in *Kennedy v. Louisiana*, regarding whether the rape but not murder of a child is unconstitutional. A discussion of the establishing of guilt emphasizes the importance of the adversary system. The chapter closes with a discussion entitled "How to Read and Interpret a Case." That section is illustrated with Focus 1.3, "The Evolution of the Right to Counsel."

Chapter 1's topics are updated with such recent crimes as those involving the murder of the University of North Carolina student body president; the murders of two young teens in Oklahoma; the 2008 terrorist acts in Mumbai, India; and recent shopping mall murders.

Chapter 2, "Elements of a Crime," analyzes the elements of criminal liability, including the criminal act (as well as the failure to act), the criminal state of mind, concurring with the act and causation, and the attendant circumstances (required for some crimes) that must accompany acts for them to be considered criminal. The discussion on legal duty is expanded, more information on general and specific intent is included, and a new discussion on *corpus delicti* is featured. The information on corporate liability is updated, including the latest information on the Enron and Anderson cases. The crimes by Debra Lafave are added to the discussion regarding charging women with violating the law by having sex with underage boys.

Chapter 3, "Anticipatory Offenses and Parties to Crimes," contains complicated concepts, and an effort was made to simplify the discussions and make criminal law relevant to modern concerns and issues. For example, the revised chapter contains the case of Warren S. Jeffs as an example of a convicted accomplice (along with the 2008 indictments against him and other polygamist sect members for allegedly engaging in "spiritual marriages" with underage girls). It also discusses the conviction of former Alabama governor, Don Siegelman, as an example of a conspiracy conviction. The chapter retains a discussion on RICO but it is shortened and simplified, with the case of convicted attorney Lynn Stewart updated.

Chapter 3 also contains a discussion of forfeiture, including the federal statute that permits forfeitures for cash smuggled into or out of the United States. The Case Analysis of this chapter features a New Hampshire accomplice liability statute, which is patterned after the Model Penal Code, thus illustrating the practicality of that Code. The case involves cruelty to animals, a topic of current interest.

Chapters 4 and 5 cover defenses to criminal acts. Chapter 4 discusses the nature of defenses and details the more traditional defenses, such as entrapment, defense of persons and property, and insanity. The section on the insanity defense analyzes the various tests used for deciding whether a defendant is insane. It includes the case of Andrea Yates, whose insanity plea at her first trial was not successful but whose conviction for drowning her five children was reversed; the case is updated. It also includes the examples of two other Texas mothers who killed their children and used the insanity defense. The information on Florida's young killers, Nathaniel Brazill and Lionel Tate, is updated, and the 2008 Arizona case in which an eight-year-old boy was charged with killing his father and another man is noted. The chapter includes more state statutes that cover the discussed defenses.

Chapter 5 covers some of the more recently recognized defenses—posttraumatic stress disorder (PTSD) and domestic authority, for example—as well as recent developments in more traditional defenses, such as intoxication and other forms of substance abuse. New information on the covered defenses includes the 2008 flight rage case of Naomi Campbell. The discussion of the battered person syndrome is enhanced with coverage of new codes permitting the introduction of such evidence at trial, examples of California's governor commuting the sentences of women convicted of killing their abusive husbands, and a case in which a court ruled that the failure of counsel to offer evidence of the battered person syndrome at trial constituted ineffective assistance of counsel. Chapter 5 also includes examples of veterans who served in Iraq and Afghanistan and suffered posttraumatic stress syndrome upon their return home.

Chapter 6, "Criminal Homicide," includes such crimes as the 2007 Virginia Tech and 2008 Northern Illinois campus shootings and the mall shootings in Omaha and in the Chicago area. The 2005 Atlanta courthouse shooting case is updated, as are all crime data and statutes. A new focus featuring the case of a surgeon charged with a felony for allegedly hastening death to perform a transplant enhances the discussion of the meaning of *death*. The Baby Moses laws are discussed in reference to the Nebraska statute that initially did not place an age limit and resulted in teens being dropped off in that state by parents who could not handle them. The 2008 change in that statute is noted. The material on physician-assisted suicide is updated, including the recently enacted statute in Washington and the judicial decision in Montana, both recognizing the practice.

Finally, Chapter 6 updates information on Dr. Jack Kevorkian (now out of prison and an unsuccessful candidate for the U.S. Congress); Marjorie Knoller (whose dog killed a neighbor; her murder charge was reversed and then reinstated, and she was sentenced to 15 years to life in prison); and the Rhode Island fire case. The latest crime data are included to enhance the discussion of murder. The inclusion of fetuses in murder statutes is discussed, including the federal 2004 Unborn Victims of Violence Act.

Chapter 7, "Assault, Robbery, Rape, and Other Serious Crimes Against the Person," continues the discussion begun in Chapter 6 on crimes against the person, focusing on assault, robbery, rape, and other crimes. This edition of Chapter 7 features the most recent FBI crime data as well as discussions of recent cases such as the rape charges (later dropped) against basketball star Kobe Bryant and, on the Duke University campus, against four former lacrosse players (also dropped).

Chapter 7 retains a discussion of date rape, but date rape drugs are moved to Chapter 11. The concept of *date rape* is expanded to include *intimate personal violence (IPV)*, which goes beyond sexual violence and includes intimates other than dates. The chapter expands the discussion of problems with data on rape, especially date rape. A new focus features California's spousal rape statute, which includes possible punishments for this crime as well as the implications for community property issues. The section on *child abuse* was revised and expanded and now includes an analysis of nonsexual as well as sexual abuse. It focuses on the 2008 Vermont case of Brooke Bennett, the 12-year-old whose body was found about a week after she disappeared, with allegations that her uncle involved her in a sex ring and then killed her. Sex pedophiles such as Dean Schwartzmiller (now serving 152 years to life in prison) and his housemate, Frederick Everts (now serving 800 years to life), are also included. An expanded discussion on statutory rape and incest is featured.

The recent Georgia case involving Genarlow Wilson, who was sentenced to 10 years in prison for oral sex with a 14-year-old when he was 17, is noted, along with the legislative and other changes regarding such acts in that state. An expanded discussion of crimes against the elderly is highlighted by Focus 7.4, the proposed Elder Justice Act of 2008, which features Congressional findings concerning crimes against the elderly. Bills before Congress to amend the Hate Crime Statistics Act are noted; recent changes in the Texas hate crime statute are recorded. The seriousness of hate crimes is illustrated by the 2008 killing of Lawrence King, 14, who was taunted by his classmates after he announced that he was gay. King was allegedly killed by a 15-year-old classmate. The discussions of hate crimes and stalking are updated.

Chapter 8, "Property and Related Crimes," includes the latest FBI trend data on serious property crimes, and Focus 8.3 presents recent shoplifting data. The latest data on financial crimes are also presented, along with enhanced discussions on these crimes. The information on arson cases is updated, as is the information on health care fraud. New cases of forgery and plagiarism are featured, along with recent information on computer crime indictments and convictions, including the case of the mother who used the Internet to bully a teen girl, who subsequently committed suicide. A new focus on identity theft contains up-to-date data on this, allegedly the fastest growing of all property crimes. It includes a discussion of a new crime, *house stealing*, in which thieves steal your identity, file fake papers, and sell your house while you are living in it. The latest on noted corporate crimes is included, as is a discussion of the CAN-SPAM Act of 2003, which concerns computer spam and, in particular, the requirement that sexually explicit material carry a warning.

Chapter 9 has a new title: "Crimes Against Public Order and Public Decency." The previous edition's chapter covered crimes against the administration of government; those crimes are now included in Chapter 10. Chapter 9 begins with a section on public order, which includes coverage of a 2007 case on whether the homeless may be prohibited from sleeping on streets. New sections in this chapter include "Public Intoxication and Drug Incapacitation," "Driving Under the Influence (DUI)," and "Alcohol Offenses and Minors," which is subdivided into discussions of the sale of alcohol to minors and minors in possession. An example of a DUI statute is included. The previous section on "Carrying Weapons" is changed to "Weapons Offenses" and contains a discussion of and excerpt from the July 2008 U.S. Supreme Court decision, *District of Columbia v. Heller*, concerning the District of Columbia's ordinance on hand guns.

Focus 9.3 (previously 9.4) contains the recent changes in the Texas statutes concerning animal abuse, thus illustrating the need to update statutes carefully. The interesting case concerning cats is used to illustrate why the statute was amended. The chapter also features new statutes prohibiting leaving animals in cars in hot or cold weather without adequate ventilation, food, and water. A new Maine statute permitting protective orders in domestic violence cases to include pets as well as humans is cited. The discussion on prostitution includes the charges against New York's former governor and also emphasizes child victims of this crime. A new focus details Congressional findings as reported in the Trafficking Victims Protection Reauthorization Act (TVPRA). The information on pornography is updated. Finally, the Case Analysis features the U.S. Supreme Court's recent decision concerning the constitutionality of the Texas sodomy statute.

Chapter 10 also has a new title, "Crimes Against the Government and Terrorism," with the information on crimes against the government moved from Chapter 9 in the previous edition and included here. The crimes of perjury, bribery, official misconduct in office, and obstruction of justice, now located in Chapter 10, are updated with such recent examples as those of Martha Stewart and "Scooter" Libby as examples of obstruction of justice. The cases of the former Detroit mayor and his mistress, also a public official, which are the subject of Focus 10.3, illustrate that individuals may be charged with more than one of the enumerated crimes against the government.

There are significant changes in the discussion of terrorism, with revisions in the examples used, some cut, and some updated; more information on weapons of mass destruction both at the national and the international level; and extensive revision of the discussion of the USA Patriot Act. The case of Jose Padilla was updated through conviction and sentencing. A new discussion of the Military Commissions Act of 2006 accompanies the discussion of the recent U.S. Supreme Court decision in *Boumediene v. Bush*. The chapter also discusses the July 2008 decision of the Fourth Circuit Court of Appeals in *ali Al-Marri v. Pucciarelli*. The U.S. Supreme Court's reaction to that case is explained; appellant's guilty plea is noted.

Chapter 10 contains more information on border security, including the Secure Fence Act of 2006; more information on the Director of National Intelligence and the new director; and a diagram of the organization of the current Department of Homeland Security (DHS) (see Focus 10.11) as well as a discussion of some of the changes in that agency.

The Case Analysis focuses on the *Hamdi* case, which concerns the manner in which enemy combatants are processed. The chapter contains updates on the subject of *enemy combatants*.

Chapter 11, "Drug Abuse and Drug Trafficking," contains a new section, "Alcohol Prohibition and Regulation," which discusses such topics as the possession of controlled substances, possession of drug paraphernalia, and the manufacture, prescription, and sale of drugs. The latest available data on drug abuse and drug offenses are included. An expanded discussion of the impact of drug abuse focuses, among other topics, on club drugs, especially on college and university campuses. The economic costs of drug abuse discussion contains the proposed 2009 federal drug budget compared to that of 2008 and notes the impact of illegal drugs on courts, law enforcement officials, and prison and jail overcrowding.

A section on drug trafficking includes the dynamics of the involved crimes and features an explanation of money laundering. The control of drug abuse and drug trafficking looks first at the federal level and contains an extensive discussion of the history and nature of the war on drugs, along with a critique of government efforts. The section on the state level of control features the New York harsh drug laws (the Rockefeller laws) and revisions to them; discusses treatment efforts, especially in California; and focuses on drug courts. Specifically, Michigan's repeal of mandatory minimum drug sentences for minor offenders is noted, as is the 2006 amendment that changes California's drug treatment statute.

The case featured in Chapter 11's Case Analysis is updated with information concerning the appellant in the case. The case centers on the 2005 U.S. Supreme Court case concerning the issue of whether the U.S. Congress, through its commerce powers, can regulate the use of marijuana for medicinal purposes. Recent updates on the issue are noted.

Chapter 12, "Sentencing and the Criminal Law," retains its previous focus on the approaches to sentencing and especially the use of sentencing guidelines, at both the federal and state levels. The eighth edition enhances the seventh edition's discussion of recent U.S. Supreme Court decisions on sentencing with those decided in subsequent terms. An excerpt from *Kimbrough v. United States*, decided in 2007, is included. Several other recent sentencing cases on sentencing are also featured. Examples are as follows: *Panetti v. Quarterman* (mental illness and the death penalty); *Kennedy v. Louisiana* (execution for rape but not murder of a child is a disproportionate punishment); and *Baze v. Rees* (upholding lethal injection as a method of capital punishment).

The discussion of sex offenders is updated with the latest in statutes as well as civil commitment procedures for these offenders. The recent changes in the crack/cocaine punishment statutes in the federal system are noted, along with data concerning minorities in criminal justice systems.

The recent statute, passed by the U.S. Congress in October 2008 and known as the Keeping the Internet Devoid of Sexual Predators Act, or KIDS Act of 2008, is discussed. This act requires registered sex offenders to register their e-mail and instant message addresses with the National Sex Offender Registry.

The many constitutional issues in sentencing remain important to this chapter, with updated coverage of the role of race as well as the new topic of the mentally challenged. The section that analyzes the relationship between sentencing and the right to a trial by jury was significantly expanded with new cases in that area.

The Case Analysis in Chapter 12 focuses on the U.S. Supreme Court's 2005 case holding that it is a violation of the federal constitution to execute juveniles. It compliments the chapter's enhanced discussion of capital punishment.

In summary, this edition includes more extensive changes than any of the previous ones, as our society has changed significantly during the past three years. It is my belief that the text depicts those changes and concerns, yet the text was carefully worded and cases were meticulously excerpted, resulting in a shorter overall book.

SUPPLEMENTS

As a full-service publisher of quality educational products, Oxford University Press does much more than just sell textbooks. The company creates and publishes an extensive array of print, video, and digital supplements for students and instructors. This edition of *Criminal Law* is accompanied by the following valuable supplements:

Instructor's Manual/Test Bank: Contains chapter outlines, key terms, chapter overviews, questions for discussion, and a complete testbank with all-new essay and multiple choice questions.

Student Study Guide: Available for download as a pdf; contains chapter outlines, key terms, chapter overviews, student learning objectives, review questions, and practice multiple choice, fill in the blank, and short answer questions.

Website: Contains a downloadable pdf version of the Student Study Guide and additional information about the new edition.

All of these supplements are provided free of charge to students and instructors. Orders of new (versus used) textbooks help us defray the cost of developing such supplements, which is substantial. Please contact your local Oxford University Press representative for more information on any of these supplements.

ACKNOWLEDGMENTS

Any text revision is a major effort, but this is particularly the case in criminal law, for the subject matter changes daily and in many jurisdictions. My work on the eighth edition of this text has been aided by family, friends, and colleagues, and I am grateful to all of them. In particular I am grateful to Heidi van Hulst, my college roommate and close friend for over 40 years, and Kerri Murray, my friend of the past few years, whose almost daily e-mails gave me encouragement and reinforcement.

As always, several professional colleagues have contributed significantly to the publication of this edition. Dr. David Fabianic of the University of Central Florida has provided almost daily encouragement. H. H. A. Cooper, Esquire, internationally recognized expert on terrorism, offered his assistance on terrorism and other issues. Chris Morales gave me advice on international issues, and my long-time friend and former colleague, Dr. Marlyn Mather, was a frequent correspondent, adding her encouragement and wisdom. As he has for many editions of all of my texts, Robin Reid solved my computer problems, most of which seemed to occur when I was facing a strict deadline. Thanks, Robin!

My weekly flights between Portland, Maine, and Tallahassee, Florida, during the school year present many challenges, but at least my cats, Kristina and Ashley, were well cared for by their cat nanny, Sandy Louis, who also compiled the case and name indexes. And after the long drive to the airport it was refreshing to know that Mike Wescott would drop me off at the terminal and take excellent care of my car, picking me back up at the airport in a warm car, free of snow, when I returned four days later. Flight problems were eased by my Delta friends. In particular I am grateful to Jeffrey P. Penzkowski and his colleagues, Bruce Moniz, Norm Pawloski, and Robert Clinard, in Crown Room A Centerpoint in Atlanta. Among other Delta Crown Room agents who were helpful during my long stopovers in Atlanta were long-time personal friends Libby Hunt and Michele Patrick.

Those weekly trips are well worth the time, expense, and, at times, problems because of my delightful students at Florida State University. To them I owe special thanks. Their enthusiasm and cooperation kept me going on some rather difficult days. I wish all of them the best in their respective future careers.

One FSU student in particular was helpful in the completion of this manuscript. John Kraniou, Ph.D. candidate in the School of Public Administration and a lawyer, assisted with the research. My thanks to John and to our school's director Frances Stokes Berry and the Ph.D. director, Robert Eger, for assigning John to this project. John also handled my classes during the time I was out for surgery.

A very special thanks to Dr. Stephen D. Trigg, orthopedic surgeon, at the Mayo Clinic Jacksonville (Florida) for his excellent work in repairing my hand and his nurse, Jacki C. Bowman, who assisted not only during surgery but promptly answered my many questions before and after surgery. My certified hand therapist, Ann S. Kemp, of the New England Rehabilitation Hospital of Portland (Maine), was in charge of my physical therapy. Without these outstanding medical persons, I would not have completed the production phase of this manuscript on time and with a minimum of problems given the difficulties of recovering from the use of my dominant hand.

My Oxford University Press editor, Sherith Pankratz, has become a friend as well as a very special editor as we combined our efforts on this, my third book under her supervision. Thanks, Sherith, for all the arrangements you and your staff made to accommodate my slow pace in returning manuscript during the production phase. Sherith was assisted by Whitney Laemmli.

Lisa Grzan, my production manager for the third time, contributed her usual superb job and frequent reinforcement as she guided the manuscript through the various production phases. The photos were secured by Linda Sykes and copyediting was completed by Michele Kornegay. My thanks also to Steven Cestaro, Director, Editorial, Design & Production.

Finally, although the final work is the responsibility of the author, the suggestions for revisions made by the following professors were greatly appreciated: Mark D. Maironis (Eastern Michigan University), Stephen O'Donnell (NHTI Concord's Community College), Karren S. Price (Stephen F. Austin State University), J. Lincoln Passmore (Mount Ida College), Michael T. Stevenson (University of Toledo), and Jennifer K. Wesely (University of North Florida).

Sue Titus Reid, J.D., Ph.D.
Professor and Director of the
Undergraduate Program
Reubin O'D. Askew School of
Public Administration and Policy
Florida State University

CHAPTER 1

An Introduction to Criminal Law

continued

INTRODUCTION

Two young Oklahomans shot several times, each with two guns, on an isolated road in rural Oklahoma in June 2008 left authorities puzzled and local citizens in fear for their lives. This crime, as well as the spring 2008 murder of the University of North Carolina student body president; the 2007 massacre of students at Virginia Tech; and shooting sprees on other school grounds and in shopping malls—along with the bombing of the federal building in Oklahoma City in April 1995; the hijacking of airplanes and deliberate crashing of them on 11 September 2001; the terrorist acts in Mumbai, India, in the fall of 2008; and many other crimes that daily victimize not only persons in the United States but those in other countries as well—has focused intense national and international attention on criminal law and criminal justice systems.

For centuries, people have been fascinated by law, particularly criminal law and violent crimes. Scholars and philosophers have written volumes in an attempt to explain the history and evolution of criminal law and the reasons for criminal behavior, and citizens have made these topics ones of political focus. Americans have supported stricter criminal laws and punishments while expressing increased fears of becoming crime victims.

The purpose of this text is to explore the dimensions of U.S. criminal laws. This chapter introduces the subject by covering the traditional reasons for imposing criminal penalties on those who violate society's laws. It includes a discussion of the extent to which the criminal law should be used to regulate behavior. Specific attention is given to the inclusion in the criminal law of behavior that some people consider private.

The chapter examines the nature and purpose of U.S. court systems, focusing on both the federal and state systems as well as trial and appellate courts. It summarizes the nature and impact of the Model Penal Code and English common law on U.S. court systems.

The sources of criminal law, the nature of discretion in criminal law, and the classification of crimes and related offenses are examined. Also included is an analysis of the constitutional limitations that are placed on criminal laws in the United States. The chapter contains a brief discussion of the establishment of guilt within the adversary system and concludes with a discussion of how to read and interpret a judicial opinion.

A night time vigil was held at Virginia Tech University in Blacksburg, Virginia, after the April 2007 shooting massacre that resulted in the murders of 32 victims, followed by the suicide of the gunman, Cho Seung-Hui, a 23-year-old student of the university. (David Howells/Corbis)

The day following the mass killings at Northern Illinois University in DeKalb, a memorial was established in memory of the five who were killed by a former student, who then killed himself. The t-shirts at the right memorialize the 32 victims of the 2007 massacre at Virginia Tech and the 13 victims of the 1999 shootings at the Columbine High School in Littleton, Colorado. (Ralf-Finn Hestoft/Corbis)

THE EMERGENCE OF LAW

Why is law important? In small groups, particularly in primitive societies, formal laws are not necessary because human behavior can be regulated through informal methods of social control. From infancy, children are taught proper behavior by their families and through other social institutions such as churches and schools. Penalties exist for violating society's norms, but those penalties are informal. They range from a disapproving glance to social ostracism or physical expulsion from the community. In most cases the threat of being banished from the community is sufficient to ensure proper behavior. The key to the success of such informal social controls is the cohesiveness of the group or society. Most members accept and follow the norms; those who do not are detected easily and can be punished swiftly and effectively without formal criminal laws.

As societies become more complex, informal social controls become less effective. With increasing numbers of people comes a decrease in the power of major social institutions to control human behavior. More conflicts arise among members and between groups, and a more formal, rationally thought-out method of social control is necessary. Although there is disagreement over how laws evolved, it is clear that at some point law emerged as a formal method by which conflicts are resolved and behavior is controlled.

CIVIL AND CRIMINAL LAW DISTINGUISHED

Both **civil law** and **criminal law** are designed to control behavior to protect the interests of society and of individuals. Both types of law prohibit or require specific actions and permit the government to assess penalties, and both may result in social stigma, but there are basic differences between civil and criminal law.

✪ A private party brings the lawsuit in a civil case.

✪ The state is the accusing party and initiates the charges in a criminal case.

✪ Different rules of evidence and procedure apply, and those rules are stricter in criminal cases.

✪ Although there are exceptions, normally society's moral condemnation is greater against those who violate the criminal law.

✪ The emphasis in civil law is on compensating the wronged person; the emphasis in criminal law is on punishing the offender.

⭐ Criminal law carries more serious penalties, such as incarceration or even the death penalty.

⭐ Civil penalties usually consist of payment to the wronged parties.

The case at the close of this chapter illustrates the differences between civil and criminal law, while noting that confinement may occur with both.

Civil laws embrace a variety of interests, such as maintaining the family (as in divorce law), protecting business relationships (such as contract law), preserving property rights, and protecting many personal interests. The last includes freedom from slander and libel, as well as from personal injury or wrongful death resulting from negligence, intentional behavior, or improperly designed or manufactured products. Some acts, such as assault and battery, may involve both civil and criminal law. Such cases may involve lawsuits in both areas of law.

THE NATURE AND PURPOSE OF CRIMINAL LAW

It is important to analyze the punishment philosophies that have provided the historical justification for criminal law. Although the emphasis on each has varied over time, there has been some consistency in the punishment philosophies advanced to support criminal law.

Criminal Law as Punishment

Punishing individuals through the criminal law is a serious act and should be based on reasons presumed to assist society in meeting worthy goals, such as the maintenance of social solidarity and the protection of citizens. Throughout history the basic punishment goals of criminal law have been **retribution** (or **revenge**), **incapacitation**, **deterrence**, and **rehabilitation** (or **reformation**), which are defined in Focus 1.1 for easy reference.

Retribution or Revenge

In early times crime victims were permitted (and expected) to take direct action against criminal offenders, and private revenge or retribution could take such extreme forms as murder. The philosophy of revenge permitted victims to inflict on offenders the same acts they had suffered. In comparison, *retribution*, which has been referred to as public or legal revenge, permits the society's governing body to impose punishment on criminal offenders. Retribution is based on the belief that offenders should be given the punishment they deserve.

In a 1972 landmark capital punishment case, *Furman v. Georgia*, the U.S. Supreme Court recognized retribution as an appropriate reason for punishment.[1] In 1976, the Supreme Court said that retribution is neither "a forbidden objective nor one inconsistent with our respect for the dignity of men."[2] The modern retributive concept of "just deserts" emphasizes that people should be punished only because they have committed a criminal act for which the state has provided punishment; hence, they deserve punishment.[3]

Incapacitation

Historically incapacitation was employed literally in some societies. The hands of a thief were cut off to prevent further thefts, and sex offenders were castrated. Although such practices are not commonly endorsed today, it has been suggested that sexual castration might be offered as an alternative to jail or prison for sexual offenders. Most courts, however, have not accepted this sentence even when it is voluntary, although the issue arose in Texas in 1996 when Larry Don McQuay, a 32-year-old offender who had almost completed his term for child molesting, volunteered to be castrated. McQuay claimed that he had molested at least 240 children and that castration would be the only way to keep him from committing similar sexual offenses upon his release. He asked the state to castrate him, but his request was denied. In August 1996, McQuay was charged with three counts of indecency that had allegedly occurred in 1989 with a 9-year-old girl. In June 1997, McQuay was found guilty of this charge and sentenced to an additional 20 years in prison.[4]

Texas law permits the *voluntary* castration of repeat sex offenders, provided they are 21 years of age or older and give written consent. They must be examined by a psychiatrist, and they must be studied for 10 years after they are released. Their rates of repeat offenses are to be compared with those of released sex offenders who are not castrated. In 2004, David Wayne Jones, a notorious child molester, voluntarily submitted to the surgery.[5]

In 1996, California became the first state to provide chemical castration for repeat child molesters. The law became effective on 1 January 1997. Defendants convicted of a second offense against a child under 13 are required to receive weekly injections of Depo-Provera,

---

FOCUS 1.1 Punishment Basis of Criminal Law

The criminal law is designed to punish, but over the years the reasons given for punishment have varied. The primary reasons are defined here.

Retribution	The philosophy that offenders should receive the punishment they deserve in light of the crimes they committed.
Revenge	Historically, an act performed by a victim to punish an offender. Today public retaliation through criminal justice systems has replaced the private revenge of earlier days, which tended to get out of control.
Incapacitation	A punishment theory and a sentencing goal, generally implemented by incarcerating offenders to prevent them from committing any other crimes. In earlier times incapacitation involved such measures as removing the hands of thieves or castrating rapists.
Deterrence	A punishment philosophy that assumes that behavior may be controlled and criminal behavior prevented by the threat of punishment. *General deterrence* strives to discourage criminality by other people by intimidating them with the punishment of an offender. *Specific deterrence* focuses on preventing additional crimes by an offender by punishing that offender.
Rehabilitation	Punishment philosophy that attempts to reform the offender through education, work, or other appropriate treatment modalities.

---

a drug that reduces sexual desire. If they prefer, offenders may instead choose surgical castration.[6]

In most cases today, however, incapacitation takes the form of incarceration in a prison or jail, thus theoretically making it impossible for the offender to prey on society.

Deterrence

Deterrence is based on the assumption that behavior is rational and that criminal behavior can be prevented if people are afraid of the penalties. Punishment of a specific offender, or *specific deterrence*, may involve physical restraint or incapacitation, such as incarceration or capital punishment. But deterrence also assumes that people may be prevented from choosing to engage in criminal acts; thus, it is not necessary to amputate a thief's hands to prevent theft. In addition, one person's punishment should deter others (*general deterrence*) from committing the same or similar criminal acts.

Numerous studies have been conducted on deterrence theory, but the concept is difficult to measure. One attempt to assess the impact of punishment on deterrence was aimed at college students, who were given a series of

hypothetical situations and asked to indicate what they would have done under the circumstances. Specifically, the students were told to assume that they had been drinking at a bar and might be impaired. They knew they had to go to work the next day and would need their cars. What did they think were the chances they would be apprehended if they drove home and that, if apprehended, they would be arrested, tried, and convicted? One group of respondents was told the penalty would be a 1-month suspension of the driver's license, while the other group was told that the penalty would be a 10-month suspension, penalties one might expect in many states. The students were then asked to indicate on a scale of 0 to 100 the chances they would drive under the circumstances. They were asked other questions to measure their impulsiveness and whether they had ever driven while impaired. The investigators concluded, "38 percent of college students appeared to be unresponsive to threatened criminal sanctions for drunk driving."[7]

Reformation or Rehabilitation

While retribution and deterrence focus on crime, reformation (or rehabilitation) focuses on criminals, emphasizing the possibility of change. Those who advocate rehabilitation believe that criminals can become noncriminals with proper treatment. Rehabilitation was the dominant focus of U.S. criminal justice systems during the late 1960s and 1970s, following the classic statement of law professor Francis A. Allen, who coined the phrase *rehabilitative ideal* in 1959. In the late 1970s and 1980s, however, the trend shifted. When the public demanded harsher punishments, statutes were changed, as exemplified in the federal system. In 1984, after hearing testimony that rehabilitation had failed and was an outmoded concept on which to base sentences, Congress enacted a comprehensive federal sentencing statute and rejected rehabilitation as the primary basis for determining sentence length.[8]

Although rehabilitation has remained in vogue in some states, in most jurisdictions the philosophy has been replaced by an emphasis on deterrence and retribution. By 1981, even Allen acknowledged the demise of the rehabilitative ideal.[9]

There has been some recent support for rehabilitation, however, as manifested by the dramatic change in California law. In the fall of 2000, 61 percent of Californians who voted approved Proposition 36, which provides for treatment rather than punishment for some drug offenders. First or second nonviolent drug offenses are viewed as health issues, not as behaviors appropriate for inclusion within the criminal law. The

new approach became law in 2001.[10] In recent years, the California Department of Corrections added the words *and Rehabilitation* to reflect the change in the department's goals.

Regardless of a jurisdiction's punishment philosophy, the problem of deciding which acts should be considered criminal is an issue of controversy.

Criminal Law and Morality

The debate over whether certain acts should be included within the purview of the criminal law has gone on for some time. The distinction is made between acts that are **mala in se** (evil in themselves) and those that are considered **mala prohibita** (evil only because they are prohibited by criminal law). The first group includes crimes such as murder, forcible rape, robbery, aggravated assault, burglary, and arson—serious crimes that endanger human life or property directly. These are acts that most, if not all, people consider criminal. The second group of crimes includes acts that are considered criminal only because statutes have defined them as such. They are not universally regarded as criminal; they may not even be regarded as criminal by most people. Examples might be private sexual acts between consenting adults, use of alcohol and other drugs, prostitution, gambling, and carrying a concealed weapon. Enforcing laws against such acts may be made more difficult by the lack of agreement over whether the behaviors should be criminalized.

Subsequent chapters of this text detail some of the crimes that might be classified as private morality and perhaps therefore should not be included in criminal law. But when deciding whether these acts should be covered by the criminal law, we must consider to what extent they involve areas that are of legitimate concern to the public, such as the spread of disease or the commission of other, more serious crimes. It is also important to consider whether the criminal law is an effective way of controlling these behaviors. These decisions may change over time, and thus criminal law reform is crucial. These decisions occur at various levels, and it is important to understand the nature of U.S. criminal court systems.

THE NATURE AND PURPOSE OF U.S. COURT SYSTEMS

The U.S. Constitution provides for three branches of government: executive, legislative, and judicial. All are important for purposes of this text, but the emphasis is

There is debate over whether the criminal law should cover certain acts considered to be private matters, such as the use of alcohol and some other drugs. However, it is important that the criminal law is used to regulate the manufacture and distribution of alcoholic beverages and other drugs. Owners of bars and their employees who sell alcoholic beverages to intoxicated customers may be responsible under both the criminal and the civil law if the intoxicated patrons harm other persons. (IStockPhoto)

Federal and state courts are crucial elements of U.S. criminal court systems. Each has both civil and criminal courts, and a given act may constitute both a civil and a criminal offense. (IStockPhoto)

on the judicial branch, for that branch has the power of **judicial review**, meaning that appellate courts may interpret the acts and events that occur in the other two branches as well as in lower courts. U.S. courts exist at the federal and state levels.

The state and the federal court systems are separate systems. The highest court of each state is the final determiner of the constitutionality of ordinances and statutes under that state's constitution and procedural rules; the U.S. Supreme Court is the final determiner of whether the decisions of any lower courts violate the U.S. Constitution and federal procedures and statutes. States' rights are considered very important, and the U.S. Constitution provides that the powers that are not delegated to the federal government are reserved for the states. In fact, most crimes are violations of state, not federal, laws (although in recent years Congress has been federalizing more crimes); consequently, most criminal trials occur in state courts. Although the state and federal systems are separate, a state may not violate the federal Constitution; thus, the U.S. Supreme Court may hear some state cases.

The Dual Court System

To simplify the discussion, Figure 1.1 provides a simple diagram of this **dual court system**. Note that on the left side of that figure the levels of federal courts are listed. In the federal system, cases may move from the lowest level, the U.S. magistrates (judges who are appointed by the district courts to hear some cases), to the district courts. These are the trial courts in the federal system, and most federal cases begin there. Decisions of the district courts may be reviewed by the appropriate circuit court of appeal; those decisions may be heard by the highest court, the U.S. Supreme Court. The state courts are diagrammed on the right side of Figure 1.1 and explained in greater detail in Table 1.1.

Some important concepts must be defined at this point. The lawful right of the legislative, executive, or judicial branch to exercise official authority is called **jurisdiction**. Jurisdiction may be limited by geographical areas or by other classifications, such as subject matter or crime categories. For example, some courts may hear and decide only **misdemeanor** (less serious) cases; others may decide only **felony** (serious) cases. Courts may be empowered to decide certain types of cases, such as criminal or civil, domestic or probate (wills and estates). Generally, special courts that decide juvenile cases do not have jurisdiction to hear other types of cases. Some courts are trial courts exclusively; others are appellate only. State courts may not decide federal court cases and vice versa.

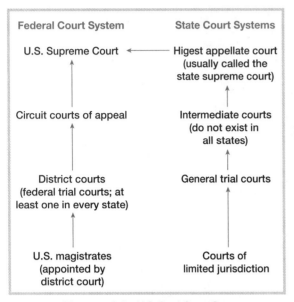

Federal Court System

U.S. Supreme Court ←

Circuit courts of appeal ↑

District courts
(federal trial courts; at
least one in every state) ↑

U.S. magistrates
(appointed by
district court) ↑

State Court Systems

Higest appellate court
(usually called the
state supreme court) ↑

Intermediate courts
(do not exist in
all states) ↑

General trial courts ↑

Courts of
limited jurisdiction

Figure 1.1 Diagram of the U.S. Dual Court System
Source: Sue Titus Reid, *Criminal Justice*, 8th ed. (Mason, Ohio: Thomson
Custom Solutions, a part of the Thomson Corporation, 2008), p. 164.

One example of jurisdiction that received extensive attention in recent years is the case of Michael Skakel, a cousin of Ethel Kennedy. Skakel was accused of murdering Martha Moxley when both were 15. Skakel was 41 and thus no longer a juvenile when he was charged with the crime, but his attorney argued that he should not be tried in an adult criminal court since the crime was committed when he was a juvenile. The judge disagreed; Skakel was tried in an adult criminal court and convicted in June 2002. He faced a life sentence for this murder, a sentence that could not have been imposed had his case been processed in a juvenile court. He was, however, sentenced to a term of 20 years to life and must serve 11 years and 10 months before he is eligible for parole. Skakel's attorney appealed on several grounds, one of which was that the adult criminal court should not have been given jurisdiction in this case. The appellate court affirmed the lower court on all issues, and the U.S. Supreme Court refused to review the case.[11]

A court may have *original jurisdiction* (the court that has the power to hear the case first), or more than one court may have *concurrent jurisdiction* (both have the power to try the case). Some courts have only *appellate jurisdiction*, and those courts hear cases that are on **appeal** from other courts. A state court decision may not be appealed to a court in another state, but if it involves a *federal* issue, it may be appealed to a federal court and eventually to the U.S. Supreme Court.

State courts may hear only cases involving issues arising from statutes or ordinances within that state, and likewise the federal system with the exception noted. There are some exceptions in civil areas, but they are not of concern in this text.

An act may violate both state and federal law, giving both the state and the federal courts jurisdiction. For example, in the Oklahoma City bombing case, Terry L. Nichols was tried in a federal court in Denver, Colorado, for violating federal murder and conspiracy statutes (he was convicted of conspiracy and involuntary manslaughter—a lesser charge within murder), and subsequently was tried for multiple counts of murder in an Oklahoma state court. He was convicted of the state charges.

Trial and Appellate Courts

Trial courts hear the facts of a case, and either a judge or a jury determines the ultimate fact: the defendant's

Michael Skakel was convicted at age 42 in an adult criminal court of killing Martha Moxley when he was 15 years old. The case raised the issue of the adult court's jurisdiction to try a case committed by a person who was a juvenile when the crime was committed. Skakel lost his appeal on all issues and remains in prison.

TABLE 1.1 Structure, Jurisdiction, and Function of State Court Systems

Court	Structure	Jurisdiction
Highest state appellate court (usually called the supreme court)	Consists of five, seven, or nine justices, who may be appointed or elected; cases decided by this court may not be appealed to the U.S Supreme Court unless they involve a federal question, and then there is no right of appeal except in limited cases.	If there is no intermediate appellate court, defendants convicted in a general trial court will have a right of appeal to this court; if there is an intermediate appellate court, this court will have discretion to limit appeals with few exceptions such as in capital cases.
Intermediate appellate court (also called court of appeals; exists in approximately half of the states)	May have one court that hears appeals from all general trial courts or may have more than one court, each with appellate jurisdiction over a particular area of the state; usually has a panel of three judges.	Defendants convicted in general trial court have right of appeal to this level.
General trial courts (also called superior courts, circuit courts, court of common pleas)	Usually state is divided into judicial districts, with one general trial court in each district, often one per county: courts may be divided by function, such as civil, criminal, probate, domestic.	Jurisdiction to try cases usually begins where jurisdiction of lower court ends, so this court tries more serious cases; may have appellate jurisdiction over cases decided in lower courts.
Courts of limited jurisdiction (also called magistrate's courts, police courts, justice of peace courts, municipal courts)	Differs from state to state; some states divide state into districts, with each having the same type of lower court; in other states, courts may be located in political subdivisions, such as cities or townships, in which case the structure may differ from court to court; may not be a court of record, in which case the system will permit trial *de novo* in general trial court; particularly in rural areas, magistrates may not be lawyers and may work only part-time.	May be limited to specific proceedings, such as initial appearance, preliminary hearing, issuing search and arrest warrants, setting bail, appointing counsel for indigent defendants; jurisdiction of cases is limited to certain types, usually the lesser criminal and civil cases; some jurisdictions may hear all misdemeanors—others are limited to misdemeanors with minor penalties.

Source: Sue Titus Reid, *Criminal Justice*, 8th ed. (Mason, Ohio: Thomson Customs Solutions, a part of the Thomson Corporation, 2008), p. 165.

guilt or innocence. Trial courts also assess the penalty for those who are convicted. Prior to trial, trial judges make other decisions, such as whether to grant bail or to deny or grant any number of motions concerning such issues as whether evidence should be admitted or excluded. A defendant who has an adverse ruling may have grounds to appeal the trial court decision to a higher court. At this point the defendant becomes the **appellant**, who argues that the lower court made a mistake that prejudiced the appellant, who now deserves a reversal of the conviction (or a change in the sentence if that is the issue). The prosecution, now the **appellee**, argues that no mistake was made at trial or, if so, it did not prejudice the appellant.

Courts, both trial and appellate, operate primarily under the criminal laws and procedures of their respective jurisdictions, although, as already noted, state statutes may not violate the federal Constitution or federal statutes. State statutes may, however, and many do, provide rights *beyond* those provided in the federal Constitution or in federal statutes.

With the extensive freedom that states have to develop and enact criminal laws, it is expected that those laws will differ from state to state. In this text we will examine a variety of state laws, but at this point it is important to understand that state legislators have been influenced by one major source in their enactment of laws, the **Model Penal Code**.

THE MODEL PENAL CODE AND CRIMINAL LAW REFORM

In recent years many states (as well as Congress) have attempted a complete revision of their criminal statutes. They have been assisted in this process by the American Law Institute (ALI), an organization of lawyers, judges, and legal scholars, who drafted a variety of model statutes that states may use in crafting their own individual statutes. States and the federal government have also been influenced by English law.

THE ENGLISH COMMON LAW AND ITS IMPACT

Before we look at the sources of U.S. criminal law, it is necessary to have an understanding of the English **common law**, from which much of our civil and criminal laws derived. In general, the term *common law* refers to those customs, traditions, judicial decisions, and other materials that guide courts in decision making but that have not been enacted by the legislatures into statutes or embodied in constitutions. The common law of England developed after the Norman Conquest in 1066. Prior to that time there was no distinction among law, custom, religion, and morality, and decisions differed from community to community. The Normans wanted to establish some unity, and to do so, the king employed representatives to travel to the various jurisdictions. These persons kept the king informed about the different jurisdictions and also carried news to each of what was happening in the others. The legal principles began to be similar, or common, throughout England, and thus the phrase, *the common law of England* or, shortened, *the common law*, was coined.

The common law was brought by the colonists to America and became the basis of much of the early law in this country. The famous jurist Oliver Wendell Holmes Jr. spoke of the common law as follows:

> The common law is not a brooding omnipresence in the sky, but the articulate voice of some sovereign or quasi-sovereign that can be identified.[12]

> The life of the law has not been logic; it has been experience. . . . In order to know what it is, we must know what it has been, and what it tends to become. . . . The very considerations which judges most rarely mention, and always with an apology, are the secret root from which the law draws all the juices of life.[13]

Common law offenses have been kept alive and interpreted by judicial decisions, which are an important part of American law today. Even when state legislatures enact laws to cover common law offenses, the interpretation of those statutes is often left to common law decisions. This is seen in federal courts, where a person cannot be punished for a common law crime today unless it is enacted into a statute. But once that occurs and Congress has provided a penalty for the offense, the courts can resort to the common law for interpretations. Likewise, even in states in which there are no longer any common law crimes, the common law may be used to *interpret* existing statutory law.

SOURCES OF CRIMINAL LAW

Law is derived from four sources: statutes, constitutions, judicial decisions, and administrative regulations.

Statutory Law

Today most states have **codified** their criminal laws, meaning that they have reduced their customs, unwritten laws, and rules to written statutes. Thus, they do not recognize an act as criminal unless it is included within the **statutory law**.

Each state's criminal statutes define the crimes and penalties applicable in that state. This text includes a sampling of state statutes at various points throughout. Although the names and citations vary, state statutes are recorded officially in publications with such names as the *Criminal Code* or *Penal Code*, preceded by the name of the state. For example, *Cal. Penal Code* refers to the criminal statutes that govern California. Congress is responsible for passing statutes that define federal crimes. These are recorded in the *United States Code*, which is also referred to as the *U.S. Code*.

A study of criminal law should distinguish between procedural and substantive law. **Substantive law** defines the elements, rights, and responsibilities of law, whereas **procedural law** defines the methods by which the law may be enforced. This text is concerned primarily with substantive criminal law.

Constitutions

To a limited extent, criminal laws are contained in constitutions. Each state's constitution may contain definitions of crimes that are applicable only to that state. The U.S. Constitution (see Appendix A) deals primarily with procedural criminal law, but the limits it establishes and the guarantees it provides are important to an understanding of criminal law. The federal and state constitutions are viewed as *minimal* protections; statutes may enhance the protections provided to individuals by the jurisdictions in which they are recognized.

Judicial Decisions and Customs

Laws come from judicial decisions as well as from customs. As noted earlier, historically common law referred to England's laws that developed through judicial decisions on a case-by-case basis (leading to the term **case law**) and that influenced the development of English and American law. But the term also applies to unwritten laws in the United States, although as noted, most laws have been codified. It is extremely important to read case law carefully, for case law is real law.

Administrative Law

A final source of law, which is often overlooked in discussions of criminal law, is **administrative law**, which consists of a body of regulations and rules that come from administrative agencies (such as the Internal Revenue Service) to which Congress and state legislatures have delegated the power to make and enforce rules and regulations. Most regulations and decisions of administrative agencies concern civil, not criminal, matters, but even violations of administrative law may constitute offenses that can be enforced through the criminal courts. Because thousands of state and federal agencies enact and enforce administrative rules that affect our daily lives in many ways, administrative law is an important method for controlling our activities; in fact, in many instances it is more effective than criminal law in controlling behavior.

English judges and English law have influenced U.S. criminal justice systems through their development of the common law. (Reuters/Corbis)

DISCRETION AND CRIMINAL LAW

A key concept that pervades the decisions and actions in U.S. criminal justice systems is **discretion**. As noted in Focus 1.2, criminal justice systems permit considerable discretion, leaving public officials and others the freedom to make independent judgments concerning the disposition of cases. This discretion is the subject of debate, much of which focuses on police discretion to stop, question, search, or arrest a person or seize property. But it also involves decisions regarding the definitions and classifications of acts that are covered by criminal statutes, constitutions, and administrative regulations.

Often overlooked but of particular significance to an understanding of criminal law is prosecutorial discretion. The **prosecutor** (or **prosecuting attorney**) is an attorney who represents the state (or federal government, in which case he or she is called a *U.S. attorney*) in a criminal case, in contrast to the **defense attorney**, who represents the accused. After police arrest a suspect, the prosecutor makes the initial decision of whether to pursue the case.

Discretion is crucial in criminal justice systems, but it must be controlled. Law enforcement officers, for example, have wide discretion in their decisions whether to arrest a person suspected of committing a crime, but they must not violate the suspect's constitutional rights in the process. (Tim Graham/Alamy)

The decision of whether to prosecute is a powerful one for which criminal justice systems provide few checks. When the prosecutor decides to pursue a case, he or she has broad discretion in deciding the offense (or offenses) with which to charge the accused. For example, a person arrested for rape might be charged with rape, aggravated assault and battery, or a lesser sexual offense. The prosecutor may make this decision for one or more legitimate reasons, such as insufficient or inadmissible evidence, refusal of witnesses or alleged victims to cooperate, lack of credibility of alleged victims and witnesses, insufficient resources within the system to devote to a long trial, societal interests, or the welfare of the accused. But some decisions may be made for extralegal reasons, such as race or gender.

Some groups may be targeted for prosecution without violating the Constitution. For example, it is common and acceptable to target dangerous offenders for priority prosecution, and prosecutors may prosecute

selectively, but the U.S. Supreme Court has held that they may not increase charges against a person in retaliation for his or her assertion of a legal right.[14]

While prosecutors are not permitted to prosecute suspects for vindictive reasons, some courts have held that certain prosecutorial decisions do not lend themselves to judicial review. This makes prosecutorial vindictiveness difficult to detect and prove. The following brief excerpt from *United States v. Richardson* illustrates this point. Defendant Richardson was accused of receiving videocassettes involving the sexual exploitation of minors. Four others arrested the same day on the same or similar charges were permitted to participate in a pretrial diversion program (such as a community sex offender treatment program) in lieu of prosecution. The defendant alleged that he was discriminated against by the prosecutor because he exercised one of his constitutional rights. The court disagreed.[15]

UNITED STATES v. RICHARDSON
856 F.2D 644 (4th Cir. 1988)

 A defendant has no right to be placed in pretrial diversion. The decision of whether a particular defendant will be allowed the opportunity to participate in the program is one entrusted to the United States Attorney. Like other prosecutorial decisions, the government has broad discretion in determining which defendants are best suited for pretrial diversion. These decisions are "particularly ill-suited to judicial review" and we are "properly hesitant to examine the decision whether to prosecute." However, prosecutorial discretion is not totally unfettered. The government may not selectively prosecute a defendant based upon arbitrary classifications such as race or religion, or the exercise of constitutional rights. . . .

In order to establish selective prosecution a defendant must show that the government was motivated by a discriminatory purpose with a resulting discriminatory effect. The defendant must establish not only that he has been singled out while others similarly situated have not been prosecuted but also that the decision to prosecute was based on impermissible considerations. A defendant challenging the government's pretrial diversion decision must set forth specific facts supporting his selective prosecution contention and may not rest on bald assertions of constitutional violations.

FOCUS 1.2   Discretion and Criminal Law

These criminal justice officials . . .	. . . must often decide whether or not or how to:
Police	• Enforce specific laws • Investigate specific crimes • Search people, vicinities, buildings • Arrest or detain people
Prosecutor	• File charges or petitions for adjudication • Seek indictments • Drop cases • Reduce charges
Judges or magistrates	• Set bail or conditions for release • Accept pleas • Determine delinquency • Dismiss charges • Impose sentences • Revoke probation
Correctional officials	• Assign to type of correctional facility • Award privileges • Punish for disciplinary infractions
Paroling authority	• Determine date and conditions of parole • Revoke parole

Source: Bureau of Justice Statistics, *Report to the Nation on Crime and Justice*: The Data, 2d ed. (Washington, D.C.: U.S. Department of Justice, 1988), p. 59.

Discretion also exists in the classification of crimes, both in deciding which classifications to use and in how to categorize crimes within those classifications.

CLASSIFICATION OF CRIMES AND RELATED OFFENSES

Before looking at the various classifications of crimes and related offenses, we must define the word **crime**. Scholars have long debated its meaning. Some definitions are concise, whereas others attempt to include all elements. Simply stated, a *crime* is the commission of an act prohibited by criminal law or the failure to act as required by criminal law. Implicit in this definition is the power of the government to impose penalties.

Two basic principles of U.S. criminal justice systems are important to an understanding of the definition of crime. The first is that the government may not punish unless there is a *law* (statutory or common) providing that an act (or a failure to act) is a crime. The second is that there is no crime without punishment. This does not mean that a state or the federal government may not decline to prosecute or refuse to punish when a person is found guilty. Rather, it means that unless the state (or the federal government) has defined an act or omission as a crime and provided **sanctions**, punishment may not be inflicted just because the act is considered to be harmful to society.

Crimes may be classified in several ways. The most common classification is by the degree of seriousness of the offense.

Grade of Offense

Although the common law classified crimes as **treason** (an attempt to overthrow the government of which one is a member or a betrayal of that government to a foreign power), felonies, or misdemeanors, most modern criminal codes divide crimes into the latter two categories.

The distinction between *felonies* and *misdemeanors* was very important under the early English common law, which held most felonies punishable by death. Misdemeanors included crimes that were not felonies. Today the categories are distinguished primarily by the sentences that may be imposed. Generally, *felonies* are crimes for which offenders may be sentenced to death or imprisoned for a long period, whereas *misdemeanors* are offenses punishable by fines, work, probation, community service, or short-term incarceration (less than one year), usually in a jail rather than a state or federal prison. Some statutes do not specify whether a particular crime is a felony or a misdemeanor; the determination is made by the punishment specified for that crime. Some statutes add a third category—*petty misdemeanors*, also called *petty offenses* in some codes. Some statutes use the terms *violation* or *infraction* to refer to less serious offenses, such as *traffic infractions.*

In addition to determining punishment, the distinction between felonies and misdemeanors (and petty offenses, where they are classified separately) may determine the court in which the case is heard. The distinction may also have a bearing on the procedures that must be followed in the criminal proceedings. Arrest rules may vary, and civil penalties that follow convictions may differ. For example, an offender might lose the right to vote upon conviction of a felony but not upon conviction of a misdemeanor.

Finally, the impact of discretion may be seen in the classification of crimes by seriousness. An act that is viewed as a felony in one state may be classified as a misdemeanor in another. Or an act that is classified as a misdemeanor the first time a person is convicted of that offense may be treated as a felony for subsequent convictions of the same offense.

Moral Turpitude

Crimes may also be classified in terms of *moral turpitude,* which refers to acts that are base, vile, and immoral. A crime of moral turpitude is "an act or behavior that gravely violates moral sentiment or accepted moral standards of the community."[16]

The distinction between crimes that do and those that do not involve moral turpitude is important. Conviction of a crime of moral turpitude may result in the disbarment of a lawyer, the revocation of a doctor's license, the dismissal of a tenured professor, or the deportation of an alien. It may also result in enhanced penalties. In many instances, however, it is difficult to define which acts are included among moral turpitude crimes.

Other Classifications

Crimes may be classified in other ways as well. Some codes distinguish between crimes that are infamous and those that are not. Included in infamous crimes are acts considered shameful or disgraceful, without fame or good report. This classification was used in common law to exclude persons from testifying in court on the belief that anyone who would commit such crimes was so depraved that he or she would not tell the truth. Included were treason, most felonies, and crimes involving dishonesty such as embezzlement, false pretense, criminal fraud, and perjury.

Other special categories may involve behaviors that technically are not criminal, such as acts committed by juveniles and processed through juvenile courts. Violations of local ordinances technically are not criminal acts, although they may resemble crimes. State legislatures delegate to municipal authorities the power to pass ordinances to regulate health, welfare, and safety. Some of these ordinances provide penalties such as short jail terms or fines, but violations of these ordinances may be considered civil, not criminal.

THE LIMITATIONS ON CRIMINAL LAW

Congress and state legislatures are limited in what they may do to define acts as criminal; similarly, courts are limited in their enforcement of criminal law. Many of the limitations are matters of criminal procedure and therefore not covered in this text, but understanding some procedural limitations is necessary for comprehending criminal law. We have already noted that courts are limited by the concept of *jurisdiction.*

Void for Vagueness and Overbreadth

Interpretations of the U.S. Constitution require that a criminal statute must be declared void for vagueness when "men of common intelligence must necessarily guess at its meaning and differ as to its application."[17] In

1983 the U.S. Supreme Court held a California statute unconstitutionally vague. *Kolender v. Lawson* involved a tall, muscular, African American man with long hair who frequently walked in an all-white neighborhood. Edward Lawson was stopped by police about 15 times between 1975 and 1977; each time he refused to identify himself.

Lawson was arrested five times, was convicted once, and served several weeks in jail. The statute under which he was arrested defined *disorderly conduct*, a misdemeanor, as the actions of one who

> loiters or wanders upon the streets or from place to place without apparent reason or business and who refuses to identify himself and to account for his presence when requested by any peace officer so to do, if the surrounding circumstances are such as to indicate to a reasonable man that the public safety demands such identification.[18]

The U.S. Supreme Court held that the statute was vague because it did not establish a standard for what a suspect must do to provide a "credible and reliable" identification. The result was that police had "virtually complete discretion . . . to determine whether the suspect has satisfied the statute." The statute permitted people to walk the streets without interference from police "only at the whim of any police officer." The Supreme Court held that the statute was unconstitutional because it failed to give adequate notice.[19]

It is not always easy to determine whether a statute may be declared void for vagueness. Laws cannot specify every prohibited act. To avoid the void for vagueness problem, statutes must have three characteristics:

1. They must give fair notice or warning to those subject to them.

2. They must guard against arbitrary and discriminatory enforcement.

3. They must not unreasonably deny people their First Amendment rights, such as the right to free speech (see Appendix A).

Consider the following fact pattern: A municipal ordinance provides that it is illegal for a person to sleep in a car parked on a public street. You are sleeping in your car parked on a public street, and you are arrested. You retain an attorney and challenge the constitutionality of the ordinance. What would you argue? Are there any circumstances under which you should be permitted to sleep in your car on a public street? Are there reasons for having an ordinance of this nature? Does *Kolender v. Lawson* apply to your case?

The Alabama Court of Criminal Appeals considered these questions, with a majority of the court holding the Montgomery ordinance unconstitutional under *Kolender v. Lawson.*[20] Consider the following brief excerpt from the majority opinion, along with the excerpt from the dissent. Which do you think is the better reasoning?

HORN v. CITY OF MONTGOMERY
619 So.2d 949 (Ala.Crim.Ct.App. 1993)

Majority Opinion

 Numerous situations could arise that would be essentially innocent—such as a driver pulling over to the curb and parking because he was too sleepy, too ill, or too tired to drive. The arresting officer recognized this possibility and admitted that he and other officers believed that they were free to decide whether to enforce the ordinance in those cases. The vagueness of the ordinance encourages arbitrary and discriminatory enforcement.

Dissenting Opinion

[The dissent argued that the discretion permitted by the statute was constitutional in that it permitted officers to distinguish between drivers who were too tired to drive and those who were too drunk to drive but might do so and become a menace to society.]

That kind of measured discretion, guided by easily ascertained criteria, simply does not constitute the "standardless sweep [that] allows policemen, prosecutors and juries to pursue their personal predilections" condemned in *Kolender*.

Ex Post Facto Laws and Bills of Attainder

The U.S. Constitution provides that "no bill of attainder or *ex post facto* law shall be passed."[21] The U.S. Supreme Court has defined an ***ex post facto*** law as one that "retroactively alter[s] the definition of crimes or increase[s] the punishment for criminal acts."[22] The *ex post facto* doctrine is interpreted to mean that although a state may change its statutes or regulations to benefit a person, it may not do so to impose punishment that did not exist at the time the act was committed or to increase the punishment.

An example of this constitutional limitation occurred in 1997, when the U.S. Supreme Court ruled that the *ex post facto* rule was violated when Florida officials canceled early release credits awarded to inmates under a statutory provision that was enacted to alleviate prison overcrowding and that was in effect when those inmates were incarcerated. In 1992 the state enacted a statute that canceled those credits for specified classes of offenders, some of whom had already been released when the state's attorney general interpreted the 1992 statute as applying retroactively. The state wanted to reincarcerate the released offenders; the Supreme Court held that such an act would be unconstitutional.[23]

In 2003, the U.S. Supreme Court upheld as constitutional the Alaska statute requiring sex offenders to register with law enforcement authorities, to provide certain personal information, and to update any changes in that information. Despite the fact that the statute was enacted after the involved offenders committed their acts, the Supreme Court held that the statute did not constitute a prohibited *ex post facto* act in that the purpose of requiring sex offenders to register in the communities in which they live after they are released from prison is to protect society, not to punish offenders.[24]

In addition to forbidding *ex post facto* laws, the U.S. Constitution prohibits the use of a **bill of attainder**, defined as a "legislative act which inflicts punishment without a judicial trial." Originally, the term referred only to the death penalty, and a bill of attainder involving lesser penalties was called a *bill of pains and penalties.*[25] Two examples are illustrative.

In 1866 a statute that prohibited from the practice of law individuals who refused to take an oath that they had not opposed the United States in the Civil War was held unconstitutional. The U.S. Supreme Court emphasized that although the legal profession could be regulated, this particular requirement bore no relationship to the fitness to practice law.[26]

In contrast, in 1977 a statute providing for governmental custody of President Richard Nixon's presidential papers was upheld. The statute dealt with the preservation of those materials and was not considered by the U.S. Supreme Court to be punitive. Although Nixon was an identifiable person, the statute did not constitute a bill of attainder.[27]

Repeal or Amendment of a Statute

If a statute is repealed or amended after the accused committed the act but before he or she is tried, may the suspect be tried for the offense specified in that statute? Under the common law, the answer was *no* unless the repeal or amendment had a "saving" provision that implied a legislative intent not to eliminate prosecutions of previous offenses. The rule applied to cases in which prosecutions had begun but had not been completed and to cases not yet begun. Prosecutions could continue or start, however, if the new statute or amendment contained a provision that had essentially all the elements of the former statute. For example, a new statute that required the same elements for first-degree sexual assault as those required for a prior rape statute would not preclude prosecution of a defendant charged under the rape statute.[28]

Double Jeopardy

The Fifth Amendment of the U.S. Constitution provides, in part, "nor shall any person be subject for the same offence to be twice put in jeopardy of life or limb." This **double jeopardy** provision is important but technically difficult. In brief, it means that once a defendant has been tried and acquitted of a crime, he or she may not be tried again for the same crime. Recall, however, that state and federal crimes might attach to the same act. Thus, as mentioned, Terry L. Nichols was tried in an Oklahoma court, under the state's murder statute, for the deaths of those who died in the bombing of the city's federal building in 1995. The state apparently did this in an effort to secure the death penalty, but that penalty was not recommended by Nichols's jury. Nichols had been convicted of manslaughter and of conspiracy, but not of murder, in the federal trial stemming from that terrorist act.

In *Blockburger v. United States*, decided in 1932, the U.S. Supreme Court interpreted the double jeopardy provision as follows:

> Each of the offenses . . . requires proof of a different element. The applicable rule is that where the same act or transaction constitutes a violation of two distinct statutory provisions, the test to be applied to determine whether there are two offenses or only one, is whether each provision requires proof of a fact which the other does not.[29]

Although the U.S. Supreme Court, along with lower courts, continues to look at the double jeopardy rule, clearly the point of the rule is to prevent the government from prosecuting defendants just to wear them down, hoping that at some point they will get a conviction.

Cruel and Unusual Punishment

The Eighth Amendment of the U.S. Constitution (see Appendix A) prohibits the imposition of **cruel and unusual punishment**, but there is little agreement on the meaning of this phrase. The U.S. Supreme Court has interpreted it in numerous cases, particularly those involving capital punishment. Although some justices disagree, the Court has not declared capital punishment per se to be cruel and unusual, but it may be held to be unconstitutional if the penalty is not proportional to the crime for which it is imposed.[30] For example, the Supreme Court has ruled that capital punishment for the rape (but not murder) of an adult woman is not proportional to the crime and thus constitutes cruel and unusual punishment.[31] In 2008 the Supreme Court ruled that the execution of an offender for the rape but not murder of a child is also cruel and unusual punishment.[32]

In addition to proportionality, there are other situations to which the prohibition against cruel and unusual punishment might apply. For example, a punishment that tortures or inflicts unnecessary pain is not permitted. This issue was raised in a 2008 case decided by the U.S. Supreme Court. In *Baze v. Rees*, the Court ruled that, in challenging Kentucky's procedures for the use of lethal injection as a form of capital punishment, the petitioners had not sustained their burden of proving "that the risk of pain from maladministration of a concededly humane lethal injection protocol, and the failure to adopt untried and untested alternatives, constitute cruel and unusual punishment." In writing for the 7–2 majority, Chief Justice John Roberts declared that there is some risk of pain in any method of execution and thus, "the Constitution does not demand the avoidance of all risk of pain in carrying out execution."[33]

Due Process and Equal Protection

The U.S. Constitution prohibits the federal government (in the Fifth Amendment) and the states (in the Fourteenth Amendment) from depriving persons of life, liberty, or property without **due process** and **equal protection** of the law (see Appendix A). Many cases have been decided by lower courts and by the U.S. Supreme Court in attempts to define these important concepts. That body of case law cannot be reviewed here, but a definition and brief interpretation of each term are important. As with statutes, the concepts of due process and equal protection refer to substantive and procedural matters.

Due process means that statutes may not be defined or enforced in an unreasonable, capricious, or arbitrary manner. People charged with crimes have a right to be notified, to be heard, and to defend themselves against the charges. Due process refers to other constitutional guarantees before, during, and after a criminal trial. The particulars of the concept may vary from case to case, as the following brief excerpt from *Burton v. Livingston* illustrates.[34]

BURTON v. LIVINGSTON
791 F.2d 97, 99-100 (8th Cir. 1986)

 Due process of law has been said to encompass a "guarantee of respect for those personal immunities which are 'so rooted in the traditions and conscience of our people as to be ranked as fundamental.'" The guarantee of due process draws a line between the power of the government, on the one hand, and the security of the individual, on the other. This line is not a fixed one like a property boundary. Its location must be surveyed anew by the court in each case through an examination of the benchmarks disclosed by the circumstances surrounding the case. Among these landmarks are the nature of the individual right, the relationship between the individual and the government, and the justification offered by the government for its conduct.

Equal protection means that no person or class of persons may be denied the same protection of law that is provided to other persons or classes of persons. The litigation in this area is extensive and arises primarily with respect to race and gender. The U.S. Supreme Court has defined some areas while leaving states considerable room to establish others.

The Right of Privacy

In the text's subsequent discussions of specific crimes, such as sexual acts between consenting adults, the right to privacy arises. At this point, however, we will look briefly at this right, which is not specified by the U.S. Constitution, although some state constitutions recognize the right specifically. For example, the Alaska constitution provides, "The right of the people to privacy is recognized and shall not be infringed."[35]

If the U.S. Constitution does not specify the right to privacy, how do we get it? This discussion emphasizes the importance of reading a case carefully to see how U.S. Supreme Court justices interpret the Constitution and statutes.

The right to privacy was articulated by the U.S. Supreme Court in its 1965 decision *Griswold v. Connecticut*.[36] The appellants in this case were the executive director of the Planned Parenthood League of Connecticut, a licensed physician, and the League's medical director, who was also a professor at the Yale Medical School. These two men "gave information, instruction, and medical advice to *married persons*. They examined the wife and prescribed the best contraceptive device or material for her use." At that time, Connecticut had the following statute:

> Any person who uses any drug, medicinal article or instrument for the purpose of preventing conception shall be fined not less than fifty dollars or imprisoned not less than sixty days nor more than one year or be both fined and imprisoned.

> [and]

> Any person who assists, abets, counsels, causes, hires or commands another to commit any offense . . . may be prosecuted and punished as if he were the principal offender.[37]

The appellants in *Griswold* were found guilty and fined $100 each. They appealed. In analyzing the issues, the U.S. Supreme Court emphasized that it did not sit in judgment of legislative enactments in business, economic, or social areas. But, said the Court, this statute interferes with the intimate relationships of married persons as well as their relationships with their physicians. And although the Constitution does not specify a right to privacy, the Supreme Court held that specific guarantees in the Bill of Rights "have penumbras, formed by emanations from those guarantees that help give them life and substance. Various guarantees create zones of privacy." Specifically, the Court listed the following constitutional amendments that create zones of privacy:

- First Amendment's right of association

- Third Amendment's prohibition against quartering soldiers in private homes during peacetime without the consent of the homeowner

- Fourth Amendment's prohibition against unreasonable searches and seizures

- Fifth Amendment's prohibition against forcing one to testify against himself to his detriment

- Ninth Amendment's provision that the "enumeration in the Constitution, of certain rights, shall not be construed to deny or disparage others retained by the people"

Justice William O. Douglas, who wrote the Court's opinion in *Griswold*, asked the question, "Would we allow the police to search the sacred precincts of marital bedrooms for the telltale signs of the use of contraceptives? The very idea is repulsive to the notions of privacy surrounding the marriage relationship." The U.S. Supreme Court reversed the convictions and established a right to privacy that has not only survived but has also been enlarged by subsequent U.S. Supreme Court decisions, as further discussions in this text demonstrate.

Other Constitutional Limitations

Criminal laws must also operate within the framework of other constitutional rights, such as freedom of religion, freedom of speech and the press, the right to assemble peacefully, the right to petition the government for redress, freedom from unreasonable searches and seizures, freedom from compulsory self-incrimination, and numerous rights that defendants have at trial, such as the right to counsel, the right not to testify against themselves, and the right to a jury trial.

THE ESTABLISHMENT OF GUILT

Although much of the law applying to the establishment of guilt in a criminal case is procedural and thus not the subject matter of this text, some points must be covered for an adequate understanding of criminal law. The adversarial nature of the U.S. system of criminal law, in contrast to the inquisitorial system of some other countries, is very important and relates to the critical issue of the burden of proof in a criminal case.

THE ADVERSARY SYSTEM

In the **inquisitorial system** defendants are presumed guilty and must prove their innocence. In the **adversary system**, the prosecutor (representing the state and the victim) and the defense counsel (representing the defendant) oppose each other in a trial if they are unable or unwilling to dispose of the case prior to a trial, and the defendant is presumed innocent. The state must prove guilt, and that is a heavy burden because of the standard of proof required in a criminal case.

The Burden of Proof

In a trial one party has the **burden of proof** on certain issues. In a civil case the person who brings the action must prove his or her case, usually by the standard of a *preponderance of the evidence*. If the other side wishes, it may present defenses, on which it will have that same standard of proof. In a criminal trial, however, the prosecution must prove its allegations **beyond a reasonable doubt**. Although this standard is usually not defined precisely, its importance in U.S. criminal trials was emphasized by the U.S. Supreme Court in *In re Winship*, decided in 1970. This case involved a juvenile, but it has been interpreted as applying to the trials of adult defendants as well.[38]

IN RE WINSHIP
397 U.S. 358, 363-364 (1970)

Justice William J. Brennan Jr. delivered the opinion of the Court. Justice John Marshall Harlan wrote a concurring opinion. Chief Justice Warren E. Burger wrote a dissent, in which he was joined by Justice Potter Stewart. Justice Hugo L. Black wrote a separate dissenting opinion.

The reasonable doubt standard plays a vital role in the American scheme of criminal procedure. It is a prime instrument for reducing the risk of convictions resting on factual error. The standard provides concrete substance for the presumption of innocence—that bedrock "axiomatic and elementary" principle whose "enforcement lies at the foundation of the administration of our criminal law." As the dissenters in the New York Court of Appeals [from which the case was being appealed] observed, and we agree, "a person accused of crime . . . would be at a severe disadvantage, a disadvantage amounting to a lack of fundamental fairness, if he could be adjudged guilty and imprisoned for years on the strength of the same evidence as would suffice in a civil case."

The requirement of proof beyond a reasonable doubt has this vital role in our criminal procedure for cogent reasons. The accused during a criminal prosecution has at stake interest of immense importance, both because of the possibility that he may lose his liberty upon conviction and because of the certainty that he would be stigmatized by the conviction. Accordingly, a society that values the good name and freedom of every individual should not condemn a man for commission of a crime when there is reasonable doubt about his guilt.

Moreover, use of the reasonable doubt standard is indispensable to command the respect and confidence of the community in application of the criminal law. It is critical that the moral force of the criminal law not be diluted by a standard of proof that leaves people in doubt whether innocent men are being condemned. It is also important in our free society that every individual going about his ordinary affairs have confidence that his government cannot adjudge him guilty of a criminal offense without convincing a proper factfinder of his guilt with utmost certainty.

There have been some problems in interpreting the meaning and extent of the beyond a reasonable doubt standard.[39] In 1994 the U.S. Supreme Court discussed the issues in two cases consolidated for argument and decision because of their similarities. The Court upheld but expressed dissatisfaction with the jury instructions concerning the reasonable doubt standard. Among other issues, the justices were concerned about the statement that a reasonable doubt exists when a juror lacks an "abiding conviction, to a moral certainty, of the truth of the charge." Because of the problems of defining *beyond a reasonable doubt*, some appellate courts have ruled that an instruction on the concept should not be given to the jury.[40]

In some instances the defendant in a criminal case may have a burden of proof, although that never applies to any of the legal elements of the offense charged. For example, some affirmative defenses require that the defendant sustain the burden of proof. Generally when the defendant has a burden of proof in a criminal case, the standard of proof will be by a preponderance of the evidence rather than the more stringent standard of beyond a reasonable doubt. Chapter 4 gives more extensive treatment to the burden-of-proof issues between prosecution and defense, while that chapter and Chapter 5 explore the matter of defenses in greater detail.

Determining Criminal Culpability: The Judge and the Jury

Although the prosecution in a criminal case has the burden of proving all elements of the crime beyond a reasonable doubt, whether the defendant is guilty is a question of fact to be determined by the jury (or by the judge if the case is not tried before a jury).

We noted earlier in this chapter that considerable discretion exists within criminal justice systems. The roles of the trial judge and the jury illustrate this discretion. If the trial judge believes that the prosecution has not proved every element of the crime beyond a reasonable doubt, he or she may grant a defense motion for a directed verdict of acquittal. In addition, during the proceeding or after all evidence is presented, the judge may dismiss the case for lack of evidence.

If certain procedural rules are violated; if the jury is unable to reach a verdict; if inadmissible evidence is introduced; if jurors, attorneys, or others in the courtroom misbehave or any of the participants in the trial become ill or cannot attend; or if any number of other reasons occur, the judge may declare a **mistrial**, which is an incomplete trial. After a mistrial, the case may be tried again before another jury (or judge), or the charges may be dismissed.

Even if there are no procedural problems and the evidence proves beyond a reasonable doubt that the defendant is guilty, the jury may refuse to return a guilty verdict—a process called **jury nullification**. In U.S. criminal justice systems, juries have wide discretion. Juries represent the community's voice in the criminal justice process, and it is understood and accepted that there are some cases in which a guilty verdict may not be returned despite the evidence. Examples are **mercy killings** or cases in which there is considerable sympathy for the defendants, such as those in which spouses or children kill spouses or parents who were abusing them over long periods of time.

HOW TO READ AND INTERPRET A CASE

Throughout this text you will have an opportunity to read and interpret edited cases. In particular, at the end of each chapter a case is presented for you to examine. How do you do this? First, each of those major cases is preceded by a Case Preview, which summarizes the case and suggests issues and questions for you to consider as you read the excerpt. Second, Appendix B details how to read a court citation. Finally, here we present some general points to consider as you read a case.

To begin, let us consider some terminology that is crucial to reading cases. First is the principal of *stare decisis*, which literally means "let the decision stand." *Stare decisis* means that although the law must be flex-

ible and change with the times, it must also be stable and predictable, and courts are reluctant to make changes. Thus, when reading opinions, you will see frequent references to other cases, or precedent, although in this text some of those references and footnotes have been deleted to simplify your reading.

Second, usually appellate judges issue written opinions when they hand down their decisions. This is particularly the case with the U.S. Supreme Court. The decision of the Court is announced and explained in the majority opinion, but some of the justices who voted with the majority may write their own opinions. Those who dissent from the majority may also write opinions. But in reading these opinions, it is critical to distinguish between the *rule of law* or the *holding* of the case—that is, the actual decision based on the facts of the case—and *dicta*, or comments, that the judges might make verbally or in writing. In their opinions, justices may make comments that represent their own views and have little or nothing to do with the holding of the case. Those comments do not constitute the law of the case, although they may be meaningful to future cases.

Another important concept is *legal reasoning*, which means that lawyers read the facts of decided cases and present the facts of undecided cases in light of those decisions—arguing that the law as decided either does or does not apply to the new fact pattern. The facts are crucial, for technically, a court decision applies only to the facts of that case.

Consider this example. Recall our previous discussion of the *Griswold* case. The persons who received contraceptives in that case were married. The next challenge heard by the U.S. Supreme Court was decided in 1972, in *Baird v. Eisenstadt*.[41] This case arose under a Massachusetts statute that provided a five-year prison term for anyone who gave away "any drug, medicine, instrument or article whatever for the prevention of conception." Excluded from the statute were registered physicians, who were permitted to "administer to or prescribe for any married person drugs or articles intended for the prevention of pregnancy or conception."[42] Registered pharmacists who were actually engaged in the pharmacy business were permitted under the law to fill those prescriptions. In effect, this statute meant that under no circumstances could contraceptives be legally available to single persons. But married persons could get them even if their purpose in securing them was to engage in illicit sexual relations. The U.S. Supreme Court held that the privacy right articulated in *Griswold* also applies to single persons.[43]

As subsequent discussions in this text show, the U.S. Supreme Court later extended the right of privacy beyond these cases, but at this point, it is relevant only to understand that *Griswold* and *Eisenstadt* underscore that court decisions are limited to the facts involved. The cases also illustrate that the law evolves over time—in some instances, such as the right to counsel, discussed in Focus 1.3, over many years.

Finally, it is important to understand that legal cases can be very difficult to read, even for skilled lawyers. Sometimes you will need to read the case more than once to understand what the justices said. The opinions do not always state with clarity the position of the writer or of the court making that decision, and they rarely say, in effect, "Dear reader, here are the facts;

here is the issue; here is the holding." Readers must glean these categories and responses on their own. In this text we help you by categorizing the opinions, but you should understand that on your own, you would be required to find the facts, the issue, the decision, and the reasons without the aids provided by this text.

SUMMARY

This chapter provided a brief overview of criminal law. In earlier times, when societies were less complex and everyone knew everyone else, human behavior could be controlled by informal means. Even the criminal law permitted people to engage in private revenge, which usually was a successful method for apprehending and

---

FOCUS 1.3   The Evolution of the Right to Counsel

The right to counsel, a critical right of defendants, is specified in the Sixth Amendment to the U.S. Constitution, which states in part, "In all criminal prosecutions, the accused shall enjoy the right . . . to have the Assistance of Counsel for his defense." This right has been litigated frequently, but a brief look at a few key cases decided by the U.S. Supreme Court emphasizes the long period of time over which the right evolved through judicial decisions. This discussion also demonstrates the issue, discussed in the text, of the importance of reading cases carefully.

Throughout most of our history, the Sixth Amendment right to counsel meant that counsel was permitted only if a defendant could afford to retain an attorney. In 1932, in *Powell v. Alabama*,[1] the U.S. Supreme Court upheld the right to appointed counsel (counsel paid for by the government). *Powell* involved several African American male youths who were accused of raping two young white women. The situation was volatile, and the state militia was ordered in to protect the defendants. The judge appointed the entire local bar to represent the youths, who were convicted. The U.S. Supreme Court recognized the "special circumstances" of this case: the youth, illiteracy, and low mentality of all the defendants. Under these circumstances and the seriousness of the crime in question, held the Court, the state had a duty to appoint effective assistance of counsel. But 10 years later, in *Betts v. Brady*,[2] the U.S. Supreme Court did not hold that the right to appointed counsel extended to an intelligent adult male with an average education. The fact that the defendant was indigent was not sufficient to warrant appointed counsel.

In 1963, 31 years after *Powell*, in *Gideon v. Wainwright*,[3] the U.S. Supreme Court held that the right to appointed counsel extended to all felony cases. Gideon, who was charged with

Clarence Earl Gideon argued that the U.S. Constitution guaranteed him the right to appointed counsel in his felony case. The Court agreed, and in subsequent cases, that right was extended to less serious offenses. (IStockPhoto)

a felony in Florida, had maintained that he was entitled to appointed counsel despite Florida's statute, which extended that right only in death penalty cases. Justice Hugo Black, who wrote the Court's opinion in *Gideon*, noted that in criminal cases, lawyers are not luxuries but necessities.

Subsequently, the right to appointed counsel has been extended beyond felony cases, and the U.S. Supreme Court has decided several cases concerning the right to effective assistance of counsel, along with numerous decisions involving when and under what circumstances the right to counsel attaches.

1. *Powell v. Alabama*, 297 U.S. 45 (1932).
2. *Betts v. Brady*, 315 U.S. 455 (1942).
3. *Gideon v. Wainwright*, 372 U.S. 355 (1963).

punishing those who did not behave within the norms. As societies grew and became more complex, informal controls were replaced with a formal system of state action; in criminal law, private revenge was replaced by what some call *public revenge*.

A brief general distinction between civil and criminal law was followed by a more extensive discussion of the nature and purpose of criminal law. Legal punishment is a serious intrusion into private lives; thus, the state needs reasonable justifications for its imposition. The reasons for criminal punishment—retribution (or revenge), incapacitation, deterrence, and rehabilitation (or reformation)—were viewed historically and discussed as the basis for punitive government action against criminal offenders.

Another issue that criminal law involves is the difficult question of which acts to include as crimes. Courts and legislators continue to debate the issue of whether certain types of behavior—such as private sexual behavior between consenting adults or the use and abuse of alcohol and other drugs—should be criminal. This chapter looked at the historical basis for the inclusion of morality within the criminal law and raised the general question of how extensive the criminal law should be. Subsequent chapters look in more detail at particular areas of concern.

To set the stage for future discussions, this chapter included an overview of courts and their functions, noting in particular the dual court nature of U.S. criminal justice systems. Trial and appellate courts were distinguished. The chapter then looked at the Model Penal Code, its meaning, and its impact on criminal law in the United States. The English common law, which has also been influential in the development of modern U.S. criminal law, was noted and discussed.

Law comes from several sources, and brief attention was given to them: statutory law, judicial decisions and customs, constitutions, and administrative law.

Because the processing of criminal law involves wide discretion, the chapter discussed the importance of discretion in U.S. criminal justice systems and focused on the extent and nature of prosecutorial discretion. Such discretion cannot and should not be eliminated, but more attention should be given to judicial review of it.

Crimes are classified in several ways; the distinctions are not always agreed on, but they are important for several reasons. The categories of felony and misdemeanor, crimes that are evil intrinsically compared to acts that are crimes primarily because they are defined as such, crimes of moral turpitude and infamous crimes, and acts that are processed in separate hearings (such as juvenile delinquency) are important in determining procedures that must be followed and in assessing punishment.

An important discussion in this chapter focused on some of the constitutional limitations on U.S. criminal laws. Statutes that are vague may not be used against the accused. Suspects may not be convicted and punished for acts that were not defined as crimes when the acts were committed. Nor is it permissible to pass statutes aimed at criminal punishment for particular categories of persons to the exclusion of others; categories such as race, ethnicity, and gender are examples. In addition, attention must be paid to statutes that have been repealed or amended and the circumstances, if any, under which people may be prosecuted in these instances.

A criminal statute may neither violate the double jeopardy protection of the U.S. Constitution nor impose cruel and unusual punishment or punishment disproportional to the crime for which it is imposed. In both substantive and procedural criminal law, due process and equal protection of the law must be observed. Other constitutional rights—such as the right to privacy, the right to free speech, and the right to the freedom of religion—must be observed but may give way to criminal prosecutions in instances that endanger the public welfare.

The establishment of guilt in an adversary system is a crucial process. In U.S. criminal justice systems, the prosecution is required to prove all elements of a crime beyond a reasonable doubt. Even when that burden of proof is met by the prosecution, the defendant may be entitled to an acquittal if the defense provides proof by a preponderance of the evidence that he or she had an adequate defense in the commission of the alleged crime.

Even if the prosecutor presents sufficient proof of all of the elements of a crime, U.S. criminal justice systems permit a jury (or a judge if the case is not tried before a jury) to ignore the evidence and decide against criminal culpability.

Finally, this chapter gave the reader a brief overview of how to read and interpret a court case.

Chapter 2 focuses in greater detail on the elements of a crime.

STUDY QUESTIONS

1. Why do we have a formal system of criminal law, and what are its advantages and disadvantages when compared with an informal system?

2. Distinguish civil law from criminal law.

3. Have criminal justice systems progressed or regressed by deemphasizing reformation or rehabilitation? Why or why not?

   Is retribution a reasonable justification for imposing the criminal law? If not, why not? If so, how far would you carry the concept?

4. Distinguish crimes that are evil in themselves from those that are considered evil primarily because the law defines them as such.

5. What is meant by this statement: "The United States has dual court systems"?

6. Distinguish between trial and appellate courts.

7. What is the importance of the Model Penal Code?

8. Define *English common law*, and discuss its importance in U.S. criminal law systems.

9. Explain the meaning and importance of case law, statutory law, and procedural law.

10. What is administrative law, and why is it important to a study of criminal law?

11. Articulate a plan for curbing prosecutorial discretion, and explain why your plan is a good one.

12. Why is it important to classify crimes, and in what ways may that be done?

13. Why do U.S. criminal justice systems provide that a statute is void if it is vague or too broad? How does the California case of *Kolender v. Lawson* illustrate these principles? What are the problems of applying this case to other fact patterns? Illustrate.

14. Distinguish between an *ex post facto* law and a bill of attainder.

15. Define *double jeopardy*, and explain its importance.

16. Do you think capital punishment is cruel and unusual? Would your answer differ if you were comparing adults and juveniles? What do you understand the concept of cruel and unusual punishment to mean in the area of sentencing? In particular, explore the concept of *proportionality*.

17. Explain due process and equal protection.

18. What do you understand the phrase *beyond a reasonable doubt* to mean? Do you think the concept should be defined for a jury?

19. If you were a criminal defendant, would you prefer to have your case decided by a judge or a jury? Give reasons for your answer.

20. What is meant by the holding or the rule of law of a case?

21. Define *legal reasoning*, and explain the importance of the facts to the interpretation of a court decision.

22. Summarize the evolution of the right to appointed counsel in felony cases.

FOR DEBATE

In this chapter we have learned that there are various ways to attempt to control behavior. This text is about criminal law, but that law may not always be the most efficient, just, or reasonable way to approach a problem. This debate topic will enable you to consider the use of the criminal law to control behavior.

Resolved: The criminal law, compared to administrative law and civil law, is a more effective way to control the following behaviors:

a. Gambling

b. Prostitution

c. The use of marijuana

d. Wearing seatbelts

e. Wearing helmets while motorcycling or bicycling

f. The use of cocaine

g. Consensual, private sex between adults

KEY TERMS

CASE ANALYSIS

KANSAS v. HENDRICKS

521 U.S. 346 (1997)

Case Preview

This case is presented to show you the difference between the civil and the criminal law in one area: the commitment to incarceration of persons thought to be dangerous to the community but who have already served their prison time.

In 1984, Leroy Hendricks was convicted of taking indecent liberties with two 13-year-old boys. After completing nearly 10 years of his prison sentence, Hendricks was scheduled for release. The state filed a petition seeking civil confinement because Hendricks was considered a sexual predator who was likely to commit future acts of sexual violence against children.

After hearing evidence of Hendricks's long history of sexual abuse against children and expert testimony on whether Hendricks was a future danger to children, a jury determined that Hendricks was a sexual predator. The judge found that Hendricks had a mental abnormality and involuntarily committed him to an indefinite period of civil confinement under the Kansas Sexually Violent Predator Act, which was invoked in 1994. That statute provides for the civil commitment of persons who, due to mental abnormality or personality disorder, are likely to engage in predatory acts of sexual violence. Under the statute *sexually violent predator* means "any person who has been convicted of or charged with a sexually violent offense and who suffers from a mental abnormality or personality disorder which makes the person likely to engage in the predatory acts of sexual violence." *Mental abnormality* is defined as a "congenital or acquired condition affecting the emotional or volitional capacity which predisposes the person to commit sexually violent offenses in a degree constituting such a person a menace to the health and safety of others." The statute is codified at K.S.A., Section 59-29a01 *et seq.* (2006).

Thus, although Hendricks was to be released from criminal confinement, he was being civilly committed because of his potential danger to society. This civil confinement was upheld by the U.S. Supreme Court.

The decision was 5–4, with Chief Justice William H. Rehnquist and Justices Clarence Thomas, Sandra Day O'Connor, Antonin Scalia, and Anthony M. Kennedy in the majority. Justices Stephen Breyer, John Paul Stevens, David H. Souter, and Ruth Bader Ginsberg dissented. Justice Clarence Thomas delivered the opinion of the Court.

Facts

[Leroy Hendricks, an inmate with a long history of sexual violence against children, was scheduled for release from prison after serving 10 years for "taking indecent liberties" with two 13-year-old boys.]

Hendricks' history of sexually molesting children dated back to 1955 and included his own stepdaughter and stepson as victims. Hendricks admitted to repeatedly sexually abusing children and stated that when he was stressed, he could not control the urge to abuse children. An expert testified that Hendricks suffered from personality trait disturbance, passive aggressive personality, and pedophilia and that it was likely he would commit sexual offenses against children in the future. Although one expert testified that it was not possible to determine the likelihood of Hendricks' future danger to children, a jury found beyond a reasonable doubt that Hendricks was a sexual predator. The trial judge found that pedophilia qualified as a mental abnormality and thus ordered Hendricks committed under the civil commitment statute.

Issue

[Whether the 1994 law providing for the civil commitment of persons violates the Federal Constitution's Due Process, Double Jeopardy and *Ex Post Facto* Clauses.]

Holding

We hold that the Kansas Sexually Violent Predator Act comports with due process requirements and neither runs afoul of double jeopardy principles nor constitutes an exercise in impermissible *ex post facto* lawmaking.

Rationale

Kansas argues that the Act's definition of "mental abnormality" satisfies "substantive" due process requirements. We agree. Although freedom from physical restraint "has always been at the core of the liberty protected by the Due Process Clause from arbitrary action". . . . that liberty is not absolute. The Court has recognized that an individual's constitutionally protected interest in avoiding physical restraint may be overridden even in the civil context:

The liberty secured by the Constitution of the United States to every person within its jurisdiction does not import an absolute right in each person to be, at all times and in all circumstances, wholly free from restraint. There are manifold restraints to which every person is necessarily subject for the common good. On any other basis organized society could not exist with safety to its members.

Accordingly, States have in certain narrow circumstances provided for the forcible civil detainment of people who are unable to control their behavior and who thereby pose a danger to the public health and safety. . . . We have consistently upheld such involuntary commitment statutes provided the confinement takes place pursuant to proper procedures and evidentiary standards. . . . It thus cannot be said that the involuntary civil confinement of a limited subclass of dangerous persons is contrary to our understanding of ordered liberty. . . .

We granted Hendricks' cross-petition to determine whether the Act violates the Constitution's double jeopardy prohibition or its ban on ex post facto lawmaking. The thrust of Hendricks' argument is that the Act establishes criminal proceedings, hence confinement under it necessarily constitutes punishment. He contends that where, as here, newly enacted "punishment" is predicated upon past conduct for which he has already been convicted and forced to serve a prison sentence, the Constitution's Double Jeopardy and Ex Post Facto Clauses are violated. We are unpersuaded by Hendricks' argument that Kansas has established criminal proceedings. . . .

As a threshold matter, commitment under the Act does not implicate either of the two primary objectives of criminal punishment: retribution or deterrence. The Act's purpose is not retributive because it does not affix culpability for prior criminal conduct. Instead, such conduct is used solely for evidentiary purposes, either to demonstrate that a "mental abnormality" exists or to support a finding of future dangerousness. We have previously concluded that an Illinois statute was nonpunitive even though it was triggered by the commission of a sexual assault, explaining that evidence of the prior criminal conduct was "received not to punish past misdeeds, but primarily to show the accused's mental condition and to predict future behavior." . . . In addition, the Kansas Act does not make a criminal conviction a prerequisite for commitment—persons absolved of criminal responsibility may nonetheless be subject to confinement under the Act. . . . An absence of the necessary criminal responsibility suggests that the State is not seeking retribution for a past misdeed. Thus, the fact that the Act may be "tied to criminal activity" is "insufficient to render the statute punitive." . . .

Moreover, unlike a criminal statute, no finding of scienter is required to commit an individual who is found to be a sexually violent predator; instead, the commitment determination is made based on a "mental abnormality" or "personality disorder" rather than on one's criminal intent. The existence of a scienter requirement is customarily an important element in distinguishing criminal from civil statutes. . . . The absence of such a requirement here is evidence

that the confinement under the statute is not intended to be retributive.

Nor can it be said that the legislature intended the Act to function as a deterrent. Those persons committed under the Act are, by definition, suffering from a "mental abnormality" or a "personality disorder" that prevents them from exercising adequate control over their behavior. Such persons are therefore unlikely to be deterred by the threat of confinement. . . .

Although the civil commitment scheme at issue here does involve an affirmative restraint, "the mere fact that a person is detained does not inexorably lead to the conclusion that the government has imposed punishment." . . .

Hendricks focuses on his confinement's potentially indefinite duration as evidence of the State's punitive intent. That focus, however, is misplaced. Far from any punitive objective, the confinement's duration is instead linked to the stated purposes of the commitment, namely, to hold the person until his mental abnormality no longer causes him to be a threat to others. . . . If, at any time, the confined person is adjudged "safe to be at large," he is statutorily entitled to immediate release. . . .

Finally, Hendricks argues that the Act is necessarily punitive because it fails to offer any legitimate "treatment." Without such treatment, Hendricks asserts, confinement under the Act amounts to little more than disguised punishment. Hendricks' argument assumes that treatment for his condition is available, but that the State has failed (or refused) to provide it. . . . Accepting the . . . apparent determination that treatment is not possible for this category of individuals does not obligate us to adopt its legal conclusions. We have already observed that, under the appropriate circumstances and when accompanied by proper procedures, incapacitation may be a legitimate end of the civil law. . . . While we have upheld state civil commitment statutes that aim both to incapacitate and to treat . . . , we have never held that the Constitution prevents a State from civilly detaining those for whom no treatment is available, but who nevertheless pose a danger to others. A State could hardly be seen as furthering a "punitive" purpose by involuntarily confining persons afflicted with an untreatable highly contagious disease. . . . Similarly, it would be of little value to require treatment as a precondition for civil confinement of the dangerously insane when no acceptable treatment existed. To conclude otherwise would obligate a State to release certain confined individuals who were both mentally ill and dangerous simply because they could not be successfully treated for their afflictions. . . .

Justice Breyer, Dissenting

I agree with the majority that the Kansas Act's "definition of 'mental abnormality'" satisfies the "substantive requirements of the Due Process Clause." Kansas, however, concedes that Hendricks' condition is treatable; yet the Act did not provide Hendricks (or others like him) with any treatment until after his release from prison and only inadequate treatment thereafter. These, and certain other, special features of the Act convince me that it was not simply an effort to commit Hendricks civilly, but rather an effort to inflict further punishment upon him. The Ex Post Facto Clause therefore prohibits the Act's application to Hendricks, who committed his crimes prior to its enactment. . . . Certain resemblances between the Act's "civil commitment" and traditional criminal punishments are obvious. Like criminal imprisonment, the Act's civil commitment amounts to "secure" confinement . . . and "incarceration against one's will." . . . In addition, a basic objective of the Act is incapacitation, which, as Blackstone [English jurist] said in describing an objective of criminal law, is to "deprive the party injuring of the power to do future mischief." . . . Moreover, the Act, like criminal punishment, imposes its confinement (or sanction) only upon an individual who has previously committed a criminal offense. . . . And the Act imposes that confinement through the use of persons (county prosecutors), procedural guarantees (trial by jury, assistance of counsel, psychiatric evaluations), and standards ("beyond a reasonable doubt") traditionally associated with the criminal law.

These obvious resemblances by themselves, however, are not legally sufficient to transform what the Act calls "civil commitment" into a criminal punishment. . . . In this circumstance, with important features of the Act pointing in opposite directions, I would place particular importance on those features that would likely distinguish between a basically punitive and a basically nonpunitive purpose. . . . When a State believes that treatment does exist, and then couples that admission with a legislatively required delay of such treatment until a person is at the end of his jail term (so that further incapacitation is therefore necessary), such a legislative scheme begins to look punitive. . . . The statutory provisions before us do amount to punishment primarily because, as I have said, the legislature did not tailor the statute to fit the nonpunitive civil aim of treatment, which it concedes exists in Hendricks' case. The Clause in these circumstances does not stand as an obstacle to achieving important protections for the public safety; rather it provides an assurance that where so significant restriction of an individual's basic freedoms is at issue, a State cannot cut corners. Rather, the legislature must hew to the Constitution's liberty-protecting line.

For Discussion

The U.S. Supreme Court makes a distinction between civil and criminal confinement to avoid the issues of due process, double jeopardy, and ex post facto. This decision will allow states to involuntarily commit sexual predators who are found to suffer a mental abnormality. Do you agree that civilly confining Hendricks is not punishment? Does this case adequately draw the line between civil and criminal law to justify the indefinite confinement of Hendricks? By focusing on retribution and deterrence, is the U.S. Supreme Court improperly ignoring the other reasons for punishment—incapacitation and rehabilitation?

INTERNET ACTIVITY

1. Go to http://www.uscourts.gov/courtlinks/ (accessed 17 June 2008), and locate your region on the U.S. map. Name the states that are included within your federal circuit court of appeals. What can you find out about the U.S. Supreme Court from this site?

2. Go online to FindLaw, http://caselaw.lp.findlaw.com/data/constitution/amendment14/ (accessed 17 June 2008), and research about the void-for-vagueness doctrine, due process, equal protection, capital punishment, and equal protection and race.

NOTES

1. *Furman v. Georgia*, 408 U.S. 238 (1972).
2. *Gregg v. Georgia*, 428 U.S. 153 (1976).
3. For a discussion, see David Fogel, *We Are the Living Proof: the Justice Model for Corrections*, 2d ed. (Cincinnati: W. H. Anderson, 1979).
4. "Molester Seeks Castration; Texas Agrees," *New York Times* (5 April 1996), p. 9; "Castration Is Allowable, Attorney General Says," *Houston Chronicle* (5 April 1996), p. 1; "Capitol Notebook: 75th Legislature," *Houston Chronicle* (4 April 1997), p. 29.
5. "Dallas Child Molester Undergoes Castration," *Dallas Morning News* (3 March 2004), p. 1. See Tex. Penal Code, Sections 501.061 and 501.062 (2008).
6. Calif. Penal Code, Section 645 (2008).
7. Greg Pogarsky, "Identifying 'Deterrable' Offenders: Implications for Research on Deterrence," *Justice Quarterly* 19, no. 3 (September 2002): 431–452, quotation is on p. 448.
8. See the Sentence Reform Act of 1984, U.S. Code, Title 18, Section 3551 *et seq.*; and U.S. Code, Title 287, Sections 991–998 (2009).
9. Compare Francis A. Allen, "Criminal Justice, Legal Values and the Rehabilitative Ideal," *Journal of Criminal Law, Criminology, and Police Science* 50 (September–October, 1959): 226–232, with Allen, *The Decline of the Rehabilitative Ideal: Penal Policy and Social Purpose* (New Haven, Conn.: Yale University Press, 1981).
10. Cal Pen Code, Section 1210.1 (2008).
11. *State v. Skakel*, 2001 Conn. Super. LEXIS 3548 (Conn. Super. Ct. 11 December 2001), *subsequent appeal*, 888 A.2d 985 (Conn. Sup. Ct., 2006), *cert. denied, Skakel v. Connecticut*, 549 U.S. 1030 (2006).
12. *Southern Pacific Co. v. Jensen*, 244 U.S. 205 (1917).
13. Oliver W. Holmes Jr., *The Common Law* (Boston: Little, Brown, 1881), pp. 1–2.
14. *Blackledge v. Perry*, 417 U.S. 21 (1974), *overruled on other grounds, Bordenkircher v. Hayes*, 434 U.S. 357 (1978).
15. *United States v. Richardson*, 856 F.2d 644 (4th Cir. 1988), case citations omitted.

16. *Lee v. Wisconsin State Board of Dental Examiners*, 139 N.W.2d 61, 65 (Wis. 1966), quoting Webster's *New International Dictionary* (3d ed.).

17. *Connally v. General Construction Co.*, 269 U.S. 385 (1926).

18. Cal Pen Code, Section 647(e) (1983). The current statute is similar, with the addition of feminine references and the changing of *reasonable man* to *reasonable person*.

19. *Kolender v. Lawson*, 461 U.S. 352 (1983).

20. *Horn v. City of Montgomery*, Ala., 619 So.2d 949 (Ala. Crim.Ct.App. 1993), cases and citations omitted.

21. U.S. Constitution, Article I, Section 9(3).

22. *Collins v. Youngblood*, 497 U.S. 37 (1990).

23. *Lynce v. Mathis*, 519 U.S. 433 (1997).

24. See *Smith v. Doe*, 538 U.S. 84 (2003). The statute in question was the Alaska Sex Offender Registration Act, 1994 Alaska Sess. Laws 41 (1994).

25. *Cummings v. Missouri*, 71 U.S. (4 Wall.) 277 (1867).

26. *Ex parte Garland*, 71 U.S. (4 Wall.) 333 (1866).

27. *Nixon v. Administrator of General Services*, 433 U.S. 425 (1977).

28. See, for example, *State v. Babbitt*, 457 A.2d 1049 (R.I. 1983).

29. *Blockburger v. United States*, 284 U.S. 299 (1932).

30. See *Weems v. United States*, 217 U.S. 349 (1910).

31. See *Coker v. Georgia*, 433 U.S. 584 (1977).

32. *State v. Kennedy*, 957 So.2d 757 (La. 2007), *rev'd*, remanded, *Kennedy v. Louisiana*, 128 S.Ct. 2641 (2008).

33. *Baze v. Rees*, 128 S.Ct. 1520 (2008). The Kentucky statute at issue is codified at K.R.S. 431.220 (2007).

34. *Burton v. Livingston*, 791 F.2d 97, 99–100 (8th Cir. 1986), citations omitted.

35. Alaska Constitution, Article I, Section 22 (2005).

36. *Griswold v. Connecticut*, 381 U.S. 479 (1965).

37. Conn. Gen. Stats., Sections 53–32 and 54–196 (1965).

38. *In re Winship*, 397 U.S. 358, 363–364 (1970), case names and citations omitted.

39. See *Mullaney v. Wilbur*, 421 U.S. 684 (1975); and *Patterson v. New York*, 432 U.S. 197 (1977).

40. *Victor v. Nebraska*, 551 U.S. 1 (1994).

41. *Baird v. Eisenstadt*, 405 U.S. 438 (1972).

42. Mass. Gen. Laws Ann., Chapter 272, Section 21 (1972).

43. *Baird v. Eisenstadt*, 405 U.S. 438 (1972).

CHAPTER 2

Elements of a Crime

INTRODUCTION

This chapter discusses the **elements of a crime** that are applicable to criminal acts in U.S. criminal justice systems. Subsequent chapters consider the elements of specific crimes. Although it is possible to explain and illustrate the general elements of a crime, interpretations may differ considerably. Thus, in the actual practice of criminal law, it is important to analyze the case law of a specific jurisdiction.

Also important to U.S. criminal law is the concept that usually only the guilty party may be punished, although this concept must be understood in the context of other legal principles, which are discussed in Chapter 3. It is also possible to be held liable for the failure to control the behavior of another, a concept discussed later in this chapter.

THE ELEMENTS OF A CRIME

In general, for an act to be a crime in U.S. criminal justices systems, four elements must be present:

1. A criminal act
2. A criminal state of mind
3. Concurrence of a criminal act and a criminal state of mind
4. Causation

Some crimes also require additional or **attendant circumstances**, which are facts surrounding a crime. A subsequent section of this chapter is devoted to attendant circumstances.

The four general elements of a crime are diagramed in Figure 2.1. The discussion of each of these elements constitutes the major focus of this chapter.

A Criminal Act

Although it might seem simplistic to state that a crime involves a criminal act, the matter is complex. The term *criminal act*, or ***actus reus***, is open to interpretation. Technically, the term means a wrongful deed that, if combined with the other elements of a crime, may result in the legal arrest, trial, and conviction of the accused. This definition eliminates the possibility of criminal punishment for one's thoughts.

There are many reasons for not punishing thoughts. Administering a system that did so would be difficult, if not impossible, because we cannot punish something about which we have no knowledge. Personal privacy, very important in U.S. criminal justice systems, would be invaded and life would be intolerable. We cherish the freedom to daydream and to fantasize even when our thoughts and fantasies concern unacceptable, perhaps illegal, behavior. It is quite another matter, however, when certain thoughts are translated into actions. Thus, it is not a crime to have obscene thoughts, but it is illegal to possess obscene materials. One may think about pornography involving children; it is illegal to possess such pornography. A college student may fantasize about drinking; it is illegal for that student to possess or drink alcoholic beverages if he or she is under the legal age for such behavior. Finally, thoughts that are translated into agreements, as in the case of conspiracy (discussed in Chapter 3), may be sufficient to constitute a criminal act.

It is also a general principle of U.S. criminal justice systems that a person may not be punished for a status, such as being a drug addict. This principle was demonstrated in the 1962 landmark case of *Robinson v. California*, in which the U.S. Supreme Court invalidated a state statute that made it a misdemeanor for a person to "be addicted to the use of narcotics." The penalty for conviction of this crime was a mandatory jail term of not less than 90 days. In its ruling, the Supreme Court emphasized that the length of that jail term was not

Figure 2.1 Elements of a Crime

cruel and unusual punishment per se, but it was cruel and unusual to make the status of being an addict a crime for which a person could be "continuously guilty . . . whether or not he has ever used or possessed any narcotics within the State, and whether or not he has been guilty of any antisocial behavior there." According to the Court, this would be the same as making it a crime "for a person to be mentally ill, or a leper, or to be afflicted with a venereal disease."[1]

Given the requirement of a criminal act, we must decide what constitutes an act. Some scholars and statutes include involuntary acts, but most require a *voluntary* act. This would exclude such actions as reflexes or convulsions, movements made during sleep or unconsciousness, and conduct engaged in while a person is under hypnosis, as well as any other movements that are made without the person's determination or effort.

The Exclusion of Involuntary Conduct

Although it is true that involuntary actions may, and often do, affect the health and welfare of others, these acts are usually not considered criminal; they may, however, result in *civil* liability. Assume, for example, that while driving your car you have an unexpected stroke, lose control, run into another car, and cause a death. This is not a voluntary act and generally you will not be charged with a criminal act, although you might be sued for the civil act of wrongful death. Because you had no reason to know that you might have a stroke, it would not be considered fair in U.S. criminal justice systems to hold you criminally responsible for your act. The situation might be different, however, if you had previously had a stroke and had reason to believe you could have another. In that situation you would have engaged in an act—driving a car—that you knew or should have known could result in the serious injury or death of another human being. The following excerpt from *People v. Decina*, decided in 1956 by the New York Court of Appeals, illustrates this concept of criminal **culpability**.[2]

PEOPLE v. DECINA
138 N.E.2d 799 (N.Y. 1956)

[The defendant drove his car on a public highway, had an epileptic seizure, lost control of his car, and killed four people. He was charged with violation of a criminal statute that provided, "A person who operates or drives any vehicle of any kind in a reckless or culpably negligent manner, whereby a human being is killed, is guilty of criminal negligence in the operation of a vehicle resulting in death." In upholding the conviction, the court made the following statement:]

[T]his defendant knew he was subject to epileptic attacks and seizures that might strike at any time. He also knew that a moving vehicle uncontrolled on a public highway is a highly dangerous instrumentality capable of unrestrained destruction. With this *knowledge*, and without anyone accompanying him, he deliberately took a chance. . . . How can we say as a matter of law that this did not amount to culpable negligence? . . .

To hold otherwise would be to say that a man may freely indulge himself in liquor in the same hope that it will not affect his driving, and if it later develops that ensuing intoxication causes dangerous and reckless driving resulting in death, his unconsciousness or involuntariness at that time would relieve him from prosecution under the statute. His awareness of a condition which he knows may produce such consequences as here, and his disregard of the consequences, renders him liable for culpable negligence, as the courts below have properly held. To have a sudden sleeping spell, an unexpected heart or other disabling attack, without any prior knowledge or warning thereof, is an altogether different situation.

The court's last sentence raises interesting legal questions, for example, in the reference to sleeping. Although committing a crime during your sleep may not subject you to the criminal law, it is not necessarily true that falling asleep at the wheel will relieve you of criminal responsibility for wrongful death or injury that results when the car crashes. The facts of each case must be examined carefully before criminal culpability is determined. That is what makes law exciting and challenging but also difficult.

Proof of an Act

Although involuntary conduct may be excluded from the act requirement of a crime, it is not always easy to determine the difference between a voluntary act and an involuntary act. Likewise, it may be difficult to prove that an act occurred even when it did.

Consider the following example, based on a 1971 case. The criminal code provided that whoever within a federal prison "conveys . . . from place to place any [specific weapons] . . . designed to kill, injure, or disable any officer, agent, employee, or inmate thereof" may be charged with an offense and, if convicted, incarcerated for not more than 10 years. How would you interpret the following facts under that statute? Greschner and Logan were inmates in a federal penitentiary. While Logan was cutting Greschner's hair, a fight between the two developed. Greschner, who swung at Logan, was seen holding a weapon at some point during the fight. A correctional officer intervened, stopped the fight, and ordered Greschner, who was not harmed, to return to his cell after surrendering a homemade knife to the officer.

Did Greschner *convey* a weapon in terms of the statute under which he was charged? Although the appellate court upheld Greschner's assault conviction, it reversed the conveying conviction for lack of sufficient evidence. The court emphasized that although the defendant possessed and used the weapon, there was no evidence that he *transported* it from place to place within the institution. Although it is possible that Greschner did convey the weapon, the government did not offer evidence of that element at trial. To the contrary, the evidence suggested that another inmate gave Greschner the weapon after he was attacked by Logan.[3]

The same court that reversed Greschner's conveyance conviction upheld that of another inmate in whose case there was evidence that he transported the weapon within the prison before being apprehended.[4] These two cases illustrate that the facts of each case must be considered carefully. There must be sufficient evidence to support each element of the crime. The prosecution has the burden of proving "beyond a reasonable doubt every element of the charged offense."[5]

A final issue that applies to proving an act but is usually associated primarily with the crime of murder is that of **corpus delicti**, which means "the body of the crime." It refers to the body or other material substance of a crime that constitutes the foundation of that particular crime. The remains of a burned building might be the *corpus delicti* of an alleged arson. The *corpus delicti* is required as **corroborating evidence** that the crime occurred. *Corroborating evidence* includes additional data to support the crime charged, especially in rape and other cases in which there were no witnesses to the alleged act, and it is crucial to proving a case. There are some exceptions to the *corpus delicti* requirement because it is difficult if not impossible to get a tangible *corpus delicti* for some crimes, such as attempt crimes, conspiracy, and income tax evasion.

Possession as an Act

An act might include possession of illegal goods, such as narcotics, alcohol, or stolen property. Possession is considered an act; however, as with other acts, possession alone may not be sufficient for a successful criminal prosecution. Generally when a criminal statute defines possession as a crime, the word is interpreted to mean *conscious* possession, although there may be some exceptions. Young people may be most familiar with the charge of MIP, minor in possession (of alcohol or other illegal drugs). It is possible that all occupants in a car who are under the legal drinking age may be charged with MIP even though they claim that they were not aware of the presence of alcohol in the car. The same could apply to a person of any age riding in a car in which illegal drugs are found by law enforcement officers. In these cases officers might rely on the concept of **constructive possession**—which technically means a person is in a position to exercise control or dominion over something—rather than actual possession.

Criminal Failure to Act

Omission or failure to act may constitute an act for purposes of criminal culpability but only when there is a **legal duty** to act. A legal duty is one imposed by statutory or case law or through an explicit or implied contract, such as the duty imposed on parents to come to the aid of their children, on physicians to aid their patients, or any duty imposed by such contracts as marriage, employment, or custody.

These teens were drinking liquor at a party after their senior prom. A person who is in illegal possession of alcohol (for example, a minor) or illegal drugs may be charged with the crime of possession. Possession may be actual or constructive. In the case of the latter, a minor may be arrested for the crime of minor in possession if he or she is a passenger in a car in which illegal drugs or alcohol are found. It is not a defense for the arrestee to claim that he or she did not know the illegal contraband was in the car. (Mark Peterson/Corbis)

A legal duty might also exist when a person takes affirmative action that creates a situation of danger to a person to whom no duty was previously allowed. For example, a California appellate court upheld the conviction of a defendant who met a man, who appeared to be drugged, at a bar. The two went to the defendant's home, and the guest asked the defendant for a spoon. The defendant gave him one, knowing that he wanted it for using drugs. Subsequently the victim passed out, and the defendant returned to the bar, leaving the victim at her home. When the defendant returned to her home, the victim was unconscious; the next morning he was dead. The defendant was charged with several crimes, including involuntary manslaughter, which under California law includes acts committed "without due caution and circumspection." The conviction was upheld by the appellate court, which emphasized that the defendant had a civil duty to exercise some care when she became aware that the victim needed medical attention.[6]

The failure to exercise due care is referred to as a **tort**, which literally means a wrong, and in law, that wrongful act may result in legal civil liability (in this case, for example, had the victim lived he could have sued the defendant; upon his death, his estate would have a cause of action for wrongful death). A tort may also be a crime, and in this case, the defendant's act of taking the victim to her home and then leaving him alone rather than seeking adequate medical help constituted criminal **negligence** (an act that a reasonable person would not do, or would not fail to do under similar circumstances) that was sufficient to sustain her criminal conviction after the victim's death.

Failure to render aid after causing a person to be injured may also create a duty to act. In 2003, Chante J. Mallard was sentenced to 50 years in prison for murder, to be served concurrently with a 10-year term for tampering with evidence. While driving, Mallard hit a homeless man, and the impact propelled the victim onto the car's windshield. Mallard drove the car home and parked it in her garage with the victim impaled on it. He bled to death. A medical expert testified at the trial that the victim could have lived had he received immediate medical attention. A jury deliberated less than an hour before voting to convict Mallard.[7]

The fact that under most criminal statutes there is no general affirmative duty to prevent crime is illus-

Chante J. Mallard is serving 50 years in prison for her failure to come to the aid of a person she injured in an automobile accident. The victim died. Mallard is also serving a 10-year sentence for tampering with the evidence in this case. (Ron Ellis/AP Images)

trated by the highly publicized case featured in Focus 2.1. The moral outrage at hearing that some people not only watched but cheered during a gang rape in New Bedford, Massachusetts, led some states to consider legislation to criminalize the failure to act to help prevent a crime. Despite the moral outrage one might develop in reading the facts of the New Bedford and other similar cases, it is important to consider why the law is reluctant to legislate affirmative action to aid others. Requiring people to take affirmative action to aid others creates problems. How much action should be required? What if the bystander is injured or killed by taking preventive action?

If you believe the law should require all of us to attempt to prevent alleged crimes, what would you require bystanders to do in a situation like the one in New Bedford? It is one thing to require people to notify law enforcement authorities, as the new California law requires, but quite another to require them to try to stop the offender. This case is easily distinguishable

from the Mallard case in that Mallard put the victim in a situation that obligated her legally to assist him or call for help.

One final point should be mentioned in this discussion of the act requirement for a crime. Failure to act when there is a legal duty to act is not a crime unless that failure *caused* the harm, injury, or death. A discussion of causation occurs later in this chapter. But first, we will consider the second major element of criminal behavior: intent.

A Criminal Intent

According to two noted legal scholars, "Deeply ingrained in human nature is the tendency to distinguish intended results from accidental happenings."[8] It makes a difference to us whether an apparent act of kindness is perceived as having been done with the appropriate feelings or accidentally. In fact, early in his classic book *The Common Law*, the late jurist Oliver Wendell Holmes stated that "even a dog distinguishes between being stumbled over and being kicked."[9]

Thus, in U.S. criminal justice systems, we do not, in most cases, impose culpability upon an act alone; a criminal state of mind must concur with the criminal act. A criminal act requires a criminal **intent** (the state of mind referring to the willful commission of an act or the omission of an act one has a legal duty to perform). The term ***mens rea*** is used even in popular writing to refer to criminal intent, yet it is one of the most debated and frequently litigated concepts in criminal law. Its literal meaning is "a guilty mind," and it refers to the intent requirement of criminal law. The statement that *mens rea* is a required element of a crime, however, is misleading if taken literally. As we discuss later in this chapter, some acts involving fault but unaccompanied by a guilty mind may constitute crimes.

The intent element required for criminal culpability is one of the most difficult to interpret and apply. Historically intent was divided into general intent and specific intent. Those concepts, however, are difficult to distinguish. Simply stated, *general intent* refers to the willful commission of an act (or the omission of an act one has a legal duty to perform); *specific intent* requires more. The difference may be illustrated by the common law crime of larceny-theft, one of the four serious property crimes as defined by the FBI's *Uniform Crime Reports* and the most frequently committed of all serious crimes as defined by that source. To establish that a defendant committed larceny-theft, the prosecution

In the spring of 1983, four men raped a young woman repeatedly in a New Bedford, Massachusetts, bar. They were indicted along with two men who were arrested for encouraging them while holding the woman down on the bar table where the acts occurred. Numerous witnesses observed the gang rape without calling the police, some reportedly yelling, "Go for it." The incident and subsequent trial received considerable media attention. The trial resulted in two acquittals and two convictions.

Public outrage at the New Bedford case led to attempts to enact statutes to require bystanders, under penalty of civil or criminal law, to come to the aid of crime victims. It was argued that at a minimum the law should require witnesses to call the police. Advocates said that the law should require affirmative action to intervene when alleged criminal acts are observed.[1]

The refusal of bystanders to come to the aid of the New Bedford rape victim was reminiscent of the widely publicized 1967 case of Kitty Genovese, whose New York neighbors refused to come to her aid while she was being stabbed repeatedly. In discussing these and other cases, criminologist Gilbert Geis stated, "It's becoming a much more anonymous society, a much more uncaring society." Many bystanders do not want to become involved in any way in alleged criminal activity. Even as a witness, a person may be threatened; it is easier to avoid involvement. In contrast, some bystanders have taken dangerous affirmative action to save the lives of victims, as illustrated by those who came to the aid of a truck driver who was beaten in Los Angeles during the riots following the acquittal in state court of four white police officers accused of using excessive force in apprehending Rodney King in 1992.[2]

Legally the issue is not whether bystanders should go to the aid of others but whether the law should *require* them to do so.

1. Summarized by the author from media accounts.
2. "Silent Crime: Bystanders Who Say, Do Nothing," *Orlando Sentinel* (11 May 1993), p. 5.

must prove that the defendant took the property of another *and* that the accused meant to carry away that property, which implies a general intent to commit the forbidden act.

An additional element of larceny-theft, however, is a specific intent, usually stated as the intent to steal the property. That is, the prosecution must prove that the defendant intended to deprive the owner of the property permanently or for an unreasonable length of time, not just that the property was taken away intentionally. Theoretically a person could intend to take property away from its lawful owner without intending to steal it, as, for example, in cases of taking an automobile for the sole purpose of a short joy ride.

Some scholars have suggested that because of the confusion, the terms *general intent* and *specific intent* be abandoned and that we refer only to the intent requirement. One solution to the confusion between the two terms is illustrated by the Model Penal Code's provision concerning the general requirements of criminal culpability, reproduced in Focus 2.2. This code utilizes four levels of culpability: purposely, knowingly, recklessly, and negligently. The Model Penal Code (MPC) defines each level of intent, ranging from the highest level (purposely) to the lowest (negligently).

In categorizing levels of culpability, the Model Penal Code distinguishes between *purposely* and *knowingly*. Both involve knowledge, but *purposely* is a stronger, more culpable intent because the defendant *consciously* intended to engage in the criminal act or to bring about a particular result, as distinct from having been "practically certain" that particular results would follow the act.

Both *purposely* and *knowingly* are to be distinguished from *recklessly*, which involves serious risks and which, according to the MPC comments, "resembles acting knowingly in that a state of awareness is involved, but the awareness is of risk, that is of a probability less than substantial certainty; the matter is contingent from the actor's point of view."[10]

To constitute recklessness, the risk must be substantial *and* unjustified. The substantial risk taken by a surgeon who knows that an operation *may* be fatal but who also knows that the patient will die without the operation does not constitute reckless behavior under this code. The MPC comments indicate that there is no way to make the definition of recklessness more specific; the jury must analyze the facts of each case in determining whether specific acts are reckless.

There is some disagreement over the inclusion within the criminal law of acts that involve negligence, the fourth level of culpability in the MPC. Negligence refers to acts that a reasonable person would not do or the failure to do something that a reasonable person would do under the same or similar circumstances. Negligence does not require a criminal intent.

FOCUS 2.2 General Requirements of Culpability

Model Penal Code, Section 2.02

(1) *Minimum Requirements of Culpability.* Except as provided in Section 2.05, a person is not guilty of an offense unless he acted purposely, knowingly, recklessly or negligently, as the law may require, with respect to each material element of the offense.

(2) *Kinds of Culpability Defined.*

   (a) *Purposely.*

   A person acts proposely with respect to a material element of an offense when:

     (i) if the element involves the nature of his conduct or a result thereof, it is his conscious object to engage in conduct of that nature or to cause such a result; and

     (ii) if the element involves the attendant circumstances, he is aware of the existence of such circumstances or he believes or hopes that they exist.

   (b) *Knowingly.*

   A person acts knowingly with respect to a material element of an offense when:

     (i) if the element involves the nature of his conduct or the attendant circumstances, he is aware that his conduct is of that nature or that such circumstances exist; and

     (ii) if the element involves the result of his conduct, he is aware that it is practically certain that his conduct will cause such a result.

   (c) *Recklessly.*

   A person acts recklessly with respect to a material element of an offense when he consciously disregards a substantial and unjustifiable risk that the material element exists or will result from his conduct. The risk must be of such a nature and degree that, considering the nature and purpose of the actor's conduct and the circumstances known to him, its disregard involves a gross deviation from the standard of conduct that a law-abiding person would observe in the actor's situation.

   (d) *Negligently.*

   A person acts negligently with respect to a material element of an offense when he should be aware of a substantial and unjustifiable risk that the material element exists or will result from his conduct. The risk must be of such a nature and degree that the actor's failure to perceive it, considering the nature and purpose of his conduct and the circumstances known to him, involves a gross deviation from the standard of care that a reasonable person would observe in the actor's situation.

It may be argued that none of the purposes of criminal punishment discussed in Chapter 1 are furthered by including negligent acts within the criminal law, but generally only conduct that is *grossly* negligent, which is conduct that is more culpable than ordinary negligence, is included. Ordinary negligence is sufficient to establish a cause of action in civil law but not in criminal law. For example, a surgeon who operates on a patient's left foot when permission had been given only for surgery on the right foot has committed an unauthorized act. This negligence may sustain a legal action for which the patient could receive civil damages, but in all probability no attempt would be made to prosecute the doctor under a criminal statute, even though technically the act constitutes a battery, which is a crime as well as a civil wrong. If, however, the surgeon had performed this surgery while under the influence of alcohol, criminal charges might be filed.

Problems of Interpretation

The MPC provisions for criminal culpability have been widely adopted, at times with modifications, but there are problems with interpretation of the levels of culpability. Some problems of applying the provisions are illustrated by a Texas case. Under the Texas statute the highest level is intentionally, rather than the MPC's purposely. Amelia Alvarado was charged with injury to a child under the Texas Penal Code, which provided as follows: "A person commits an offense if he intentionally, knowingly, recklessly or with criminal negligence engages in conduct that causes serious bodily injury . . . to a child who is 14 years of age or younger."[11]

Alvarado, who was charged with intentionally and knowingly causing serious bodily injury to her child by placing him in a tub of hot water, was convicted under this statute. On appeal her attorney argued that the trial judge was in error when he instructed the jury that a person acts intentionally, or with intent, when it is that person's "conscious objective or desire to engage in the conduct or cause the result." In other words, for a conviction in this case under this statute, the prosecution was required to prove only that the defendant knowingly or intentionally put the child in hot water.

The defense argued that the statute required the prosecution to prove that the defendant had a "conscious objective or desire to cause serious bodily injury to the child or that she was aware that putting the child in the water was reasonably certain to cause serious bodily injury to the child."[12]

The confusion arose over whether the statute meant that the required level of culpability applied only to the criminal act or also to the result of that act. The appellate court held that the prosecution had to prove that in addition to having the mental culpability required for the commission of the act, the defendant intended or knew that serious bodily injury would result from that act.

Because interpretation problems are extensive in case law, it is important to understand the impossibility of stating what is meant by *intent* in criminal law. Rather, it is necessary to analyze carefully the prior interpretations of a statute before concluding how that statute might apply to the facts of a new case. It is also necessary to consider the intent requirement in terms of state and federal constitutional law.

To illustrate, consider *United States v. X-Citement Video, Inc.*, decided in 1994. The defendant in this case was convicted of violating the federal Protection of Children Against Sexual Exploitation Act of 1977 by purchasing videotapes (and having some of those tapes shipped through interstate commerce) featuring Traci Lords, whose performance in pornographic films while she was an adolescent produced considerable litigation. On appeal the Ninth Circuit reasoned that it would be unconstitutional under the First Amendment (see Appendix A) to convict a defendant under a federal statute prohibiting the distribution, shipping, or receipt of child pornography unless the government proved that the defendant had knowledge that the material involved minority performers. The Ninth Circuit held that the statute did not contain that knowledge requirement; consequently, it was unconstitutional.[13]

The case was appealed to the U.S. Supreme Court, which disagreed that the knowledge requirement was not a part of the statute and upheld the conviction. The case involved a number of issues on appeal, but for our purposes here, only one phase of the holding is relevant. The statute and the Supreme Court's resolution of the major issue are reproduced in the following excerpt from the case.[14]

Traci Lords, who was a child porn star, turned to legitimate theater as she matured. Lords was the underage person who was featured in the pornography at issue in the case of United States v. X-Citement Video, Inc. (Neal Preston/Corbis)

UNITED STATES v. X-CITEMENT VIDEO, INC.

513 U.S. 64 (1994)

Chief Justice William H. Rehnquist delivered the opinion of the Court, in which Justices John Paul Stevens, Sandra Day O'Connor, Anthony M. Kennedy, David H. Souter, Ruth Bader Ginsburg, and Stephen G. Breyer joined. Justice Stevens filed a concurring opinion. Justice Antonin Scalia filed a dissenting opinion, in which Justice Clarence Thomas joined.

The Protection of Children Against Sexual Exploitation Act of 1977, as amended, prohibits the interstate transportation, shipping, receipt, distribution or reproduction of visual depictions of minors engaged in sexually explicit conduct. The Court of Appeals for the Ninth Circuit reversed the conviction of respondents for violation of this Act. It held that the Act did not require that the defendant know that one of the performers was a minor, and that it was therefore facially unconstitutional. We conclude that the Act is properly read to include such a requirement. . . .

[The relevant part of the statute is as follows]:

(a) Any person who—

(1) knowingly transports or ships in interstate or foreign commerce by any means including by computer or mails, any visual depiction, if—

(A) the producing of such visual depiction involves the use of a minor engaging in sexually explicit conduct; and

(B) such visual depiction is of such conduct;

(2) knowingly receives, or distributes, any visual depiction that has been mailed, or has been shipped or transported in interstate or foreign commerce, or which contains materials which have been mailed or so shipped or transported, by any means including by computer; or knowingly reproduces any visual depiction for distribution in interstate or foreign commerce or through the mails, if—

(A) the producing of such visual depiction involves the use of a minor engaging in sexually explicit conduct; and

(B) such visual depiction is of such conduct; . . .

The critical determination which we must make is whether the term "knowingly" in subsections (1) and (2) modifies the phrase "the use of a minor" in subsections (1)(A) and (2)(A). The most natural grammatical reading, adopted by the Ninth Circuit, suggests that the term "knowingly" modifies only the surrounding verbs: transports, ships, receives, distributes, or reproduces. Under this construction, the word "knowingly" would not modify the elements of the minority of the performers, or the sexually explicit nature of the material, because they are set forth in independent clauses separated by interruptive punctuation. . . .

[The Court rejected the Ninth Circuit's interpretation of the statute for several reasons, some of which are complicated constitutional law issues. The Court concluded that in its amendments to the statute Congress did not intend to remove the *mens rea* requirement and that] the term "knowingly" in Section 2252 extends both to the sexually explicit nature of the material and to the age of the performers.

In this decision, the U.S. Supreme Court interpreted the statute as containing an implicit requirement that the government must prove that the accused knew the actor was a minor; thus, the statute as written is constitutional because it does contain a *mens rea* requirement. The Court reasoned that Congress intended to include that requirement because to eliminate it could produce ridiculous consequences. For example, if knowledge of the age of the actor and the content of the material were not required, any person who received materials whose content violated the statute could be prosecuted and convicted. A new resident of an apartment might receive and hold materials for the prior occupant. If those materials violated the statute, the individual could be prosecuted for "knowing receipt" of the mail in violation of the law.

This federal case illustrates the differences in the way courts may interpret the words of statutes and the importance of those interpretations, especially on the element of intent. The next example, an excerpt from a state case, is presented to illustrate the meaning of *general intent* since some states continue to use that concept, along with that of *specific intent*. The case is from Hawaii and involves the issue of whether the appellants intended to violate the state's statute concerning creating a common nuisance by appearing nude in public. The elements of the crime are:

1. The defendant exposes himself or herself

2. In a public place where he or she may be seen by others

3. Under circumstances under which a reasonable trier of fact could conclude there was an intent to offend the community's sense of common decency.

In this case, the appellants were sunbathing on a public beach. One was on his back, the other on his stomach. There were no allegations of specific acts of indecent behavior. The appellants were observed by police officers responding to a call.

ROCKER v. STATE
475 P.2d 684 (1970)

Appearing in the nude is not per se illegal. It must be coupled with the intent to indecently expose oneself. Intent is an element of the crime of common nuisance defined by [the statute]. The intent necessary is a general intent, not a specific intent; i.e., it is not necessary that the exposure be made with the intent that some particular person see it, but only that the exposure was made where it was likely to be observed by others. Thus, the intent may be inferred from the conduct of the accused and the circumstances and environment of the occurrence.

The defendants argue that there is no circumstantial evidence in the record from which a trier of fact could conclude that the element of intent had been proved beyond a reasonable doubt. The issue, therefore, is whether defendants' nude sunbathing at Puu Olai beach at Makena, Maui, was at a place so public that a trier of fact could infer it was intended to be seen by others. The prosecution offered testimony of one of the arresting police officers that the beach was a popular location for fishermen and was in fact one of his favorite fishing spots. Defendants testified that the public in general used the beach, that it was used by fishermen and local residents, and that they observed between 20 and 25 people on the beach over a two-month period. Although the Puu Olai beach is isolated by a hill and a ledge, away from the view of the public road and adjoining beaches, it is accessible by a well-worn path and known to be a favorite location of fishermen to cast and throw fish nets. In view of this and other evidence in the record, we cannot agree with defendants' argument that the trier of fact could not find the beach so public as to justify an inference of intent on the part of defendants to be seen by others.

Additional problems with interpreting the intent requirement are contained in the Case Analysis presented at the end of this chapter.

Proving Criminal Intent

Proving that a defendant intended to commit a crime is not always an easy task, but the law permits an **inference** of intent from relevant facts, as illustrated by *Rocker v. State*. If sufficient **circumstantial evidence** (evidence of facts other than those on which proof is needed but from which deductions or inferences may be drawn concerning the facts in dispute) is presented, the jury may be permitted to infer intent from that evidence. Thus, in the 2002 conviction of Michael Skakel, discussed in Chapter 1, the jury was permitted to find the defendant guilty of killing Martha Moxley 27 years earlier even though the prosecution did not introduce any physical evidence that placed Skakel at the crime scene. There was, however, in the minds of the judge and jury, sufficient circumstantial evidence to lead to the conclusion beyond a reasonable doubt that Skakel committed the crime. Among that evidence were the testimonies of witnesses, a tape recording of a conver-

sation Skakel had with a friend (Skakel did not take the stand to testify), and inconsistent statements concerning Skakel's alibi for the night of the murder. As noted in Chapter 1, the case was upheld on appeal.

Intent must be distinguished from **motive**, which refers to the *why* of a defendant's actions. Hungry parents who steal bread from the local store may do so to feed their families, but that motive does not negate the crime, although in some cases necessity might be a defense (such as breaking into a structure to use a phone to report an emergency; you might not be charged with a crime but probably would have to pay for the cost of the property damage). In general, the state does not have to prove a bad motive to get a conviction, although it may be helpful to do so. As a 1914 California case held, "Proof of motive, while never indispensable in a murder prosecution, is always permissible and often valuable."[15]

The Concurrence of a Criminal Act and a Criminal Intent

It is a general principle of U.S. criminal law that the state of mind, or *mens rea*, and the act, *actus reus*, must coincide. This principle is illustrated by the California Penal Code, which states: "In every crime or public offense there must exist a union, or joint operation of act and intent, or criminal negligence."[16] In addition, there must be evidence that the criminal act is attributable to the *mens rea*. If Susan intends to kill John, buys a gun, fires at John, misses, and then decides not to make another attempt to kill him but later does so accidentally, she has not committed murder. The criminal state of mind required for murder did not coincide with the act that caused John's death.

It is not required, however, that the final result of the criminal act occur at the time of the criminal state of mind. This principle may be illustrated by the common law **year-and-a-day rule**. If a person with the requisite criminal mind struck a victim on the head with the intent to kill but death did not result until later, that person could be charged with murder (assuming sufficient evidence of all other elements of murder) as long as the victim died within one year and a day of the attack. This rule was intended to prevent murder charges from being brought long after the criminal attack, the assumption being that medical science was not advanced sufficiently to determine the cause of remote death. The longer the time period, the more likely it was that the victim died of other causes. With advances in medical science, many jurisdictions have extended or abolished this rule, but its continued importance to the crime of murder is discussed in Chapter 6.

Causation

Even if all of the elements discussed so far are proved beyond a reasonable doubt, defendants may not be held criminally responsible unless it can be shown that their acts *caused* the injury, death, or property damage to the victims. **Causation** is a complicated term, for it has different meanings depending on the circumstances and the type of law involved. In criminal law the search for cause is not easy, but generally we are looking for the *legal* cause of the harm, which technically means the act that is nearest in the order of causation. This does not necessarily mean the act occurs closest to the result. For example, a criminal act committed against a victim who dies later may be followed by other noncriminal acts that contribute to the victim's death. But if the crime is a **substantial factor** (one that a reasonable person might conclude was sufficient to support the resulting injury or death) contributing to that death, it may be judged the legal cause.

In contrast, an **intervening act** (one that occurs after an alleged criminal act and the resulting injury) may be judged the legal cause—or at least a contributing cause—of the injury or death. This, too, can be complicated. For example, a person with the *mens rea* for murder who fires a gun at the victim, misses the heart (for which the bullet was aimed), and hits the arm should not be charged with murder when the targeted victim dies of cancer in two weeks. The actor may, however, be charged with attempted murder. He or she had the requisite intent and committed the criminal act, even if that act was not the cause of death. If, however, the victim is taken to the hospital after being shot in the arm and death ensues as the result of negligently performed surgery, the actor may be held criminally responsible for murder unless the doctor's actions are grossly negligent or intentional. In this hypothetical case, it is also possible that the doctor's acts may be considered an independent intervening cause, relieving the original actor of criminal responsibility for murder, but not of attempted murder.

These principles are illustrated in *People v. Stewart*, in which the defendant was convicted of criminal homicide after stabbing a victim. While operating on the victim's wound, a surgeon discovered a hernia and decided to correct it. During the hernia operation, the victim had a heart attack and died. There was evidence that the anesthesiologist's failure to provide sufficient oxygen caused the heart attack. The jury's guilty verdict on the murder charge against the defendant was reversed on appeal, with the appellate court holding that the anesthesiologist's negligence was a sufficient independent intervening cause to relieve the defendant of criminal responsibility for murder.[17]

The defendant's criminal culpability may also be reduced or eliminated if the victim engages in actions that could contribute to increased injuries or death. Consider the case of a robbery and stabbing victim whose injuries required surgery. After surgery the patient-victim was disoriented and resisted treatment. On four occasions the patient removed the tube that had been inserted into his stomach; he subsequently died. Was his death caused by the robbery and stabbing or by the victim's own acts? A Pennsylvania appellate court upheld the murder conviction, giving the following reason:

> The fact that the victim, while in weakened physical condition and disoriented mental state, pulled out the tubes and created the immediate situation, which resulted in his death, is not such an intervening and independent act sufficient to break the chain of causation of events between the stabbing and the death.[18]

The case might have been decided differently, however, if the deceased had not been disoriented and there was evidence that he was in full control of his actions and had committed suicide.

It is possible that an act not caused by an offender may combine with the offender's act to produce a harmful result. The other causes may be the result of the negligence or criminal activities of other parties or of natural causes such as a storm. When multiple causes occur, it may be difficult to determine whether the offender should be held criminally responsible for the harmful results. *People v. Arzon*, decided by the New York Supreme Court in 1978, illustrates this situation. The defendant in this case was indicted for second-degree murder and third-degree arson after he allegedly set fire to a couch, causing a serious fire on the fifth and sixth floors of an abandoned building. When firefighters found it impossible to bring the fire under control, they left the building. Another fire on the second floor (also thought to be arson but not connected with the defendant) combined with the smoke from the fifth and sixth floors, making evacuation dangerous. One firefighter died. In the following brief excerpt from the case, the court explains its decision to uphold the conviction.[19]

PEOPLE v. ARZON
401 N.Y.S.2d 156 (1978)

[T]he defendant was accused of murder in the second degree, for having, "under circumstances evincing a depraved indifference to human life, recklessly engaged in conduct which created a grave risk of death to another person," thereby causing the death of Martin Celic, and with felony murder [in which death occurs as the result of another felony—usually required to be a serious one, such as robbery or, as in this case, arson]. . . .

There is remarkably little authority on precisely what sort of behavior constitutes "depraved indifference to human life." In the leading case on the subject, the Court of Appeals affirmed the conviction of defendants who had abandoned their helplessly intoxicated robbery victim by the side of a dark road in subfreezing temperature, one-half mile from the nearest structure, without shoes or eyeglasses, with his trousers at his ankles, his shirt pulled up and his outer clothing removed. The court held that while the deceased was actually killed by a passing truck, the defendants' conduct was a sufficiently direct cause of the ensuing death to warrant criminal culpability and that "it is not necessary that the ultimate harm be intended by the actor. It will suffice if it can be said beyond a reasonable doubt . . . that the ultimate harm is something which should have been foreseen as being reasonably related to the acts of the accused."

Clearly, an obscure or merely probable connection between the defendant's conduct and another person's death is not enough to support a charge of homicide. . . .

[T]he defendant's conduct need not be the sole and exclusive factor in the victim's death . . . [but] an individual is criminally liable if his conduct was a sufficiently direct cause of the death, and the ultimate harm is something which should have been foreseen as being reasonably related to his acts. It is irrelevant that, in this instance the fire which had erupted on the second floor intervened, thus contributing to the conditions that culminated in the death of Fireman Celic. . . . Certainly it was foreseeable that firemen would respond to the situation, thus exposing them, along with the persons already present in the vicinity, to a life-threatening danger. The fire set by the defendant was an indispensable link in the chain of events that resulted in the death. It continued to burn out of control, greatly adding to the problem of evacuating the building by blocking off one of the access routes. At the very least, the defendant's act . . . placed the deceased in a position where he was particularly vulnerable to the separate and independent force, in this instance, the fire on the second floor.

ATTENDANT CIRCUMSTANCES

Some crimes have an additional element (or elements) that must accompany the criminal act and the criminal mind. *Attendant circumstances* are facts surrounding an event. This means that a criminal act may not be prosecuted as a crime—even if the guilty mind is present and the act caused the injury, death, or property loss—unless the specified circumstances coexist with the act and guilty mind. For example, under the common law a man could not be prosecuted for raping his wife. Rape statutes excluded marital sexual relations even when they involved force. Thus, to prove rape, it was necessary to prove (in addition to other elements of the crime) that the defendant raped someone who was not his wife. This common law approach to rape has been changed in most U.S. jurisdictions. Other examples of statutes that require attendant circumstances are listed in Focus 2.3.

LIABILITY WITHOUT FAULT

Criminal culpability is imposed in some situations even though no fault or evil intent can be shown on the part of the accused. The three categories of liability without fault—strict liability, vicarious liability, and enterprise liability—are justified on the grounds that:

- In many cases in which they are applied, only minor penalties are assessed.

- Proof of intent is difficult if not impossible to obtain.

- Criminal culpability is essential for compensation of victims as well as for deterrence of others.

Strict Liability

The first type of liability without fault, **strict liability,** is illustrated by the provision in most jurisdictions that selling alcoholic beverages to a minor is a strict liability crime. It is not necessary to prove a criminal intent

---

FOCUS 2.3   **Examples of Statutory Requirements of Attendant Circumstances**

Tex. Penal Code, Chapter 8 (2009)

Section 37.02 Perjury

(a) A person commits an offense if, with intent to deceive and with knowledge of the statement's meaning:

  (1) he makes a false statement under oath or swears to the truth of a false statement previously made and the statement is required or authorized by law to be made under oath; . . .

Attendant Circumstance—Actor must be under oath.

Tex. Penal Code, Chapter 6 (2009)

Section 25.01 Bigamy

(a) An individual commits an offense if:

  (1) he is legally married and he:

    (A) purports to marry or does marry a person other than his spouse . . . under circumstances that would, but for the actor's prior marriage, constitute a marriage; or

    (B) lives with a person other than his spouse in this state under the appearance of being married; . . .

Attendant Circumstance—Proof required of actor's prior marriage.

---

to sell to a minor. Proof that the liquor was sold to the minor is sufficient.

Statutory rape (sexual intercourse, or, in some jurisdictions, other sexual acts as well, with an underage person even though that person allegedly consented) is also a strict liability offense in most jurisdictions. Historically, it made no difference that the minor victim appeared to be of age or that she initiated the activity. The crime of statutory rape was intended for the protection of girls considered to be too young to consent to sex. In recent years some jurisdictions have included boys in their definitions of statutory rape victims. Thus, when a Seattle teacher, Mary Kay Letourneau, age 34, married, and the mother of four children, had sex with a 12-year-old male student, it made no difference whether the student was a willing participant. Washington state law provides the following:

> A person is guilty of rape of a child in the second degree when the person has sexual intercourse with another who is at least twelve years old but less than fourteen years old and not married to the perpetrator and the perpetrator is at least thirty-six months older than the victim.[20]

If the victim is under 12, not married to the perpetrator, and the latter is at least 24 months older than the victim, the crime is that of rape of a child in the first degree.[21]

Over the years the rationale that young people need to be protected from sexual experiences has been questioned in cases involving persons close to the age (usually 16) at which they may legally consent to sex. Today some exceptions are made to the strict liability approach to statutory rape prosecutions, with a few courts allowing the defense that a reasonable person would have thought the alleged victim was of legal age.[22] Because prison sentences for statutory rape may be long, the use of the strict liability approach in this crime is an exception to the rationale that most convictions for strict liability crimes result in relatively minor penalties.

Some jurisdictions distinguish strict liability crimes from related crimes. For example, a New York statute illustrates the distinction between *strict liability crimes* and crimes involving *mental culpability*. Note the first sentence in the following statement concerning the *voluntary act* requirement.

> The minimal requirement for criminal liability is the performance by a person of conduct which includes a voluntary act or the omission to perform an act which he is physically capable of performing. If such conduct is all that is required for commission of a particular offense, or if an offense or some material element thereof does not require a culpable mental state on the part of the actor, such offense is one of "strict liability." If a culpable mental state on the part of the actor is required with respect to every material element of an offense, such offense is one of "mental culpability."[23]

Vicarious Liability

The second type of liability without fault, **vicarious liability**," in contrast to strict liability, dispenses with the requirement of the *actus reus* and imputes the criminal act of one person to another."[24] Vicarious liability is illustrated by the following brief excerpt from a classic case, *Commonwealth v. Koczwara*, decided by the Pennsylvania Supreme Court in 1959. The U.S. Supreme Court refused to review the case, leaving the lower court decision standing. Koczwara, a tavern owner, was convicted, fined $500, and sentenced to three months in prison for vicarious liability when one of his employees sold liquor to a minor. Koczwara had not authorized his employees to violate the Pennsylvania statute prohibiting the sale of liquor to minors, nor did he know the violation had occurred. On appeal, the court upheld the fine but not the prison term, thus illustrating the general principle that persons convicted of crimes under the concept of vicarious liability are usually not sentenced to jail or prison.[25]

COMMONWEALTH v. KOCZWARA

155 A.2d 825 (Pa. 1959), cert. denied, 363 U.S. 848 (1960)

The distinction between respondeat superior in tort law and its application to the criminal law is obvious. In tort law, the doctrine is employed for the purpose of settling the incidence of loss upon the party who can best bear such loss. But the criminal law is supported by totally different concepts. We impose penal treatment upon those who injure or menace social interest, partly in order to reform, partly to prevent the continuation of the anti-social activity and partly to deter others. If a defendant has personally lived up to the social standards of the criminal law and has not menaced or injured anyone, why impose penal treatment? . . .

The Courts of the Commonwealth have already strained to permit the legislature to carry over the civil doctrine of respondeat superior as a means of enforcing the regulatory scheme that covers the liquor trade. We have done so on the theory that the Code established petty misdemeanors involving only light monetary fines. It would be unthinkable to impose vicarious criminal responsibility in cases involving true crimes. . . . Liability for all true crimes, wherein an offense carries with it a jail sentence, must be based exclusively upon personal causation. . . . A man's

 liberty cannot rest on so frail a reed as whether his employee will commit a mistake in judgment.

In *United States v. Park*, decided in 1975, the U.S. Supreme Court emphasized the reasons for vicarious liability. In *Park*, the president of Acme Markets, a major supermarket chain, and the corporation were charged with violations of the federal Food, Drug and Cosmetic Act. Due to the presence of rats in the warehouse, food packaged and shipped by Acme was contaminated. The U.S. Supreme Court rejected the defendant's argument that he should not be found guilty because he did not consciously do any wrong. According to the Supreme Court, the only defense permitted in such cases is for the defendant to produce evidence that he was powerless to correct or prevent the violation. The following brief excerpt explains the Court's reasoning.[26]

UNITED STATES v. PARK

421 U.S. 658 (1975)

Chief Justice Warren E. Burger delivered the opinion of the Court, in which Justices William O. Douglas, William J. Brennan Jr., Byron R. White, Harry A. Blackmun, and William H. Rehnquist joined. Justice Potter Stewart filed a dissenting opinion, in which Justices Thurgood Marshall and Lewis F. Powell Jr. joined.

[Cases] reveal that in providing sanctions which reach and touch the individuals who execute the corporate mission—and this is by no means necessarily confined to a single corporate agent or employee—the Act imposes not only a positive duty to seek out and remedy violations when they occur but also, and primarily, a duty to implement measures that will ensure that violations will not occur. The requirements of foresight and vigilance imposed on responsible corporate agents are beyond question demanding, and perhaps onerous, but they are no more stringent than the public has a right to expect of those who voluntarily assume positions of authority in business enterprises whose services and products affect the health and well-being of the public that supports them. . . .

The duty imposed by Congress on responsible corporate agents is, we emphasize, one that requires the highest standard of foresight and vigilance; but the Act, in its criminal aspect, does not require that which is objectively impossible. The theory upon which responsible corporate agents are held criminally accountable for "causing" violations of the Act permits a claim that a defendant was "powerless" to prevent or correct the violation.

Enterprise Liability

The third type of liability without fault is **enterprise liability**. Under the common law, corporations could not be charged with crimes. This position rested on the argument that corporations had no mind (thus there could be no intent) and no bodies (thus there could be no imprisonment). As the criminal law broke away from that position, the first impositions of criminal responsibility on corporations or other business enterprises were criminal fines. The charges were limited to social welfare situations, such as the mislabeling of drugs or the packing and distribution of adulterated products. Today most courts rule that corporations or business enterprises may be held criminally culpable for the criminal acts (or omissions) of their agents who are acting on behalf of the enterprise.

The U.S. Supreme Court has upheld the constitutionality of criminal laws that impute the acts of agents to their corporations, holding the latter responsible. In *New York Central and Hudson River Railroad Co. v. United States*, the Court said, "The act of agent, while exercising the authority delegated to him . . . may be controlled, in the interest of public policy, by imputing his act to his employer and imposing penalties upon the corporation for which he is acting."[27] This case has been interpreted to mean that the mental state as well as the act of the agent may be imputed to the corporation.

There are limitations to enterprise liability. Corporations are held responsible for the criminal acts of their agents only when those agents are acting within the scope of the corporate employment. Further, if the statute in question provides only for the punishments of death or imprisonment, corporations cannot be held liable, as those punishments would not be applicable. Some courts have ruled that crimes that may be considered inherently personal, such as perjury, rape, murder, or bigamy, are not included within enterprise liability.

One final point regarding enterprise liability is that the previously successful argument by corporations that they should be liable only for property crimes has been challenged. For example, one court emphasized the potential harm to society of personal crimes committed by corporate agents. In *Granite Construction Co. v. Superior Court,* the Fifth District Court of Appeals emphasized the economic benefits that corporations might enjoy if they were not responsible for damages and personal injuries (or deaths) caused by their defective products. The court reasoned, "To get these economic benefits, corporate management may shortcut expensive safety precautions, respond forcibly to strikes, or engage in criminal anticompetitive behavior."[28]

With the increasing number of serious injuries and deaths caused by defectively designed products, we can expect to see more prosecutions under the enterprise theory of criminal culpability. The arguments against criminal culpability are, however, quite strong. In addition to giving serious consideration to the policy aspect of enterprise liability in criminal law, we should consider empirical research on whether the use of the criminal law is a deterrent in these cases or whether such cases are best left to civil law.

In recent years federal prosecutors have gone after corporate executives whom they believe have engaged in significant crimes against the public. But corporate crime is difficult to prosecute, as some of these trials demonstrate. Focus 2.4 summarizes some of the completed and ongoing attempts to bring alleged corporate criminals to justice.

SUMMARY

This chapter focuses on the four general elements of criminal responsibility: a criminal act, a criminal intent, the concurrence of the act and the intent, and causation. Some crimes also require attendant circumstances in addition to these four elements. These elements are discussed in more detail in subsequent chapters in connection with specific crimes, such as murder, but the purpose of this chapter is to establish the foundation for an understanding of the general elements of a crime.

All crimes must involve a criminal act or a failure to act where there is a legal duty to act. We may not be prosecuted for our criminal thoughts, but criminal culpability may exist once we take a substantial step toward a criminal act. Involuntary reflexes or convulsions, bodily movements during sleep or unconsciousness, or conduct during hypnosis are not considered voluntary acts, as they do not occur with the volition of the actor. Some voluntary acts may be criminal but may not result in criminal culpability because of recognized defenses, which are discussed in Chapters 4 and 5. But critical here is the understanding that the act (or failure to act) must have occurred through the volition of the actor.

The second general element of a crime is that a criminal intent, or *mens rea*, must be proved. The

FOCUS 2.4 Government Prosecutions of High-Profile Corporate Executives

In recent years, corporate crime has become a high priority of U.S. attorneys, who have brought prosecutions against corporate executives accused of looting their companies and the public. The December 2001 bankruptcy filing by the Houston, Texas, energy giant Enron, resulting in the loss of jobs and retirement pensions of over 4,500 workers, led the government to investigate possible criminal actions that caused or at least contributed to the downfall of Enron, once listed as the seventh-largest company on the Fortune 500 list of corporations. Enron's founder, Kenneth L. Lay, was convicted, but he died unexpectedly prior to his sentencing; under the laws of federal criminal procedure, his conviction was vacated since he could not appeal.

Enron's former chief financial officer (CFO), Andrew Fastow, pleaded guilty to two charges of conspiracy and agreed to forfeit $23.8 million of the funds he received as a result of his illegal activities at Enron. Fastow was to be sentenced to 10 years in prison, but the trial judge sentenced him to only 6 years, stating that 10 was unreasonable.[1] Fastow and his wife, Lea, who pleaded guilty to one misdemeanor count of filing a false tax return, asked for and received permission to serve their prison sentences so that their two small children would have one parent at home. Lea Fastow, who was sentenced to 1 year, served her term first and was released in July 2005, after which her husband began serving his prison term.

Enron's former chief executive officer (CEO), Jeffrey Skilling, was convicted and sentenced to 24.3 years in prison. With good behavior and participation in a substance abuse program, Skilling could reduce the time he must serve by 54 days a year. At

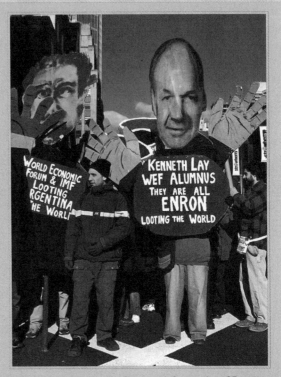

Kenneth L. Lay, founder and former chief executive of Enron Corporation, was charged with defrauding the company's investors, leading to the collapse of the company. Lay was convicted but died before he could appeal; under federal criminal procedural laws, his conviction was vacated. (David Grossman/ The ImageWorks)

problems with interpreting and proving criminal intent were discussed.

The third element of a crime requires concurrence of the criminal act and the criminal intent. And finally, the fourth general element requires that the criminal act and intent, occurring together, must have caused the result in question. All intervening variables must be excluded. Causation involves one of the most difficult areas of proof, often because we do not know enough about the problem, we cannot get sufficient evidence, or there may be more than one actual cause.

In addition to these four elements, some crimes require the proof of attendant circumstances. Normally these circumstances are specified by the statute establishing the crime, and they may not always require the same level of criminal intent as that required to prove the act and the state of mind.

The final section of this chapter discussed those areas of criminal liability that are considered to be liability without fault. Some acts are considered so important that the criminal law imposes liability even when the actors do not realize they are violating a law, such as an adult who engages in sex with a minor, even if the adult thinks the minor is of legal age to consent and even if the minor did consent. This section discussed the three types of liability without fault: strict liability, vicarious liability, and enterprise liability.

Even if all of the elements of a crime are proved beyond a reasonable doubt, as we noted in Chapter 1, the jury (or judge if the case is not tried before a jury) may return a verdict of not guilty. In addition, by presenting an adequate defense, the defendant may avoid (or reduce the level of) criminal responsibility, despite the prosecution's successful presentation of sufficient evi-

Skilling's sentencing, the trial judge stated that Skilling's crimes "imposed on hundreds if not thousands a life sentence of poverty" [as the result of losing their jobs and pensions.][2]

Former Enron treasurer Ben Gilsan Jr. is serving a five-year term at a low-security federal institution near Austin, Texas, after pleading guilty to conspiracy to commit wire and securities fraud. Other former Enron employees have also been convicted, but one conviction associated with the Enron scandal is of particular importance to corporate liability.

After a six-week trial, federal prosecutors won a conviction against Arthur Andersen, one of the world's largest accounting firms, for obstruction of justice in shredding documents in the case of their client, Enron. The company was placed on five years' probation and fined $500,000. In June 2004, a federal court upheld the conviction, but in July 2005, the U.S. Supreme Court reversed on the grounds that the jury instruction was defective. Chief Justice William H. Rehnquist delivered the opinion for a unanimous court, noting that the jury instruction dealt with the issue of what is meant by "knowingly . . . corruptly persuade" another person "with intent to . . . cause" that person to "withhold" documents from, or "alter" documents for use in, an "official proceeding." The Supreme Court held that in order to "knowingly corruptly persuade," one must be "conscious of wrongdoing," in contrast to the jury instruction, which, in effect, permitted the jury to find guilt without the accounting firm being conscious of wrongdoing. The jury was told that it could convict "if it found petitioner intended to 'subvert,

undermine, or impede' governmental factfinding by suggesting to its employees that they enforce the document retention policy. . . . "Dishonesty' was no longer necessary to a finding of guilt, and it was enough for petitioner to have simply 'impeded' the Government's factfinding ability."[3]

In Andersen, the Supreme Court referred to *United States v. X-Citement Video, Inc.*, excerpted earlier in this chapter. Recall that in that case the issue was whether the word *knowingly* referred to only those words that immediately followed, such as sells, ships, transports, and so on, or also applied to later words referring to a minor. The Supreme Court held that *knowingly* applied both to the sexually explicit nature of the material and to the age of the performers as well as the verbs immediately following the word. Likewise, in Andersen, the U.S. Supreme Court held that *knowingly* is an important element in the case and that the jury should have been so instructed. Said the Supreme Court, "We hold that the jury instructions failed to convey properly the elements of a 'corrupt persuasion.'"[4] This does not mean that the firm's officials are innocent. It only means that the trial court's instructions did not hold the jury to a high enough measure of intent.

1. "Fastow Sentenced to 6 Years," *New York Times* (27 September 2006), p. 1C.
2. "Skilling Sentenced to 6 Years," *New York Times* (27 September 2006), p. 1C.
3. *Arthur Andersen, LLP v. United States*, 544 U.S. 696 (2005).
4. *Arthur Andersen, LLP v. United States*, 544 U.S. 696 (2005).

dence of all elements of the crime. Defenses in criminal law are so important that Chapters 4 and 5 are devoted to them. First, however, it is necessary to look at anticipatory offenses and parties to crimes, the focus of Chapter 3.

STUDY QUESTIONS

1. Explain the meaning of the terms *actus reus* and *mens rea*.

2. When is a behavior not an act in the criminal law? Explain.

3. Distinguish between failure to act (or omission) and act. Under what circumstances do you think failure to act should be a crime? Relate your answers to cases discussed in the text.

4. List the four levels of criminal intent or culpability in the Model Penal Code, and define each.

5. What are the difficulties with trying to prove criminal intent? Illustrate.

6. What is meant by the following quote from the U.S. Supreme Court: "The law presumes that a person intends the ordinary consequences of his voluntary acts"?

7. How does *motive* differ from *intent* in criminal law?

8. What is meant by *causation* in criminal law?

9. How does the concept of intervening causes influence legal causation? How does multiple causation affect criminal responsibility?

10. What is meant by *attendant circumstances*, and how do you know when they exist?

11. Distinguish strict liability, vicarious liability, and enterprise liability. Would you exclude any of these from the criminal law? Why or why not?

12. What was the intent issue in the case involving the Arthur Andersen accounting firm?

FOR DEBATE

Discuss the issues surrounding the following debate topics, giving special attention to the reasons for (or the lack of) such statutes historically, along with the societal changes that might make it reasonable to revise or abolish (or create) the statutes.

Resolved: All persons who witness a crime should be required to report that incident to law enforcement officials as soon as reasonably possible. Proof of the failure to do so should constitute a felony.

Resolved: Laws that criminalize sexual behavior between adults and consenting teenagers between the ages of 12 and 16 should be abolished.

KEY TERMS

CASE ANALYSIS

APPRENDI v. NEW JERSEY

530 U.S. 466 (2000)

Case Preview

This case is cited frequently as a key case involving sentencing issues, but it also raises the questions of intent and the burden of proof, both of which are applicable to Chapter 2 and are the focus here. The case involves two New Jersey statutes, one of which is a hate crime statute. A *hate crime* is one that is associated with prejudice that may be based on any or all of the following, depending on the jurisdiction's approach: race, religion, disability, gender, national origin, sexual orientation, or ethnicity. In most jurisdictions, including New Jersey, there are special hate crime statutes, providing for enhanced penalties for those convicted of such crimes. Although New Jersey has a hate crime statute, Charles C. Apprendi was not charged with a hate crime, but the state's hate crime statute came into play at sentencing. That statute provides for an "extended term" of imprisonment if the court finds by a preponderance of the evidence that "the defendant, in committing the crime acted with a purpose to intimidate an individual or group of individuals because of race, color, gender, handicap, religion, sexual orientation or ethnicity" [N.J. Stat. Ann., Section 2C:44–3(e) (2000)]. This statute permits an enhancement of between 10 and 20 years for a second-degree offense. This statute was not mentioned in the charges against Apprendi, but notice how the trial judge sentences the defendant. In reading the case, recall our discussion of the difference between *intent* and *motive* and consider whether those are confused by the Court. Also recall our discussion of the burden of proof, and analyze what the Supreme Court says about that crucial issue.

One final note: Actual cases may be very long and filled with complicated legal issues and citations to many cases. *Apprendi* is an example. What you see here is a very small part of the opinions, and they have been edited carefully to eliminate parts of law and reasons that are not relevant to our points in this chapter. Nor are all of the opinions represented.

Chief Justice William H. Rehnquist delivered the opinion of the Court, joined by Justices Antonin Scalia, David H. Souter, Clarence Thomas, and Ruth Bader Ginsburg. Justice Scalia wrote a concurring opinion. Justice Thomas wrote a concurring opinion, in which Justice Scalia joined in part. Justice Sandra Day O'Connor wrote a dissenting opinion, in which Chief Justice Rehnquist and Justices Anthony M. Kennedy and Stephen G. Breyer joined. Justice Breyer wrote a dissenting opinion, in which Chief Justice Rehnquist joined.

Facts

At 2:04 a.m. on December 22, 1994, Charles C. Apprendi fired several .22-caliber bullets into the home of an African-American family that had recently moved into a previously all-white neighborhood in Vineland, New Jersey. Apprendi was promptly arrested, and at 3:05 a.m. admitted that he was the shooter. After further questioning, at 6:04 a.m., he made a statement—which he later retracted—that even though he did not know the occupants of the house personally, "because they are black in color he does not want them in the neighborhood." A New Jersey grand jury returned a 23-count indictment charging Apprendi with four first-degree, eight second-degree, six third-degree, and five fourth-degree offenses. None of the counts referred to the hate crime statute, and none alleged that Apprendi acted with a racially biased purpose.

[Apprendi pleaded guilty to three counts, and the prosecutor dismissed the other 20 counts.] As part of the plea agreement, however, the State reserved the right to request the court to impose a higher "enhanced" sentence on count 18 (which was the December 22 shooting) on the ground that that offense was committed with a biased purpose . . . . Apprendi, correspondingly, reserved the right to challenge the hate crime sentence enhancement on the ground that it violates the United States Constitution. . . .

[After an evidentiary hearing, the trial judge] found "by a preponderance of the evidence" that Apprendi's actions were taken "with a purpose to intimidate" as provided by the [hate crimes] statute, [and] the trial judge held that the hate crime enhancement applied. [The conviction was upheld by the Appellate Division of the Superior Court of New Jersey and affirmed by a divided New Jersey Supreme Court. The U.S. Supreme Court granted *Certiorari* and reversed the lower court's decision.]

Issue

[After noting that the issue of an enhanced sentence for racial bias was not argued before the U.S. Supreme Court, although it was argued in the lower courts, the U.S. Supreme Court stated clearly that was not the issue in this case.] The question presented is whether the Due Process Clause of the Fourteenth Amendment requires that a factual determination authorizing an increase in the maximum prison sentence for an offense from 10 to 20 years be made by a jury on the basis of proof beyond a reasonable doubt.

Holding

In sum, our reexamination of our cases in this area, and of the history upon which they rely, confirms . . . [that] [o]ther than the fact of a prior conviction, any fact that increases the penalty for a crime beyond the prescribed statutory maximum must be submitted to a jury, and proved beyond a reasonable doubt.

Rationale

In his 1881 lecture on the criminal law, Oliver Wendell Holmes, Jr., observed: "The law threatens certain pains if you do certain things, intending thereby to give you a new motive for not doing them. If you persist in doing them, it has to inflict the pains in order that its threats may continue to be believed." New Jersey threatened Apprendi with certain pains if he unlawfully possessed a weapon and with additional pains if he selected his victims with a purpose to intimidate them

because of their race. As a matter of simple justice, it seems obvious that the procedural safeguards designed to protect Apprendi from unwarranted pains should apply equally to the two acts that New Jersey has singled out for punishment. Merely using the label "sentence enhancement" to describe the latter surely does not provide a principled basis for treating them differently.

At stake in this case are constitutional protections of surpassing importance: The proscription of any deprivation of liberty without "due process of law" . . . and the guarantee that "in all criminal prosecutions, the accused shall enjoy the right to a speedy and public trial, by an impartial jury." . . . Taken together, these rights indisputably entitle a criminal defendant to "a jury determination that [he] is guilty of every element of the crime with which he is charged, beyond a reasonable doubt." . . .

If a defendant faces punishment beyond that provided by statute when an offense is committed under certain circumstances but not others, it is obvious that both the loss of liberty and the stigma attaching to the offenses are heightened; it necessarily follows that the defendant should not—at the moment the State is put to proof of those circumstances—be deprived of protections that have, until that point, unquestionably attached. . . .

By its very terms, [the hate crimes] statute mandates an examination of the defendant's state of mind—a concept known well to the criminal law as the defendant's *mens rea*. . . . [T]he fact that the language and the structure of the "purpose to use" criminal offense is identical in relevant respects to the language and structure of the "purpose to intimidate" provision demonstrates to us that it is precisely a particular criminal *mens rea* that the hate crime enhancement statute seeks to target. The defendant's intent in committing a crime is perhaps as close as one might hope to come to a core criminal offense "element." . . .

[Whether the required finding is characterized as one of "elements" or "sentencing factors" is determined not by form, but by effect.] [D]oes the required finding expose the defendant to a greater punishment than that authorized by the jury's guilty verdict? . . . .

Indeed, the effect of New Jersey's sentencing "enhancement" here is unquestionably to turn a second-degree offense into a first-degree offense, under the State's own code.

Justice O'Connor, with whom Chief Justice Rehnquist and Justices Kennedy and Breyer join, dissenting

Our Court has long recognized that not every fact that bears on a defendant's punishment need be charged in an indictment, submitted to a jury, and proved by the government beyond a reasonable doubt. Rather, we have held that the "legislature's definition of the elements of the offense is usually dispositive." Although we have recognized that "there are obviously constitutional limits beyond which the States may not go in this regard," and that "in certain limited circumstances [the] reasonable-doubt requirement applies to facts not formally identified as elements of the offense charged," we have proceeded with caution before deciding that a certain fact must be treated as an offense element despite the legislature's choice not to characterize it as such. We have therefore declined to establish any bright-line rule for making such judgments and have instead approached each case individually, sifting through the considerations most relevant to determining whether the legislature has acted properly within its broad power to define crimes and their punishments or instead has sought to evade the constitutional requirements associated with the characterization of a fact as an offense element.

In one bold stroke the Court today casts aside our traditional cautious approach and instead embraces a universal and seemingly bright-line rule limiting the power of Congress and state legislatures to define criminal offenses and the sentences that follow from convictions thereunder. The Court states: "Other than the fact of a prior conviction, any fact that increases the penalty for a crime beyond the prescribed statutory maximum must be submitted to a jury, and proved beyond a reasonable doubt." In its opinion, the Court marshalls virtually no authority to support its extraordinary rule. Indeed it is remarkable that the Court cannot identify a single instance, in the over 200 years since the ratification of the Bill of Rights, that our Court has applied, as a constitutional requirement, the rule it announces today.

For Discussion

This case is usually cited along with discussions of hate crimes, and that topic does occur later in this text. Here, however, it is cited as an example of the U.S. Supreme Court's emphasis on the importance of the test of beyond a reasonable doubt. The chapter notes that this test is required for *all* elements of a crime. *Apprendi* holds that the beyond a reasonable doubt test also applies in some sentencing measures—specifically, an enhancing measure.

Do you agree with the majority's analysis, or with that of the dissent, concerning the legislative characterization of the elements of the hate crime statute? Do you think the jury should play a role in determining the punishment enhancement of a hate crime?

INTERNET ACTIVITY

Although *mens rea* is an element of most crimes, criminal culpability varies with the type of crime being charged. For example, in cases of manslaughter prosecutors would not have to prove intent to kill but some other guilty state of mind such as gross negligence or recklessness. The Crime Library is available on the Court TV website, located at http://www.trutv.com/library/crime/index.html (accessed 8 December 2008). This library is a collection of more than 500 nonfiction feature stories on major crimes, criminals, trials, forensics, and criminal profiling.

1. Review five of the available stories, and identify the levels of culpability and burdens of proof for the types of offenses depicted on the website.

2. Although motive is not an element of a criminal offense, many prosecutors believe that motive is essential to getting a conviction. What are the various motives for some of the crimes depicted in the Crime Library? Do you think having a motive helps to get a conviction for a crime? Why or why not?

NOTES

1. *Robinson v. California*, 370 U.S. 660 (1962).
2. *People v. Decina*, 138 N.E.2d 799 (N.Y. 1956).
3. *United States v. Greschner*, 647 F.2d 740 (7th Cir. 1981).
4. *United States v. Fountain*, 642 F.2d 1083 (7th Cir. 1981), cert. *denied*, 451 U.S. 993 (1981).
5. *In re Winship*, 397 U.S. 358, 364 (1970).
6. *People v. Oliver*, 258 Cal.Rptr. 138 (Cal.App.1st Dist. 1989).
7. "Woman Is Sentenced to 50 Years in Case of Man in Windshield," *New York Times* (28 June 2003), p. 1.
8. Rollin M. Perkins and Ronald N. Boyce, *Criminal Law*, 3d ed. (Mineola, N.Y.: Foundation Press, 1982), p. 826.
9. Oliver Wendell Holmes Jr., *The Common Law* (Birmingham, Ala.: The Legal Classics Library, 1982, originally published in 1881 by Little Brown), p. 3.
10. Commentary to Section 2.02, Model Penal Code (1985).
11. Tex. Penal Code, Title 5, Section 22.04 (1985). Subsequently this statute was amended as follows: "(a) A person commits an offense if he intentionally, knowingly, recklessly, or with criminal negligence, by act or intentionally, knowingly, or recklessly by omission, causes to a child, elderly individual, or disabled individual: (1) serious bodily injury; (2) serious mental deficiency, impairment, or injury, or (3) bodily injury. . . . [The act applies to an actor who has] a legal or statutory duty to act [or one who has] assumed care, custody, or control of a child, elderly individual, or disabled individual. . . . [A child is defined as] a person 14 years of age or younger." Tex. Penal Code, Title 5, Section 22.04 (2008).
12. *Alvarado v. State*, 704 S.W.2d 36 (Tex. Crim. App. 1985).
13. *United States v. X-Citement Video, Inc.*, 982 F.2d 1285, 1291 (9th Cir. 1992), *reversed*, 513 U.S. 64 (1994).

14. *United States v. X-Citement Video, Inc.*, 513 U.S. 64 (1994), cases and citations omitted. The statute is codified at U.S. Code, Title 18, Section 2251 *et seq.* (2009).
15. *People v. Rongo*, 145 P. 1017 (Cal. 1914).
16. *Calif. Penal Code*, Section 20 (2008).
17. *People v. Stewart*, 40 N.Y.2d 692 (N.Y. App. 1976).
18. *Commonwealth v. Cheeks*, 223 A.2d 291 (Pa. 1966).
19. *People v. Arzon*, 401 N.Y.S.2d 156 (1978), citations omitted.
20. RCWA, Section 9A.44.076 (2008).
21. RCWA, Section 9A.44.073 (2008).
22. See *People v. Hernandez*, 393 P.2d 673 (Cal. 1964), and the discussion in Chapter 7 of this text.
23. N. Y. Penal Code, Section 15.10 (2008).
24. *State v. Beaudry*, 365 N.W.2d 593 (Wis. 1985).
25. *Commonwealth v. Koczwara*, 155 A.2d 825 (Pa. 1959), *cert. denied*, 363 U.S. 848 (1960).
26. *United States v. Park*, 421 U.S. 658 (1975), cases and citations omitted.
27. *New York Central and Hudson River Railroad Co. v. United States*, 212 U.S. 481 (1909), footnotes and citations omitted.
28. *Granite Construction Co. v. Superior Court*, 149 Cal. App.3d 465 (5th Dist. 1983).

CHAPTER 3

Anticipatory Offenses and Parties to Crimes

INTRODUCTION

C hapters 1 and 2 introduced criminal law, including the elements of a crime. Subsequent chapters discuss particular crimes, such as murder and nonnegligent manslaughter, rape, robbery, aggravated assault, larceny-theft, burglary, motor vehicle theft, and arson, the eight serious crimes as defined by the FBI. These and other crimes of violence and of property exist only when the criminal act and the criminal state of mind concur to produce a result.

It is possible, however, that individuals may engage in acts that are dangerous to society because they imply an *inclination* to commit a crime even though the target crime is never accomplished. For example, an attempt to commit rape is a serious threat to the potential victim and to society even if the rape is not committed. Anticipatory, uncompleted, or incipient crimes are called **inchoate crimes.** These crimes are important not only because, in and of themselves, they are threatening but also because they may lead to other crimes. Since inchoate crimes are considered threats to society, it is important to consider them in light of the purposes of criminal law discussed in Chapter 1.

For example, if deterrence is a goal, will it be accomplished by criminalizing inchoate crimes? Is deterrence more likely if the criminal code permits a **defense** (a legal challenge by the defendant) of abandonment or renunciation to any or all of the inchoate crimes? Is it reasonable for society to demand retribution from those who plan to commit a crime or who conspire with another to commit a crime but never go any further? What about an **attempt** crime, which is defined as an act involving two basic elements—a step toward the commission of a crime and a specific intent to commit that crime? If those elements are met but the crime is not actually committed, should the actor be prosecuted? Does the lack of success in attempted murder threaten the targeted victim and society to the extent that it should be considered a crime?

In reviewing the purposes of criminal law, it is also important to consider whether all who are involved in a crime should have the same criminal responsibility. Should punishment be more severe for the individual who instigates, plans, leads, and makes arrangements to commit a crime than it is for a person whose only function is to assist during one or more stages of that crime? The role of various parties to crimes is another focus of this chapter.

SOLICITATION

The asking, inciting, ordering, urgently requesting, or enticing of another person to commit a crime is known as **solicitation**. The solicited crime does not have to be committed for the crime of solicitation to occur. Perhaps the most familiar solicitation crime is that of soliciting for purposes of prostitution.

Some states divide solicitation into degrees, with the crime considered more serious as the crime solicited becomes more serious. Others consider the relative ages of the solicitor and the solicitee. New York, for example, defines *solicitation in the first degree*, a class C felony, as follows:

A person is guilty of criminal solicitation in the first degree when, being over eighteen years of age, with intent that another person under sixteen years of age engage in conduct that would constitute a Class A felony, he solicits, requests, commands, importunes or otherwise attempts to cause such other person to engage in such conduct.[1]

Pennsylvania's solicitation statute is illustrative of a comprehensive statute that does not break the crime down into degrees:

(a) DEFINITION OF SOLICITATION. A person is guilty of solicitation to commit a crime if with the intent of promoting or facilitating its commission he commands, encourages or requests another person to engage in specific conduct which would constitute such crime or an attempt to commit such crime or which would establish his complicity in its commission or attempted commission.[2]

These and similar solicitation statutes recognize that when one person entices another to commit a crime, that act constitutes sufficient danger to society that criminal culpability should ensue.

Elements of Solicitation

The crime of solicitation has essentially two elements:

1. An act: commanding, encouraging, or demanding that another person engage in conduct that constitutes a crime.
2. An intent: having the purpose of promoting or facilitating that person to commit a crime.

Thus, criminal solicitation requires a purpose to promote or facilitate the commission of a crime as well as a command, encouragement, demand, request, or other means of enticing another to commit the crime. That incitement may be directed at a crowd and not just a particular individual.

In some jurisdictions the communication of criminal solicitation may qualify even if it is not accomplished. For example, the Model Penal Code (MPC) provides as follows:

It is immaterial under [the section defining solicitation] that the actor fails to communicate with the person he solicits to commit a crime if his conduct was designed to effect such communication.[3]

Some jurisdictions classify *uncommunicated solicitation* as *attempted solicitation*, as illustrated by the following excerpt from *State v. Lee*, decided by the Oregon Court of Appeals in 1991.[4] Notice as you read this case that the court refers to common law in its efforts to interpret the crime of solicitation. Recall our earlier discussion concerning the use of the common law for this purpose. Notice also the mention of the MPC as providing a basis for the Oregon solicitation statute but differing in one key element from that code. Finally, this case demonstrates that even when a lower court is in error, a new trial may not be required.

STATE v. LEE

804 P.2d 1208 (Or. App. 1991), review denied,
812 P.2d 827 (Or. 1991)

Defendant appeals his conviction for solicitation to commit robbery in the first degree. He argues that a letter that was not delivered can support, at most, a conviction for attempted solicitation. We agree.

In July, 1989, defendant, while in jail, wrote letters to an acquaintance who was in the Hillcrest Juvenile Center, outlining plans to rob a store and a residence. The letters were intercepted by Hillcrest personnel and never reached their intended recipient. The first intercepted letter stated:

I wrote about two weeks ago. I guess you didn't get it. So, I'll tell you again. The job I got set up will get us some guns. On the other page is a picture of the place. And then I want to go to Washington. Okay.

The letter also described plans for robbing a store and burglarizing a residence. The other letter intercepted at Hillcrest also discussed plans for a "job." Defendant admitted that he wrote the letters.

Defendant first argues that there was insufficient evidence to convict him of solicitation. He contends that the evidence was insufficient for the court to find that he had the requisite "intent of causing another to engage in specific conduct constituting a crime" [as required by statute]. . . .

Defendant next contends that, because the letters were never received by the addressee, he did not commit the crime of solicitation, but only attempted solicitation. Solicitation is defined in [the state statute as follows]:

A person commits the crime of solicitation if with the intent of causing another to engage in specific conduct constituting a crime punishable as a felony or as a Class A misdemeanor or an attempt to commit such felony or Class A misdemeanor the person commands or solicits such other person to engage in that conduct.

The statute contains two elements: *mens rea* and *actus reus*. Defendant was found by the trial court to have the specified state of mind. He argues, however, that the *actus reus* proved by the state was insufficient to support a conviction, because the intercepted letters do not constitute a completed solicitation. The statute provides that a person is guilty of solicitation if that person "commands or solicits" another to engage in criminal conduct constituting a felony or a Class A misdemeanor. However, the terms "command" or "solicit" are not defined in the statute, and it is unclear whether they include circumstances where a communication is not received. Our function is to construe the statute to carry out the legislature's intent. . . .

[The court then reviewed the legislative history of the statute, along with that of the common law and the Model Penal Code.]

We conclude that a completed communication is required to prove the crime of solicitation. Accordingly, defendant's conviction for solicitation was error. An attempt to solicit is necessarily included in the completed crime. Because the trial court found defendant guilty of acts constituting attempted solicitation, no new trial is required.

Some jurisdictions require that the crime solicited must be a serious one—for example, a felony—whereas others include any crime. Recall the difference between the New York and Pennsylvania statutes, cited earlier, concerning the crime that must be solicited. New York requires for the crime of first-degree solicitation that the solicited crime must be a Class A felony, which is the highest category of felony in that state. Pennsylvania requires only that a crime be solicited; this could apply to any crime.

Penalties for solicitation vary, with some statutes providing a lesser penalty for solicitation than for the solicited crime. Others provide the same penalty as that for the most serious crime solicited, with the exception of capital crimes and first-degree felonies. In those cases, the attempt may be punished as a second-degree felony. Some jurisdictions require corroboration of witnesses or circumstances to substantiate the criminal intent for solicitation.

The criminal intent for solicitation is one of specific intent. Thus, it is not sufficient to joke to another about committing a crime, even if that person commits the crime suggested. To constitute solicitation, the communication must be made with the intent to entice the target party to commit the crime.

Defenses to Solicitation

Some states permit the defense of renouncing solicitation. For example, Arizona permits the defense but requires that there must be a voluntary and complete renunciation of the criminal intent, which

may be shown by meeting both of the following requirements:

1. Notifying the person solicited.
2. Giving a timely warning to law enforcement authorities or otherwise making a reasonable effort to "prevent the conduct or result solicited."[5]

Some jurisdictions require that for renunciation to be acceptable, the solicitor of the crime must persuade the solicitee not to commit the crime or must in some other way prevent the crime from occurring. Presumably this action means that the solicitor is no longer dangerous to society and therefore punishment is not necessary. An example of this type of statute is that of Pennsylvania:

> It is a defense that the actor, after soliciting another person to commit a crime, persuaded him not to do so or otherwise prevented the commission of the crime, under circumstances manifesting a complete and voluntary renunciation of his criminal intent.[6]

ATTEMPT

In some states that do not have solicitation statutes, earlier courts held that soliciting could be penalized as an attempt crime, defined earlier. The crime of *attempt* requires that the actor go beyond mere preparation to commit a crime, and this is not true of solicitation. According to one court, "To constitute an attempt there must . . . be an act of perpetration. . . . However, solicitation is preparation rather than perpetration."[7] Because attempt requires going beyond mere preparation, it may be viewed as a serious act for which criminal punishment should be provided.

Early English cases recognized the crime of attempt. For example, one court stated that an "intent may make an act, innocent in itself, criminal; nor is the completion of an act, criminal in itself, necessary to constitute criminality."[8] Another English court stated, "All offenses of a public nature, that is, all such acts or attempts as tend to the prejudice of the community, are indictable."[9] Attempt was considered to be a misdemeanor whether the attempt was to commit a misdemeanor or a felony.

Most U.S. jurisdictions have statutes criminalizing attempt crimes, although the nature of the statutes varies. Some refer to *any* crime, while others limit the crime to an attempt to commit a serious crime, a felony, or any of an enumerated list of serious crimes. Many jurisdictions have one statute that covers all attempt crimes, while some include a separate statute for each attempt crime, for example, attempted rape, attempted robbery, and so on.

Elements of Attempt

The crime of attempt has two elements:

1. A criminal intent
2. A criminal act

The first element of attempt is that the defendant must have had the requisite criminal intent. The intent required for attempt is a *specific intent*. As one court concluded, "One cannot attempt to commit an act which one does not intend to commit."[10] Thus, criminal attempt excludes acts that are the result of a general intent, negligence, or recklessness.

The Model Penal Code definition of criminal attempt, reprinted in Focus 3.1, emphasizes the intent requirement by requiring that the intent must be done *purposely*. Notice also that under the MPC criminal attempt includes an omission, or failure to act where there is a legal duty to act.

One problem with the intent requirement occurs when the defendant has been charged with attempted murder but the victim has not died. One may be convicted of murder without proof of a specific intent to kill a particular victim. As stated previously, a conviction is appropriate in some cases in which the defendant has not exhibited an intent to kill but has engaged in reckless behavior reflecting indifference to human life or has manifested an intent only to inflict great bodily harm but death resulted. With these same facts and a victim who does not die, however, a charge of attempted murder is inappropriate.

Under these facts, attempted murder requires a higher intent than would be required for a murder

---

FOCUS 3.1 Criminal Attempt: The Model Penal Code

Section 5.01. Criminal Attempt

(1) *Definition of Attempt.* A person is guilty of an attempt to commit a crime if, acting with the kind of culpability otherwise required for commission of the crime, he:

(a) purposely engages in conduct which would constitute the crime if the attendant circumstances were as he believes them to be; or

(b) when causing a particular result is an element of the crime, does or omits to do anything with the purpose of causing or with the belief that it will cause such result without further conduct on his part; or

(c) purposely does or omits to do anything which, under the circumstances as he believes them to be, is an act or omission constituting a substantial step in a course of conduct planned to culminate in his commission of the crime.

(2) *Conduct Which May Be Held Substantial Step Under Subsection (1)(c).* Conduct shall not be held to constitute a substantial step under Subsection (1)(c) of this Section unless it is strongly corroborative of the actor's criminal purpose. Without negating the sufficiency of other conduct, the following, if strongly corroborative of the actor's criminal purpose, shall not be held insufficient as a matter of law:

(a) lying in wait, searching for or following the contemplated victim of the crime;

(b) enticing or seeking to entice the contemplated victim of the crime to go to the place contemplated for its commission;

(c) reconnoitering the place contemplated for the commission of the crime;

(d) unlawful entry of a structure, vehicle enclosure in which it is contemplated that the crime will be committed;

(e) possession of materials to be employed in the commission of the crime, which are specially designed for such unlawful use or which can serve no lawful purpose of the actor under the circumstances;

(f) possession, collection or fabrication of materials to be employed in the commission of the crime, at or near the place contemplated for its commission, where such possession, collection or fabrication serves no lawful purpose of the actor under the circumstances;

(g) soliciting an innocent agent to engage in conduct constituting an element of the crime.

(3) *Conduct Designed to Aid Another in Commission of a Crime.* A person who engages in conduct designed to aid another to commit a crime which would establish his complicity under Section 2.06 if the crime were committed by such other person, is guilty of an attempt to commit the crime, although the crime is not committed or attempted by such other person. . . .

conviction had the victim died. This situation has been questioned because of the threat to individuals and to society that may result when people who are grossly negligent in their conduct escape criminal responsibility because the attempt statutes do not cover their acts.

Another issue arises with regard to attempted murder. As subsequent discussions will note, in some jurisdictions one may be convicted of murder when death occurs during the commission of another felony (or at least a serious felony). Thus, if a victim dies of a heart attack while being subjected to armed robbery, the offender may be charged with murder in some jurisdictions. In contrast, some courts have held that the intent requirement for attempted murder is not present in such circumstances.[11] Although attempt crimes require a specific rather than a general intent, it may be confusing to apply that requirement to some crimes, as illustrated by a Washington Supreme Court case. The defendant in *State v. Chhom* was a 16-year-old who was charged with the attempted rape of a child. The evidence at trial showed that Sarun Chhom and several of his companions approached a 9-year-old boy and grabbed him off his bicycle. While the companions held the boy, Chhom dropped his pants, exposed his penis, and attempted to force it into the victim's mouth. Chhom was charged with attempted rape of a child and unlawful imprisonment. The latter charge was dropped.

Based on a prior case, Chhom argued on appeal that he could not be charged with attempting to commit a crime that does not require proof of intent and thus his conviction was improper. The state supreme court disagreed: "When coupled with the attempt statute, the intent required for attempted rape of a child is the intent to accomplish the criminal result: to have sexual intercourse. . . . We hold that rape of a child can serve as the base crime for a charge of attempt." The case was remanded for a new trial.[12]

The second element of attempt is that there must be a criminal act. Most courts require that the defendant goes beyond preparation and moves toward perpetration of the crime. The difference between *preparation* and *perpetration* is of critical legal significance in that unless perpetration has occurred, there is no criminal attempt. In the following excerpt from *United States v. Cartlidge*, the appellate court discusses various tests for making this determination. The defendant in *Cartlidge* was a former law enforcement officer who argued that the evidence used to convict him of taking a bribe to provide protection for a purported marijuana smuggling operation was not sufficient to support his conviction for attempting to **aid and**

abet (assisting or facilitating the commission of a crime; discussed later in this chapter) in the possession and distribution of marijuana. The court disagreed.

The court held that the defendant's acts of "silence and providing warnings when needed, promising assistance, assurances of ability to provide protection against law enforcement interference, and supplying information about a convenient time for the operation, coupled with the acceptance of payment for these services," went beyond preparation and supported an attempt to aid and abet a federal crime. The court's discussion of the issue is enlightening.[13]

UNITED STATES v. CARTLIDGE
808 F.2d 1064 (5th Cir. 1987)

A recurrent problem in determining whether a defendant has committed an attempt is "pinpointing the time in the unfolding of a criminal plan at which the actor becomes liable for an attempt." The execution of a crime, other than one committed impetuously, involves planning and preparation. Like the jurisprudence of most states, federal law defines the threshold of criminality as the time when the defendant has gone beyond those preliminary activities and committed the additional act that constitutes the proscribed attempt even though he has not yet committed the contemplated crime. . . .

Most states have adopted the subjective [in contrast to the objective] criminality approach. . . . [T]his approach emphasizes what the defendant has already done rather than what remains to be done, imposes liability only if some firmness of criminal purpose is shown, and permits the defendant's conduct to be assessed in the light of the statements. It also recognizes that an attempt to aid in the commission of a crime is sufficient for criminal sanction, and several statutes explicitly condemn such conduct. . . .

Cartlidge contends that the evidence against him, even if wholly believed, was sufficient only to prove that he took a bribe, not that he attempted to aid and abet in the distribution of marijuana. Cartlidge's acceptance of three payments was evidence of receipt of a bribe, but it was also a step in a plan to aid in the distribution of a controlled substance. Cartlidge also gave information about the propitiousness of the planned date, furnished information, albeit erroneous, that federal agents could not conduct an investigation without his knowledge, and promised to shield those whom he thought to be drug dealers. These activities are sufficient to show that he had moved beyond preparation. They were substantial steps strongly corroborative of criminal intent.

In this case, the court refers to an "additional step" and a "substantial step" that are sufficient to indicate that preparation has occurred. Note in Focus 3.1 that the MPC, Section 5.01(1)(c), also requires a substantial step. The Code then defines in the following section what is meant by a substantial step.

A 1996 case decided by the Tennessee Supreme Court draws a distinction between a substantial step and mere preparation. The case involved two 12-year-old girls who plotted to kill their teacher with rat poison. One of the girls took the poison in her purse to school that day. She showed it to another student on the bus, and after they arrived at school that student told the homeroom teacher, who told the principal.

The two defendants were leaning over the teacher's desk near her coffee cup when the teacher walked into the room. They giggled and ran back to their seats. The teacher saw a purse lying next to her coffee cup. Shortly thereafter the student who owned the purse was called to the principal's office, where the purse was searched and the rat poison found. Subsequently both girls gave written statements to the sheriff concerning their plans to poison their teacher.

The court noted that under the prior Tennessee statute and a previous court ruling in that state, in all probability there would have been no attempt crime unless the poison had already been placed in the cup. At that point, however, it might have been too late. The teacher might have consumed the drink with the poison and died. The court held that the facts were sufficient for a trier of fact to conclude that the offender had taken a substantial step (as required by the new statute) toward committing second-degree murder. The court stated that

> when an actor possesses materials to be used in the commission of a crime, at or near the scene of the crime, and where the possession of those materials can serve no lawful purpose of the actor under the circumstances, the jury is entitled, but not required, to find that the actor has taken a "substantial step" toward the commission of the crime if such action is strongly corroborative of the actor's overall criminal purpose.[14]

Focus 3.2 contains quotations from several courts that have drawn the line between preparation and perpetration. A close reading of those statements shows the difficulty one might have in making a decision, since the guidelines are not clear.

The substantial step requirement is particularly difficult in attempt cases involving sex crimes. Compare the following two cases: In the first, the defendant was convicted of attempted rape after he ordered a woman to take off her clothes. She was wearing jeans and could not get them off over her boots; so he ordered her to

---

FOCUS 3.2   Preparation or Attempt? Courts Seek a Definition

When faced with the issue of whether a defendant has gone beyond preparation and committed an act sufficient to constitute the crime of attempt, courts must devise tests. The following are a few of the guidelines articulated by various courts over the years:

1. "The act must reach far enough towards the accomplishment of the desired result to amount to the commencement of the consummation."[1]
2. "[W]here the intent to commit the substantive offense is . . . clearly established . . . , acts done toward the commission of the crime may constitute an attempt, where the same acts would be held insufficient to constitute an attempt if the intent with which they were done is equivocal and not clearly proved."[2]
3. "Acts in furtherance of a criminal project do not reach the stage of an 'attempt' unless they carry the project forward within dangerous proximity to the criminal end to be attained."[3]
4. "The question whether an accused is guilty of an attempt to commit a crime is determined by his intentions and actions, and is unaffected by the circumstance that by reason of some unforeseen obstacle he was prevented from achieving his purpose. He is guilty if he has with criminal intent made some positive steps, beyond mere preparation, looking to the performance of an act which, if perpetrated, would be a crime."[4]

1. *People v. Miller*, 42 P.2d 308, 309 (Cal. 1935).
2. *People v. Berger*, 280 P.2d 136, 138 (Cal.Ct.App. 1955).
3. *People v. Ditchik*, 41 N.E.2d 905 (N.Y. 1942), citations omitted.
4. *People v. Sullivan*, 75 N.E. 989, 992 (N.Y. 1903).

perform oral sex on him. He put her in the trunk of his car, drove around for several hours, and let her out. He was convicted of assault and battery with intent to kill, attempted rape, forcible sodomy, robbery with a firearm, and kidnapping. The appellate court upheld all but the conviction for attempted rape, which it reversed on the grounds that the defendant did not take a substantial step toward committing rape. The court explained, "It must be such act or acts as will apparently result, in the usual and natural course of events, if not hindered by extraneous causes, in the commission of the crime itself."[15] As subsequent discussions will note, the forced act in this case may constitute rape today, but this was not the case at that time.

In the second case, the defendant stopped a 13-year-old girl who was riding her bicycle from her parents' home, where she had been helping her mother with a garage sale, to another garage sale down the street. The defendant asked the girl to help him find his dog; she refused. He offered her money to do so; she refused. He offered more money; she refused. He said he would go to her home and ask her parents if she could help him and asked her to get into his truck so he could drive her home. She refused.

The defendant followed the girl to her home. The girl told her mother what had happened, and the police were called. The defendant denied that he had any improper intentions, but the evidence showed that he did not have a dog and that previously he had been convicted of raping a 13-year-old girl. Do you believe the facts constitute sufficient evidence to convict him of attempted kidnapping and attempted rape? The Oregon Court of Appeals upheld the conviction for attempted kidnapping in the second degree but reversed the conviction for attempted rape. The Oregon Supreme Court reversed, leaving both convictions standing.[16]

One final point on the act element for attempt crimes is that the offender's act does not have to be the last act in the chain of causation to constitute an attempt. The case law of the state in which the alleged attempt occurs must be consulted to understand how that state's courts have reacted to the causation issue in attempt cases.

Defenses to Attempt

Two defenses available in attempt cases are:

1. Abandonment
2. Impossibility

If two of the purposes of criminal law are to deter people from committing criminal acts and to punish those who commit crimes, what position should the law take when people abandon their plans to commit a crime? Should it make a difference whether the abandonment is voluntary or involuntary? Do you agree with one court's ruling that "anywhere between the conception of the intent and the overt act toward its commission, there is room for repentance; and the law in its beneficence extends the hand of forgiveness?"[17]

The following case excerpt presents some of the basic issues involved in deciding whether an attempt occurred or whether there has been sufficient abandonment that the crime was not committed.

PEOPLE v. STAPLES
85 Cal. Rptr. 589 (Cal.Ct.App. 1970)

 The facts of this case are as follows. Staples, under an assumed name and while his wife was out of town, rented an office located over the mezzanine of a bank from 23 October 1967 to 23 November 1967. The defendant knew that the bank's vault was below the mezzanine.

The landlord had ten days before commencement of the rental to complete repairs and painting, but during that period, defendant Staples took some items into the office, including drilling tools, two acetylene gas tanks, a blow torch, a blanket, and a linoleum rug. The landlord saw these items from time to time when he checked on repairs.

The defendant found out that no one was in the building on Saturdays. On Saturday, 14 October 1967, he drilled two groups of holes into the floor of the office above the mezzanine room. He stopped drilling before the holes went through the floor. He came back to the office several times, thinking he would slowly drill down farther. Each time he left he covered the holes with the linoleum rug.

The defendant installed a lock on the closet and intended to, and perhaps did, place his tools in that closet. But he left the keys to the lock on the premises. Around the end of November and apparently after November 23, the landlord notified the police of the tools and turned the office over to them. The defendant was arrested on 22 February 1968. After he was told his rights, he gave a statement that included the following.

> Saturday, the 14th . . . I drilled some small holes in the floor of the room. Because of tiredness, fear, and the implications of what I was doing, I stopped and went to sleep.

> At this point I think my motives began to change. The actual . . . commencement of my plan made me begin to realize that even if I were to succeed a fugitive life of living off of stolen money would not give the enjoyment of the life of a mathematician however humble a job I might have.
>
> I still had not given up my plan however. I felt I had made a certain investment of time, money, effort and a certain psyhological [*sic*] commitment to the concept.
>
> I came back several times thinking I might store the tools in the closet and slowly drill down (covering the hole with a rug of linoleum square). As time went on
>
> (after two weeks or so), my wife came back and my life as bank robber seemed more and more absurd.

Do you think the defendant abandoned his attempt to commit burglary, for which he was convicted? The appellate court noted that the case was unusual in that in the typical attempt case the defendant is intercepted or caught in the act, but that did not appear to have occurred in this case.

On the one hand, if on his own the defendant in *Staples* abandoned the intent to commit burglary, why should he be punished? On the other hand, if his statements about abandonment were merely self-serving, why not punish him? Does his abandonment create in your mind a reasonable doubt about whether he intended to commit burglary? Was he fantasizing about committing the perfect crime without really intending to carry it out? Recall that criminal intent is a necessary element of attempt. Would you argue that this defendant never went beyond mere preparation and therefore the second element of attempt, an act, did not occur? The appellate court in *Staples* took the position that when the defendant started drilling, he began the breaking element requirement for burglary and thus had committed an act in preparation for that crime. The attempt conviction was upheld.

Some courts do recognize abandonment as a defense if there is evidence that abandonment is voluntary and complete. Most courts do not recognize this defense when abandonment is the result of getting caught or of someone finding out about the act. When the defense is allowed, it is interpreted strictly, and most defendants do not succeed with it.

The Arizona statute illustrates most of these points. It refers to the renunciation of attempt as well as to two other crimes, conspiracy and facilitation, both of which are discussed later in this chapter:

In a prosecution for attempt, conspiracy or facilitation, it is a defense that the defendant, under circumstances manifesting a voluntary and complete renunciation of his criminal intent, gave timely warning to law enforcement authorities or otherwise made a reasonable effort to prevent the conduct or result which is the object of the attempt, conspiracy or facilitation.[18]

A more plausible defense to attempt is **factual impossibility** (meaning there are circumstances, unknown to the actor, that prevented the commission of an attempt) or **legal impossibility** (no crime would have been committed even if the defendant's intentions had been fully performed or set in motion). Most U.S. courts hold that a defendant may be charged with an attempt crime when physical or factual impossibility exists, but not when legal impossibility exists. Although it may be difficult to determine the difference in any particular case, the following case excerpt refers to some examples.

BOOTH v. STATE
398 P.2d 863 (Okla.Crim.App. 1984)

 What is a "legal impossibility" as distinguished from a "physical or factual impossibility" has over a long period of time perplexed our courts and has resulted in many irreconcilable decisions and much philosophical discussion by legal scholars.

The reason for the "impossibility" of completing the substantive crime ordinarily falls into one of two categories: (1) Where the act if completed would not be criminal, a situation which is usually described as a "legal impossibility," and (2) where the basic or substantive crime is impossible of completion, simply because of some physical or factual condition unknown to the defendant, a situation which is usually described as a "factual impossibility." . . .

Examples of the so-called "legal impossibility" situations are:

(a) A person accepting goods which he believes to have been stolen, but which were not in fact stolen goods, is not guilty of an attempt to receive stolen goods. . . .

(c) An accused who offers a bribe to a person believed to be, but who is not, a juror is not guilty of an attempt to bribe a juror.

(d) A hunter who shoots a stuffed deer believing it to be alive is not guilty of an attempt to shoot a deer out of season.

Examples of cases in which attempt convictions have been sustained on the theory that all that prevented the consummation of the completed crime was a "factual impossibility" are:

(a) The picking of an empty pocket.

(b) An attempt to steal from an empty receptacle or an empty house.

(c) Where defendant shoots into the intended victim's bed, believing he is there, when in fact he is elsewhere.

(d) Where the defendant erroneously believing that the gun is loaded points it at his wife's head and pulls the trigger.

(e) Where the woman upon whom the [illegal] abortion operation is performed is not in fact pregnant.

The defense of impossibility might be raised in relationship to the actor's state of mind, that is, whether the actor had the required *mens rea* to commit the attempt. Thus, in most cases impotency is considered a factual impossibility and therefore not a defense to attempted rape. Impossibility might be a defense, however, if the would-be rapist had known for some time that he was impotent and not capable of having sexual intercourse. In jurisdictions in which the traditional definition of rape is still in effect, he might not have the requisite *mens rea* for attempted rape.

One final type of impossibility is *inherent impossibility*, usually illustrated by the hypothetical case of the doctor who comes to the United States from another country and attempts to use voodoo to kill a person. Because murder by voodoo is impossible, the doctor should not be charged with attempted murder even though his act might be considered wrong or even sinful. As one court noted, "It is true the sin or wickedness may be as great as an attempt or conspiracy by competent means; but human laws are made, not to punish sin, but to prevent crime and mischief."[19]

The Spread of AIDS: An Attempt Crime?

The rapid spread of the human immunodeficiency virus (HIV), which causes the deadly **acquired immune deficiency syndrome (AIDS)**, has affected all of our social institutions, including our legal systems. Some state legislatures have enacted statutes criminalizing the knowing exposure of another to HIV or AIDS. An example is that of Michigan, which provides as follows:

(1) A person who knows that he or she has or has been diagnosed as having acquired immunodeficiency syndrome or acquired immunodeficiency syndrome related complex, or who knows that he or she is HIV infected, and who engages in sexual penetration with another person without having first informed the other person that he or she has acquired immunodeficiency syndrome or acquired immunodeficiency syndrome related complex or is HIV infected, is guilty of a felony.

(2) As used in this section, "sexual penetration" means sexual intercourse, cunnilingus, fellatio, anal intercourse, or any other intrusion, however slight, of any part of a person's body or of any object into the genital or anal openings of another person's body, but emission of semen is not required.[20]

That statute was upheld by the Michigan Court of Appeals in 1998 when it was challenged by a woman who appealed her three convictions for engaging in sexual acts without informing her partner of her HIV status. The defendant was sentenced to concurrent terms of two years and eight months to four years of imprisonment on each of the three counts.[21]

Another issue, however, is whether criminal culpability for attempt crimes may be imposed on those who knowingly engage in acts that could result in the transmission of HIV. A Maryland appellate court held that the intent required for attempted second-degree murder cannot be inferred from the fact that a defendant knowingly exposes others to a risk of HIV infection. *Smallwood v. State* involved a defendant who knew that he was HIV-positive and had been told he must use condoms to protect his sexual partners from the infection. Dwight Ralph Smallwood was accused, among other crimes, of raping three women and not using condoms during those attacks. He was indicted on three charges of attempted second-degree murder, attempted first-degree rape, robbery with a deadly weapon, assault with intent to murder, and reckless endangerment. He entered guilty pleas to some of these charges; the only ones on appeal were Smallwood's convictions for attempted murder in the second degree and assault with intent to murder; those charges were reversed.

The court distinguished this case from other cases in which offenders expressed a desire to transmit the HIV virus and concluded that conviction for second-degree murder requires that the state must show that the defendant had a *specific intent* to kill the victim. Excerpts from the opinion follow.[22]

SMALLWOOD v. STATE
680 A.2d 512 (Md. 1996)

Death by AIDS is clearly one natural possible consequence of exposing someone to a risk of HIV infection, even on a single occasion. It is less clear that death by AIDS from that single exposure is a sufficiently probable result to provide the sole support for an inference that the person causing the exposure intended to kill the person who was exposed. While the risk to which Smallwood exposed his victims when he forced them to engage in unprotected sexual activity must not be minimized, the State has presented no evidence from which it can reasonably be concluded that death by AIDS is a probable result of Smallwood's actions to the same extent that death is the probable result of firing a deadly weapon at a vital part of someone's body. Without such evidence, it cannot fairly be concluded that death by AIDS was sufficiently probable to support an inference that Smallwood intended to kill his victims in the absence of other evidence indicative of an intent to kill.

In this case, we find no additional evidence from which to infer an intent to kill. Smallwood's actions are wholly explained by an intent to commit rape and armed robbery, the crimes for which he has already pled guilty. . . .

In contrast with these [other cited] cases, the state in this case would allow the trier of fact to infer an intent to kill based solely upon the fact that Smallwood exposed his victims to the risk that they might contract HIV. Without evidence showing that such a result is sufficiently probable to support this inference, we conclude that Smallwood's convictions for attempted murder and assault with intent to murder must be reversed.

As this discussion suggests, the intent requirement for attempt crimes is complicated and often difficult to prove. This may also be the case with the next inchoate crime we discuss—conspiracy.

CONSPIRACY

Like solicitation and attempt, **conspiracy** is an inchoate crime. *Conspiracy* means agreeing with another to join together for the purpose of committing an unlawful act or agreeing to use unlawful means to commit an act that would otherwise be lawful. The unlawful act does not have to be committed; the crime of conspiracy involves the *agreement* to engage in the unlawful act.

Unlike the other inchoate crimes, however, conspiracy permits criminal prosecution for the behavior of others as well as for one's own acts. A further distinction between attempt and conspiracy is that, unlike attempt, which merges into the crime (thus, a defendant cannot be convicted of both attempt to commit robbery and robbery of the same person), in most jurisdictions a defendant can be convicted of conspiracy and of the crime that was its object. Some jurisdictions do not permit two convictions.

Conspiracy may also be distinguished from attempt in that attempt requires an *act* of preparation, whereas the agreement may be sufficient to constitute the act requirement in conspiracy. Therefore, it is possible that a defendant could be convicted of conspiracy to commit robbery under circumstances that would not justify a conviction for attempted robbery.

In 2008 Rod R. Blagojevich, former Illinois governor, was arrested and indicted for conspiracy and soliciting bribes. It was alleged that Blagojevich, who as governor had the power to appoint a person to the U.S. Senate seat vacated when Barack Obama was elected president of the United States, attempted, in effect, to "sell" that seat. Blagojevich was impeached by the Illinois House of Representatives. (Tannen Maury/epa/Corbis)

Conspiracy is a favorite crime of many prosecutors, and as far back as 1925 it was called "the darling of the prosecutor's nursery."[23] Conspiracy received this label because of procedural reasons that are beyond the scope of this text but also because the definition of the crime permits prosecutions in cases in which it would be impossible to prove the elements of attempt. Because it is defined broadly, conspiracy is a useful tool for prosecutors. The role that conspiracy charges can play in today's world is illustrated in Focus 3.3, which examines some of the latest corporate financial scandals, and in Focus 3.4, which discusses a recent U.S. Supreme Court case on conspiracy.

In 2008 Rod R. Blagojevich, former Illinois governor, was arrested and indicted for conspiracy and soliciting bribes. It was alleged that Blagojevich, who as governor had the power to appoint a person to the U.S. Senate seat vacated when Barack Obama was elected president of the United States, attempted, in effect, to "sell" that seat. Blagojevich was impeached by the Illinois House of Representatives.

The Problem of Definition

Many students become frustrated by the lack of agreement in law. The study of law would be so much easier if there were fewer ambiguities. Conspiracy is no exception to this problem. It would be a misrepresentation of the facts to suggest a simple and definite statement defining the crime of conspiracy.

FOCUS 3.3   Conspiracy in the Corporate World

In recent years several major corporations (such as Enron, ImClone, WorldCom, Tyco International, and Adelphia Communications) reported financial losses, leading to criminal allegations, indictments, and arrests of company officials as well as the loss of millions of dollars in investments, jobs, and retirement funds for employees. The charges against corporate officials were numerous and involved several crimes discussed in the text, including conspiracy, which is a focus of this chapter. Focus 2.4 discussed the Enron scandal briefly and noted that Andrew Fastow and Ben Gilsan Jr., former executives of that company, were convicted of conspiracy, among other crimes. Enron has been described as a "company where fraud and deceit were the workaday mechanisms used to disguise the failings of a corporation secretly spinning out of control."[1]

In October 2002, Timothy N. Belden, a former senior trader at Enron, pleaded guilty to conspiracy with regard to illegally manipulating the California power crisis and thus making money for his company. According to the prosecution, "Belden and others conspired to defraud California electricity consumers and customers through a variety of schemes designed to artificially increase payments from the California power manager to Enron." This conspiracy, said the prosecutor, "allowed Enron to exploit and intensify the California energy crisis and prey on energy consumers at their most vulnerable moment."[2]

ImClone Systems is another corporation whose executives faced prosecutions. Shortly before the Federal Drug Administration's (FDA) announcement in late December 2001 that it would reject the company's application to market an experimental cancer drug, Samuel D. Waksal, the company's founder and chief executive, and several of his family and friends, sold large amounts of ImClone stock. The announcement of the FDA decision sent the company's stock prices down significantly. In October 2002, Waksal pleaded guilty to some charges, including conspiracy. Waksal was sentenced to over seven years in prison and ordered to pay $4 million in back taxes and fines.

The corporate scandals of recent years have reached beyond those who were employed by the corporation in question. For example, Martha Stewart, founder of Martha Stewart Omnimedia, a billion-dollar business empire, sold 4,000 shares of ImClone stock shortly before the aforementioned announcement. She was convicted of several federal charges, including conspiracy, and served five months in prison, followed by a five months of house arrest. Peter Bacanovic, Stewart's stockbroker at Merrill Lynch, was convicted, among other crimes, of conspiring with Stewart to lie about her sale of ImClone stock. He received the same sentence as Stewart.

Richard M. Scrushy, founder of HealthSouth Corporation, a company that he and others almost bankrupted during an accounting fraud, was convicted of conspiracy and other crimes and is serving seven years in a federal prison. Don Siegelman, former Alabama governor, was also convicted of conspiracy and other crimes based upon allegations that Siegelman offered Scrushy a seat on a state hospital licensing board in exchange for paying off a $500,000 debt from a lottery campaign initiated by the former governor.

1. "An Ex-Official Faces Charges in Enron Deals," *New York Times* (3 October 2002), p. 1.
2. "Enron Trader Pleads Guilty to Conspiracy," *New York Times* (16 October 2002), p. 1C.
3. "Ex-Governor Says Conviction Was Political," *New York Times* (27 June 2007), p. 15.

FOCUS 3.4   The U. S. Supreme Court Looks at Conspiracy

In 2003, the U.S. Supreme Court decided a conspiracy case that might have implications for efforts to combat terrorism. *United States v. Recio* involved a drug transaction in which four men were charged and convicted in a case involving the illegal transportation of $12 million worth of cocaine and marijuana. Government officials seized the truck and arrested the two original drivers, who then cooperated with law enforcement and drove the truck to their original destination, at which point the truck was taken over by Jimenez Recio and Adrian Lopez-Meza, the other two alleged conspirators. Recio and Lopez-Meza were arrested, charged, and convicted of conspiracy to possess with intent to distribute a controlled substance. Recio was also convicted of possession with intent to distribute.

Recio and Lopez-Meza argued successfully on appeal that their conspiracy convictions should be reversed because, based on a precedent case decided by that appellate court, a conspiracy ends when it becomes impossible to achieve the object of that conspiracy because of intervention by law enforcement of-

ficials.[1] Here, the government had already seized the truck when the appellants took possession; thus, they argued, they could not continue with the "object" of the alleged conspiracy.

The court agreed, but the U.S. Supreme Court reversed and remanded the case, holding that a conspiracy does not end because its "object" is thwarted by law enforcement officials. The U.S. Supreme Court noted that it has "repeatedly said that the essence of a conspiracy is 'an agreement to commit an unlawful act.'" The agreement is a "distinct criminal evil," which is punishable.[2]

This case has implications for efforts to combat terrorism as well as drug trafficking, both discussed later in this text. The government argued that it needs to cast a wide net to combat such crimes.

1. *United States v. Jimenez Recio*, 258 F.3d 1069 (9th Cir. 2002), *rev.d., remanded,* 537 U.S. 270 (2003).
2. *United States v. Jimenez Recio*, 537 U.S. 270 (2003).

A good starting point is a brief look at common law conspiracy. Conspiracy was not a recognized crime in early common law. When it emerged, it was defined narrowly, but over the years the definition was expanded. For purposes of this discussion, an 1832 definition is significant. In that year, an English lord stated that an indictment for conspiracy required that a defendant must be charged either with conspiracy "to do an unlawful act or a lawful act by unlawful means."[24] Although the word *unlawful* could have been understood as meaning *criminal*, the English and American courts interpreted it more broadly, to include acts that are "corrupt, dishonest, fraudulent, immoral, and in that sense illegal, and it is in the combination to make use of such practices that the dangers of this offense consist."[25]

Some jurisdictions retained this common law definition when drafting their statutes. Where that occurs, *conspiracy* is defined broadly as an agreement (or combination or confederation) to engage in an unlawful act or to engage in a lawful act by unlawful means. Some jurisdictions specify only that the conspiracy must be to commit a crime, whereas others specify the type of crime.

The New York Penal Code contains an example of a modern conspiracy statute. New York provides for six degrees of conspiracy, with the definition of each spec-

ifying the type of crime that must be the subject of the conspiracy and the type of felony that this conspiracy would be. For example, New York defines *conspiracy in the first degree* as follows:

> A person is guilty of conspiracy in the first degree when, with intent that conduct constituting a class A felony [the most serious of felonies] be performed, he, being over eighteen years of age, agrees with one or more persons under sixteen years of age to engage in or cause the performance of such conduct.[26]

The purpose of adding multiple degrees of conspiracy was to decrease the number of adults who use juveniles in criminal activities to limit their own exposure to prosecution. Conspiracy in the sixth degree in New York, for example, constitutes only the lowest form of punishment for conspiracy in that state, and it does not require the use of juveniles specifically. Conspiracy in the sixth degree, a class B misdemeanor, is defined as follows:

> A person is guilty of conspiracy in the sixth degree when, with intent that conduct constituting a crime be performed, he agrees with one or more persons to engage in or cause the performance of such conduct.[27]

Not all jurisdictions separate conspiracy into degrees, but most consider conspiracy to be a serious crime. For example, Pennsylvania defines the crime as follows:

> A person is guilty of conspiracy with another person or persons to commit a crime if with the intent of promoting or facilitating its commission he:
>
> (1) agrees with such other person or persons that they or one or more of them will engage in conduct which constitutes such crime or an attempt or solicitation to commit such crime; or
>
> (2) agrees to aid such other person or persons in the planning or commission of such crime or of an attempt or solicitation to commit such crime.[28]

Note that the Pennsylvania definition of conspiracy incorporates references to both solicitation and attempt.

Elements of Conspiracy

The crime of conspiracy consists of two basic elements:

1. A criminal act, which may be an agreement (some statutes require an act plus an agreement)
2. A criminal intent

The Act or Agreement

The first element of conspiracy is that there must be a criminal act. The act may be the agreement, which is the essence of conspiracy. The agreement does not have to be a written one; usually it is not. It may be inferred from the facts and circumstances of the case, but close analysis of the alleged agreement is important to determine:

✪ Whether more than one party was involved

✪ Whether the requisite criminal intent was present

✪ Whether there was one or more than one conspiracy

New York and some other jurisdictions require that the act must be an overt one. Thus, under that state's law, a person "shall not be convicted of conspiracy unless an overt act is alleged and proved to have been committed by one of the conspirators in furtherance of the conspiracy."[29]

Proving the existence of an agreement to commit an act may be difficult. One method is the objective standard, articulated by one court as whether any *rational* trier of fact (*e.g.*, a judge or juror) could conclude beyond a reasonable doubt that an agreement existed. The objective standard may be distinguished from the subjective standard, which asks in effect whether *you*, the trier of fact, could conclude that there was an agreement.[30]

The Problem of Multiple Agreements

An issue that may be even more complicated than whether an agreement existed is that of whether more than one agreement was in effect. If the prosecutor charges the defendants with more than one conspiracy but can prove only one of the charges and there is evidence of more than one, the defendants may be entitled to an acquittal. The number of agreements may also be important in the imposition of punishment.

It is not always easy to determine whether one or more conspiracies existed. Consider, for example, a complex series of transactions, such as occurred in *United States v. Bruno*, a frequently cited case despite the fact that it was decided in 1939 and reversed on other grounds. *Bruno* can be analyzed by two methods of determining the nature and scope of a conspiracy and whether one or more conspiracies existed: the chain or the wheel (or circle).[31]

In *Bruno*, 88 defendants were indicted for conspiracy to import, possess, and sell narcotics over a long period. The evidence showed that smugglers in New York City imported the drugs and sold them to intermediaries who distributed the drugs to two groups of retailers, one in Texas and Louisiana and the other in New York. These transactions are diagrammed in Figure 3.1.

The smugglers in *Bruno* committed the crime of importing. The intermediaries committed the crime of illegal distribution, and the two groups of retailers committed the crime of selling drugs illegally. The retailers argued that because there was no evidence that they had any contact with one another or with the smugglers, they were not involved in a conspiracy with them.

The U.S. Supreme Court held that only one conspiracy existed and that despite the lack of contact between the retailers and the smugglers, they each knew the other had to exist in order to complete the acts of smuggling, possessing, and distributing drugs. This chain of activities implies the existence of only one large conspiracy. Each retailer could be held criminally liable for every sale of narcotics made by other retailers as well as for the crime of smuggling.

In the second method of determining the extent of a conspiracy or the number of conspiracies—the

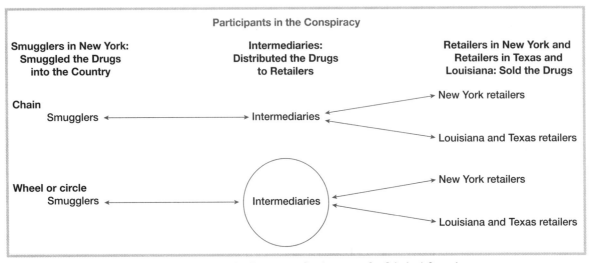

FIGURE 3.1 The Wheel and Chain Approach to the Agreement Rquirement of a Criminal Conspiracy

Source: Diagrammed by the author from the facts of *United States v. Bruno*, 105 F.2d 921 (2d Cir. 1939), *rev'd. on other grounds*, 308 U.S./ 287 (1939).

wheel or circle—the intermediaries (distributors) may be viewed as the central hub of the wheel, with the smugglers and each group of retailers constituting spokes on the wheel. Although in *Bruno* there was no communication between the New York retailers and the Texas and Louisiana retailers or between either of those groups of retailers and the smugglers, all communicated with the distributors. The U.S. Supreme Court held that such communication would be sufficient to establish an agreement to violate drug laws.

The retailers in *Bruno* argued unsuccessfully that there could not be only one conspiracy, as the government had charged, because neither group of retailers knew of the existence of the other and neither had communicated with the smugglers. The U.S. Supreme Court held that only one conspiracy existed. The Court ruled that, although it was of no concern to the smugglers who or how many retailers were involved, they knew there had to be retailers for the drugs to be sold.

The U.S. Supreme Court also held that each retailer knew he was a necessary part of "a scheme of distribution, and the others [the other retailers], whom he knew to be convenient to its execution, were as much parts of a single undertaking or enterprise as two salesmen in the same shop."[32]

The Requirement of an Act Plus an Agreement

Another element of conspiracy may be an act in addition to the agreement. Under some state statutes the agreement alone is sufficient; no further act is required. Other statutes, however, require that in addition to the agreement there must be an overt (open, public) act. When that is the case, normally the requirement is not as stringent as that required for an attempt. Often it is intended to permit any of the actors a chance to abandon their participation and avoid prosecution. An example of a sufficient overt act is the purchase of stamps to carry out a conspiracy to commit murder by poison sent through the mail.

Some states specify that an act in addition to an agreement is required only for some conspiracy crimes. Consider the Arizona statute:

> A person commits conspiracy if, with the intent to promote or aid the commission of an offense, such person agrees with one or more persons that at least one of them or another person will engage in conduct constituting the offense and one of the parties commits an overt act in furtherance of the offense, except that an overt act shall not be required if the object of the conspiracy was to commit any felony upon the person of another, or to commit an offense under [two other sections, defining the crimes of burglary and arson].[33]

When an overt act is required, it is not always necessary that all alleged co-conspirators engage in the overt act; an act on the part of one may be sufficient to establish this element of the crime.[34]

The Intent

The second element required for conspiracy is, of course, the *mens rea* or criminal intent. It is not sufficient to show that the conspirators intended to agree. It must be proved that they intended to accomplish an unlawful (or criminal) objective, which was the object of the conspiracy. The elements of the objective must be met. Consider the following example: Suppose A and B plan to bomb a building to destroy the structure. They know there are people inside and that in all probability these people will be killed by the explosion. A and B do not intend to kill the occupants. If they do bomb the building and people inside die as a result, the conspirators may not be convicted of conspiracy to commit murder (although they might be convicted of murder), only of conspiracy to bomb the building.[35]

Another problem that exists with regard to the *mens rea* requirement of conspiracy is what to do with alleged conspirators who merely provid goods or services that are used by others for unlawful (or criminal) purposes. Conspiracy requires intent, not just knowledge, so it would seem that knowledge that the goods and services would be used for unlawful purposes would not be sufficient.

U.S. Supreme Court cases on this point may seem inconsistent. In 1940 in *United States v. Falcone*, the Supreme Court held that selling sugar and yeast to buyers known to be engaging in a conspiracy to make illegal liquor was not sufficient to make the sellers part of the conspiracy.[36] But in 1943, in *Direct Sales Co. v. United States*, the Supreme Court upheld the conspiracy conviction of a drug manufacturer and wholesaler who sold large quantities of morphine to a specific doctor over a long period of time and must have known that the doctor could not have needed that amount of the drug for legal prescriptions.[37]

In later cases other courts have found the intent required for conspiracy by emphasizing the facts of *Direct Sales*, along with additional facts such as inflated prices, failure to keep required records of sales of restricted products (such as drugs), and the percentage of a seller's business accounted for by the illegal sales.[38]

One final *mens rea* requirement in conspiracy cases in some jurisdictions is that the parties must have had a corrupt motive, a person's reason for engaging in an act. Thus, if the parties did not know they were violating a statute, they might argue successfully that they were not guilty of conspiracy, which, by definition, implies that the agreement "must have been entered into with an evil purpose, as distinguished from a purpose to do the act prohibited, in ignorance of the prohibition."[39]

Not all courts agree, however, noting that normally ignorance of the law is not an excuse. Others take the position that if the conspiracy is to commit an act that is not generally agreed to be a crime but has been defined as such, the corrupt motive doctrine applies. This is based on the assumption that a person should be aware that there are laws against the more serious acts (such as murder, rape, robbery) but might not be aware that acts such as gambling or using some drugs are crimes.

Limitations on Parties to Conspiracy

The law establishes four limitations on parties to the crime of conspiracy:

✪ Wharton rule

✪ Husband-and-wife rule

✪ Two-or-more rule

✪ Corporation rule

Some jurisdictions, however, do not accept all of these limitations.

The **Wharton rule**, named after its author, Francis Wharton, specifies that when individuals engage in crimes that by definition require more than one person, they may not be prosecuted for conspiracy to commit those crimes; a third party must be involved for a conspiracy to exist. Crimes that qualify under this rule are acts such as adultery, bigamy, and incest. The Wharton rule has been rejected in some jurisdictions.

A second limitation is the *husband-and-wife rule*. Under the common law a husband and wife were considered to be one person, and because conspiracy requires two or more persons, they could not conspire to commit a crime. This position was accepted in the United States in earlier days, based primarily on the assumption that the husband "owned" his wife, who was under his control. As other laws concerning the relationship between husband and wife have changed, so has the law of conspiracy. Today a wife may legally act independently of her husband, so the two of them may commit conspiracy.

A third limitation on parties to conspiracy is the *two-or-more rule*, requiring that for a conspiracy to exist two or more persons must be involved. Although it is obvious that the definition of conspiracy precludes one person from conspiring alone, courts have taken different positions on what happens if, for example, one

Under the common law a husband and wife were considered as one person and thus did not constitute two people for the purposes of committing conspiracy. This rule, along with many other common law rules attaching to marriage, has been changed in most jurisdictions. (Jennifer Trenchard/IStockPhoto)

of two alleged conspirators is acquitted. Technically, if there are only two alleged conspirators and one is acquitted, the other may not be convicted, as there would be only one party to the conspiracy. Some courts have taken this position, while others look to the *reason* why a second alleged co-conspirator was not convicted. For example, if one alleged co-conspirator agreed to testify against the other alleged co-conspirator(s) in exchange for not being prosecuted, a conspiracy conviction may be upheld on the defendant who did not cooperate with the prosecution.

Although it might seem unfair to uphold the conspiracy convictions of a defendant whose alleged co-conspirators were acquitted in separate trials but not uphold those convictions if those acquittals occur in the same trials, the argument for taking this position is that it is necessary to maintain internal consistency. Logically, the same jury could not acquit one of two alleged conspirators and convict the other, for the second one would not have had anyone with whom to conspire. But if two juries reach different conclusions, internal consistency is not compromised. These issues are not problems, of course, in those jurisdictions that do not recognize the two-or-more rule.

A similar issue arises when the person charged with conspiracy allegedly conspired with a person who had

no intention of carrying out the conspiracy—for example, a police officer. Modern cases have held that this situation does not preclude a conspiracy conviction against the party with the criminal intent.[40]

The fourth limitation on parties to conspiracy is the *corporation rule*. Corporations may commit conspiracy with other corporations or with a natural person, although there may be problems with the two-or-more rule when that occurs. When two corporations and an officer of each are charged, there is no problem, for there are two or more separate persons involved in the conspiracy. Likewise, when a corporation is indicted for conspiracy, along with one of its officers and an officer from another corporation, the two-or-more requirement is met.

The problem arises when a corporation and one of its officers is charged with conspiracy. Very early cases established that this does not constitute a conspiracy.[41] Nor is there a conspiracy in a case involving two corporations and one agent acting for both corporations. In both of these cases, only one human actor is involved, so there can be no agreement between two or more persons.

The two-or-more requirement also arises when two or more agents of the same corporation are involved. Courts have differed on whether this situation meets the two-or-more requirement for conspiracy.

Defenses to Conspiracy

Most courts hold that impossibility is not a defense to conspiracy. Some, using the analogy of attempt, hold that legal but not factual impossibility is a defense. In many jurisdictions withdrawal or renunciation is permitted as a defense to conspiracy. Recall the earlier notation of the Arizona statute concerning renunciation as a defense to attempt, solicitation, conspiracy, or facilitation. Consider also this Pennsylvania statute:

> It is a defense [to conspiracy] that the actor, after conspiring to commit a crime, thwarted the success of the conspiracy, under circumstances manifesting a complete and voluntary renunciation of his criminal intent.[42]

Renunciation or abandonment of a conspiracy might be difficult to prove. Jurisdictions vary on their statutory requirements to prove the defense, and courts vary on their interpretations of the statutes.

In reacting to a requirement that the defense of withdrawal occurs only when alleged conspirators either communicate their withdrawal intentions to the persons with whom they had agreements or inform law enforcement authorities of the agreements and their intentions to abandon, the U.S. Supreme Court stated,

> Affirmative acts inconsistent with the object of the conspiracy and communicated in a manner reasonably calculated to reach co-conspirators have generally been regarded as sufficient to establish withdrawal or abandonment.[43]

Other Issues in Conspiracy

An important issue that arises in conspiracy cases is the extent to which the actor is liable for the crimes of his or her co-conspirators. In the leading case, *Pinkerton v. United States*, the U.S. Supreme Court established that a co-conspirator may be held accountable for the acts of fellow conspirators even though the requirements of criminal culpability for the acts of others involved in the crime are not met. Some of the offenses for which Pinkerton was convicted were committed without his knowledge and while he was in prison.[44]

The **Pinkerton rule** has been criticized as one that could result in gross distortion. If anyone who gets involved in a conspiracy is responsible for all criminal acts of co-conspirators, a relatively uninvolved person could become criminally culpable for many crimes.

Some courts dodge this problem by limiting criminal culpability for crimes of co-conspirators to reasonably foreseeable acts.

Another issue concerns the duration of the conspiracy. Culpability for the crimes of co-conspirators lasts only as long as the conspiracy. The conspiracy is considered to continue "up to the abandonment or success."[45] In a particular case, that point might be hard to determine, but it is very important, as a number of procedural issues are affected by the time at which the conspiracy ended. Both the duration of the conspiracy and the extent of culpability for the crimes of co-conspirators, in the case of a particular defendant, are affected by whether that defendant withdraws successfully or abandons the conspiracy.

Statutes concerning the duration of a conspiracy vary. The Pennsylvania statute offered here is one example.

> (g) DURATION OF CONSPIRACY . . .
>
> (1) conspiracy is a continuing course of conduct which terminates when the crime or crimes which are its object are committed or the agreement that they be committed is abandoned by the defendant and by those with whom he conspired;
>
> (2) such abandonment is presumed if neither the defendant nor any one with whom he conspired does any overt act in pursuance of the conspiracy during the applicable period of limitation; and
>
> (3) if an individual abandons the agreement, the conspiracy is terminated as to him only if and when he advises those with whom he conspired of his abandonment or he informs the law enforcement authorities of the existence of the conspiracy and of his participation therein.[46]

One final point of importance in conspiracy cases is that they may be (and usually are) extremely complicated. Frequently conspiracy charges are combined with charges for substantive crimes, many of which involve illegal drug sales. There may be multiple defendants (even scores of them in some instances), which means multiple attorneys if the cases are tried together. In addition, numerous substantive crimes may be alleged, with the charges differing by defendants. These cases may take weeks, even months, to try, resulting in enormous expense to the government as well as to

PARTIES TO CRIMES

The law has long recognized criminal culpability for people other than those who commit criminal acts. Individuals may assist, aid and abet, incite, or encourage others to commit criminal acts. The word **complicity** means association in a wrongful act. Thus, a person who shares in the guilt even though he or she did not engage in the crime is an **accomplice** to the crime, meaning that the individual shares in the responsibility for the crime but not in the criminal act itself. Such a person assumes criminal culpability in terms of the degree of involvement in the criminal act.

An example of this crime is illustrated by the 2007 conviction of Warren S. Jeffs, 51, leader of a 10,000-person polygamist cult, who was found guilty of aiding in the forced marriage of an underage girl, age 14, to her cousin. Jeffs was sentenced to up to life in prison. Even though he was not accused of having sexual relations with the underage girl, he was held criminally responsible for those illegal acts. In 2008, Jeffs and several members of a Texas polygamist sect were indicted on charges related to the so-called spiritual marriages with girls between the ages of 12 and 15, which is underage for consenting to sexual relations. The state had previously seized 440 children from the Texas ranch, alleging that they were abused and in danger if they continued to live there. After a court ruling that the state had overstepped its authority, most of the children were returned to their families. Strict rules and court oversight were required, but many of the charges were dropped. Jeffs and the others who were indicted face felony charges and will be tried.[47]

Various terms are used to describe the type and degree of accomplice involvement. Not all jurisdictions have all of these categories, and they may differ in definitions as well.

Under the common law a **principal** was the person who committed the crime, in contrast to the accessory, who assisted in the crime or who encouraged another to commit a crime. Most modern statutes do not make this distinction. Both the principal and the accessory are treated as principals, and accessories may be con-

Warren S. Jeffs, leader of a 10,000-person polygamist cult, was convicted in 2007 of aiding and abetting in the forced marriage of an underage girl. He was sentenced to up to life in prison. In 2008 Jeffs and others were indicted on charges related to "spiritual marriages" with underage girls. In 2007, Texas law enforcement officials seized 440 children from the cult's Texas ranch, alleging that the children had been abused. After various court battles, most of those children were returned to the custody of their mothers, although monitoring is required. (Steve Marcus/Reuters/Corbis)

victed even if the principal has not been convicted. Some jurisdictions, however, distinguish between types of principals. A **principal in the first degree** is one who perpetrates a crime either through his or her own act or by use of inanimate objects or innocent people. A **principal in the second degree** incites or abets the commission of a crime and is present actually or constructively. A person is present constructively when, without being present, he or she assists the principal of the first degree at the moment the crime is being committed. In many crimes, it is common for the principal in the second degree of a bank robbery to be posted away from the bank, ready to signal when the coast is clear.

An **accessory before the fact** incites or abets but is not present actually or constructively when the crime is committed. An example is someone who provides information or tools used in the commission of a crime. An **accessory after the fact** is one who, knowing that a felony has been committed, receives, relieves, comforts, or assists the perpetrator of the criminal act for the purpose of hindering the apprehension and conviction of that person.

Most modern statutes do not distinguish between principals of either degree and accessories before the fact; all three are treated as principals. Consider, for example, the Michigan statute entitled *Abolition of distinction between accessory and principle*:

> Every person concerned in the commission of an offense, whether he directly commits the act constituting the offense or procures, counsels, aids, or abets in its commission may hereafter be prosecuted, indicted, tried and on conviction shall be punished as if he had directly committed such offense.[48]

Accessories may be convicted even if the principal has not been convicted, although there are some exceptions. Many current statutes simply specify that an accomplice is accountable legally for the conduct of another, without referring to any of the categories used historically and defined here. One example of a statute that takes this position is that of New Hampshire, which is reproduced in full in Focus 3.5. In addition to providing an illustration of a modern complicity statute, the New Hampshire statute is important to the Case Analysis at the end of this chapter. Read the statute carefully as you digest this discussion on parties to crimes and consider, in particular, the type of intent that it requires.

Elements of Accomplice Liability

In general there are three elements to accomplice liability:

1. Whether it is necessary to find the principal guilty before convicting the accomplice
2. The act
3. The mental state

Often a fine line is drawn between doing enough and not doing enough to constitute the act required for accomplice liability. The easier cases are those in which the alleged accomplice provides a hotel room for a prostitute, provides a gun for a murderer, drives the getaway car for a robber, or supplies the necessary technological information for a computer thief. More difficult is the person who is present and appears to approve and who has some legal duty to act but does not do so.

Each case must be decided on its facts. *Pace v. State*, decided by the Indiana Supreme Court in 1967, illustrates the problem, while giving some general statements about guidelines for determining whether the alleged accomplice has committed the requisite act.[49]

PACE v. STATE
224 N.E.2d 312, 313 (Ind. 1967)

[The appellant was convicted of aiding and abetting a robbery.]

[T]he record shows the following: appellant, his wife and two infant children were in a car driving from South Bend to LaPorte. Eugene Rootes was riding with them. The appellant was driving with his wife and one child in the front seat. Rootes and appellant's other child were in the back seat. While in South Bend, appellant after asking his wife for permission stopped to pick up a hitchhiker, [Richard Leon] Reppert, who sat next to Rootes in the back seat with one of appellant's infant children. Later Rootes pulled a knife and took Reppert's wallet. After driving further, Reppert got out of the car. Rootes then took his watch. The appellant said nothing during the entire period and they continued driving. . . .

The main question . . . is what evidence beyond the mere presence of a person at the scene of a crime is sufficient to sustain a conviction as an accessory before the fact? This court has previously stated that negative acquiescence is not

FOCUS 3.5 Accomplice Liability in New Hampshire

N.H. Rev. Stats. Ann. (2008), Section 626:8. Criminal Liability for Conduct of Another

I. A person is guilty of an offense if it is committed by his own conduct or by the conduct of another person for which he is legally accountable, or both.

II. A person is legally accountable for the conduct of another person when:

    (a) Acting with the kind of culpability that is sufficient for the commission of the offense, he causes an innocent or irresponsible person to engage in such conduct; or

    (b) He is made accountable for the conduct of such other person by the law defining the offense; or

    (c) He is an accomplice of such other person in the commission of the offense.

III. A person is an accomplice of another person in the commission of an offense if:

    (a) With the purpose of promoting or facilitating the commission of the offense, he solicits such other person in committing it, or aids or agrees or attempts to aid such other person in planning or committing it; or

    (b) His conduct is expressly declared by law to establish his complicity.

IV. Notwithstanding the requirement of a purpose as set forth in paragraph III(a), when causing a particular result is an element of an offense, an accomplice in the conduct causing such result is an accomplice in the commission of that offense, if he acts with the kind of culpability, if any, with respect to that result that is sufficient for the commission of the offense. In other words, to establish accomplice liability under this section, it shall not be necessary that the accomplice act with a purpose to promote or facilitate the offense. An accomplice in conduct can be found criminally liable for causing a prohibited result, provided the result was a reasonably foreseeable consequence of the conduct and the accomplice acted purposely, knowingly, recklessly, or negligently with respect to that result, as required for the commission of the offense.

V. A person who is legally incapable of committing a particular offense himself may be guilty thereof if it is committed by the conduct of another person for which he is legally accountable, unless such liability is inconsistent with the purpose of the provision establishing his incapacity.

VI. Unless otherwise provided, a person is not an accomplice in an offense committed by another person if:

    (a) He is the victim of that offense; or

    (b) The offense is so defined that his conduct is inevitably incident to its commission; or

    (c) He terminates his complicity prior to the commission of the offense and wholly deprives it of effectiveness in the commission of the offense or gives timely warning to the law enforcement authorities or otherwise makes proper effort to prevent the commission of the offense.

VII. An accomplice may be convicted on proof of the commission of the offense and of his complicity therein, though the person claimed to have committed the offense has not been prosecuted or convicted or has been convicted of a different offense or degree of offense or has an immunity to prosecution or conviction or has been acquitted.

enough to constitute a person guilty of aiding and abetting the commission of a crime. Consequently, this court has always looked for affirmative conduct either in the form of acts or words from which reasonable inferences of a common design or purpose to effect the commission of a crime might be drawn. . . .

In the facts at bar we have found no evidence or reasonable inferences therefrom which might demonstrate that the appellant aided and abetted in the alleged crime. While he was driving the car, nothing was said, nor did he act in any manner to indicate his approval or countenance of the robbery. While there is evidence from which a jury might reasonably infer that he knew the crime was being committed, his situation was not one which would demonstrate a duty to oppose it. We do not intend to draw any hard and fast rules in this area of the law. Each case must be reviewed on its own facts; in so doing we hold that the verdict is not sustained by substantial evidence of probative value and is therefore contrary to law.

Judgment reversed.

Jurisdictions also differ regarding the *mens rea* requirement of complicity. Generally alleged accomplices are required at a minimum to have the *mens rea* required for the offenses for which they are alleged to be accomplices. In addition, most jurisdictions specify that the acts must be accompanied by an intent to aid in the commission of the crime, although in many cases it is difficult to distinguish between one who intends only to sell a product or a service and one who intends to do that to facilitate a crime. For example, if a motel owner rents rooms to individuals, knowing that they intend to use those rooms for illegal purposes, has the owner intended to facilitate a crime as well as to engage in a financial transaction?

Few cases have been decided on this issue, and the two leading ones disagree. *Backun v. United States*, decided in 1940, provides that the "seller may not ignore the purpose for which the purchase is made if he is advised of that purpose, or wash his hands of the aid that he has given the perpetrator of a felony by the plea that he has merely made a sale of merchandise."[50]

An earlier case, *United States v. Peoni*, concluded, "All the words used—even the most colorless, 'abet'— carry an implication of purposive attitude towards" the crime.[51] That decision is cited with approval in a 1990 Idaho case, stating that aiding and abetting "requires some proof that the accused either participated in or assisted, encouraged, solicited, or counseled the crime." Further,

> [m]ere knowledge of a crime and assent to or acquiescence in its commission does not give rise to accomplice liability. Failure to disclose the occurrence of a crime to authorities is not sufficient to constitute aiding and abetting. Rather, under the Idaho Criminal Code, failure to report a felony makes a person guilty only as an accessory, not as an accomplice.[52]

Several ways to solve the conflict between *Peoni* and *Backun* have been suggested. Accomplice liability may be limited to instances in which there exists "the purpose of promoting or facilitating the commission of an offense." Thus, it must be shown that the accomplice affirmatively desired to encourage or assist the principal.[53]

Second, some courts have held that it is sufficient that accomplices *know* their acts will assist in the commission of crimes, although they do not necessarily *desire* that result. Third, some jurisdictions permit finding that accomplices have the requisite criminal intent if they act recklessly, knowing that their behavior will facilitate the commission of a crime. These people may be just as dangerous to society as those who intend the harmful result. Some courts acknowledge this scenario only in the case of serious crimes.

Some jurisdictions have specified other conditions that must be considered, such as what stake the accomplice has in the outcome of the venture. For example, a defendant who will share in the financial proceeds of the venture presumably would have the intent to aid.

One other approach to the intent issue in accomplice liability is to enact a statute for criminal **facilitation**, which means to make it easier for another person to engage in a criminal act. New York has four degrees

of criminal facilitation, with *criminal facilitation in the first degree* defined as follows:

> A person is guilty of criminal facilitation in the first degree when, believing it probable that he is rendering aid to a person under sixteen years of age who intends to engage in conduct that would constitute a class A felony, he, being over eighteen years of age, engages in conduct which provides such person with means or opportunity for the commission thereof and which in fact aids such person to commit such a class A felony.[54]

Analogous to its statute that covers conspiracy in the first degree, discussed earlier in this chapter, New York drafted this criminal facilitation statute in an attempt to curb the increasing number of adults who were using young people in criminal activities to minimize or limit their own exposure to prosecution.

One final point with regard to complicity is that the penalty may be assessed in terms of the seriousness of the target crime. Notice in the following Kentucky criminal facilitation statute that the penalty for the facilitated crime increases as the facilitated crime increases; thus, the penalty for facilitating a misdemeanor is less than that of facilitating a felony.

> (1) A person is guilty of criminal facilitation when, acting with knowledge that another person is committing or intends to commit a crime, he engages in conduct which knowingly provides such person with means or opportunity for the commission of the crime and which in fact aids such person to commit the crime.
>
> (2) Criminal facilitation is a:
>   (a) Class D felony when the crime facilitated is a Class A or Class B felony or capital offense;
>   (b) Class A misdemeanor when the crime facilitated is a Class C or Class D felony;
>   (c) Class B misdemeanor when the crime facilitated is a misdemeanor.[55]

Other Issues of Accomplice Liability

Three other issues regarding accomplice liability should be mentioned briefly:

⬤ Whether the Wharton rule applies

⬤ Defenses

⬤ The scope of the crime

The Wharton Rule

As in the Wharton rule in conspiracy, in most cases of accomplice liability individuals are not held criminally culpable as accomplices when they assist principals to commit crimes that by definition require two people, such as prostitution, which requires a prostitute and a customer.

Defenses to Accomplice Liability

Generally abandonment is recognized as a defense to accomplice liability, but to sustain this defense, the defendant must show that the complicity was abandoned in a timely manner.

The Scope of Accomplice Liability

Traditionally an accomplice has been held criminally responsible for all crimes that might reasonably result in complicity, even though the principal's crimes go beyond those crimes contemplated by the accomplice. It may be argued, however, that this position extends criminal culpability beyond the requirement of a criminal state of mind; consequently, some jurisdictions reject the traditional rule.

PROSECUTING ANTICIPATORY OFFENSES AND PARTIES TO CRIMES

In the discussions of anticipatory offenses and parties to crimes, state and federal statutes have been mentioned. However, the crimes discussed in this chapter are also brought under the federal **Racketeer Influenced and Corrupt Organizations Act (RICO)**, which was part of the Organized Crime Control Act of 1970. This statute has been called the new darling of the prosecutor's nursery, replacing conspiracy in that position. RICO got this title because it is written broadly and therefore constitutes a potentially powerful prosecutorial tool. In enacting RICO, Congress stated: "It is the purpose of this Act to seek the eradication of organized crime in the United States . . . by providing enhanced sanctions and new remedies to deal with the unlawful activities of those engaged in organized crime."[56]

Although RICO was designed primarily to prosecute organized crime, the broadness of the statute enables prosecutors to use it effectively to prosecute the crimes discussed in this chapter. Unlike other statutes, RICO does not create specific individual offenses but operates on a *pattern* of offenses, most generally, those involving **racketeering**, which is a process of engaging in a racket, such as conspiracy, to obtain an illegal goal by means of threats. In addition, RICO allows enhanced penalties, as in the **forfeiture** provision, which provides that when a person is convicted under RICO, "any interest he has acquired or maintained in violation of" the RICO statute may be subjected to forfeiture. This means the government may order that the personal or real property acquired from money derived through RICO acts be forfeited to the government. That includes houses, cars, boats, and other assets as well as money paid for defense attorney fees, if the assets were secured from the alleged criminal acts. The forfeiture provision, as well as the threat of prosecution, has led many defense attorneys to decline to defend persons accused of drug trafficking or terrorist acts, for it may be impossible to determine whether the money the defendants use for lawyer fees came from illegal sources.

RICO also differs from other statutes in that penalties may be cumulative. Defendants may receive penalties for the underlying crime as well as for the RICO violation. One final distinction is that RICO provides different civil penalties, such as permitting some plaintiffs to recover treble damages. This means that instead of the usual procedure of permitting successful plaintiffs to recover the extent of their business and property losses from defendants who violated RICO, they may recover three times those damages.

Despite the focus on organized crime, RICO has also been used to prosecute doctors, lawyers, labor union leaders, government officials, and many other professionals, as well as business people charged with civil and criminal acts covered by the statute. Focus 3.6 illustrates the success that U.S. attorneys have had using RICO to prosecute lawyers who represented persons charged with such offenses as illegal drug trafficking or terrorism. Often the attorneys are accused of aiding and abetting their clients in some of their illegal activities. Attorney Lynne Stewart, whose case is discussed in that focus, is an example. Her attorney defended Stewart in these words:

> My client denies that she committed crimes. She denies that she did anything wrong. . . . I think [the prosecution of Stewart is] an attempt to send a message to the legal community. "If you represent people who we, the Justice Department, determine to be social pariahs, whether we call them terrorists or predators, there's going to be a price to pay."[57]

FOCUS 3.6   Good Defense or Illegal Activities: A Look at the Prosecution of Lawyers

"These lawyers defended clients charged with drug crimes aggressively. They did all the things lawyers are supposed to do and now they're charged." Those words of noted Miami defense attorney Roy Black were disputed by representatives of the Drug Enforcement Administration (DEA) and federal prosecutors. Black was referring to two of his firm's clients and others who were indicted in a 1995 drug case.[1]

Many defense lawyers will no longer defend persons accused of trafficking in drugs because of the fear that they will be charged with aiding and abetting or that the fees paid will be forfeited. According to Roy Black, "It is a frightening thought that lawyers can now be charged with crimes of their clients." But U.S. attorney Kendall Coffey of Miami, Florida, saw it differently: "This is not a case of lawyers falling into ethical gray areas. . . . It would be criminal if a truck driver had done these things."[2]

The charges against the attorneys in this case raised critical legal issues of how far an attorney may go in defending a client. Defense attorneys believe that the government charged the attorneys because of an overzealous attempt to crack down on drug trafficking in South Florida. A writer for the *American Bar Association Journal* stated it this way:

> A federal indictment of a handful of lawyers on charges of aiding and abetting their drug-dealing clients has sent shock waves throughout the defense bar, and left many wondering where good lawyering ends and criminal activity begins.[3]

Federal attorneys have also gone beyond drug cases in their pursuit of complicity charges against defense lawyers. For example, in April 2002 prosecutors secured an indictment against New York lawyer Lynne Stewart, who represented Sheik Omar Abdel-Rahman, known as the "blind cleric" who was convicted of leading the first World Trade Center bombing. Stewart was accused of aiding her client "in continuing to direct the terrorist activities of the Islamic Group from his prison cell in the United

States." Rahman is serving a life sentence for his 1995 conviction for plotting to blow up several New York City landmarks, including the World Trade Center.

In a speech before the New Jersey state bar in October 2002, Stewart proclaimed that what happened to her "could happen to anyone, at any time, anyplace and anywhere for lawyers who represent clients charged with heinous crimes."[4] Stewart, who was charged with aiding and abetting a terrorist organization, has represented terrorists, political radicals, and mob figures. In February 2005, Stewart, co-conspirator Ahmed Abdel Sattar, and Stewart's Arabic translator, Mohammed Yousry, were convicted of defrauding the government and aiding an imprisoned terrorist. Specifically, Stewart was portrayed as the mastermind in a conspiracy to evade the special prison administrative restrictions concerning the contacts that Stewart's client was permitted with the outside world and in lying to the government in a written statement that she would observe those restrictions. In October 2005, Stewart's motion for a new trial was denied; in 2007 she was disbarred.[5] Stewart was sentenced to 28 months in prison and was free pending the federal prosecutors' appeal of that sentence, which could have been as long as 30 years.

1. "Lawyer Indicted on Drug Charges Recognized as Brilliant by Peers," *Los Angeles Times* (7 June 1995), p. 20.
2. Ibid.
3. Henry J. Reske, "Defense Lawyers Fear Impact of Cali Case," *American Bar Association Journal* 81 (September 1995): 16.
4. "Indicted Lawyer: It Could Happen to You: Terrorists' Attorney Paints a Chilling Picture," *New Jersey Lawyer* (7 October 2002): 4.
5. "Proof Sufficient to Convict Lynne Stewart, Judge Holds," *New York Law Journal* 234 (26 October 2005): 1; *United States v. Sattar*, 395 F.Supp.2d 79 (S.D.N.Y. 2005), *and related proceeding, Matter of Stewart*, 834 N.Y.S.2d 157 (1st Dept. 2007).

Prosecutors and the jury saw it differently; Stewart was believed to have been providing material to terrorists.

Federal RICO Statute

The federal RICO statute begins by listing the crimes that may form the basis of a RICO offense. Twenty-four federal and eight state crimes are included. These crimes are referred to as *predicate crimes* because they constitute a predicate, or basis, for a RICO violation.

Each predicate crime may constitute a racketeering activity, but the RICO statute requires a *pattern* of racketeering activity. It is not aimed at individual violators but rather at those who have committed at least two predicate offenses within a 10-year period, one of which occurred after RICO became effective.

Specifically, RICO prohibits the following:

1. The use of income derived from a *pattern of racketeering* to acquire an interest in an enterprise

The federal RICO statute has been used to indict and convict defense attorneys, such as Lynne Stewart, who was convicted of aiding and abetting clients who were involved in terrorist acts. Stewart was sentenced to 28 months in prison and was free pending the federal prosecutor's appeal of that sentence, which could have been as long as 30 years. (Chet Gordon/The Image Works)

2. Acquiring or maintaining an interest in an enterprise through a pattern of racketeering activity

3. Conducting or participating in an enterprise's affairs through a pattern of racketeering activity

4. Conspiring to commit any of these offenses[58]

The RICO statute does not, however, specify what is necessary to make two or more federal crimes a pattern. In *H.J. Inc. v. Northwestern Bell Telephone Company*, the U.S. Supreme Court faced that issue in a civil RICO action. RICO is used frequently as a basis for civil cases because of the potentially high penalties (treble damages) plus court costs and attorney fees. Although trial procedures and proof distinguish civil

and criminal RICO actions, the Court's interpretation of the meaning of the pattern requirement in a civil case has applicability to a criminal RICO case.[59]

In this case the U.S. Supreme Court noted that Congress had not specified what it meant by *pattern*, looked at the legislative history of the statute, and concluded that Congress intended the RICO statute to cover continuing racketeering activity. The key phrase in the Court's analysis is *continuity plus relationship*. The Supreme Court held as follows:

> In order to prove a pattern of racketeering activity, a plaintiff or prosecutor must show at least two racketeering predicates that are related *and* that amount to, or threaten the likelihood of, continued criminal activity. Proof of neither relationship nor continuity requires a showing that the racketeering predicates were committed in furtherance of multiple criminal schemes.[60]

The statute specifies that an enterprise includes "any individual, partnership, corporation, association or other legal entity, and any union or group of individuals associated in fact although not a legal entity." According to the U.S. Supreme Court in *United States v. Turkette*, the enterprise must have an ongoing formal or informal organization whose associates function as a continuing unit. Legal enterprises are included.[61]

Litigation under RICO may be complex, but it is important to understand that RICO was intended by Congress to reach serious cases—major violators who engage in a pattern of racketeering activity. As noted, however, the statute is worded broadly, and the U.S. Supreme Court has found it necessary to place some limits on the interpretation of some of the broad language. In 1993 the Supreme Court held that generally, professional advisers to businesses, such as accountants, do not participate in those businesses to the extent that they should be included within the reach of RICO.[62]

State RICO Statutes

States also have RICO statutes. For example, Georgia's criminal code has a chapter entitled "Racketeer Influenced and Corrupt Organizations." One section enumerates the following *prohibited activities*:

(a) It is unlawful for any person, through a pattern of racketeering activity or proceeds derived therefrom, to acquire or maintain, directly or indirectly, any interest in or control of any enterprise, real property, or personal property of any nature, including money.

(b) It is unlawful for any person employed by or associated with any enterprise to conduct or participate in, directly or indirectly, such enterprise through a pattern of racketeering activity.

(c) It is unlawful for any person to conspire or endeavor to violate any of the provisions of subsection (a) or (b) of this Code section.[63]

In 1986, the Georgia Supreme Court held that Section (b) was not unconstitutionally vague or overbroad; the U.S. Supreme Court declined to review the case.[64]

Forfeitures

In the preceding discussion it was mentioned that the government may require forfeitures of personal and real property acquired or maintained by money secured through illegal patterns of racketeering. RICO is not the only federal statute that permits forfeitures; about 100 statutes contain a forfeiture provision. It is estimated that 80 percent of individuals who lose property through forfeiture laws are never charged with crimes. The government seizes not only the means of the illegal production of goods and the illegal goods (such as drugs) but also the homes in which the illegal materials are found and the vehicles used to transport them. These forfeitures may occur without prior notice, and the individual who wants the property back has the burden of proving that it should not have been confiscated. Before a hearing will be held on that issue, the owner of the forfeited property must post a bond of 10 percent of the value of the property.[65]

The U.S. Supreme Court has shown some concern with the potential unfairness of forfeitures, as illustrated by two recent decisions. The Court has ruled that the value of seized property must not be excessive when compared to the seriousness of the crimes in question. The Court views the forfeiture of property as punishment and applies the cruel and unusual punishment clause of the Eighth Amendment (see Appendix A) to the analysis of forfeitures.[66] In a Florida case involving civil forfeiture proceedings in which the government had taken a house alleging that it was purchased with money from drug trafficking, the U.S. Supreme Court bolstered the right of persons to appeal when the government seizes their property.[67] In a subsequent case the Court held that unless there are exigent circumstances, the government must give no-

tice and allow the opportunity for a hearing before real property subject to civil forfeiture is seized.[68]

But in a 1996 decision the U.S. Supreme Court upheld the forfeiture of an innocent person's property. In *Bennis v. Michigan* the Court ruled that the Fourteenth Amendment's due process clause (see Appendix A) does not forbid a forfeiture of property belonging to an innocent owner who was not aware that the property would be used in a crime. The Supreme Court referred to precedent cases, holding that "an owner's interest in property may be forfeited by reason of the use to which the property was put even though the owner did not know that it was to be put to such use." *Bennis* involved a petitioner who was co-owner of a car in which her husband was apprehended while having sex with a prostitute. The state forfeited the wife's interest as well as her husband's interest in the car even though she did not know of her husband's illegal acts.[69]

The U.S. Supreme Court has, however, placed limits on how much can be forfeited. In 2001, in *United States v. Bajakajian*, a sharply divided Court, by a 5-4 vote, held that a forfeiture intended as punishment is unconstitutional if the amount is "grossly disproportional" to the offense. Specifically, the Court held that it was unconstitutional to require a forfeiture of $357,144 in undeclared cash that a Los Angeles man and his family were carrying in their suitcases on a flight to Cyprus. The family violated the statute that requires that a person who transports over $10,000 in cash out of the United States to another country, or from another country into the United States, or who receives money so transported by another, must report that transaction. Failure to do so subjects one to a charge of bulk cash smuggling, which can lead to forfeiture of the funds that were not reported.[70]

SUMMARY

After two chapters that discussed the meaning and purpose of the criminal law and the general culpability of persons for criminal acts, this chapter focused on anticipatory crimes and the criminal responsibility of people who are connected to crimes but who are not participants in the traditional sense. An understanding of the crimes discussed in this chapter provides additional reasons for thinking about the meaning and purpose of the criminal law and for reexamining how far that law should go to deter, to promote justice, to punish, or to accomplish any other relevant purpose.

Some of the crimes discussed in this chapter may be categorized as inchoate or anticipatory in that the actual crime is never committed. Inchoate crimes are important, however, for in many cases they lead to the commission of other crimes. An individual who is thwarted in an attempted robbery may try again—and succeed. But even the failures are threats to society, as well as to potential victims.

The crime of solicitation permits punishing people who are the instigators of crimes but who do not commit those crimes. The solicitor may be the prime reason the crime is committed. Because of the potential seriousness of solicitation, some states have very strict requirements for a successful abandonment or renunciation defense.

It is not always easy to distinguish *solicitation*, which involves preparation, from *attempt*, which involves perpetration along with the required criminal state of mind. The facts of each case must be analyzed carefully to determine whether there is any direct movement toward committing a crime—in other words, whether there is an attempt.

Abandonment and legal impossibility are two defenses that may be permitted in attempt cases. Both require careful consideration of the facts. Frequently it is difficult to determine whether the accused abandoned the attempt or just failed to achieve the goal of committing a crime successfully. Likewise, it may be difficult to determine the difference between factual impossibility, which usually is not a defense, and legal impossibility, which may be a valid defense.

This chapter contained a discussion of criminalizing the knowing transmission of HIV, which causes AIDS. The use of attempt crimes in these cases has been challenged in the courts, with some upholding the convictions and others rejecting them.

Conspiracy occupied a significant portion of this chapter, for it is a crime that is prosecuted frequently today and, most recently, has involved top executives in large corporations. Because some jurisdictions permit prosecution and conviction for a substantive crime (such as murder) and conspiracy (such as conspiracy to commit murder), conspiracy is a very important tool for prosecutors. Conspiracy is important, too, because this crime may be prosecuted successfully even when the predicate crime did not occur. A person may be found guilty of conspiracy to commit burglary even though the burglary was not committed. Conspiracy is a favorite charge of prosecutors also because it is defined broadly. Most conspiracy statutes are precise enough to pass constitutional scrutiny but sufficiently broad to encompass a wide range of acts.

Conspiracy requires an agreement between two or more parties. In most jurisdictions the agreement is sufficient to constitute the act required for a crime, but some jurisdictions require an overt act in addition to the agreement. The agreement required for conspiracy is not an easy element to prove. It does not have to be a written agreement; in fact, conspiracy agreements are seldom written. Nor does the agreement have to be communicated to each person in the alleged conspiracy.

The wheel and the chain methods may be used to decide whether an agreement existed between parties that have had no contact with one another. If all of the parties had contact with a central hub (the wheel approach), in some cases it can be inferred that a reasonable person in that situation would know there were others involved.

Conspiracies may be limited by the Wharton rule, referring to crimes that require a specific number of people. Adultery, for example, requires two people; therefore, if only two people are involved, under the Wharton rule there cannot be a conspiracy to commit adultery. Although in the past husbands and wives could not conspire because legally they were one person, that rule has been changed.

Corporations may be charged with conspiracy provided the two-or-more rule is not violated. The key is to determine whether one or two human actors were involved in the alleged criminal agreements. Although any alleged conspiracy may have begun with more than one party to the agreement, that may change when one party is acquitted. If only one party is left without an acquittal, that individual may not be tried for conspiracy in many jurisdictions. Exceptions may be made, depending on the nature of the acquittal.

The *mens rea* requirement for conspiracy presents problems. The conspirators must have not only an intent to agree but also an intent to accomplish the criminal purpose. Usually the degree of intent required is that required for the substantive crime. Intent may be inferred, however, from the alleged conspirator's knowledge of the situation. In addition, some jurisdictions require an evil purpose or motive.

One reason that conspiracy is a popular crime with prosecutors is that it permits punishment of individuals for crimes committed by others. Some of these crimes may go beyond the original agreement. This rule, called the Pinkerton rule, has been criticized. Some jurisdictions handle the Pinkerton rule problem by limiting criminal liability of an individual for the criminal acts of a co-conspirator only if those acts are reasonably foreseeable.

The next section of this chapter focused on parties to crimes. Jurisdictions differ in how they categorize such crimes, but generally the following categories exist: principal in the first degree, principal in the second degree, accessory before the fact, and accessory after the fact. Today most jurisdictions do not distinguish among either degree of principals and accessories before the fact; all three are treated as principals.

As with other crimes included in this chapter, defining the elements of a principal may be difficult. An act is required. Usually courts look for affirmative acts in contrast to mere acquiescence to an act. The *mens rea* required for a principal may be hard to determine, but usually it will require at least the level of *mens rea* required for the offense to which the actor is an alleged accomplice. Some jurisdictions require proof of an intent to aid. Some look to see what stake the accomplice has in the outcome of the illegal venture. Others try to avoid these problems by drafting a separate statute to cover criminal facilitation.

The chapter then focused on the prosecution of the crimes discussed in the chapter, including the prosecution of attorneys and others under the Racketeer Influenced and Corrupt Organizations Act (RICO). RICO permits prosecution for both the individual predicate crimes as well as for the enterprise activities if a sufficient pattern of activities can be established.

RICO also permits forfeitures (as do many other federal as well as state statutes), and the chapter noted examples of some recent efforts of U.S. officials to apply this provision, as well as court restrictions on the amounts that may be forfeited.

All of the crimes discussed in this chapter may be related to the rest of a jurisdiction's criminal code. It is important to check that code carefully before deciding how anticipatory crimes and parties to crimes are applied. The crimes discussed in this chapter may also be related to the crimes covered in subsequent chapters, such as crimes of violence, property crimes, or drug trafficking.

STUDY QUESTIONS

1. Why does a criminal code need to include solicitation?

2. Comment in detail on this statement: A person charged with solicitation to burn a house may not be convicted of that crime if the house does not burn.

3. Discuss the elements and the defenses for solicitation.

4. Distinguish between solicitation and attempt.

5. Explain how the act and intent elements of a crime relate to the crime of criminal attempt. Explain what is meant by the "substantial step" requirement imposed by some attempt statutes or judicial interpretations of those statutes.

6. What must occur for a defendant to establish abandoning an attempt? What is the difference between voluntary and involuntary abandonment?

7. What is meant by *impossibility* in criminal law? Distinguish between factual impossibility and legal impossibility.

8. What do you think is the most appropriate charge to bring against persons who know they are HIV-positive or already have AIDS and who engage in activities, such as sexual intercourse or biting, that may spread the virus to others?

9. Why are prosecutors so fond of conspiracy statutes?

10. Discuss the requirement of an act as an element of conspiracy.

11. What is the difference between the wheel and the chain analogies? How do they relate to conspiracy?

12. What is meant by the *Wharton rule*? Should it be abolished?

13. Under what circumstances may corporations be prosecuted for conspiracy?

14. Briefly discuss the problems with requiring a criminal intent, or *mens rea*, for conspiracy.

15. To what extent may conspirators be held criminally responsible for the crimes of their co-conspirators? How does the Pinkerton rule apply to this question? Do you think this rule should be followed? Why or why not?

16. How long does a conspiracy last? How do you know when it ends? Why are conspiracy cases so complicated?

17. Discuss recent conspiracy cases in the corporate world.

18. Explain the differences among the following: principal in the first degree, principal in the second degree, accessory before the fact, and accessory after the fact. Should any of these categories be abolished? Why or why not?

19. Explain the elements in accomplice liability crimes.

20. When prosecutors bring charges against people allegedly involved in organized or business crimes, why might they prefer RICO to statutes defining specific crimes, such as conspiracy?

21. Explain what is meant by *predicate crimes* and *criminal enterprise* under RICO. What is a pattern of activity?

22. Under what theory have some defense lawyers been convicted of complicity crimes?

22. Define *forfeiture*, and apply it to recent conspiracy or related cases.

23. What is the purpose of the statute that requires persons to report transporting (or receiving) over $10,000 in cash when leaving or entering the United States? Is all of the money subject to forfeiture? Explain the basis for your answer.

FOR DEBATE

Later in this text we will explore in detail the crimes of drug trafficking and terrorism. It is relevant here, however, to consider the current efforts by the U.S. Department of Justice to prosecute lawyers in their defense of individuals accused of these major categories of crimes. This chapter's debate topic is based on this area of concern.

Resolved: That the U.S. Department of Justice should pursue vigorously by use of RICO and other statutes the prosecution of defense attorneys who represent persons accused of drug trafficking, terrorist acts, or other major crimes, if there is any evidence those attorneys may have been involved in acts of complicity.

KEY TERMS

CASE ANALYSIS

STATE v. ETZWEILER

480 A.2d 870 (N.H. 1984), and superseded by statute as stated in State v. Anthony, 861 A.2d 773 (N.H. 2004)

Case Preview

Chapter 2 analyzed the issue of intent and noted the four types of intent that the Model Penal Code (and subsequently many states) requires: purposely, knowingly, recklessly, and negligently. That discussion noted that some scholars question the inclusion of *negligently* in the definition of intent. This chapter explained inchoate crimes, which illustrate that some acts are considered criminal even though specific individuals may not have been directly involved in the actual commission of those acts. The last section of the chapter analyzed parties to crimes, one of which is an accomplice to a crime.

The case presented here raises the issue of whether one may be held accountable as an accomplice in a case of alleged negligent homicide. *Negligent homicide* is recognized by the Model Penal Code and many state statutes. It requires that a death occur as the result of a negligently driven motor vehicle but does not require that the driver have a purposeful or knowingly intent to kill or even have engaged in reckless behavior.

Under the common law, if a person was present and involved in aiding and abetting a crime, that individual could be charged as a principal in the crime. Under that theory, the owner of an automobile who loaned his car to a drunk person and rode in the car with that individual could be held criminally culpable for damage, injuries, or death caused by that drunk driver. Likewise, under the common law, a bar owner could be held responsible for injuries, deaths, or property damage caused by persons who caused an accident after leaving a bar and getting into a car to drive it while under the influence of alcohol. This would be the case even if the owner was not present at the bar when the liquor was consumed.

In 1973, the State of New Hampshire enacted the statute in question in this case, thereby abrogating the common law of that state by creating a statute of *accomplice liability*. In so doing, the state legislature gave a much more narrow definition of those cases in which a person could be held criminally culpable for the conduct of another person. Consider carefully the statute in this case, analyze the facts, and decide whether the court is reasonable in its interpretation of the statute and, if so, whether that is a good statute or should be changed.

The decision by the New Hampshire Supreme Court was 3-2, with Judges Batchelder, Brock, and Souter in the majority and Judges Douglas and King dissenting. Judge Batchelder wrote the opinion for the court.

Facts

On July 30, 1982, the defendants, Mark Etzweiler and Ralph Bailey, arrived in Etzweiler's automobile at the plant where both were employed. Bailey had been drinking alcoholic beverages and was, allegedly, intoxicated. Etzweiler, allegedly knowing that Bailey was intoxicated, loaned his car to Bailey and proceeded into the plant to begin work. Bailey drove Etzweiler's car away. Approximately 10 minutes later, Bailey, driving recklessly, collided with a car driven by Susan Beaulieu. As a result of the accident, two passengers in the Beaulieu car, Kathryn and Nathan Beaulieu, were killed.

[Etzweiler was indicted on two counts of negligent homicide and, subsequently, two counts of negligent homicide as an accomplice. The New Hampshire Supreme Court ordered all of the indictments against Etzweiler dismissed. Bailey was indicted on two counts of manslaughter in the deaths of the two children, who were passengers in the other car. Bailey was convicted of the lesser offenses of negligent homicide and sentenced to prison; those convictions were upheld on appeal.]

Issue

[W]hether the legislature . . . intended to impose criminal culpability upon a person who lends his automobile to an intoxicated driver but does not accompany the driver, when the driver's operation of the borrowed automobile causes death.

Holding

[W]e hold, as a matter of law [decided by the court rather than a matter of fact determined by a jury after hearing the evidence in the case], that, in the present context of the Criminal Code, an individual may not be an accomplice to negligent homicide.

Rationale

Accomplice liability under [New Hampshire law] is defined in two parts . . . "A person is an accomplice of another person in the commission of an offense if: (a) With the purpose of promoting or facilitating the commission of the offense, he solicits such other person in committing it, or aids or agrees or attempts to aid such other person in planning or committing it; . . . " Under [this] section, the State has the burden of establishing that the accomplice acted with the purpose of promoting or facilitating the commission of the substantive offense. This encompasses the requirement that the accomplice's acts were designed to aid the primary actor in committing the offense . . . , and that the accomplice had the purpose to "make the crime succeed". . . . [In addition] . . . the State has the burden of establishing . . . [that] the accomplice must act "with the kind of culpability, if any, with

respect to that result that is sufficient for the commission of the offense." . . .

Our interpretation of the accomplice liability statute effectuates the policy that an accomplice's liability ought not to extend beyond the criminal purposes that he or she shares. Because accomplice liability holds an individual criminally liable for actions done by another, it is important that the prosecution fall squarely within the statute. . . .

[U]nder our statute, the accomplice must aid the primary actor in the substantive offense with the purpose of facilitating the substantive offense—in this case negligent homicide. . . . To satisfy the requirements [of New Hampshire law] the State must establish that Etzweiler's acts were designed to aid Bailey in committing negligent homicide. Yet under the negligent homicide statute, Bailey must be unaware of the risk of death that his conduct created. We cannot see how Etzweiler could intentionally aid Bailey in a crime that Bailey was unaware he was committing.

For Discussion

The legal citation to this case ends with the following information: *and superseded by statute as stated in State v. Anthony*, 861 A.2d 773 (NH 2004).

Consider the facts of this later case. Virginia Anthony was indicted for being an accomplice to her husband's act of committing cruelty toward an animal (a felony) by aiding him in binding the legs of a colt together and leaving it to suffer and cause injury. The jury was instructed that they could also convict her of the lesser charge of being an accomplice to negligent cruelty toward an animal. Anthony was acquitted on the felony charge but convicted of the lesser charge of being an accomplice to negligent cruelty toward an animal. She argued on appeal that according to *Etzweiler*, New Hampshire does not recognize the crime of being an accomplice to a negligent act, such as cruelty to an animal. In *State v. Anthony*, the New Hampshire Supreme Court rejected Anthony's appeal, emphasizing that in 2001, New Hampshire revised the complicity statute and added Section IV (reprinted in Focus 3.5) and that this section, following the Model Penal Code's intent requirements of purposely, knowingly, recklessly, or negligently, includes the conduct in question.

After a long discussion of all the intent meanings, the court in *Anthony* concluded:

> Accordingly, under our interpretation of [the revised New Hampshire statute] the crime of accomplice to negligent cruelty to animals exists under New Hampshire law.

Which of the two cases, *Etzweiler* or *Anthony*, do you think states the most reasonable position? Do you think the facts of the two cases are clearly distinguishable? Would you find it reasonable to deny criminal culpability in either or both case but permit the victims to sue for civil damages? Consider the following Internet Activity.

INTERNET ACTIVITY

Dram shop laws that provide civil liability for those who allow a visibly intoxicated person to drive are in place in a number of states. The following University of Delaware website is dedicated to a variety of issues related to alcohol and the consumption of alcohol by college students. This particular page will allow you to access research and data about alcohol and the dram shop laws: http://www.udel.edu/brc/research_statistics/reviews.html (accessed 9 December 2008).

Review the information available about the dram shop laws, and consider the following question: Do you think it is more effective to use the criminal law or the civil law against bartenders in an effort to deter drunk drivers? Consider the website's discussion of *social hosts*, and decide whether you think dram shop laws should include them as well as bartenders.

NOTES

1. NY CLS Penal, Title G, Section 100.13 (2008).
2. Pa.C.S., Title 18, Section 902(a)(b)(2008).
3. American Law Institute, Model Penal Code, Section 5.02 (b), Official Draft, 1985.
4. *State v. Lee*, 804 P.2d 1208 (Or. App. 1991), *review denied*, 812 P.2d 807 (Or. 1991).
5. Ariz. Rev. Stat., Title 13, Section 13-1005B (2008).
6. Pa.C.S., Title 18, Section 902(B)(2007).
7. *Gervin v. State*, 371 S.W.2d 449 (Tenn. 1963).
8. *Rex v. Scofield*, Cald. 397 (1784).
9. *Rex v. Higgins*, 2 East 5 (1801).
10. *People v. Terry*, 479 N.Y.S.2d 278, 279 (N.Y.App.Div. 1984).
11. See, for example, *Gray v. State*, 654 So.2d 552 (Fla. 1995).
12. *State v. Chhom*, 911 P.2d 1014 (Wash. 1996).
13. *United States v. Cartlidge*, 808 F.2d 1064 (5th Cir. 1987), footnotes and citations omitted.
14. *State v. Reeves*, 916 S.W.2d 909 (Tenn. 1996). The Tennessee criminal attempt statute is codified at Tenn. Code Ann., Section 39-12-101 (2008).
15. *Schultz v. State*, 749 P.2d 559 (Okla.Crim.App. 1988).
16. *State v. Walters,* 783 P.2d 531 (Or.App. 1989), *reversed*, 804 P.2d 1164 (Ore. 1991), *cert. denied*, 501 U.S. 1209 (1991).
17. *State v. Hayes*, 78 Mo. 307 (1883).
18. Ariz. Rev. Stat., Section 13-1005 (2008).
19. *Attorney General v. Sillem*, 159 Eng. Rep. 178 (1863).
20. Mich. Comp. Laws, Title 333, Section 333.5210 (2008).
21. *Jensen v. Michigan*, 586 N.W.2d 748 (Mich.App. 1998).
22. *Smallwood v. State,* 680 A.2d 512 (Md. 1996).
23. *Harrison v. United States*, 7 F.2d 259 (2d Cir. 1925).
24. *Rex v. Jones,* 110 Eng. Rep. 485 (1832).
25. *State v. Burnham*, 15 N.H. 396 (N.H. 1844).
26. NY CLS Penal, Title G, Section 105.17 (2008).
27. NY CLS Penal, Title G, Section 105.00 (2008).
28. Pa.C.S., Title 18, Section 903(a)(1)(2) (2008).
29. NY CLS Penal, Title G, Section 105.20 (2008).
30. *United States v. Brown*, 776 F.2d 397 (2d Cir. 1985), *cert. denied*, 475 U.S. 1141 (1986).
31. *United States v. Bruno*, 105 F.2d 921, 922 (2d Cir. 1939), *rev'd. on other grounds*, 308 U.S. 287 (1939).
32. *United States v. Bruno*, 105 F.2d 921, 922 (2d Cir. 1939), *rev'd. on other grounds*, 308 U.S. 287 (1939).
33. Ariz. Rev. Stat., Title 13, Section 13-1003.A. (2008).
34. *United States v. Robinson*, 503 F.2d 208 (7th Cir. 1974), *cert. denied*, 420 U.S. 949 (1975).
35. See Model Penal Code comment to Section 5.03, p. 403.
36. *United States v. Falcone*, 311 U.S. 205 (1940).
37. *Direct Sales Co. v. United States*, 319 U.S. 703 (1943).
38. See, for example, *People v. Lauria*, 59 Cal.Rptr. 628 (Cal. Ct.App. 1967).
39. *People v. Powell*, 63 N.Y. 88 (1875).
40. *State v. St. Christopher,* 232 N.W.2d 798 (Minn. 1975).
41. *Union Pacific Coal Co. v. United States*, 173 F. 737 (8th Cir. 1909).
42. Pa.C.S., Title 18, Section 903(f) (2008).
43. *United States v. United States Gypsum Co.*, 438 U.S. 422 (1978).
44. *Pinkerton v. United States*, 328 U.S. 640 (1946).
45. *United States v. Kissel*, 218 U.S. 601 (1910).
46. Pa.C.S., Title 18, Section 903(g)(1)(2)(3) (2008).
47. "Polygamist Ranch Three Sect Members Surrender, Post Bond: All Face Sexual Assault Charges; Two also Accused of Bigamy," *Dallas Morning News* (30 September 2008), p. 3.
48. MCLS, Section 767.39 (2008).
49. *Pace v. State*, 224 N.E.2d 312, 313 (Ind. 1967).
50. *Backun v. United States*, 112 F.2d 635, 637 (4th Cir. 1940).
51. *United States v. Peoni*, 100 F.2d 401, 402 (2d Cir. 1938).
52. *State v. Randles*, 787 P.2d 1152, 1155 (Idaho 1990).
53. Model Penal Code, Section 2.06(3)(a).
54. NY CLS Penal, Title G, Section 115.08 (2008).
55. KRS, Title L, Section 506.080 (2008).
56. Section 1 of Public Law 91-452, 84 Stat. 922 (1994). The statute is codified at U.S. Code, Title 18, Sections 1961–1968 (2009).
57. "DOJ Says Four Lawyers Broke Anti-Terror Rules," *Fulton County Daily Report* (18 April 2002), n.p.
58. U.S. Code, Title 18, Section 1962 (2009).
59. *H. J. Inc. v. Northwestern Bell Telephone Company*, 492 U.S. 229 (1989).
60. *H. J. Inc. v. Northwestern Bell Telephone Company*, 492 U.S. 229 (1989).

61. *United States v. Turkette*, 452 U.S. 576 (1981).

62. See *Reves v. Ernst & Young*, 507 U.S. 170 (1993).

63. O.C.G.A., Title 16, Chapter 14, Section 16-14-4(a)(b)(c) (2008).

64. *Chancey v. State,* 349 S.E.2d 717 (Ga. 1986), *cert. denied,* 481 U.S. 1029 (1987).

65. "A Law Run Wild: Conservative Lawmaker Seeks Asset Forfeiture Limits," *American Bar Association Journal* 79 (October 1993): 24.

66. See *Austin v. United States,* 509 U.S. 602 (1993); and *Alexander v. United States,* 509 U.S. 544 (1993).

67. *Republic National Bank v. United States,* 506 U.S. 80 (1992).

68. See *United States v. James Daniel Good Real Property,* 510 U.S. 43 (1993).

69. *Bennis v. Michigan,* 516 U.S. 442 (1996).

70. *United States v. Bajakajian,* 524 U.S. 321 (2001). The statute is codified at U.S. Code, Title 31, Section 5316 (2009).

CHAPTER 4

Defenses to Criminal Culpability: Part I

INTRODUCTION

In U.S. criminal justice systems, the prosecution is required to prove beyond a reasonable doubt that the defendant is guilty of the crime (or crimes) charged. All elements of the crime must be proved. The prosecution must prove that a particular defendant committed a specified criminal act, with the requisite intent, that any attendant circumstances required by the statute were present, and that the act was the legal cause of the harm in question. It is possible, however, that proof on all of these elements may not be sufficient for a conviction.

In criminal law, a successful defense may result in a reduced charge or an acquittal. A *defense* is a legal challenge by the defendant. It may consist only of a denial of the factual allegation of the prosecution, or it may offer new factual allegations in an effort to negate the charges, in which case it is called an **affirmative defense**. For example, a defendant might respond that in effect, yes, I committed that crime, but I did not have the requisite intent for the act because I was suffering from insanity.

Defenses are very important, but they are not always easily understood. Because of the possible confusion between a defense and an element of a crime, it is necessary to analyze the issues involved in distinguishing these terms and allocating the burden of proof between the prosecution and the defense. Placing the burden of proof on one side means that side is responsible for producing the evidence that will convince the trier of fact of the truth of the allegation. Thus, with regard to all elements of a crime, the prosecution has the burden of offering enough proof to convince the trier of fact (beyond a reasonable doubt) that all elements exist. The defense has no burden of proof with regard to those elements.

This discussion is important not only in distinguishing elements from defenses but also in illustrating the necessity of analyzing the facts of each criminal case. It is not possible to make categorical statements that may be memorized and applied in all circumstances. Each case requires an analysis of general legal principles to determine whether they are or are not applicable. Such uncertainty makes the law difficult but challenging.

Defenses may be *partial* or *complete*, meaning that they serve to reduce (partial defense) or to defeat (complete defense) the charge. A partial defense to the charge of murder might result in a manslaughter conviction because it defeats one of the elements of murder. A successful complete defense, such as insanity, may lead to a verdict of not guilty. As with most concepts in criminal law, the difference between partial and complete defenses may be difficult to ascertain.

The defendant may elect not to present a defense, and in some cases this is a successful strategy.

THE BURDEN OF PROOF AND PRESUMPTIONS

Chapter 2 discussed the *elements* of a crime, noting that the term refers to what the prosecution must prove to sustain a conviction. Included are an act and a criminal state of mind that concur to produce a harmful result. In addition, some crimes require proof of attendant circumstances. Chapter 1 emphasized that the prosecution must prove these elements beyond a reasonable doubt. Chapter 1 also pointed out that even in a criminal case the defendant has the burden of proof in some instances. When that occurs, the usual standard is a **preponderance of the evidence**, a lower standard than the prosecution's burden of proof beyond a reasonable doubt. This concept refers to evidence showing that, on the whole, it supports the fact in question.

Although it is tempting to make statements such as, "The prosecution must prove all elements of a crime beyond a reasonable doubt" and "The defense must prove all defenses by a preponderance of the evidence," in reality the issues are more complicated and may be affected by a **presumption**, which is an assumption of a fact that is based on other facts; it is not a fact but an inference from a fact. A presumption may be either *conclusive*, in which case it is accepted by law, or *rebuttable*, in which case the opposing party may offer evidence to refute it.

Some of the problems that arise in allocating the burden of proof may be illustrated by a look at the presumption of innocence. According to this crucial principle, in U.S. criminal justice systems everyone charged with a crime faces the judicial system as an innocent person. The prosecution has the difficult burden of proving beyond a reasonable doubt all of the required elements of the crime or crimes charged. To ease the prosecutor's burden, the legislature could draft a statute that would shift the burden of proof on an element of the crime from the prosecution to the defense.

That is not permitted constitutionally, but the problem arises when a statute does so by the use of presumptions or by its definition of defenses. This situation and others have led to several major court decisions that are critical to an understanding of matters relating to the burden of proof in a criminal case.

Major Court Decisions

The U.S. Supreme Court has decided several key cases involving presumptions, defenses, elements of a crime, and the allocation of the burden of proof in criminal cases. Six of these cases, along with one from a lower federal court, are summarized briefly in Focus 4.1. As the following discussion demonstrates, however, it is important to view these summaries in light of the facts of each case.

FOCUS 4.1   Defenses, Elements, and the Burden of Proof in a Criminal Case: A Summary of Cases

The discussion in this chapter raises some of the problems of allocating the burden of proof in a criminal case. This focus lists the major cases, along with a brief statement of the importance of each. The first six cases were decided by the U.S. Supreme Court.

In re Winship[1]
The prosecution in a criminal case must prove its case by the standard of *beyond a reasonable doubt*. Although this case involved issues in a juvenile court, the holding is also generally considered applicable to adult criminal courts.

Mullaney v. Wilbur[2]
The proof standard of beyond a reasonable doubt established by *Winship* applies to *all* elements of a crime.

Patterson v. New York[3]
The New York murder statute did not involve shifting the burden of proof on an element of second-degree murder from the prosecution to the defense when it required the defendant to prove the defense of being "under the influence of extreme emotional disturbance."

Sandstrom v. Montana[4]
Instructing the jury that the law "presumes that a person intends the ordinary consequences of his voluntary acts" is unconstitutional because it might lead a juror to think the defendant rather

than the prosecution has the burden of proof on the issue of criminal intent.

Francis v. Franklin[5]
A jury instruction that the defendant, found in possession of stolen property, was presumed to have stolen that property unless a satisfactory explanation had been offered for its possession was held unconstitutional because it shifted the burden of proof and denied the presumption of innocence.

Martin v. Ohio[6]
It is permissible to place on the defendant the burden of proving the affirmative defense of self-defense.

United States v. Byrd[7]
The Insanity Defense Reform Act in the federal system does not shift to the defendant the burden of proof on the intent element of a crime when it requires the defendant to prove the insanity defense by clear and convincing evidence.

1. *In re Winship*, 397 U.S. 358 (1970).
2. *Mullaney v. Wilbur*, 421 U.S. 684 (1975).
3. *Patterson v. New York*, 432 U.S. 197 (1977).
4. *Sandstrom v. Montana*, 442 U.S. 510 (1979).
5. *Francis v. Franklin*, 471 U.S. 307 (1985).
6. *Martin v. Ohio*, 480 U.S. 228 (1987).
7. *United States v. Byrd*, 834 F.2d 145 (8th Cir. 1987).

In *Mullaney v. Wilbur*, decided in 1975, the defendant was charged under a Maine statute that recognized two categories of homicide, murder and manslaughter. Both of these statutes required that the prosecution prove the elements of an unlawful, intentional killing. Murder involved the additional element of **malice aforethought** (the murder was predetermined and intentional and without legal justification or excuse), but the statute provided that malice aforethought could be presumed if the state proved an unlawful, intentional killing. In addition, Maine provided a heat-of-passion defense to a murder charge, but the defendant had the burden of proving that defense by a preponderance of the evidence. Defendant Wilbur was accused of killing a man who made sexual advances toward him. Wilbur argued that allowing the prosecution to presume malice aforethought on sufficient proof of an unlawful, intentional killing—and therefore permitting a murder conviction unless the defense proved that the unwanted sexual advances supported a heat-of-passion defense—in reality removed from the prosecution the burden of proving (beyond a reasonable doubt) an element of murder (malice aforethought). The U.S. Supreme Court agreed.

Against the argument that the prosecution had to prove only those elements that would require an acquittal if not proved, the U.S. Supreme Court held that the burden of proof required of the prosecution means that it must prove *all* elements of a particular crime beyond a reasonable doubt. The Court ruled that the Maine approach shifted the burden of proof to the defendant and thus increased "the likelihood of an erroneous murder conviction."[1] The Supreme Court did not, however, answer the question of whether it would be permissible constitutionally to place on the defendant the burden of proving *all* affirmative defenses.

The issue of the burden of proof in criminal cases received further attention in *Patterson v. New York*, decided by the U.S. Supreme Court in 1977.[2] Patterson was charged with second-degree murder after allegedly shooting and killing the man with whom he saw his partially clothed and estranged wife. Patterson confessed to the killing but reasoned that he was "under the influence of extreme emotional disturbance," which constituted a defense under New York law. He argued that the charge should have been manslaughter, not second-degree murder.

Under New York law, the charge of second-degree murder required the prosecution to prove that the defendant intended to cause the death of another and did cause that death. Malice aforethought was not an element, as it was in the Maine statute involved in the case of *Mullaney v. Wilbur.*

The U.S. Supreme Court upheld Patterson's conviction, distinguishing the case from *Mullaney v. Wilbur* by the fact that the Maine statute required malice aforethought as an *element* of murder; the New York statute did not have that requirement. The Court viewed the New York affirmative defense of extreme emotional disturbance as "a substantially expanded version of the older heat-of-passion concept." The Court concluded that the New York statute in *Patterson* did not involve a "shifting of the burden to the defendant to disprove any fact essential to the offense charged since the New York affirmative defense of extreme emotional disturbance bears no direct relationship to any element of murder." In the following brief excerpt from the case, the U.S. Supreme Court articulated limits to its holding concerning the standard of beyond a reasonable doubt and the allocation of the burden of proof on elements and defenses in a criminal case.

PATTERSON v. NEW YORK
432 U.S. 197 (1977)

Justice Byron White delivered the opinion of the Court, in which Chief Justice Warren E. Burger and Justices Potter Stewart, Harry A. Blackmun, and John Paul Stevens joined. Justice Louis F. Powell Jr. filed a dissenting opinion, in which Justices William J. Brennan Jr. and Thurgood Marshall joined. Justice William H. Rehnquist took no part in the consideration or decision of the case.

 The requirement of proof beyond a reasonable doubt in a criminal case is "bottomed on a fundamental value determination of our society that it is far worse to convict an innocent man than to let a guilty man go free." The social cost of placing the burden on the prosecution to prove guilt beyond a reasonable doubt is thus an increased risk that the guilty will go free. While it is clear that our society has willingly chosen to bear a substantial burden in order to protect the innocent, it is equally clear that the risk it must bear is not without limits; . . . Due process does not require that every conceivable step be taken, at whatever cost, to eliminate the possibility of convicting an innocent person. . . .

We . . . decline to adopt as a constitutional imperative, operative countrywide, that a State must disprove beyond a reasonable doubt every fact constituting any and all affirmative defenses related to the culpability of an accused. Traditionally, due process has required that only the most basic procedural safeguards be observed; more subtle balancing of society's interests against those of the accused have been left to the legislative branch. We therefore will not disturb the balance struck in previous cases holding that the Due Process Clause requires the prosecution to prove beyond a reasonable doubt all of the elements included in the definition of the offense of which the defendant is charged. Proof of the nonexistence of all affirmative defenses has never been constitutionally required; and we perceive no reason to fashion such a rule in this case and apply it to the statutory defense at issue here.

Mullaney and *Patterson* illustrate some of the problems involved in allocating the burden of proof on defenses in a criminal case. Clearly, before the burden of proof may be placed on the defendant, a defense must be a real defense and not a shifting of the burden of proof for an element of the crime. The problem arises in determining when the state has worded a statute (or a judge instructed a jury) in such a way that the defendant's burden of proof involves an element of the crime. The required element of *mens rea* provides the framework in which to analyze this possibility.

The Element of Intent

Criminal intent, or *mens rea*, is an element of a crime and therefore must be proved beyond a reasonable doubt by the prosecution. The U.S. Supreme Court has decided numerous cases on this issue, two of which are important to this discussion.

In *Sandstrom v. Montana*, the U.S. Supreme Court overturned a murder conviction because the trial court had instructed the jury that "the law presumes that a person intends the ordinary consequences of his voluntary acts." This instruction is unconstitutional because it could lead a jury to conclude that once the prosecution proves the defendant has committed the killing voluntarily, the jury should convict even if the prosecution has not proved the element of criminal intent.[3] The result would be to compromise or nullify the presumption of innocence.

A second U.S. Supreme Court decision related to the intent element is *Francis v. Franklin*, in which the Supreme Court considered the issue of a jury instruction that could lead a juror to conclude that the defen-

dant had the burden of proof on intent. In *Franklin* the jury was instructed that "a person of sound mind and discretion is presumed to intend the natural and probable consequences of his acts, but the presumption may be rebutted." The Court held that this instruction was unconstitutional because it relieved the state of its burden of proving beyond a reasonable doubt every element of a charged crime.[4]

The Burden of Proof and Self-Defense

Elements of a crime have been distinguished from affirmative defenses in self-defense cases. In *Martin v. Ohio* the U.S. Supreme Court upheld an Ohio statute that required the defendant to sustain the burden of proof on self-defense. Under the statute self-defense was an affirmative defense. The case involved a defendant who was charged with aggravated murder, defined as "purposely, and with prior calculation and design, causing the death of another." The defendant testified that she shot and killed her husband after he struck her.[5]

In *Martin*, the U.S. Supreme Court ruled that the Ohio statute requiring a defendant who raises the defense of self-defense to sustain the burden of proving that defense does not shift from the prosecution to the defendant either of the two required elements of aggravated murder, which are that the defendant committed the murder and that she had the specific purpose and intent to cause the death or that she did so with prior calculation and design.

The Burden of Proof and the Insanity Defense

Criminal cases involving the insanity defense have tested the issues regarding the burden of proof. In these cases the allocation of the burden of proof raises the issue of whether insanity is an affirmative defense to be proved by the defendant or whether it negates intent, a required element that the prosecution must prove. The U.S. Supreme Court views insanity as an affirmative defense.[6]

The issue of whether insanity is an affirmative defense or a negation of *mens rea* is important particularly in the federal system because the federal criminal code's Insanity Defense Reform Act places on the defendant the burden of proving insanity by clear and convincing evidence, a standard that is stricter than a preponderance of the evidence but not as strict as beyond a reasonable doubt.[7]

Prior to the passage of the Insanity Defense Reform Act, the defendant had the burden of *introducing* the insanity defense, after which the prosecution had the burden of *proving* beyond a reasonable doubt that the defendant was sane when the crime was committed. These rules were in effect during the trial of John W. Hinckley Jr., who, in attempting to assassinate President Ronald Reagan as he left a Washington, D.C., hotel on 30 March 1981, wounded Reagan and three others.

At his trial, Hinckley's attorneys presented evidence that Hinckley thought that if he killed the president he would win the favor of actress Jodie Foster, with whom he was obsessed. According to the psychiatric experts presented by the defense, the defendant's beliefs were based on his viewing of a movie, *Taxi Driver*, in which Foster played the part of a 12-year-old prostitute. The lead character was a lonely taxi driver who became so obsessed with the prostitute that he stalked a U.S. senator with a gun to gain publicity and the attention of the character played by Foster. At the end of the movie, the taxi driver killed the prostitute's pimp and became a hero.

At Hinckley's trial, the prosecution could not prove beyond a reasonable doubt that Hinckley was sane when he attempted to assassinate President Ronald Reagan; thus, Hinckley's insanity defense was successful.

The federal standard of requiring the defense to prove insanity by clear and convincing evidence, adopted after the Hinckley trial, was upheld by a federal court in 1987.[8]

TYPES OF DEFENSES

An analysis of scholarly writings in criminal law, along with various state codes, shows little agreement on how to classify or categorize defenses. A review of the various approaches contributes confusion and adds little in a positive way, other than to permit dividing the discussion into sections or chapters. Thus, this text makes no attempt to classify or categorize types of defenses, nor does it discuss all defenses. For example, a defendant may establish an *alibi* by offering proof that he or she was in another state at the time the crime in question was committed. One might question whether this is a defense or a method of attacking the prosecution's case. In any event, an alibi is not included here as a defense.

In studying defenses, it is important to recall what we have learned about the meaning and purpose of criminal law. The moral or blameworthy element of punishment through the criminal law is critical to the topic of defenses, for by recognizing defenses we are saying that some criminal acts will not be punished or that punishment may be reduced because of a defense. As with most issues in criminal law, the lines are hard to draw in particular cases. Likewise, jurisdictions differ in their statutory definitions and judicial interpretations of these defenses.

Ignorance or Mistake

Although generally ignorance of the law is no excuse, under some circumstances ignorance of the law, mistake of fact, and mistake of law are recognized defenses to criminal culpability.

In criminal law, the defense of **mistake** refers to a situation in which actors commit criminal acts that they would not have committed had they had knowledge of the law or the facts. At issue may be a *mistake of law* or a *mistake of fact*; the difference between these two categories has been stated as follows:

> Mistake and ignorance of *fact* involve perceptions of the world and empirical judgments derived from those perceptions. Mistake and ignorance of *law* involve assessment of whether, given a certain set of acts, the actor would or would not be violating the law.[9]

The mistake defense may be used to negate a mental element of the crime, such as the knowledge or belief requirement. For example, a good-faith belief with regard to an income tax deduction may negate the federal statute's intent requirement of *willful* as an element of the crime of income tax evasion.

The mistake defense may be applied in two situations. In the first, individuals do not know the law exists. Normally this is not an excuse, although in rare cases it may be, as illustrated by *Lambert v. California*, a landmark case decided by the U.S. Supreme Court in 1957. In *Lambert* the Supreme Court invalidated a Los Angeles municipal ordinance that forbade any convicted person to be or remain in the city for more than five days without registering. The Supreme Court emphasized that the law requires reasonable notice, and because most people would not expect this ordinance to exist, actual knowledge of the duty to register and meet other requirements of the ordinance is required for the ordinance to be constitutional. The Court stated: "Were it otherwise, the evil would be as great as it is when the law is written in print too fine to read or in a language foreign to the community."[10]

The second type of mistake occurs when individuals are mistaken about a collateral element, such as the legality of a previous divorce, which causes them to misunderstand the legal significance of their conduct, such as remarrying. Although bigamy is a strict liability crime in most jurisdictions, some jurisdictions recognize an honest and reasonable mistake as a partial or complete defense to bigamy.

The use of mistake of fact as a partial rather than a complete defense may be applicable to statutory rape cases in some jurisdictions. This position is illustrated in a Washington case in which a 20-year-old male defendant had sexual intercourse with a 13-year-old female. The defendant proved that he had a reasonable belief that the alleged victim was between 14 and 16 years of age. The state statute defines *statutory rape in the second degree* as sexual intercourse committed by one who is over 16 with a person who is 11 or older but less than 14. A reasonable mistake is not a complete defense; thus, the defendant is not entitled to an acquittal but may be convicted of a lesser offense. The Washington Court of Appeals upheld the conviction of statutory rape in the *third* degree, a less serious offense, which includes sexual intercourse committed by a person over 18 with one 14 or older but less than 16.[11]

As noted in Chapter 2, many jurisdictions retain the position that statutory rape is a strict liability crime and that a reasonable mistake of fact regarding the age of the victim is not a defense. Some jurisdictions permit the mistake of fact (to age) as a defense but restrict this defense to specified ages. Consider, for example, the following Pennsylvania statute:

> Except as otherwise provided, whenever in this chapter the criminality of conduct depends on a child being below the age of 14 years, it is no defense that the defendant did not know the age of the child or reasonably believed the child to be the age of 14 years or older. When criminality depends on the child's being below a critical age older than 14 years, it is a defense for the defendant to prove by a preponderance of the evidence that he or she reasonably believed the child to be above the critical age.[12]

Duress or Necessity

Defendants may succeed in defending their criminal acts if they can show that they acted under **duress**. In

criminal law, *duress* refers to a condition in which an individual is coerced or induced by the wrongful act of another to commit a criminal act. To succeed with a duress defense, defendants must prove that when they committed the crimes for which they are advancing the defense, they were threatened by unlawful force. Not many defendants attempt this defense; thus, the case law is limited. Most cases hold that the force must be such that would cause serious bodily injury or death, and the threat of harm must be imminent. Most states require that the threat be to the actor rather than to a third party, although a few permit the defense in the case of a threat to a close relative of the actor. One must have acted reasonably to assert the duress defense, which is usually not permitted in murder cases.

The duress defense may not be available when defendants recklessly place themselves in positions in which it is probable that they will be subjected to duress. In addition, it may not be available for persons who negligently place themselves in such circumstances if negligence is the basis of culpability for the crime in question.

A defense related to duress is that of **necessity**. In criminal law, the *necessity defense* refers to an act that, though criminal in other circumstances, may not be considered criminal because of the compelling force of the circumstances. The necessity defense differs from the duress defense in that, in most cases, the coercive forces are forces of nature rather than of humans. In actual cases, however, the distinction is not always clear. Like duress, the necessity defense is based on the assumption that a person ought to be free to commit some crimes in order to prevent greater harm. Thus, breaking into the home of another to secure shelter or food in a crisis or to telephone the police during an emergency may constitute a defense to the crime of breaking and entering, although the person who commits this act may be required to pay for the resulting damages.

Unlike duress, a successful necessity defense need not be based on avoiding human injury or death; avoiding property damage may be acceptable. In rare cases, the defense permits serious crimes, such as intentional homicide, when that act is necessary to avoid a greater harm, such as killing one person to avoid the deaths of two others. The actor must have the intent to avoid a greater harm. The decision regarding whether a greater or lesser harm was avoided is left to the court, not to defendants.

Two additional points regarding the necessity defense are important. First, a defendant is not permitted to use the defense if another alternative is available that would prevent the greater harm and still be legal. For example, it is not permissible to steal clothes for needy children if free clothing may be secured from local institutions. Second, the necessity defense is not available to defendants who created the necessity to choose between two evils, although the defense may be permitted to prevent a greater evil. Chapter 11's Case Analysis features the use of marijuana for medicinal purposes as a defense.

Infancy

In November 1999, the *New York Times* printed an article entitled "Fear of Crime Trumps the Fear of Lost Youth." The article featured four young persons who had been convicted of murders they committed while they were under 16. The one that was particularly shocking was the case of Nathaniel Abraham of Michigan, who was convicted of fatally shooting a stranger. Abraham, who was 11 at the time of the crime, could have received up to life in prison. He was sentenced to custody until he is 21, spent almost a decade in a juvenile correctional facility at a cost of almost $1 million to the state, and in 2008, just 22 months after his

release, was charged with possession of a controlled substance (Ecstasy) and entered a guilty plea. It was predicted that Abraham would be sentenced to two years in prison.[13]

A more recent crime committed by an 8-year-old that drew shock and concern was the 2008 killings of men in the small Arizona community of St. Johns. The child's name was withheld, but in 2009 the accused, then age 9, entered a plea agreement in which he admitted that he killed his father's friend but was not required to admit that he killed his father. The plea means that the child will not be tried and thus we may never know the reasons for his actions that resulted in the deaths of his father, Vincent Romero, and his friend, Timothy Romans. At the time of this writing the judge had not acted on the plea deal and thus the child had not been sentenced, but it was anticipated that the youngster would not be incarcerated but would be required to undergo years of therapy and counseling.[14]

Two Florida youths have also been in the news in recent years for committing murder. Lionel Tate, who was 12 when he killed his 6-year-old playmate, claiming that he was play wrestling, was convicted in 2001 (when he was 14) in an adult criminal court of

David McMillan of St. John the Baptist Church in St. Johns, Arizona, speaks to the media after the 2008 funeral service for Vincent Romero. Romero and his friend Timothy Romans were shot and killed in a double murder. Romero was shot four times and Romans was shot six times. Romero's 8-year-old son was accused of both murders, but in early 2009, when the youngster was 9, he accepted a plea offer that would permit him to enter a guilty plea in the death of Romans and thereby escape a public trial in an adult court. The young offender was not sentenced to prison but will be required to undergo counseling and therapy for years. (Dana Felthauser/AP Images)

Lionel Tate, who was 14 when he was convicted of murdering a little girl when he was 12, is the youngest person ever sentenced to life in prison without the possibility of parole. After his conviction was reversed on appeal, the state again offered the plea bargain agreement that Tate had refused before trial. Tate accepted the plea agreement but was subsequently charged with armed robbery and other offenses, to which he eventually entered a guilty plea and was sentenced to 30 years in prison. (Broward Sheriff's Department/AP Images)

first-degree murder and sentenced to the state's mandatory penalty for that crime: life in prison with no chance of parole. Tate was thought to be the youngest person in the United States to receive life without parole. In December 2003, a Florida appellate court reversed Tate's conviction and sentence, ruling that because of his youth, he was constitutionally entitled to a hearing to determine whether he fully understood the charges against him and could reasonably participate in his defense. Because he did not have that hearing, he was entitled to a new trial.

The prosecution offered Tate its original plea bargain: Plead guilty to second-degree murder and serve only 3 years in a juvenile detention center, followed by 10 years on probation. This time Tate accepted the offer, and because of his time served, he was released in 2004 with the provision that he would be under house arrest (released to his mother) for 1 year, followed by 10 years on probation. But in May 2005, Tate was accused of committing armed robbery of a pizza deliveryman. He received a 10-year prison sentence in a plea deal, and that sentence is being served concurrently with the 30 years he was assessed for violating

the terms of his probation on the murder conviction. In 2007, that 30-year sentence was upheld by an appellate court.[15]

The second Florida youth, Nathaniel Brazill, also 14 at his trial, was only 13 when he killed his favorite teacher. Brazill was convicted of second-degree murder and thus avoided Florida's mandatory penalty of life without parole. Brazill, who faced a sentence of from 25 years to life, was sentenced to a mandatory term of 28 years in prison for the murder charge and 5 years (with a 3-year mandatory term) for an assault charge. The sentences were upheld, but Brazill's petition filed on his own, for a hearing on the issue of ineffective assistance of counsel, rejected by the trial court, was reversed and remanded by the appellate court, thus giving Brazill an opportunity to present evidence on his allegations.[16]

These convictions of teens probably would not have occurred under the early common law, which provided that children below age 7 could not be convicted of a crime because of a conclusive presumption that they were not capable of forming the requisite criminal intent. It was also assumed that young persons could be rehabilitated. Under the common law a **rebuttable presumption** (a presumption that is subject to being refuted by evidence) of incapacity governed children who were between the ages of 7 and 14, with the exception that boys under 14 were conclusively presumed incapable of rape. A rebuttable presumption of criminal intent existed for children 14 and over, and they could be charged as adults.

Although most U.S. jurisdictions retain some of these distinctions, they are less important now than under the common law because of the prevalence of the juvenile court, which has jurisdiction over children of specified ages. Many states, however, permit waivers to adult criminal courts of juveniles who commit serious crimes. Some limit waivers to serious violent crimes. Jurisdiction may also be waived when it appears to be in the best interests of society, when the children are thought to be beyond rehabilitation, or when they have committed several serious crimes. Some states specify by statute that juveniles who are accused of committing serious crimes may be tried in criminal courts without the requirement of waiver hearings and procedures.

Insanity

The **insanity** defense (a defense involving a state of mind or mental condition that negates a defendant's responsibility for his or her actions) is a controversial

FOCUS 4.2   The Insanity Defense and Mothers Who Kill Their Children

The insanity defense has been in the spotlight in recent years in Texas. In 2002 Andrea Yates, who drowned her five children in the family bathtub and was tried for capital murder, was unsuccessful in the use of the defense in her first trial. One of Yates's treating physicians described her as one of the sickest patients he had ever treated, but Yates was convicted although not sentenced to death. Rather, she was given a life sentence, but in January 2005 her conviction was reversed. She was tried again and was successful in her insanity defense, but she remains hospitalized for treatment in a Texas mental facility.[1]

The insanity defense was also successful in a second Texas case in which a mother killed her children. Deanna Laney was acquitted of stoning to death two of her children, ages 6 and 8; she "could not bring herself to complete the task on their 2-year-old brother." She reportedly said she told God that he would just have to finish that job. In Laney's case, psychiatrists testified that the defendant was severely mentally ill and thought that, as a test of her faith, God had selected her to kill her children. Laney was perceived as a woman so mentally ill that she did not understand the wrongness of her acts and did not plan them. Laney was committed to a psychiatric facility and probably faces a lifetime of monitored treatment.[2]

In a third Texas case, which occurred in 2008, Valeria Maxon, 33, was found not guilty by reason of insanity after she admitted that she drowned her son, Alexander Maxon, in a hot tub. Her husband, Michael Maxon, 54, was facing criminal charges of abandoning the child after he left his wife alone with the child even though he knew the wife was mentally ill. Valeria Maxon was released from a mental hospital just 14 days prior to killing her son. She had been diagnosed with several types of mental illness. According to her attorney, the child's death by her mother was "a clear case of insanity. . . . Valeria is a sweet lady who loved her son more than anything in the world. This mental illness was so powerful that it caused her to kill her son."[3]

Andrea Yates entered an insanity plea to murder charges involving the drowning deaths of her five children. Yates, who was found guilty at her first trial, went on trial again in May 2006 after an appeals court reversed her conviction and she refused a plea bargain. Yates's insanity defense was successful in her second trial. She is now hospitalized for treatment in a Texas facility. (Texas Department of Criminal Justice/Ap Images)

1. See *Yates v. Texas*, 171 S.W.3d 215 (Tex. App. 1st Dist. 2005), excerpted in the Case Analysis at the end of this chapter.
2. See "Civil Commitment vs. Life in Prison: What Andrea Yates Knew that Deanna Laney Didn't," *Texas Lawyer* 20, no. 6 (12 April 2004): 27; "Guilty but Insane in the Legislature," *Texas Lawyer* 20, no. 12 (24 May 2004): 1.
3. "Woman Not Guilty in Son's Drowning: Judge Gives Reason of Insanity; Husband Faces Abandonment Charges," *Dallas Morning News* (2 May 2008), p. 1B.

defense despite the fact that it is used in less than 1 percent of all felony cases, and most defendants who assert the defense are unsuccessful.

Technically, *insanity* is a social and legal term, but usually it is assumed to be a medical term, often used synonymously with *mental illness*. When used successfully in criminal law, the insanity defense results in an acquittal. But unlike other defenses, the successful use of the insanity defense does not always result in the release of a defendant. Most defendants found not guilty by reason of insanity are confined to a mental hospital for treatment, as illustrated by the case of John W.

Hinckley Jr., mentioned earlier in this chapter, and by the cases discussed in Focus 4.2.

Insanity Tests

Over the years several tests have been developed to define and measure insanity. The elements of these tests are stated in Focus 4.3, and each test is discussed briefly in the text.

The M'Naghten Rule

The traditional, most frequently used insanity test, the **M'Naghten rule**, or the *right-versus-wrong test*, comes

---

FOCUS 4.3 Insanity Tests

M'Naghten Rule—The Right-versus-Wrong Test

A defendant may be found not guilty by reason of insanity if, as the result of a defect of reason from disease of the mind, the defendant either

- Did not know the nature and quality of the act committed, or
- Did not know that the act was wrong

The Irresistible Impulse Test

The defendant's state of mind is such that he or she may know the nature and quality of an act and that it is wrong but cannot forbear from committing the act.

The Durham Rule: The Product Rule

If the unlawful act was the product of mental disease or defect, the accused is not criminally responsible for his or her conduct.

The ALI Test of the Model Penal Code: The Substantial Capacity Test, Section 4.01. Mental Disease or Defect Excluding Responsibility

(1) A person is not responsible for criminal conduct if at the time of such conduct as a result of mental disease or defect he lacks substantial capacity either to appreciate the criminality [wrongfulness] of his conduct or to conform his conduct to the requirements of law.

(2) As used in this article, the terms "mental disease or defect" do not include an abnormality manifested only by repeated criminal or otherwise antisocial conduct.

---

from an 1843 English case. Under this rule a defendant may be found not guilty by reason of insanity if it can be shown that, as a result of a defect of reason from disease of the mind, the defendant (1) did not know the nature and quality of the act committed or (2) did not know that the act was wrong.[17]

In the English case, defendant Daniel M'Naghten was found not guilty by reason of insanity after he argued successfully that the criminal act of which he was accused was caused by his delusions. M'Naghten was accused of shooting and killing the British prime minister's secretary, thinking the secretary was the prime minister, whom M'Naghten believed was heading a conspiracy to take his life.

The main problems with the M'Naghten rule have centered on definitions. There is little case law on the meaning of the phrase *disease of the mind*. Most courts have not seemed too concerned about the issue and, without defining the phrase, tell the jury that they must find that the defendant suffered from a mental disease. The meaning of the word *know* is a more serious problem. Does it mean that the defendant has cognitive knowledge or that he or she has a moral understanding of the nature and quality of the act? In most courts the M'Naghten rule is stated without a definition of *know*.

The M'Naghten rule has other words and phrases that may also present interpretation problems, such as the *nature and quality of the act* and *wrong*. Does

the former mean that the defendant understands both the physical nature and the physical consequences of an act—for example, that putting a match to kerosene will cause a fire that will burn a building and kill people sleeping inside? Does *wrong* mean knowing that an act is legally wrong, morally wrong, or both? The M'Naghten rule is criticized for these and other ambiguities.

Some argue that the M'Naghten rule emphasizes the cognitive part of the personality to the exclusion of the emotional elements, that the ability to control one's behavior is not determined solely by cognition. It is also argued that the M'Naghten rule poses impossible questions for psychiatrists and other experts when they testify and that the rule is not an adequate way to identify defendants who should not be subjected to criminal punishments.

An example of a statute following the M'Naghten rule is the Texas statute that was in effect at the time of the Andrea Yates trial, discussed in Focus 4.2.

(A) It is an affirmative defense to prosecution that, at the time of the conduct charged, the actor, as a result of severe mental disease or defect, did not know that his conduct was wrong.

(B) The term "mental disease or defect" does not include an abnormality manifested only by repeated criminal or otherwise antisocial conduct.[18]

This version of the Texas statute was enacted after the John Hinckley case. After Hinckley was found not guilty by reason of insanity, the District of Columbia and other jurisdictions, including Texas, revised their statutes governing the insanity plea. Previously Texas required that in order to succeed in an insanity defense, defendants had to prove that because of a mental disorder they could not *conform* their behavior to the law. The Texas requirement currently in effect is that defendants must prove that they did not know they were engaging in a criminal or wrongful act at the time the alleged crime was committed. Yates might have been successful in her insanity defense at her first trial prior to this change. The evidence indicated that Yates apparently believed that she had to drown her children to save their souls from Satan, but the prosecution argued successfully that she *knew* when she drowned them that she was committing a crime. The jury concluded that on the basis of Yates's 911 call to the police and her admission to them that she expected criminal punishment as a result of her deeds, she was not insane under the provisions of Texas law.

The Yates jury also may have based its decision in the first trial on the **expert testimony** presented by the state. *Expert testimony* is opinion evidence given under oath by a person who possesses technical knowledge or skill that is both relevant to the case and not possessed by the average person. In the first *Yates* trial, an expert testified concerning a television program about a mother who drowned her children and was acquitted on an insanity defense. There was testimony that Yates usually watched that program. The jury may have concluded that she watched that episode and planned her criminal acts as a result. This would have been evidence of premeditation and negated the insanity defense. Yates's conviction was reversed on these grounds, and the case is presented at the close of this chapter in the Case Analysis section. As noted in Focus 4.2, Yates was acquitted in her second trial.

The Irresistible Impulse Test
A second insanity test is the **irresistible impulse test**, which is a test for insanity stating that defendants may or may not be found guilty for criminal acts if they were unable to control the actions leading to a crime even though they may have known the act(s) was wrong. This test has been adopted in some states either by statute or by court decision.[19]

The definition of *irresistible impulse* varies from case to case, with one court stating that it means a defendant would commit a crime even if there were a "policeman at his [or her] elbow."[20] It is argued that this instruction is too restrictive. Some people might be able to exercise self-control in the presence of a police officer but be unable to control their behavior in other circumstances.

The Durham Rule
The third insanity test, the **Durham rule**, comes from a 1954 District of Columbia case, *Durham v. United States*. In *Durham*, Judge David L. Bazelon, who wrote numerous opinions in which he attempted to integrate law and the social sciences, viewed the insanity defense as an opportunity for psychiatrists to offer their insights into mental disease to assist in determining insanity. Judge Bazelon maintained that the right-versus-wrong test did not take "sufficient account of psychic realities and scientific knowledge" and that "it is based upon one symptom and so cannot validly be applied in all circumstances." A broader test was needed, articulated as follows: "An accused is not criminally responsible if his unlawful act was the product of mental disease or mental defect."[21] The Durham rule became known as the *product rule*.

Judge Bazelon distinguished *disease*, which is "capable of either improving or deteriorating," from *defect*, a "condition which is not considered capable of either improving or deteriorating and which may be either congenital, or the result of injury, or the residual effect of a physical or mental disease." He emphasized that this rule would assist in eliminating from criminal culpability those people who are not punishable in U.S. criminal justice systems because they lack moral blame.

As articulated by Judge Bazelon, the Durham rule was not precise enough to convince many states to adopt it. Critics argued that the test left too much influence to expert witnesses and too much discretion to the jury. In addition, no standards were set by courts. In 1972, the *Durham* case was overruled in the District of Columbia, where it originated, and the court adopted a modified version of the American Law Institute's test of insanity, which is discussed in the following section.[22]

The Substantial Capacity Test
A fourth insanity test is the **substantial capacity test**, which was developed by the scholars of the American

Law Institute (ALI), who drafted the Model Penal Code. The ALI rejected the Durham rule and proposed a modified version of the M'Naghten and irresistible impulse tests. The substantial capacity test provides as follows:

(1) A person is not responsible for criminal conduct if at the time of such conduct as a result of mental disease or defect he lacks substantial capacity either to appreciate the criminality [wrongfulness] of his conduct or to conform his conduct to the requirements of law.

(2) As used in this article, the terms "mental disease or defect" do not include an abnormality manifested only by repeated criminal or otherwise antisocial conduct.[23]

The ALI test is broader than the M'Naghten rule in its substitution of *appreciate* for *know*. Thus, under the ALI test, a defendant who knows the difference between right and wrong but who does not appreciate that difference may be successful with the insanity defense. It is appropriate to introduce expert testimony, such as that provided by psychiatrists and psychologists, to provide evidence of the defendant's emotional and intellectual capacity. In establishing a substantial capacity test, the ALI test appears to be compromising between what has been interpreted as the total impairment requirement of the M'Naghten and irresistible impulse tests and the apparent requirement of only slight impairment in the Durham rule.

The second paragraph of the ALI test was written to exclude sociopathic or psychopathic personalities (these terms are difficult to distinguish but both refer to the lack of the development of a moral sense—also called an antisocial personality) because of disagreement among authorities over whether such personalities suffer from a mental disease. The paragraph is controversial and has been rejected by some jurisdictions, but it has been adopted by most jurisdictions that use the ALI test.

These four insanity tests and other issues, such as the jury verdict of not guilty by reason of insanity in the trial of John W. Hinckley Jr., led to strong public support for changes in the insanity defense. Some jurisdictions followed the Michigan plan, discussed in the next section, while others abolished the insanity defense.

Guilty but Mentally Ill

Since 1975 a defendant who raises the insanity defense in Michigan, in addition to being found guilty, not guilty, or not guilty by reason of insanity, may be found **guilty but mentally ill (GBMI)**.

The Michigan statute distinguishes insanity from mental illness and provides for a finding of GBMI if the jury is convinced beyond a reasonable doubt of *all* of the following:

(a) The defendant is guilty beyond a reasonable doubt of an offense.

(b) The defendant has proven by a preponderance of the evidence that he or she was mentally ill at the time of the commission of that offense.

(c) The defendant has not established by a preponderance of the evidence that he or she lacked the substantial capacity either to appreciate the nature and quality or the wrongfulness of his or her conduct or to conform his or her conduct to the requirements of the law.[24]

Under the Michigan statute, a defendant who pleads guilty or who is found after a trial to be mentally ill may receive the sentence that could be imposed under a guilty plea alone. The difference is that a verdict of GBMI obligates the Department of Mental Health to provide psychiatric treatment while the defendant is on probation or in prison.

Other states adopted various versions of the Michigan statute, but the constitutionality of GBMI statutes has been challenged. Here are a few examples:

- The Michigan Supreme Court has upheld this statute, stating that the major purpose of the GBMI verdict is "to limit the number of persons who . . . were *improperly* being relieved of all criminal responsibility by way of the insanity verdict."[25]

- The South Carolina Supreme Court upheld that state's GBMI statute.[26]

- The Illinois statute was upheld by that state's supreme court, although the case was remanded on another issue.[27]

Abolition of the Insanity Defense

Dissatisfaction with the insanity defense has led some jurisdictions to abolish it. The Idaho Code states: "Mental condition shall not be a defense to any charge of criminal conduct." The code does, however, permit the admission of expert testimony to negate the *mens rea* required for the charged offense and provides that a person found to have a mental condition, if incarcerated, shall be placed in a correctional facility that has treatment facilities.[28] Some states permit evidence of mental illness to be admitted only for the purpose of determining the appropriate sentence.

Support for abolishing the insanity defense is related in some cases to the unrealistic assumption that all or most persons found not guilty by reason of insanity are released back into society. This is not always the case. John Hinckley Jr., for example, has been given permission to leave the medical facility and visit his parents, but he has not been released unconditionally. As noted, Andrea Yates is in a treatment facility in Texas. In fact, most defendants who are acquitted by reason of insanity are confined in mental institutions or hospitals. But there are legal limitations on this practice.

In 1983, the U.S. Supreme Court upheld a District of Columbia statute that provides for the indefinite commitment in a mental hospital of a criminal defendant found not guilty by reason of insanity, under the following provisions. Within 50 days of commitment, the individual is entitled to a judicial hearing to determine release eligibility. The patient must prove by a preponderance of the evidence that he or she is ready for release. Failure to do so results in continued commitment. In *Jones v. United States*, the U.S. Supreme Court said, "A verdict of not guilty by reason of insanity is sufficiently probative of mental illness and dangerousness to justify commitment of the acquittee for the purposes of treatment and the protection of society." The Court held that this is true even if the commitment is longer than would have been the case had the individual been found guilty and sentenced under the applicable statute.[29]

In contrast, in 1992, by a 5-4 vote, the U.S. Supreme Court limited Louisiana's indefinite commitment of persons found not guilty by reason of insanity. In *Foucha v. Louisiana*, the Court's majority invalidated the statute that permitted the state to continue confining insanity acquittees even if they were no longer mentally ill as long as they were judged by a court to be dangerous to themselves or others.[30] To be released, the insanity acquittee had to prove that he or she was not dangerous.

Foucha was found to be dangerous based on the testimony that he had an antisocial personality, a condition that is not treatable and does not constitute a mental disease. The U.S. Supreme Court emphasized that in order to detain Foucha when he no longer had a mental disease, the state would have to go through civil commitment proceedings and prove current mental illness and dangerousness. The state had not done that. Although the state may punish or even imprison criminals for reasons of deterrence, Louisiana could not do so in the case of Foucha, who had not been convicted of a crime.

The U.S. Supreme Court distinguished *Foucha* from a pretrial detention case in which the Court permitted preventive detention of persons accused of crimes. In *United States v. Salerno* the Court upheld the pretrial detention of a dangerous person awaiting trial, but the circumstances are narrowly limited and a full adversary hearing is required. In *Salerno* the Supreme Court said, "In our society liberty is the norm, and detention prior to trial or without trial is the carefully limited exception."[31]

Diminished Capacity or Partial Responsibility

Some defendants who are not insane may establish the defense of diminished capacity or partial responsibility. This defense is available when it can be shown that the mental illness of the defendant, though not sufficient to establish insanity, caused such lack of capacity that the defendant could not have achieved the requisite intent at the time of the crime. The defense may be used, for example, to show that a defendant charged with first-degree murder did not have the requisite intent for that crime, although he or she might be convicted of the lesser crime of manslaughter.

Some states, such as California, have abolished the defense of diminished capacity. According to the California Penal Code, "As a matter of public policy there shall be no defense of diminished capacity, diminished responsibility, or irresistible impulse in a criminal action or juvenile adjudication hearing."[32] Despite this, California provides that "evidence of diminished capacity or of a mental disorder may be considered by the court only at the time of sentencing or other disposition or commitment."[33]

Automatism

Also similar to the insanity defense is the **automatism defense**, which may be raised by defendants who have evidence that they were unconscious or semiconscious when the alleged crimes were committed. For example, a physical problem—such as an epileptic seizure, a concussion, or an unexplained blackout—that results in an accident that kills someone might support a complete defense for a driver charged with manslaughter. However, as mentioned in Chapter 2, if the driver knew or should have known that the physical problem existed, probably the defense would not be applicable.

Emotional trauma might be another acceptable reason for the automatism defense, but brainwashing is not a sufficient basis for asserting the defense. Nor is unconsciousness caused by voluntary intoxication sufficient.

From the defendant's point of view, automatism as a defense is to be preferred over that of insanity because acquittal based on the automatism defense is complete and the defendant is released, although civil commitment proceedings might follow.

Entrapment

The **entrapment** defense, which applies only to actions by government agents or their employees, may be used when a defendant was induced to commit a crime that he or she would not have been inclined to commit without the government agent's actions. A successful defense requires proof of two elements:

1. A government agent induced the defendant to commit the crime.
2. The defendant was not otherwise predisposed to commit the crime.

It is obvious that one of the best ways for police to gather evidence against offenders is to be present when the crimes are committed. Since this rarely occurs, police may go under cover or use informants to gain information about criminal activity. Both practices are acceptable as long as government agents do not go too far in their activities. In 1932 in *Sorrells v. United States*, the U.S. Supreme Court stated, "Society is at war with the criminal classes, and courts have uniformly held that in waging this warfare the forces of prevention and detection may use traps, decoys, and deception to obtain evidence of the commission of crime."[34]

In a later case the U.S. Supreme Court said, "It is clear that the government may supply drugs to a suspect in a drug investigation."[35] But there are limits to what the government may do without committing entrapment. As the Supreme Court said in 1958 in *Sherman v. United States*, "To determine whether entrapment has been established a line must be drawn between the trap for the unwary innocent and the trap for the unwary criminal."[36]

The entrapment defense is frequently raised in cases involving alleged illegal drug sales or sex offenses. For example, the defense was successful in the case of a defendant with whom a government informant became a friend over a period of six months. The informant requested several times that the defendant help him to procure illegal drugs. Eventually the defendant succumbed. The court held that the defendant "was not predisposed to commit this offense." Thus, the defendant was entrapped.[37]

An example of the successful use of the entrapment defense in a case involving sex-related issues is presented in Focus 4.4. That case was brought under the federal code. The following is an example of a state entrapment defense statute (Indiana).

(a) It is a defense that:
   (1) The prohibited conduct of the person was the product of a law enforcement officer, or his agent, using persuasion or other means likely to cause the person to engage in the conduct; and
   (2) The person was not predisposed to commit the offense.

(b) Conduct merely affording a person an opportunity to commit the offense does not constitute entrapment.[38]

Outrageous Government Conduct

A defense similar to entrapment is that of outrageous government conduct. The defense is based on the assumption that some behavior is so offensive and so outrageous that when it is committed by a government agent it cannot be the basis for collecting evidence to convict a suspect.

In the outrageous government conduct defense, the emphasis is on the behavior of the government rather than the mind of the defendant, as in the entrapment defense. "When the government's conduct . . . is sufficiently outrageous, the courts will not allow the government to prosecute offenses developed through that conduct."[39] In making that statement in 1992, a federal appellate court noted that outrageous government conduct is a viable defense that may be raised even when the accused may not succeed in the entrapment defense because of a predisposition to commit

JACOBSON v. UNITED STATES
503 U.S. 540 (1992)

Justice Byron White delivered the Court's opinion, in which Justices Harry A. Blackmun, John Paul Stevens, David H. Souter, and Clarence Thomas joined. Justice Sandra Day O'Connor filed a dissenting opinion, in which Chief Justice William H. Rehnquist and Justice Anthony M. Kennedy joined, and in which Justice Antonin Scalia joined in part. The following opinion is by Justice White.

 In February 1984, petitioner, a 56-year-old veteran-turned-farmer who supported his elderly father in Nebraska, ordered two magazines and a brochure from a California adult bookstore. The magazines, entitled Bare Boys I and Bare Boys II, contained photographs of nude preteen and teenage boys. The contents of the magazines startled petitioner, who testified that he had expected to receive photographs of "young men 18 years or older." . . . The young men depicted in the magazines were not engaged in sexual activity, and petitioner's receipt of the magazine was legal under both federal and Nebraska law. Within three months, the law with respect to child pornography changed; Congress passed the Act illegalizing the receipt through the mails of sexually explicit depictions of children. In the very month that the new provision became law, postal inspectors found petitioner's name on the mailing list of the California bookstore that had mailed him Bare Boys I and II.

There followed over the next 2 1/2 years, repeated efforts by two Government agencies, through five fictitious organizations and a bogus pen pal, to explore petitioner's willingness to break the law by ordering sexually explicit photographs of children through the mail. . . .

[The Court described the government's actions in detail.]

There can be no dispute about the evils of child pornography or the difficulties that laws and law enforcement have encountered in eliminating it. Likewise, there can be no dispute that the Government may use undercover agents to enforce the law. . . .

In their zeal to enforce the law, however, Government agents may not originate a criminal design, implant in an innocent person's mind the disposition to commit a criminal act, and then induce commission of the crime so that the Government may prosecute. . . .

By the time the petitioner finally placed his order, he had already been the target of 26 months of repeated mailings and communications from Government agents and fictitious organizations. Therefore, although he had become predisposed to break the law by May 1987, it is our view that the Government did not prove that this predisposition was independent and not the product of the attention that the Government had directed at petitioner since January 1985.

1. *Jacobson v. United States*, 503 U.S. 540 (1992), cases and citations omitted.

---

the defense. The "thrust of [the defense as articulated in other cases] is that the challenged conduct must be shocking, outrageous, and clearly intolerable." The court went on to note that cases

> make it clear that this is an extraordinary defense reserved for only the most egregious circumstances. It is not to be invoked each time the government acts deceptively or participates in a crime that it is investigating. Nor is it intended merely as a device to circumvent the predisposition test in the entrapment defense.[40]

Some states recognize the defense of outrageous government conduct. For example, in September 1996, for the first time in its history, the Washington Supreme Court held that a police informant's conduct was so objectively outrageous that it violated the Fourteenth Amendment's due process clause (see Appendix A). In *State v. Lively* the police informant's conduct was described as "trolling for targets." The informant attended meetings of Alcoholics Anonymous/Narcotics Anonymous and developed a romantic relationship with a lonely alcoholic defendant who claimed that the informant was emotionally supportive and that they lived together and had a sexual relationship. The defendant had attempted suicide prior to her attendance at the therapeutic meetings. She stated that after a few months the informant told her that he had a friend who wanted to buy cocaine and inquired whether she knew a source. He asked her repeatedly each day for two weeks before she agreed to buy the drugs. The entrapment defense was raised, with the court holding that the defendant was required to prove her lack of a predisposition to commit the offense. The prosecution did not have the burden of proving that the defendant was predisposed to sell the drugs.[41]

In 1993 that same federal appeals court held that the outrageous conduct prohibition would not preclude a government agent from supplying some drugs to addicts while working under cover, but that

> [a]t a certain threshold, the government's conduct would violate due process. For instance, we speculate that if a government agent entered a drug rehabilitation treatment center and sold heroin to a recovering addict, and the addict was subsequently prosecuted for possession of a controlled substance, the outrageous government conduct defense might properly be invoked.[42]

Defense of Persons and Property

The law permits people to defend themselves, other people, and property under certain circumstances. The defense of persons or property is one of the most controversial defenses today, as more people are buying guns and using them defensively. (The controversial U.S. Supreme Court case on the issue is discussed in Chapter 9 of this text.) Defense of self, defense of others, and defense of property may not be separated in all cases; some cases involve all three. To the extent that these defenses are separable, the rules differ with regard to acts that are permitted.

Self-Defense and the Defense of Others

The defense of self and of others is permitted under some circumstances. The general rule on self-defense is that a person is permitted to use force to repel the actions of another under the following circumstances, which constitute the elements of self-defense:

1. The individual has an honest and reasonable belief that he or she is

2. Facing an unlawful threat of imminent death or serious bodily injury

3. By an aggressor (i.e, no provocation on the part of the one who asserts self-defense) and

4. The force used was reasonable under the circumstances.

In the first and fourth elements, the word *reasonable* is important, for it establishes an *objective* rather than a subjective standard, meaning that the accused acted as a reasonable person would have acted under the circumstances. If the belief was a reasonable one, it would not matter that it was inaccurate. That is, if it can be shown that most people would reasonably believe they were in danger of immediate physical harm, use of force is justified.

In some jurisdictions the rules regarding self-defense may be different for police officers, who may be held to a *subjective* rather than an objective standard, in which case the issue is whether *that* officer believed he or she was in danger, not whether a reasonable person would have had that belief. Finally, the threatened harm must be imminent and unlawful, and the actor must not have provoked the attack.

The right to use force does not always include the right to use **deadly force**. The use of deadly force to protect oneself or others may be limited to situations in which the actors have reasonable beliefs that deadly force is necessary to protect them from harm that might cause serious bodily injury or death. The Model Penal Code permits the use of deadly force when "the actor believes that such force is necessary to protect himself against death, serious bodily injury, kidnapping, or sexual intercourse compelled by force or threat." The code does not permit the use of deadly force as a defense if, in the same encounter, the actor provoked the incident that led to the threat of harm or death.[43]

Some jurisdictions require a person to retreat before using deadly force, although some limit that duty to situations in which retreat can be accomplished with safety. The Model Penal Code requires retreating if it can be done with "complete safety," although, with a few exceptions, the code does not require actors to retreat within their own homes.[44]

The exclusion of the home from the duty to retreat is known as the *castle doctrine*, and according to the Rhode Island Supreme Court, a "majority of American jurisdictions recognize [this doctrine] pursuant to which a person attacked in his dwelling is not required to retreat before using fatal force to repel the attack." The Rhode Island court extended the castle doctrine in a case involving a social guest who had been asked to leave. "We now hold that one who is attacked in his dwelling by one who initially entered as a social guest

Although most jurisdictions require that, if it is safe to do so, a person must retreat before using force for self-defense, retreat is not usually required if the threat occurs in one's home. This lack of a duty to retreat within one's home is referred to as the castle doctrine. (IStockPhoto)

but who has become a trespasser by remaining after being ordered to leave is similarly absolved from the duty to retreat."[45]

Subsequently the Rhode Island Supreme Court decided a case involving a woman who stabbed her husband in their home. The husband died shortly thereafter, and the wife was charged with murder. The defendant claimed that her husband had beaten her for years and that on the occasion in question, he was threatening her life. She was convicted of manslaughter, and she appealed on several issues, one of which was the court's instruction that there is a duty to retreat even in your own home if you are being threatened by a co-occupant. The appellate court upheld that instruction.[46]

One final point on self-defense involves the fact that jurisdictions differ with regard to whether force may be used to resist arrest. The traditional position is that a person may use force to resist an unlawful arrest, although some jurisdictions reject that rule and provide, either through statutes or case law, that it is never permissible to use force to resist a person one knows or should know is a law enforcement officer. This position may be taken to avoid the potential escalation of violence that may occur when a person resists arrest and the officer must use force to effect the arrest. This position is also advanced to prevent citizens from making their own judgments about the legality of arrests. It is argued that if the arrest is illegal, citizens may use civil avenues for redress in the courts.

The rules governing the use of force to protect others are similar to those for self-defense. The actor is justified in using force to protect others if conditions exist that would justify the use of force for self-defense for the actor and for the threatened person and if the actor believes it is necessary to use force to protect the other person. Generally it is not required that a special relationship exist between the parties before the use of force is justified to protect another.

Finally, some jurisdictions specify by statute that self-defense is permitted against certain felonies, such as sexual assault.

Some of the preceding points are illustrated by North Dakota's self-defense statute, which is as follows:

A person is justified in using force upon another person to defend himself against danger of imminent unlawful bodily injury, sexual assault, or detention by such other person, except that:

1. A person is not justified in using force for the purpose of resisting arrest, execution of process, or other performance of duty by a public servant under color of law [acting in the capacity of one's job as a public official], but excessive force may be resisted.

2. A person is not justified in using force if:

   a. He intentionally provokes unlawful action by another person to cause bodily injury or death to such other person; or

   b. He has entered into a mutual combat with another person or is the initial aggressor unless he is resisting force which is clearly excessive in the circumstances. A person's use of defensive force after he withdraws from an encounter and indicates to the other person that he has done so is justified if the latter nevertheless continues or menaces unlawful action.[47]

Defense of Property

Even though defense of property is permitted, the rules are more stringent than those for self-defense or for the defense of others. Some of these rules differ among the jurisdictions, although it is well accepted that unless property occupiers need to protect themselves, they are not privileged to use deadly force to protect property. Otherwise, if it is reasonably necessary to use force to protect property from the immediate criminal acts of others, reasonable force is permitted. The force is limited to the amount needed to prevent the criminal acts; it is not reasonable to use any force if the acts can be prevented by asking the intruder to stop. The property owner is not privileged to use force against a **trespasser** (one who has no legal or implied right to be on the property of another), if that person would be placed in substantial danger of serious bodily injury upon being excluded from the property. For example, this rule prohibits the use of booby traps or other such devices designed to cause serious bodily harm or death.

In most instances the use of devices that are not designed to cause serious bodily injury or death is justified for the protection of property. Devices that are not designed to cause serious bodily injury or death may be used if they are reasonable under the circumstances and if those devices are used customarily or reasonable care is taken to inform potential intruders that the devices are present.

Law Enforcement

A final defense against criminal conduct included in this chapter is that of law enforcement. Conduct that is criminal under most circumstances may be justified and therefore not criminal when committed by a law enforcement officer or by a private citizen attempting

Court decisions and departmental policies limit the circumstances under which law enforcement officers may use force, especially deadly force. Some departmental policies do not permit high speed chases, the results of which are depicted here, because of the danger these chases may create for innocent bystanders, as well as the participants. (AP Images)

to enforce the law. New York's statute illustrates this. It provides that conduct is not criminal when "such conduct is required or authorized by law or by a judicial decree, or is performed by a public servant in the reasonable exercise of his official powers, duties, or functions."[48] Thus, a police officer may possess narcotics for the purpose of law enforcement as long as the officer does not engage in acts that might be classified as outrageous, as discussed earlier in this chapter. The statute also has a provision that acts that might otherwise be illegal might not be illegal in emergency situations.

There is a reasonable limit to the acts (otherwise criminal) that may be committed to gain evidence of other crimes. The highly controversial practice of police officers' getting involved in morality offenses is an example. Some activities are permitted, depending on how far the officers go in those activities, but it would not be permissible for an officer to engage in sexual intercourse with a prostitute, commit an armed robbery, or hire someone to commit a murder.

Force, including deadly force, may be used by private citizens as well as by police officers in certain circumstances without incurring criminal responsibility. Police officers and people aiding them may use force to effect an arrest. Under some circumstances an arrest warrant is necessary for a legal arrest; the exceptions are matters of criminal procedure and are not discussed here. Authorities may use force to prevent an arrested person from escaping or to protect officers and other people. The most critical issues arise over the use of deadly force.

Under the common law, police were permitted to shoot any **fleeing felon** (a person who allegedly had committed a felony and was eluding arrest). This rule developed over a period of time when all felonies were capital offenses and felons were likely to get away if not apprehended quickly. Many states codified the common law rule, although some limited the shooting to fleeing felons who were accused of more serious felonies, such as murder or forcible rape. This practice was changed as the result of a 1985 U.S. Supreme Court decision.

In *Tennessee v. Garner* police dispatched to a "prowler inside call" were told by a neighbor that she heard a glass break in the house next door. An officer went to the back of the house, heard a door slam, and saw a man running toward the fence. The officer, with the aid of his flashlight, saw the man's face and hands and said the person looked to be about 17 or 18 years old and about 5 feet 5 to 5 feet 7 inches tall. The suspect was actually 15 and 5 feet 4 inches tall.

The officer yelled, "Police, halt," but the suspect did not stop. The officer testified that although apparently the suspect was not armed, he thought that if the suspect got over the fence, he would elude police officers. The officer fired, hit the suspect in the back of the head, and killed him. The Tennessee statute permitted a law enforcement officer to fire under such circumstances after giving a warning. After acknowledging the importance of crime prevention, the U.S. Supreme Court ruled that the Tennessee statute was unconstitutional as implemented in this case. The Court gave reasons and guidelines for the use of deadly force when police are attempting to arrest a suspect.[49]

TENNESSEE v. GARNER
471 U.S. 1 (1985)

Justice Byron White delivered the opinion of the U.S. Supreme Court, in which Justices William J. Brennan Jr., Thurgood Marshall, Harry A. Blackmun, Louis F. Powell Jr., and John Paul Stevens joined. Justice Sandra Day O'Connor filed a dissenting opinion, in which Chief Justice Warren E. Burger and Justice William H. Rehnquist Jr. joined.

The use of deadly force to prevent the escape of all felony suspects, whatever the circumstances, is constitutionally unreasonable. It is not better that all felony suspects die than that they escape. Where the suspect poses no immediate threat to the officer and no threat to others, the harm resulting from failing to apprehend him does not justify the use of deadly force to do so. . . . A police officer may not seize an unarmed, nondangerous suspect by shooting him dead. . . .

[The Court noted that the statute, although unconstitutional as applied to the facts of this case, is not unconstitutional on its face, which means it could be upheld under some circumstances.]

Where the officer has probable cause to believe that the suspect poses a threat of serious physical harm, either to the officer or to others, it is not constitutionally unreasonable to prevent escape by using deadly force. Thus, if the suspect threatens the officer with a weapon or there is probable cause to believe that he has committed a crime involving the infliction or threatened infliction of serious physical harm, deadly force may be used when necessary to prevent escape and when some warning has been given where feasible. Ap-

 plied in such circumstances, the Tennessee statute would pass constitutional muster.

Under restricted conditions (usually a requirement that the suspect committed a dangerous felony, such as murder), a private person may use deadly force to effect an arrest. Most statutes permit people who are not assisting peace officers to use deadly force only when they are protecting themselves or others.

SUMMARY

This chapter began a discussion of the major defenses that may be raised to negate a crime or some element of a crime. Chapter 5 completes the discussion. These defenses are very important, but they are complicated. The case law on defenses is immense, and new challenges continue to arise in the interpretations of long-used defenses.

The introduction to this chapter set the stage for discussing individual defenses by illustrating that it is not easy to distinguish some defenses from the required elements of a crime and that the allocation of the burden of proof is not a simple matter.

Although it is not possible to write a simple statement or draft a list of what can and cannot be done on these issues, it is possible to make general statements. It must be understood, however, that these principles may lead to different legal conclusions, depending on a particular fact pattern.

With these limitations in mind, we may state that generally, the prosecution must prove all elements of a crime beyond a reasonable doubt and the defense must prove all affirmative defenses by a preponderance of the evidence. Defenses must be defined so that they do not shift from the prosecution to the defendant the burden of proof on any element of a crime. A defense that shifts to defendants the burden of proving they are innocent may be viewed as relieving the prosecutor of the burden of proving guilt. This is unconstitutional in U.S. criminal justice systems.

The section on types of defenses began with a discussion of ignorance or mistake. Despite the commonly held belief that ignorance of the law is no excuse, the law recognizes the mistake of ignorance defense under some circumstances. In addition, the law recognizes that some otherwise criminal acts are committed under duress; in those cases the actors are not criminally responsible. In other circumstances someone may need to commit an otherwise criminal act to prevent a greater harm, in which case the defense of necessity is permitted.

Infancy is another factor in determining criminal culpability. Children are not normally held to criminal liability even when they commit serious crimes. Statutes differ on how they define *juvenile* and *adult*. All states have a juvenile court system that differs significantly from adult criminal court systems. More and more states are changing their statutes to permit the prosecution to try juveniles in adult criminal courts when they are charged with serious violent felonies such as robbery, rape, or murder.

The insanity defense, although used infrequently, is one of the most controversial defenses, illustrated by reactions to its successful use in the trial of John Hinckley Jr. In a more recent case, in which a Texas mother, Andrea Yates, drowned her five children, the defense was not successful at her first trial, but after her case was reversed on appeal, Yates was acquitted at her second trial. The *Yates* case is the basis of the chapter's Case Analysis at the end of the chapter.

The insanity defense raises the problems of defining the term *insanity* and, once the defense is introduced, deciding whether the prosecution must prove that the defendant was sane at the time of the alleged act or whether the defense has the burden of proving insanity. Because the U.S. Supreme Court has held that insanity is an affirmative defense (in contrast to requiring the prosecution to prove sanity as an *element* of the crime at issue), it is permissible to place the burden of proof on the defendant. When this occurs, generally the standard of proof required for the insanity defense is the civil standard of a preponderance of the evidence. The federal criminal code, however, requires proof by clear and convincing evidence, which is a higher standard than the usual civil one.

Several tests are used to define insanity. The one used most frequently, the M'Naghten rule, is referred to as the *right-versus-wrong rule*. This rule permits finding a defendant not guilty by reason of insanity if it can be shown that, at the time the crime was committed and as the result of a defect of reason caused by a disease of the mind, the defendant did not know the nature and quality of the act or did not know that the act was wrong.

There was dissatisfaction with the M'Naghten rule because it did not apply to defendants who knew the nature, quality, and illegality of their acts but could not control themselves and keep from committing the crimes. Some jurisdictions combined the M'Naghten rule with the irresistible impulse test, which was drafted to include this situation.

Dissatisfaction with both of these rules led the District of Columbia to draft the Durham rule, which is also called the *product rule*. The test of insanity under the Durham rule is whether the defendant's act is the product of mental disease or mental defect. The difficulty of defining *product, mental disease*, and *mental defect* led the District of Columbia courts to abolish the Durham rule, which was never widely adopted in other jurisdictions.

Another insanity test, the *substantial capacity test*, has been widely adopted in those jurisdictions that have an insanity defense. This test permits the insanity defense in cases in which mental disease or defect results in the lack of a substantial capacity to appreciate the criminality of an act or to conform one's behavior to the law. This test, in substituting the word *appreciate* for the word *know*, is broader than the M'Naghten rule. Generally the substantial capacity tests exclude sociopathic or psychopathic personalities from their definitions of insanity.

Dissatisfaction with the insanity defense has led a few states to legislate a provision for the defense of guilty but mentally ill (GBMI). Michigan led the way with this approach, which applies to a person who is guilty of an offense and mentally ill when the offense is committed but who is not legally insane at that time. A defendant found GBMI may receive the same sentence as a defendant found guilty, but generally the state is required by statute to provide treatment for the GBMI defendant. The Michigan Supreme Court and other state supreme courts have upheld GBMI statutes. Some states have abolished the insanity defense rather than make this or other changes.

The diminished capacity or partial responsibility defense is similar to the insanity defense and may be used by defendants who are not insane but who suffer from such mental impairment that they cannot form the required criminal intent for a particular crime. The defense of automatism is available to defendants who are not in control of their actions because they are either unconscious or semiconscious.

One of the most litigated defenses is entrapment. Despite numerous attempts to define the term, case law illustrates that it remains unclear when the defense is applicable. In general, the defense may be used by defendants who can prove that their criminal acts were the result of inducement by a government official or employee and that they were not otherwise predisposed to commit the crimes. This defense is used frequently in cases involving drugs or sex. The entrapment defense may be distinguished from the less frequently used defense of outrageous government conduct, which focuses on the actions of a government official rather than on the predisposition of a suspect.

Individuals are permitted to defend themselves, their property, and other persons, but self-defense is another frequently litigated defense that raises considerable controversy. Although the defense must be analyzed in light of the facts of a particular situation, usually it is available when a person is threatened with unlawful force that would cause immediate harm. However, the threatened person may use only as much force as is reasonably necessary for protection. Defense of property permits less use of force than defense of persons, and usually the use of deadly force is permissible only when someone is threatened with death or serious bodily injury.

Police officers are permitted to use deadly force in some instances without incurring criminal responsibility. The common law rule that permitted police to shoot and kill a fleeing felon was changed by ordinances and statutes in some jurisdictions prior to the U.S. Supreme Court's ruling in *Tennessee v. Garner*. Today police and private persons may not use deadly force except under restricted conditions (usually those involving a dangerous felony).

One of the fascinating and challenging aspects of the law is that despite its stability and predictability, the law also changes. One might say there are fads and fashions in criminal law and in criminology just as there are in clothing and other areas of life. Defenses that are used frequently today may not be as popular in the future. Furthermore, the specific uses of any given defense may change, and the laws regarding those uses continue to develop and grow. It is important in the practice or enforcement of law to be aware of the latest changes in one's jurisdiction. Chapter 5 discusses some defenses that are relatively new or that have been expanded in recent years.

STUDY QUESTIONS

1. Why is it necessary to distinguish elements of a crime from defenses to a crime?

2. How does the standard of proof required of the prosecution differ from that required of the defense?

3. How might a presumption affect the burden of proof?

4. How did the Supreme Court distinguish *Mullaney v. Wilbur* from *Patterson v. New York*? Do you find this distinction meaningful? If so, why? If not, why not?

5. What is wrong with telling the jury in a murder case that "the law presumes that a person intends the ordinary consequences of his or her voluntary act"? Discuss applicable case law.

6. Who has the burden of proof in self-defense, and why? In the insanity defense?

7. When would ignorance or mistake be a defense? Should a reasonable mistake of age be a defense to statutory rape?

8. Distinguish the defense of automatism from that of duress or necessity.

9. Should the age of an accused person have any bearing on our reaction to serious crimes that person is alleged to have committed?

10. Define and compare the major tests of insanity, and contrast the insanity defense and the irresistible impulse defense. Do you think either of these defenses should be abolished? Is guilty but mentally ill an improvement over the traditional defenses involving mental illness?

11. What are the key elements of an entrapment defense? Do you agree with the Court's decision in *Jacobson v. United States*?

12. Distinguish the outrageous government conduct defense from the entrapment defense. Should either be abolished?

13. Under what circumstances may one defend person or property, and how much force may be used?

14. Compare the position taken by the U.S. Supreme Court in *Tennessee v. Garner* to the traditional common law approach to the use of deadly force by police officers.

FOR DEBATE

When the law states that sex with an underage person is a crime even if that person appears to be of legal age and is the aggressor, a perpetrator who has sex with the underage person may be convicted of a sex crime, be sent to prison, and be required to register (perhaps even for life) as a sex offender. Consider whether this approach to sexual behavior should be continued by debating this issue.

Resolved: A reasonable and good-faith belief that a consensual sexual partner is of legal age should be a complete defense to the crime of statutory rape.

A significant change in U.S. criminal justice systems has occurred in recent years, and that involves the refusal to recognize the common law rules concerning criminal liability of young people. Many jurisdictions now permit the trial in adult criminal courts of juveniles who commit violent crimes. In light of this change, debate this issue.

Resolved: Any person under the age of 14 who commits a crime, even if that crime is violent, should be processed through a juvenile court rather than an adult criminal court. There should be a strong presumption that a person between the ages of 14 and 16 who commits a serious violent crime should be processed through the juvenile court system.

KEY TERMS

affirmative defense, 83	irresistible impulse test, 93
automatism, 95	malice aforethought, 85
deadly force, 98	mistake, 87
duress, 88	M'Naghten rule, 91
Durham rule, 93	necessity, 88
entrapment, 96	preponderance of the evidence, 83
expert testimony, 93	presumption, 84
fleeing felon, 101	rebuttable presumption, 90
guilty but mentally ill (GBMI), 94	substantial capacity test, 93
insanity, 90	trespasser, 100

CASE ANALYSIS

YATES v. TEXAS

171 S.W.3d 215 (Tex. App. Houston, 1st Dist., 2005)

Case Preview

The nation was shocked, horrified, and outraged at the recitation of the facts of this case: A Texas mother drowned each of her five children in the bathtub and admitted that she did so. The nation wept as five little coffins with the children's bodies were laid to rest. To many, this appeared to be an easy case to prosecute; the state asked for the death penalty. Others argued that Andrea Yates must have been insane to commit these atrocious acts. As more facts were disclosed, some wondered why her treating physicians and Yates's family, especially her husband, did not realize the seriousness of her illness.

The jury found Yates guilty but did not recommend the death penalty. Yates was incarcerated but appealed. That appeal was successful in January 2005, and in November 2005, the Texas Court of Criminal Appeals (the highest Texas court for criminal appeals) refused the state's petition for discretionary review. At her second trial, Yates was successful in her insanity defense (some of the evidence presented during the first trial was excluded from the second trial, as noted in this chapter). She remains in a Texas treatment facility.

Justice Sam Nuchia delivered the opinion of the court.

Overview by the Court

Appellant, Andrea Pia Yates, was charged by two indictments with capital murder for the drowning deaths of three of her five children. Rejecting appellant's insanity defense, the jury found her guilty and, having answered the special issue regarding appellant's continuing threat to society "No," assessed punishment at life in prison. Following the verdict and before the punishment phase of the trial, appellant learned that the State's expert witness, Dr. Park Dietz, had presented false testimony. Appellant moved for mistrial, but the trial court denied the motion. Appellant asserts 19 points of error in which she challenges, among other things, the factual sufficiency of the evidence to support the verdict rejecting the insanity defense, the denial of a motion for mistrial based on false testimony, and the denial of her right to due process by the use of false or perjured testimony. We reverse and remand.

Facts

Appellant and Russell Yates were married on April 17, 1993. Their first child, Noah, was born in February 1994; their second child, John, was born in December 1995; and their third child, Paul, was born in September 1997. During this time, the Yates family moved from Friendswood to Florida and back to the Houston area, living in a recreational vehicle. In 1998, they

moved from the recreational vehicle to a converted bus and continued to live in a trailer park. At one point, appellant told her husband she felt depressed and overwhelmed, and he suggested that she talk to her mother and a friend.

In February 1999, a fourth child, Luke, was born. On June 18, 1999, appellant suffered severe depression and tried to commit suicide by taking an overdose of an antidepressant that had been prescribed for her father. She was admitted to the psychiatric unit of Methodist Hospital. After her release six days later, she began seeing a psychiatrist, Dr. Eileen Starbranch, as an outpatient. On July 20, 1999, Yates found appellant in the bathroom, holding a knife to her neck. Dr. Starbranch recommended that appellant be admitted to Spring Shadows Glen Hospital. Appellant was admitted, against her wishes, the next day. At Spring Shadows Glen, appellant told a psychologist, Dr. James Thompson, that she had had visions and had heard voices since the birth of her first child. Dr. Starbranch ranked appellant, at the time of her admission to Spring Shadows Glen, among the five sickest patients she had ever seen. Before discharging appellant from the hospital, Dr. Starbranch told appellant and Yates that appellant had a high risk of another psychotic episode if she had another baby.

In August 1999, the Yates family moved from the converted bus to a house that Yates had bought while appellant was in the hospital. That fall, appellant began home-schooling Noah. Appellant saw Dr. Starbranch for the last time on January 12, 2000. She told Dr. Starbranch that she had stopped taking her medication in November 1999. In November 2000, appellant's fifth child, Mary, was born. In March 2001, appellant's father died. This death seemed to precipitate a decline in appellant's functioning, and she began to suffer from depression. On March 28, 2001, Yates contacted Dr. Starbranch and told her that appellant was ill again. Dr. Starbranch wanted to see appellant immediately, but Yates said he could not bring her in until the next Monday.

Appellant was not taken to Dr. Starbranch's office, but was admitted to Devereux Hospital in League City on March 31, 2001. There, she was observed as being catatonic or nearly catatonic and possibly delusional or having bizarre thoughts. She was treated by Dr. Mohammed Saeed and was placed on a suicide watch. Appellant was discharged on April 13, 2001, upon her own and Yates's request. She began an outpatient program at Devereux, and Dr. Saeed recommended that someone stay with her at all times and that she not be left alone with her children.

On April 19, Yates's mother came for a visit. She had intended to stay for about one week, but, when Yates told his mother that appellant was suffering from depression, his mother decided to stay longer and moved to a nearby extended stay hotel.

Yates's mother went to appellant's home every day. She observed that appellant was almost catatonic, did not respond to conversation or made a delayed response, stared into space, trembled, scratched her head until she created bald spots, and did not eat. On May 3, appellant filled a bathtub with water, but could not give a good reason for doing so. When asked, she said, "I might need it." On May 4, appellant was re-admitted to Devereux, and on May 14, she was discharged, seeming to be better. Dr. Saeed had prescribed the medication, Haldol, and appellant continued to take it after her discharge. Dr. Saeed also recommended electroconvulsive therapy, but appellant rejected that recommendation.

After her second discharge from Devereux, appellant was able to take care of her children, but was still uncommunicative and withdrawn. She smiled infrequently and seemed to have no emotions, but Yates did not think it was unsafe to leave her alone with the children. On June 4, appellant had a follow-up appointment with Dr. Saeed, who decided to taper her off of Haldol. Appellant denied having any suicidal or psychotic thoughts. Appellant met with Dr. Saeed again on June 18, and she again denied having any psychotic symptoms or suicidal thoughts. She was no longer taking Haldol, and Dr. Saeed adjusted the dosages of her other anti-depressant medications.

On June 20, 2001, at 9:48 a.m., appellant called 9-1-1 and told the operator, Sylvia Morris, that she needed the police. Morris transferred the call to the Houston Police Department, and appellant told the police operator that she needed a police officer to come to her home. Appellant also called Yates at his work and told him that he needed to come home, but would not say why. As Yates was leaving, he called her and asked if anyone was hurt, and she said that the kids were hurt. He asked, "Which ones?" She responded, "All of them."

Within minutes of appellant's 9-1-1 call, several police officers arrived at appellant's home. They discovered four dead children, soaking wet and covered with a sheet, lying on appellant's bed. The fifth child, Noah, was still in the bathtub, floating face down. Appellant was quiet and cooperative with the police officers.

At trial, ten psychiatrists and two psychologists testified regarding appellant's mental illness. Four of the psychiatrists and one of the psychologists had treated appellant either in a medical facility or as a private patient before June 20, 2001. They testified regarding the symptoms, severity, and treatment of appellant's mental illness. Five psychiatrists and one psychologist saw appellant on or soon after June 20 for assessment and/or treatment of her mental illness. Four of these five psychiatrists and the psychologist testified, in addition to their observations and opinions regarding appellant's mental illness, that appellant, on June 20, 2001, did not know right from wrong, was incapable of knowing what she did was wrong, or believed that her acts were right.

The tenth psychiatrist, Dr. Park Dietz, who interviewed appellant and was the State's sole mental-health expert in the case, testified that appellant, although psychotic on June 20, knew that what she did was wrong. Dr. Dietz reasoned that because appellant indicated that her thoughts were coming from Satan, she must have known they were wrong; that if she believed she was saving the children, she would have shared her plan with others rather than hide it as she did; that if she really believed that Satan was going to harm the children, she would have called the police or a pastor or would have sent the children away; and that she covered the bodies out of guilt or shame.

On cross-examination, appellant's counsel asked Dr. Dietz about his consulting work with the television show, "Law & Order," which appellant was known to watch. . . . [Among other statements, Dr. Dietz made the following]:

As a matter of fact, there was a show of a woman with postpartum depression who drowned her children in the bathtub and was found insane and it was aired shortly before the crime occurred. . . .

In his final argument at the guilt-innocence phase of the trial, appellant's attorney referred to Dr. Dietz's testimony by stating, "Or maybe even we heard some evidence that she saw some show on TV and knew she could drown her children and get away with it."

The prosecutor, in his final argument, made the following reference to Dietz's testimony about the "Law & Order" episode:

She gets very depressed and goes into Devereux. And at times she says these thoughts came to her during that month. These thoughts came to her, and she watches "Law & Order" regularly, she sees this program. There is a way out. She tells that to Dr. Dietz. A way out.

After the jury had returned a guilty verdict, appellant's counsel discovered that Dr. Dietz had given false testimony. The producer of "Law & Order" spoke to counsel by telephone and said he could not recall such an episode. An attorney representing the producer, after talking to Dr. Dietz and researching the shows, verified to counsel that there was no show with a plot as outlined by Dr. Dietz. Dr. Dietz acknowledged that he had made an error in his testimony. . . .

Appellant moved for a mistrial based on Dr. Dietz's false testimony, and the trial court denied the motion. . . .

Issue

[As stated by the appellant's counsel] [T]he issue is not whether or not the State was aware and we have no reason to believe the State was aware that such a program did not exist. The issue is that the defense of insanity was rebutted by the testimony of Dr. Dietz relative to an act of premeditation, that is a planned and/or a deceptive act on Mrs. Yates' part, that is something that would give her an idea, a way out of these particular allegations. And that was relayed to this jury and we believe that the jury relied upon the presentation of Dr. Dietz as well as the cross-examination by [the State's attorney] of [another expert witness, called by the defense] relative to this particular issue.

Rationale

It is uncontested that the testimony of Dr. Dietz regarding his consultation on a "Law & Order" television show having a plot remarkably similar to the acts committed by appellant was untrue and that there was no "Law & Order" television show with such a plot. . . . The record reflects that the State used Dr. Dietz's testimony twice. First [the testimony was used in the cross-examination of an expert.] . . . Second, the State connected the dots in its final argument by juxtaposing appellant's depression, her dark thoughts, watching "Law & Order," and seeing "a way out." Thus, the State used Dr. Dietz's false testimony to suggest to the jury that appellant patterned her actions after that "Law & Order" episode. We emphasize that the State's use of Dr. Dietz's false testimony was not prosecuto-

rial misconduct. Rather, it served to give weight to that testimony. . . .

Five mental health experts testified that appellant did not know right from wrong or that she thought what she did was right. Dr. Dietz was the only mental health expert who testified that appellant knew right from wrong. Therefore, his testimony was critical to establish the State's case. Although the record does not show that Dr. Dietz intentionally lied in his testimony, his false testimony undoubtedly gave greater weight to his opinion.

Holding

We conclude that there is a reasonable likelihood that Dr. Dietz's false testimony could have affected the judgment of the jury. We further conclude that Dr. Dietz's false testimony affected the substantial rights of appellant. Therefore, the trial court abused its discretion in denying appellant's motion for mistrial.

Accordingly, we . . . reverse the trial court's judgment and remand the cause for further proceedings.

For Discussion

After this appellate decision, which ordered a new trial, Yates and her attorney rejected a plea bargain offer from the prosecution. The offer required Yates to plead guilty to lesser charges in exchange for a 35-year sentence. According to Yates's attorney, the offer did not provide that Yates would get adequate psychiatric treatment and not be placed in the general prison population.

In the second trial, prosecutors agreed that Yates was mentally ill but argued that she knew what she was doing, that she planned the drowning of her children, and that she knew those acts were wrong. Thus, she was not insane under the provisions of the Texas statute. The jury found otherwise; Yates was found not guilty by reason of insanity. She was not released; nor did her attorneys or family request that. She continues to be confined in a medial facility for treatment.

If you were the prosecutor, would you have made the plea bargain offer of 35 years for a plea to a lesser charge than murder? If you were the defense attorney, would you have accepted that offer or go to trial, hoping for an acquittal but taking the risk that your client could get a life sentence?

Postscript on the Yates Case

In July 2004 a criminal defense attorney, Elizabeth Kelley, published a review of a book on the Yates case,

Are You There Alone? The Unspeakable Crime of Andrea Yates, authored by a reporter who covered the case, Suzanne O'Malley, and published by Simon & Schuster. The review appears in the official publication of the Association of American Trial Lawyers (now called American Association for Justice), *Trial*, no. 7 (July 2004): 86–87.

One juror (in the first trial) was quoted as saying, "There's no doubt in anyone's mind that she [Andrea Yates] was mentally ill, but that wasn't the question asked us. Did she know right from wrong? That was all we talked about in deliberation."

O'Malley interviewed jurors and numerous others associated with the Yates case and concluded that if anything good could come from this tragedy, it would be that we put more resources into the treatment of mental illness and that our criminal justice systems provide greater care for mentally ill defendants.

INTERNET ACTIVITY

1. For a brief overview of the usual defenses that are available in one state (Wisconsin) for specific crimes, look at the following website of the law firm of Van Wagner and Wood: http://www.vanwagnerwood.com/CM/Custom/Mitigating-Circumstances.asp (accessed 9 December 2008). What defenses are available in that state for driving under the influence (DUI)?

What information does this source provide on the following?

⭐ Diminished capacity

⭐ Coercion or necessity

⭐ Self-defense

⭐ Provocation

⭐ Mitigating circumstances

2. The insanity defense remains controversial. Some states have opted for a different version of the defense—guilty but mentally ill. Others, as noted in the text, have abolished the defense. Check the website of the American Psychiatric Association: http://www.healthyminds.org/insanitydefense.cfm (accessed 9 December 2008). See what additional information you can find about the insanity defense.

NOTES

1. *Mullaney v. Wilbur*, 421 U.S. 684, 701 (1975).
2. *Patterson v. New York*, 432 U.S. 197 (1977), cases and citations omitted.
3. *Sandstrom v. Montana*, 442 U.S. 510 (1979).
4. *Francis v. Franklin*, 471 U.S. 307 (1985).
5. *Martin v. Ohio*, 480 U.S. 228 (1987).
6. See *Rivera v. Delaware*, 429 U.S. 877 (1976).
7. See U.S. Code, Title 18, Section 17(b) (2009), formerly at Section 20.
8. See *United States v. Byrd*, 834 F.2d 145 (8th Cir. 1987).
9. Kenneth W. Simons, "Mistake and Impossibility, Law and Fact, and Culpability: A Speculative Essay," *Journal of Criminal Law & Criminology* 81 (Fall 1990): 469, emphasis in the original.
10. *Lambert v. California*, 355 U.S. 225 (1957).
11. *State v. Dodd*, 765 P.2d 1337 (Wash.App. 1989).
12. Pa.C.S., Title 18, Chapter 31, Section 3201 (2008).
13. "Fear of Crime Trumps the Fear of Lost Youth," *New York Times* (21 November 1999), p. 3, Week in Review; "Abraham Pleads Guilty to Drug Charges," *Detroit News* (18 November 2008), Metro Section; "Nathaniel Abraham Sentenced to Four Years in Prison on Drug Charge," *Detroit News* (6 January 2009), Metro Section.
14. "Nobody Seems to Know Why," *Los Angeles Times* (23 November 2008), p. 14; "Deal Lets Young Killer's Motives Stay Hidden," *New Zealand Herald* (23 February 2009), n.p.
15. "Documents: Tate Left with Guns," *Orlando Sentinel* (2 July 2005), p. 6B; "Probation Hearing Delayed," *Orlando Sentinel* (12 October 2005), p. 5B; "Two Reprieves Lost: Tate Gets 30 Years," *Los Angeles Times* (20 May 2006), p. 8; "Hearing Held for Suspect in Tot's Beating Death," *Miami Herald* (18 January 2008), n.p. Tate's last appeal, in which his 30-year sentence was upheld, was published without an opinion. *Tate v. State*, 967 So.2d 214 (Fla.Dist.Ct.App. 4th Dist. 2007).
16. *Brazill v. State*, 845 S.2d 282 (Fla.Dist.Ct.App. 4th Dist. 2003), *review denied*, 876 So.2d 561 (Fla. 2004), and *post conviction proceeding, remanded,* 937 So.2d 272 (Fla. Dist.Ct.App. 4th Dist. 2006); "Brazill Will Get an Appeal Hearing," *Sun-Sentinel* (Fort Lauderdale, Florida) (31 May 2007), p. 2B.
17. *M'Naghten's Case*, 8 Eng. Rep. 718, 722 (H.L. 1843).
18. Tex. Penal Code, Title 2, Section 8.01 (2007).
19. See, for example, *State v. Thompson*, Wright's Ohio Rep. 617 (1834).
20. *United States v. Kunak*, 5 U.S.C.M.A. 346 (1954).
21. *Durham v. United States*, 214 F.2d 862 (D.C.Cir. 1954), *overruled in part, United States v. Brawner*, 471 F.2d 969 (D.C.Cir. 1972).
22. *United States v. Brawner*, 471 F.2d 969 (D.C.Cir. 1972).
23. Model Penal Code, Section 4.01.

24. Mich. Comp. Laws, Chapter 760-777, Section 768.36(a)(b)(c) (2008).

25. *People v. Ramsey*, 375 N.W.2d 297 (Mich. 1985), emphasis in the original.

26. *State v. Hornsby*, 484 S.E.2d 869 (S.C. 1997).

27. *People v. Lantz*, 712 N.E.2d 314 (Ill. 1999), *on remand, remanded sub nom.*, 733 N.E.2d 438 (Ill. App. 2d Dist. 2000), *appeal denied*, 742 N.E.2d 333 (Ill. 2000).

28. Idaho Code, Title 18, Section 18-207 (2008).

29. *Jones v. United States*, 463 U.S. 354 (1983).

30. *Foucha v. Louisiana*, 504 U.S. 71 (1992).

31. *United States v. Salerno*, 481 U.S. 739, 755 (1987).

32. Cal Pen Code, Section 28(b)(2008).

33. Cal Pen Code, Section 25(c) (2008).

34. *Sorrells v. United States*, 287 U.S. 435, 453–454 (1932).

35. *Hampton v. United States*, 425 U.S. 484 (1976).

36. *Sherman v. United States*, 356 U.S. 369 (1958).

37. *State v. Grenfell*, 564 P.2d 171 (Mont. 1977).

38. Ind. Code Ann, Title 35, Section 35-41-3-9 (2008).

39. *United States v. Mosley*, 965 F.2d 906, 909 (10th Cir. 1992).

40. *United States v. Mosley*, 965 F.2d 906, 910 (10th Cir. 1992).

41. *State v. Lively*, 921 P.2d 1035 (Wash. 1996).

42. *United States v. Harris*, 997 F.2d 812, 818 (10th Cir. 1993).

43. Model Penal Code, Section 3.04(2)(b).

44. Model Penal Code, Section 3.04(2)(b)(ii)(A).

45. *State v. Walton*, 615 A.2d 469 (R.I. 1992).

46. *State v. Ordway*, 619 A.2d 819 (R.I. 1992).

47. N.D. Cent. Code, Title 12, Section 12.1-05-03 (2008).

48. NY CLS Penal, Title C, Section 35.05(1) (2008).

49. *Tennessee v. Garner*, 471 U.S. 1 (1985), citations and footnotes omitted.

CHAPTER 5

Defenses to Criminal Culpability: Part II

INTRODUCTION

We have learned that in a criminal case the prosecution must prove all *elements* of a charged crime beyond a reasonable doubt and that this burden of proof may not be shifted to the defendant. Chapter 4 pointed out that even if the prosecution sustains this burden of proof, a defendant may not be criminally responsible for the crime if an affirmative defense is proved. Chapter 4 also explored some of the more traditional affirmative defenses.

This chapter continues the discussion of affirmative defenses in criminal law by looking at some additional ones, such as intoxication, which has received an increasing amount of attention recently; domestic authority; and consent, condonation, or victim's conduct. The increased use of the battered person syndrome is included, with an extensive analysis of that defense, followed by discussions of other stress defenses, such as extreme emotional disturbance and various post-traumatic stress disorders. A variety of miscellaneous defenses that have been proposed but have not received wide acceptance by courts are mentioned in closing.

INTOXICATION

Chapter 1 contained a brief analysis of the issues concerning the role that criminal law should play in attempts to control what some people consider moral, not legal, issues. The use of alcohol and other drugs is often included in this category. This section focuses on whether substance abuse should be a factor in criminal defenses.

Intoxication, which refers to the condition that exists when a person consumes alcohol or other drugs to the extent that his or her mental or physical abilities are significantly affected, is recognized as a defense in criminal law under some circumstances. The intoxication defense, however, is not recognized in situations in which intoxication is an *element* of the crime, as, for example, in the case of driving while intoxicated. The defense is permitted in some instances in which there is evidence that intoxication created a state of mind similar to that of an insane person and thus the defendant could not form the requisite intent required for the crime at issue. In jurisdictions that recognize the irresistible impulse test, the intoxication defense may be used when defendants offer evidence that as a result

Intoxication may be a defense to criminal acts under restricted circumstances. It is not a defense to the crime of driving while impaired. (Jan Greune/Getty Images)

of intoxication they were unable to control themselves and thus engaged in criminal behavior although they knew that behavior was wrong.

It is widely known that alcohol and other drugs are involved in many crimes. However, that fact reveals only part of the picture. Of interest in this chapter is whether substance abuse constitutes a *defense* to criminal behavior, and the answer is that the issue requires a consideration of whether substance abuse is a disease or a moral problem.

Substance Abuse: Disease or Moral Problem?

The law has long recognized that there is a difference between consuming alcohol and other drugs voluntarily and doing so because one has no control—as, for example, being forced to use drugs (which might raise a defense of coercion or duress, both discussed in Chapter 4). It has been argued, however, that alcoholism and drug addiction are diseases. In support of this position, in 1997 the director of the National Institute on Drug Abuse (NIDA) made this statement:

> Dramatic advances over the past two decades in both the neurosciences and the behavioral sciences have revolutionized our understanding of drug abuse and addiction. Scientists have identified neural circuits that are involved in the actions of every known drug of abuse, and they have specified common pathways that are affected by almost all such drugs. Research has also begun to reveal major differences between the brains of addicted and nonaddicted individuals and to indicate some common elements of addiction, regardless of the substance.[1]

At the 2001 annual meeting of the National Association of Addiction Treatment Providers the issue of whether chemical abuse is a form of obsessive-compulsive disorder (OCD), a mental disease, was discussed. One researcher proclaimed, "Chemical dependency satisfies all the criteria of OCD" and "Drug dependence satisfies all *Diagnostic and Statistical Manual of Mental Disorders* criteria for OCD." Another emphasized the importance of identifying bad genes and concluded that in the future "gene therapy will eradicate the disease of addiction."[2]

If substance abuse is a disease rather than a moral problem, this has implications for criminal law, and the resolution of the issue is important to a discussion of the intoxication defense and may be expected to influence changes in legislation and court decisions concerning that defense.

Experts debate whether addiction to alcohol or other drugs is a disease or a moral problem, and the answer to the issue has significant implications regarding how criminal justice systems respond to criminal acts committed by persons under the influence. (Peter Dazeley/Photodisc/Getty Images RF)

In 1988 the U.S. Supreme Court considered a related issue in *Traynor v. Turnage*, a case that involved the Veterans Administration benefits that are provided by law to eligible veterans. Most of the facts are not important to this discussion, and the technical issues were resolved by the Veterans' Judicial Review Act of 1988, but what is important is the issue of whether alcoholism constitutes willful misconduct.[3]

After analyzing the history of congressional statutes concerning the use of the words *willful misconduct*, particularly with regard to Veterans Administration legislation, the U.S. Supreme Court held that alcoholism constitutes willful misconduct. The Court emphasized, however, that it was not deciding the disease issue: "This litigation does not require the Court to decide whether alcoholism is a disease whose course its victims cannot control. It is not our role to resolve this medical issue on which the authorities remain sharply divided." But the Court did agree with the Veterans Administration legislation that primary alcoholism (alcoholism that is not "secondary to and a manifestation of an acquired psychiatric disorder") is the result of the veteran's "own willful misconduct."[4] With regard to the issue of whether alcoholism is a disease, note that in the excerpt from *People v. Tocco* (see p. 113), decided in 1998, the New York Supreme Court stated that for 30 years the medical community had uniformly agreed that alcoholism is a disease.

Intoxication as a Legal Defense

The intoxication defense is divided into two types: involuntary and voluntary. **Involuntary intoxication** (intoxication without choice or will, such as that which occurs when someone slips drugs into the food or drink of an unsuspecting person), a seldom-used defense, is appropriate when a defendant has acted under intoxication that was compelled or coerced by another or when a defendant became intoxicated as the result of deception, mistake, or ignorance. The latter category might involve a defendant who is allegedly unaware of the side effects of a prescription drug, as illustrated by the *Pittman* case discussed in Focus 5.1, along with other cases involving drug-related defenses.

Involuntary intoxication might include *pathological* intoxication, which has been defined as "intoxication grossly excessive in degree, given the amount of the intoxicant, to which the actor does not know he is susceptible." One approach is to permit involuntary intoxication and pathological intoxication to serve as affirmative defenses "if by reason of such intoxication the actor at the time of his conduct lacks substantial capacity either to appreciate its criminality [wrongfulness] or to conform his conduct to the requirements of law."[5]

Georgia permits the defense of involuntary intoxication as follows:

(a) A person shall not be found guilty of a crime when, at the time of the act, omission, or negligence constituting the crime, the person, because of involuntary intoxication, did not have sufficient mental capacity to distinguish between right and wrong in relation to such act.

(b) Involuntary intoxication means intoxication caused by:

(1) Consumption of a substance through excusable ignorance; or

(2) The coercion, fraud, artifice, or contrivance of another person.[6]

In most cases **voluntary intoxication**, which refers to intoxication brought on by free will, is not a defense. Georgia criminal statutes, for example, provide, "Voluntary intoxication shall not be an excuse for any criminal act or omission."[7]

Voluntary intoxication is a defense in some jurisdictions if it negates an element of the offense, but at best it is only a partial defense, meaning that it cannot negate general intent but may negate specific intent. Even though intoxication releases some inhibitions and may cause a person to behave in a way he or she would not have behaved in a nonintoxicated state, that is not a defense. However, the law may recognize intoxication as a defense to the *specific* intent required for a crime such as first-degree murder, in which case the defendant might be convicted of second-degree murder. For example, Kansas law provides as follows:

An act committed while in a state of voluntary intoxication is not less criminal by reason thereof, but when a particular intent or other state of mind is a necessary element to constitute a particular crime, the fact of intoxication may be taken into consideration in determining such intent or state of mind.[8]

In some jurisdictions intoxication may negate a specific but not a general intent. Other jurisdictions generally refuse to recognize that voluntary intoxication can negate a specific intent, although they may permit the court to examine the facts of a particular case and decide whether under those circumstances voluntary intoxication should be permitted as a defense.

In most jurisdictions voluntary intoxication cannot negate recklessness or negligence when those elements, rather than purpose or knowledge, are required for the crime.

The following excerpt from *People v. Tocco*, decided by the New York Supreme Court, illustrates the use of the intoxication defense and gives a historical overview of the issue of whether alcoholism is a disease.[9]

PEOPLE v. TOCCO

525 N.Y.S.2d 137 (N.Y.Sup. 1988)

The defendant here is charged with arson in the second degree and reckless endangerment in the first degree. More specifically, he is alleged to have set fire to the apartment in which he resided with his ex-wife and children. . . .

The defense admits the act. It contends that the defendant, who testified that he did not remember his arrest on the occasion for which he was being tried by reason of his intoxicated state, was incapable of formulating the requisite intent necessary to subject him to liability for the crime of arson in the second degree. . . .

Alcoholism is generally defined as the chronic, pathological use of alcohol. There is a 30 year consensus in the

FOCUS 5.1   Should Prescription Drug Use Be a Legal Defense to Illegal Behavior?

In recent years, considerable attention has been given to the effect that prescription drugs have on behavior. In particular, defense attorneys have sought to introduce the possible effects as reasons to explain the violent behavior of their clients, especially in cases in which the prosecution must prove a specific intent to commit the crime in question. Thus, it is argued that, in effect, the drugs prevented the defendant from having the mental capacity to develop that specific intent.

To illustrate, in a widely publicized murder trial in February 2005, defense attorneys argued that their client, Christopher Pittman, who was only 12 when he killed his grandparents, was unable to control his actions because of the effect of Zoloft, an antidepressant drug, which had been prescribed shortly before the killings. The defense argued that Pittman did not have the specific intent required for convictions of first-degree murder.

The Pittman case is significant because the federal Food and Drug Administration (FDA) had recently issued an order requiring a warning label on all antidepressants, stating that such drugs might carry an increased risk of suicidal thoughts when taken by young people.

Pittman's defense requested, and the judge granted, a jury instruction on the defense of involuntary intoxication. The jury was told that three conditions must occur for this defense to be successful and that the defense must prove all of the following:

- The defendant must have been unaware of the potentially intoxicating effect of Zoloft.

- The defendant was taking Zoloft under a doctor's prescription.

- The drug Zoloft rendered the defendant unable to tell the difference between right and wrong.

The essential facts of the Pittman case were as follows. Pittman's mother left him when he was a child. He lived with various relatives, including briefly with his father; his mother reappeared and then disappeared again, after which Pittman ran away. He was placed in a Florida behavioral facility, where he was taking Paxil, also an antidepressant drug. He was released from that facility and went to live with his grandparents in South Carolina, enrolled in school, and began taking Zoloft under a physician's prescription. Prosecutors argued that, after his grandfather dis-

ciplined him for getting into trouble at school, Pittman shot his grandparents, set the house on fire, and stole their car. The jury convicted Pittman of two counts of first-degree murder; he was sentenced to two 30-year sentences with no chance of parole.

When questioned after the trial, some jurors said they thought Zoloft may have influenced Pittman's behavior but that it was not what caused him to murder his grandparents. Despite the lack of success of the Zoloft defense in the Pittman case, it is significant that the trial judge permitted the defense, as have other judges. This sends mixed signals to the public. On the one hand, even the FDA is suggesting a careful look at this and other antidepressant drugs before prescribing them for young people. On the other, many people suffering from depression, including young persons, have been helped by Zoloft and other drugs.[1]

On appeal, Pittman's attorneys raised several issues, including the argument that the prosecution had not sufficiently rebutted the presumption of infancy. That presumption, which states that a child between 7 and 14 is presumed to lack the mental capacity to commit a crime, is rebuttable and does not, as the defense argued, require expert testimony to be refuted. The state appellate court rejected all issues raised on appeal and upheld the convictions and sentences.[2]

In a Michigan case, however, a defendant was found not guilty by reason of insanity after he claimed that he shot his estranged wife because of the influence of the prescription drug Halcion. In his first trial in 1990, John Caulley was convicted of first-degree murder and sentenced to life in prison. He was granted a retrial after an appellate court ruled that the jury should have been permitted to consider the effect of Halcion on his behavior. Caulley claimed the drug, which he took as a sleeping aid, caused him to shoot his wife.[3]

1. "Boy's Murder Case Entangled in Fight over Antidepressants," *New York Times* (23 August 2004), p. 1; "Boy Who Took Antidepressant Is Convicted in Killings," *New York Times* (16 February 2005), p. 12.
2. *Pittman v. South Carolina*, 647 S.E.2d 144 (S.C. 2007), *cert. denied,* 128 S.Ct. 1872 (2008).
3. "Man Who Killed His Wife Found Insane: Had Blamed Sleep Aid," *Phoenix Gazette* (21 October 1993), p. 10; *State v. Caulley*, 494 N.W.2d 853 (Mich.App. 1992), *appeal denied*, 502 N.W.2d 39 (Mich. 1993).

medical profession that such pathological use of alcohol is a disease. . . .

Even were our courts inclined to accept the disease thesis advanced by the medical profession, ignorance largely prevails as to its etiology. . . .

At common law, intoxication was never a defense to criminal misconduct. Instead, it was viewed as an aggravating circumstance which heightened moral culpability. "The common law courts viewed the decision to drink to excess with its attendant risks to self and others, as an independent culpable act." Later cases allowed evidence of intoxication to be introduced for limited purposes, such as to negative proof that the defendant possessed the physical capacity to commit the crime.

Under the present state of the law, voluntary intoxication is not a defense to a criminal charge; however, in crimes that have specific intent as an essential element, voluntary intoxication has been found to negative such intent, thereby rendering the defendant not guilty of the crime charged. . . .

And while intoxication may negative the *mens rea* in a crime requiring specific intent, it may not negative the lower culpable mental state required in crimes of recklessness. . . .

Involuntary intoxication is a defense if it deprives the intoxicated person of understanding the nature and quality of his act or the knowingness that the act is wrong. . . .

[T]here is a recognition among physicians that alcoholism is a disease characterized by loss of control over the consumption of alcoholic beverages. Can then an alcoholic's inebriated state(s) ever be considered truly voluntary? This question and a related one dealing with narcotic addiction have been dealt with by some courts. . . . [The court discusses *Robinson v. California* and *Powell v. Texas*.]

Some commentators have speculated that courts will be required, some time in the future, to meet the argument that the intoxication of a chronic alcoholic, is . . . involuntary. If such were the case, the chronic alcoholic could never be held liable for crimes that he committed while in a severely intoxicated state. As of yet, no court has extended the defense to preclude prosecution of an alcoholic for non-alcohol related crimes committed while in an intoxicated state. And, presently, alcoholism is not a defense even to alcohol related crimes that punish more than mere status. . . .

[I]t would appear that any change in the law would find basis only in conclusive medical evidence spurred by growing social concern, rather than constitutional pivots. Yet, if alcoholism is a disease characterized by an inability to control the consumption of alcoholic beverages, then the imposition of criminal liability for acts performed while drunk would at first blush defy logic.

Separating the physical act of drinking from the causative condition, alcoholism, is the distinguishing factor to which we must pay heed. Alcoholics should be held responsible for their conduct; they should not be penalized for their condition. An enlightened society cannot otherwise justify itself.

If an alcoholic knows that he is prone to commit criminal acts while drunk and that the consumption of even one drink will destroy his ability to resist further drinking, to the point of intoxication, as in the instant case, it must follow that his voluntarily imbibing of the first drink is the very initiation of a reckless act—and the concomitant disregard of the substantial and unjustifiable risk attendant thereto. If so, under our law the consumption of said drink by such alcoholic raises the act to the level of recklessness per se, subjecting him to strict accountability for crimes such as reckless arson and/or reckless endangerment now before the Court. No case has been uncovered imposing liability at this early threshold.

Arguendo, if we accept alcoholism as a disease, the hypothesis suggests that some (though probably not all) alcoholics lack the ability to control the taking of even the first drink. . . .

[U]pon the evidence adduced at the trial of this action, this Court finds the defendant not guilty of arson in the second degree, which is defined as "intentionally damag[ing] a building . . . by starting a fire" as he lacked the specific intent to damage a building. However, the Court finds: the defendant guilty of the lesser included offense of arson in the fourth degree, which is defined as "recklessly damag[ing] a building . . . by intentionally starting a fire."

Further, and likewise, the Court finds the defendant guilty of reckless endangerment in the first degree. Here, the defendant voluntarily commenced a reckless course of action (i.e., the act of his taking an alcoholic beverage), a risk in itself, the natural consequences of which, the unjustifiable endangerment of the lives of others thus being intended.

People v. Tocco raises a number of important issues. Note the references to *Powell and Robinson*, U.S. Supreme Court decisions that relate to the issue of punishing people for an act versus a status. "Powell was convicted not of being a chronic alcoholic, but for being drunk in a public place on a particular occasion. Thus, he was being punished for the performance of an act, rather than for mere status." The U.S. Supreme Court said that when Powell took a drink while sober, he was exercising free will. What if scientific evidence shows that this is not the case and that, to the contrary, people who have certain genes cannot control their actions with regard to drinking alcohol (or taking other drugs)? Should that evidence change our practices regarding intoxication as a defense to criminal acts? Should it change the results in the cases discussed in Focus 5.1? If so, to what extent? Should intoxication be a complete defense to a criminal act? These are crucial questions that courts continue to face in the light of new scientific evidence.

Earlier decisions showed some unwillingness to integrate research findings into legal issues. In his dissenting opinion in *Powell*, Justice Abe Fortas, joined by three other justices, emphasized that one important issue is to distinguish between a criminal act and a condition. *Powell* did not involve a criminal act but rather "the mere *condition* of being intoxicated in public." The opinion continued as follows.[10]

POWELL v. TEXAS
392 U.S. 514 (1968)

Justice Thurgood Marshall wrote the opinion of the Court, joined by Chief Justice Warren E. Burger and Justices Hugo L. Black and John Marshall Harlan; Justice Black wrote a concurring opinion, joined by Justice Harlan. Justice Byron White concurred in the result and wrote a separate opinion. Justice Abe Fortas wrote a dissent, joined by Justices William O. Douglas, William J. Brennan Jr., and Potter Stewart.

Justice Fortas, Dissenting
The questions for this Court are not settled by reference to medicine or penology. Our task is to determine whether the principles embodied in the Constitution of the United States place any limitations upon the circumstances under which punishment may be inflicted. . . .

[The justice distinguished *Robinson* and *Powell*.]

Robinson stands upon a principle which, despite its subtlety, must be simply stated and respectfully applied because it is the foundation of individual liberty and the cornerstone of the relations between a civilized state and its citizens. Criminal penalties may not be inflicted upon a person for being in a condition he is powerless to change. In all probability, Robinson at some time before his conviction elected to take narcotics. But the crime as defined did not punish this conduct. The statute imposed a penalty for the offense of "addiction"—a condition which Robinson could not control. Once Robinson had become an addict, he was utterly powerless to avoid criminal guilt. He was powerless to choose not to violate the law.

In the present case, appellant is charged with a crime composed of two elements—being intoxicated and being found in a public place while in that condition. The crime, so defined, differs from that in *Robinson*. The statute covers more than mere status. But the essential constitutional defect here is the same as in *Robinson*, for in both cases the particular defendant was accused of being in a condition which he had no capacity to change or avoid. . . .

[The opinion states the trial court judge's findings regarding Powell's drinking and continues as follows:] I read these findings to mean that appellant was powerless to avoid drinking: that having taken his first drink, he had "an uncontrollable compulsion to drink" to the point of intoxication; and that once intoxicated, he could not prevent himself from appearing in public places.

Two additional points about the alcoholism defense should be noted. First, intoxication may be grounds for mitigating a sentence. For example, Texas provides that "[e]vidence of temporary insanity caused by intoxication may be introduced by the actor in mitigation of the penalty attached to the offense for which he is being tried."[11] Second, in crimes such as public drunkenness, for which intoxication is an element of the crime, generally the intoxication defense is not recognized unless the defendant can prove involuntary intoxication.

It may be more difficult to use an intoxication defense now that the U.S. Supreme Court has reinstated a Montana statute that prohibited the consideration of evidence of voluntary intoxication when determining whether a defendant possessed the requisite mental state for homicide. In 1996 the Supreme Court decided *State v. Egelhoff*, in which the defendant was convicted of knowingly or purposefully killing two traveling companions after a day of drinking. He was permitted to introduce evidence that his alcohol consumption on the day in question prevented him from engaging in the physical acts required for the killings. The trial court instructed the jury that they could not consider intoxication in their discussion of the mental state required for the crime.[12]

The Montana Supreme Court had held that a defendant has a due process right "to present and have considered by the jury all relevant evidence to rebut the State's evidence on all elements of the offense charged." The U.S. Supreme Court disagreed, reviewed the history of due process in regard to this case, reinstated the statute, and noted that approximately one-half of all homicides are committed by persons under the influence of alcohol. That Court assumed a deterrent effect of the statute, too, as seen in the following excerpt.[13]

STATE v. EGELHOFF
518 U.S. 37 (1996)

Justice Antonin Scalia, joined by Chief Justice William H. Rehnquist and Justices Anthony M. Kennedy and Clarence Thomas, delivered the opinion of the Court. Justice Ruth

Bader Ginsburg concurred in the approval of the statute; Justice Sandra Day O'Connor wrote a dissenting opinion, joined by Justices David H. Souter, Stephen G. Breyer, and John Paul Stevens, with Justices Souter and Breyer also writing dissenting opinions.

Disallowing consideration of voluntary intoxication has the effect of increasing the punishment for all unlawful acts committed in that state, and thereby deters drunkenness or irresponsible behavior while drunk. The rule also serves as a specific deterrent, ensuring that those who prove incapable of controlling violent impulses while voluntarily intoxicated go to prison. And finally, the rule comports with and implements society's moral perception that one who has voluntarily impaired his own faculties should be responsible for the consequences.

There is, in modern times, even more justification for laws such as [the Montana statute in question] than there used to be. Some recent studies suggest that the connection between drunkenness and crime is as much cultural as pharmacological—that is, that drunks are violent not simply because alcohol makes them that way, but because they are behaving in accord with their learned belief that drunks are violent. This not only adds additional support to the traditional view that an intoxicated criminal is not deserving of exoneration, but it suggests that juries—who possess the same learned belief as the intoxicated offender—will be too quick to accept the claim that the defendant was biologically incapable of forming the requisite *mens rea*. Treating the matter as one of excluding misleading evidence therefore makes some sense.

. . . Although the rule allowing a jury to consider evidence of a defendant's voluntary intoxication where relevant to *mens rea* has gained considerable acceptance, it is of too recent vintage, and has not received sufficiently uniform and permanent allegiance to qualify as fundamental, especially since it displaces a lengthy common-law tradition which remains suported by valid justifications today.

Four justices disagreed with the U.S. Supreme Court's decision, with three of them writing dissenting opinions. The opinions reflect the lack of agreement on medical as well as legal issues, and we can expect further developments with regard to the intoxication defense.

DOMESTIC AUTHORITY

The defense of *domestic authority* stems from ancient laws that gave husbands the legal right to discipline their wives with a "whip or rattan no bigger than [a] thumb, in order to enforce the salutary restraints of domestic discipline."[14] The husband's right to administer such discipline is not recognized under modern common or statutory law. The law does, however, recognize the right of parents to discipline their children. Under some circumstances, those acting in the place of parents may do likewise.

Teachers may also discipline their students. Discipline under the domestic authority provision must be reasonable, however, or it will constitute assault and battery or a violation of civil rights. Some states specify by statute that teachers may not use corporal punishment, interpreted by a Nebraska court to mean "the infliction of bodily pain as a penalty for disapproved behavior."[15] That state's statute provides that "Corporal punishment shall be prohibited in public schools."[16] The statute does state, however, that teachers and administrative personnel "may take actions regarding student behavior . . . which are reasonably necessary to aid the student, further school purposes, or prevent interference with the educational process." Examples of permitted behavior include but are not limited to:

- ✪ Counseling with students

- ✪ Conferences with parents

- ✪ Requiring a student to remain after school to do extra work

- ✪ Rearranging student schedules

- ✪ Restricting a student's extracurricular activities

- ✪ Requiring that a student receive psychological or psychiatric counseling and evaluation[17]

Although Nebraska (along with some other states) prohibits corporal punishment of students, the U.S. Supreme Court has ruled that disciplining of schoolchildren may include paddling. According to the Court, the Eighth Amendment's prohibition against cruel and unusual punishment (see Appendix A) applies to criminals, not to school students. The U.S. Supreme Court emphasized, however, that any punishment that goes beyond that which is reasonably necessary to maintain discipline in the classroom may result in civil and criminal culpability.[18]

Domestic authority exists in other situations as well. Persons in charge of trains, theaters, boats, airplanes (see Focus 5.2), and other similar places have the right to use reasonable force to control persons who are disruptive. Prison officials may discipline

FOCUS 5.2 Airline Rage

Airline personnel have a legal right to exercise limited authority over passengers in order to ensure security and order within airports and on airplanes. This is not always easy.

The terms *flight rage* or *air rage* are familiar to many people even though they do not appear in most dictionaries. They refer to persons who become angry and create disruptions during a flight or in airports. The problems frequently occur when a passenger has been denied a request of a flight attendant, such as for a drink, but flight rage may also occur when passengers become upset with other passengers. Airline officials on the aircraft have the legal authority to use reasonable force to restrain the unruly passenger. After the terrorist attacks of 11 September 2001, however, some other passengers also take action.

Although in some venues flight rage incidents have decreased since 9/11, they have increased in others. In fact, some security experts warn us to expect just that. In 2002, security expert H. H. A. Cooper stated that air rage "is no passing fad or fancy. On even the most cursory examination, the potential for disaster is evident. Even a slight acquaintance with the elements of the phenomenon suggests that it is going to become even more of a problem in the not too distant future."[1]

A study by criminal psychologists in Britain found an increase in air rage events (from 80 in 2000–2001 to 696 in 2003–2004 in that country alone) and in the need of its victims for counseling, leading one travel agency in that country to offer insurance policies to cover the costs of counseling for persons who are victimized by air rage. According to this study, many persons who are victims of these incidents need professional counseling and suffer from severe stressors. The researchers concluded that "Air rage is a growing problem that can manifest itself in some bizarre and truly frightening ways."[2]

The American Psychological Association (APA) estimated in 2008 that one-third of Americans suffer from extreme stress, which has increased over the past five years. The APA referred not only to flight or air rage but to computer rage, road rage, and even shopping rage.[3]

It is predicted that flight rage will become more of a problem if the government and airlines permit cell phone use during flights. In fact, some lawmakers introduced a bill in April 2008 to prevent cell phone use during flights in an effort to avoid increased flight rage. As one representative stated, we need to ban such calls before the airlines become accustomed to the money they could make from such calls. We should ban "loud and incessant talking" on airlines because it may enrage other passengers.[4]

Flight rage was in the news in the summer of 2008, when model Naomi Campbell pleaded guilty to assaulting two police officers, swearing repeatedly, and yelling loudly at a British Airways flight captain after she was told that her bag would not be on the flight she was taking from London to Los Angeles. Campbell was sentenced to 200 hours of community service.

In June 2008, numerous business class passengers had to be restrained when a Quantas airlines flight was 24 hours late leaving Sydney, Australia, and the passengers began swearing at the staff in the airline's private lounge.[5]

In 2004, a passenger flying from South Africa to the United Kingdom admitted that he was drunk on the flight and that he disobeyed airline personnel and engaged in abusive and threatening behavior.[6]

In June 2002, a British citizen who lived in Houston, Texas, entered a plea to simple assault resulting from his striking a flight attendant in October 2001. The attendant was trying to calm the passenger. And in August 2003, a 30-year-old woman, at the end of a flight from Newark, New Jersey, to Shannon, Ireland, was arrested for assaulting a member of the Continental Airlines crew on board and of engaging in behavior that could cause serious offense or annoyance to others on the flight. Claribel Delgado entered guilty pleas to both charges.[7]

In March 2005, Australian police reported that a woman on a flight from Bali, who was apparently refused alcohol, struck an airline attendant and spat on passengers. She also allegedly paced

---

inmates, but they may not inflict punishment that violates the Eighth Amendment's prohibition against cruel and unusual punishment. Ship captains, service officers, and others may discipline those who serve under them. In all of these situations the discipline must be reasonable. If unreasonable force is used, the actors may be subject to criminal prosecution if the act constitutes a crime.

Many cases have interpreted what *reasonable* means regarding control and punishment in these and other contexts, particularly punishment inflicted on inmates. Recently there have been numerous cases of alleged child abuse by parents and those acting in the role of parents. The concern here is with whether the inflicted punishment falls within the domestic authority defense when a criminal charge is brought against the person inflicting it. That question cannot be answered unless we can determine what constitutes *reasonable punishment*. We consider the issue in the context of parental punishment of children.

Passengers, realizing they may miss their flights as the result of the longer lines and frustrated by the increased intrusion, may react in anger. As with onflight airline personnel, however, airport security (and other) personnel may use reasonable force to restrain passengers who become disruptive.

Source: Summarized by the author from media sources.

1. H. H. A. Cooper, "Air Rage Is All the Rage," *Journal of Police Crisis Negotiations* 2, no. 2 (2002): 3.
2. "Air-Rage Victims Are Covered," *Sunday Times* (Perth, Australia) (12 December 2004), n.p.
3. "Stress and Mental Health," *The Oklahoman* (25 May 2008), n.p.
4. "Congress Zeros In on In-Flight Cell Calls," *St. Louis Post-Dispatch* (16 April 2008), p. 2.
5. "Delays Spark Air Rage," *Daily Telegraph* (Australia) (4 June 2008), p. 11, Local section.
6. "Man Pleads Guilty to 'Air Rage' on Virgin Atlantic Flight," *Airline Industry Information* (26 February 2004), n.p.
7. "Guilty of Air Rage on Flight from US to Shannon," *Irish Times* (City edition; home news) (26 August 2003), p. 2.
8. "Air Rage on Flight," *The Advertiser* (29 March 2005), p. 9.

the aisles for more than two of the flight's three and a half hours of flying time.[8]

In addition to the problems that may be created by flight rage are those that may occur before passengers board planes. In 2002 several reports of attacks by passengers against airport security guards underscored the increasing frustration with new security rules that had gone into effect and perhaps not been publicized sufficiently.

The Model Penal Code (MPC) stipulates that the force a parent may use on a child is limited to force that "is not designed to cause or known to create a substantial risk of causing death, serious bodily injury, disfigurement, extreme pain or mental distress or gross degradation." In addition, the parental force must be used for the purpose "of safeguarding or promoting the welfare of the minor, including the prevention or punishment of his misconduct."[19] Of course, each of those terms must be interpreted.

How far should the domestic authority defense go to protect parents from criminal culpability in disciplining their children? In an Illinois case, a father was charged with aggravated battery and cruelty to children after he whipped his two sons, ages 12 and 9, with an electrical extension cord. The children had stolen money from their mother's purse. The mother-wife testified that she did not realize the extent of the injuries until she examined the children the next morning. When she found red marks on their backs, she took them to the hospital.

The father appealed his conviction for cruelty to children on the one count that involved the son who did not sustain permanent injuries. The appellate court refused to reverse that conviction, holding that the force used fell within the statutory provisions that prohibited a person from willfully and unnecessarily injuring a child under his legal control.[20]

We turn now to three other defenses that have been used historically: consent, condonation, and victim's conduct.

CONSENT, CONDONATION, AND VICTIM'S CONDUCT

Usually a person's consent to a crime, negligence in bringing about that crime, or forgiveness of that act is not a defense. The issue of consent frequently arises in cases of **euthanasia**, a term applied to the act of killing someone, often at that person's request, because of a terminal illness, considerable pain, or a dibilitating handicap. Often the person killed is a relative—frequently a spouse—who has allegedly begged the actor to end his or her pain and misery with death. The law does not permit this cooperation and agreement to negate the criminal act, just as the law does not permit a patient to agree to malpractice or a sports star to agree to bribery. It is not uncommon in cases of euthanasia, however, that prosecutors refuse to bring charges, grand juries refuse to indict, or juries refuse to convict.

In other cases, consent may negate an element of a crime. For example, by definition, *forcible rape* is sexual intercourse without the victim's consent. If the victim consents, the act is not forcible rape provided the alleged victim is of legal age and capacity to consent. If the alleged victim is under the legal age of consent, sexual intercourse may constitute *statutory rape*, which is also a felony.

Consent may be a defense to less serious acts, such as those that might occur in a lawful sports activity, in which a person might be hurt by the nature of the game. An act that might constitute a criminal assault and battery under other circumstances might not be considered criminal during a sporting event. In any case in which consent is a defense to the crime, the consent must have been given voluntarily (not the product of force, duress, or deception) and knowingly by a legally competent person.

Condonation, or forgiveness of a criminal act by an alleged victim, is not generally a defense to a crime in the United States, although in other countries it may be. For example, a few countries drop forcible rape charges against men whose alleged victims agree to marry them. But in the United States a victim's forgiveness does not eliminate the criminal responsibility of the perpetrator, for crimes are considered offenses against society as well as against individual victims. Under some circumstances, however, victims of less serious crimes are permitted to negotiate a civil settlement with their assailants, after which the court may dismiss the criminal charges.

Finally, a victim's conduct is not normally acceptable as a defense to a crime. Persons who hitchhike, are picked up, and are subsequently murdered may have been foolish in their actions, but those actions do not excuse the person who murdered them.

THE BATTERED PERSON SYNDROME DEFENSE

The **battered person syndrome** is a recently recognized condition used in some jurisdictions as a criminal defense analogous to self-defense, which was discussed in Chapter 4. The difference is that evidence of the battered person syndrome is permitted in some courts as a defense to criminal acts even though the element of imminent danger, required for self-defense, is not present. Indeed, in some cases in which evidence of the defense has been admitted at trial, the assailant, usually a woman, injured or murdered her lover or spouse in a situation in which he was not a threat, as, for example, when he was sleeping.

The *battered person syndrome* arises from a cycle of abuse by a special person, often a parent or a spouse, that leads the battered person to perceive that violence against the offender is the only way to end the abuse. Most commonly the term *battered woman syndrome* is used, but the extension of the concept to others, such as adult males as well as children who murder their parents after years of alleged physical or sexual abuse, has led to the use of the more neutral term *battered person syndrome*, although the term *battered child syndrome* is used in some jurisdictions. In this discussion, *battered person syndrome* is used in referring to all cases in which evidence of long-term battering is introduced in defense of a criminal act, in mitigation of a sentence for a conviction, or as evidence that a

Persons who have suffered abuse for long periods of time may perceive that the only way to protect themselves is to kill their abusers. An increasing number of courts permit expert testimony on the battered person syndrome as a partial, or even a complete, defense in such cases. Prevention of domestic violence is important. This violence victim is wearing an AWARE (Abused Women's Active Response Emergency) alarm necklace that silently signals police if the woman is in danger. (Vivianne Moos/Corbis)

convicted person should receive leniency or **clemency** (mercy, kindness, or leniency when granted by the governor or the U.S. president).

Lenore Walker, a psychologist who testifies about the battered woman syndrome, defined the battered woman as one who is

> repeatedly subjected to any forceful physical or psychological behavior by a man in order to coerce her to do something he wants her to do without concern for her rights. . . . Furthermore . . . the couple must go through the battering cycle at least twice. . . . [If] she remains in the situation, she is defined as a battered woman.[21]

It is the *perceived* threat of imminent danger that is a crucial element in the battered person syndrome defense, and it is this element that requires expert testimony to assist the jury in understanding why the abused person remains in the relationship. Although not all courts faced with the issue have permitted expert witnesses to testify about the battered person syndrome, an increasing number are doing so. The evidence was first held admissible in 1979.[22]

The excerpt that follows from *State v. Koss*, decided by the Ohio Supreme Court in 1990, may represent a modern trend toward acceptance of expert testimony on the battered person syndrome and possibly even an expansion of the self-defense argument. Note that the case overrules a 1981 decision concerning some of these issues.

In *State v. Koss*, the defendant, who had allegedly been abused physically by her husband on many occasions, testified that on the day her husband was killed she went to their bedroom where he was sleeping. As she undressed, he "hauled off and hit her." The next thing she remembered was "a noise or something." She grabbed a holster she saw on the floor, left the house, picked up her son at her daughter's house, and drove to her mother's home in another city. When asked if she shot her husband while he slept, she replied, "No." A patrol officer responding to a "man shot" call discovered the deceased in the couple's bedroom, dressed in his Coast Guard uniform, with his head lying over one edge of the bed and his feet lying over the other edge. The cause of death was one gunshot wound to his head.[23]

STATE v. KOSS

551 N.E. 2d 970 (Ohio 1990)

 We shall first address whether the trial court erred in refusing to admit evidence of the battered woman syndrome. The trial court excluded the testimony based on the earlier decision of this court in *State v. Thomas*. . . .

In *Thomas*, we stated that "such expert testimony is inadmissible because it is not distinctly related to some science, profession or occupation so as to be beyond the ken of the average lay person. Furthermore, no general acceptance of the expert's particular methodology has been established." However, since 1981, several books and articles have been written on this subject. In jurisdictions which have been confronted with this issue, most have allowed expert testimony on the battered woman syndrome. . . .

Expert testimony regarding the battered woman syndrome can be admitted to help the jury not only to understand the battered woman syndrome but also to determine whether the defendant had reasonable grounds for an honest belief that she was in imminent danger when considering the issue of self-defense.

Expert testimony on the battered woman syndrome would help dispel the ordinary lay person's perception that a woman in a battering relationship is free to leave at any time. The expert evidence would counter any "common sense" conclusions by the jury that if the beatings were really that bad the woman would have left her husband much earlier. Popular misconceptions about battered women would be put to rest, including the beliefs that the women are masochistic and enjoy the beatings and that they intentionally provoke their husbands into fits of rage. . . .

A history of physical abuse alone does not justify the killing of the abuser. Having been physically assaulted by the abuser in the past is pertinent to such cases only as it contributes to the defendant's state of mind at the time the killing occurred; e.g., in that it formed the basis for the woman's perception of being in imminent danger of severe bodily harm or death at the hands of her partner.

We believe that the battered woman syndrome has gained substantial scientific acceptance to warrant admissibility. . . .

Accordingly, we overrule *State v. Thomas* to the extent that it holds that expert testimony concerning the battered woman syndrome may not be admitted to support the affirmative defense of self-defense. Where the evidence establishes that a woman is a battered woman, and when the expert is qualified to testify about the battered woman syndrome, expert testimony concerning the syndrome may be admitted to assist the trier of fact [the judge or jury] in determining whether the defendant acted in self-defense.

The excerpt emphasizes the importance of evidence on the battered person syndrome. Technically, the murders for which the evidence is submitted are not committed in true self-defense, as there is no imminent threat of danger. If there were, self-defense would be a sufficient defense. The evidence of battering helps to establish that the defendant *perceived* that she (or he) was in imminent danger.

The importance of the battered person syndrome as a defense is underscored by the California Evidence Code, which since 1992 has permitted the introduction of evidence regarding this syndrome. California also provides that any person convicted of a homicide prior to 1992, for whom the evidence of a battered person syndrome might have been relevant, may petition for a new trial and submit that evidence. The California Supreme Court underscored the importance of this evidence in a 1996 case in which it stated that evidence of a battered person syndrome is relevant

> to explain a behavior pattern that might otherwise appear unreasonable to the average person. . . . [It] not only explains how a battered woman might think, react, or behave, it places the behavior in an understandable light. . . . [The evidence can] disabuse jurors of commonly held misconceptions.[24]

In 2007, after three previous vetoes, California's governor Arnold Schwarzenegger did not oppose the parole board's recommended release of Flozelle Woodmore, who had served more than half of her life in prison for murdering her husband. Woodmore was, of course, convicted prior to the state's admission of evidence on the battered person syndrome, which, in California, is referred to as *intimate partner battering*.

The Extension of the Defense

The expanding number of jurisdictions that recognize the battered person syndrome defense has led to concerns about the nature of some of the proposed uses. For example, in an Illinois murder case the defendant-wife wanted to use the battered person syndrome in defense of an act she committed *after* she killed her husband. According to the defendant, her husband came home one night with a male prostitute, placed heavy barbells across her legs so that she could not move, and forced her to watch the two men engage in sexual acts. Then each man attacked her sexually. Later her husband attacked her again and tried to drown her by holding her head in the toilet. He also tried to choke her. She pushed him back in self-defense, and he fell to the floor dead. She dismembered his body. The defendant wanted to introduce evidence of the battered woman syndrome to justify the dismemberment. The trial court refused, holding that such evidence is admissible only on the question of why the killing was committed and therefore is not relevant to acts that occurred later.[25]

The prosecution used the dismemberment evidence to prove the defendant's consciousness of guilt. The appellate court held that the defendant was entitled to introduce evidence of the battered woman syndrome to refute that inference. The expert witness would have testified that the battered person syndrome is relevant to conduct *after* as well as *at* the time of the killing.

The battered person syndrome was at issue in a 1992 lower California appellate court case involving a woman who was convicted of killing her live-in boyfriend. The appellate court ruled that the woman had received ineffective assistance of counsel because her attorney did not introduce evidence of the battered woman syndrome.[26]

More recently, in 2007, the Oklahoma Court of Criminal Appeals (the highest court in the criminal system in that state, with the Oklahoma Supreme Court hearing only appeals in civil cases) ruled that the failure to offer evidence of the battered woman syndrome in the case of Pearl Smith,—who murdered her husband, was convicted of second-degree murder, and sentenced to 28 years in prison,—was evidence of ineffective assistance of counsel. Thus, Smith was entitled to a new trial. At that trial, she was convicted of a lesser offense of first-degree manslaughter and sentenced to four years in prison.[27]

The battered person syndrome has been extended to situations other than the abuse or killing of the abuser. An unusual case in that regard is the focus of the Case Analysis at the end of this chapter.

Evidence of the battered person syndrome is also permitted at the sentencing phase to show mitigation. In one case, for example, the judge sentenced a woman to probation after her conviction for shooting and killing her husband. The defendant pleaded guilty to first-degree manslaughter after testifying that her husband had abused her for 25 years. In assessing the light penalty, which included a $2,000 fine and a $500 payment to the state victims' compensation fund, the judge responded to requests for leniency from the defendant's children and her late husband's sisters, stating, "Unusual facts often bring unusual sentences."[28]

A California judge imposed probation on a woman who shot and killed her husband while he slept. The judge said he was not sending a message to anyone but that he could not "in good conscience send her to jail." The defendant testified that her husband had abused her physically for 25 years.[29]

Children as Battered Persons Who Murder

Increasing attention has been given in recent years to children who murder their parents after years of alleged abuse. In some jurisdictions evidence of the battered person syndrome has been permitted in such cases, as this discussion explains.

In 1993, in what was said to be the first recognition of the battered child defense, a Washington appellate court reversed the second-degree murder conviction of a youth who shot his stepfather, whom he claimed had abused him for years. The court ruled that the trial court erred in refusing to admit evidence of the battered child syndrome, holding that sufficient evidence exists to extend the battered woman syndrome to "analogous situations affecting children." According to the court, the battered child fears reprisal of the battering parent, feels helpless, has low self-esteem, thinks it is futile to resist, and believes in the omnipotence of the parent. The court noted, however, that evidence of battering alone was not sufficient; there also has to exist a "perceived imminence of danger, based on the appearance of some threatening behavior."[30]

On appeal, the Washington Supreme Court held that evidence of the battered child syndrome is admissible

> to help prove self-defense whenever such a defense is relevant. The underlying principles of the battered child syndrome are generally accepted in the scientific community and satisfy the [evidence] requirements by helping the trier of fact to understand a little-known psychological problem.[31]

The court went further, however, and ruled that evidence of the battered child syndrome alone is not sufficient to ensure that the defendant had the reasonable belief that he or she was in imminent danger, an element of self-defense. The court remanded the case to the trial court to reconsider the impact of evidence of the battered child syndrome on its decision to deny a self-defense instruction.[32]

The Ohio Supreme Court ruled in 1988 that a child who killed his drunken mother after several years of alleged abuse should have been permitted to introduce evidence of the battered person syndrome to support his claim of self-defense and his request for a jury instruction on the lesser included offense of voluntary manslaughter. The appellant had been convicted of murder after the trial court judge refused to admit the evidence to support the requested jury instruction.[33]

Focus 5.3 states the facts of two recent cases in which attempts have been made to introduce the battered child syndrome defense.

It is important to understand that when expert testimony on the battered person, or any other syndrome or type of evidence, is involved, there are two key issues. The first is whether the expert testimony should be admitted; the second is whether the evidence supports the issue for which it is proposed.

OTHER STRESS DISORDERS

A number of other disorders associated with stress are recognized by some courts as a partial or complete defense to criminal acts.

Extreme Emotional Disturbance

Oregon provides that extreme emotional disturbance may constitute a partial defense to intentional murder but not to aggravated felony murder or other crimes. The Oregon statute provides as follows:

> It is an affirmative defense to murder . . . that the homicide was committed under the influence of extreme emotional disturbance when such disturbance is not the result of the person's own intentional, knowing, reckless or criminally negligent act, and if there is a reasonable explanation for the disturbance. The reasonableness of the explanation for the disturbance must be determined from the standpoint of an ordinary person in the actor's situation under the circumstances that the actor rea-

---

FOCUS 5.3   Abused Children Who Kill Their Parents

Should children be justified in killing parents who abuse them? If so, under what circumstances? If not, why not? A number of cases have occurred in recent years. In many of these cases self-defense is not an appropriate defense, and therefore efforts have been made to introduce the battered child syndrome as a defense.

The discussion begins with *State v. MacLennan*, which was decided by the Minnesota Supreme Court in 2005. This case involved Jason MacLennan, who, at the age of 17, shot his self-made-multimillionaire father six times after his father yelled at him. Jason's attorney, Andrew Pearson, petitioned the Minnesota trial court to permit him to introduce expert testimony on the battered child syndrome to support his client's self-defense argument. The judge refused, and that refusal was the only issue on appeal.

In pretrial motions, Pearson argued that the jury needed evidence from an expert witness to explain why a child, abused by his father for years, would perceive that he had no option but to kill his father. And, as the state had recognized the battered woman syndrome (since 1989, accepted by the state supreme court), it should also permit expert testimony concerning the battered child syndrome. The trial judge refused and Jason was convicted of first-degree murder and sentenced to life in prison. On appeal, the state's supreme court held that although the in-

correct standard was used for determining the admission of the disputed evidence at trial, the trial court did not err in its decision to exclude the specific offered testimony. After hearing that evidence, the trial judge determined correctly that the defense had not met its burden of showing that the evidence was generally accepted in the psychiatric and psychological communities *and* that the defendant had suffered severe emotional abuse.[1]

In 2001, an Illinois appellate court reversed the first-degree murder conviction of a young man who killed his father, Anthony Shanahan, with a pipe. The son admitted the killing, but his request to present expert testimony on the battered child syndrome in order to support the requisite mental state for self-defense was denied by the trial court. The defendant was permitted to introduce evidence of abuse by his father, along with a written report by the expert, but the expert was not permitted to testify. The appellate court, in reversing the conviction, held that the trial judge abused his discretion when he refused to grant the defendant's motion for a continuance to provide time to bring in an expert to testify.[2]

1. *State v. MacLennan*, 702 N.W.2d 219 (Minn. 2005).
2. *People v. Brendan Shanahan*, 753 N.E.2d 1028 (1st Dist. Ill. 2001).

sonably believed them to be. Extreme emotional disturbance does not constitute a defense to . . . any other crime.[34]

Posttraumatic Stress Disorder (PTSD)

A variety of relatively recently developed defenses may fall under the category of **posttraumatic stress disorder (PTSD)**. PTSD is a disorder in which stress is experienced by people who have suffered severe trauma, such as during war or rape. Symptoms include nightmares, feelings of guilt, disorientation, and reliving the traumatic event(s). It is argued that victims of this disorder should not be held accountable for their criminal acts because they cannot control their behavior.

PTSD can cause other anxiety disorders, depression, substance abuse, poor physical health, or psychosocial impairment. During World War I, the syndrome was called *shell shock*. Other terms have been used, such as *operational fatigue*, *combat fatigue*, and *war neurosis*. Whatever the term, the earlier reaction to the syndrome (particularly by officers in the military) was that those who manifested it were cowardly; treatment was not provided. By 1952, however, the American Psychiatric Association recognized the need to provide diagnosis and treatment for war-related stress.[35]

Approximately 10 million Americans will develop PTSD at some point in their lives. Among women the most frequent cause is rape or other sexual trauma. Among military women the most frequent cause is war.[36]

Several stress syndromes are included in this discussion.

The Combat Stress Syndrome

The war in Iraq raised the problems of reactions to combat. The recentness of this war, however, limits the number of cases in which attempts have been made to raise the issue of posttraumatic stress disorder resulting from combat as a defense in criminal cases. A few cases have occurred.

In January 2005, a soldier pleaded guilty to drug charges and to being absent without leave (AWOL) from Fort Carson, Colorado, when he left the base in the summer of 2004. Pvt. Andrew Martinez, 25, said that he started using illegal drugs when he could not get the "grisly battlefield images from Iraq" out of his mind. He checked into a Veterans Affairs (VA) hospital, where he was diagnosed with posttraumatic stress disorder. Martinez was sentenced to the time he had already served in jail (116 days), ordered to forfeit his pay, and given a bad conduct discharge, which elimi-

Many men and women who have returned from the war in Iraq or Afghanistan have been diagnosed with some form of posttraumatic stress disorder. It is too early to know whether the combat stress syndrome defense will be successful in those cases in which these veterans are charged with crimes. (Scott Olson/Getty IMages)

nated his eligibility for VA benefits. Despite the fact that this defendant did not succeed with his attempts at a PTSD offense (there was testimony to rebut his statements supporting the defense), his attorney insisted that we must do a better job with soldiers who return from combat and that the criminal law may not be the best way to process their crimes. The executive director of the Gulf War Resource Center emphasized that combat may not excuse subsequent criminal behavior, but we need to understand that if we do not provide treatment for soldiers who suffer PTSD, we can expect problems.[37]

During the past two years, however, more reports have surfaced about increased stress within the military. The Army's installation at Fort Hood, Texas, one of the largest in the world, is experiencing more signs of war stress, including more requests for marriage counseling for spouses, especially when their loved ones volunteer for additional tours of combat duty. An Army survey revealed that soldiers are 50 percent more likely to report posttraumatic stress if they serve more than one tour of duty. The Army also reported in 2008 that in recent years soldiers have exhibited a 30 percent increase in binge drinking, a doubling of the use of illegal drugs, and close to a doubling of suicides in Iraq and Kuwait. Equipment shortages for training at Fort Hood, along with housing issues and redeployments, create additional stress.[38]

The most frequent use of the PTSD defense in a criminal case involving defendants who experience combat has been by those who fought in Vietnam. In that war, compared to previous ones, stress problems were magnified by new types of warfare that killed or maimed quickly, but advances in medical technology saved many who would have died in previous wars. Multiple amputees, paraplegics, and soldiers with other problems returned home. One result was a greater understanding of stress syndromes during and after the Vietnam War, and treatment became available. Some examples of PTSD involving Vietnam War veterans and criminal acts are discussed in Focus 5.4, along with comments concerning the mental health issues of today's soldiers.

For some Vietnam veterans, problems arose when they returned home and confronted protestors who argued that the war was immoral. Some veterans suffered problems that were diagnosed as caused by the Vietnam War stress syndrome. Marital problems, poor job performance, and general adjustment problems were typical reactions to the stress resulting from the war. Many veterans suffered sudden feelings of being in combat, sleep disturbances, survival guilt, catastrophic dreams, intrusive memories, anger, isolation, and alienation.

In 1980 the American Psychiatric Association defined these reactions as PTSD, caused by trauma that "is generally outside the range of . . . common experiences" and "that would evoke significant symptoms of distress in most people." Such traumas include combat, some natural disasters, bombing, torture, and death camps but exclude simple bereavement, marital conflicts, or business losses.[39]

Some courts have admitted expert testimony on PTSD. In many cases this evidence is used to show that the defendant was in a dissociative state. For example, one defendant claimed that he believed he was in North Vietnam when he shot a police officer. Another, who escaped from prison, testified that he thought he was in Vietnam and that he was running back home.[40]

In another case, the Kansas Supreme Court upheld the convictions of a defendant who was unable to show that he was in a dissociative state caused by PTSD at the time he committed the crimes of kidnapping, aggravated assault, aggravated burglary, and criminal damage to property, but portions of the case are reprinted here to show the court's review of PTSD and its importance. In *State v. DeMoss*, the defendant's use of expert testimony on PTSD was weakened by testimony that voluntary intoxication, not PTSD, caused him to engage in the criminal acts in question. But the use of the PTSD syndrome as a defense is growing, and there is reason to believe that as medical researchers discover more evidence of the impact of PTSD and attorneys gain greater understanding of the syndrome, expert testimony on PTSD will become even more important in the criminal courtroom.[41]

STATE v. DeMOSS

770 P.2d 441, 442 (Kan. 1989)

[A] brief discussion of the nature of P.T.S.D is required. The American Psychiatric Association classifies P.T.S.D. as an anxiety disorder. This disorder is one which may be suffered following a traumatic event which is outside the normal realm of human experiences. These events, known as "stressors," include both natural disasters and deliberate man-made disasters such as military combat, rape, assault, torture, bombing, and death camps. Stressors of

FOCUS 5.4 The War Stress Syndrome as a Legal Issue

The stress of combat has been recognized for years, but it was the Vietnam War that gave impetus to a renewed recognition of the impact war stresses can have on young people. The average age of those who served in Vietnam was only 19, younger than in previous wars, "and while combat in other wars was often intense but relatively brief, in Vietnam the threat of attack or ambush was nearly constant for many soldiers." The strong antiwar feelings of many U.S. citizens made the impact of the war stresses even more significant.[1]

In January 2002, a Vietnam veteran who was unsuccessful in his use of his posttraumatic experiences to support an insanity defense was executed in Missouri. James Johnson murdered three law enforcement officers and the wife of a sheriff on 8 December 1991. When the case was heard before the Missouri Supreme Court, Justice Ronnie White recommended a new trial on the grounds that Johnson's attorneys were incompetent in their presentation of the insanity plea. His colleagues did not agree and the conviction stood.[2]

In 1988, the first person in Louisiana to use his Vietnam service as a basis for a criminal insanity plea was electrocuted for murdering a police officer who was taking him to jail for drunkenness.[3]

In Florida in 1993, considerable sympathy was expressed for a Vietnam veteran condemned to die for killing a gas station attendant 14 years previously. Governor Lawton Chiles blocked the execution of Larry Joe Johnson in early 1993, but after a study of the case, a new execution date was set. The Florida Supreme Court turned down Johnson's appeal, with three justices agreeing reluctantly on the basis of procedures in effect at the time of the original sentencing. Justice Gerald Kogan, writing for those three justices, said, "When this death warrant is executed, Florida will electrocute a man injured and most probably maimed psychologically while serving in his nation's military in Vietnam and elsewhere." The U.S. Supreme Court refused to review the case, and Johnson was executed.[4]

In 1992, five Florida prisons became centers for treating posttraumatic stress disorder among veterans, along with assisting Vietnam veterans with military benefits and issues related to Agent Orange, a defoliant used during the war. It was estimated

that between 3,200 and 3,500 Vietnam veterans were incarcerated in Florida prisons.[5] But in 1994 the Florida Supreme Court upheld a trial court's refusal to admit evidence on the Vietnam War stress syndrome, noting that it is not a commonly understood condition. The U.S. Supreme Court refused to review the case. The defendant in *Reaves v. State* was convicted of first-degree murder and sentenced to death.[6]

As the text notes, posttraumatic stress disorders (PTSD) are also characteristic of today's soldiers. In 2008, the Pentagon reported that 40,000 veterans who served in Iraq or Afghanistan in recent years had been diagnosed with PTSD. That figure, which includes only the *reported* cases, was estimated by a Rand Corporation study to be as high as 300,000.[7]

Studies also show that within recent years, between 12 and 15 percent of soldiers deployed to Iraq and Afghanistan are medicated for stress, including drugs to regulate depression and anxiety. Some of these men and women are redeployed after being treated for PTSD.[8]

1. "Sheriff Will Witness Execution of Man Who Killed His Wife," *St. Louis Post-Dispatch* (7 January 2002), p. 1A; "Missouri Executes Convicted Murderer," *Agence France Presse* (9 January 2002), n.p.
2. "Sympathy for Killer Claiming Post-Vietnam Stress," *New York Times* (14 February 1993), p. 16.
3. "Five Die in Chicago Shootings," *Tallahassee Democrat* (23 September 1988), p. 1.
4. "Court: Justice Not Served by Execution," *Miami Herald* (30 April 1993), p. 5B. See *Johnson v. Singletary*, 618 So.2d 731 (Fla. 1993), *cert. denied*, 466 U.S. 963 (1993).
5. "Man Guilty of Killing Mom: Vietnam-Era Veteran Said He Suffered from Stress Disorder," *Sun-Sentinel* (Fort Lauderdale) (1 May 1996), p. 3B.
6. *Reaves v. State*, 639 So.2d 1 (Fla. 1994), *cert. denied*, 513 U.S. 990 (1994).
7. "Army's Battle: Mental Illness; Military Tries to Balance Caring for True PTSD Patients, Keeping an Eye out for Malingering Soldiers," *Chicago Tribune* (23 June 2008), p. 9C.
8. "Suicides in Army Increase by 13 Percent," *Baltimore Sun* (30 May 2008), p. 1A.

human origin, such as war and military combat, produce more severe and longer lasting disorders than do natural disasters.

Perhaps the best known symptom of P.T.S.D. is the reexperiencing of the traumatic event, which can occur either through recollections of the event, recurrent dreams of the event, or a sudden acting out or feeling that the traumatic

event is actually occurring at the moment. This last possibility is known as a "dissociative state" and is the rarest symptom of P.T.S.D., occurring only in extreme cases. Dreams and recollections are far more common.

Additional symptoms include numbing of responsiveness to, or involvement in, the outside world; hyperalertness or exaggerated startle response; sleep disturbances;

guilt about the person's own survival or about the tactics which the person used in order to survive; memory impairment and difficulty concentrating; and avoidance of activities which may cause the person to recall the stressful event. Any and all symptoms may also be intensified by exposure to events which resemble the stressor. This becomes particularly important in terms of the dissociative state and criminal behavior. Other problems associated with P.T.S.D. which become significant when viewed in the context of criminal behavior are the person's tendency toward increased irritability, impulsive behavior, and unpredictable explosions of aggression with little or no provocation.

On a positive note, in May 2008, the philanthropic and educational arms of the American Psychiatric Association (APA) outlined a major expansion of efforts to offer mental health services to military persons returning from Iraq and Afghanistan. According to the announcement,

> [e]fforts will be made to create a large, national, volunteer network over the next three years to address postwar mental health issues such as post-traumatic stress disorder (PTSD), traumatic brain injury (TBI), drug abuse, anxiety and depression. . . . [The goal is to recruit] 10 percent of the 400,000 mental health professionals in the United States by 2015 to assist in this effort.[42]

Rape Trauma Syndrome (RTS)

Another stress disorder that is being increasingly introduced in courtrooms is the **rape trauma syndrome (RTS)**, which is a type of PTSD that follows forced sex. The term was coined by Ann Wolbert Burgess and Lynda Lytle Holmstrom in their study of women who claimed to be rape victims,[43] and it is now considered a posttraumatic stress disorder.

In general, evidence of RTS will not be admitted to support the factual issues of whether a rape occurred. But it may be allowed to support (or reject) related issues, such as the credibility of the alleged victim, the reason for delaying reporting the incident to the police, the significance of a lack of a struggle, and the behavior of the alleged victim after the incident. Judges vary in their reasons for admitting or excluding RTS evidence.

The importance of RTS evidence was emphasized in the following excerpt from a 2003 New York case. The case involved a 21-year-old woman with an IQ of 70 who shot and killed her alleged rapist, whom she had known for years as a friend. There was evidence that the defendant and the alleged victim had engaged in consensual sex on previous occasions. The complainant testified that when she saw the defendant a few days after the alleged rape and confronted him about it, he laughed at her and suggested that he could do it again, whereupon she shot and killed him. She was tried for murder. The prosecution's motion to exclude testimony of the RTS was denied, and the defense presented such evidence. Two weeks into the trial the judge ruled that RTS evidence would not be permitted. That decision was made after evidence was presented that the defendant lied to the state's psychiatrist who examined her. The defendant was convicted of second-degree murder and sentenced to 25 years to life in prison. She appealed and her conviction was reversed on the grounds that she could not have had an adequate defense with the change in evidence during the trial, that RTS evidence was admissible, and that the sentence was excessive. Following are excerpts from that case, *Pulinario v. Goord*, which was affirmed on appeal after the appellant's conviction and the exclusion of evidence had been confirmed by a state appellate court.[44] Petitioner then filed a **writ** (an order from the court) of *habeas corpus* (a petition asking a court to take—or order—specified action; often filed by inmates questioning the legality of their confinement). The court granted the writ.[45]

PULINARIO v. GOORD

291 F.Supp. 2d 154 (E.D.N.Y. 2003), aff'd,
2004 U.S. App. LEXIS 26803 (2nd Cir. 2004)

Imagio Santana was, the evidence could be construed as showing, a drug dealer who had pulled a knife. Without Dr. Ledray's testimony to rebut its arguments, the prosecution was permitted to thoroughly exploit the jurors' misconceptions about the conduct of rape victims and argue, among other things, that petitioner's seemingly calm demeanor after the rape and her untruths to the psychiatrists—which appear to be not typical of rape victims—were evidence that she had not been raped.

At trial, petitioner testified that during her childhood and teenage years, she was the frequent victim of sexual and physical abuse. Between the ages of seven and eleven years old, she was sexually abused by three older cousins and she was later physically abused by multiple boyfriends. . . .

Post-traumatic stress disorder is a psychological reaction to an extreme traumatic event such as rape. Those suffering from PTSD are said to typically exhibit symptoms such as the re-experiencing of the trauma through memories, nightmares and flashbacks, feelings of numbness or detachment, and insomnia, irritability, impaired concentration, and hypervigilance. The Diagnostic and Statistical Manual of Mental Disorders notes that "the disorder may be especially severe or long lasting when the stressor is of human design (e.g. torture, rape)." Courts in New York have recognized . . . that rape is a stressor that may cause PTSD. PTSD is an accepted ground for asserting a defense of extreme emotional disturbance under [N.Y. statute] and a "mental disease or defect" defense under [another N.Y. statute] the latter of which, if accepted by a jury, constitutes a complete defense to a crime.

"Rape trauma syndrome" is a mental health term that describes the typical behavioral responses of rape victims. In the long term, victims suffer through nightmares and phobias. . . . Although experiencing common physical and emotional reactions to rape, [research has found that] victims overtly respond to rape in different ways. Some victims exhibit an "expressed style" response, which is characterized by emotional behavior, such as crying, sobbing and feelings of anxiety. Other victims exhibit a "controlled style" response, where none of these symptoms are manifested, and the victim appears calm and rational, which might lead an uniformed observer to conclude that no rape has occurred.

Rape is an under-reported crime. . . . Studies have shown that rape victims do not report rape, or delay in reporting, because of fear of mistreatment by police and hospital personnel, lack of support by family and friends, fear of rapist retaliation, and feelings of guilt. . . . A rape victim's fear that her accusations will be greeted with skepticism is particularly acute where she knew the attacker or had a prior consensual sexual relationship. Studies have shown that a rape victim who has a prior sexual relationship with her attacker is less likely to be believed by others and she may be blamed for having brought the rape upon herself. Studies have shown that one of the most popular misconceptions about rape is that the victim by behaving in a certain way brought it on herself. For that reason, studies have demonstrated that jurors will under certain circumstances blame the victim for the attack and will refuse to convict the man accused. Studies have also shown that jurors will infer consent where the victim has engaged in certain types of behavior prior to the incident.

Many rape victims, in light of these popular misconceptions, delay in reporting a rape or falsely deny a prior relationship with their attacker. . . .

Had Dr. Ledray [the defense expert on RTS] been allowed to testify at trial concerning petitioner's mental condition at the time of the shooting, arguably she would have testified that it is not uncommon for rape victims to tell untruths and withhold information because they feel that "others will judge them and not believe they were raped. . . . If they were doing something illegal, or something they believe may be used against them, they will often leave these details out to prevent additional blame and shame."

Because rape victims often act in such counter-intuitive ways, and because jurors may misconceive such behavior as evidence that the victim was not raped, the New York Court of Appeals held that expert testimony concerning RTS is admissible to explain the conduct of rape victims. In [that case] the complainant did not immediately report the rape to law enforcement and lied to the police about her relationship to her attacker on two separate occasions by denying a prior association with her assailant although the complainant had actually known defendant for years and had seen him the night before the attack. The court admitted expert testimony concerning RTS because it would help the jury understand that "a rape victim who knows her assailant is more fearful of disclosing his name to the police and is in fact less likely to report the rape at all." Courts have admitted RTS testimony to explain the conduct of rape victims both in cases where the rape victim is the complainant, as well as in cases where the victim is the defendant who is accused of a crime against her attacker. . . .

The essence of petitioner's defense at trial was that on the night she shot Imagio Santana, her childhood friend, she was attempting to seek from him an explanation as to why he had raped her several days before. During their conversation, the jury could have found that Imagio reacted violently and threatened to rape her again. When Imagio ignored petitioner's warnings to stay away from her, she shot him. The prosecution presented no direct evidence contradicting any of petitioner's testimony. Her testimony was corroborated by the discovery of a folding knife, with the blade in the open position, ready for use, near Imagio's body. There were drugs in one of Imagio's hands when the police found him and an autopsy revealed that Imagio had used drugs shortly before his death. There was also testimony at trial indicating that Imagio had previously raped a fourteen year old girl. Given this evidence corroborating petitioner's account of the shooting, her lack of any history of violent conduct, her close relationship to the Santana family, and Imagio's checkered past and prior violent conduct towards petitioner and others, the defense, on these historical facts, presented a significant issue as to whether petitioner was guilty of intentional murder. . . .

In light of petitioner's impaired mental condition on the night of the shooting, she sought to present to the jury the defenses of mental disease or defect, extreme emotional disturbance, and justification. Each of these defenses relied on proof that petitioner was suffering from PTSD at the time of the shooting, to which Dr. Ledray was prepared to testify. When Dr. Ledray's testimony concerning PTSD was entirely precluded, all three of petitioner's defenses were fatally undermined.

"Courts . . . must consider the facts of the individual case in evaluating the Government's interest [and procedures] in prosecution" when it is dealing with a person claiming mental illness. Here the state courts severely inhibited a defense by unconstitutionally preventing the jury from learning that a person in petitioner's position might lie because the rape itself causes her to lie.

The petition for a writ of habeas corpus is granted. Petitioner is to be released unless state criminal proceedings are commenced against petitioner within sixty days. This judgment is stayed until appeals are completed.

In other jurisdictions, the Kansas Supreme Court held that when a defendant claims the alleged victim consented to the sexual act, expert testimony on the RTS may be admitted to support the contention that consent was not given.[46]

The Indiana Supreme Court held that if evidence of the RTS is admitted by the prosecution, the defense may also introduce RTS evidence. In *Henson v. State,* the trial judge refused the defense's request to introduce evidence of RTS after the defendant had presented testimony that the night after the alleged rape the complainant was seen dancing and drinking at the same bar in which the defendant had first met her. The defense wanted to introduce the evidence to show that the behavior of the complainant was inconsistent with that of one who had been raped the night before. The appellate court agreed that the evidence was relevant to that point and ruled that it should have been admitted. The court noted that in other cases it had permitted the use of evidence on the RTS to be introduced by the prosecution and concluded that it would be unfair not to permit the defense to do likewise.[47]

Rape victims may not have consistent recountings of the events, and evidence of the RTS may be introduced to explain this to the jury. As one federal court noted, the reactions of a rape victim before, during, and after the crime "include not immediately reporting the rape or telling anyone of the assault and the inability to form clear and vivid memories of the event."[48]

Another point about RTS is important. Although the syndrome is normally associated with women, there is evidence that men who are raped may also suffer from the RTS. One corrections journal reported a study in which prison rapes of male inmates revealed such symptoms as "nightmares, deep depression, shame, loss of self-esteem, self-hatred and considering or attempting suicide."[49]

Postpartum Depression (PPD) Syndrome

A final PTSD defense involves evidence of **postpartum depression (PPD) syndrome**. *Postpartum depression* is a disorder that some women experience after giving birth. Mothers who kill their children may use a variety of reasons in their defenses, but those who kill shortly after their babies are born may have a case for using the PPD syndrome defense.

The problem of PPD gained worldwide recognition in the aftermath of the *Yates* case discussed in Chapter 4. Evidence introduced in those trials disclosed that Andrea Yates had suffered from PPD and had been under the care of a psychiatrist.

The American Psychiatric Association reports that approximately three-fourths of all women suffer "baby blues" after giving birth, but most women recover in a few days. Between 10 and 20 percent of women experience depression for a longer period after giving birth. Only approximately 1 or 2 of every 1,000 new mothers experience PPD to the extent suffered by Yates, but an assistant professor of obstetrics and psychiatry at Duke University refers to PPD as "the most under-recognized, under-diagnosed, and under-treated obstetrical complication in America."[50]

At a meeting of the Royal Australian and New Zealand College of Psychiatrists, experts noted that approximately 41 percent of depressed mothers have thoughts of harming their small children; between 8 and 22 percent of new mothers experience postnatal depression. The medications for treatment for this mental illness are quite good; however, the problem lies in the failure to diagnose the mental condition and recommend treatment in time.[51]

After their babies are born, some women suffer postpartum depression (PPD) syndrome, but most recover quickly. If the problem persists and the mother engages in criminal behavior, she may be entitled to have an expert present evidence of PPD at her trial. (IStockPhoto)

The *Yates* and other recent cases have renewed interest in PPD, and it may be expected that the associated legal defense will be used more frequently in the future as we gain a greater understanding of this traumatic time in the lives of some new mothers.

MISCELLANEOUS DEFENSES

In addition to those already discussed in this and the previous chapter, numerous other defenses are recognized in various jurisdictions. Some of these defenses have been raised in U.S. courts and rejected, although they have been successful in other countries. Others are being used today more frequently or more successfully than before. A few are mentioned in this section.

Premenstrual syndrome (PMS) (which refers to the physiological changes that occur in a woman before menstruation) has been used successfully in a few other countries but has had very limited success in the United States. Over 150 symptoms of PMS have been identified, but most are not thought to be associated with criminal behavior. The most prevalent PMS symptoms that might be associated with criminal behavior are depression, irritability, and temporary psychosis. In severe cases, medical treatment is required and consists mainly of hormone therapy.

According to drug manufacturer Eli Lilly, about 3 to 5 percent of menstruating women in the United States are affected by PMS. "The symptoms include severe mood swings, irritability, depression, decreased interest in usual activities and difficulties in concentration, as well as sleeping problems and physical symptoms such as breast tenderness and bloating."[52]

Some physicians believe that PMS is related to behavior; one who concluded that PMS should be a recognized legal defense stated:

> It is unfortunate that many PMS sufferers may have been imprisoned because the law does not recognize PMS as a valid defense. This injustice must be corrected. Premenstrual syndrome is real. Its effects on many women can be catastrophic and must be taken into account by the criminal justice system. It is grossly improper to make moral judgments about a condition which may have such devastating effects on individuals and society.[53]

Another defense is that of *public duty*. If public officers are executing a court order, performing public duties required for their offices, or engaging in certain military duties, they may be justified in taking certain actions that would not otherwise be permitted. In general, statutes specify the situations in which the law may be violated by public officials or military officers. The defense issue arises when it is not clear that the action taken falls within the *public duty defense* exception.

A defense that is recognized but has not been very successful in recent years is that of *superior orders*. Employees, especially in the military, argue that they should not be responsible for otherwise criminal acts if they were following the orders of their superior officers when they engaged in those acts. One of the most famous and unsuccessful tests of this defense occurred after the Vietnam War when Lieutenant William Calley was convicted of murder for the execution of unresisting Vietnamese at My Lai. It was estimated that Calley and others killed up to 250 or more My Lai villagers. Calley was the only person tried for those murders.

Calley defended that he was following orders and thus should be acquitted of murder charges because "an obedient subordinate should be acquitted so long as he did not personally know of the order's illegality." The military court did not agree, and Calley was convicted. Calley was sentenced to life at hard labor, which was reduced. After he had served only four and a half months in prison, Calley was pardoned by President Richard M. Nixon.[54]

A defense that is gaining in use, although not necessarily in success, is the *rough sex defense*. In previous times, "She asked for it" was a common defense to rape, and in many cases it was successful. In most rape cases today this is not an issue because statutes in most jurisdictions make it difficult or impossible to introduce evidence of the alleged victim's prior sexual experience in an effort to justify the she-asked-for-it defense. However, a new defense has evolved—the rough sex defense. According to Alan M. Dershowitz, noted Harvard University law professor and appellate attorney, "The she-asked-for-it defense doesn't exist anymore. . . . So now we're hearing she demanded it."[55]

The rough sex defense, used primarily in murder or attempted murder cases, is based on the use of rough physical action during sex. It is assumed that such actions heighten sexual pleasure. In his murder trial for the 1986 death of Kathleen Holland, for example, Joseph Porto testified that Holland asked him to tie a rope around her neck and pull. He became very excited, pulled too hard, and she died. The prosecutor called it the "oops" defense, but the jury may have been impressed. The defendant was convicted of criminally negligent homicide, a lesser charge, punishable by no more than four years in prison. In January 1991, after serving two and a half years, Porto, age 22, was released from prison.[56]

Another type of defense to criminal activities is that of *religious beliefs*. This defense arises most frequently in cases in which parents, presumably for religious reasons, refuse to obtain necessary medical care for their children, who die as a result. The defense of religious beliefs was used by William and Christine Hermanson, Christian Scientists, who were convicted of third-degree murder and felony child abuse when their seven-year-old daughter died after they refused to obtain medical care for her. The religious belief defense

was not successful in this case, but the case was "the first case in the United States in 22 years in which Christian Scientists have been held criminally responsible for the death of a child after relying solely on prayer to cure an illness." The Hermansons were sentenced to 15 years' probation and ordered to secure medical care when needed for their other two children. On appeal, the case was reversed by the Florida Supreme Court.[57]

These and other defenses may be expected to gain even more attention in the future as we continue to explore human behavior and its causes—or, as some would argue, we become less willing to assume responsibility for acts we engage in voluntarily.

SUMMARY

This chapter continued Chapter 4's discussion of defenses to criminal acts. Chapter 4 included the more traditional defenses. This chapter focused on some traditional ones, such as intoxication, that may gain greater acceptance with increased understanding of the human body or lesser acceptance as a result of the get-tough theme in criminal justice systems today. The chapter also included some new defenses that are gaining in acceptance, along with some that have not yet been successful but may be in future cases.

Recent scientific studies question the belief that substance abuse, at least in the case of alcohol, is solely a moral problem. Rather, it may be the result of genetics; if that is true and if individuals cannot control the abuse, the intoxication defense must take on a greater role in criminal law. It would mean that the distinction the U.S. Supreme Court has made between a condition (or status) and a voluntary act is meaningless in the area of substance abuse. Furthermore, it would constitute cruel and unusual punishment to punish a person for the status of being intoxicated if that condition is not subject to individual control.

Despite the reluctance of the U.S. Supreme Court and other courts to view alcoholism or addiction to other drugs as an illness or condition rather than the result of free will, intoxication is recognized as a partial defense in some situations, particularly when it negates a specific intent required to prove the crime in question.

Acts that would be criminal in other circumstances may not be so when committed under domestic authority, such as a parent disciplining a child or a teacher disciplining a pupil. This area is controversial, and the laws and rules are not clear, leaving room for interpretation.

In some cases, consent, condonation, or the victim's conduct may provide a defense to criminal acts. Euthanasia was cited as an example. Technically one cannot consent to be killed, but when that happens in cases of terminally ill patients, prosecutors may not bring charges; if they do charge, some juries do not convict. Consent may negate an element of some crimes, such as rape, for which lack of consent is an element of the crime.

The increased attention in recent years to the extent and nature of domestic violence has led to the recognition of a defense in this area. The battered person syndrome defense recognizes the lack of appropriateness of the traditional self-defense approach when serious injury or murder occurs after repeated acts of domestic violence over an extended period. In such cases, when the perpetrator is not threatened with imminent harm, some defense attorneys have been successful in their arguments that a person who has suffered abuse over a long period of time may reasonably believe he or she is in danger of imminent harm or death even though that is not actually the case. Because this is not a matter of common knowledge, some jurisdictions permit experts to testify concerning the battered person syndrome. This evidence informs the jury of how a person may be expected to react to years of violence. The battered person syndrome may be a complete or partial defense; it may also be used in mitigating a sentence. The defense has been extended to include children who kill parents who have allegedly abused them for years.

Various other stress disorders are being advanced as defenses today. Extreme emotional disturbance is one example, as illustrated by the Oregon statute.

The return of many Vietnam War veterans with psychological and emotional problems led to a greater awareness of posttraumatic stress disorder (PTSD). As a result, courts have been more receptive to admitting expert testimony on this disorder. Another form of PTSD is rape trauma syndrome. Although courts do not recognize evidence of the syndrome to prove that rape occurred, expert testimony on the condition is recognized in an increasing number of jurisdictions to explain the delay in reporting the rape as well as the alleged victim's general behavior after the rape.

Other defenses, such as that of rough sex, may be expected to receive increasing attention in the future as we expand our knowledge of human behavior and our willingness to permit experts to testify in court about that behavior.

With the conclusion of our examination of criminal defenses to crime, we turn in the following chapters to an analysis of the major acts covered by criminal statutes.

STUDY QUESTIONS

1. What is meant by *substance abuse*?

2. Do you think alcoholism (or any other type of substance abuse) is a disease or a moral problem or both? Explain your answer.

3. Discuss the nature and extent of the intoxication defense, and indicate whether you agree with the current general legal position with regard to this defense.

4. Under what circumstances, if any, should condonation and consent be defenses to criminal behavior?

5. Discuss the meaning of the battered person syndrome along with the extent to which you think it should or should not constitute a defense to a criminal act, such as murdering a spouse, lover, child, friend, or parent. Do you think the law should distinguish categories of battered persons? Should the defense extend to psychological battering? If so, where would you draw the line?

6. What is the relationship between the battered person syndrome defense and self-defense?

7. Should extreme emotional disorder be a defense? Discuss.

8. What is PTSD, and how does it relate to combat? Should it be a viable defense?

9. Discuss the use of the rape trauma syndrome as a defense. How far should this defense be extended?

10. What is the PMS defense, and what is the general position of U.S. courts on this defense?

11. Should rough sex ever be a defense? Why or why not?

FOR DEBATE

It has been argued that in today's U.S. criminal justice systems, defendants have too many freedoms and do not take sufficient responsibility for their acts. It is the tradition of our systems, however, that people who do not have control over their acts should not be held criminally culpable for them. Consider both sides of this issue in the following debate topic.

RESOLVED: U.S. courts should not permit defenses associated with the use of prescription drugs or related to emotional or environmental factors.

KEY TERMS

CASE ANALYSIS

COMMONWEALTH V. CONAGHAN

740 N.E. 2d 956 (Mass. 2000)

Case Preview:

This case is presented to show the possible impact of the battered woman syndrome on a defendant's competency to participate in her defense. Deborah Conaghan entered a guilty plea to manslaughter in the death of her son after her request to present information on the battered woman syndrome was denied. Four and a half years after that plea, Conaghan petitioned the Massachusetts Superior Court to order the trial court to provide her a competency examination and to permit her to withdraw her guilty plea. Conaghan argued that at the time she entered her guilty plea she was suffering from battered woman syndrome caused by beatings by her boyfriend, and as the facts in the excerpt here indicate, she claimed that she entered the guilty plea because of the effects of the syndrome. Her petitions were denied by the superior court. On appeal, the Supreme Judicial Court of Massachusetts held that Conaghan was entitled to an examination by an expert to determine whether she suffered from battered woman syndrome and, if so, whether her guilty plea was the result of this syndrome.

This case illustrates that the battered woman syndrome can be used to support a defendant's assertion of incompetency. The highest court in Massachusetts emphasized that a guilty plea is not valid unless it is made voluntarily, "with sufficient awareness of the relevant circumstances, and with the advice of competent counsel," and that a voluntary plea might be impossible for one suffering from the battered woman syndrome.

Facts

Conaghan's plea hearing. At the plea hearing, the assistant district attorney read Conaghan's statement to the police concerning the events surrounding her son's death. Conaghan told the police that no one else was in the house when she pushed her son and that she previously had pushed him in the same manner four or five other times. Additionally, she stated that these punishments had begun in September, 1991, and that there was no one else present when they took place. Conaghan also stated twice in response to the judge's questions that she was pleading guilty out of her own free will. The trial judge specifically asked her whether anybody had threatened her or made promises in order to get her to plead guilty and she replied, "No."

(a) Materials in support of motion to withdraw guilty plea and for new trial. In support of her motion to withdraw the guilty plea and for a new trial, Conaghan filed supplementary materials regarding Paul Haynes's violent conduct with other women and children, an affidavit narrating her own history of physical and psychological abuse, and some of her psychiatric and medical records since her incarceration. The [trial] judge concluded that there was nothing in Conaghan's affidavit creating a substantial issue that would require a psychiatric examination or examinations and an evidentiary hearing.

(b) Conaghan's affidavit. In 1991, Conaghan met Paul Haynes. Shortly after beginning a relationship with Haynes, he moved in with her. Because Haynes was unemployed, Conaghan used her earnings and child support payments to pay his rent and bills. Haynes told Conaghan that he worked for an individual named "Tony" who was affiliated with the mafia. Haynes would often threaten Conaghan with Tony if she did not obey him or if she displeased him in any way. While she was living with Haynes, she learned that Haynes also owned a gun. Haynes ordered Conaghan to punish her son physically in order to cure his behavioral problems and illnesses. Haynes also physically punished Conaghan's son. At Haynes's direction, Conaghan assisted him. According to Conaghan, prior to Haynes's moving in she had only punished her son through nonphysical means. Conaghan stated in her affidavit that Haynes instructed her to lie to the authorities about her son's death. Haynes told her to "cover for him" because, if charged, he would receive life imprisonment given his prior criminal record. Haynes also instructed Conaghan to kill herself. When she refused, Haynes instructed her to turn herself in to the authorities; Conaghan did so. In addition, Haynes continued to instruct her on what to tell her lawyer and the authorities. According to Conaghan, Haynes also told her to plead guilty in order to avoid further investigation which might result in his being charged.

(c) Conaghan's psychiatric records. Conaghan submitted some of her mental treatment records since her incarceration. She has received extensive therapy for severe bipolar disorder [a psychiatric disorder, formerly known as manic depression, which is characterized by periods of mania followed by depression, but with normal periods in between]. These records also make references to her "past tendencies to be lorded over by abusive males." Conaghan has not been evaluated for battered woman syndrome while at the Massachusetts Correctional Institution at Framingham, because diagnosis of and treatment for battered woman syndrome is beyond the mandate of the prison's medical services department.

(d) Evidence at Paul Haynes's trial. One year and eleven months after Conaghan's plea, Haynes was convicted by a jury of forcible rape of a child, indecent assault and battery on a child under fourteen years of age, assault and battery, and assault and battery by means of a dangerous weapon in connection with his abuse of James and Joyce Sanford. The partial transcript of that trial submitted by Conaghan in support of her motion to withdraw her guilty plea and for a new trial reveals the violent and abusive personality of Paul Haynes.

Haynes moved in with Rebekah Sanford. He brought Conaghan with him and told Sanford that Conaghan was his sister. His testimony reveals that the Sanford children, especially James, were continually "disciplined" by Haynes. The testimony revealed the Sanfords' fear of Haynes and fear of being killed. Conaghan's affidavit expressed the same fear.

Conaghan testified at Haynes's trial. She said Haynes would beat the Sanford children and afterward show her the bruises to humiliate the children. According to Conaghan, Haynes was particularly violent toward James.

Haynes also would talk to Conaghan about Tony who was involved in the mafia and was "very mean and . . . when he wanted something, he got it and didn't care how he got it." Conaghan also said that Haynes had a gun in his briefcase and that he would carry his briefcase with him "all the time." After Conaghan and Haynes separated in May, 1992, they continued to exchange letters until sometime in October, 1992, after Conaghan's plea to manslaughter. At Haynes's trial, Conaghan stated that she "still loved him in a sense because of what we shared but that he was now in her past."

(e) Investigative reports from the district attorney's office. The district attorney's office interviewed friends of Rebekah and various other women involved with Haynes prior to his trial. These reports reveal Paul Haynes as a violent and abusive person, especially toward women and children.

Issue

We granted the defendant's application for further appellate review to determine, among other issues whether Conaghan's motion for a competency examination or examinations pursuant to [the statute] was erroneously denied.

Holding

The order denying Conaghan's motion for a court-appointed expert under [the statute] is vacated, the case is remanded to the Superior Court for an examination or examinations by an expert on battered woman syndrome to determine (1) whether Conaghan was suffering from battered woman syndrome; (2) whether, if she were suffering from battered woman syndrome, Conaghan had the ability at the time of that plea to assist her attorney in preparing her defense; (3) whether, if she were suffering from battered woman syndrome, Conaghan was competent voluntarily to plead guilty; and (4) whether, if she were suffering from battered woman syndrome, Conaghan pleaded "with a reasonable degree of rational understanding" and with a "rational as well as factual understanding of the proceedings against [her]."

The order denying the motion for a competency examination or examinations is vacated. The matter is remanded to the Superior Court proceeding consistent with this opinion and for such further proceedings as may be needed after the expert has rendered an opinion.

So ordered.

Rationale

The Commonwealth asserts that Conaghan's delay makes her claim not credible. The Commonwealth also asserts that Conaghan is not credible because she did not come forward until after Haynes's trial. Where, as here, the claim is that Conaghan was not competent rationally to assist her counsel in her defense or to meet the constitutional requirement that a plea must be voluntary with "sufficient present ability to consult with [her] lawyer with a reasonable degree of rational understanding and whether [she] has rational as well as factual understanding of the proceedings against [her]," expert testimony is required.

Evidence of battered woman syndrome is "material to the issue whether [Conaghan] could assist her counsel in preparing a defense that served her best interests." A common characteristic of battered women is a learned helplessness which manifests itself in the inability to perceive herself as abused and to communicate the abuse to others. Evidence of battered woman syndrome may be considered newly discovered evidence warranting a new trial because usually there is delay in coming forward with information on the abuse, even if there were some knowledge of the abuse at trial. . . . Therefore, the fact that Conaghan was not able to come forward with claims of abuse at the hands of Haynes until 1997 does not render her allegations less credible, if she suffered from battered woman syndrome.

Conclusion. Conaghan's motion raises a serious question as to her mental competency to assist her attorney in establishing a defense and to plead guilty voluntarily. On this record, Conaghan is entitled to an examination or examinations by an expert in battered woman syndrome under [the statute] as to her competency to assist counsel in her defense and to enter a voluntary plea due to battered woman syndrome. [The statute] provides that "whenever a court of competent jurisdiction doubts whether a defendant in a criminal case is competent to stand trial or is criminally responsible by reason of mental illness or mental defect, it may at any stage of the proceedings . . . order an examination of such defendant to be conducted by one or more qualified . . . psychologists . . . when an examination is ordered, the court shall instruct the examining physician or psychologist in the law for determining mental competence to stand trial and criminal responsibility." Nothing in the statute limits the time within which this must be done.

For Discussion

The decision in this case returns the case to the trial court with instructions to order a competency hearing. Conaghan was entitled to be examined by an expert on battered woman syndrome, who should be instructed to determine whether Conaghan suffered from the syndrome and, if so, whether that would have rendered her incapable of entering a guilty plea intelligently and voluntarily. The battered woman syndrome is not accepted evidence in all jurisdictions. Should it be? Why or why not? Should the defense be extended to battered males? Battered children? Explain your answers.

INTERNET ACTIVITY

In this chapter it was shown that many defendants are the victims of a variety of abuses and disorders that may or may not relieve them of responsibility for their crimes. The following is a short list of websites, all accessed on 27 November 2008 (there are many more that you can find using any search engine), that focus on crime victims:

http://www.ncvc.org/
http://www.ojp.usdoj.gov/ovc/
http://www.ocva.wa.gov/
http://www.musc.edu/cvc/

Visit these websites, and critique the information provided in terms of resources for victims, information about the criminal justice system, and the use of victimization as a defense to criminal liability. How informative are these sites? Do they discuss the potential negative and criminal consequences of victimization? Is there any discussion of insanity, substance abuse, battering, or stress disorders as the result of victimization? Conduct more specific Web-based searches using a variety of search engines, and examine how much (or how little) information is available concerning victimization as a defense to criminal responsibility.

NOTES

1. Alan I. Leshner, "Addiction Is a Brain Disease—and It Matters," *National Institute of Justice Journal* 237 (Washington, D.C.: U.S. Department of Justice, October 1998), p. 2.
2. "Is Chemical Dependence an Obsessive-Compulsive Disorder?" *Alcoholism & Drug Abuse Weekly* 13 (28 May 2001): 1.
3. *Traynor v. Turnage*, 485 U.S. 535 (1988), *superseded by statute*, Veterans' Judicial Review Act of 1988, USCS, Title 38, Section 7105 (2009), which defines the scope of reviewability and procedures for appealing VA benefits decisions.
4. *Traynor v. Turnage*, 485 U.S. 535 (1988), *superseded by statute*, Veterans' Judicial Review Act of 1988, USCS, Title 38, Section 7105 (2009).
5. Model Penal Code, Sections 2.08(5)(c) and 2.08(4).
6. O.C.G.A., Title 16, Section 16-3-4 (a)(b) (2007).
7. O.C.G.A., Title 16, Section 16-3-4 (c) (2007).
8. K.S.A., Chapter 21, Section 21-3208(2) (2006).
9. *People v. Tocco*, 525 N.Y.S.2d 137 (N.Y.Sup. 1988), footnotes and citations omitted.
10. *Powell v. Texas*, 392 U.S. 514 (1968), dissenting opinion.
11. Tex. Penal Code, Title 2, Section 8.04(b) (2009).
12. *State v. Egelhoff*, 518 U.S. 37 (1996).
13. *State v. Egelhoff*, 518 U.S. 37 (1996), citations and footnotes omitted.
14. *Bradley v. State*, Walker 156, 157 (Miss. 1824).
15. *Daily v. Board of Education of Merrill School District*, 588 N.W.2d 813 (Neb. 1999).
16. R.R.S. Neb., Chapter 79, Section 79-295 (2005).
17. R.R.S. Neb., Chapter 79, Section 79-258 (2005).
18. *Ingraham v. Wright*, 430 U.S. 651 (1977).
19. Model Penal Code, Section 3.08(1)(a)(b).
20. *People v. Johnson*, 479 N.E.2d 481 (Ill.Ct.App. 1985).
21. *Quoted in State v. Kelly*, 478 A.2d 364 (N.J. 1984).
22. See *Ibn-Tamas v. United States*, 407 A.2d 626 (D.C.Cir. 1979).
23. *State v. Koss*, 551 N.E.2d 970 (Ohio 1990), footnotes and citations omitted.
24. *People v. Humphrey*, 56 Cal. Rptr. 2d 142 (Cal. 1996). The California Evidence Code that provides for the introduction of evidence concerning the battered person syndrome is codified at Calif. Evid. Code, Section 1107 (2008).
25. *People v. Minnis*, 455 N.E.2d 209, 214-215 (Ill.App.4th Dist. 1983).
26. *People v. Day*, 2 Cal.Rptr. 2d 916 (Cal.App. 1992), *review denied sub nom.*, 1998 Cal. LEXIS 234 (Cal. 1998).
27. *Smith v. State*, 144 P.3d 159 (Okla. Crim. App. 2006). The case is discussed in "Stilwell Woman's Sentence Reduced from 28 to 4 Years," *The Oklahoman* (Oklahoma City, OK) (17 June 2007), p. 20A.

28. "Woman Gets Probation after Fatally Shooting Abusive Spouse," *Dallas Morning News* (30 May 1987), p. 37.

29. "Abused Wife Gets Break in Slaying of Husband," *Miami Herald* (14 June 1990), p. 2.

30. *State v. Janes*, 822 P.2d 1238 (Wash.App. 1992), *rev'd.*, 850 P.2d 495 (Wash. 1993).

31. *State v. Janes*, 850 P.2d 495, 503 (Wash. 1993).

32. *State v. Janes*, 850 P.2d 495 (Wash. 1993).

33. *State v. Nemeth*, 694 N.E.2d 1332 (Ohio 1998).

34. ORS, Chapter 16, Section 163.135 (2007).

35. See American Psychiatric Association, *Diagnosis and Statistical Manual of Mental Disorders* (Washington, D.C.: American Psychiatric Association, 1952).

36. *Today's School Psychologist* 4 (5 July 2001), n.p.

37. "GI Pleads Guilty to AWOL, Drug Charges," *Denver Post* (26 January 2005), p. 3B.

38. "Pressed by the Demand of Two Wars, Plus Mandates to Expand, Reorganize, and Modernize, the Army Is Nearing Its Breaking Point," *National Journal* (7 April 2007), n.p.

39. American Psychiatric Association, *Diagnostic and Statistical Manual of Mental Disorders*, 3d ed. rev. (Washington, D.C.: American Psychiatric Association, 1987), Section 309.89.

40. *State v. Felde*, 422 So.2d 370 (La. 1982); and I, 338 N.W.2d 673 (S.D. 1983).

41. *State v. DeMoss*, 770 P.2d 441, 444 (Kan. 1989), cases and citations omitted.

42. American Psychiatric Foundation, http://www.psych foundation.org/, accessed 27 November 2008.

43. Ann Wolbert Burgess and Lynda Lytle Holmstrom, "Rape Trauma Syndrome," *American Journal of Psychiatry* 131 (1974): 981.

44. *People v. Pulinario*, 720 N.Y.S.2d 382 (2d Dep't. 2001), *appeal denied*, 754 N.E.2d 214 (2001), and *habeas corpus granted*, *Pulinario v. Goord*, 291 F. Supp. 2d 154 (E.D.N.Y. 2003), *aff'd.*, 2004 U.S. App. LEXIS. 26803 (2d Cir. 2004).

45. *Pulinario v. Goord*, 291 F. Supp. 2d 154 (E.D.N.Y. 2003), *aff'd.*, 2004 U.S. App. LEXIS 26803 (2d Cir. 2004), case names and citations omitted.

46. *State v. Marks*, 647 P.2d 1292 (Kan. 1982).

47. *Henson v. State*, 535 N.E.2d 1189 (Ind. 1989).

48. *Beauchamp v. City of Noblesville*, 320 F.3d 733 (7th Cir. 2003).

49. "Progression to Sexual Slavery," *Corrections Professional* 6 (4 May 2001), n.p.

50. "Bye Bye Blues: Falling Apart and Picking Up the Pieces with Postpartum Depression," *San Antonio Current* (25 April–1 May 2002), n.p.

51. "Baby Blues under Microscope at Conference," AAP Newsfeed (29 April 2002), n.p.

52. "Lilly's Fluoxetine Approved in USA for Severe Premenstrual Syndrome," *IAC Newsletter Database* (17 July 2000), n.p.

53. Thomas L. Riley, "Premenstrual Syndrome as a Legal Defense," *Hamline Law Review* 9 (February 1986): 193–202; quotation is on pp. 201–202.

54. *Calley v. Callaway*, 382 F.Supp. 650 (M.D.Ga. 1974), *rev'd.*, 519 F.2d 184 (5th Cir. 1975), *cert. denied*, 425 U.S. 911 (1976).

55. "The Rough-Sex Defense: When Killers Blame Erotic Impulses, Does Rough Justice Result?" *Time* (23 May 1988), p. 55.

56. "The Rough-Sex Defense"; "Released," *Newsweek* (7 January 1991), p. 57.

57. "Religion Is Rejected as Murder Defense," *New York Times* (20 April 1989), p. 12; "Beliefs Tested by Girl's Death," *St. Petersburg Times* (1 December 1991), p. 1. The case is *Hermanson v. State*, 604 So.2d 775 (Fla. 1992).

CHAPTER 6

Criminal Homicide

INTRODUCTION

The April 2007 shooting deaths of 32 students and faculty members at Virginia Tech University by a lone gunman, Cho Seung-Hui, 23, a student, who also killed himself, reminded us that mass murder is still a threat. The deaths of thousands during the 11 September 2001 terrorist attacks in the United States left us to ponder whether we are ever safe from violence. But this 2007 massacre on one of our university campuses made it clear that death can occur anywhere and quickly. The students and faculty at Virginia Tech had no warning; most were barricaded in classrooms by the gunman before he began firing. The Virginia Tech massacre led other colleges and universities to develop or improve their internal warning systems, but in February 2008, shortly before the end of class in a lecture hall on a campus in Northern Illinois, a lone gunman dressed in black appeared on stage and began firing. Five students were killed and 18 were injured before Steve Kazmierczak, 27, an excellent student academically, turned one of his four weapons on himself and ended his life. Reports that the gunman had recently stopped taking his antidepressant medication renewed discussions of the possible side effects of such drugs. Recall that Chapter 5 discussed this issue (see again Focus 5.1).

Shopping malls and department stores are also targets for mass violence, illustrated by the December 2007 shootings in the Von Maur department store in Omaha, Nebraska, where Robert A. Hawkins, 19, fired at shoppers before taking his own life. Just two months later, five women were shot to death in a department store in the Chicago, Illinois, area.

The fall 2008 terrorist acts in Mumbai, India, killing over 100 persons and wounding scores more, along with the 7 July 2005 terrorist bombings of three London subway trains and one bus, resulting in the deaths of at least 56 people and injuries to 700 or more, demonstrated to us that other countries are not safe either. Earlier that year we realized that even our courthouses can be places of violence, as illustrated by the March killing spree at the Fulton County Court House in Atlanta, Georgia. In 2008 Brian Nichols was convicted of those murders. Nichols was sentenced to life in prison after the jury deadlocked 9-3 in favor of the death penalty.

These and other killings illustrate several points about murder. First, the randomness of some murders means that many people may lose their lives simply by being in the wrong place at the wrong time. Of particular concern is that even schools are not safe places for children or teachers. Second, although most of today's murders are not committed by adolescents or children, the fact that any of them are is disturbing, especially when we see multiple murders committed on our school grounds. Finally, violence occurs in the home as well as in public places and is committed by family members as well as by strangers.

This chapter focuses on murder, the most serious of the violent crimes. First, it is useful to look at a brief overview of violent crimes.

AN OVERVIEW OF VIOLENT CRIMES

In reading about these crimes and others, it is probably of little comfort to most people that overall **violent crime** data in the United States decreased during 2007 after rising between 2004 and 2006. However, the decease in 2007 was only approximately 0.7 percent. Figure 6.1 depicts these changes.[1]

In the United States, crime data come from various sources, but the primary source is the Federal Bureau of Investigation (FBI), which requests the cooperation of states in reporting crimes. The FBI's annual publication, *Crime in the United States: Uniform Crime Reports*—usually referred to as the **Uniform Crime Reports**, or the **UCR**, reports the national data the FBI has compiled and analyzed. The *UCR* recording system in-

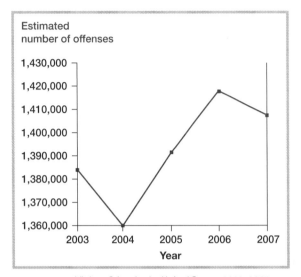

FIGURE 6.1 *Violent Crime in the United States, 2003-2007*
Source: Federal Bureau of Investigation, *Crime in the United States: Uniform Crime Reports, 2007*, http://www.fbi.gov/ucr/cius2007/offenses/violent_crime/index.html, accessed 30 November 2008.

cludes four crimes in the category of serious violent crimes. Those crimes are discussed in this chapter and in Chapter 7, with this chapter focusing on murder and nonnegligent manslaughter. For convenience, the four serious violent crimes and their definitions are reprinted in Focus 6.1.

The FBI records the volume and the rate of serious crimes. The **crime rate** refers to the number of crimes per 100,000 in the population. The *UCR* also reports the **crimes known to the police**, which includes all serious offenses that have been reported to the police and for which the police have sufficient evidence to believe were actually committed. The *UCR* also reports arrests. In addition to the four serious violent crimes, the *UCR* reports data on serious property crimes as well as less serious violent and property crimes. Definitions of these crimes are noted where appropriate throughout the text.

HOMICIDE

The term that refers to all cases in which a human being kills another human being by his or her own act, omission, or procurement is **homicide**. The state of Washington defines the term as follows:

> Homicide is the killing of a human being by the act, procurement, or omission of another, death occurring at any time, and is either (1) murder, (2) homicide by abuse, (3) manslaughter, (4) excusable homicide, or (5) justifiable homicide.[2]

Not all killings or homicides carry criminal culpability. A killing committed in self-defense or by accident or any other circumstance that the law permits is called an **excusable homicide**. Excusable homicides involve some fault but not enough that the law considers them worthy of criminal culpability. Another category is **justifiable homicide**, which is a killing that is intentional but carries no evil intent and is permitted by law, such as one involving capital punishment or a killing by a law enforcement officer in the line of duty when attempting to prevent a felony. Because the law permits justifiable homicides, no fault is assigned to these killings. For example, it is permissible for a designated person to perform whatever tasks are necessary to carry out a legal death penalty; that is a planned killing that does not constitute criminal homicide. Likewise, under some circumstances, police may kill in the line of duty, and citizens may kill in self-defense without incurring criminal responsibility.

In many cases it is difficult to distinguish excusable from justifiable homicide. Persons threatened with immediate great bodily harm or death are permitted to use reasonable means to prevent an attack. If the threatened person has legal cause to kill in self-defense and does so intentionally, the result is justifiable (rather than excusable) homicide. For example, Mary McIntyre, 35, who was held hostage at her Concord, California, business, was not charged with murder when she killed Jociel Bulawin, a former employee who told her she would have to shoot him or he would kill her. He held her hand on a gun aimed at his head and told her to fire.[3]

If the actor does not intend to kill but causes the death of another while engaging in the proper use of self-defense, the act is excusable homicide. If the actor is sufficiently negligent, however, the killing may be considered negligent homicide (discussed later), for which he or she could be criminally culpable.

Because of the problems of distinguishing justifiable homicide from excusable homicide, some jurisdictions do not use those terms. They may use only one term, such as *criminal homicide*, which may be further divided into categories, such as murder and manslaughter. Some jurisdictions define criminal homicide along the lines used by the Model Penal Code, with the intent categories of purposely, knowingly, recklessly, or negligently causing the death of another human being (see again Focus 2.2 in Chapter 2). Other jurisdictions use the term *intentionally* in place of *purposely* but the result is essentially the same: a categorization of murder by the seriousness of the act.

FOCUS 6.1	*Uniform Crime Report (UCR)* Definitions of Serious Violent Crimes
Murder and Nonnegligent Manslaughter	[T]he willful (nonnegligent) killing of one human being by another.
Forcible Rape	[T]he carnal knowledge of a female forcibly and against her will. Assault or attempts to commit rape by force or threat of force are also included; however, statutory rape (without force) and other sex offenses are excluded.
Robbery	[T]he taking of or attempting to take anything of value from the care, custody, or control of a person or persons by force or threat of force or violence and/or by putting the victim in fear.
Aggravated Assault	[A]n unlawful attack by one person upon another for the purpose of inflicting severe or aggravated bodily injury. . . . [T]his type of assault is usually accompanied by the use of a weapon or by other means likely to produce death or great bodily harm. Attempted aggravated assault that involves the display of—or threat to use—a gun, knife, or other weapon is included in this crime category because serious personal injury would likely result if the assault were completed. When aggravated assault and larceny-theft occur together, the offense falls under the category of robbery.

Source: Federal Bureau of Investigation, *Crime in the United States, Uniform Crime Reports 2004* (Washington, D.C.: U.S. Government Printing Office, 2005), pp. 15, 27, 31, 37.

GENERAL DEFINITIONAL ISSUES

States differ in how they define homicide and its categories. In general, however, state homicide statutes have common definitional issues, two of which are analyzed in detail in the following sections.

Another Human Being Requirement

The first issue is that of *another human being.* Use of the word *another* precludes listing suicide within the definition of homicide, although historically it was included in some jurisdictions, along with the act of counseling another to take his or her own life.

The second term, *human being,* has been interpreted to be a *living* human being. The Texas Penal Code uses the term *individual,* which it defines as "a human being who is alive, including an unborn child at every stage of gestation from fertilization until birth."[4] Two definitional problems are raised here: the meaning of *living* (or alive) and the meaning of *human being* or *person.*

The requirement of a *living human being* becomes an issue when a fetus dies as the result of a crime against a pregnant woman. Under the common law the fetus was not considered to be a person or a human being. It had to be born alive before its death could be classified as a homicide. Most state statutes followed this rule, although there were some exceptions, such as permitting a charge of manslaughter but not of murder.

A Florida case illustrates this position. A pregnant Florida teenager who shot herself in the stomach (because she said she was too poor to get an abortion), killing her fetus, was charged with manslaughter and third-degree murder. A Florida district court of appeal held that the third-degree murder charge was not permissible but that Kawana M. Ashley could be tried for manslaughter, based on the fact that the fetus was born alive and then died, presumably as the result of the mother's criminal negligence when she shot herself. (Criminal negligence can support a manslaughter charge.) The Florida Supreme Court ruled that an expectant mother may not be charged with criminal responsibility for the death of her fetus under the facts of this case.[5] (See the Case Analysis at the end of this chapter.)

But what does it mean to be born alive? Some states require that the fetus be expelled from the mother's body and be breathing on its own. Others require that the baby cry or that the umbilical cord is severed. Some courts, such as the California Supreme Court, have held that if the birth process has started and the fetus is viable, the baby is considered to have been born alive.[6]

The born-alive requirement may affect other crimes, such as **infanticide**, which refers to killing a child at or soon after its birth. Historically, infanticide was acceptable in some societies; parents were permitted to kill deformed children and, in some cases, female children, since male children were preferred. Where infanticide has been a crime, it has not been considered as serious as murder.

Decriminalizing abortion has resulted in a problem when, during an abortion process, a fetus is born alive. To cover this situation some states, such as Pennsylvania, have enacted statutes requiring health care professionals to do what they can to save the life of the fetus. A Pennsylvania physician was convicted of infanticide when he failed to take positive steps to preserve the life of a fetus born alive during an abortion. The baby survived for about 90 minutes. The physician, who could have been sentenced to three and a half to seven years in prison, was placed on three years' probation and ordered to perform 300 hours of community service. In sentencing the defendant, the judge said that she did not wish to make an example of him, that prison and a heavy fine would serve no purpose, but that the doctor had made a "criminal mistake."[7]

Some states have made statutory changes in the common law requirement of being born alive and include the fetus within their murder statutes, as noted in the Texas statute cited earlier in this chapter. Texas previously defined *individual* in its murder statute as "a human being who has been born and is alive." Other states define killing a fetus as manslaughter, discussed later in this chapter.

California amended its murder statute, which defined the crime as "the unlawful killing of a human being, with malice aforethought," to state, "Murder is the unlawful killing of a human being, or a fetus, with malice aforethought." The statute excludes acts such as legal abortions. In 1994, the California Supreme Court held that in an assault on a pregnant woman who subsequently loses her baby, the assailant may be prosecuted for murder even if the fetus was not viable at the time of the assault.[8]

In 2004, the California Supreme Court held that the act of killing a fetus constituted second-degree murder in a case in which the defendant did not know the woman he killed was pregnant. The court stated that by engaging in the violent conduct that killed the deceased, the perpetrator "demonstrated a conscious disregard for all life, fetal or otherwise, and hence is liable for all deaths caused by his conduct."[9]

The Minnesota first- and second-degree murder statutes were amended in 1986 and now contain a provision prohibiting the murder of an unborn child. The new crime, *murder of an unborn child*, is defined as follows when it involves first-degree murder:

> Whoever does any of the following is guilty of murder of an unborn child in the first degree and must be sentenced to imprisonment for life:
>
> (1) causes the death of an unborn child with premeditation and with intent to effect the death of the unborn child or of another;
>
> (2) causes the death of an unborn child while committing or attempting to commit sexual conduct in the first or second degree with force or violence, either upon or affecting the mother of the unborn child or another; or
>
> (3) causes the death of an unborn child with intent to effect the death of the unborn child or another while committing or attempting to commit burglary, aggravated robbery, kidnapping, arson in the first or second degree, tampering with a witness in the first degree, or escape from custody.[10]

This change in the Minnesota statutes has been tested in the courts, as explained in Focus 6.2, which also discusses the meaning of the word *living*. Within recent years, a number of other states have enacted legislation that includes the killing of a fetus (apart from abortion) as homicide. Some of those statutes limit the homicide to cases involving a viable fetus, generally considered to be an embryo at 28 weeks (earlier in some jurisdictions) of development.

These statutory changes may result in criminal charges against pregnant women who take cocaine or some other illegal substance that results in fetal death or injury, but prosecutors have usually not been successful in prosecuting these cases. Perhaps the most cited example was that of the 1996 case of Deborah J. Zimmerman. Zimmerman was charged with attempted first-degree intentional homicide and first-degree reckless injury after giving birth to a baby with **fetal alcohol syndrome**, which refers to a cluster of abnormalities that a fetus may have due to the fact that its mother consumed alcohol during her pregnancy. The effects include growth deficiencies, facial abnormalities, and mental retardation. Zimmerman arrived at a hospital one week before her due date, announcing that she wanted to "kill this thing." She had previously been seen in bars drinking and suggesting that she would like to "drink the baby to death." At birth the

FOCUS 6.2   Should Killing a Fetus Constitute Murder?

The question of the legal status of a fetus in California, as noted in the text, is clear: It is a person. The issue gained international attention in April 2003 when the bodies of Laci Peterson and her unborn son were washed ashore in California. Laci, age 27 and eight months pregnant, according to her husband, left home on Christmas Eve 2002 to walk the family dog. After the discovery of the bodies, Laci's husband, Scott, who said he was fishing the day Laci disappeared, was charged with two counts of capital murder and held without bail. Peterson was convicted of first-degree murder for Laci's death and second-degree murder in the death of the fetus. He was sentenced to death.

The issue of the legal status of a fetus was debated and litigated prior to the Peterson case. In 1985 the Minnesota Supreme Court held that the Minnesota statute defining the crime of murder of an unborn child was constitutional and that the state could proceed with its prosecution of Sean Merrill for the murder of Gail Anderson and her 27- or 28-day-old embryo. It was unclear whether the defendant knew that Anderson was pregnant.

In *State v. Merrill*, the court held that the phrase "causes the death of an unborn child" was not vague and that the use of the word *living* in the statute presented no problem, in that living is nothing more than the property of growing or becoming, a characteristic of all living things. The dissent argued that the statute was vague, led to arbitrary and discriminatory interpretation, and therefore was unconstitutional.

The Minnesota statute was enacted by the legislature after the state's supreme court ruled in a 1985 case that the homicide statutes did not apply to the death of a viable fetus.[1] Merrill claimed unsuccessfully that the statute was vague because it did not define when life begins or when death occurs. In reaction to that argument, the court responded as follows:

> The difficulty with this argument, however, is that the statutes do not raise the issue of when life as a human person begins or ends. The state must prove only that the implanted embryo or the fetus in the mother's womb was living, that it had life, and that it has life no longer. To have life, as that term is commonly understood, means to have the property of all living things to grow, to become. It is not necessary to prove, nor does the statute require, that the living organism in the womb in its embryonic or fetal state be considered a person or a human being. People are free to differ or abstain on the profound philosophical and moral questions of whether an embryo is a human being, or on whether or at what stage the embryo or fetus is ensouled or acquires "personhood." These questions are entirely irrelevant to criminal liability under the statute. Criminal liability here requires only that the genetically human embryo be a living organism that is growing into a human be-

Scott Peterson, here led into a California court, was sentenced to California's death row for the murder of his wife, Laci, who was pregnant with their son. California state law includes a fetus within its murder statutes, and Scott was convicted of second-degree murder in the death of his unborn son. (Reuters/Corbis)

> ing. Death occurs when the embryo is no longer living, when it ceases to have the properties of life.[2]

In July 1993, two charges of first-degree murder and two charges of second-degree murder were filed against Chao Yang, accused in the stabbing deaths of a 29-year-old Rochester, Minnesota, woman and her eight-month-old fetus. Blood tests disclosed that Yang was the father of the fetus. Yang was tried and convicted of two counts of second-degree murder, sentenced to 51 years in prison, and faced with deportation. The Minnesota Court of Appeals upheld the convictions.[3]

1. *State v. Soto*, 378 N.W.2d 625 (Minn. 1985).
2. *State v. Merrill*, 450 N.W.2d 318, 323 (Minn. 1990), *cert. denied*, 496 U.S. 931 (1990).
3. See "Man Charged in Stabbing Death of Rochester Woman, Her Fetus," *Star Tribune*, Metro edition (3 July 1993), p. 5B; "Suspect in Rochester Slaying Is Arrested," *Star Tribune*, Metro edition (9 October 1993), p. 1B; "Man's Double Murder Conviction Is Upheld," *Star Tribune* (20 June 1995), p. 8B. The case is *State v. Yang*, 533 N.W.2d 81 (Minn.Ct.App. 1995).

baby was very small, intoxicated, and suffering from mild alcohol-related abnormalities. However, a Wisconsin court ruled that the charges against Zimmerman should be dismissed because both state statutes in effect at that time were limited to offenses against "a human being," defined as "one who has been born alive." In this case the fetus was not born at the time the mother consumed the alcohol.[11]

The Zimmerman case, however, sparked interest in the statutory protection of the unborn from the substance abuse of their mothers, leading Wisconsin to enact a provision allowing the taking of an adult expectant mother into custody under a judicial order based on a finding that the woman has exhibited a significant lack of self-control in the use of "alcohol beverages, controlled substances or controlled substance analogs," and as a result

> there is a substantial risk that the physical health of the unborn child, and of the child when born, will be seriously affected or endangered unless the adult expectant mother is taken into custody and that the adult expectant mother is refusing or has refused to accept any alcohol or other drug abuse services offered to her or is not making or has not made a good faith effort to participate in any alcohol or other drug abuse services offered to her.[12]

Although Zimmerman's acts did not fall within the Wisconsin statutes, those statutes do provide that, under some circumstances, causing the death of a fetus constitutes homicide. Wisconsin's *first-degree intentional homicide* statute includes causing "the death of an unborn child with intent to kill that unborn child, kill the woman who is pregnant with that unborn child or kill another." The state's *reckless homicide* statute includes a person who "recklessly causes the death of an unborn child under circumstances that show utter disregard for the life of that unborn child, the woman who is pregnant with that unborn child, or another."[13]

Another approach to classifying killing a fetus is to consider intentionally causing the death of a pregnant woman as murder but classify the death of the fetus as the lesser charge of manslaughter. For example, a Michigan statute enacted in 1931 and still in effect provides the following:

> The willful killing of an unborn quick child by any injury to the mother of such child, which would be murder if it resulted in the death of such mother, shall be deemed manslaughter.[14]

In 2004, the U.S. Congress passed, and President George W. Bush signed, the Unborn Victims of Violence Act of 2004 (also known as Laci and Connor's

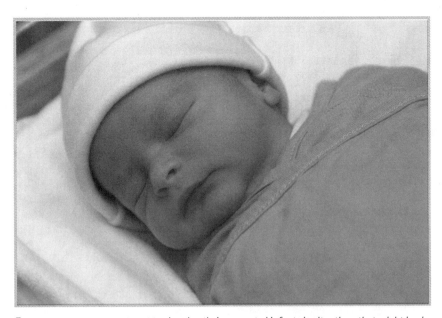

To encourage young parents not to abandon their unwanted infants in situations that might lead to their deaths, some states, such as Texas, have enacted Baby Moses laws. These laws provide immunity to parents who abandon their infants at designated safe places, from which the babies are taken and placed with foster parents or within institutions to await adoption. (IStockPhoto)

Act, after Laci, pregnant wife of Scott Peterson, who is under a death sentence for her death and that of their unborn but named son, Connor), which provides that the death of a fetus resulting from a crime against its mother is a separate crime, provided the accused "had knowledge or should have had knowledge that the victim of the underlying offense was pregnant; or . . . intended to cause the death of, or bodily injury to, the unborn child." The death penalty is not permitted for this crime.[15]

Finally, some jurisdictions have established by law a system permitting persons to leave their newborns at *safe places* (e.g., fire stations, police departments, hospitals or clinics) and not be subject to criminal prosecution. In most jurisdictions this policy applies only to the period 72 hours after the birth of the child, but others permit a longer period (such as 30 days) after the infant's birth for turning him or her over to medical or other designated personnel. According to the American Bar Association, these **Baby Moses laws** are gaining ground in the United States,[16] but some problems have occurred. In 2008, for example, Nebraska faced an unexpected result from its law: Parents left teens at safe places. Some parents even drove from out of state to leave their teens in Nebraska under the Nebraska Safe Haven Act, which had no termination date. In November 2008 Nebraska amended the statute to include a limit of 30 days after the birth of the child in question. The statute became effective immediately; however, 36 older children were left at Nebraska safe havens between the effective date of the original statute in July 2008 and the revised version in November of that year. The last child to be left was a 14-year-old boy from California.[17]

The Texas Criminal Code provides an example of this type of statute. Its section entitled *Abandoning or Endangering Child* enumerates the conditions under which one may be criminally charged but states this final provision: "It is an exception to the application of this section that the actor voluntarily delivered the child to a designated emergency infant care provider under Section 262.302, Family Code."[18] That section provides that a designated emergency infant care provider shall take possession of a child who appears to be 60 days old or younger if that child is delivered voluntarily by the child's parent and that parent does not express an intent to return for the child. The care provider has no legal duty to obtain information from the parent and may not do so unless it appears that the child has been abused or neglected. "However, the parent may be given a form for voluntary disclosure of the child's medical facts and history." The infant care provider is not liable for any injuries to the child unless due to the provider's negligence. The provider is under a legal duty to take care of the child's welfare and safety.[19]

The Definition of Death

A second issue that homicide statutes raise is the definition of *death*. Historically the term was not defined legally; this was not an issue because there was general agreement that death meant the cessation of breathing and heartbeat. Today, however, the definition of death has become a critical issue in many homicide cases, in part because of doctors' ability to keep patients functioning with the aid of life-support systems. Further, organ transplantation has created a need to define when death occurs. For some organs to be viable for successful transplants, they must be removed before all body functions have ceased, and they must be preserved carefully until quick transplantation occurs.

The issue of when death occurs arose in a Florida case involving an anencephalic child who was born with a functioning brain stem; the child's heart was beating, and she was breathing. (*Anencephaly* is a congenital absence of all or part of the brain.) The child's parents wanted their baby declared dead so that her functioning organs could be transplanted to other children. The Florida Supreme Court ruled that donation of the child's organs would not be legal. The court noted that there was no agreement on the utility of the desired transplants and that the ethical, legal, and constitutional issues had not been resolved.[20]

The issue of when death occurs for purposes of transplants was raised in February 2008, when a California doctor was accused of accelerating the death of a patient in order to harvest his kidneys and liver for transplants. The case is discussed in Focus 6.3.

The problem of when death occurs is further complicated by the growing number of living wills. These wills are formal written statements made by legally competent individuals about the action they want taken if they require life-support systems or organ transplants in order to live. The statutes vary, but in general, when a living will is executed properly, termination of life-support systems, resulting in the death of a patient, will not constitute homicide.

The issue of when death occurs gained national and international attention in recent years, when the parents

FOCUS 6.3   Organ Transplants and Death

A critical question in the medical world of organ transplants is: When does death occur for purposes of harvesting organs from a potential donor? It is common knowledge that an effective transplant must take place quickly after a donor dies, but doctors are not permitted to hasten death to secure viable organs. It is estimated that 18 people die each day while awaiting organ transplants; the pressure to secure viable organs is thus intense.

In the first U.S. case in which a transplant surgeon has been charged with criminal behavior for hastening the death of a potential donor, Dr. Hootan C. Roozrokh, a San Francisco surgeon whose transplant training occurred at the Stanford Medical School, faced three felony counts. Dr. Roozrokh was accused of administering excessive and improper doses of drugs to Ruben Navarro, 25, who was near death when he was admitted to a California hospital in 2006. Navarro, who suffered from a neurological condition, apparently had a heart attack and was rushed to the hospital in a comatose condition.

Dr. Roozrokh faced a possible prison term of eight years and a $20,000 fine if convicted. Two of the charges against him were dismissed by the judge who stated a lack of evidence, but according to the judge, conflicting testimony with regard to the third charge, felony dependent adult abuse, a felony that could result in up to 4 years in prison, warranted a trial. After a two-month trial, the jury acquitted the doctor in December 2008.

In June 2008, the Medical Board of California was seeking to revoke or suspend the surgeon's medical transplant license based on allegations that, in violation of state law, the doctor was in the patient's hospital room ordering drugs prior to a declaration of death and "actively monitoring the patient's vital signs for a determination of death." The Medical Board also accused the surgeon of administering painkillers to Navarro even though the doctor had not been granted staff privileges at that hospital. Experts indicated that the amount of painkillers administered was excessive. Finally, according to the Medical Board, Dr. Roozrokh used inappropriate and unprofessional language when he asked a nurse whether the patient had received his "candy," apparently referring to pain medications.

Dr. Roozrokh apparently administered massive doses of morphine, a painkiller, along with an antianxiety drug, Ativan, to speed up the comatose man's death. The potential donor's mother had given permission for organ transplants from her son, but he lived another seven hours after his ventilator was removed, and that period was much too long for his organs to be viable for transplants.

Dr. Roozrokh's attorney declared that his client had not committed any "unethical, illegal, immoral or medically inappropriate" acts. Although the case resulted in an acquittal, the filing of felony charges, although short of murder charges, may result in a decrease in surgeons willing to perform transplants and potential donors agreeing to donate their organs. As stated by the president of the American Society of Transplant Surgeons, "If you think a malpractice lawsuit is scaring surgeons off, wait to see what happens when people see a surgeon being charged criminally and going to jail."[1]

1. Quoted in "Surgeon Is Accused of Hurrying Death of Patient to Get Organs," *New York Times* (27 February 2008), p. 1. The information in this focus is summarized from that source and the following: "Board Targets Doctor's License," *Los Angeles Times* (6 June 2008), p. 3B; "Transplant Surgeon Faces Trial on Abuse Charges," *Los Angeles Times* (20 March 2008), p. 4B; and "Transplant Surgeon Acquitted," *Los Angeles Times* (19 December 2008), p. 3B.

of Terri Schiavo wanted to leave their daughter attached to life support systems; her husband, Michael Schiavo, wanted to disconnect them. Terri, 39 at the time of her death in 2005, had been in a vegetative state since 1990, when she suffered a heart attack and lapsed into a coma. Terri's parents, friends, some politicians, and many other people, including some physicians, argued that Terri was responsive and that, with proper therapy and treatment, she would improve. Michael Schiavo and his supporters argued that she was brain dead and, according to Michael, would not have wanted to live that way. He wanted to remove the tubes that provided food and hydration, while his opponents argued that removal would starve Terri to death. The case went through numerous legal decisions in Florida, resulted in a special emergency session in the U.S. Congress (which drafted a special bill to "save Terri") and a special bill in Florida, removing and then reinserting the tubes, and numerous protests before it was resolved with the final removal of Terri's tubes and her subsequent death. But the case continued to generate controversy even after the autopsy report that Terri had been hopelessly brain damaged and that, contrary to accusations that her husband abused her, there was no evidence of abuse. The case highlighted the need for living wills that clearly state what their authors wish to happen in such cases.

The resolution of issues regarding the definition of *death* relates to the *causation* element of homicide.

The controversies surrounding whether life support systems should be removed from Terri Schiavo made national and international headlines for months. Schiavo, who did not have a written living will, was in a vegetative state for 15 years before she died in 1995. Her husband, Michael Schiavo, who argued that Terri would not have wanted to live in that condition, finally won the legal battles against her parents and others; Terri's life support systems were removed, and she died. (Getty Images)

Causation

An important element the prosecution must prove in homicide cases is that the alleged crime and not some other act *caused* the victim's death. This issue may be resolved by case law or by statute.

The Year-and-a-Day Rule

Because of the difficulties in determining the cause of death, the common law utilized a *year-and-a-day* rule. If death did not occur within a year and a day after an alleged criminal act, the defendant could not be convicted of criminal homicide. Some state legislatures incorporated this rule into their homicide statutes. Others, in moving from the common law to statutory law, did not mentioned the year-and-a-day rule. Failure to include the rule in a statute may be interpreted as an abandonment of the rule, as illustrated by the following case.

A Georgia father, David Lebron Cross, was indicted for the death of his child. Cross admitted that he shook his daughter but said he did so because she was choking on her bottle. Prosecutors claimed successfully that the defendant inflicted such injury that the child sustained brain damage and became coma-

tose. Seventeen months after the alleged child abuse, at the request of the mother and over the objection of the father, a judge ruled that the child could be taken off life support. Within a few weeks she died. The father was charged with murder. A Georgia judge granted the defense motion to dismiss, based on the argument that death did not occur within a year and a day after the alleged criminal abuse. The prosecutor appealed that ruling to the Georgia Supreme Court, which invalidated the state's year-and-a-day rule and ordered the father to stand trial for murder. According to the court, the year-and-a-day rule was eliminated when the legislature rewrote the criminal code in 1968 and did not include the common law rule.[21]

In 1999, the Tennessee Supreme Court held that the year-and-a-day rule no longer existed in that state. Even though it had not been abandoned by the legislature, the court emphasized that the reasons for the rule no longer exist, with, among other changes, the expansion of life due to medical advancements and the greater accuracy of determining the cause of death.[22]

California retained the theory of the year-and-a-day rule but expanded the time period. According to the California Penal Code,

To make the killing either murder or manslaughter, it is requisite that the party die within three years and a day after the stroke received or the cause of death administered. If death occurs beyond the time of three years and a day, there shall be a rebuttable presumption that the killing was not criminal. The prosecution shall bear the burden of overcoming this presumption. In the computation of such time, the whole of the day on which the act was done shall be reckoned the first.[23]

Two words in the California statute need to be defined at this point. As noted in Chapter 4, a presumption is an assumption of a fact that is based on other facts. A *rebuttable presumption* is one that can be refuted with evidence, in contrast to a *nonrebuttable presumption*, which cannot be refuted. An example of a rebuttable presumption is the presumption of innocence. We presume innocence, but the prosecution may refute that as long as the proof is beyond a reasonable doubt.

Multiple Causation

The year-and-a-day (or similar) rule does not always solve the causation problem because a victim who dies within that time period may have been subjected to more than one cause of death. Assume, for example, that a person who is injured severely by a criminal act is taken to the hospital, where a doctor performs surgery required by the injury, and that the doctor's surgery constitutes medical malpractice. The patient dies two days after being stabbed. Who is responsible for the death?

Usually a negligent act by a third party occurring after a criminal act does not relieve the original wrongdoer of criminal culpability if the first act was a substantial factor in causing the death. An Arizona case states: "Medical malpractice will break the chain of causation and constitute a defense only if death is attributable solely to the medical malpractice and not induced at all by the original wound." This case involved the victim of a criminal stab wound. The attending physician who conducted exploratory surgery to determine the extent of the wound unknowingly perforated the lower intestine and did not discover his mistake. The patient developed peritonitis, which led to his death. The court upheld the offender's conviction.[24]

Causation also presents problems when two or more parties commit separate acts, neither one of which would have been sufficient alone to cause the victim's death. In those cases many courts look carefully at the intent of the individuals who committed the acts. If the prosecution can prove that a defendant intended to cause death, most courts find that intent sufficient for a conviction for criminal homicide unless the second act clearly broke the chain of causation between the defendant's act and the victim's death.

Many state statutes do not define causation for criminal homicide cases and rely instead on court interpretations of the word *cause*. It is not uncommon, however, for courts to neglect to define *cause* other than to say that the defendant's act must have caused the victim's death. It is assumed that everyone knows the meaning of the word. Not so, said the U.S. Court of Appeals for the Second Circuit, in the following fact pattern.

Barry Warren Kibbe and his co-defendant, Roy Krall, first met George Stafford, who was drunk, at a bar. The bartender refused to serve Stafford another drink, although Stafford flashed a $100 bill, which Kibbe and Krall saw. When Stafford began soliciting a ride from patrons, Kibbe and Krall offered. They drove to another bar, in which Stafford was refused a drink, and then to a third bar, where drinks were served. After leaving that bar, Kibbe and Krall demanded Stafford's money, received it, and then forced him to lower his pants and remove his boots to prove that he did not have more money. They abandoned Stafford by the side of the road, placing his boots and jacket on the shoulder of the road.

Shortly thereafter Michael Blake, a college student who was speeding down the rural road, saw Stafford sitting in the middle of the road with his hands in the air. Blake testified that he did not have time to react; thus, he did not try to avoid hitting Stafford, who died shortly after the collision. The autopsy showed that the deceased had a high alcohol concentration (0.25 percent) in his blood. The medical examiner testified that Stafford died of wounds suffered from the impact of Blake's truck. The jury convicted Kibbe and Krall of second-degree murder, second-degree robbery, and third-degree grand larceny.

In the following excerpt from the case, the federal appellate court explained why it reversed the second-degree murder conviction. The issue hinged on the state's requirement to prove beyond a reasonable doubt all of the elements of the crime: that the defendants exhibited a depraved indifference to Stafford's life, that they engaged recklessly in conduct that created a grave risk of death to him, and that their actions caused his death.[25]

KIBBE v. HENDERSON

534 F.2d 493 (2d Cir. 1976)

[The appellate court noted that the trial court did not instruct the jury on the meaning of causation, and continued as follows:] The omission of any definition of causation, however, permitted the jury to conclude that the issue was not before them or that causation could be inferred merely from the fact that Stafford's death succeeded his abandonment by Kibbe and Krall.

Even if the jury were aware of the need to determine causation, the court's instruction did not provide the tools necessary to that task. The possibility that jurors, as laymen, may misconstrue the evidence before them makes mandatory in every case instruction as to the legal standards they must apply. . . . It has been held that where death is produced by an intervening force, such as Blake's operation of his truck, the liability of one who put an antecedent force into action will depend on the difficult determination of whether the intervening force was a sufficiently independent or supervening cause of death. The few cases that provide similar factual circumstances suggest that the controlling questions are whether the ultimate result was foreseeable to the original actor and whether the victim failed to do something easily within his grasp that would have extricated him from danger.

If you had been on that jury, do you think you would have concluded that the defendants should have foreseen that Stafford would not take action to protect himself and that approximately half an hour after they abandoned him he would be hit and killed by a speeding truck? On appeal, the U.S. Supreme Court reversed the lower appellate court's decision, holding that no evidence had been presented that the lack of an instruction on causation prejudiced the defendants. Thus, the second-degree murder conviction was reinstated. According to the U.S. Supreme Court, "A person who is 'aware of and consciously disregards' a substantial risk must also foresee the ultimate harm that the risk entails. Thus, the jury's determination that the respondent acted recklessly necessarily included a

determination that the ultimate harm was foreseeable to him."[26]

Corpus Delicti

A final legal concept important to all crimes but especially to homicides is *corpus delicti*, which means the "body of the crime" and refers to the body or other material substance of a crime that constitutes the foundation of that particular crime. The remains of a burned house might be the *corpus delicti* in an arson case. In criminal homicide cases, *corpus delicti* includes much more than the body of the deceased, although to prosecute a defendant for any category of criminal homicide, theoretically the prosecutor has to produce the dead body or evidence that one exists.

The *corpus delicti* is required as corroborating evidence that the crime occurred. *Corroborating evidence* includes additional data to support the crime charged, especially in rape and other cases in which there were no witnesses to the alleged act, and it is crucial to proving a case. Thus, even if the accused confesses to a murder, if the body cannot be found or there is no evidence of a dead body, that confession is not sufficient for a conviction. In many cases the prosecutor will not file charges until the body is found. There are some exceptions to the *corpus delicti* requirement. Some courts have abandoned this requirement because it is difficult if not impossible to get a tangible *corpus delicti* for some crimes. Examples would be attempt crimes, conspiracy, and income tax evasion.

The *corpus delicti* rule does not require that the actual body be produced. An example was that of the prosecution of David Waters, charged with the murder of atheist leader Madalyn O'Hair (who successfully challenged the legality of prayer in public schools), her son, and a granddaughter, who had been missing since 1995 and were presumed dead when Waters was arrested in May 2000. Waters, who had a prior criminal record but hid that from O'Hair, was one of her employees and apparently knew that she had money, most of which came from contributions to her atheist organizations. Waters and two accomplices kidnapped O'Hair, her son, and her granddaughter and murdered them. In January 2001, Waters and prosecutors entered into a plea agreement, and Waters led authorities to the buried and dismembered bodies of the three missing persons. Waters, who pleaded guilty to extorting $600,000 from O'Hair, is serving a 20-year prison sentence in the federal prison in Leavenworth, Kansas.[27]

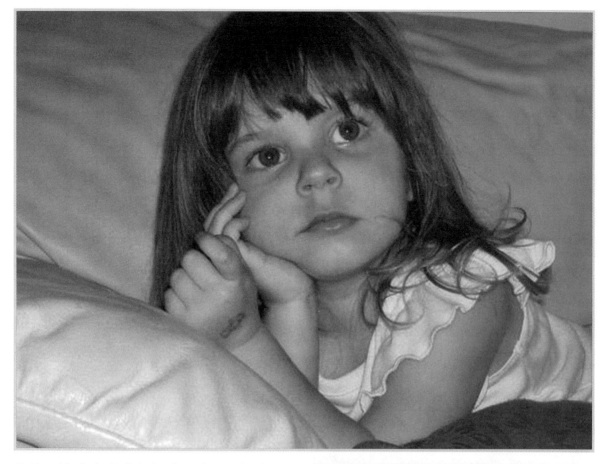

Florida toddler Caylee Marie Anthony's remains were found months after her disappearance in 2008 . Her mother, Casey Anthony, pictured at right during a court appearance, gave numerous and conflicting stories concerning her child's disappearance. The child's remains were discovered just a short distance from the grandparents' home, where the child and her mother had lived. Casey Anthony had already been charged with first-degree murder and aggravated manslaughter of a child. She pleaded not guilty and was scheduled for trial in September 2009. (AP images)

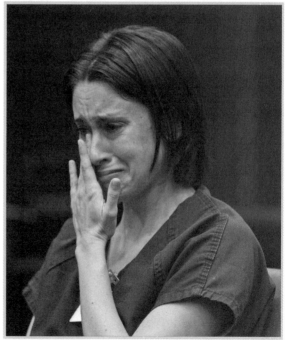

MURDER

Although it is a commonly recognized crime, **murder** is difficult to define. In general, *murder* is the unlawful and unjustified killing of another human being (or a fetus in some jurisdictions) with malice aforethought. Murder includes several types, such as the intent to kill, the intent to do great bodily harm, an act done in willful disregard of the strong likelihood that death or great injury would result, or a killing committed during the commission of another felony. In the FBI's *Uniform Crime Reports (UCR)*, the offense of murder also includes nonnegligent manslaughter, which is discussed separately in this chapter. The FBI data for 2007, compared to 2006, showed a slight decline (0.6 percent) in the United States, accounting for 1.2 percent of the overall serious violent crimes that year. The 2007 figure was 2.4 percent below that of 2003. Most of the 2007 murders (89.9 percent) occurred within Metropolitan Statistical Areas.[28] Finally with regard to data, although murder is the most serious of the four violent crimes recorded by the FBI, it has the highest clearance rate (61.2 percent) of all serious crimes, as graphed in Figure 6.2. A crime is considered cleared if an arrest is made or, if no arrest is made, exceptional means are present. Before an agency can confirm that a crime has been cleared by exceptional means, the agency must have met all of the following four circumstances.

⚙ "Identified the offender.

⚙ Gathered enough evidence to support an arrest, make a charge, and turn over the offender to the court for prosecution.

⚙ Identified the offender's exact location so that the suspect could be taken into custody immediately.

⚙ Encountered a circumstance outside the control of law enforcement that prohibits the agency from arresting, charging, and prosecuting the offender."[29]

Elements of Murder

Regardless of the definition, all acts classified as murder generally require the following elements:

1. There must be an unlawful act (or omission) committed by a human being.

2. The act must be accompanied by the requisite *mens rea*.

3. The act must be the legal cause of the victim's death.

4. The victim must be a living human being. (As noted earlier, some jurisdictions now include a fetus.)

5. Death must occur within a reasonable period (usually specified, such as a year and a day under the common law; now extended under some modern statutes).

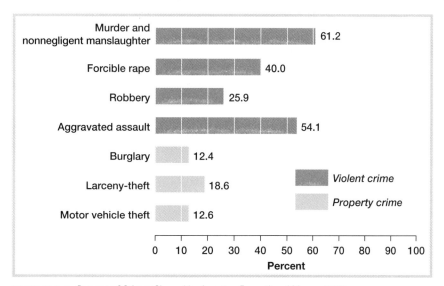

FIGURE 6.2 *Percent of Crimes Cleared by Arrest or Exceptional Means, 2007*
Source: Federal Bureau of Investigation, *Crime in the United States: Uniform Crime Reports, 2007,* http://www.fbi.gov/ucr/cius2007/offenses/clearances/index.thml, accessed 30 November 2008.

Chapter 2 contained a general discussion of most of these elements. Some—for example, the year-and-a-day rule—were discussed earlier in this chapter. Others, such as the *mens rea* requirement for murder, need further elaboration, and that may be done in the context of the common law development of the crime of murder.

Common Law Murder

The common law crime of murder developed over several centuries. Some states follow the common law definition (an unlawful killing of another human being with malice aforethought). Others have modified that definition (e.g., to include the killing of a fetus.) There is so much confusion over the meaning of the crime of murder, however, that some commentators have suggested that, rather than dwelling on the common law definition, states should emphasize categories or types of murder. That is the approach this chapter takes, but first it is important to understand the traditional approach and its influence on current statutes.

Under the common law and many modern statutes, murder requires *malice aforethought*, which means that the killing must be predetermined and intentional and without legal justification or excuse. Malice aforethought, however, is not used literally, and over time the concept has eroded. Common law judges interpreted the term so differently that in many cases it bore no resemblance to its ordinary usage.

When the term *malice aforethought* is used, it must be defined. A typical traditional murder statute that includes the concept provides that malice may be *express* or *implied*. Those terms are distinguished in the California statute as follows:

> It [malice aforethought] is express when there is manifested a deliberate intention unlawfully to take away the life of a fellow creature. It is implied, when no considerable provocation appears, or when the circumstances attending the killing show an abandoned and malignant heart.[30]

Defendants who claim that because they had no malice toward anyone in the area they should not be charged with murder after firing into a crowd at a shopping center will find judges unsympathetic to their arguments. Malice may be inferred from the facts of such a case. More specifically, one court has held that "[m]alice aforethought may be inferred from the intentional use of a deadly weapon in a deadly and dangerous manner."[31]

Some jurisdictions have abandoned the malice aforethought requirement in favor of categories that define the various types of murder in terms of the type of mental element or intent involved. They may use the term *malice aforethought*, however, to distinguish between first- and second-degree murder. Other jurisdictions avoid the use of this confusing terminology altogether.

An example of a short, straightforward definition of murder is that of Iowa, which defines murder as follows: "A person who kills another person with malice aforethought either express or implied commits murder."[32] The code then defines the acts that constitute the highest form of murder, first degree, and that list includes some of the types we discuss here.

Types of Murder

Jurisdictions may vary significantly in the ways in which they categorize murder. A few categories are distinguished here. The names of these categories are used to describe the type of murder. Some states use the types but give them a different name. For example, Oregon's *aggravated murder* statute includes murder for hire (discussed later in this chapter). In addition, it includes homicide of a person under the age of 14. It also includes the killing of any of the following types of persons if the killing is related to that individual's official position: police officers, judicial officers, jurors or witnesses in a criminal proceeding, employees or officers of a court of justice, and members of the parole board or board of postprison supervision. Homicides by persons who escape from incarceration, persons who use explosives, and persons who kill to conceal a crime also fall within this statute. Finally, aggravated murder includes multiple killings, killings that involve torture or maiming, and killings by persons previously convicted of certain homicides.[33]

Intent to Kill

The most common murders involve the intent to kill. If there are no mitigating circumstances to reduce the charge to manslaughter and if the killing is not excusable or justifiable, the defendant who intends to kill may be convicted of murder. Intent-to-kill murders do not require acts; omissions are sufficient, provided there is a legal duty to act. The intent to kill may be shown when the killing takes place under circumstances that would likely result in a death, as well as in those rare cases in which the defendant articulates an intent to kill.

The intentional (as opposed to negligent) use of a deadly weapon may be introduced as evidence from which an inference of an intent to kill may be made, although the defendant may refute that inference. The intent to kill must be shown. It is possible, for example, that a person might shoot at another person with the intention of scaring, not killing. The real intent, of course, may not be known. The jury must infer intent or lack of intent by analyzing the evidence presented at the trial.

The common law provision that the intent to kill had to be premeditated is no longer required. For this type of murder it is sufficient to show an unpremeditated intent to kill.

Intent to Inflict Great Bodily Harm

Death that results from serious bodily injuries may be murder when it can be shown that the defendant intended to inflict serious or great bodily harm, even though there was no intent to kill. The phrase *great bodily harm* means harm greater than plain bodily injury (which must be interpreted) but less than death. This is to avoid murder convictions when death occurs from simple injury. In the language of an early American case, "Every assault involves bodily harm. But any doctrine which would hold every assailant as a murderer where death follows his act would be barbarous and unreasonable."[34] In such a case, however, a manslaughter charge might be appropriate.

An example of a state statute that covers intent to kill, intent to commit great bodily harm, and intent to commit a felony (discussed later) is that of California. Notice the other specifics in this statute, such as drive-by shootings as well as the use of weapons of mass destruction.

> All murder which is perpetrated by means of a destructive device or explosive, a weapon of mass destruction, knowing use of ammunition designed primarily to penetrate metal or armor, poison, lying in wait, torture, or by any other kind of willful, deliberate, and premeditated killing, or which is committed in the perpetration of, or attempt to perpetrate, arson, rape, carjacking, robbery, burglary, mayhem, kidnapping, train wrecking, or any act punishable under [specific statutes], or any murder which is perpetrated by means of discharging a firearm from a motor vehicle, intentionally at another person outside of the vehicle with the intent to inflict death, is murder of the first degree.

All other kinds of murders are of the second degree. . . .

[The statute defines some of the preceding terms and concludes with the following words:]

To prove the killing was "deliberate and premeditated," it shall not be necessary to prove the defendant maturely and meaningfully reflected upon the gravity of his or her act.[35]

Depraved Heart

Depraved heart murders are killings resulting from the extremely reckless conduct of the defendant. This type of murder is said to be the result of a depraved mind, an abandoned and malignant heart, or wickedness. For depraved heart murder, the defendant must *create* the risk, but courts differ in their holdings concerning whether the defendant must be *aware* of the risk (the subjective test) or whether it is sufficient that a reasonable person would have been aware of the risk (the objective test).

The risk required for a depraved heart murder must be greater than that required in negligence cases, with some jurisdictions requiring circumstances that manifest "extreme indifference to the value of human life." The firing of a loaded gun into an occupied automobile that results in death to one or more persons is an example of creating a risk that exhibits extreme indifference to the value of human life.[36]

Mississippi includes depraved heart murder in its homicide statute, which is as follows:

(1) The killing of a human being without the authority of law by any means or in any manner shall be murder in the following cases:

(a) When done with deliberate design to effect the death of the person killed, or of any human being;

(b) When done in the commission of an act eminently dangerous to others and evincing a depraved heart, regardless of human life, although without any premeditated design to effect the death of any particular individual;

(c) When done without any design to effect death by any person engaged in the commission of any felony other than rape, kidnapping, burglary, arson, robbery, sexual battery, unnatural intercourse with any child under the age of twelve (12), or nonconsensual unnatural intercourse with mankind, or felonious abuse and/or battery of a child in violation of [another statute], or in any attempt to commit such felonies;

(d) When done with deliberate design to effect the death of an unborn child.[37]

The second section of this statute defines *capital murder*.

Intent to Commit a Felony

An unintended death resulting from the commission of a felony may be classified as a **felony murder**. Under the common law, these deaths were considered murders, but over the years the felony murder doctrine developed by statute, and it differs among the jurisdictions. Some limit felony murder to deaths resulting from the more serious felonies (such as armed robbery) or state that the doctrine is limited to "inherently dangerous felonies." Others limit the time period involved; some are more restrictive on legal cause. Still others require that the killing be independent of the felony. Maine's *felony murder* statute is one example:

A person is guilty of felony murder if acting alone or with one or more other persons in the commission of, or an attempt to commit, or immediate flight after committing or attempting to commit, murder, robbery, burglary, kidnapping, arson, gross sexual assault, or escape, the person or another participant in fact causes the death of a human being, and the death is a reasonably foreseeable consequence of such commission, attempt or flight.[38]

Maine includes attempt crimes, too, but the felony murder statute contains four circumstances that together may constitute an affirmative defense to prosecution. The defendant:

2A. Did not commit the homicidal act, aid, or in any way solicit, command, induce, procure or aid the commission thereof;

B. Was not armed with a dangerous weapon, or other weapon under circumstances indicating a readiness to inflict serious bodily injury;

C. Reasonably believed that no other participant was armed with such a weapon; and

D. Reasonably believed that no other participant intended to engage in conduct likely to result in death or serious bodily injury.[39]

Some states do not enumerate the felonies that can be the basis for felony murder when death results. Massachusetts, for example, defines *murder as follows:*

Murder committed with deliberately premeditated malice aforethought, or with extreme atrocity or cruelty, or in the commission or attempted commission of a crime punishable with death or imprisonment for life is murder in the first degree. Murder which does not appear to be in the first degree is murder in the second degree. Petit treason shall be prosecuted and punished as murder. The degree of murder shall be found by the jury.[40]

Focus 6.4 contains several examples of cases involving felony murders.

There is considerable debate over the felony murder rule. The doctrine may have made sense under the common law when all felonies were punishable by death. Then it made little difference whether the defendant was convicted of murder or of another felony. Today, because capital punishment may be imposed only in murder cases and because some states consider felony murder a capital offense, it is argued that it is unconstitutional to impose the death penalty on those who were involved in the felony but did not commit the killing.

The U.S. Supreme Court appeared to agree with this position in 1982 (see again Focus 6.4), when it held that it was unconstitutional to impose the death penalty on a defendant who drove the getaway car in an armed robbery in which his cohorts killed the robbery victims. In *Enmund v. Florida*, the Court ruled that it would be cruel and unusual punishment to impose the death penalty on one "who aids and abets a felony in the course of which a murder is committed by others but who does not himself kill, attempt to kill, or intend that a killing take place or that lethal force will be employed."[41] But in 1987, in *Tison v. Arizona* (also noted in Focus 6.4) the U.S. Supreme Court held that under some circumstances it is permissible to impose the death penalty in felony murder cases.[42]

Causation may be difficult to establish in felony murder cases, as in the following instance: The defendant raped and severely beat an 85-year-old woman. The woman was moved to a nursing home after the attack, but she was so depressed she would not eat. She could not be fed through a nasal tube because of her facial injuries. When nurses were trying to feed her, she died of asphyxiation because, due to a broken rib that limited lung capacity, she was unable

FOCUS 6.4　Felony Murder Cases

The legality of felony murder statutes has been tested in several cases. The first discussed here occurred in Maryland, where one spring morning William Henry Jackson and James Wells Jr. set out to rob a jewelry store in Baltimore. Apparently the plan was to take as much jewelry as possible and then get away; there were to be no killings.

Acting on a tip, police surrounded Jackson and Wells in the store. In a desperate attempt to escape, the two robbers took the owners hostage. Using them as shields, Jackson and Wells escaped temporarily when they commandeered a police car. A lengthy car chase ended in a hail of gunfire at a police road-block. During the shoot-out one of the store owners was killed accidentally by police gunfire.

Jackson and Wells were convicted of first-degree murder under the Maryland felony murder statute. The Maryland Court of Appeals, in affirming the conviction, found that the acts of Jackson and Wells "established such a causal relationship with respect to the death as to make them criminally liable therefor."[1]

This case contrasts with the decision reached by the California Supreme Court in *People v. Phillips*. In *Phillips* the defendant, a chiropractor, persuaded a couple to remove their daughter from a hospital where she was scheduled to undergo cancer surgery. He assured them he could cure her without surgery. After the daughter died, the state charged the chiropractor, who had received $500 in compensation, with felony grand theft and felony murder. The California Supreme Court struck down the defendant's murder conviction, holding that grand theft was not an inherently dangerous crime and therefore could not be the basis for a felony murder conviction.[2]

In *Tison v. Arizona*, a felony murder case decided by the U.S. Supreme Court, two brothers helped free their father and another convict from prison. When their car broke down, one of the brothers stopped another car. Both brothers watched and did nothing to stop their father from killing the four members of the family in the other car. The brothers and their father were convicted of capital murder and sentenced to death. The Tison brothers appealed to the U.S. Supreme Court, claiming that their participation in the murders was so minor that the imposition of the death penalty would not serve its purposes of retribution and deterrence. The Supreme Court responded that the brothers' participation was "anything but minor" but that even if a defendant's participation in a crime is minor and his mental state is one of "reckless indifference," the death penalty is not precluded.[3]

In an earlier case, *Enmund v. Florida*, the U.S. Supreme Court had considered facts similar to those in *Tison*. In *Enmund* the petitioner received the death sentence despite the fact that he had done nothing more than drive a getaway car. The lower court held that it was irrelevant to this case that when the killings took place the petitioner was not present and that he did not anticipate or intend the killings. The Supreme Court reversed the lower court, holding that the death penalty should be imposed only in situations where the defendant "intended, contemplated or anticipated that lethal force would or might be used or that life would or might be taken in accomplishing the underlying felony."[4]

The differences between *Tison* and *Enmund* may be explained by a closer examination of the facts in the two cases: In *Tison* the brothers looked on and made no effort to prevent their father from killing the victims. In *Enmund* the petitioner sat in a car alongside the road, unaware that the victims were being executed. His involvement in the murders was too remote to justify capital punishment.

A recent case that has not been tested on appeal but which provides a dramatic example of the impact of the felony murder doctrine is that of Juan M. Alvarez, 29, who parked his sport utility vehicle on a California rail line and then fled. A passenger train hit the vehicle, struck a parked freight train, and crashed into an oncoming commuter train, killing 11 people. Alvarez was convicted of arson and 11 counts of first-degree murder under California's felony murder statute, which permits a murder conviction when one is convicted of a serious felony (in this case, arson) that causes the death of another even though the defendant did not intend to cause that death. Prosecutors in this case argued that Alvarez intended to kill commuters to get attention from his estranged wife. The defense argued that the defendant aborted a suicide attempt and never intended to harm anyone. The jury spared Alvarez the death penalty. His estranged wife said she would tell their two children, ages 7 and 10, that their father was spending the rest of his life in prison because he was unfairly convicted.[5]

1. *Jackson v. State*, 408 A.2d 711 (Md. 1979).
2. *People v. Phillips*, 414 P.2d 353 (Cal. 1966).
3. *Tison v. Arizona*, 481 U.S. 137 (1987).
4. *Enmund v. Florida*, 458 U.S. 782 (1982).
5. "Jury Spares Killer's Life in Rail Crash," *Los Angeles Times* (16 July 2008), p. 1B.

to expel food aspirated into her trachea. The defendant was convicted of murder. Would you uphold that conviction?

If the woman had died during the rape and beating, the defendant could have been charged with murder. But was her death by asphyxiation a reasonably foreseeable result of his criminal act? The court said yes, that even though an intervening event may relieve a defendant of murder after the commission of another felony, in this case the defendant's criminal acts set in motion a series of events that caused the victim's death, and thus his murder conviction was proper.[43]

Several cases demonstrate developments in the law of felony murder. The New Mexico Supreme Court has held that kidnapping is an inherently dangerous crime on which felony murder may be based.[44] The California Supreme Court established that supplying cocaine to a user who dies after it is ingested may constitute the predicate crime for felony murder but only if the drug has a "high probability" of resulting in death. This position goes further in interpreting the "inherently dangerous to human life" approach, which in many jurisdictions has looked only to the inherent nature of the predicate crime—thus, rape and kidnapping are inherently dangerous crimes. Supplying cocaine may not always be inherently dangerous, but under some circumstances it may fall within this traditional category.[45]

One final example is more unusual. In 1999, the North Carolina Court of Appeals held that a defendant (with a prior drunk driving conviction) who, while driving drunk, caused a collision that resulted in two deaths was properly convicted under the state's felony murder statute. That statute defines *murder in the first or second degree* as including, among other acts, a killing "committed in the perpetration or attempted perpetration of any arson, rape or a sex offense, robbery, kidnapping, burglary, or other felony committed or attempted with the use of a deadly weapon." The issue on appeal in this case was whether an automobile constitutes a deadly weapon, and the court held that it does. The defendant had been convicted of first-degree murder, assault with a deadly weapon inflicting serious bodily injury, assault with a deadly weapon, and driving while impaired. The court held that it was not proper to convict the defendant of first-degree murder under the felony murder statute because he did not have the specific intent to commit any of the underlying felonies, and all required that element. The court

upheld the other convictions. The defendant was sentenced to life without parole.[46]

Murder for Hire

A final type of murder is *murder for hire*, defined by the state of Utah as one type of aggravated murder, specifically a murder involving a person who intentionally or knowingly "committed, or engaged or employed another person to commit the homicide pursuant to an agreement or contract for remuneration or the promise of remuneration for commission of the homicide."[47]

It is not uncommon that a murder for hire statute is not called by that name, as illustrated by the preceding. In Washington, for example, the definition of *aggravated first-degree murder* includes, among others, the following circumstances:

> (4) The person committed the murder pursuant to an agreement that he or she would receive money or any other thing of value for committing the murder;

> (5) The person solicited another person to commit the murder and had paid or had agreed to pay money or any other thing of value for committing the murder;[48]

This statute was utilized in a case that involved two adults and five teens. A live-in caretaker, Barbara Marie Opel, 37, and her daughter's 17-year-old boyfriend, Jeffrey James Grote, were accused of enlisting five teenagers, including Opel's 13-year-old daughter, to kill Jerry Duane Heimann, 64, the son of Evelyn Heimann, 89, for whom Opel was a care provider. The elderly woman, who had Alzheimer's and could not speak, barely survived by eating newspapers during the days she was neglected after the killing. Allegedly Opel and Grote planned to steal $40,000 from Mr. Heimann. Both of the accused were charged with aggravated first-degree murder, for which they entered not guilty pleas.

Investigators reported that Opel offered Grote a car and clothing; the teens were offered about $300 each. Police alleged that the five teens beat Mr. Heimann to death with bats while Opel waited in the basement with her two younger children, ages 11 and 7, both of whom then helped clean the house after the murder.

A jury found Opel guilty of aggravated first-degree murder but could not reach the required unanimous verdict for the death penalty. Opel was sentenced to life without parole and told that she could have no contact with her children.

In a plea arrangement, Grote pleaded guilty to the lesser charge of first-degree murder and agreed to testify against Opel in exchange for a recommended 50-year sentence, which was later imposed. Because of his age, he could not be sentenced to death under Washington law. Kyle Boston, a friend of Grote, pleaded guilty to second-degree murder and was sentenced to 22 years in prison. A fourth person, who was only 13 at the time of the crime, was treated as a juvenile and thus his name is confidential; he is a cousin of Boston. He admitted his guilt in the murder and told the judge that he received about $100 for his participation, with which he bought a sweatsuit. This teen was sentenced to confinement until age 21, at which time the jurisdiction of the juvenile court ends. Marriam Oliver, 15, who lost her plea to be processed through the juvenile rather than the adult criminal court, was found guilty and sentenced to 22 years in prison.[49]

Degrees of Murder

Although the common law had no degrees of murder, most modern statutes divide murder into at least two categories (first-degree murder and second-degree murder) in order to assess different penalties. Some jurisdictions, such as Texas, have a separate category for murders that carry the death penalty.[50]

First-degree murder includes deliberate, premeditated, intent-to-kill murders as well as felony murders committed during the commission of enumerated felonies such as rape, arson, robbery, or kidnapping. The enumerated felonies differ from jurisdiction to jurisdiction, as already noted.

Some states include as first-degree murder those murders committed by use of poison, lying in wait, or bombing. More recently, some states, such as California,[51] have included murders that involve torture.

One of the key elements of first-degree murder is **premeditation**, which refers to the act of planning, deliberating, designing, or thinking out in advance an intention to kill another person. The time required for premeditation for murder may be short, and courts differ on their interpretation of this concept. The following excerpt from an Arizona Supreme Court case illustrates the issue. Defendant Henry Daniel Guerra was convicted of premeditated first-degree murder. The jury instruction gives one approach to defining premeditation.[52]

STATE v. GUERRA
778 P.2d 1185 (Ariz. 1989)

According to Guerra's own testimony, he went to the alley armed with a mace and a hunting knife, dressed in camouflage clothing, and planning to do some "pranks." While there, he overheard and witnessed the confrontation between McMahon and Cox. Aware of the volatile situation [based on previous confrontations about which Guerra had knowledge], Guerra, carrying his "perpetrator" and knife, walked a considerable distance down the alley to confront McMahon. [Guerra stabbed McMahon to death.] We believe this provides substantial evidence to support a guilty verdict on premeditated murder. A reasonable mind could find that Guerra, even if he did not premeditate a murder before he went to the alley, had sufficient time to reflect and premeditate a murder after McMahon confronted Cox.

Premeditation requires a length of time to permit reflection. The trial judge instructed the jury as follows:

> Premeditation means that the defendant's intention or knowledge existed before the killing long enough to permit reflection.
>
> *The time for reflection need not be prolonged and there need be no appreciable space of time between the intention to kill unlawfully and the act of killing.*
>
> *It may be as instantaneous as the successive thoughts of the human mind,* however it must be longer than the time required to form the intent or knowledge that such conduct will cause death.
>
> An act is not done with premeditation if it is the instant effect of a sudden quarrel or heat of passion.

Generally, *second-degree murder* is defined as any murder not included in first-degree murder. The Iowa statute is an example: "A person commits murder in the second degree when the person commits murder which is not murder in the first degree."[53]

Second-degree murder includes intent-to-kill murders that are not deliberate or premeditated; felony murders that are not considered first-degree murders (such as killings committed during larceny-theft); depraved heart murders; and intent-to-inflict-serious-bodily-harm murders, whether or not premeditated or deliberate.

The difficulty of distinguishing between first- and second-degree murder in some cases is illustrated by the following excerpt from *State v. Bingham*, in which the Washington Court of Appeals discussed the concept of premeditation. The victim in this case was a retarded adult who was last seen with the defendant. Her body was found three days later. She had been raped and strangled. The defendant was convicted of aggravated first-degree murder, with rape considered the aggravating circumstance. The defendant agreed that a murder conviction was appropriate but argued on appeal that it should have been second-degree, not first-degree, murder, since he lacked premeditation. The appellate court agreed and reversed the first-degree murder conviction and remanded the case for appropriate sentencing for second-degree murder.[54]

STATE v. BINGHAM

699 P.2d 262 (Wash.Ct.App. 1985)

 We are asked to decide whether the time to effect death by manual strangulation is alone sufficient to support a finding of premeditation in the absence of any other evidence supporting such a finding. . . .

Premeditation is a separate and distinct element of first-degree murder. It involves the mental process of thinking over beforehand, deliberation, reflection, weighing or reasoning for a period of time, however short, after which the intent to kill is formed. The time required for manual strangulation [three to five minutes in this case] is sufficient to permit deliberation. However, time alone is not enough. The evidence must be sufficient to support the inference that the defendant not only had the time to deliberate but that he actually did so. To require anything less would permit a jury to focus on the method of killing to the exclusion of the mental process involved in the separate element of premeditation. . . .

Unless evidence of both time for and fact of deliberation is required, premeditation could be inferred in any case where the means of effecting death requires more than a moment in time. For all practical purposes it would merge with intent; proof of intent would become proof of premeditation. However, the two elements are separate. Premeditation cannot be inferred from intent.

Premeditation can be proved by direct evidence [evidence offered by an eyewitness who testifies to what he or she saw, heard, tasted, smelled, or touched; any other evidence that directly shows the existence of a disputed fact and therefore requires no inferences], or it can be proved

by circumstantial evidence [evidence that may be inferred from a fact or a series of facts] where the inferences drawn by the jury are reasonable and the evidence supporting the jury's findings is substantial. There was no such evidence here, either direct or circumstantial.

The *Bingham* case illustrates the difficulty of proving premeditation. Thus, in murder cases, some jurisdictions permit convictions for a **lesser included offense**, which is a crime that is less serious than the one with which a defendant is charged. For first-degree murder, a lesser included offense could be second-degree murder or manslaughter. Other uses of the concept of lesser included offense are important, too, as noted in the following discussion.

Lesser Included Offenses

In *State v. Bingham* the appellate court held that the defendant could be sentenced for second-degree murder even though his conviction for first-degree murder was overturned. This was because the jury had been instructed on lesser included offenses—offenses that have some though not all of the elements of the charged offense. All of the elements required for conviction of second-degree murder are included within those of first-degree murder, but premeditation is not required for second-degree murder. Thus, the lack of evidence for premeditation, although precluding a conviction for first-degree murder, does not preclude a finding of second-degree murder, provided the jury has been properly instructed on that issue.

One final issue with regard to acts that might be considered murder is that of a physician aiding a patient to commit suicide.

PHYSICIAN-ASSISTED SUICIDE

In 1997, in *Washington v. Glucksberg*, the U.S. Supreme Court upheld the Washington and New York statutes that criminalized the act of a physician's aiding or abetting a suicide.[55] The Court ruled that the statutes at issue did not violate due process or equal protection. However, the Court left open the possibility that states may provide for physician-assisted suicide legislation if they choose, which Oregon has done, and in the fall 2008 election, Washington also enacted a physician-assisted suicide statute. The New York, Oklahoma, and Alaska statutes, none of which permits physician-

FOCUS 6.5   Laws Regarding Assisting Suicide

State of New York
NY CLS Penal Law, Section 125.15 (2008). Manslaughter in the Second Degree
A person is guilty of manslaughter in the second degree when . . . .

   (3) He intentionally causes or aids another person to commit suicide.

State of Oklahoma.
   In Oklahoma the Assisted Suicide Prevention Act is part of the public health and safety code.

Okl. St. Title 63, Section 3141.1 (2008)
Short title—Legislative intent

   B. It is the intent of the Oklahoma Legislature to protect vulnerable persons from suicide, to reduce the cost to taxpayers of en-
       forcing the assisted-suicide laws by promoting civil enforcement and providing for reimbursement of attorney fees by those
       found to be violating the law.

Section 3141.3. Violations
A person violates the Assisted Suicide Prevention Act when the person, with the purpose of assisting another person to commit or to
attempt to commit suicide, knowingly either:

   1. Provides the physical means by which another person commits or attempts to commit suicide; or
   2. Participates in a physical act by which another person commits or attempts to commit suicide.

State of Oregon
Oregon was the first state to permit physician-assisted suicide, which is defined in the state's Death with Dignity Act, codified at ORS
127.880 *et seq.* (2007).

Section 314. Construction of Act.
Nothing in [the statute sections detailing Death with Dignity] shall be construed to authorize a physician or any other person to end a
patient's life by lethal injection, mercy killing or active euthanasia. Actions taken in accordance with [Death with Dignity] shall not, for
any purpose, constitute suicide, assisted suicide, mercy killing or homicide, under the law.

State of Alaska
Alaska Stat., Section 11.41.120(a)(2) (2008)
A person commits the crime of manslaughter if the person . . . .

   (2) intentionally aids another person to commit suicide.

---

assisted suicide, are included in Focus 6.5. Note that in Alaska the crime is that of manslaughter, which under the laws of that state is a class A felony. Focus 6.5 also includes a portion of Oregon's statute concerning physician-assisted suicide (PAS).

In 1994, Oregon became the first state to enact a statute permitting physicians to assist others in committing suicide. The Oregon statute, referred to as the *Death with Dignity Act*, permits physicians to prescribe lethal drugs to persons with less than six months to live, provided that those persons request the drugs and are making an informed decision. The statute was opposed by the Bush White House and challenged by the U.S. attorney general, but in 2006, the U.S. Supreme Court held that the federal controlled substances act does not permit the U.S. attorney general to take action against a physician who prescribes drugs for assisted suicide in a state that legalizes physician-assisted suicide.[56]

In the fall elections of 2008, Washington became the second state to permit physician-assisted suicide by statute, and the following month, Montana became the first state to recognize PAS through case law. Judge Dorothy McCarter issued a ruling, stating that "The Montana constitutional rights of individual privacy and human dignity, taken together, encompass the right of a competent terminally (ill) patient to die with dignity" and, said the judge, that involves PAS.[57]

In the United States, attention to PAS followed the actions of Dr. Jack Kevorkian, who was prosecuted on murder charges stemming from his assistance to patients who committed suicide. The first murder charges were dropped in 1991 after a judge noted that Michigan, where the suicides were committed, had no law against physician-assisted suicides. According to the judge, Kevorkian's acts of hooking patients up to a "suicide machine" did not meet the elements of first-degree murder.[58]

Between 1991 and 1999, Dr. Kevorkian was in and out of court and jail during a series of charges, trials, court decisions, and statutory measures, all of which culminated in his 1999 convictions for second-degree murder and delivering a controlled substance, for his role in the death of Tom Youk, a patient dying from Lou Gehrig's disease. Dr. Kevorkian videotaped the steps leading to and including the patient's death; that tape, which was aired on CBS's *60 Minutes*, provided the evidence the prosecution needed to secure a conviction of the "suicide doctor," as Kevorkian was called.

Kevorkian was sentenced to 10 to 25 years in prison by a judge who told him, "You had the audacity to go on national television, show the world what you did and dare the legal system to stop you. Well, sir, consider yourself stopped."[59] Kevorkian lost his appeals, with the Michigan Court of Appeals rejecting his argument that his nationally televised assistance at the death of 52-year-old Youk was not second-degree murder but euthanasia, which, he claimed, is legal. Kevorkian alleged that he was not taking a life but rather providing "a medical service for an agonized human being." In 2002 the U.S. Supreme Court refused to consider his appeal.[60] In 2007, Kevorkian was released from prison, and in 2008, he announced that he was running as an independent for a seat in the U.S. Congress. The so-called Dr. Death campaigned on the basis of the Ninth Amendment to the U.S. Constitution, which, he claimed, by protecting rights not otherwise specified, implies a right to choose to die. He lost the election.

MANSLAUGHTER

A second but less serious category of homicide is **manslaughter**, which traditionally has been defined as an unlawful killing without malice aforethought. For example, California defines *manslaughter* as "the unlawful killing of a human being without malice"[61] and then designates three types, as we will see in the following discussion.

Although manslaughter generally refers to homicides that are not as serious as those that constitute first- or second-degree murder, in many cases it is difficult to distinguish the crimes murder and manslaughter. For example, consider the California case involving the second-degree murder conviction of Marjorie Knoller and the conviction of her husband and law partner, Robert Noel, for involuntary manslaughter. The couple owned a dog that mauled and killed a neighbor in their apartment building. Many legal authorities questioned whether the elements for murder were present, but the judge did permit the case to go to the jury, and Knoller was convicted of second-degree murder. Subsequently, that murder conviction was dismissed by the judge, who ruled there was not sufficient evidence to support it. However, in April

Marjorie Knoller was convicted of second-degree murder after her dog mauled and killed a neighbor. The conviction was subsequently dismissed by the trial judge, who said there was insufficient evidence to support the charge. The California Supreme Court reinstated the murder charge and remanded the case with sentencing instructions. In 2008, the trial court sentenced Knoller to 15 years to life in prison. (AP images)

2003, prosecutors asked an appellate court to reinstate the murder conviction, arguing that the judge was improper in second-guessing the jury when he overruled the conviction. Further, it was alleged that the judge used the wrong legal test for murder and should not have compared the wife's guilt with that of her co-defendant husband and law partner, Noel, who was not charged with murder. Both defendants were sentenced to four years in prison.[62]

In 2005 a panel of three judges on the First District Court of Appeals held that the trial judge had not properly interpreted the law. The appellate court sent the case back to the trial court for reconsideration. The appellate court held that the prosecutor was not required by law to prove that the defendant knew that the dog might kill but only that she knew that by taking the dog "outside of her apartment without a muzzle, she was endangering the life of another. The key to the issue is her conscious disregard for the life of another person." In 2007, the California Supreme Court reversed the decision of the intermediate appellate court and remanded the case to that court with instructions to send it back to the trial court with instructions to reconsider.[63] That was done; the second-degree murder charge was reinstated in 2008, and Knoller was sentenced to from 15 years to life in prison.

Types of Manslaughter

Under the common law, manslaughter was divided into two types for the purpose of distinguishing different kinds of conduct but not for the purposes of differential punishment. Some jurisdictions have retained these categories, while others define *manslaughter* in terms of degrees; still others use only the one term *manslaughter*. The types of manslaughter are examined more closely in the following sections.

Voluntary Manslaughter

An unlawful killing that does not involve malice aforethought but that occurs after adequate provocation may be classified as **voluntary manslaughter**, in which the killing must occur after such provocation by the victim that even reasonable people could be expected to react violently. It must be proved that the particular defendant was provoked, that a reasonable person would not have cooled off between the time of the provocation and the killing, and that the defendant did not cool off. For example, California defines *voluntary manslaughter* as an unlawful killing of a human being

without malice committed "upon a sudden quarrel or heat of passion."[64]

This discussion of voluntary manslaughter includes an explanation of the types of the crime plus an analysis of the reasonable person standard used to determine whether a specific killing falls within the category of voluntary manslaughter.

Heat-of-Passion Manslaughter

Voluntary manslaughter may be called *heat-of-passion homicide* or *heat-of-passion voluntary manslaughter*. *Heat of passion* was the term used under the common law (and followed by some states) to describe this type of voluntary manslaughter. Some states also include extreme emotional or mental disturbance within this form of manslaughter.

A Utah case, *State v. Standiford*, illustrates a modern reaction to these concepts. Fred W. Standiford was convicted of second-degree murder after he killed a person, whom he "claimed came after him with a gun, screaming in Japanese, and grabbed him. He [Standiford] seized the closest weapon, a kitchen knife, intending only to scare her, and since the threat of the knife did not stop her, he just started swinging the knife." Standiford appealed on several grounds, including his argument that the trial court erred in refusing to give his requested heat-of-passion manslaughter instruction. In the full opinion the Utah Supreme Court criticized the common law term malice aforethought, which it described as "a confusing carry-over from prior law [that] . . . can lead to confusion, if not error [and that] should no longer be used." The court said that other mental state requirements should be used, and the following excerpt begins with a listing of the requirements for second-degree murder, stating why these are preferable to the concept of malice aforethought. The court explained heat-of-passion manslaughter before upholding the trial court in its refusal to give a jury instruction on the latter.[65]

STATE v. STANDIFORD
769 P.2d 254 (Utah, 1988)

 [T]he culpable mental states included in the second degree murder statute are (1) an intent to kill, (2) an intent to inflict serious bodily harm, (3) conduct knowingly engaged in and evidencing a depraved indifference to human life, and (4) intent to commit a felony other than murder.

These terms are comparable to the old malice afore-thought, but are much more precise and less confusing. The statute treats these forms of homicide as having similar culpability. Second degree murder is based on a very high degree of moral culpability. That culpability arises either from an actual intent to kill or from a mental state that is essentially equivalent thereto—such as intending grievous bodily injury and knowingly creating a very high risk of death. The risk of death in the latter two instances must be so great as to evidence such an indifference to life as to be tantamount to that evidenced by an intent to kill. In contrast, the felony-murder provision of the second degree murder statute is something of an exception to the above principle, as it does not require an intent to kill or any similar mental state. . . .

Defendant also challenges the trial court's refusal to give his requested heat-of-passion manslaughter instruction. The common law, and our previous law, defined manslaughter, *inter alia* [among other things], as a killing committed without malice, and the term *without malice* meant a homicide committed either (1) in the "heat of passion" for which there was an adequate provocation, or (2) by an unduly dangerous or otherwise unlawful act. Instead of incorporating the "heat of passion" standard, the current criminal code redefined that type of manslaughter to describe the conduct of one who "causes the death of another under the influence of extreme emotional disturbance for which there is a reasonable explanation or excuse." . . . This definition reformulates and enlarges the heat-of-passion standard to include any extreme emotional disturbance based on a reasonable excuse or explanation that mitigates the blameworthiness of the homicide.

 [The court held that Standiford's contention that this killing fell within the "extreme emotional disturbance" category was "without merit."]

Manslaughter in Domestic Relations
The difficulty of drawing the line between murder and voluntary manslaughter is illustrated by the approach taken by the common law and many modern statutes to cases in which a husband killed his wife when he caught her engaging in the act of adultery. It was assumed that seeing one's wife in such a compromising situation was sufficient provocation for killing the lover or the wife. The Texas statute, which was not repealed until 1974, provided as follows:

> Homicide is justifiable when committed by the husband upon one taken in the act of adultery with the wife, provided the killing take place before the par-

ties to the act have separated. Such circumstance cannot justify a homicide where it appears that there has been, on the part of the husband, any connivance in or assent to the adulterous connection.[66]

A few jurisdictions extended this rule to women who caught their husbands in the act of adultery and killed the husband or his lover, but most considered these acts murder. These provisions are no longer in existence. A 1977 Georgia decision explains why: "Any idea that a spouse is ever justified in taking the life of another—adulterous spouse or illicit lover—to prevent adultery is uncivilized."[67]

Some jurisdictions that treated domestic homicides as manslaughter (or justifiable homicide) rather than murder required that the exception was appropriate only when the offended spouse caught the spouse and his or her lover in the adulterous act and the killing followed immediately. Other jurisdictions extended the concept of voluntary manslaughter to spousal killings that followed being told of adultery, even if that report was erroneous but reasonable.[68]

In 1989 the Illinois Supreme Court held that a confession of adultery is not sufficient to reduce a killing from murder to manslaughter. In *People v. Chevalier*, the court refused to reverse the convictions in two cases in which persons killed their adulterous spouses. In one case the defendant killed his wife after she jeered at his sexual abilities and confessed that she had committed adultery. In the other case the defendant killed his wife after she confessed to having committed adultery in their bed.[69]

Despite the demise of adultery as a condition for reducing murder to manslaughter, other circumstances may warrant a manslaughter rather than a murder charge. Words, fights, and other situations that would lead a reasonable person to kill may suffice, depending on the jurisdiction's statutes and case law.

It is important to understand that in these circumstances the law is not meant to imply that it is permissible to kill (as it is permissible to do in self-defense or to protect the life of another). Manslaughter statutes recognize that it is reasonable to be provoked to kill under circumstances that do not warrant justifiable or excusable homicide. The person who kills is criminally responsible, though not to the extent of murder. The concept of reasonableness is crucial in deciding whether a killing constitutes murder or manslaughter. The concept of the reasonable person requires further explanation.

The Reasonable Person Standard

The reasonable person (or objective) standard is critical in deciding whether a homicide constitutes voluntary manslaughter or murder. Two English cases illustrate the difference. In the first case an impotent defendant, who had killed a prostitute when she laughed at his unsuccessful attempts to have sexual intercourse with her, argued unsuccessfully that his behavior should be measured by what a reasonable impotent man would do. The House of Lords held that the behavior of a reasonable person, not a reasonable person with the peculiar characteristics of the defendant, is the test. It upheld the jury's verdict for murder, despite the defendant's argument that, had the jurors been instructed that the standard is how a reasonable impotent man would react to such provocation, they might have returned a verdict of manslaughter.[70]

In 1978 the House of Lords reached a different result in a case involving a 15-year-old who killed an older man who sexually molested and then mocked him. The jury was instructed to view the defendant's behavior in terms of how a reasonable adult would act under the same or similar circumstances. The House of Lords ruled that the jury should have been instructed to consider how a reasonable person of the same age would have acted under the same or similar circumstances.[71]

The two English cases raise the issue of whether the reasonable person standard in a criminal case should be interpreted to mean that a defendant should be judged in terms of the reasonable person endowed with all of that defendant's characteristics. The reasonable person standard is important in manslaughter cases because the rationale behind a manslaughter (as opposed to a murder) charge is that reasonable people, when sufficiently provoked, will react without thinking. If they kill, they should be responsible for the death, but not to the extent of murder.

In some cases, courts have held that provocation resulting from battery, adultery, mutual combat, assault, injury to third parties, illegal arrest, or fighting words constitutes adequate provocation to reduce a killing from murder to manslaughter. Various courts interpret these categories differently. Attempts have been made to define the relevant terms in the statutes. Two examples are noted. Do they make it clear to you which facts would fall within these definitions?

> *Heat of passion* . . . means that at the time of the act the reason is disturbed or obscured by passion to an extent which might [make] ordinary men of fair, average disposition liable to act irrationally without due deliberation or reflection, and from passion rather than judgment.
>
> [*Sudden provocation* was defined as follows:]
>
> [H]eat of passion will not avail unless upon sudden provocation. Sudden means happening without previous notice or with very brief notice; coming unexpectedly, precipitated, or unlooked for. . . . It is not every provocation, it is not every rage of passion that will reduce a killing from murder to manslaughter. The provocation must be of such a character and so close upon the act of killing, that for a moment a person could be considered as not being the master of his own understanding.[72]

Some jurisdictions have extended voluntary manslaughter beyond the heat-of-passion or extreme emotional problem situations. Most of these extensions have occurred by statute rather than by case law. Examples are situations in which defendants advance defenses such as self-defense, the right to prevent a felony, or acting under coercion or duress, but cannot prove all of the elements of the defense. In these cases, murder may be reduced to manslaughter.

As with most crimes, attempt crimes are permissible with voluntary manslaughter (although not with involuntary manslaughter, which by definition is not an intentional killing).

Involuntary Manslaughter

The crime of **involuntary manslaughter** is a killing that is committed recklessly but unintentionally, as when one is under the influence of alcohol or other drugs. Usually this category of manslaughter applies to a killing that results when the defendant is engaged in a criminal act that is less serious than a felony.

The California Penal Code defines *involuntary manslaughter* as an unlawful killing of a human being without malice "in the commission of an unlawful act, not amounting to felony; or in the commission of a lawful act which might produce death, in an unlawful manner, or without due caution and circumspection."[73]

Misdemeanor or Negligent Manslaughter

In some jurisdictions involuntary manslaughter is called *misdemeanor manslaughter*. Involuntary manslaughter may also include deaths that occur as the result of **negligent manslaughter**, which is a killing that is not lawful or justified but does not involve malice, only negligence. For example, Alaska criminal statutes provide: "A person commits the crime of criminally negligent homicide if, with criminal negligence, the person causes the death of another person."[74] In addition, misdemeanor or negligent manslaughter charges may be brought in cases in which a parent's negligence results in a child's death.

An example of a case involving multiple counts of involuntary manslaughter occurred in Rhode Island after a fatal nightclub fire in 2003. Jeffrey A. Derderian and his brother Michael A. Derderian, owners of the nightclub, were indicted for involuntary manslaughter, along with Daniel M. Biechele, who was the tour manager for the band Great White. The fire started when Biechele set off three pyrotechnic devices, creating sparks, which ignited the polyurethane that had been installed to reduce sound. Approximately 400 people were inside the building, which quickly burst into flames, killing 100 people and injuring 200. According to the state's attorney general, the brothers were charged with criminal negligence based on the way in which they operated the club and misdemeanor manslaughter because they allegedly did not maintain the soundproofing in a fireproof manner. The criminal negligence charges against Biechele stemmed from allegations that he discharged the devices negligently. The manslaughter charges were based on the failure of the band to get a permit to use fireworks inside the building.[75]

Biechele, who agreed to testify against the Derderian brothers, pleaded guilty to 100 counts of involuntary manslaughter, after which the criminal negligence charges were dropped. Biechele, who was sentenced to four years in prison, was released on parole in March 2008 after serving 22 months. His request for parole was supported by numerous relatives of the fire's victims. The Derderian brothers entered no contest pleas to involuntary manslaughter charges. Jeffrey Derderian was sentenced to 500 hours of community service and three years on probation. Michael Derderian was sentenced to four years in prison. He will be paroled in October 2009.[76]

Vehicular and DUI Manslaughter

Another type of manslaughter is *vehicular manslaughter*, which usually encompasses numerous types of vehicular homicides, including those caused by gross negligence. Some states include within this category a killing that results from an accident while the driver is intoxicated (driving under the influence, or DUI; if death results, the act may be charged as a DUI manslaughter). California, for example, has a statutory provision for the crime of *gross vehicular manslaughter while intoxicated*, a felony punishable by imprisonment in the state prison for 4, 6, or 10 years. This statute, however, requires more than just being over the legal drinking limit, just as gross negligence in speeding requires more than being slightly over the speeding limit.[77]

California also has a statute for *vehicular manslaughter,* which involves—except as provided in the statute regarding gross vehicular manslaughter—"operating a vessel in the commission of an unlawful act, not amounting to felony, and with gross negligence; or operating a vessel in the commission of a lawful act which might produce death, in an unlawful manner, and with gross negligence."[78]

Recall the discussion earlier in this chapter concerning the inclusion of a fetus in a murder statute. Florida has a statute on *vehicular homicide*, defined as "the killing of a human being, or the killing of a viable fetus by any injury to the mother, caused by the operation of a motor vehicle by another in a reckless manner likely to cause the death of, or great bodily harm to, another."[79]

Deaths that result from accidents occurring while defendants are under the influence of alcohol or other drugs may also be prosecuted as involuntary manslaughter if the state does not have a vehicular homicide or DUI manslaughter statute. Such acts may also be prosecuted as murder if the prosecution has evidence that would take the case beyond that of manslaughter and shows evidence of intent. Thus, Dallas County (Texas) jurors convicted Sarah Foust of murder in a case in which she backed her car at a waitress (who chased after Foust, who was legally drunk, and her friends when they left the restaurant without paying a $135 bill); the waitress was thrown on top of the car; Foust accelerated; the victim was thrown off the car and killed after Foust turned the car sharply.[80] Two of Foust's friends were each sentenced to 30 days in jail; a third was given a 30-day jail sentence. Foust was sentenced to life in prison. A murder conviction for automobile accidents is very unusual.

In cases involving negligent drivers, it is important to recall earlier discussions of discretion in criminal justice systems. Prosecutors have wide discretion in deciding whether to prosecute these cases. They may, and frequently do, decline to prosecute drivers whose negligence causes death to others when the drivers were neither speeding excessively nor driving under the influence of alcohol or other drugs.

Failure-to-Act Manslaughter

Manslaughter charges may be brought when failure to act is the crime, as illustrated by a California case in which an appellate court upheld the manslaughter conviction of a petitioner who did not summon help for an obviously intoxicated guest in her home. The guest had injected himself with heroin in the petitioner's presence, and she made no attempt to stop him. The defendant had met the victim at a bar, invited him to her home, given him a spoon, and let him use her bathroom for the injection. She knew that he intended to inject himself with the drug. After the victim emerged from the bathroom and collapsed on the floor and the defendant tried unsuccessfully to rouse him, she conferred with the bartender by phone and then returned to the bar.

The petitioner's daughter returned home later that afternoon, found the unconscious guest, called the bar, and was told by her mother to drag him outside and hide him behind the shed so neighbors could not see him. The daughter and two friends did so. They checked on him that night and found that he still had a pulse and was snoring, but by the next morning he was dead. An autopsy revealed that the cause of death was morphine poisoning, resulting from the heroin he had injected. The petitioner's argument that she did not cause the death because she did not cause his condition was unsuccessful. The court noted that the deceased was extremely drunk when the petitioner took him from a public place to her home, a private place, in which only she could provide assistance. Thus, she owed him a legal duty and, having breached that duty, was criminally responsible for his death.[81]

SUMMARY

This chapter focused on the violent acts of murder and manslaughter, two types of homicide. Homicide occurs when a human being kills another human being by his or her own act, omission, or procurement. Thus, homicide refers to killings that are justifiable or excusable (such as killings by police officers under some circumstances and killings by anyone when the use of deadly force is necessary for self-defense or the defense of others) as well as to killings that are not legally acceptable and thus may result in criminal responsibility.

Confusion over the differences among justifiable, excusable, and criminal homicides, the three categories of the common law, has led some jurisdictions to abandon those categories. Most divide homicides into two categories: murder and manslaughter, the approach taken in this chapter. Some states follow the common law distinctions, while others have a mixture of both or some other version.

In some cases confusion may arise over what is meant by *human being* and what is meant by *death*, for criminal homicide must involve a person who was alive at the time the alleged criminal act occurred. These issues are particularly confusing with the advent of modern medicine that prolongs life, the desire of some to be able to terminate (or have terminated) their lives, and the legalization of abortion.

Causation is frequently a difficult problem in homicide cases, especially when two or more acts may contribute to the victim's death. Some courts look to the intent of the offender; evidence of a criminal intent may be sufficient to establish criminal culpability when actual causation is mixed. Some states require that the defendant's act must have been a substantial factor in the victim's death.

The difficulties of determining the cause (or causes) of death led the common law to adopt the year-and-a-day rule. Modern science gives us greater accuracy and speed in determining the cause of death; thus, some states have abandoned the rule, while others, such as California, have retained it but extended the rule to a longer time period.

Distinguishing between murder and manslaughter may present problems in homicide prosecutions. Usually murder requires premeditation and malice aforethought, which may be expressed or implied from other facts. Manslaughter is an unlawful killing without malice. But the word *malice* is confusing, too, because it does not necessarily mean hatred or ill will but, rather, an evil motive. Some jurisdictions have abandoned this requirement, but even in those that no longer require the element of malice aforethought, the concept may be used to distinguish first-degree from lesser degrees of murder. In general, first-degree murder includes deliberate, premeditated, intent-to-kill murders as well as felony murders.

Second-degree murder may be defined in terms of murder that is not first-degree. Included might be deaths that occur while an offender is engaged in another criminal act that is not included in the felony-murder category. Also included might be intent-to-kill murders that are not deliberate or premeditated, depraved heart murders, and intent-to-inflict-serious-bodily-harm murders.

Acts that under other circumstances might be considered murder may not be classified as such if they involve physician-assisted suicide. The U.S. Supreme Court has upheld the right of states to ban physician-assisted suicide, but Oregon and Washington have enacted statutes permitting such actions.

Second-degree murder may be difficult to distinguish from manslaughter, which may be divided into two categories. *Voluntary manslaughter* is a killing that would be murder except that it is committed under circumstances of extreme mental or emotional disturbance (or in the heat of passion); *involuntary manslaughter* is a criminal killing that is committed recklessly but unintentionally, usually during the commission of an unlawful act, such as driving while intoxicated. In addition, acts that do not reach the level of voluntary manslaughter may be called *misdemeanor manslaughter*, *vehicular manslaughter*, or *failure-to-act-manslaughter*.

This chapter is not meant to be exhaustive in its discussion of murder and manslaughter. Both crimes involve many legal fine points that are beyond the scope of this text. Nor is it meant to suggest that these crimes are more important or create more fear than other violent crimes. In many cases the emotional and psychological scars may be far greater for victims of less violent or even nonviolent crimes.

Chapter 7 focuses on assault and battery, rape, and other violent crimes, as well as less violent crimes. Some of these crimes against the person involve consent and are considered by many people to be private matters that should be beyond the reach of the criminal law; others involve the exploitation of victims and engender little dispute when they are defined as crimes, especially when the victims are children.

STUDY QUESTIONS

1. Define *homicide,* and distinguish justifiable and excusable from criminal homicide.

2. What are the three types of criminal homicide?

3. What is infanticide, and how is it related to modern criminal law? What is the meaning of *born alive*? How has its meaning changed in recent years?

4. What is the meaning of *person* in homicide statutes?

5. Define *death* for legal purposes.

6. What causation problems does homicide present?

7. What is the year-and-a-day rule? Why have some states abandoned or revised it?

8. What is *corpus delicti*? How important is that concept today compared to the past?

9. Distinguish between murder and manslaughter.

10. List and define the basic elements of murder.

11. What is meant by *malice aforethought*?

12. Explain what is meant by these types of murder: intent to kill, intent to inflict great bodily harm, and depraved heart.

13. What is felony murder? Murder for hire?

14. Distinguish between first- and second-degree murder.

15. What is meant by *lesser included offense*? How does that concept apply to murder?

16. What are the legal and moral issues surrounding physician-assisted suicide? How should they be resolved?

17. Name and define the types of manslaughter.

18. Explain the application of the reasonable person concept to manslaughter cases.

FOR DEBATE

As medical science improves our chances of living longer, some people are questioning whether they wish to do so if they are suffering from painful diseases. A few have chosen to take their own lives or have asked others, even physicians, to help them. Only one jurisdiction in the United States, Oregon, permitted physician-assisted suicide until November 2008, when the state of Washington also approved it. The U.S. Supreme Court has upheld the right of a state to permit physician-assisted suicide, but it has refused to recognize a constitutional right to the practice. This debate issue is designed to assist students in exploring the legal, practical, moral, and ethical implications of physician-assisted suicide.

Resolved: Physician-assisted suicide should be considered a constitutionally protected right; in the alternative, states should enact statutes to permit it, but strict safeguards should be part of the provisions.

KEY TERMS

Baby Moses laws, 145

crime rate, 140

crimes known to the police, 140

excusable homicide, 140

felony murder, 154

fetal alcohol syndrome, 142

homicide, 140

infanticide, 141

CASE ANALYSIS

STATE V. ASHLEY

670 So.2d 1087 (Fla.App.2d Dist. 1996),
quashed, in part, certified question answered,
701 So.2d 338 (Fla. 1997).

Case Preview

This chapter discussed the meaning of a person for purposes of murder and manslaughter statutes. Recall that under the common law a fetus was not considered a person but that some states (such as California) have changed their statutes to include a fetus. Thus, Scott Peterson was found guilty of two murders in the death of his wife and their unborn son: first-degree murder in the case of Laci, his wife, and second-degree murder for the death of her fetus.

This case presents a rather unusual situation in that the pregnant woman, Kawana Ashley, was not injured by another person. Rather, she sought to end her pregnancy by shooting herself in the stomach. When the injuries to her fetus resulted in its death, the state of Florida charged Ashley with manslaughter and third-degree murder. The murder charge was dismissed; the state appealed and Ashley cross-appealed. The issues before the Florida Supreme Court were certified questions from the District Court of Appeal for the Second Circuit. The Florida Supreme Court answered the questions. The decision was *per curiam*, which means by the whole court, or a decision in which all the justices joined, in contrast to an opinion that is authored by one (or more) justice(s).

Ashley was charged with third-degree murder, which Florida defines as "[t]he unlawful killing of a human being, when perpetrated without any design to effect death, by a person engaged in the perpetration of, or in the attempt to perpetrate, any felony other than any" of several listed serious felonies. Ashley was also charged with manslaughter, which the state statute defines as "[t]he killing of a human being by the act, procurement, or culpable negligence of another, without lawful justification according to the provisions of [the statute] and in cases in which such killing shall not be excusable homicide or

murder." Finally, Ashley was charged with violating the state's abortion statute.

The state's argument was that when Ashley attempted to perform an abortion on herself, she violated the provisions of the abortion law and that because the fetus died as a result, she committed third-degree murder.

When reading the excerpted opinion, note the discussion of the common law. In its opinion the court stated, "Our review of the present record reveals no novel legislative intent to trump the common law and pit woman against fetus in criminal court."

Per Curiam

Facts

Although Kawana Ashley, an unwed teenager, was in her third trimester of pregnancy (she was twenty-five or twenty-six weeks pregnant), she had told no one. Her three-year old son was being raised by her grandmother, Rosa, with whom Ashley lived, and Rosa had told Ashley that she would not care for another child if Ashley were to become pregnant again. On March 27, 1994, Ashley obtained a gun and shot herself. She was rushed to the hospital, underwent surgery, and survived. The fetus, which had been struck on the wrist by the bullet, was removed during surgery and died fifteen days later due to immaturity. Ashley had given conflicting reasons for her actions. She initially told officers that she had been the victim of a drive-by shooting, but later said she had shot herself "in order to hurt the baby." She told another officer, however, that she had not tried to kill the baby and wanted the baby, and told a friend that the gun had discharged accidently. As a result of the death of the fetus, the State Attorney charged the teenager with alternative counts of murder and manslaughter, with the underlying felony for the murder charge being criminal abortion.

Issues

We have for review . . . the following questions:

1 May an expectant mother be criminally charged with the death of her born alive child resulting from self-inflicted injuries during the third trimester of pregnancy?

2 If so, may she be charged with manslaughter or third-degree murder, the underlying predicate felony being abortion or attempted abortion?

Holding

We answer the first question in the negative as explained below, and this renders the second question moot.

Rationale

At common law, while a third party could be held criminally liable for causing injury or death to a fetus, the pregnant woman could not be. . . .

The woman was viewed as the victim of the crime. The criminal laws were intended to protect, not punish her.

The common law that was in effect on July 4, 1776, continues to be the law of Florida to the extent that it is consistent with the constitutions and statutory laws of the United States and Florida. . . .

The presumption is that no change in the common law is intended unless the statute is explicit and clear in that regard. Unless a statute unequivocally states that it changes the common law, or is so repugnant to the common law that the two cannot coexist, the statute will not be held to have changed the common law.

In the present case, none of the statutes under which Ashley was charged "unequivocally" state that they alter the common law doctrine conferring immunity on the pregnant woman. In fact, none even hint at such a change. Nor are any of the statutes so repugnant to the common law that the two cannot coexist. Accordingly, we conclude that the legislature did not abrogate the common law doctrine of immunity for the pregnant woman. . . .

The State's reading of the present statutes has other flaws. First, the concept of a self-induced abortion via .22 caliber bullet is dubious in itself and is highly questionable as a procedure intended to be regulated by [the statute]. Second, prosecution for third-degree murder based on the unenumerated felony of criminal abortion is an oxymoron—i.e., the third-degree murder statute requires an accidental killing, while the criminal abortion statute requires an intentional termination of pregnancy. Under the State Attorney's scenario, a woman could be charged with, and face imprisonment for, an "accidental intentional" crime—whatever that phrase might mean. And third, to allow prosecution for manslaughter would require that this Court extend the "born alive" doctrine in a manner that has been rejected by every other court to consider it. . . .

We reached a similar result in [another case] wherein we held that a pregnant woman cannot be held criminally liable for passing cocaine in utero to her fetus. The relevant statutory section, we concluded, contained no indication of legislative intent to prosecute the woman. Medical science prescribes rehabilitation, not imprisonment, for the offender: [Various] considerations have led the American Medical Association Board of Trustees to oppose criminal sanctions for harmful behavior by a pregnant woman toward her fetus and to advocate that pregnant [offenders] be provided with rehabilitative treatment appropriate to their specific psychological and physiological needs. This prescription for rehabilitation applies to not just the mature woman, but the wayward teenager as well.

For Discussion

The Florida Supreme Court is essentially saying that in order to prosecute a woman for self-inflicted injuries that kill her fetus, the legislature must specifically create a law that abrogates the common law immunity provided to pregnant women in these circumstances. Do you agree or disagree with the outcome of this case? Other states have passed these types of laws; for example, in Oklahoma a statute provides: "Every woman who solicits of any person any medicine, drug, or substance whatever, and takes the same, or who submits to any operation, or to the use of any means whatever, with intent thereby to procure a miscarriage, unless the same is necessary to preserve her life, is punishable by imprisonment."[82]

If you were a legislator would you pass such a law to allow future prosecutions? This law would apply to drug-addicted women as well. Would that result in prosecuting pregnant women for their status, that is, being drug addicts? Would you support that interpretation of the statute? Why or why not? What problems or issues concerning criminal intent and causation might arise in prosecuting a case similar to the *Ashley* case under the Oklahoma law?

INTERNET ACTIVITY

To find out more about different types of murders, serial killers, notorious killers, and the criminal mind, go to Court TV's Crime Library website at http://www.crimelibrary.com/index.html (accessed 30 November 2008). Choose a murderer or a murder investigation, and examine the information. Based on your understanding of the murder or murder investigation and the information from this chapter, determine whether the murder described would qualify as an aggravated murder, whether there was an intent to kill, whether there was intent to inflict great bodily harm, whether the murder resulted from a depraved heart, whether there was an intent to commit a felony, and/or whether it was a murder for hire. What evidence supports your finding?

NOTES

1. Federal Bureau of Investigation, *Crime in the United States: Uniform Crime Reports* 2007," http://www.fbi.gov/ucr/cius2007/offenses/violent_crime/index.html, accessed 30 November 2008.
2. Rev. Code Wash., Title 9A, Section 9A.32.010 (2008).
3. "Hostage Kills Captor—at His Pleading," *San Francisco Chronicle* (26 March 1996), p. 13.
4. See Tex. Penal Code, Title 1, Section 1.07(26) (2009).
5. "Pregnant Woman's Shot Not Murder," *St. Petersburg Times* (23 March 1996), p. 1. The case is *State v. Ashley*, 670 So.2d 1087 (Fla.App.2d Dist. 1996), *quashed, in part, certified question answered*, 701 So.2d 338 (Fla. 1997).

6. See *People v. Chavez*, 176 P.2d 92 (Cal. 1947).

7. "Doctor Sentenced in Infant's Death," *New York Times* (20 December 1989), p. 14. The case is *Brokans v. Melnick*, 569 A.2d 1373 (Pa.Super.Ct. 1989), *appeal denied*, 584 A.2d 310 (Pa. 1990).

8. *People v. Davis*, 872 P.2d 591 (Cal. 1994). The revised statute is Calif. Penal Code, Section 187(a) (2008).

9. *Taylor v. State*, 86 P.3d 881 (Cal. 2004).

10. Minn. Stat. Section 609.2661 (2007). Second-degree murder of an unborn child is codified at Minn. Stat., Section 609.2662 (2007).

11. *State v. Deborah J.Z.*, 596 N.W.2d 490 (Wis.App. 1998), *review denied*, 604 N.S.2d 570 (Wis. 1999).

12. Wis. Stat., Section 48.193 (2007).

13. Wis. Stat., Section 940.01 (2007) (first-degree intentional homicide); Wis. Stat., Section 940.02 (2007) (first-degree reckless homicide).

14. MCLS, Section 750.322 (2008).

15. Unborn Victims of Violence Act of 2004, U.S. Code, Chapter 18, Section 90A (2009).

16. "Texas Idea Takes Off: States Look to Safe Haven Laws as a Protection for Abandoned Infants," *American Bar Association Journal* 87 (September 2001), p. 30.

17. "National Briefing/Nebraska: California Teen Is Last to Be Abandoned Under Law," *Los Angeles Times* (23 November 2008), p. 28A. See also the Nebraska Safe Haven Act, 2007 Bill Tracking Report, NE L.B. 3A.

18. Tex. Penal Code, Section 22.041(h) (2009).

19. Tex. Fam. Code, Section 262.302 (2009).

20. *In re T.A.C.P.*, 609 So.2d 588 (Fla. 1992).

21. *State v. Cross*, 401 S.E.2d 510 (Ga. 1991).

22. *State v. Rogers*, 992 S.W.2d 393 (Tenn. 1999), *aff'd.*, 532 U.S. 451 (2001).

23. Cal Pen Code, Section 194 (2008).

24. *State v. Hills*, 605 P.2d 893, 894 (Ariz. 1980), citing *State v. Sauter*, 585 P.2d 242 (Ariz. 1978).

25. *Kibbe v. Henderson*, 534 F.2d 493 (2d Cir. 1976), *rev'd.*, *Henderson v. Kibbe*, 431 U.S. 145 (1977), footnotes and citations omitted.

26. *Henderson v. Kibbe*, 431 U.S. 145, 156 (1977).

27. "Leader of O'Hair Plot Admits to Another Slaying," *Austin American Statesman* (18 April 2002), p. 2B.

28. Federal Bureau of Investigation, *Crime in the United States: Uniform Crime Reports* 2007: Murder," http://www.fbi.gov/ucr/cius2007/offenses/violent_crime/murder_homicide.html, accessed 30 November 2008.

29. Federal Bureau of Investigation, *Crime in the United States: Uniform Crime Reports* 2007: Clearances," http://www.fbi.gov/ucr/cius2007/offenses/clearances/index.html, accessed 30 November 2008.

30. Cal Pen Code, Section 188 (2008).

31. *Keys v. State*, 766 P.2d 270, 271 (Nev. 1988), quoting *Moser v. State*, 544 P.2d 424, 426 (Nev. 1975).

32. Iowa Code, Title 16, Section 707.1 (2008).

33. ORS, Title 16, Section 163.095 (2007).

34. *Willar v. People*, 30 Mich. 16 (1874).

35. Calif. Penal Code, Section 189 (2008).

36. See Model Penal Code, Section 210.2, Comment 1, pp. 13–15.

37. Miss. Code Ann., Section 97-3-19 (2008).

38. M.R.S., Title 17-A, Section 202 1. (2008).

39. M.R.S., Title 17-A, Section 202 2. A, B, C, D (2008).

40. ALM GL, Chapter 265, Section 1 (2008).

41. *Enmund v. Florida*, 458 U.S. 782 (1982).

42. *Tison v. Arizona*, 481 U.S. 137 (1987).

43. *People v. Brackett*, 510 N.E.2d 877 (Ill. 1987).

44. *State v. Pierce*, 788 P.2d 352 (N.M. 1990).

45. *People v. Patterson*, 778 P.2d 549 (Cal. 1989).

46. *State v. Jones*, 516 S.E.2d 405 (N.C.Ct.App. 1999), *aff'd. in part and rev'd. in part, remanded*, 538 S.E.2d 917 (N.C. 2000). The felony murder statute is N.C. Gen. Stat, Section 14–17 (2008).

47. Utah Criminal Code, Section 76-5-202(h) (2008).

48. ARCW, Section 10.95.020(4)(5)(2008).

49. "Seattle Times Staff and News Services," *Seattle Times* (6 April 2002), p. 3B; "Grote Gets 50 Years in Heimann Slaying," *Seattle Times* (24 April 2003), p. 2B. The case is *State v. Oliver*, 2003 Wash. App. LEXIS 2337 (Wash.Ct.App. 2003), reported at *State v. Oliver*, 118 Wn. App. 1067 (2003), *review denied*, 94 P.3d 959 (Wash. 2004).

50. Tex. Penal Code, Title 5, Section 19.03 (2009).

51. Cal Pen Code, Section 189 (2008).

52. *State v. Guerra*, 778 P.2d 1185, 1189-1190 (Ariz. 1989), emphasis not in the original jury instruction but added by the appellate court in this opinion.

53. Iowa Code, Title 16, Section 707.3 (2008).

54. *State v. Bingham*, 699 P.2d 262, 265 (Wash.Ct.App. 1985), *aff'd.*, 719 P.2d 109 (Wash. 1986).

55. *Washington v. Glucksberg*, 521 U.S. 702 (1997); *Vacco v. Quill*, 521 U.S. 793 (1997).

56. *Oregon v. Ashcroft*, 368 F.3d 1118 (9th Cir. 2004), *aff'd.*, 546 U.S. 243 (2006).

57. The Washington statute that prohibited physician-assisted suicide, Wash. Rev. Code 70.122.100 (2008), entitled "Mercy Killing or Physician Assisted Suicide not Authorized," was rewritten by Initiative Measure 1000, adopted at the 4 November 2008 election and now permits physician-assisted suicide. For the Montana case adoption of physician-assisted suicide, see *Baxter v. State*, 2008 Mont. Dist. Lexis 482 (5 December 2008).

58. "Suicide Doctor Wins Dismissal," *American Bar Association Journal* 77 (February 1991): 22.

59. "Kevorkian Sentenced to 10 to 25 Years in Prison," *New York Times* (14 January 1999), p. 1.

60. "Kevorkian Conviction Upheld by Mich. App. Court,"

Nursing Home Litigation 3, no. 7 (February 2002): 4. The case is *People v. Kevorkian*, 639 N.W.2d 291 (Mich. App. 2001), *cert. denied sub nom.*, 537 U.S. 888 (2002).

61. Calif. Penal Code, Section 192 (2008).

62. "Appeal for Murder Rap in Dog-Maul Case," *San Francisco Chronicle* (12 April 2003), p. 15.

63. *People v. Noel*, 2005 Cal.App.LEXIS 725 (Cal.App.1st Dist., 6 May 2005), and *rev'd., remanded, superseded sub nom.*, 158 P.3d 731 (Cal 2007).

64. Calif. Penal Code, Section 192(a) (2008).

65. *State v. Standiford*, 769 P.2d 254, 259, 268 (Utah 1988), citations omitted.

66. Tex. Crim. Code, Article 1220, repealed in 1974. See *Shaw v. State*, 510 S.W.2d 926 (Tex.Crim.Ct.App. 1974).

67. See, for example, *Burger v. State*, 231 S.E.2d 769 (Ga. 1977).

68. See, for example, *State v. Yanz*, 50 A. 37 (Conn. 1901).

69. *People v. Chevalier*, 544 N.E.2d 942 (Ill. 1989).

70. *Bedder v. Director of Public Prosecutions*, 2 All E.R. 801 (House of Lords, 1954).

71. *Director of Public Prosecutions v. Camplin*, 2 All E.R. 168 (House of Lords 1978).

72. Maine trial court's instructions as quoted by the U.S. Supreme Court in *Mullaney v. Wilbur*, 421 U.S. 684, 687 (1975).

73. Calif. Penal Code, Section 192(b) (2008).

74. Alaska Stat., Section 11.41.130(a) (2008).

75. "3 Men Are Indicted in Fire at Rhode Island Nightclub," *New York Times* (10 December 2003), p. 14.

76. "Tentative Settlement Is Reached with TV Station in Fatal Nightclub Fire," *New York Times* (3 February 2008), p. 20.

77. Calif. Penal Code, Title 8, Section 191.5(c) (2008).

78. Calif. Penal Code, Title 8, Section 192.5 (2008).

79. Fla. Stat., Title 46, Section 782.071 (2009).

80. "Woman Who Hit Waitress Found Guilty of Murder," *Dallas Morning News* (20 July 2003), Domestic news section, n.p.

81. *People v. Oliver*, 258 Cal. Rptr. 138 (Cal.Ct.App. 1989), *review denied*, 1989 Cal. LEXIS 4188 (Cal. 1989).

82. Okla. Stat., Title 21, Section 862 (2008).

CHAPTER 7

Assault, Robbery, Rape, and Other Serious Crimes Against the Person

INTRODUCTION

Discrete, easily differentiated definitions of crimes are impossible. Perhaps this fact is illustrated most clearly by some of the crimes discussed in this chapter, for there is overlap between such crimes as forcible rape and forcible sodomy and the crimes of assault and battery. More specifically, some of the crimes against the person, such as aggravated sexual assault, may be indistinguishable from others, such as aggravated assault, except that they focus on sex. Likewise, robbery, which is discussed in this chapter, is a violent personal crime but is also a property crime.

Among the variety of crimes against the person included in this chapter, some are violent and some are consensual but occur in situations in which the law does not permit consent, such as sex with minors or others considered by law to be incapable of granting consent. Sex crimes against adults and children have become issues of national concern in recent years. Crimes that previously were considered either improper for discussion (such as sex with children) or merely a domestic concern (such as sexual violence in intimate personal relationships) are now viewed as serious violent crimes against the person.

In addition to discussing the historical approach to violent crimes against the person, this chapter focuses on some of the recent changes in legislation and case law in these areas. Although this text focuses on criminal law rather than criminal procedure, some procedural changes provide the basis for the criminal law prosecution. Where that occurs, they are noted.

The analysis begins with assault and battery, two crimes against the person whose treatment under law provides a basis for the modern-day approach to some of the other crimes analyzed in this chapter. The discussion continues with the violent crime of robbery. Forcible rape (and sodomy) complete the coverage of the violent personal crimes as categorized by the *Uniform Crime Reports (UCR)*. The chapter then turns to a look at child abuse and elder abuse.

The crimes of false imprisonment and kidnapping, although they are not by definition violent, often become so, and they are thus discussed in this chapter. Hate crimes, a relatively newly named type of crime, are also frequently violent. Likewise, although stalking does not require violence, it is a serious crime because it threatens the safety of its victims.

ASSAULT

The terms **assault** and **battery** are used together or interchangeably, but historically they were different crimes; each could occur without the other. *Assault* referred to the unlawful attempt or threat to inflict immediate harm or death, whereas *battery* referred to the unauthorized harmful or offensive touching of another. Under this approach, it is incorrect to say that A assaulted B when describing a physical attack by A on B. That is the battery, although it is quite possible that the battery was preceded by an assault, that is, a threat by A to inflict an immediate battery on B.

Under the common law assault and battery were misdemeanors. In most modern statutes, these crimes are categorized by degrees or types, and in many jurisdictions assault and battery are merged into one crime. Generally assault is categorized as simple or aggravated, and both categories may be subdivided.

SIMPLE ASSAULT

An example of a statute covering simple assault and battery—although referring to it only as *assault*—is that of Texas, which defines an *assault* as an act committed by one who:

(1) intentionally, knowingly, or recklessly causes bodily injury to another, including the person's spouse;

(2) intentionally or knowingly threatens another with imminent bodily injury, including the person's spouse; or

(3) intentionally or knowingly causes physical contact with another when the person knows or should reasonably believe that the other will regard the contact as offensive or provocative.[1]

Some jurisdictions require that for an act to be an assault there must be a threat of immediate harm or, as the Texas statute provides, *imminent* harm; an intent to frighten in the future will not be sufficient. Some jurisdictions require the present ability to succeed in carrying out the threat.

Simple assaults and batteries include acts that do not involve aggravation. The law recognizes that some unauthorized touchings are offensive even if they are not dangerous. For example, it has long been considered a battery to spit in the face of another. But not every offensive touching constitutes a battery. As with most areas of law, the difficulty is in drawing the line, particularly when the law permits the use of force to control people in some circumstances.

The case of *Government of Virgin Islands v. Stull* is illustrative. It involved a man who was disruptive in a bar described by its owner's attorney as "a waterfront saloon and poolroom which cannot be expected to attract clientele always likely to maintain the highest degree of order." On previous occasions the man had been told to leave because he was disruptive. On the occasion in question, when the customer refused to leave, Ray Stull grabbed him by the arm and led him to the door. The customer alleged that he was kicked. That claim was in dispute, but the trial court found Stull guilty of simple assault and battery. The appellate court vacated that decision with instructions to enter a verdict of not guilty. The following excerpt from the United States District Court for the District of the Virgin Islands opinion gives some of the reasons.[2]

GOVERNMENT OF VIRGIN ISLANDS v. STULL

280 F.Supp. 460 (V.I.Dist.Ct. 1968)

The Municipal Court apparently recognized, as this court does, that the owner of a bar or other public or semi-public place has the right to eject unwanted or disorderly persons from the premises. Indeed, the law is rather clear on this point:

> The owner, occupant, or person in charge of any public or semipublic place of business may request the departure of a person who does not rightfully belong there or who by his conduct has forfeited his right to be there, and may treat him as a trespasser, using reasonable force to eject him from the premises. . . .

Under the circumstances of the present case, the Court cannot see how appellant could have used any lesser degree of force in removing Matthew [a customer] from the premises, an act which he had the right to do. Matthew, in Stull's view, was causing a disturbance. He was told to leave. He objected. Whereupon Stull took him by the arm and led him out. It was not incumbent upon Stull to argue or plead with Matthew. His license to remain on the premises had been terminated, and reasonably so, as the court views the facts. His failure to leave when requested to do so authorized Stull to exercise a reasonable degree of force. Had Stull kicked Matthew, as Matthew alleged, this would be a different case, but the taking of Matthew by the arm and pushing, pulling, or leading him to the door was, in the Court's opinion, entirely reasonable and in fact the minimal amount of force employable under the circumstances.

Aggravated Assault

The most frequently committed of the four serious crimes as categorized and reported by the FBI's *UCR* is that of **aggravated assault**, which accounted for 60.7 percent of the four serious violent crimes reported by the FBI in 2007.[3] The volume of aggravated assaults in 2007 were down less than 1 percent over the 2006 volume but represented a 12.4 percent decline from 1998 and a 21.5 percent decline in the rate of aggravated assaults for that year.[4]

Aggravated assault may involve acts performed with the intention of committing another crime or acts accompanied by particularly outrageous or atrocious circumstances. This may include assault with a dangerous weapon. Notice that the District of Columbia statute does not require a weapon; the Florida statute, which follows, requires the use of a deadly weapon.

The District of Columbia Penal Code defines *aggravated assault* as follows:

(a) A person commits the offense of aggravated assault if:

(1) By any means, that person knowingly or purposely causes serious bodily injury to another person; or

(2) Under circumstances manifesting extreme indifference to human life, that person intentionally or knowingly engages in conduct which creates a grave risk of serious bodily injury to another person, and thereby causes serious bodily injury.[5]

In some cases aggravated assault charges are brought in conjunction with attempt crimes, such as aggravated assault with an attempt to commit rape, in which an assailant beats a victim brutally but does not complete the attempted rape. The degree of assault and the subsequent penalty may be greater when the accused is charged with an attempt to commit another felony. This is true particularly when a dangerous weapon is involved in the commission of an assault. The District of Columbia, for example, provides a maximum penalty of a $5,000 fine or up to five years in prison (or both) for attempted aggravated assault, which is less than the penalties provided for completing the crime.[6]

If the use of a deadly weapon is a required element for an aggravated assault, the court must define *deadly weapon* if the statute does not do so. A Florida case, *Dixon v. State*, illustrates the issue. The appellant was charged with attempted murder but convicted of the lesser included charge of aggravated battery. He appealed, arguing that the use of his hands did not meet the statutory definition of a deadly weapon. The case, excerpted later in this chapter, is based on the Florida statute, which provides that

(1) (a) A person commits aggravated battery who, in committing battery:

1. Intentionally or knowingly causes great bodily harm, permanent disability, or permanent disfigurement; or

2. Uses a deadly weapon.

(b) A person commits aggravated battery if the person who was the victim of the battery was pregnant at the time of the offense and the offender knew or should have known that the victim was pregnant.[7]

The *Dixon* appeal was heard by a three-judge appellate panel, which affirmed the conviction, upholding the jury instruction that hands may constitute a deadly weapon. The appellant requested a hearing before the full court, which granted the request and reversed and remanded the case. The complaining witness, Juanita Dixon, testified at trial that she "had separated from appellant, her husband of twenty-two years, for a few years before May 1990, when she lived with him for a few days." She stated that on 18 August 1990 at approximately 4:30 in the afternoon, appellant arrived with her daughter. They talked for a while, and she asked him whether he was going to stay or leave with her daughter. He said he would stay, and she told him to leave. They argued, and eventually Dixon said, "Well, the heck with it. . . . Just stay because I don't feel like arguing." The daughter left, and, according to Dixon, appellant then said to her, "I'm going to kill you." Dixon testified that she thought he "was jiving," since they were watching television when the statement was made.

Dixon testified that the appellant went to the kitchen. When he returned he grabbed her by placing his hands around her neck, at which point she decided, "Oh my gosh he is for real." He hit her several times in the jaw and ribs. She testified that she passed out for about 10 minutes as a result of the choking and that when she came to, appellant was going through her purse. She ran to a neighbor's house and dialed 911.

Defense counsel argued that no aggravated assault occurred, as the injuries described in Section 1 of the statute were not met. There was no deadly weapon, so Section 2 was not met. The three-judge panel reviewed Florida case law as well as the case law of other jurisdictions and concluded that

circumstances surrounding the actual use of the hands must be taken into consideration on a case-by-case basis, and that where there are facts sufficient upon which a jury could reasonably find an object, such as a person's hand, to be a deadly weapon based upon the manner in which it was used, the jury should be so instructed.

The panel noted that the

> fact that the object, such as a hand, is not a conventional deadly weapon, such as a firearm, does not mean that the object was used in a manner that could not be considered deadly. . . . Where an individual uses his hands to strangle a person, the use of his hands in such a manner turns his hands into a deadly weapon.

The full court of the Fifth District Court of Appeal of Florida disagreed, as the following excerpt shows. The Florida Supreme Court declined to review the case, thus leaving the lower appellate court's decision standing.[8]

DIXON v. STATE

603 So.2d 570 (Fla.Dist.Ct.App. 5th Dist. 1992).

We are reluctant to overturn Dixon's conviction for aggravated battery, since proof that he brutally attacked his wife was clear. However, it is axiomatic in our legal system that a defendant cannot be convicted of a crime unless the state proves all the necessary elements of the crime, and that crime must be properly charged.

The trial court reasoned that depending on how they are used, fists and hands can be considered to be deadly weapons. If the circumstances are such that bare hands inflict deadly force, this issue is one which should be resolved by the jury. Although there is some out-of-state authority for this view, we have found no Florida appellate case that so holds.

We think that view is contrary to good public policy, the law in this district, and the law in most other jurisdictions. . . .

We conclude that, in general, bare hands (like bare feet) are not deadly weapons for purposes of alleging or proving the crime of aggravated battery. The issue of whether the bare hands or feet of a person specially skilled or trained in martial arts to kill or inflict deadly force with them can be deemed "deadly weapons" is reserved for future consideration. But, in this case, there was no allegation or proof Dixon had any such skills or training.

Accordingly, we reverse Dixon's conviction for aggravated battery and we direct that it be reduced to simple

battery. We remand to the lower court for resentencing on simple battery.

The *Dixon* case emphasizes in the first paragraph of this excerpt that the state must prove all elements of a crime. One of the elements of the crime of aggravated battery in that jurisdiction was the use of a deadly weapon. As we have emphasized, cases are decided on their individual facts. Thus, it is possible that if the defendant in this case had been a major prizefighter, his hands might have been considered to be a deadly weapon. Normally, however, that will not be the case.

Some jurisdictions list other crimes that might be considered a type of aggravated assault. For example, Washington, D.C., has a statute referred to as *assault with intent to* . . . and then names specific crimes, all of which are serious. That statute provides:

> Every person convicted of any assault with intent to kill or to commit first degree sexual abuse, second degree sexual abuse, or child sexual abuse, or to commit robbery, or mingling poison with food, drink, or medicine with intent to kill, or wilfully poisoning any well, spring, or cistern of water, shall be sentenced to imprisonment for not less than 2 years or more than 15 years.[9]

One final comment on aggravated assault is that this crime, as well as simple assault, often occurs within the home. Today we speak of **domestic violence** or **intimate personal violence (IPV)**, but many jurisdictions do not have specific criminal statutes with these terms; thus assault and battery and other crimes are used to prosecute these offenses. The term *domestic violence* refers to the infliction of physical and other forms of harm on members of the family, including spouses, children, parents, and, in some cases, friends who have close personal relationships and perhaps even live together. IPV refers to violence toward a current or former spouse, girlfriend, or boyfriend.

Reckless Assault

Another category of assault is an assault, usually a misdemeanor, involving reckless behavior, defined by the Model Penal Code as follows:

> A person commits a misdemeanor if he recklessly engages in conduct which places or may place another person in danger of death or serious bodily

injury. Recklessness and danger shall be presumed where a person knowingly points a firearm at or in the direction of another, whether or not the actor believed the firearm to be loaded.[10]

Some jurisdictions divide assault into degrees and include reckless acts within the lowest of those degrees. Alaska, for example, has four degrees of assault, with assault in the fourth degree, which is a misdemeanor, defined as follows:

(a) A person commits the crime of assault in the fourth degree if

(1) that person recklessly causes physical injury to another person;

(2) with criminal negligence that person causes physical injury to another person by means of a dangerous instrument; or

(3) by words or other conduct that person recklessly places another person in fear of imminent physical injury.[11]

But Alaska also has a statutory provision for the crime of *reckless endangerment*, which it defines as follows:

(a) A person commits the crime of reckless endangerment if the person recklessly engages in conduct which creates a substantial risk of serious physical injury to another person.[12]

Mayhem

Some jurisdictions include within assault statutes the offense of **mayhem**, which refers to permanent injury inflicted on a victim with the intent to injure and which may disable or disfigure that person. Other jurisdictions define *mayhem* as a separate crime. To illustrate, consider the Rhode Island statute entitled *Mayhem*, with the lead to the following section referring to *mutilation or disabling*. The statute was originally enacted in 1896.

Every person who shall voluntarily, maliciously, or of purpose put out an eye, slit the nose, ear, or lip, or cut off, bite off, or disable any limb or member of another, shall be imprisoned not exceeding twenty (20) years nor less than one year.[13]

Under the common law, *mayhem* referred to rendering a person less able to fight. Mayhem could occur by dismemberment or disablement. Later the crime was extended to include disfigurement that did not disable the victim.

Today some jurisdictions retain the crime of mayhem without reference to the ability to fight but with reference to disfigurement, which refers to a battery that changes the appearance of a person. For example, the District of Columbia statute prohibiting *mayhem or maliciously disfiguring* has been interpreted to require *permanent* disfigurement, defined as follows:

To be permanently disfigured means that the person is appreciably less attractive or that a part of his body is to some appreciable degree less useful or functional than it was before the injury.[14]

Some statutes require the prosecution to prove that the defendant accused of mayhem had the intent to injure, and some require an intent to disable or disfigure. Some statutes list the body parts that are included, as illustrated by the Rhode Island statute reprinted earlier.

Under early common law, mayhem was a felony punishable by causing the perpetrator to lose the same body part that the victim lost, but that punishment gave way to imprisonment (or in some cases capital punishment). Under most modern statutes mayhem is a felony, but the punishment is not as severe as it was under the common law.

ROBBERY

The FBI categorizes **robbery** as one of the four serious violent crimes. This crime involves the taking or attempting to take anything of value from the care, custody, or control of a person or persons by force or threat of force or violence or by putting the victim in fear. Today the trend is to consider robbery as a violent crime against the person, but it is also a crime of property. It is the fear element that makes robbery a crime against the person; it is the items taken that make the crime similar to theft crimes.

Although robberies increased by 3.9 percent from 2004 to 2005 and 7.2 percent from 2005 to 2006, the last year of available data, 2006–2007, showed a decline of 0.5 percent in the volume of robberies (1.2

percent decrease in the rate), but that represented a 7.5 percent increase in 2007 robberies compared to those recorded in 2003. In 2007 robbery victims collectively lost $588 million, with an average of $4,201 loss per victim.[15]

Although most robberies may not involve the actual use of violence, the threat is there—and some robberies are violent and result in death. Consider, for example, the bank robbery in a small Nebraska town in September 2002, resulting in the shooting and killing of four employees and one customer in the largest bank robbery attempt in the state's history. Residents were terrorized; schools were closed; streets were empty. The president of the Norfolk Chamber of Commerce noted that such a crime would be tragic in any town, but in this small town, "It affects everybody." A long-time resident of the town stated it this way: "We have accidents and drunk driving and shoplifting and a drug problem like everyone else, but the senseless killing of five innocent people, that's kind of hard to explain." Shortly after the robbery, one of the deadliest bank robberies in U.S. history, four men were arrested. All were convicted and sentenced to death or consecutive life sentences.[16]

The Elements of Robbery

The elements of robbery are as follows:

1. A trespassory taking
2. A carrying away
3. Of the personal property
4. Of another
5. With the intent to steal

Historically and in many modern statutes, the first element, a trespassory taking, meant that the stolen property had to be taken from the person or presence of the victim by force or intimidation. The requirement of *from the person or presence of the victim* means that the possessor of the property must be close enough that he or she could exercise control over the property and prevent the robbery except for the presence of force or intimidation.

Not all jurisdictions agree with that requirement, as illustrated by the New York robbery statutes in Focus 7.1. In 1965, the New York legislature changed that state's robbery statute to accommodate the problem

that some types of forcible thefts were excluded under the common law requirement. Here are some of the considered circumstances:

✪ A person, wishing to steal property from a farm house, encounters the owner in the field, knocks him unconscious, and proceeds to the house to steal.

✪ A person takes a victim at gunpoint and forces him to call his office and instruct an employee to remove money from the company safe and deliver it to a designated person.[17]

These and other similar circumstances that involve stealing but are actually robberies, although excluded from the common law definition, are covered under the revised New York robbery statutes.

The second element, the process of carrying away, is known as **asportation**, which simply means the act of moving things or people from one place to another.

The third element requires that items taken must constitute **personal property**, not real property. Technically, in the law, *property* refers to anything that belongs exclusively to an individual. It is divided into two types: personal and real. *Personal property* refers to property that can be moved. The concept is probably best understood by those who have sold homes and have been informed by their agents that although the drapes may be personal property, the brackets nailed into the walls or window casings constitute real property because, although they can be removed, to do so would cause damage.

The fourth element, *of another*, means that the personal property that is carried away belongs to another person. The fifth element, *with the intent to steal*, requires that the perpetrator had the requisite mental element to deprive the owner of property permanently or for an unreasonable period of time.

Some robbery statutes do not enumerate all of these elements; they may be included by reference to theft. Consider, for example, the Pennsylvania robbery statute:

(1) A person is guilty of robbery if, in the course of committing a theft, he:

    (i) inflicts serious bodily injury upon another;

    (ii) threatens another with or intentionally puts him in fear of immediate serious bodily injury;

(iii) commits or threatens immediately to commit any felony of the first or second degree;

(iv) inflicts bodily injury upon another or threatens another with or intentionally puts him in fear of immediate bodily injury; or

(v) physically takes or removes property from the person of another by force however slight.

(2) An act shall be deemed "in the course of committing a theft" if it occurs in an attempt to commit theft or in flight after the attempt or commission.[18]

The requirement of force or intimidation causes difficulty in distinguishing *robbery* from *theft*. For example, is a quick purse snatching robbery or theft? Cases differ, but generally it depends on how quickly the snatching occurs. If the purse is grabbed so quickly that the victim does not even miss it, the act may be interpreted as theft, not robbery. But if the victim is aware of the act and struggles to retain the purse, the act may be classified as a robbery.

Pickpocketing is generally included in the category of theft crimes, although if the victim realizes what is happening and struggles to prevent the crime but is overcome by the actor, the offender may be charged with robbery. If the offender uses force to render the victim helpless and then steals, the act may be robbery.

The use of intimidation to commit a theft may constitute robbery. Actual violence is not required; a threat will suffice. The threat need not be directed at the victim. It could be directed at the victim's family, but the threat must be of an *immediate* injury. It is not sufficient that the offender issued a general threat to harm the victim's family at some point in the future.

Unlike theft statutes, most robbery statutes do not distinguish acts by the value of what is taken. In robbery it is the threat or actual use of violence that is crucial. Robbery statutes, however, may grade the crime in terms of aggravating factors, such as the aid of an accomplice, actual injury, or the use of a dangerous weapon. Simple robbery may be distinguished from aggravated robbery, which requires an aggravating circumstance. Robbery statutes may also be classified by degrees, as they are in New York, which has robbery in the first, second, and third degrees, as noted in Focus 7.1.

FOCUS 7.1 **Robbery in the State of New York, NY CLS Penal, Title J, Article 160 (2008)**

Section 160.15. Robbery in the First Degree

A person is guilty of robbery in the first degree when he forcibly steals property and when, in the course of the commission of the crime or of immediate flight therefrom, he or another participant in the crime:

1. Causes serious physical injury to any person who is not a participant in the crime; or

2. Is armed with a deadly weapon; or

3. Uses or threatens the immediate use of a dangerous instrument; or

4. Displays what appears to be a pistol, revolver, rifle, shotgun, machine gun or other firearm; except that in any prosecution under this subdivision, it is an affirmative defense that such pistol, revolver, rifle, shotgun, machine gun or other firearm was not a loaded weapon from which a shot, readily capable of producing death or other serious physical injury, could be discharged.

Section 160.10. Robbery in the Second Degree

A person is guilty of robbery in the second degree when he forcibly steals property and when:

1. He is aided by another person actually present; or

2. In the course of the commission of the crime or of immediate flight therefrom, he or another participant in the crime:

    (a) Causes physical injury to any person who is not a participant in the crime; or

    (b) Displays what appears to be a pistol, revolver, rifle, shotgun, machine gun or other firearm; or

3. The property consists of a motor vehicle, as defined in section one hundred twenty-five of the vehicle and traffic law.

Section 160.05. Robbery in the Third Degree

A person is guilty of robbery in the third degree when he forcibly steals property.

Another approach is that of the Texas Penal Code, which defines two crimes: robbery and aggravated robbery. *Robbery*, which is a second-degree felony, includes intentionally, knowingly, or recklessly causing bodily injury or placing another in fear of imminent bodily injury or death. The act escalates to *aggravated robbery*, a first-degree felony, if a deadly weapon is used or exhibited or if actual bodily harm is caused. The act of threatening imminent bodily harm or death without causing harm is also aggravated robbery if committed upon a person who is 65 years of age or older or who is disabled (meaning one "with a mental, physical, or developmental disability who is substantially unable to protect himself from harm").[19]

Some interesting litigation occurs over the elements of robbery. If an aggravated robbery statute requires the use of a dangerous weapon but does not define those words, what is included? One court held that, because it was used to inflict serious bodily harm on the robbery victim, a stapler qualified as a dangerous weapon.[20] Another held that a toy gun would suffice.[21]

Is an unloaded gun a dangerous weapon? The U.S. Supreme Court has held that it is, giving three reasons, "each independently sufficient," for its decision. In the first place, a gun is "typically and characteristically dangerous," and it is manufactured and sold for purposes that are dangerous. Thus, it is reasonable to assume that the gun is to be used for dangerous purposes "even though it may not be armed at a particular time or place." In the second place, "the display of a gun instills fear in the average citizen." Thus, it creates in a reasonable person an immediate fear that danger will occur. Third, "a gun can cause harm when used as a bludgeon."[22] And recall our earlier discussion in this chapter regarding the issue of whether hands could constitute a dangerous weapon in the crime of assault.

Home-Invasion Robbery

Robbery of persons within their own homes is a particularly fear-creating event; thus, special statutes have been enacted to cover this act, which is usually referred to as **home-invasion robbery**. Most states now have such statutes, and a typical one is that of Florida, which provides as follows:

(1) "Home-invasion robbery" means any robbery that occurs when the offender enters a dwelling with the intent to commit a robbery, and does commit a robbery of the occupants therein.[23]

Robbery is a serious crime when committed with the use of a dangerous weapon. The crime, however, does not necessarily require the use of a weapon; it is the fear instilled by the act that distinguishes robbery from larceny-theft, which is also a serious crime. (IStockPhoto)

The statute further provides that home invasion is a first-degree felony. In enacting this statute (along with one on carjacking, discussed in Chapter 8), the legislature amended several Florida statutes to include these crimes. For example, the murder statute was amended to provide that both carjacking and home-invasion robbery are considered murder when death results.[24]

The FBI's four most serious crimes also include sexual violence, as illustrated in the next section.

FORCIBLE RAPE

The FBI's *UCR* includes **forcible rape** as one of the four serious violent crimes for which it collects data. The crime is defined as "the carnal knowledge of a female forcibly and against her will" and includes assaults and attempts.[25] Under the common law, *rape* was defined as the unlawful carnal knowledge of a female without her consent. The word *unlawful* meant that the act was not authorized by law. For centuries that definition was interpreted to preclude applying the law to a husband who had forced sexual intercourse with his wife. (See the discussion of marital rape later in this chapter.) *Carnal knowledge* is synonymous with *sexual intercourse*, but under the common law the term was limited to acts involving the penis and the vagina. Today, in many jurisdictions, other sex acts, such as anal and oral sex, usually referred to as **sodomy**, may also be included, along with **rape by instrumentation**, the penetration of any body opening by a foreign object for the purpose of sexual gratification or humiliation. Under the common law, forcible rape required *penetration*, which was defined as the insertion of the penis into the vagina to any extent; emission did not have to occur for the crime to be complete.

The final element of the common law definition of rape is that intercourse occurred without the consent of the victim. Proving the lack of consent was a factual problem, which led to many interesting statutory and case law rules about evidence in rape cases. Only within recent years have these been changed in some jurisdictions.

The discussion in this section is limited to *forcible* rape and sodomy. Both of these crimes could be included within the crime of *assault and battery*, for each constitutes offensive, unauthorized applications of force to the person of another, usually preceded by a threat. But forcible rape and sodomy are considered so serious that traditionally they have been defined as separate crimes rather than included within assault and battery statutes.

Today, however, the terms *rape* and *sodomy* are not always included in statutes drafted to prosecute these crimes. Rather, such words as *sexual assault* or *sexual battery*, *deviate sexual behavior*, or simply *sexual conduct* are used. In some cases the definition of the more serious crimes is accompanied by the word *aggravated* or even *repeated*.

Data on Forcible Rape

Data on forcible rape are probably among the most inaccurate of all crime data. In the *UCR*, for example, rape data are based on *crimes known to the police*, and many victims are unwilling to report being raped because of the shame the victimization may elicits. Further, the rigors of cross-examination in a rape trial can be quite challenging as well as embarrassing. The confusion over terminology may lead some rape victims to misunderstand what constitutes an illegal sexual act, or they may fear retaliation by the rapists or others if they report the crime. They may think that law enforcement authorities will not do anything if they do report the rape. According to researchers, these reasons result in a *significant* underreporting of forcible rape.[26]

A victimization study survey conducted by the National Institute of Justice, the first National Violence Against Women Survey, found approximately twice as many rapes (defined as oral, anal, or vaginal intercourse) as reported by official reports. At the time of their first rape, 54 percent of the victims were under 18; 21 percent were under age 12. The typical female rape victim reported being raped three times a year. Approximately 111,000 men reported that they were rape victims, with the perpetrators in most of those cases being other men. Many of the female victims indicated they were raped by someone they knew, and of those who were raped after they were 18 years old, three-fourths said the offender was a date or an intimate partner.[27]

Researchers have also found that acknowledging a rape is a difficult problem for many victims, with studies of college women reporting that approximately one-half of rape victims acknowledge the rape as just that: rape. They think it was a simple assault or even a "mistake" but not a serious crime.[28]

Despite the questionable accuracy of the *UCR* reportings, that publication is the official source of data on this crime and other serious crimes. In 2007, the *UCR* reported an estimated 90,427 forcible rapes, a decrease of 2.6 percent over the 2006 estimates and 3.7 percent down from 2003. Rapes by force accounted for 92.2 percent of reported rapes in 2007, while attempts to rape comprised the remained of the reported offenses.[29]

The violence of rape and the outrage it can bring from society were illustrated by the allegations against Duke lacrosse players in the spring of 2006, when an African American female dancer claimed that while she was in a home in which the players, who had hired her to dance, were having a party, she was raped by three white players. The allegations polarized the campus and the town and captured extensive national and international media attention. Some claimed the alleged victim was lying and tried to discredit her; the prosecutor was accused of bringing the charges for political reasons (he was running for reelection); many argued that the allegations underscored long-standing racial and economic divisions within the community. The lacrosse coach resigned; the program was dropped for that year. Additional details of this case are featured in Focus 7.2, along with other cases of alleged rape.

FOCUS ON FORCIBLE SODOMY

Closely related to forcible rape and, in some jurisdictions, a form of that crime is the crime of *sodomy*. Sodomy was not a common law crime in England, but it was later defined by statute. It was an American common law crime, later defined by statute, and generally included both the ancient and religious crimes (punishable by ecclesiastical courts) of bestiality (sex with a beast) and buggery (sexual intercourse *per anum*, or per anus), later defined to include sex *per os* or oral sex. The sex acts involved in these offenses were considered to be unnatural. A few current statutes retain the definition of sodomy in terms of "that abominable crime against nature." For example, Idaho prohibits "the infamous crime against nature, committed with mankind or with any animal." The penalty for this crime is not less than five years in prison.[30]

Likewise, Massachusetts statutes refer to *sodomy* and *buggery* as that "abominable and detestable crime against nature," for which an offender can be sent to prison for up to 20 years. The state also criminalizes "unnatural and lascivious acts" with other persons. Massachusetts courts have interpreted those phrases to include anal penetration and bestiality (as crimes against nature) and oral-genital and oral-anal contact (as unnatural and lascivious acts),[31] although in 2002 the state's highest court held these statutes inapplicable to private behavior between consenting adults.[32]

Some jurisdictions include fellatio (oral stimulation of the penis) either within sodomy statutes or within the interpretation of those statutes. Oral sexual stimulation of a woman is included by some but not all courts that have interpreted similar statutes.[33] Some have introduced a term such as *deviant sexual behavior* to encompass oral and anal sex and excluded deviant sexual behavior with consent from the coverage of the criminal law, thus legalizing those forms of sexual behavior when engaged in by consenting adults in private.

This section's focus, however, is on *forced* behavior. The crime of forcible sodomy has been in the national news since 1997, when members of the New York City Police Department were accused of sodomizing a Haitian immigrant, Abner Louima, as noted in Focus 7.3.

Another method of categorizing sexual offenses in recent criminal law revisions is to establish *degrees* of criminal sexual conduct, with declining seriousness and penalties. Examples might be first-degree sexual assault, second-degree sexual assault, and so on. Or they might include only the term *sexual assault*, with a second category of *aggravated sexual assault*. To complicate matters further, some jurisdictions retain the term *rape* and add another, such as *criminal sexual assault*, but define the latter as a separate and serious crime, not a lesser offense within rape. Or *aggravated sexual assault* may be defined as a more serious crime than *aggravated assault*. Some of these approaches are illustrated by Texas statutes.

Texas categorizes *aggravated assault* as a *second-degree felony* (unless the act involves public officials in the line of duty, and so on),[34] but *aggravated sexual assault* is a first-degree felony. The Texas statutes do not include the word *sodomy*, but they refer to the acts traditionally covered by that term. They also deviate from the traditional position that sexual offenses may be committed only against women or girls. By using such terminology as "causes the penetration of the anus or the sexual organ of another," the state permits males to be considered victims of sex crimes. In previous versions, this statute contained the word *female* before sexual organ. The Texas statutes, like those of many states, are lengthy; thus, only the first part of the sexual assault statute is included in Focus 7.4. But the reprinted part shows the extent of the acts that are covered as well as the change in the historical approach to who may be victims.

The Texas statute covering *aggravated sexual assault* is similar to the one for *sexual assault* in its definition of the acts covered. But it enumerates several additional circumstances that make the acts more serious, such as the abuse of a child under 14 or an elderly or disabled person or the use of a weapon or drugs to effectuate the act or acts.[35]

The Elements of Forcible Rape and Sodomy

Despite the problems of definition and of interpreting the elements of forced sexual acts, there are some general elements of these offenses, listed here and discussed individually.

1. Female gender (extended to males in some jurisdictions today)

2. Penetration

3. Lack of consent

FOCUS 7.2   Rape and Wrongful Convictions

Historically, rape has been a difficult crime to prove, as usually there are no witnesses and traditionally courts permitted the introduction of evidence calling into question the sexual history of the alleged victim. Today, with the use of DNA evidence permitted in most U.S. courts, it is often possible to introduce scientific evidence that connects the alleged rapist to the crime. DNA evidence has also been used to exonerate those who have been convicted of rape and other crimes. There are many cases of such exonerations on record today. In other cases, complaining witnesses refused to cooperate after they were harassed by the media and others. A few examples illustrate the issues.

In 2003, Kobe Bryant, a superstar basketball player with the Los Angeles Lakers, was accused of raping a young woman in a resort hotel in a small Colorado town. Bryant admitted that he had sexual relations with his accuser but insisted that the acts were consensual.

Media attention to the Bryant case was extensive, and the accuser's sexual history, although normally not admissible in court because of the Colorado rape shield statute (see the text for a discussion of *rape shield statutes*), was discussed in the media. Eventually, the judge ruled that the evidence of any sexual conduct the complainant might have had shortly before and after the encounter with Bryant was relevant to the issue of injuries she claimed were caused by forced sex with the defendant. Thus, that evidence could be admitted. The trial judge also ruled that the complainant could not be referred to as the *victim* during court proceedings. The accuser's name and picture were published on the Internet and in the tabloid press despite the custom of not publishing the name of alleged rape victims. Finally, some of the documents in the case were (allegedly) inadvertently released. These and perhaps other factors (such as death threats) led the accuser to withdraw her willingness to go forward with the case, leading the prosecutor to ask for and the judge to grant a dismissal in the case. The alleged victim did, however, continue with her civil case against Bryant. Legal commentators had pointed out that the filing of that case before the conclusion of the criminal case hurt the prosecution because it suggested a financial motive. The civil case was settled out of court, and the terms were confidential.

Rape counselors and others were concerned that the media coverage in the Bryant case, along with the subsequent dismissal of the case, would discourage future victims from reporting to the police that they have been raped by well-known men. They may be correct, as the following information suggests.

Reporters for a New Jersey newspaper consulted four members of a local rape victim support group and also talked with the district attorney who prosecuted a high-profile rape and sodomy case (discussed next) involving a mentally impaired 17-year-old Glen Ridge, New Jersey, rape victim and several high school men. The prosecutor noted that information that was supposed to be the subject of private hearings in the Bryant case was being leaked to the media and that "This has a chilling effect on rape victims coming forth. . . . They are playing fast and loose with the rape shield law." The legal director of the Pennsylvania Coalition Against Rape proclaimed: "Because defense attorneys are trying to pierce the rape shield law, we are seeing the trial before the trial. The problem, even if information is not revealed in court, is that it's already been leaked and most people have heard of it. You can't unring the bell."[1]

The New Jersey report on rape victims quoted one alleged victim, a 20-year-old woman, as saying that the media coverage of the Kobe Bryant case kept her from filing a complaint after she was raped. "I can't watch the news. . . . [I]t aggravates the hell out of me. . . . People try to find something wrong with rape victims. . . . I don't want people looking at me differently or opening the wound that still hasn't healed about my being molested as a child."[2]

There are two sides to rape allegations. There is the possibility of a false claim against specific individuals, whose lives may be ruined in the process. In the spring of 2006, Durham, North Carolina, prosecutor Mike Nifong brought charges against three Duke University lacrosse players who were accused of raping a woman at a team party on 13 March 2006. The three denied the charges, and one produced evidence that he was not at the party at the time of the alleged sexual assaults. The media became intensely involved in this event and may have been partially responsible for the eventual outcome: The state's attorney general, after investigation of the allegations, determined that there was no credible evidence that the defendants committed the alleged

Gender of the Actor and of the Victim

The common law limitation of rape to male perpetrators and female victims has been changed in most jurisdictions, with many of them adopting gender-neutral language for both perpetrators and victims. For example, California's former requirement that rape is "an act of sexual intercourse . . . accomplished with a female" has been changed to provide that rape is "an act of sexual intercourse accomplished with a person not the spouse of the perpetrator."[36]

The Requirement of Penetration

Under the common law, penetration was usually interpreted to mean any penetration, and this approach has

Mike Nifong, center, answers questions from reporters in 2006. Nifong, who prosecuted false rape allegations against three Duke University lacrosse players, was accused of maliciously prosecuting a case that he knew was unfounded. Nifong lost his job, was disbarred, was convicted of lying in court, and was ordered to serve one day in jail. The falsely accused defendants sued the university and the city for malicious prosecution. (AP Images)

acts. Roy A. Cooper took the unusual act of announcing that Nifong was overzealous and that the players were *innocent*. Cooper considered filing criminal charges against the accuser but decided not to do that, stating that she may really believe that the alleged acts occurred. Nifong was disbarred after the state bar found that he repeatedly lied and misrepresented facts in the case. He was convicted of lying in court and ordered to serve one day in jail, which he served in September 2007. Nifong was forced to resign his office. The three accused men filed charges against Nifong and the city for malicious prosecution; they settled with Duke for an undisclosed amount of money.

The former Duke lacrosse players were fortunate; they had attorneys who could uncover evidence and put pressure on the prosecution. Not all defendants have this opportunity; many are convicted and serve time in prison before they are exonerated for crimes they never committed, as illustrated by the case of

Ronald Cotton, who served 11 years in prison for two rapes that he did not commit. He was subsequently granted a pardon by the state's governor.

Cotton was misidentified by one of the rape victims as the man who raped her. He was released from prison after DNA evidence revealed that he could not have committed either of the two rapes for which he was serving time. The DNA evidence pointed to another man, who confessed and was sentenced for the crimes.

Sources: Adapted from Sue Titus Reid, *Crime and Criminology* (New York: Oxford University Press, 2009), Media Focus 7.1, p. 197, and Exhibit 11.1, p. 348, and updated from various media sources.

1. "Kobe Bryant Rape Case Seen Having a Chilling Effect: Some Fear Fewer Women Will Report Assaults," *The Record* (Bergen County, NJ) (15 June 2004), p. 1.
2. "Kobe Bryant Rape Case."

been followed in most U.S. jurisdictions. For example, a California statute provides as follows: "The essential guilt of rape consists in the outrage to the person and feelings of the victim of the rape [*victim of the rape* replaced *of the female* in 1979]. Any sexual penetration, however slight, is sufficient to complete the crime."[37] As noted earlier, this may include rape by instrumentation.

The penetration requirement has been one of the most difficult and frequently litigated elements of rape and sodomy. In a Kansas case in which the defendant who committed oral sex on his daughter was convicted of aggravated criminal sodomy (among other offenses), the appellate court reversed his conviction for sodomy (but upheld his conviction for indecent

FOCUS 7.3 New York City Police Officer Convicted of Sodomy

In 1997 Abner Louima, a Haitian immigrant, accused officers of the New York City Police Department of beating him in a stationhouse bathroom, sodomizing him with a broom handle, and then forcing the broom into his mouth. After three weeks of trial, during which damaging testimony was presented, Justin A. Volpe

New York police officer Justin A. Volpe was sentenced to 30 years in prison for beating and sodomizing Abner Louima in a stationhouse bathroom. (Mark Lenniham/AP Images)

entered a guilty plea. Volpe is serving a 30-year prison term for his crime.

Charles Schwarz was found guilty of aiding Volpe and of perjury. Schwarz, his attorney, his family, and his friends maintained that he was not the officer in the bathroom assisting Volpe. His case captured the attention of the national media, with, for example, a feature on CBS's *60 Minutes*. In March 2002 an appellate court overturned (on technical grounds) the perjury charge as well as the obstruction of justice convictions of Schwarz and two other officers. Schwarz was retried in the summer 2002 and found guilty of perjury, but the jury deadlocked on three other counts, including two civil rights charges.

Prosecutors announced plans to try Schwarz again, but shortly before the trial a plea agreement was reached. Schwarz pleaded guilty to perjury in exchange for a prison sentence of up to five years. This ended the case but did not resolve the identity of the accomplice. Under the terms of the plea agreement, Schwarz, his wife, and his attorneys may not make statements regarding the sexual or other assaults of Louima, and prosecutors may not debate the issue of whether Schwarz was the accomplice. In May 2007 Schwarz was released from custody.

In 2001 Louima settled a civil suit with New York City for $8.7 million.

Sources: Summarized from media sources.

---

liberties with a child, a less serious crime, carrying a much shorter prison term than aggravated criminal sodomy) because there was no evidence of penetration or oral copulation. The court also held that "cunnilingus is not an act of 'sodomy' as that term is defined by statute." The state statute was revised subsequently, and today defines *sodomy* as "oral contact or oral penetration of the female genitalia or oral contact of the male genitalia; anal penetration, however slight, of a male or female by any body part or object; or oral or anal copulation or sexual intercourse between a person and an animal." The statute does not include anal penetration conducted for recognized health care or other recognized practices, such as body cavity searches in penal systems.[38]

Lack of Consent

A conviction for forcible rape or forcible sodomy requires that the victim did not consent to the sexual act. Lack of consent is another element that is difficult to

prove because in most cases there are no witnesses. Consent is not legal if obtained by duress, threats of harm if one refuses, or fraud or if it is given by a person who cannot consent legally (e.g., mentally incompetent or underage persons).

Because of the difficulty of proving consent or lack of consent, evidence of a struggle was a common requirement in rape cases in the past. Today in many jurisdictions it is not necessary to prove that the victim risked great bodily injury or death by struggling with the assailant, thus showing resistance. Generally the requirement is that the resistance was reasonable in light of the victim's age and strength, the surrounding facts, and all attendant circumstances, or that no resistance need be shown. The issue is whether or not consent was given.

A 1994 Pennsylvania Supreme Court decision in a controversial rape case, *Commonwealth v. Berkowitz*, alarmed and dismayed victims' rights advocates. The

---

FOCUS 7.4 Sexual Assault Crime Statute

Texas Penal Code, Title 5, Chapter 22, Section 22.011 (2009). Sexual assault.

(a) A person commits an offense if the person:

(1) intentionally or knowingly:
  (A) causes the penetration of the anus or sexual organ of another person by any means, without that person's consent;
  (B) causes the penetration of the mouth of another person by the sexual organ of the actor, without that person's consent; or
  (C) causes the sexual organ of another person, without that person's consent, to contact or penetrate the mouth, anus, or sexual organ of another person, including the actor; or

(2) intentionally or knowingly:
  (A) causes the penetration of the anus or sexual organ of a child by any means;

(B) causes the penetration of the mouth of a child by the sexual organ of the actor;

(C) causes the sexual organ of a child to contact or penetrate the mouth, anus, or sexual organ of another person, including the actor;

(D) causes the anus of a child to contact the mouth, anus, or sexual organ of another person, including the actor; or

(E) causes the mouth of a child to contact the anus or sexual organ of another person, including the actor.

[The statute then enumerates the situations in which an act is committed "without the consent" of the other person. These circumstances include acts that are compelled, forced, or involve a person with a mental disease or defect or who is unaware of the act; an act by a clergyman or a public servant; and so on.]

---

case involved a sexual act between a man and a woman in the man's dormitory room. The woman had consumed a mixed drink previously in her room, to "relax a little" before she met her boyfriend, with whom she had previously had an argument. When she saw that her boyfriend was not in his room, she decided to visit another friend nearby. She entered this friend's room and saw someone on the bed with a pillow over his head; she walked over and removed the pillow, later testifying that she thought the person was her friend. According to the woman, the man initiated sexual intercourse by shoving her to the bed (not a big shove but not a romantic one either) and getting on top of her. She did not resist physically because he was on top of her, but she did say no. The male student testified that the woman came to his room and awakened him and consented willingly to sexual intercourse. He claimed that she said no, but in a "moaning way," which he took to communicate consent. He testified that on previous occasions they had discussed sex, in particular the size of his penis, and that she had asked him to show it to her.

The Pennsylvania Supreme Court held that under the facts of the case, sufficient physical force as required by the state statute was not shown. The court noted that the statutory requirement of "forcible compulsion" or "threat of forcible compulsion that would prevent resistance by a person of reasonable resolution" did not require physical force. The phrase includes "moral, psychological or intellectual force used to compel a person to engage in sexual intercourse against that person's will." The court found no evidence of such coercion and discharged the rape conviction while reversing and remanding on the charge of indecent exposure.[39]

Where physical resistance is required to show lack of consent, proof of resistance may be offered by showing evidence of torn clothing, bruises or cuts, broken bones, and other evidence of a possible struggle. The modern trend, however, is that the victim's testimony is sufficient on the consent issue, although, in reality, it may not be sufficient for a conviction.

Another common practice for showing consent has been to permit the defense to introduce evidence of the victim's prior sexual experiences, the assumption being that someone who had engaged in sexual acts previously, or who was promiscuous, would be more likely to have consented during the act at issue. This evidence might be considered important particularly if, on a prior occasion, the complainant had engaged in sex with the defendant. Evidence of prior sexual experience, however, is highly prejudicial as well as embarrassing to victims, who may refuse to report rapes rather than submit to such questioning. The evidence may have no relevance to the case, and in most jurisdictions today, such evidence is generally not admissible under what is referred to as a **rape shield statute** unless it can be shown that the evidence is relevant in that particular case.

One final issue regarding consent is whether an alleged victim's request that the perpetrator use a condom is evidence of consent. Cases involving this issue have led to statutes such as that of California, which provides that in sex cases in which consent is at issue, "evidence that the victim suggested, requested, or otherwise communicated to the defendant that the defendant use a condom or other birth control device, without additional evidence of consent, is not sufficient to constitute consent."[40]

Date Rape

As noted earlier, data show that many rapes occur in situations in which the parties know each other. Forced sexual intercourse or sodomy that occurs within a social situation outside of marriage is often referred to as **date rape**. The alleged victim may have agreed to some intimacy but not to the activities defined in that jurisdiction as constituting the elements of rape or sodomy. There is evidence that alcohol and other drugs play a major role in these incidents, and more attention is given to that issue in Chapter 11. At this point, however, it is important to understand that legally, forced sexual relations, even within a social situation, constitute *forcible rape* or *sodomy* and should be prosecuted as such.

Date rape is a cause for concern. In the past, such behavior was frequently ignored by law enforcement officials, based on the assumption that the alleged victim encouraged, enticed, or in some other way "asked for" the sexual acts. The issue, however, is not whether the two people knew each other but whether the complainant consented to the sexual relations that allegedly occurred. There is no legal concept of *real rape* versus *date rape*. If the elements of forcible rape are present, the crime is rape, whether the parties are strangers, acquaintances, casual dates, steady lovers, or, in most jurisdictions today, spouses, as discussed in the next section.

Marital Rape

Another type of forced sex that historically was not viewed as rape occurs within marriage. As prosecu-

One of the nation's most notorious convicted date rapists is Andrew Luster, grandson of the founder of the cosmetic firm Max Factor. Luster was charged with 87 counts of date rape, which were accomplished after he laced his dates' drinks with a date rape drug. Luster, who fled the country during his trial, was found guilty in his absence. He was subsequently located in Mexico and extradited to the United States, where he is serving a 124-year prison sentence. (Getty Images)

tions for **marital rape** (forced sexual intercourse with a spouse) have increased, courts and legislatures have had to reevaluate the common law position that a husband could not legally rape his wife, with the exception of his aiding another person to have intercourse with her. Implicit in the marriage contract was a willingness on the part of the wife to participate in sexual intercourse at her husband's desire. Most rape statutes excluded the wife as a rape victim. And some religions took literally the scripture, "Wives submit yourselves unto your husbands." In fact, it was not until 1999 that the Baptist General Convention of Texas, representing 2.7 million members, repudiated its position calling for married women to "submit graciously" to the desires of their husbands.[41]

Some states have revised their rape statutes to include marital rape victims of both genders. The Texas statute reproduced in Focus 7.4 does not specify gender or marital relationship but refers to committing the forbidden acts on "another person," which presumably could include a male spouse. A similar statute in Arkansas, which we discuss next, was interpreted as including marital rape.

In May 2002 the Arkansas Supreme Court upheld a rape conviction even though the appellant argued that state's statute should be interpreted as following the historical English position that a man's sexual relations with his wife could not be prosecuted as rape. The estranged husband admitted that he broke into his wife's trailer, put duct tape over her mouth, and threatened to harm the children and that they had sex, which she engaged in out of fear and against her will. Yet, he argued, his actions did not fall within the state's rape statute. When a woman marries, she contracts to any and all sexual relations her husband desires. A unanimous court disagreed, holding that the appellant's actions fell within the state's prohibition against forced sex "with another person." The defendant was sentenced to 10 years in prison.[42]

Other state courts have also extended the crime of forcible rape to include marital rape. For example, the Georgia statute that defines rape as "carnal knowledge of a female forcibly and against her will" was interpreted by the Georgia Supreme Court to include marital rape. The court held that when a woman says "I do," she does not mean "I always will" as far as sexual intercourse is concerned. In *Warren v. State*, decided in 1985, the Georgia Supreme Court upheld the conviction of a man accused of raping and sodomizing his wife while they were living together. "Certainly no normal woman who falls in love and wishes to marry . . . would knowingly include an irrevocable term to her revocable marriage contract that would allow her husband to rape her."[43]

In 1992 an Illinois appellate court ruled that a sexual assault committed by a person against his or her spouse is not a less serious threat than one committed by another person; the marital rape exemption was ruled unconstitutional.[44]

Other states, such as California, have enacted specific statutes that prohibit marital rape and classify both husband and wife as potential rape victims. The statute is reproduced in Focus 7.5. Note the penalties that are provided and the implications for the couple's community property.[45]

In 1991 the House of Lords, Great Britian's highest court, overturned 250 years of common law when it upheld the conviction and sentencing of a man who assaulted and attempted to rape his estranged wife at the home of her parents.[46]

Changes in legislation, however, may not be very effective in reality. Even when the law recognizes marital rape as a crime, convictions are difficult, as illustrated by the 1992 South Carolina case involving a woman who was tied up, with her eyes and mouth taped, and videotaped while her husband assaulted her. The tape was shown to the jury, but the husband testified that his wife liked rough sex and that the cries they heard on the tape when he slapped her were cries of joy, part of a sex game. He was acquitted.[47]

CHILD ABUSE

Any of the violent personal crimes discussed previously in this text may constitute **child abuse**, which refers to the physical, emotional, psychological, and sexual abuse of a child by parents, other relatives, acquaintances, or strangers. Some crimes against children could be prosecuted through the state's murder, rape, assault and other statutes, but most jurisdictions also have special statutes aimed at the prosecution of child abuse. These statutes vary in wording and coverage, but they are based on federal guidelines. The federal statute defines *child abuse and neglect* as:

- Any recent act or failure on the part of a parent or caretaker which results in death, serious physical or emotional harm, sexual abuse or exploitation; or

- An act or failure to act which presents an imminent risk of serious harm.[48]

Some state statutes clearly permit physical punishment of children. Of note is the Florida statute, which defines *child abuse* as

> any willful act or threatened act that results in any physical, mental, or sexual injury or harm that causes or is likely to cause the child's physical, mental, or emotional health to be significantly impaired. Abuse of a child includes acts or omissions. Corporal discipline of a child by a parent or legal custodian for disciplinary purposes does not in itself constitute abuse when it does not result in harm to the child.[49]

FOCUS 7.5 Marital Rape

Calif. Penal Code, Title 9, Chapter 1, Section 262 (2008), Section 262. Spousal Rape

(a) Rape of a person who is the spouse of the perpetrator is an act of sexual intercourse accomplished under any of the following circumstances:

(1) Where it is accomplished against a person's will by means of force, violence, duress, menace, or fear of immediate and unlawful bodily injury on the person or another.

(2) Where a person is prevented from resisting by any intoxicating or anesthetic substance, or any controlled substance, and this condition was known, or reasonably should have been known, by the accused.

(3) Where a person is at the time unconscious of the nature of the act, and this is known to the accused. As used in this paragraph, "unconscious of the nature of the act" means incapable of resisting because the victim meets one of the following conditions:

(A) Was unconscious or asleep.

(B) Was not aware, knowing, perceiving, or cognizant that the act occurred.

(C) Was not aware, knowing, perceiving, or cognizant of the essential characteristics of the act due to the perpetrator's fraud in fact.

(4) Where the act is accomplished against the victim's will by threatening to retaliate in the future against the victim or any other person, and there is a reasonable possibility that the perpetrator will execute the threat. As used in this paragraph, "threatening to retaliate" means a threat to kidnap or falsely imprison, or to inflict extreme pain, serious bodily injury, or death.

(5) Where the act is accomplished against the victim's will by threatening to use the authority of a public official to incarcerate, arrest, or deport the victim or another, and the victim has a reasonable belief that the perpetrator is a public official. As used in this paragraph, "public official" means a person employed by a governmental agency who has the authority, as part of that position, to incarcerate, arrest, or deport another. The perpetrator does not actually have to be a public official.

(b) As used in this section, "duress" means a direct or implied threat of force, violence, danger, or retribution sufficient to coerce a reasonable person of ordinary susceptibilities to perform an act which otherwise would not have been performed, or acquiesce in an act to which one otherwise would not have submitted. The total circumstances, including the age of the victim, and his or her relationship to the defendant, are factors to consider in apprising the existence of duress.

(c) As used in this section, "menace" means any threat, declaration, or act that shows an intention to inflict an injury upon another.

(d) If probation is granted upon conviction of a violation of this section, the conditions of probation may include, in lieu of a fine, one or both of the following requirements:

(1) That the defendant make payments to a battered women's shelter, up to a maximum of one thousand dollars ($1,000).

(2) That the defendant reimburse the victim for reasonable costs of counseling and other reasonable expenses that the court finds are the direct result of the defendant's offense. [The statute contains specific information concerning the payment of restitution.]

Varying definitions and reporting issues result in data problems. With that in mind, consider that the Child Protective Services (CPS) agencies in the United States reported that almost 3.6 million children were investigated or assessed in 2006, and an estimated 905,000 children were abuse victims. The breakdown of those data is as follows:[50]

○ Neglected   64.1 percent

○ Physically abused   16.0 percent

○ Sexually abused   8.8 percent

○ Psychologically mistreated   6.6 percent

○ Medically neglected   2.2 percent

Of the reported cases, 48.2 percent of the victims were boys; 51.5 percent were girls. The rate of victimization was highest in the younger age groups, with a rate of 24.4 per 1,000 children in the birth to one year age group. The victimization *rates* were higher among children of color than among white children, but white children constituted 48.8 percent of the reported victims.[51]

It is important to emphasize that these data represent *reported* cases of child abuse and are probably understated and may overrepresent the gender or race of the victims as a result of reporting issues.

This discussion of child abuse is divided into two major categories: (1) nonsexual abuse and neglect and (2) sexual abuse.

Nonsexual Abuse and Neglect

As the Florida statute cited previously notes, mental and emotional health as well as physical and sexual acts are covered under the term *child abuse*. Note that the Florida statute permits some corporal punishment by parents and others in control of children, as do most jurisdictions. The problem arises in determining what is and what is not permitted. If you think the Florida statute is vague, read the entire statute, which is quite lengthy and specific, citing such examples of abuse as acts that produce specific results, such as sprains, disfigurement, bone or skull fractures, brain damage, and many other results. Prohibited acts also constitute a long list and include giving a child poison, alcohol, drugs, or other substances that result in injury or sickness or affect the child's behavior, judgment, or motor coordination. The statute prohibits abandoning or neglecting the child, again giving specific details and a lengthy list of definitions.

It is, however, difficult at times to know just how far one can go in physically disciplining a child without violating the child abuse statutes. A recent New York case demonstrates excessive punishment. Cesar Rodriguez was charged with second-degree murder in the death of his stepdaughter, Nixzmary Brown. Rodriguez admitted that he routinely beat the 7-year-old child with a belt, hit her with his hands, threw her on the floor, duct-taped her to a chair, and tied her with bungee cords. On the night the child died, Rodriguez severely beat her and held her head under cold running water because she jammed his computer with her toys. The jury convicted him of first-degree manslaughter and unlawful imprisonment. The jurors commented that they could not find the "depraved indifference" required for a second-degree murder conviction. Rodriguez was sentenced to 26 1/3 to 29 years in prison. The child's mother, Nixzaliz Santiago, 29, was acquitted of second-degree murder but convicted of manslaughter and two counts of assault and sentenced to 40 1/3 to 43 years in prison.[52]

Neglect as child abuse also takes many forms, ranging from failure to obtain proper medical care for a child to a failure to provide sufficient and nutritious food, adequate shelter and clothing, education, and so on. Children, depending on their ages, may be considered neglected if they are left unsupervised at home or in any other building or in a vehicle.

Despite the fact that both neglect and physical abuse can and do lead to death, it is perhaps the sexual abuse of children that is most shocking. Although in many cases of child sexual abuse there is no violence and children are alleged to have consented, these acts are criminal because children are not legally capable of consenting. A closer look at sex crimes against children explains why.

Sexual Abuse

Children are abused sexually in many ways; several cases are discussed in Focus 7.6.

Statutory Rape

Unlike forcible rape, *statutory rape* (sexual intercourse, and in some jurisdictions, other sexual acts, with an underage person even though that person consented) was not an early common law crime, although in 1275 English common law criminalized it, setting the age at 12 and lowering that to 10 in 1576. In the 1700s and 1800s statutory rape laws in the United States set the age of consent at 10 or 12, but between 1885 and 1900 those ages were raised to 16 or even higher in most states. Historically statutory rape included only sexual intercourse with an underage girl, but today some statutes are gender-neutral. The philosophy behind these statutes is that minors may be taken advantage of sexually and that they are not old enough to know how to avoid sexual predators. The age under which minors may not give legal consent to sexual relations varies among jurisdictions.

In most jurisdictions statutory rape is a strict liability crime, meaning that the perpetrator does not have to be aware of the minor's age. However, a reasonable mistake of fact concerning the minor's age may constitute a defense in some jurisdictions.[53]

Statutory rape was a media focus for weeks in 2008, when state officials raided a polygamist compound in West Texas and removed all the children, alleging that the adults in that religious sect were abusing the children. Particular attention was given to alleged statutory

FOCUS 7.6   Child Abuse: Recent Cases

Child Abuse in Sex Rings and Trafficking

In early July 2008, after a massive search by local and state police in Vermont, aided by the FBI, the body of 12-year-old Brooke Bennett was found about one mile from the home of her uncle, Michael Jacques, 42, who was quickly charged by the FBI with kidnapping Brooke and with possession of child pornography, which was found on his computer. Jacques was the last person known to have seen Brooke alive, as he allegedly dropped her off at a convenience store to meet a friend; they were seen on the store's surveillance tape. A few days later he was arrested and jailed on charges of sexually abusing another child. Law enforcement officers were tipped off by a 14-year-old, who told them she was with the two on June 25, the day Brooke disappeared, and that Jacques tricked Brooke into thinking she was going to a party but took her back to his house, where she and the 14-year-old watched television for a while. According to this witness, Jacques then told her to leave as he took Brooke upstairs. The witness, who told authorities that she had been having sex with Jacques as part of a sex ring since she was 9 years old, left the house with her boyfriend and never saw Brooke again. Brooke's former stepfather, Raymond Gagnon, was arrested on charges of obstructing justice in the case. Kevin D. Grosenheider, 58, was charged with misprision of felony for assisting Gagnon covering up evidence.[1]

The allegation of a sex ring in this case came shortly after the FBI announced in late June 2008 that it had arrested 399 persons in multiple states and charged them with trafficking children for prostitution. This was believed to be the largest law enforcement case of its type. FBI director Robert S. Mueller III stated, "The sex trafficking of children remains one of the most violent and unforgivable crimes."[2] These crimes are easier to commit today because of the Internet, and more attention is given to that in subsequent chapters.

Child Abuse in Day Care Centers

In 2007, Khemwatie Bedessie, 38, was sentenced to 20 years in prison for rape, sexual assault, and child endangerment of a four-year-old boy in her day care center. Some of the parents of children enrolled in that center continued to support her through the trial and sentencing, leaving the judge to question openly whether they had "lost every grasp of our moral compass." He continued by declaring that we do not need experts to tell us that

> our children are our greatest blessing. . . . Don't harm them, don't abuse their trust, don't take advantage of their

affection. This court has no doubt that Ms. Bedessie did all those things.[3]

This case resulted in a conviction, but that is not always the case. In 1983 the reported allegations of a two-and-one-half-year-old child led to lengthy and expensive investigations in the McMartin Preschool in a Los Angeles suburb. In January 1990, the longest trial in U.S. history, which had already cost over $15 million, ended with acquittals on 52 counts of molesting young children. The jury deadlocked on one count of conspiracy against both defendants, Peggy McMartin and her son Raymond Buckey, and on 12 molestation charges against Buckey. His second trial, which began in April 1990 and was expected to continue into 1991, ended with a mistrial in July 1990.

Sexual Abuse of Children by the Clergy and Teachers

Throughout the United States in recent years, the media has carried reports of alleged sexual abuse of children, usually young boys, by Catholic priests. Some of these acts were alleged to have occurred many years previously; others were recent. Some of the alleged perpetrators were removed from office but did not face criminal charges. Some were charged and acquitted; others were convicted. Among the most cited allegations were those against John J. Geoghan, 66, who was convicted in 2002 in Boston of sexually abusing a young male in 1991 while Geoghan was a priest. Geoghan was sentenced to 9 to 10 years in prison, where he was strangled by another inmate. Also in 2002, the Reverend Paul R. Shanley, age 71, one of the key figures in the Roman Catholic Church scandal in the Boston area, was convicted of sexually abusing children and sentenced to 12 to 15 years in prison.

Schoolteachers have also been convicted of sexually abusing children, and in recent years, an increasing number of female teachers have been in the news as child predators. Mary Kay LeTourneau, 34, married and with four children, had two children by her student, Vili Fualaau, who was 13 at the time the relationship began. For her crime, LeTourneau served seven and one-half years in prison; after her release, she and Vualaau married. The parade of female teachers having sex with young male students continued through the highly publicized case of Debra Lafave (now divorced from her former husband and going by the name Debra Beasley), who pleaded guilty in 2004 to having sex with a 14-year-old male student. Unlike LeTourneau, Lafave did

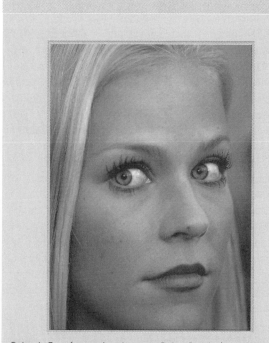

Debra LaFave (now using the name Debra Beasley) was charged with having sex with a 14-year-old student in two separate jurisdictions. After numerous negotiations between the defense and the prosecution, it was agreed that LaFave would not be tried but, rather, would plead guilty to lewd and lascivious behavior and be placed on house arrest and probation. This action came after the boy's parents insisted that he not be subjected to the physically, psychologically, and emotionally draining experience of a public trial. (AP Images)

not serve prison time but, rather, was placed on house arrest followed by probation.

Child Abuse by Repeat Sex Offenders

The reoffending by convicted sex offenders after they are released from prison has led to numerous statutes designed to reduce such offenses. In particular, long prison sentences are implemented, as illustrated by the case of convicted pedophile Dean Schwartzmiller, who was sentenced to 152 years to life in prison for sexually abusing two boys in the California home he shared with Frederick Everts. Schwartzmiller had a manuscript of 1,500 pages detailing sexual acts with 100 boys, but he claims to have had numerous other victims. Everts, said to have been diagnosed as a sexual sadist, had sex with much younger children, including a stepson, whom he abused after tying the

child to a bed when the little boy was between 3 and 5 years old. According to the prosecutor in Everts's most recent case, the defendant molested his 3-month-old biological son prior to his 1993 conviction for sodomizing children. Law enforcement authorities found over 100,000 images of child pornography in the home occupied by these two sexual predators. Everts admitted that he married one woman so he could molest her son. In 2007 Everts and was found guilty of molesting three boys and sentenced to 800 years to life in prison. As for treatment, Everts claims that he wanted treatment and that if necessary, he should spend his life in prison to keep from reoffending.[4]

In February 2008, Corey Saunders, a convicted sex offender, was accused of raping a 6-year-old boy in the New Bedford public library in Massachusetts. The child's mother was within feet of the encounter, the boy allegedly having been lured away by Saunders, asking him if he could show him something. Reportedly the little boy thought he was to be shown a book. A librarian, who saw Saunders talking to the little boy, remembered Saunders' name from a previous visit, looked it up in the registry of sex offenders, found that he was listed, told the mother, and called the police. Saunders was released from prison in 2006 after serving his sentence resulting from his 2001 guilty plea to a charge of attempted rape of a child. Although prosecutors and experts recommended that he be civilly committed as a dangerous sex offender, the judge ruled that they did not prove that allegation, and he was released on probation and required to register as a sex offender. Further attention is given to this issue in Chapter 12.[6]

Sources: Unless otherwise noted by endnotes, the information was summarized by the author from media sources.

1. "Dead Girl Linked to Uncle and Sex Ring," *Star-Ledger* (Newark, NJ) (3 July 2008), p. 14; "FBI Links S.A. Man to Girl's Assault," *San Antonio Express-News* (18 October 2008), p. 2B.
2. "Hundreds Seized in Sweep Against Child Prostitution," *New York Times* (26 June 2008), p. 15.
3. "Queens Day Care Worker Gets 20 Years in Rape of 4-Year-Old," *New York Times* (1 August 2007), Late edition—final, p. 2B.
4. "Large Number of Files Found in Los Gatos Porn Case Could Be a Trend," *San Jose Mercury News* (California) (5 April 2007), n.p.
5. "Sex Offender Accused of Raping Boy, 6, in Public Library," *New York Times* 2 February 2008), p. 8.

rape under the guise of forcing young girls into so-called *spiritual marriages* with much older men. It was also alleged that some of the teens in the compound gave birth to children conceived while their mothers were underage for consenting to sex. Over 400 children were removed from the compound and placed in foster homes and group homes throughout the state for weeks while lawyers for the Yearning For Zion Ranch of the Fundamentalist Church of Jesus Christ of Latter-day Saints in Eldorado, Texas, battled the legal issues in court and state attorneys fought to prove their allegations. A Texas appellate court ruled that the children had been illegally seized and sent the case back to the lower court for resolution in keeping with the appellate ruling. Most of the children were returned to their homes, but the court placed their parents under some restrictions and required future monitoring. Several of the male leaders who allegedly participated in or arranged the marriage of underage girls to older men were prosecuted, as discussed in Chapter 3's analysis of complicity crimes.

National data on statutory rape are not reported by the FBI in its annual *Uniform Crime Reports*, but the agency does collect and report statutory rape data in its **National Incident Based Reporting System (NIBRS)** (a method of collecting crime data on 22 crimes; the system views crimes as involving numerous elements). An analysis of information on statutory rapes known to law enforcement between 1996 and 2000, the latest data available from this source, lists the following.

✪ "Most (95%) statutory rape victims were female. . . .

✪ More than 99% of the offenders of female statutory rape victims were male.

✪ Of all offenders of male statutory rape victims, 94% were female. . . .

✪ Three of every 10 statutory rape offenders were boyfriends or girlfriends and 6 in 10 were acquaintances.

✪ An arrest occurred in 42% of all statutory rape incidences with the probability of arrest declining as victim age increased."[54]

The report noted that the traditional stereotype of a statutory rape victim as a young girl whose perpetrator was a much older man is being challenged by the number of cases involving female perpetrators and younger male victims, especially in school venues. Two of those cases are discussed in Focus 7.6, along with other types of child abuse (see again Focus 7.6).

The increase in teacher/student abuse reportings, especially of sexual abuse, may only represent an increase in the willingness of alleged victims to report. But in 2007, the New York State Board of Education reported that in recent years the number of reported cases of complaints by students or their parents against teachers or administrators (referred to as *moral fitness cases*) had tripled and that most of the complaints were of sexual behavior. The increasing number of such complaints may also be related to the successful civil suits, resulting in significant monetary damages, in sexual harassment cases, especially those against the Catholic Church.[55]

Not all jurisdictions have statutory rape laws as such, but they may have statutes that cover the behavior, and they may have degrees of the crime and specify ages of the perpetrator and the victim. For example, Washington defines *rape of a child in the first degree* as involving "sexual intercourse with another who is less than twelve years old and not married to the perpetrator and the perpetrator is at least twenty-four months older than the victim." *Rape of a child in the second degree* occurs when "the person has sexual intercourse with another who is at least twelve years old but less than fourteen years old and not married to the perpetrator and the perpetrator is at least thirty-six months older than the victim."[56]

Statutory rape laws were enacted to protect innocent young girls from sexual exploitation. They have been used, however, to prosecute sexual acts between teens close in age. In 2007, a Georgia case challenged these traditional laws. Genarlow Wilson, 17, received consensual oral sex from a 15-year-old female teen. Wilson was sentenced to 10 years in prison without parole after his conviction for aggravated child molestation, a felony. Wilson was an honors student and a star athlete in high school. His legal appeals were widely supported, including by such persons as former president Jimmy Carter. Wilson's lawyers argued on appeal that the young man was being subjected to cruel and unusual punishment, convicted under a statute intended for adult sexual predators. Primarily because of this case, Georgia amended its aggravated child molestation statute in 2006 to include the following exception:

(2) A person convicted of the offense of aggravated child molestation when:

Genarlow Wilson was sentenced to 10 years in prison for receiving oral sex from a 14-year-old girl when Wilson was 17. The Georgia legislature amended its aggravated child molestation statute to include exceptions but did not apply the changes retroactively. The Georgia Supreme Court ordered Wilson released from prison on the grounds that his sentence was grossly disproportionate to his crime; Wilson had already served two years. (AP Images)

(A) The victim is at least 13 but less than 16 years of age;

(B) The person convicted of aggravated child molestation is 18 years of age or younger and is no more than four years older than the victim; and

(C) The basis of the charge of aggravated child molestation involves the act of sodomy shall be guilty of a misdemeanor and shall not be subject to the sentencing and punishment provisions of Code Section 17-10-6.1.[57]

The legislature did not, however, apply this amendment retroactively, so Wilson was not released from prison until the state's supreme court ruled in his favor. In a 4-3 ruling, that court held that the 10-year sentence in Wilson's case was "grossly disproportionate to his offense." Wilson was released within 10 hours, but he had already served two years in prison.[58]

The Georgia statute retains this definition of *child molestation:*

A person commits the offense of child molestation when he or she does any immoral or indecent act to or in the presence of or with any child under the age of 16 years with the intent to arouse or satisfy the sexual desires of either the child or the person.[59]

Incest

A second type of child sexual abuse is that of **incest**, which refers to sexual relations between children and family members or relatives who are legally too close to marry. Incest may be classified as a separate crime by that name or included within other sex crimes. Incest victims are not all children, but it is discussed here in that capacity, as most victims are under the legal age of consent. The New Mexico and Minnesota statutes illustrate two ways of defining *incest*. The New Mexico statute provides as follows:

Incest consists of knowingly intermarrying or having sexual intercourse with persons within the following degrees of consanguinity: parents and children including grandparents and grandchildren of every degree, brothers and sisters of the half as well as of the whole blood, uncles and nieces, aunts and nephews.[60]

The Minnesota statute takes a different approach while achieving the same result:

Whoever has sexual intercourse with another nearer of kin to the actor than first cousin, computed by rules of the civil law, whether of the half or the whole blood, with knowledge of the relationship, is guilty of incest and may be sentenced to imprisonment for not more than ten years.[61]

Incest may also be prosecuted as a sex crime or along with other sex crimes. For example, in a Tennessee case a father raped and sodomized his daughter, forced her to look at sexually explicit pictures in a magazine, and then forced her to observe him and her mother engaging in sodomy and sexual intercourse. The father was prosecuted for aggravated sexual abuse, which may carry a more severe penalty than incest.[62]

Although data are an issue and must be examined carefully and in light of an understanding that reporting a sex crime is problematic, the National Center for Victims of Crime (NCVC) reports that incest is committed in all income groups, by all races and ethic groups, by both genders, and includes grandparents, nieces, nephews, uncles, aunts, and so on. Approximately 46 percent of child rape victims are victimized by family members, thus committing the crime of *statutory rape* as well as that of *incest*. The NCVC estimates that there are as many as 10 million incest victims in the United States. The most common forms of incest reported are father-daughter and stepfather-daughter, but there are also reported cases of mother/stepmother and daughter/son/or stepchildren. The NCVC also cites research concluding that incest is particularly damaging because the perpetrators are persons that the children have been taught to trust and when it occurs, there is often pressure from the family to remain silent. Incest may cause severe mental and emotional problems for its victims, including eating disorders, amnesia, low self-esteem, depression, nightmares, flashbacks, posttraumatic stress disorders, and self-destructive behavior. There is also research indicating that a significant number of inmates report having been sexually victimized by their families as well as by others.[63]

Trafficking in Child Prostitution

Children are also abused by being lured or forced into prostitution, and Focus 7.6 features examples of this practice (see again Focus 7.6). With wide access to the Internet, children are easier targets today than in previous times, and sexual predators take advantage of this fact. Chapter 9 gives further attention to crimes committed by use of the Internet, along with the illegal involvement of children in pornography.

One final comment: The sexual abuse of children is serious and should, in most cases, be prosecuted, but attention should also be given to false accusations made against parents and others accused of such serious crimes. In a landmark California case in 1994, a jury awarded Gary Ramona $500,000 against a psychotherapist whom he had accused of "conning his adult daughter into remembering childhood incidents of incest" that the father claimed never occurred. The trial took two months and was the first in which a therapist who used the controversial technique of recovered memory was challenged by a nonpatient claiming to have been abused as the result of that procedure's use on a patient.[64]

ELDER ABUSE

As Americans live longer due primarily to medical advances, the problem of abusing the elderly gains more attention. **Elder abuse** takes many forms, ranging from emotional abuse by family and caretakers to sexual and other forms of physical abuse and including financial scams.

Some jurisdictions have specific statutes aimed at preventing elder abuse. For example, Missouri has three degrees of elder abuse, with *elder abuse in the first degree* defined as follows:

> A person commits the crime of elder abuse in the first degree if he attempts to kill, knowingly causes or attempts to cause serious physical injury, . . . to any person sixty years of age or older or an eligible adult as defined in [another statute.][65]

Another approach is to define elder abuse along with the abuse of other so-called protected categories of persons. The Alabama code provides an example, as follows:

> It shall be unlawful for any person to abuse, neglect, exploit, or emotionally abuse any protected person. For purposes of this section, residence in a nursing home, mental institution, developmental center for the mentally retarded, or other convalescent care facility shall be prima facie [on its face sufficient to establish a fact] evidence that a person is a protected person.[66]

Elderly people are also the victims of sexual abuse, although this type of abuse is often hidden. But in 2005, researchers published the results of their study of the sexual abuse of the elderly in Virginia. The most common type of abuse they found involved women as victims of sexualized kissing and fondling (79 percent of the reported cases), followed by the abuse of an unwelcome sexual interest in the older person's body (43 percent of the reported cases). Many of the perpetrators were other residents of the care facilities, although there were also cases of abuse by caretakers.[67]

Although data on elder abuse are scarce, a bill introduced into both houses of the U.S. Congress cites some figures, along with concerns about elder abuse. The findings that are part of the Elder Justice Act are reprinted in part in Focus 7.7. That bill has not been enacted into law, but in 2008, the U.S. House of Representatives passed a bill entitled The Elder Abuse Victims Act of 2008. That bill, which was referred to the Senate House Judiciary Committee in October 2008, is designed to

> protect seniors in the United States from elder abuse by establishing specialized elder abuse prosecution and research programs and activities to aid victims of elder abuse, to provide training to prosecutors and other law enforcement related to elder abuse prevention and protection, and for other purposes.[68]

FOCUS 7.7 Elder Justice Act

2008 Senate 1070, Section 2.

To amend the Social Security Act [USCS, Title 42, Section 301 *et seq.* (2008)] to enhance the social security of the Nation by ensuring adequate public-private infrastructure and to resolve to prevent, detect, treat, intervene in, and prosecute elder abuse, neglect, and exploitation, and for other purposes. [The bill was introduced in 2007 and on 17 September 2008 referred to the U.S. Senate Committee on Finance. No further action had been taken as of March 2009].

Findings.

Congress finds the following:

(1) The proportion of the United States population age 60 years or older will drastically increase in the next 30 years as more than 76,000,000 baby boomers approach retirement and old age.

(2) Each year, anywhere between 500,000 and 5,000,000 elders in the United States are abused, neglected, or exploited.

(3) Elder abuse, neglect, and exploitation have no boundaries, and cross all racial, social class, gender, and geographic lines.

(4) Victims of elder abuse, neglect, and exploitation are not only subject to injury from mistreatment and neglect, they are also 3.1 times more likely than elders who were not victims of elder abuse, neglect, and exploitation to die at an earlier age than expected.

(5) There is a general dearth of data as to the nature and scope of elder abuse, neglect, and exploitation. . . .

(6) Despite the dearth of data in the field, experts agree that most cases of elder abuse, neglect, and exploitation are never reported and that abuse, neglect, and exploitation shorten a victim's life, often triggering a downward spiral of an otherwise productive, self-sufficient elder's life. . . .

(9) No Federal law has been enacted that adequately and comprehensively addresses the issues of elder abuse, neglect, and exploitation and there are very limited resources available to those in the field that directly deal with the issues.

(10) Differences in State laws and practices in the areas of elder abuse, neglect, and exploitation lead to significant disparities in prevention, protective and social services, treatment systems, and law enforcement, and lead to other inequities.

(11) The Federal Government has played an important role in promoting research, training, public safety, and data collection, and the identification, development, and dissemination of promising health care, social, and protective services, and law enforcement practices, relating to child abuse and neglect, domestic violence, and violence against women. The Federal Government should promote similar efforts and protections relating to elder abuse, neglect, and exploitation. . . .

(16) All elements of society in the United States have a shared responsibility in responding to a national problem of elder abuse, neglect, and exploitation.

FALSE IMPRISONMENT AND KIDNAPPING

Two other serious crimes against the person are **false imprisonment** and **kidnapping**. These are similar crimes in that both require restricting victims' freedom. They differ in the elements required to establish the crimes, the seriousness of the offenses, and the punishments.

Under common law, *kidnapping* (restricting the freedom of a victim against his or her will and removing the victim from one place to another) required the asportation (the removal from one place to another) of a victim from his or her own country to another. *False imprisonment* (the unlawful and knowing restraint of a person against his or her wishes so as to deny freedom) did not require asportation. Sometimes called *false arrest*, false imprisonment referred only to the unlawful confinement of another person. Thus, kidnapping was the same as false imprisonment with the added element of asportation. Some jurisdictions do not define a separate crime of false imprisonment; likewise, some states do not define kidnapping as a separate crime if it is committed incidental to another crime.

Asportation remains a required element of kidnapping in most jurisdictions. Consider the following portion of the California kidnapping statute:

Every person who forcibly, or by any other means of instilling fear, steals or takes, or holds, detains, or arrests any person in this state, and carries the person into another country, state, or county, or into another part of the same county, is guilty of kidnapping.[69]

Under the California statute, asportation might not be required if it can be shown that the offender had an intent to take the victim out of the state.[70]

The following excerpt contains comments by the Michigan Court of Appeals concerning the asportation issue in that state.[71]

PEOPLE v. ADAMS
205 N.W.2d 415 (Mich. 1973)

The harm sought to be prevented is not movement of the victim, but his removal from one place to another and attendant increased risks to the victim. The actual distance the victim is transported does not necessarily correspond with the invasion of his physical interest. An asportation of 50 feet may in some cases expose the victim to precisely those abuses which kidnapping statutes are designed to prevent; in other cases, an asportation of 500 feet may alter the victim's situation not at all. . . .

[The court continued with its analysis by concluding that moving the victim does not constitute asportation unless] it has significance independent of the assault. And, unless the victim is removed from the environment where he is found, the consequences of the movement itself to the victim are not independently significant from the assault—the movement does not manifest the commission of a separate crime—and punishment for injury to the victim must be founded upon crimes other than kidnapping.

On appeal, that decision was affirmed in part and reversed in part, with the Michigan Supreme Court agreeing with the requirement of asportation but disagreeing that the victim had to be removed from the original environment. According to that court, "In one sense you can change the environment of the smallest room by intruding a criminal with a weapon, although in another sense it is still the same room."[72]

What is the purpose of this exercise in deciding when asportation has occurred? The courts are trying to avoid making the lesser crime of false imprisonment into the more serious crime of kidnapping by finding the asportation element when it has nothing to do with the crime of kidnapping or by creating two crimes (false imprisonment and kidnapping) when only one actually occurred.

Some kidnapping statutes require that the victim be isolated in a *secret* place; others require only proof

that there was an intent to isolate the victim. Some statutes define more than one degree of kidnapping, requiring aggravating circumstances for the more serious offense of first-degree kidnapping. Kidnapping a child for purposes of prostitution or pornography is an example of an aggravating circumstance; kidnapping for ransom is another. Frequently the classic kidnapping is accompanied by other crimes, such as extortion, sexual assault, ransom demands, terrorism and torture, and murder.

Some jurisdictions define a separate crime of *child stealing* or *parental kidnapping*. Congress passed the Parental Kidnapping Prevention Act of 1980, which permits federal authorities to issue warrants for parents who flee a state's jurisdiction to avoid prosecution for parental kidnapping. The statute also obligates states, under specified circumstances, to recognize child custody determinations of other states.[73] The U.S. Supreme Court has held, however, that this statute does not give federal courts the power to resolve conflicting custody battle disputes between states. That problem is for Congress to decide through appropriate legislation if states refuse to cooperate with the provisions of the federal act. Thus, if two states disagree in a child custody case, federal courts cannot solve that dispute in a civil action. Critics argue that this ruling makes U.S. courts powerless to deter parental kidnapping, for it does nothing to prevent a parent from kidnapping a child and going to another jurisdiction to avoid the custody decision of the home state.[74]

The problem with child kidnapping cases, however, is that parents who take children illegally from a custodial parent may be difficult, if not impossible, to locate. Some move to other countries, while others begin a new life, with successful disguises for themselves and for their children.

Parental kidnapping cases are difficult to win, and lower courts have disagreed over whether a natural parent may be convicted of kidnapping his or her child under the various state statutes. The Arizona Supreme Court upheld a father's convictions for sexual conduct with a minor, kidnapping, and child abuse. Under Arizona law, a conviction of kidnapping requires that the victim be restrained with the intent to commit a further act. The court held that child abuse met the predicate crime requirement for a kidnapping conviction.[75]

One final method of handling these types of cases within the criminal law is the approach taken by Ohio, which has a statute entitled *Interference with custody*. That statute includes children "under the age of eighteen, or a mentally or physically handicapped child under the age of twenty-one" as well as adults institutionalized for mental retardation or mental illness and children under the state's juvenile custody. It is a crime for anyone "knowing the person is without privilege to do so or being reckless in that regard" to "entice, take, keep, or harbor" persons in the enumerated categories.[76, 77]

Two final, often violent, crimes against the person are discussed in the following two sections.

HATE CRIMES

In 1990 Congress called for the collection of data on crimes involving bias against persons, and in 1994 Congress amended the statute to include physical and mental disabilities. These crimes, usually called **hate crimes**, represent traditional crimes (e.g., assault and battery, rape, and murder) that are motivated in whole or in part by a person's actions toward another based on certain characteristics. At present, those characteristics include race, religion, disability, sexual orientation, or ethnicity.[78] Some state hate crime statutes include gender. In many cases, however, hate crimes are not prosecuted under hate crime statutes but under traditional crimes (such as aggravated assault or murder) that are committed with an improper bias or motivation.

Since hate crimes as such are relatively new, we do not have trends in crime rates on these crimes, but the *UCR* does report some data, with the most recent, the 2007 data, showing that most hate crimes are motivated by racial bias (50.8 percent), followed by religious bias (18.4 percent), sexual-orientation bias (16.6 percent), ethnicity/national origin bias (13.2 percent), and disability bias (1 percent). Of the hate crimes reported in 2007, 60 percent were against persons, with 39.7 percent against property. The most single reported hate crime against persons in 2007 was intimidation, accounting for 47.4 percent. Most of the hate crimes directed at property consisted of destruction, damage, or vandalism.[79]

Various hate crime bills to amend the federal hate crime statutory provision were under consideration in the U.S. Congress in 2007 and 2008. These bills, if enacted, would require the collection of data on hate crimes committed against persons based on their gender or homeless person status.[80]

Hate crimes resulting in deaths in the United States gained significant national and international attention in recent years.

Most recently, 15-year-old Lawrence King of Oxnard, California, suffered harassment from his classmates after he stated that he was gay. He was shot to death in the computer lab. Brandon McInerney, 14, was charged with murder and a hate crime, for which he could, if convicted, receive a prison sentence of 51 years. His attorney was challenging the decision to try the youth in the adult criminal court.[81]

In 1998, Matthew Shepard, 21, a university student in Wyoming, died after a severe beating in what was thought to be the result of bias against him because of his lifestyle, the only reference the judge made to Shepard's sexual orientation when he sentenced Russell A. Henderson to life in prison for Shepard's murder. Henderson entered a guilty plea shortly before his scheduled trial. He is serving two life sentences. Subsequently a jury found Henderson's friend, Aaron J. McKinney, guilty of aggravated robbery, kidnapping, and murder; McKinney faced the death penalty but was sentenced to two life terms without parole. Shepard's parents started a foundation in their son's name with the purpose of combating hatred and bigotry through educational programs.

In another widely discussed hate crime case, James Byrd Jr., a 49-year-old African American, was tortured and dragged to his death behind a truck in Texas in June 1998. Three white men were tried and convicted for the crime. Russell Brewer, 32, and Bill King, 25, were convicted of capital murder, while the third defendant, Shawn Berry, 24, who was sentenced to life, will serve at least four decades in prison for his role in this hate crime. Texas had no specific hate crime statute at the time (the governor signed the James Byrd Hate Crime Act in May 2001), but it did permit enhanced sentencing if during the punishment phase "the court determines that the defendant intentionally selected the victim primarily because of the defendant's bias or prejudice against a group." Note, however, that no *specific* groups were enumerated in that statute. Today the statute provides enhanced sentencing if the trier of fact

> determines beyond a reasonable doubt that the defendant intentionally selected the person against whom the offense was committed or intentionally selected property damaged or affected as a result of the offense because of the defendant's bias or prejudice against a group identified by race, color, disability, religion, national origin or ancestry, age, gender, or sexual preference.[82]

Hate crime statutes have been challenged in the courts. Some have been upheld, while others have been voided as violating the First Amendment right to free speech (see Appendix A). The Oregon Supreme Court upheld a state statute that makes it a crime for two or more people to injure another "because of their perception of that person's race, color, religion, national origin or sexual orientation." The court held that this statute is directed against conduct rather than speech. The U.S. Supreme Court refused to hear the case, thus permitting the ruling to stand.[83]

The California hate crime statute was upheld against claims of vagueness and equal protection.[84] In 1995 the statute was upheld against First Amendment claims.[85] In June 1993 the U.S. Supreme Court upheld a state statute that provided for enhanced sentences for persons convicted of crimes motivated by racial or other bias.[86]

An example of an ordinance that did not survive a constitutional challenge is seen in a case that illustrates the difference between conduct and speech. In *R.A.V. v. St. Paul*, the U.S. Supreme Court invalidated a St. Paul, Minnesota, ordinance that prohibited displaying on public or private property a symbol that a person knew or should have known would arouse alarm, anger, or resentment on the basis of race, color, creed, religion, or gender. In *R.A.V.*, a white teenager was accused of burning a cross in the yard of an African American family. The Court found that the ordinance could have a chilling effect on the right to free speech because it permitted the expression of only one side of an issue.[87]

In 2003 the U.S. Supreme Court upheld the Virginia Supreme Court in its ruling that the state's statute concerning cross burning was unconstitutional. *Virginia v. Black* involved three defendants, one of whom was convicted of violating the state statute that prohibited cross burning with the intent to intimidate. A second defendant entered a guilty plea to attempted cross burning and conspiracy to commit cross burning. The third defendant was convicted of attempted cross burning. The convictions were affirmed by the Virginia Court of Appeals but reversed by the state supreme court, which ruled that the statute violated the First Amendment because it punished individuals for engaging in symbolic speech, which may be infringed upon by the government only if the speech involves obscenity, defamation, and fighting words. Eight of the U.S. Supreme Court justices viewed cross burning under the facts of this case as constituting free speech and

ruled that in order for the prosecution to prevail under the Virginia statute, it must prove beyond a reasonable doubt that the speech in question was intended to intimidate rather than to express an opinion. The lone dissenter, Justice Clarence Thomas, declared, "There is no other purpose to the cross, no communication, no particular message. . . . It was intended to cause fear and to terrorize a population."[88]

STALKING

Some forms of behavior that do not rise to the level of physical injury or fall within traditional criminal definitions of serious crime but that may be frightening for the targeted person may now be covered under statutes designed to prevent **stalking**, which most states have enacted in recent years. According to a 2006 publication of the *American Journal of Preventive Medicine*, 1 in 14 women and 1 in 50 men in the United States have been stalked at some time in their lives. Prior to that release the limited data on stalking came from the National Violence Against Women Survey and the Sexual Victimization of College Women Survey, both funded by the National Institute of Justice (NIJ). Among other data, those two sources reported the following:

- "1 out of every 12 United States women (8.2 million) and 1 out of every 45 United States men (2 million) has been stalked at some point in their lives.

- An estimated 1.4 million individuals are stalked annually in the United states.

- 13.1% of college women were stalked during the school year.

- 78% or four out of five stalking victims were women.

- Overall, 87% of stalkers were men.

- Female victims most often were stalked by an intimate partner.

- 80.3% of women attending college or universities who were being stalked knew their stalkers."[89]

Stalking statutes vary considerably, but primarily they are designed to punish people who watch, follow, and harass others repeatedly over a period of time. Some of the statutes are too broad and cannot pass constitutional tests. Others are narrowly drawn and have been upheld.

Florida provides that "any person who willfully, maliciously, and repeatedly follows or harasses another person" may be charged with *stalking*. The state's trial courts split over the issue of whether this law is constitutional, but a state appellate court upheld the statute and the state supreme court affirmed.[90]

New Hampshire provides the following definition of stalking:

I. A person commits the offense of stalking if such person:

(a) Purposely, knowingly, or recklessly engages in a course of conduct targeted at a specific person which would cause a reasonable person to fear for his or her personal safety or the safety of a member of that person's immediate family, and the person is actually placed in such fear;

(b) Purposely or knowingly engages in a course of conduct targeted at a specific individual, which the actor knows will place that individual in fear for his or her personal safety or the safety of a member of that individual's immediate family; or

(c) After being served with, or otherwise provided notice of, a protective order . . . that prohibits contact with a specific individual, purposely, knowingly, or recklessly engages in a single act of conduct that both violates the provisions of the order and is listed in paragraph II(a).[91]

The following section of this statute defines terms, including that of *code of conduct* (which refers to two or more acts "over a period of time, however short, which evidences a continuity of purpose"). Note however, that section (c) provides that a single stalking act will be sufficient if the actor has been served with a *protective order*, which is a court order to protect a person who has been threatened. Such orders are often issued in domestic situations.

Stalking statutes have been challenged in the courts with some success; however, some statutes have also been upheld. Consider these examples. An Ohio court of appeals held that the law prohibiting a person from engaging in a "pattern of conduct" that he or she knows will "cause another to believe that the offender will cause physical harm to the other person or cause mental distress to the other person" is not vague or

too broad. A "pattern of conduct" is defined as "two or more incidents closely related in time."[92]

In contrast, the Kansas antistalking statute was invalidated. That statute defined stalking as follows: "an intentional and malicious following or course of conduct directed at a specific person when such following or course of conduct seriously alarms, annoys, or harasses the person, and which serves no legitimate purpose."[93]

The Kansas Supreme Court held that the statute was void for vagueness because *alarms* and *annoys* are subjective terms and thus open to many interpretations. The court noted that there were no guidelines to enlighten persons on the meaning of when following a person becomes "alarming, annoying, or harassing." As defined, the crime of stalking, according to the court, "depends upon the sensitivity of the complainant." The court did hold, however, that the word *following* is not vague.[94]

The Kansas statute was changed to read as follows:

Stalking is an intentional, malicious and repeated following or harassment of another person and making a credible threat with the intent to place such person in reasonable fear for such person's safety.[95]

North Carolina has a similar statute, which is as follows:

(A) Offense.—A person commits the offense of stalking if the person willfully on more than one occasion follows or is in the presence of, or otherwise harasses, another person without legal purpose and with the intent to do any of the following:

(1) Place that person in reasonable fear either for the person's safety or the safety of the person's immediate family or close personal associates.

(2) Cause that person to suffer substantial emotional distress by placing that person in fear of death, bodily injury, or continued harassment, and that in fact causes that person substantial emotional distress.[96]

A final type of stalking statute is new and does not yet exist in many jurisdictions: electronic stalking, or **cyberstalking**. On 1 January 1999 California's *computer stalking statute* became effective. It constitutes an amendment to the state's stalking statute by

Computers may be used in the commission of property crimes, such as identity theft, but they are also used in personal crimes, such as stalking, leading some jurisdictions to enact specific statutes aimed at such crimes. (IStockPhoto)

adding that the term *credible threat* in the original statute means

> a verbal or written threat, including that performed through the use of an electronic communication device, or a threat implied by a pattern of conduct or a combination of verbal, written, or electronically communicated statements and conduct made with the intent to place the person that is the target of the threat in reasonable fear for his or her safety or the safety of his or her family and made with the apparent ability to carry out the threat so as to cause the person who is the target of the threat to reasonably fear for his or her safety or the safety of his or her family. It is not necessary to prove that the defendant had the intent to actually carry out the threat.[97]

The first charge under this new statute came just a few weeks after the statute became law, when Gary Steven Dellapenta, a 50-year-old security guard, was accused of sending out an advertisement, via electronic mail, in which he described the alleged victim and listed her name, address, and phone number, along with information on how to bypass her home security system. The alleged victim, who did not even own a computer, was not injured, but six men showed up at her house over a period of several months. The men stated that they were responding to her advertisement. Dellapenta, who had been rebuffed by the victim, was impersonating her in the advertisement, which stated that she fantasized about being raped.[98] Dellapenta pleaded guilty to three counts of solicitation for sexual assault and one count of stalking. He was sentenced to six years in prison.

SUMMARY

In one sense every crime is a crime against a person. This chapter continued the discussion in Chapter 6 of the serious, violent crime of homicide by focusing on assault and battery, robbery, and forcible rape. It also discussed other crimes against a person, including those against children (e.g., incest and statutory rape) and the elderly. Still other crimes are considered serious, though they may or may not be violent, because they infringe on personal freedom (e.g., kidnapping and false imprisonment) or intentionally cause fear in victims (e.g., hate crimes and stalking). Some of the crimes discussed in this chapter are either more prevalent or more obvious today than previoiusly because of increased reporting by victims. Most represent recent and significant changes in legislation and case law. These changes may contribute to increased reporting by victims.

Assault, battery, and mayhem are violent crimes that involve inflicting bodily injury on others in an unlawful manner. These crimes may be minor or very serious, such as dismemberment in the case of mayhem or serious beatings in the case of aggravated assault. A simple assault may not involve any real physical injury but is a crime because it involves an unauthorized, offensive touching. Many cases of assault are in the context of domestic violence, and only recently have we begun to recognize these acts as violent crimes rather than solely as domestic problems.

Robbery was the next serious violent crime discussed. Scholars and law enforcement agencies differ in their treatment of this crime, with some counting it as a serious *property* crime. The FBI lists robbery as a serious *violent* crime, which is the position taken in this text. Although robbery involves all of the elements of larceny-theft (discussed in Chapter 8), it has the added element of putting the victim in fear of imminent harm. It is that element that calls for the categorization of robbery as a serious violent crime. Robberies within homes are particularly frightening, and recently home-invasion robbery statutes have been enacted in many jurisdictions to cover this crime.

Forcible rape, which under the common law was defined as the unlawful carnal knowledge of a female without her consent, has been changed by statute in some jurisdictions to include male victims and female offenders and to expand the definition of *carnal knowledge* beyond that of penile-vaginal intercourse. In many recent statutory changes, forcible rape and forcible sodomy are combined into crimes with such names as *aggravated sexual assault* or *aggravated sexual abuse*.

Forcible rape and sodomy, as well as assault, have been recognized recently in many jurisdictions as including acts that occur within the domestic setting. Some states have repealed their marital rape and sodomy exemptions through legislation, while others have done so through case law.

Date rape is another violent crime that received little attention until recently. Today it is recognized that, in a criminal case of alleged sexual assault, the issue is not whether the victim knew the assailant but whether the victim consented to the sex acts at issue in the allegations. This official recognition of date rape as a violent crime does not mean, however, that victims have become necessarily more willing to report the crimes. Nor does it mean that police, prosecutors, judges, and jurors are more willing to believe that rape may occur within a marriage or other situation in which the complaining witness agreed to some social interaction with the alleged offender.

Physical abuse of children is a personal crime that is gaining more attention as we see such dramatic events as the drowning of all of her children by Andrea Yates, whose case was the subject of Chapter 4's Case Analysis.

A crime against children that has surfaced only recently as one that occurs with some regularity is the sexual abuse of children. Today an alarming number of adults are reporting that they were abused as children, many by members of their own families or by church officials. Sexual abuse may, and usually does, cause serious psychological and physical problems for children, and some of those problems do not surface until later in life. Thus, it is important to prevent this crime as well as to detect it when it occurs and to assist the victims in their adjustments. However, false allegations of sexual abuse have occurred and may be devastating for the innocent parents or other accused persons. Sorting out falsehoods from truth is extremely important but exceedingly difficult.

At the opposite end of the age spectrum from children are the elderly, who are the targets of physical abuse, including sexual abuse. The chapter noted recent Congressional attempts to enact legislation in this area aimed at the prevention of elder abuse.

Kidnapping is another serious crime against the person. In one sense, it is identical to false imprisonment but with the added element of asportation. Modern kidnapping statutes do not require that the victim be taken to another country, as under the common law, but there is no general agreement on what is meant by the *asportation* element.

Neither kidnapping nor false imprisonment necessarily involves physical violence. However, both are serious crimes against the person because they may involve violence, usually create fear in their victims, and by definition involve restraint against the person's will. These crimes, like robbery, illustrate the problem of placing crimes in discrete categories.

Two final crimes against the person, both of which create fear, are *hate crimes* and *stalking*. These acts have only recently been defined specifically as crimes, and data are scarce, but they both create fear and may result in serious physical harm or even death to victims. Stalking may be even more dangerous when it occurs by means of the Internet; thus, attention was given to the recently defined crime of *cyberstalking*.

This concludes our discussion of individual serious crimes against the person, but it is important to understand that violence occurs in many settings, and it is thought by some that violence in many if not all areas is increasing. That is difficult to know because of inaccurate data, but clearly, violence remains a serious problem in the United States and in many other countries. The immediate reaction is to change the law. That may be functional in some cases, but it does not work in others. In addition, harsher laws may create other problems, such as overcrowded court dockets, jails, and prisons as well as overworked law enforcement and other criminal justice system personnel.

Chapter 8 continues our discussion of the major serious crimes as defined in U.S. criminal justice systems, along with some less serious crimes. From the crimes against the person in Chapters 6 and 7, we now move to crimes against property.

STUDY QUESTIONS

1. Distinguish among assault, battery, and mayhem. Distinguish between simple and aggravated battery.

2. How does domestic violence compare to assault and battery?

3. What is meant by *reckless assault and battery*?

4. How would you define a dangerous weapon?

5. Why is robbery a violent crime against the person?

6. What is meant by *home-invasion robbery*? Why do we need a separate statute for this crime?

7. How do modern statutes and the common law differ in their definition of forcible rape? Of sodomy?

8. Should date rape and rape by strangers be processed in different ways? How about marital rape?

9. Should men be considered rape victims when they suffer sexual assaults that otherwise meet the definition of rape? If so, under which circumstances? If not, why not?

10. What is statutory rape, and what are its elements? Should any changes be made in the traditional statutory rape statutes? Why or why not?

11. Define *incest*.

12. Do you believe convictions for incest and statutory rape should carry the same penalties as those for sexual assault by strangers? Why or why not?

13. What is *elder abuse*? Do we need separate statutes to cover this crime?

14. Should parental child kidnapping be a separate crime, or should it be prosecuted as kidnapping, requiring the same elements and carrying the same penalties as provided for any kidnapping?

15. Explain the importance of asportation in kidnapping cases.

16. List and discuss ways in which men and women, adults and children can prevent becoming kidnap victims.

17. What are hate crimes? Why are statutes covering these crimes so recent? Do we need these statutes?

18. Define *stalking* and *cyberstalking*, and analyze efforts to deter these crimes by statute.

FOR DEBATE

In recent years, several kidnappings captured national attention, some featured nightly for days or even weeks. A few kidnappings involve positive endings in the sense that the child is returned alive although harmed by the trauma of the kidnapping and perhaps sexually abused or physically and psychologically injured in other ways. But most kidnapping victims are found dead, some having been raped or tortured prior to their deaths. This debate topic is designed to encourage students to evaluate the role of the media in kidnappings, considering that role along with the constitutional right of free speech and of the press to publish information as well as the privacy rights discussed in previous chapters.

Resolved: The media should be encouraged to reduce its coverage of missing children cases and to show more respect for the privacy rights of the alleged victims and their families.

KEY TERMS

aggravated assault, 174

asportation, 177

assault, 172

battery, 172

child abuse, 187

cyberstalking, 199

date rape, 186

domestic violence, 175

elder abuse, 194

false imprisonment, 195

forcible rape, 179

hate crime, 197

home-invasion robbery, 179

incest, 193

intimate personal violence (IPV), 175

kidnapping, 195

marital rape, 186

mayhem, 176

National Incident Based Reporting System (NIBRS), 192

personal property, 177

CASE ANALYSIS

STATE v. STARK

832 P.2d 109 (Wash. App. 1992)

Case Preview

This case raises several legal issues. Two of the issues are mentioned but not discussed here. Students may wish to read the case to see the resolution of these issues, which are not central to this chapter but are important to criminal law. The first involves the issue of sentencing; the second involves privacy. The defendant argued that he was told when tested for HIV that the test results would remain confidential and thus, the testimony of the expert, Dr. Locke, should have been excluded from the trial. The appellate court did not agree, upholding the admission of that testimony. The portion of the case considered here concerns the intent requirement for assault, along with the issue of whether the assault statute was void for vagueness, a concept covered in earlier discussions as well as in this chapter.

Some jurisdictions cover the matter of unprotected sex by a person who knows he or she is HIV-positive by using attempted murder statutes, while some jurisdictions have statutes specific to the issue. In this case, however, the statute utilized is that of second-degree assault and battery, which under the Washington Code, which governs this case, states as follows, in relevant part:

> (1) A person is guilty of assault in the second degree if he or she, under circumstances not amounting to assault in the first degree: . . . (e) With intent to inflict bodily harm, exposes or transmits human immunodeficiency virus as defined in [another section of the state statute.][99]

This case involved a bench trial (a trial before the judge only) on one count and a jury trial on two counts; the defendant was convicted of all counts, which were joined in this appeal.

Opinion by Judge Petrich, with Judges Alexander and Seinfeld Concurring

Facts

On March 25, 1988, Calvin Stark tested positive for HIV, which was confirmed by further tests on June 25 and on June 30, 1988. From June 30, 1988, to October 3, 1989, the staff of the Clallam County Health Department had five meetings with Stark during which Stark went through extensive counseling about his infection. He was taught about "safe sex," the risk of spreading the infection, and the necessity of informing his partners before engaging in sexual activity with them. On October 3, 1989, Dr. Locke, the Clallam County Health Officer, after learning that Stark had disregarded this advice and was engaging in unprotected sexual activity, issued a cease and desist order as authorized by [the statute].

Stark did not cease and desist, and, consequently, on March 1, 1990, Dr. Locke went to the county prosecutor's office intending to seek the prosecutor's assistance, pursuant to [another statute], in obtaining judicial enforcement of the cease and desist order. The prosecutor instead had Dr. Locke complete a police report. The State then charged Stark with three counts of assault in the second degree under [the statute]. Each count involved a different victim:

Count 1: The victim and Stark engaged in sexual intercourse on October 27 and October 29, 1989. On both occasions, Stark withdrew his penis from the victim prior to ejaculation. The victim, who could not become pregnant because she had previously had her fallopian tubes tied, asked Stark on the second occasion why he withdrew. He then told her that he was HIV positive.

Count 2: The victim and Stark had sexual relations on at least six occasions between October 1989, and February 1990. Stark wore a condom on two or three occasions. . . . When she told Stark that she had heard rumors that he was HIV positive, he admitted that he was and then gave the victim an AZT pill "to slow the process of the AIDS."

Count 3: The victim and Stark had sexual relations throughout their brief relationship. It was "almost nonstop with him," "almost every night" during August 1989. Stark never wore a condom and never informed the victim he was HIV positive. When pressed, Stark denied rumors about his HIV status. The victim broke off the relationship because of Stark's drinking, after which Stark told her that he carried HIV and explained that if he had told her, she would not have had anything to do with him.

Issue

1. [Whether the evidence presented was sufficient to sustain a finding of "intent to inflict bodily harm."]
2. [Whether the statute in question was void for vagueness.]

Holding

1. [The evidence presented was sufficient to support a finding of "intent to inflict bodily harm."]
2. [The statute was not vague.]

Rationale

[With regard to the sufficiency of the evidence:] In determining whether sufficient evidence supports a conviction, "[t]he standard of review is whether, after viewing the evidence in a light most favorable to the State, any rational trier of fact could have found the essential elements of the charged crime beyond a reasonable doubt." Under this standard, we resolve all inferences in favor of the State.

Stark contends that there is insufficient evidence to prove that he "exposed" anyone to HIV or that he acted with intent to inflict bodily harm. Since Stark is undisputedly HIV positive, he necessarily exposed his sexual partners to the virus by engaging in unprotected sexual intercourse. The testimony of the three victims supports this conclusion.

The testimony supporting the element of intent to inflict bodily harm includes Dr. Locke's statements detailing his counseling sessions with Stark. With regard to the first victim, we know that Stark knew he was HIV positive, that he had been counseled to use "safe sex" methods, and that it had been explained to Stark that coitus interruptus will not prevent the spread of the virus. While there is evidence to support Stark's position, all the evidence viewed in a light most favorable to the State supports a finding of intent beyond a reasonable doubt. . . .

With regard to the later victims, we have, in addition to this same evidence, Stark's neighbor's testimony that Stark, when confronted about his sexual practices, said, "I don't care. If I'm going to die, everybody's going to die." We also have the testimony of the victim in count 2 that Stark attempted to have anal intercourse with her and did have oral sex, both methods the counselors told Stark he needed to avoid. . . . [The court cited numerous cases from other jurisdictions supporting a finding of intent sufficient for the crime charged with regard to an HIV-positive person engaging in acts that might spread the virus to others.]

[With regard to the vagueness issue:] Stark contends that this court should dismiss his convictions because [the statute] is unconstitutionally vague. He contends that the statute does not define the prohibited conduct with sufficient specificity to put an ordinary citizen on notice as to what conduct he or she must avoid.

Statutes that are susceptible to arbitrary and discriminatory enforcement are invalid. Criminal statutes must contain ascertainable standards for consistent adjudication.

To succeed on his claim, Stark must prove beyond a reasonable doubt that the statute is unconstitutionally vague, thereby defeating the presumption of constitutionality. . . . If persons of common intelligence must necessarily guess at a statute's meaning and differ as to its application, the statute is unconstitutionally vague.

When a defendant asserts that a statute is unconstitutionally vague on its face, as opposed to vague as applied, the reviewing court must still look to the facts of the case before looking for hypothetically constitutional situations. If the defendant's conduct fits within the proscribed conduct of the statute, the defendant cannot assert other hypothetical applications of the law.

"[I]mpossible standards of specificity are not required." "[A] statute is not unconstitutionally vague merely because a person cannot predict with complete certainty the exact point at which his actions would be classified as prohibited conduct." "[I]f men of ordinary intelligence can understand a penal statute, notwithstanding some possible areas of disagreement, it is not wanting in certainty."

Where as here, the statute requires proof of specific criminal intent, the remaining terms are less vague or indefinite than they might otherwise be considered. Moreover, because the assault statute does not implicate any First Amendment rights, Stark cannot claim the statute is facially vague; he may only argue that it is vague as applied to him. It is therefore irrelevant whether the statute gives adequate notice that the hypothetical conduct he describes is prohibited.

Stark complains that the statute "nowhere defines the term expose, nor does it state that it is a crime to transmit the HIV virus to another human being." No reasonably intelligent person would think the statute criminalizes the transmission of HIV to nonhumans. Stark's argument regarding the term "expose" is also unpersuasive. Any reasonably intelligent person would understand from reading the statute that the term refers to engaging in conduct that can cause another person to become infected with the virus. Stark engaged in unprotected sexual intercourse with other human beings after being counseled on several occasions that such conduct would expose his partners to the virus he carries. He was not forced to guess at what conduct was criminal.

For Discussion

Do you agree that Stark's behavior should be construed as a violation of the criminal code, specifically as a form of assault? Would your answer remain the same if Stark did not know that he was HIV-positive? Review this chapter's discussion of assault and the elements of the crime of assault. Based on this information, do you think Stark's behavior amounts to assault? Does his behavior result in the threat of immediate harm? If you contend that Stark's behavior amounts to assault, would you consider charging him with the more serious crime of aggravated assault? Why or why not? Do you think Stark's behavior is more like reckless assault? Why or why not?

Subsequent to this case, the Washington Code was revised to include exposing one to the HIV virus as a first-degree assault, defined in relevant part as follows:

(1)   A person is guilty of assault in the first degree if he or she, with intent to inflict great bodily harm: . . .

(b) Administers, exposes, or transmits to or causes to be taken by another, poison, the human immunodeficiency virus as defined in [another statute]; or any other destructive or noxious substance.[100]

Do you agree with this change in the statute? Why or why not?

INTERNET ACTIVITY

1. Although rape (sexual battery) is a very serious crime, it is one of the most underreported crimes, and myths about rape abound. Find out how much you know about the crime of rape by taking the quiz at http://www.justicewomen.com/cj_rapequiz_en.html (accessed 30 November 2008).

2. The Administration for Children and Families (ACF) of the U.S. Department of Health and Human Services provides information on child abuse and neglect. For frequently asked questions about this topic, access its website at http://www.acf.hhs.gov/ (accessed 30 November 2008).

NOTES

1. Tex. Penal Code, Title 5, Chapter 22, Section 22.01 (2009).
2. *Government of Virgin Islands v. Stull*, 280 F.Supp. 460 (V.I. Dist. Ct. 1968), footnotes and citations omitted.
3. Federal Bureau of Investigation, *Preliminary Annual Uniform Crime Report, January–December 2007*, http://www.fbi.gov/ucr/2007prelim/table3.htm, accessed 30 June 2008.
4. Federal Bureau of Investigation, *Crime in the United States: Uniform Crime Reports 2007: Aggravated Assault*, http://www.fbi.gov/ucr/cius2007/offenses/violent_crime/aggravated_assault.html, accessed 28 November 2008.
5. D.C. Code, Title 22, Section 22-404.01 (2009).
6. D.C. Code, Title 22, Section 22-404.01(c) (2009).
7. Fla. Stat., Title 46, Section 784.045 (2009).
8. *Dixon v. State*, 1992 Fla. App. LEXIS 2481 (Fla.Dist.Ct. App. 1992). This opinion of the three-judge panel was withdrawn by the full court, which substituted its opinion, excerpted in the text and published at 603 So.2d 570 (Fla.Dist.Ct.App. 1992), footnotes and citations omitted, *review denied*, 613 So.2d 9 (Fla. 1992).
9. D.C. Code, Title 22, Section 22-401 (2009).
10. Model Penal Code, Section 211.2.
11. Alaska Stat., Title 11, Chapter 41, Section 11.41.230 (2008).
12. Alaska Stat., Title 11, Chapter 41, Section 11.41.250 (2008).
13. R.I. Gen. Laws, Title 11, Chapter 29, Section 11-29-1 (2008).
14. *Perkins v. United States*, 446 A.2d 19 (D.C.Ct.App. 1982). The D.C. statute is codified at D.C. Code, Section 22-406 *et seq.* (2009).
15. Federal Bureau of Investigation, *Crime in the United States: Uniform Crime Reports 2007: Robbery*, http://www.fbi.gov/ucr/cius2007/offenses/violent_crime/robbery.html, accessed 28 November 2008.
16. "Five People Shot to Death in Nebraska Robbery," *New York Times* (27 September 2002), p. 18; "Nebraska Robbers Entered Shooting, Police Say," *New York Times* (28 September 2002), p. 12; "Judge Rules Vela Eligible for Death," *Omaha World-Herald* (4 May 2006), p. 1B.
17. NY CLS Penal, Article 160, Note (2009). From Commission Staff notes.
18. Pa.C.S. Title 18, Category C, Section 3701 (2008).
19. Tex. Penal Code, Title 7, Chapter 29, Sections 29.02 and 29.03 (2009).
20. *Cummings v. State*, 384 N.E.2d 605 (Ind. 1979), *aff'd. without opinion, Cummings v. Duckworth*, 843 F.2d 500 (7th Cir. 1988).
21. *United States v. Martinez-Jimenez*, 864 F.2d 664 (9th Cir. 1989), *cert. denied*, 489 U.S. 1099 (1989).
22. *McLaughlin v. United States*, 476 U.S. 16 (1986).
23. Fla. Stat., Title 46, Chapter 812, Section 812.135 (2009).
24. The Florida murder statute is codified in Fla. Stat., Title 46, Chapter 782, Section 782.04 (2009).
25. Federal Bureau of Investigation, *Uniform Crime Reports: Crime in the United States 2007, Forcible Rape*, http://www.fbi.gov/ucr/cius2007/offenses/violent_crime/forcible_rape.html, 30 November 2008.
26. Eric P. Baumer, Richard B. Felson, and Steven F. Messner, "Changes in Police Notification for Rape, 1973–2000," *Criminology* 41, no. 3 (August 2003): 841–872.
27. Patricia Tjaden and Nancy Thoennes, *Full Report of the Prevalence, Incidence, and Consequences of Violence Against Women: Findings from the National Violence Against Women Survey* (Washington, D.C.: National Institute of Justice, 2000).
28. See Bonnie S. Fisher et al., "Acknowledging Sexual Victimization as Rape: Results from a National-Level Study," *Justice Quarterly* 20, no. 3 (September 2003): 536–574.
29. Federal Bureau of Investigation, *Crime in the United States 2007, Forcible Rape*.
30. Idaho Criminal Code, Section 18-6605 (2008).
31. See *Commonwealth v. Gallant*, 369 N.E.2d 707 (Mass. 1977); and *Commonwealth v. Balthazar*, 318 N.E.2d (Mass. 1974).
32. The case is *Gay & Lesbian Advocates & Defenders v. AG*, 763 N.E.2d 38 (Mass. 2002). The statutes are codified at ASM GL Chapter 272, Sections 34 and 35 (2008).

33. See, for example, *State v. Tarrant*, 80 N.E.2d 509 (Ohio Ct.App. 1948), excluding cunnilingus from the sodomy statute. Including the act was *Locke v. State*, 501 S.W.2d 826 (Tenn.Crim. 1973).

34. Tex. Penal Code, Title 5, Chapter 22, Section 22.02 (2009).

35. Tex. Penal Code, Title 5, Chapter 22, Section 22.021 (2009).

36. Cal Pen Code, Title 9, Chapter 1, Section 261 (2008).

37. Cal Pen Code, Title 9, Chapter 1, Section 263 (2008).

38. *State v. Moppin*, 783 P.2d 878 (Kan. 1989), *superseded by statute as stated in Norton v. State*, 1991 Kan. App. LEXIS 796. (Kan.Ct.App. 1991). The new statute is K.S.A., Chapter 21, Article 35, Section 21-3501 (2006).

39. *Commonwealth v. Berkowitz*, 609 A.2d 1338 (Pa.Super. 1992), *aff'd. in part and vacated in part*, 641 A.2d 1161 (Pa. 1994).

40. Cal Pen Code, Title 9, Chapter 1, Section 261.7 (2008).

41. "Baptists in Texas Reject a Call for Wives to 'Submit' to Husbands," *New York Times* (10 November 1999), p. 20.

42. "Law Does Not Allow Man to Rape Wife, State High Court Says," *Arkansas Democrat-Gazette* (20 May 2002). The state statute is codified at Ark. Code Ann., Section 5-14-103 (a)(1) (2008). The case is *Jones v. State*, 74 S.W.3d 663 (Ark. 2002).

43. *Warren v. State*, 336 S.E.2d 221 (Ga. 1985).

44. *People v. M.D.*, 595 N.E.2d 702 (Ill.Ct.App. 1992), *appeal denied*, 602 N.E.2d 467 (Ill. 1992).

45. Cal Pen Code, Title 9, Chapter 1, Section 262 (2008). For more information on marital rape, see Article: "Contest and Consent: A Legal History of Marital Rape," *California Law Review* 88 (October 2000): 1373.

46. *R. v. R., House of Lords* (1991), 4 All ER 481; 3WLR 767; 94 CR App. Rep. 216 (1992).

47. "Marital-Rape Acquittal Upsets Activists," *Miami Herald* (19 April 1992), p. 11.

48. U.S.C.A., Title 42, Section 5106g (2009).

49. Fla. Stat., Title 5, Chapter 39, Section 39.01(2) (2009).

50. U.S. Department of Health & Human Services, Administration for Children & Families, *Child Maltreatment 2006*, Chapter 3, pp. 1, 2, http://www.acf.hhs.gov/programs/cb/pubs/cm06/chapter3.htm, accessed 5 July 2008.

51. U.S. Department of Health & Human Services, *Child Maltreatment 2006*, p. 2.

52. "Maximum Term for Stepfather in Death of Girl," *New York Times* (4 April 2008), Late edition—final, p. 1B; "Seeing Failure of Mother as Factor in Sentencing," *New York Times*, Late edition, final (17 November 2008), p. 24A.

53. See *People v. Hernandez*, 393 P.2d 673 (Cal. 1964).

54. Karyl Troup-Leasure and Howard N. Snyder, Office of Juvenile Justice and Delinquency Prevention, Office of

Justice Programs, *Statutory Rape Known to Law Enforcement* (Washington, D.C.: U.S. Department of Justice, September 2005), p. 1.

55. "Between Teacher and Student: Sex Cases and the Suspicions Are Increasing," *New York Times* (20 June 2007), p. 20.

56. ARCW, Section 9A.44.073 (first degree) and Section 9A.44.976 (second degree) (2008).

57. O.C.G.A., Title 16, Chapter 6, Section 16-6-4(d)(2) (2009).

58. "Man Convicted as Teenager in Sex Case Is Ordered Freed by Georgia Court," *New York Times* (27 October 2007), p. 9. The case is *Humphrey v. Wilson*, 652 S.E.2d 501 (Ga. 2007).

59. O.C.G.A., Title 16, Chapter 6, Section 16-6-4(a) (2009).

60. N.M. Stat. Ann., Chapter 30, Article 10, Section 30-10-3 (2008).

61. Minn. Stat., Section 609.365 (2008).

62. *Donegan v. McWherter*, 676 F.Supp. 154 (M.D.Tenn. 1987).

63. National Center for Victims of Crime, "Incest," http://www.ncvc.org/ncvc/main.aspx?dbName=DocumentViewer&DocumentID=32360, accessed 7 July 2008.

64. "Jury Awards Father Accused of Incest in Memory Therapy," *New York Times* (14 May 1994), p. 1. The case is *Ramona v. Isabella*, 66 Cal.Rptr. 2d 766 (Cal.App.2d Dist. 1997).

65. R.S.Mo., Title 38, Chapter 565, Section 565.180 (2008). For a discussion, see Elizabeth Rathbone-McCuan, "Elder Abuse Within the Context of Intimate Violence," *UMKC Law Review* 69 (Fall 2000): 215.

66. Code of Ala., Title 38, Chapter 9, Section 38-9-7 (2008).

67. "When Elders Are Molested: Sexual Abuse of Nursing Home Residents Too Often Goes Unreported," *Legal Times* (27 June 2005), n.p.

68. Elder Abuse Victims Act of 2008, HR 5352, passed in the House on 23 September 2008.

69. Cal Pen Code, Part I, Title 8, Chapter 3, Section 207(a) (2008).

70. See Cal Pen Code, Section 207(d) (2008).

71. *People v. Adams*, 192 N.W.2d 19 (Mich.Ct.App. 1971), *aff'd. in part, rev'd. in part*, 205 N.W.2d 415 (Mich. 1973), citations omitted.

72. *People v. Adams*, 205 N.W.2d 415, 421 (Mich. 1973).

73. U.S. Code, Title 28, Section 1738A (2009).

74. *Thompson v. Thompson*, 484 U.S. 174 (1988).

75. *State v. Viramontes*, 788 P.2d 67 (Ariz. 1990).

76. Ohio Rev. Code Ann., Title 29, Chapter 2929, Section 2919.23 (2008).

77. "Warrants Say North Carolina College Student Was Kidnapped, Robbed and Shot," *New York Times* (29 June 2008), p. 18.

78. U.S.C.A, Title 28, Section 534 (2009).

79. Federal Bureau of Investigation, *Uniform Crime Reports: Crime in the United States* 2007: Hate Crime Statistics, *Incidents and Offenses*, http://www.fbi.gov/ucr/hc2007/incidents.htm, accessed 2 November 2008.

80. See, for example, H.R. 226 (to include homeless persons) and H.R. 1164 (to include gender) (2008).

81. "A Deadly Clash of Emotions: A Gay Teen Is Taunted at His Oxnard School. He Pushes Back by 'Flirting.' Next, Gunfire," *Los Angeles Times* (8 March 2008), p. 1; "Defense: No Trial As Adult for Teen," *Los Angeles Times* (19 January 2009), p. 1B.

82. Tex. Code of Crim. Proc., Chapter 40, Article 42.014(a) (2009), as amended. See also Tex. Penal Code, Title 3, Subchapter D, Section 12.47 (2009).

83. *State v. Plowman*, 838 P.2d 558 (Ore. 1992), *cert. denied*, 508 U.S. 974 (1993).

84. See *In re Joshua H.*, 13 Cal.App.4th 1734 (1993), *review denied*, 1993 Cal. LEXIS 3412 (Cal. 1993); and *People v. MacKenzie*, 34 Cal.App. 4th 1256 (6th Dist. 1995). The California hate crime statute is codified at Cal Pen Code, Section 422.6 (2008).

85. *In re M.S.*, 896 P.2d 1365 (Cal. 1995).

86. *State v. Mitchell*, 508 U.S. 476 (1993).

87. *R.A.V. v. St. Paul*, 505 U.S. 377 (1992).

88. *Virginia v. Black*, 538 U.S. 343 (2003).

89. Office on Violence Against Women, U.S. Department of Justice, *Report to Congress on Stalking and Domestic Violence*, 2005 Through 2006," p. 1, http://www.ncjrs.gov/pdffiles1/ovw/220827.pdf, accessed 8 July 2008.

The original sources are as follows: Patricia Tjaden and Nancy Thoennes, *Stalking in America: Findings from the National Violence Against Women Survey*, U.S. Department of Justice, National Institute of Justice and the Centers for Disease Control and Prevention (April 1998); and Bonnie Fisher, Francis T. Cullen, and Michael G. Turner, *Sexual Victimization of College Women*, U.S. Department of Justice, National Institute of Justice (December 2000).

90. *Pallas v. State*, 636 SO.2d 1358 (Fla.Dist.Ct.App. 1994), *aff'd.*, 654 So.2d 127 (Fla. 1995), *approved*, 754 So.2d 127 (Fla. 1995).

91. RSA 633:33-a (2008).

92. *State v. Dario*, 665 N.E.2d 759 (Ohio App. 1995). The statute is codified at ORC, Title 29, Chapter 2903, Section 2903.211 (2008).

93. Kan. Stat. Ann., Section 21-3438 (1999).

94. *State v. Bryan*, 910 P.2d 212 (Kan. 1996).

95. K.S.A., Chapter 21, Article 34, Section 21-3438 (2008).

96. N.C. Gen. Stat., Chapter 14, Article 35, Section 14-277.3 (2008).

97. Cal Pen Code, Part I, Title 15, Chapter 2, Section 646.9(g) (2008).

98. "Computer Stalking Case a First for California," *New York Times* (25 January 1999).

99. Rev. Code Wash. (ARCW), Title 9A, Chapter 9A.36, Section 9A.36.021(1)(e) (1992).

100. Rev. Code Wash. (ARCW), Title 9A, Chapter 9A.36, Section 9A.36.011 (2008).

CHAPTER 8

Property and Related Crimes

continued

INTRODUCTION

Modern property law cannot be fully understood without looking at its history, particularly in the English common law. Life was much simpler when property laws first emerged. That simplicity is important in understanding how and why certain rules developed concerning property crimes and why some acts included in criminal laws today were considered acceptable business practices under the common law.

The influence of early English common law on the development of common law and statutory law in the United States was particularly strong in the area of property law. Although U.S. criminal laws have embraced some acts that were not considered crimes in England historically, they have retained many of the elements of the English common law. Thus, some sections in this chapter look briefly at English common law definitions and interpretations before discussing modern property law. They also look at some generalities about each crime, as well as examples of current property crime statutes.

The first part of the chapter focuses on the four **property crimes** categorized by the Federal Bureau of Investigation (FBI) as serious crimes: larceny-theft, burglary, motor vehicle theft, and arson, for which the FBI publishes data on occurrences as well as on arrests. For crimes categorized as less serious property offenses, the FBI reports only arrest data. Some of those crime categories are discussed in the second part of the chapter. Particular attention is given to several types of **fraud**, as some of those crimes are capturing considerable national attention today. The chapter looks at various types of computer crimes, which can involve the theft of property as well as

of identity and even encompass stalking, which was discussed in Chapter 7. Significant attention is given to identity theft, thought to be the fastest growing type of crime in the United States today. The chapter closes with a relatively newly defined crime, that of carjacking.

SERIOUS PROPERTY OFFENSES

The official FBI crime data, published in the agency's annual *Uniform Crime Reports (UCR)*, list four serious property offenses: larceny-theft, burglary, motor vehicle theft, and arson. The *UCR's* definitions of those crimes are reproduced in Focus 8.1. The latest FBI dated on the percent change for these four crimes for each year from 2003 through 2007 are presented in Figure 8.1.[1]

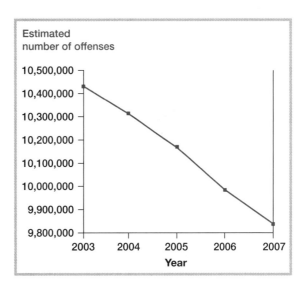

FIGURE 8.1 *Property Crime in the United States, 2003–2007*
Source: Federal Bureau of Investigation, *Crime in the United States: Uniform Crime Reports, 2007*, http://www.fbi.gov/ucr/cius2007/offenses/property crime/index.html, accessed 28 November 2008.

FOCUS 8.1	Serious Property Crimes: *UCR* Definitions
Burglary	"The unlawful entry of a structure to commit a felony or theft."
Larceny-Theft	"The unlawful taking, carrying, leading, or riding away of property from the possession or constructive possession of another."
Motor Vehicle Theft	"The theft or attempted theft of a motor vehicle."
Arson	"Any willful or malicious burning or attempt to burn, with or without intent to defraud, a dwelling house, public building, motor vehicle or aircraft, personal property of another, etc."

Source: Federal Bureau of Investigation, *Crime in the United States: Uniform Crime Reports 2004* (Washington, D.C.: U.S. Government Printing Office, 2005), pp. 45, 49, 55, 61.

Larceny-Theft

The oldest common law theft crime is **larceny-theft**, which is the most frequently committed serious crime in the United States, accounting for over 60 percent of the four serious property crimes in the United States in any given year. The number of larceny-theft crimes in 2007 decreased by 0.6 percent from 2006. Larceny-thefts accounted for an estimated 66.7 percent of all property crimes in 2007.[2]

The contribution of the common law to the evolution of modern theft crime statutes is important; thus, we will take a closer look at the common law.

Common Law Larceny-Theft

Under early common law, larceny-theft was the only type of theft punishable as a crime, and its elements were interpreted narrowly. *Larceny-theft* was defined as the unlawful taking, carrying, leading, or riding away of property from the possession of another with the intent to steal. Many actions that we consider theft today were not included under that definition and its interpretations through case law. As one early case noted, it was not a crime to "make a fool of another" by deliberately delivering fewer goods than the purchaser had ordered.[3]

Also under English common law, because of the seriousness of larceny-theft (which at times carried the death penalty), the elements of the crime were enumerated carefully. Despite this fact, many judges were reluctant to convict. Consequently, technicalities crept into the law, making some of the elements a disgrace and embarrassment. Attempts to erase these loopholes led one scholar to conclude that the "intricacies of this patchwork pattern are interesting as a matter of history but embarrassing as a matter of law-enforcement."[4]

The elements of larceny-theft are as follows:

1. A trespassory taking
2. A carrying away (asportation)
3. Of the personal property
4. Of another
5. With the intent to steal

Under the common law, technically no act could be larceny-theft unless all of these elements were present. Modern statutes make some exceptions.

Trespassory Taking

The critical element of larceny-theft is the requirement of a *trespassory taking*, a phrase used in the common law to refer to the unlawful taking away of goods from the owner's possession. Apparently the common law crime of larceny-theft was developed to deter people from committing thefts that might cause personal retaliation. It was assumed that if an owner saw someone taking away his property, he would react in a way that might lead to violence. If no trespassory taking occurred but someone outsmarted him and thereby misappropriated his personal property, the owner might be angry but the offender would not likely be available for immediate retaliatory action. The peace of society was less likely to be challenged and, consequently, the common law provided civil but not criminal remedies.

As society became more complex, especially in business transactions, judges thought it necessary to expand larceny-theft to cover thefts that did not involve trespassory takings. But instead of abolishing trespassory taking as a requirement of larceny, judges developed fictions in which a taking was assumed.

The judicial fiction might operate like this: When a master delivered property to his servant to be used for the benefit of the master, it was argued that the servant had *custody* of the property but that the master retained *possession*, which in this situation was called **constructive possession**. *Constructive possession* is a legal doctrine that refers to the condition of having the power to control an item along with the intent to do so. Other fictions developed, but the following example illustrates the problems created when judges began trying to expand the law of larceny-theft without developing new offense categories.

In *Hufstetler v. State*, decided by the Alabama Court of Appeals in 1953, the defendant stopped at a service station and asked to have the gas tank of his car filled. The attendant pumped 61/2 gallons of gas into the tank. At that time the total value of the gas was $1.94, which was below the requirement for **grand larceny**. The defendant drove off without paying for the gas. He was convicted of **petit larceny** (*petit* means small, and in this context, it refers to a smaller theft than that of grand larceny; the two crimes are distinguished only by the amount stolen, and that amount is generally specified by statute) and appealed, arguing that because the station attendant parted voluntarily with the possession and ownership of the gasoline, he was not guilty of petit larceny, one element of which is a trespass. In upholding the conviction, the court emphasized that the owner retained constructive possession because actual possession was obtained by trick. The court stated: "The obtaining of the property by the consent of the owner under such conditions will not necessarily prevent the taking from being larceny. . . . The trick or fraud vitiates the transaction, and it will be deemed that the owner still retained the constructive possession."[5] Larceny in this manner is called **larceny by trick**, which refers to deceptively obtaining possession of goods from a victim who surrenders possession voluntarily and without knowledge of the deceit involved. Larceny by trick, in the *Hufstetler* case, established the element of *taking* from the possession of the owner.

Another exception to the requirement of actual possession crept into the law as judges attempted to deal with the problem that occurred when a **bailee**, a person to whom goods are entrusted by a **bailor** (a person who entrusts goods to a bailee), converted those goods to his own use. Technically the bailee was not taking the goods from the possession of the owner; thus, larceny-theft had not occurred. The master-servant exception did not apply because the bailee was an independent contractor.

New provisions were needed. The first solution was to rule that the bailee could be convicted of larceny-theft if he broke open a case of goods and took some of the contents. Some judges reasoned that once the bailee broke the bulk, possession returned to the owner, whereas others argued that the bailee never had possession of the contents, only of the container. The practical result was that a bailee who misappropriated the entire package could not be charged with larceny-theft because he had not taken the package unlawfully from the owner's possession. But if he broke open the package and took part of the contents, larceny-theft was an appropriate charge, provided the other elements of larceny-theft were present.[6]

These and other fictions led to changes in the law of larceny-theft. Today, when a bailee misappropriates property, some states treat that act as larceny-theft if the package is broken but as embezzlement if it is not broken. Other states have a separate crime, *larceny by bailee*, to cover the misappropriation whether or not there was a breaking. Some have a general crime called *theft* that covers all of these situations.

The importance of the taking element of larceny-theft is illustrated by the crime of shoplifting. Suppose a student enters the university bookstore, picks up several pens, and puts them in his or her pocket before leaving. Has the element of taking occurred? May the student be charged with larceny-theft before leaving the premises? This issue arose in three New York cases. The facts differed in each case, but essentially all involved acts that might be considered shoplifting except that in each case the accused had not left the store when he or she was apprehended. For example, in one of the cases the suspect took a book from the shelf of a bookstore, put it in his briefcase, and continued to browse. When confronted by an employee, he reacted by hitting that person with the briefcase. It fell open, and the book fell out. In the following excerpt, the New York Court of Appeals explains its reasons for upholding the shoplifting convictions. The court discussed the common law of property with its requirement of a taking, and then the modern evolution of the law away from actual taking to a requirement that the individual exercised control over the property "inconsistent with the continued rights of the owner," noting, however, that it is expected that customers may examine or even try on articles.[7]

PEOPLE v. OLIVO
420 N.E.2d 40 (N.Y. 1981)

In many cases, it will be particularly relevant that defendant concealed the goods under clothing or in a container. Such conduct is not generally expected in a self-service store and may in a proper case be deemed an exercise of dominion and control inconsistent with the store's continued rights. Other furtive or unusual behavior on the part of the defendant should also be weighed. Thus, if the defendant surveys the area while secreting the merchandise or abandons his or her own property in exchange for the concealed goods, this may evince larcenous rather than innocent behavior. Relevant too is the customer's proximity to or movement towards one of the store's exits. Certainly it is highly probative of guilt that the customer was in possession of secreted goods just a few short steps from the door or moving in that direction. Finally, possession of a known shoplifting device actually used to conceal merchandise, such as a specially designed outer garment or false-bottomed carrying case, would be all but decisive.

Of course, in a particular case, any one or any combination of these factors may take on special significance. And there may be other considerations, not now identified, which should be examined. So long as it bears upon the principal issue—whether the shopper exercised control wholly inconsistent with the owner's continued rights—any attending circumstance is relevant and may be taken into account. . . .

Quite simply, a customer who crosses the line between the limited right he or she has to deal with merchandise

 and the store owner's rights may be subject to prosecution for larceny.

A Carrying Away

The second element of larceny-theft is that the goods must be taken away; this is called *asportation*, which means moving a thing (or a person) from one place to another. This element may be satisfied by the slightest movement. If the defendant attempts to take the article away and does not succeed, the asportation element is not complete and larceny-theft has not occurred. Thus, a defendant who removed a coat from a store dummy and tried to take it away but could not do so because it was attached by a chain was not guilty of larceny-theft.[8]

Personal Property of Another

The third and fourth elements of common law larceny-theft are that the article must be the *personal property of another person*. The phrase *of another* means that abandoned property and wild animals were not included. Under the common law, personal property referred only to tangible personal property. Trees, minerals, crops, and other items of real property were not included.

Today some statutes include trees and other items of real property within the definition of theft and therefore do not require separate actions to constitute the crime. In most cases, electricity and gas are considered property subject to larceny-theft, but labor and services are not covered unless specified by statute, which some jurisdictions have done.[9]

Theft of a service, such as boarding a chair lift at a ski resort without a lift ticket, is covered under some modern theft statutes. (IStockPhoto)

With the Intent to Steal

The final element of common law larceny-theft was that the defendant must have had an intent to "wholly and permanently deprive the owner thereof."[10] In current statutes, however, some jurisdictions provide that taking some vehicles, such as a car, a bicycle, or a boat, for temporary use or operation constitutes a crime, but such acts may be categorized as misdemeanors rather than as felonies, which is typical of larceny-theft.[11]

Modern Theft Codes

We have analyzed the common law elements of larceny-theft because most of those elements are retained in modern theft statutes, and frequently the common law is used to interpret those statutes. In recent years many jurisdictions have enacted legislation more specific than common law larceny-theft. These specific statutes reflect the problems that arose when attempts were made to apply the common law definition of larceny-theft to modern theft crimes.

Some of the problems have been noted already. For example, services were excluded from the personal property requirement of larceny-theft. Some jurisdictions have included theft of services under a special statute, while others have expanded their existing statutes to include theft of services.

Another way to distinguish theft crimes is illustrated by New York's penal code and is similar to the common law distinction between grand larceny and petit larceny. Under the English common law the difference between the two types of larceny was determined by the value of the goods, a practice followed by some states today. New York, however, differentiates grand and petit larceny by elements other than, or in addition to, the monetary value of the stolen property. In New York, *petit larceny* is defined as follows: "A person is guilty of petit larceny when he steals property. Petit larceny is a class A misdemeanor." Petit larceny is "in essence, simply the basic crime of larceny." The term encompasses all thefts, including grand larceny, regardless of amounts or type of property stolen. In practice, however, New York's petit larceny statute is used to encompass thefts that do not amount to grand larceny.[12]

The New York Penal Code delineates four degrees of grand larceny, all of which are felonies. Grand larceny in the first degree, the most serious larceny offense, requires obtaining property valued at more than $1 million by extortion in which the victim is placed in fear of any one of several enumerated possibilities. The next three degrees require various attendant circumstances or value minimums, with the value decreasing to $50,000 (second degree), $3,000 (third degree), and $1,000 (fourth degree). Examples of attendant circumstances are seen in the definition of *grand larceny in the fourth degree*, which includes the theft of secret scientific materials, credit or debit cards, firearms, public records, and so on.[13]

Another modern approach regarding larceny-theft crimes is to combine all, or at least most, theft-related crimes into one crime of theft. In the Texas Penal Code's chapter on theft, for example, one section is entitled *Consolidation of theft offenses*. This section, reprinted in Focus 8.2, states that the section that follows it is a general theft statute, combining several types of theft that

---

FOCUS 8.2   A Modern Theft Statute

Texas Penal Code, Title 7, Chapter 31, Section 31.02 (2009). Consolidation of Theft Offenses.

Theft as defined in Section 31.03 constitutes a single offense superseding the separate offenses previously known as theft, theft by false pretext, conversion by a bailee, theft from the person, shoplifting, acquisition of property by threat, swindling, swindling by worthless check, embezzlement, extortion, receiving or concealing embezzled property, and receiving or concealing stolen property.

Texas Penal Code, Title 7, Chapter 31, Section 31.03 (2009). Theft.

(a) A person commits an offense if he unlawfully appropriates property with intent to deprive the owner of property.

(b) Appropriation of property is unlawful if:

(1) it is without the owner's effective consent;

(2) the property is stolen and the actor appropriates the property knowing it was stolen by another; or

(3) property in the custody of any law enforcement agency was explicitly represented by any law enforcement agent to the actor as being stolen and the actor appropriates the property believing it was stolen by another.

were previously defined as separate crimes. The Texas approach illustrates one modern approach to defining larceny-theft crimes. Section 31.03's statement of the elements of theft contains a lengthy list of situations and characteristics that are important to the crime of theft. One final point, however, is that the Texas Penal Code does contain some separate theft crimes, such as the following:

⊛ Theft of service

⊛ Theft of trade secrets

⊛ Presumption for theft by check

⊛ Unauthorized use of a vehicle

⊛ Tampering with identification numbers

⊛ Unauthorized use of a television decoding and interception device or a cable descrambling, decoding, or interception device

⊛ Manufacturing, selling, or distributing the devices listed in the previous crime concerning decoding[14]

Some jurisdictions continue to have numerous larceny-theft statutes covering the various types of larceny-theft. This approach, however, may result in a lack of coverage for some theft crimes. In these cases, it may be necessary to have specific theft crimes to cover the particular type of theft rather than rely on a general theft crime statute. Examples of such crimes are computer crimes, identity theft, and carjacking, each of which is discussed separately later in this chapter.

FOCUS 8.3 Shoplifting: A Frequent Theft Crime

- "More than $13 billion worth of goods are stolen from retailers each year. That's more than $35 million per day.
- There are approximately 27 million shoplifters (or 1 in 11 people) in our nation today. More than 10 million people have been caught shoplifting in the last five years.
- Shoplifting affects more than the offender. It overburdens the police and the courts, adds to a store's security expenses, costs consumers more for goods, costs communities lost dollars in sales taxes and hurts children and families.
- Shoplifters steal from all types of stores including department stores, specialty shops, supermarkets, drug stores, discounters, music stores, convenience stores and thrift shops.
- There is no profile of a typical shoplifter. Men and women shoplift about equally as often.
- Approximately 25 percent of shoplifters are kids, 75 percent are adults. 55 percent of adult shoplifters say they started shoplifting in their teens.
- Many shoplifters buy and steal merchandise in the same visit. Shoplifters commonly steal from $2 to $200 per incident depending upon the type of store and item(s) chosen.
- Shoplifting is often not a premeditated crime. 73 percent of adult and 72 percent of juvenile shoplifters don't plan to steal in advance.
- 9 percent of kids say they know other kids who shoplift. 66 percent say they hang out with those kids.
- Shoplifters say they are caught an average of only once in every 48 times they steal. They are turned over to the police 50 percent of the time.
- Approximately 3 percent of shoplifters are 'professionals' who steal solely for resale or profit as a business. These include drug addicts who steal to feed their habit, hardened professionals who steal as a life-style and international shoplifting gangs who steal for profit as a business. 'Professional' shoplifters are responsible for 10 percent of the total dollar losses.
- The vast majority of shoplifters are 'non-professionals' who steal, not out of criminal intent, financial need or greed but as a response to social and personal pressures in their life.
- The excitement generated from 'getting away with it' produces a chemical reaction resulting in what shoplifters describe as an incredible 'rush' or 'high' feeling. Many shoplifters will tell you that this high is their 'true reward,' rather than the merchandise itself.
- Drug addicts, who have become addicted to shoplifting, describe shoplifting as equally addicting as drugs.
- 57 percent of adults and 33 percent of juveniles say it is hard for them to stop shoplifting even after getting caught.
- Most non-professional shoplifters don't commit other types of crimes. They'll never steal an ashtray from your house and will return to you a $20 bill you may have dropped. Their criminal activity is restricted to shoplifting and therefore, any rehabilitation program should be 'offense-specific' for this crime.
- Habitual shoplifters steal an average of 1.6 times per week."

Source: Information is reproduced verbatim from the National Learning & Resource Center of the National Association for Shoplifting Prevention (NASP), a nonprofit organization. The data are based on "years of research with thousands of shoplifting offenders." The data and other relevant information on shoplifting may be found at the association's website, http://www.shopliftingprevention.org (accessed 10 December 2008). Click on shoplifting statistics.

A frequently committed type of larceny-theft is shoplifting, which is featured in Focus 8.3.

Burglary

A major property crime similar to but distinct from larceny-theft is **burglary**, which refers to the breaking and entering of an enclosed structure without consent and with the intent to commit a felony therein. It is important to note that burglary does not require an actual theft, as does larceny-theft. Estimated burglaries in 2007 showed a decrease of 0.2 percent from 2006, accounting for 22.1 percent of the estimated serious property crimes in 2007.[15]

Along with arson, common law burglary was classified as an offense against the habitation and occupancy. Today both arson and burglary are statutory crimes. The statutory definitions of burglary and arson go far beyond the common law definitions and elements, which, however, are important to an understanding of modern statutes.

Before examining the elements of common law burglary, it is necessary to distinguish residential burglary from robbery, discussed in Chapter 7. Robbery requires a taking of property from the person or presence of the victim by the use of force or threat of force, elements that are not required for burglary.

Burglary of a home may and often does occur when no one is home. But burglary may lead to robbery if the offender encounters the victim while committing the crime. Household burglary is one of the most serious of crimes, not only because of the illegal entry into the home but also because violence may occur if the home is occupied. Burglary is also serious because burglars may be involved in crime for many years.

Common Law Burglary

Common law burglary referred to breaking and entering the dwelling of another during the night with the intent to commit a felony. Thus, its elements were as follows:

1. A breaking and entering
2. Of the dwelling of another
3. During the nighttime
4. With the intent to commit a felony therein

Each element is important in the understanding of modern burglary statutes. First, the requirement of *breaking and entering* did not require destruction of any part of the property in order to enter, but it did require a "breaking, removing, or putting aside

Common law burglary required the breaking and entering of a dwelling place during the nighttime, with the intent to commit a felony. Modern burglary statutes are not as strict and may differ from state to state. (iComstock RF/Jupiter Images)

of something material, which constitutes a part of the dwelling house, and is relied on as a security against intrusion."[16] The emphasis on security is important. If the door was already open, entering by that means did not constitute a breaking. If the door was closed but unlatched, opening the door constituted a breaking. In some jurisdictions, if the door was open partially and if it was necessary to open it further to enter, breaking was deemed to have occurred.[17]

A 1994 Nebraska case underscores the importance of the element of breaking. A defendant who was convicted of burglary appealed his case on the grounds that when he jumped over a fence to steal transmission casings from a storage yard, he did not commit burglary because no breaking occurred. The Nebraska Supreme Court agreed and reversed his conviction. The court emphasized that burglary requires a forceful breaking and entering with the intent to commit any felony or steal property, that breaking is an essential element of the crime, and that it requires a removal of some obstruction.[18] As we shall note later, not all states require this traditional element for burglary.

Under some circumstances, such as obtaining entry by fraud, by threatening to use force, by going through a chimney, or by having a servant or some other person within the structure open the door, it was argued that constructive force sufficient to constitute a breaking had occurred. The breaking had to involve a **trespass**, a crime referring to the entering or remaining unlawfully in or on the premises (including land, boats, or other vehicles) of another under certain circumstances as specified by statute. Trespass is discussed in more detail later in this chapter. In addition to a trespass, the entry must have been accomplished by means of the breaking. Therefore, it would not be sufficient if the offender broke a window but then entered the dwelling through a door that had been left open by the owner.

Under common law burglary the requirement of entry could be satisfied if any part of the person (e.g., a hand or foot) entered; it was not necessary that the person's whole body enter the dwelling. The entry requirement could also be accomplished by the use of a tool, provided that the tool was for the purpose of committing the intended felony. Using an auger (a boring tool) to drill a hole through a floor to steal grain by letting the grain fall into a sack constituted an entry. It would not be an entry, however, if the offender inserted a tool into the dwelling to effect his or her own entry but did not actually enter.[19] Nor could entry be accomplished constructively by sending in someone who was not legally capable of committing a crime, such as a child, an insane person, or a trained monkey or other animal to commit the felony.

The second element of common law burglary required that the *dwelling of another* be entered. Under the common law, burglary was limited to acts that occurred within the home, referred to as the *dwelling* or the *dwelling place*. There was some precedent that a church could be the subject of burglary, because it was the home of the Almighty, and this common law position was accepted in a 1964 Maryland case.[20] Usually a dwelling was a place where someone slept regularly; occasional sleeping was not sufficient. If the building was used regularly during one season (e.g., a summer home), that would suffice, provided the possessor intended to return another summer. The dwelling requirement was met if someone slept regularly in an office or other structure; it was the regular sleeping that was critical to this element of the offense.

Included within the definition of *dwelling* were pertinent buildings that were "within the **curtilage**," such as the enclosed ground, garage, barn, stable, cellar, or other buildings immediately surrounding the dwelling. If there was no fence, the buildings considered to be within the curtilage would have to be reasonably close enough to the dwelling to be fenced.

One final requirement was that the dwelling place had to be that of *another person*. Burglary did not encompass breaking and entering your own property with the intent to commit a felony. This element was raised in a case in which an estranged husband entered the separate apartment occupied by his wife and was charged with burglary and trespass. The husband argued on appeal that because he and his wife were legally married he had a right to the dwelling and thus he could not be convicted of burglary since the element that the dwelling be another's place was not present. The Colorado Supreme Court disagreed and upheld the conviction. The court said that at most the fact of marriage would give the estranged husband an economic interest in the lease, but it would not give him a possessory interest in the apartment. According to the court, the "controlling question is occupancy rather than ownership." There was no evidence that the husband had a legal right to occupy the apartment even though the wife did not have a **restraining order** (a judicial order forbidding one to do something, as for example, in this situation, to go near the estranged wife) against him.[21]

Common law burglary also required that the crime occur during the night, usually defined as from sunset, or when the countenance of a person could not be discerned, until sunrise. Both the breaking and the entering had to occur at night, although they did not have to occur on the same night; a person might break on one night and enter on a subsequent night.

The final element of common law burglary was that of the *intent to commit a felony*, usually larceny-theft, but any felony would suffice. It was sufficient if one entered the building to commit the felony but did not actually do so. It was the unlawful breaking and entering with the intent of committing the felony that constituted burglary. If the felony (e.g., larceny-theft) was completed, the offender could be charged with and convicted of both larceny-theft and burglary. It is important to understand, however, that although larceny-theft always required that something be stolen, that was not the case with burglary.

Finally, if the individual entered the dwelling without an intent to commit a felony and once inside decided to commit a felony, he or she might be convicted of that felony but not of burglary. To constitute common law burglary, the intent to commit the felony must have been present at the time of the unlawful breaking and entering. The intent to commit a misdemeanor would not be sufficient; there must have been an intent to commit a felony.

Statutory Burglary

Most, if not all, of the common law requirements are retained in modern burglary statutes, some with modification. Although they may require unlawfully remaining, most statutes no longer require a breaking: Any illegal entrance may be sufficient. The Pennsylvania burglary statute is illustrative:

> A person is guilty of burglary if he enters a building or occupied structure, or separately secured or occupied portion thereof, with intent to commit a crime therein, unless the premises are at the time open to the public or the actor is licensed or privileged to enter. [The statute provides that it is a defense if the building is abandoned.][22]

The Pennsylvania criminal code defines *occupied structure* as: "Any structure, vehicle or place adapted for overnight accommodation of persons, or for car-

rying on business therein, whether or not a person is actually present."[23]

Notice that the Pennsylvania burglary statute requires only the intent to commit a *crime*, not the intent to commit a *felony* within the building or structure.

Some state statutes are more specific with regard to the structure involved. Consider, for example, the California statute, which lists numerous structures. The parts of the statute referring to other statutes that define some of these structures have been omitted here.

> Every person who enters any house, room, apartment, tenement, shop, warehouse, store, mill, barn, stable, outhouse or other building, tent, vessel, . . . floating home, . . . railroad car, locked or sealed cargo container, . . . trailer coach, . . . any house car, . . . inhabited camper, . . . aircraft, . . . or mine or any underground portion thereof, with intent to commit grand or petit larceny or any felony is guilty of burglary. . . . [The statute defines *inhabited* as meaning] currently being used for dwelling purposes, whether occupied or not.[24]

Even if they are not as specific as the California statute, most state burglary statutes do expand the common law requirement of a dwelling to include any structure, although they may provide greater penalties for persons who burglarize a dwelling. The distinction between night and day is retained in some statutes; in others it is eliminated or made relevant only to punishment.

Some jurisdictions define grades of burglary, such as aggravated burglary or burglary of the first and second degree; or they classify certain types of burglary as a felony of the first, second, or third degree and provide differential sentences depending on the perceived seriousness of the type of burglary.

New York's burglary statutes illustrate some of these points. In New York, where there are three degrees of burglary, *unlawfully remaining* is an alternative to *entering*, permitting a charge of burglary when a person "knowingly enters or remains unlawfully in a building with intent to commit a crime therein." While this phrase refers to all three degrees, it is the sole definition of third-degree burglary; to constitute first- or second-degree burglary, other elements must be met. Those elements range from being "armed with explosives or a deadly weapon" to displaying "what appears to be a pistol, revolver, rifle, shotgun, machine gun or other firearm," with some exceptions that may reduce a first-degree charge to second-degree burglary. In essence, the New York statute grades burglary in terms of the total circumstances in which it occurs, with special reference to the potential for danger. All three degrees of burglary are felonies in New York.[25]

The New York statute deviates from the common law requirement of intent to commit a felony in that it refers only to the intent to commit a crime. Thus, a burglary conviction could be based on an intent to commit a misdemeanor. Other statutes, such as Montana's, use terminology such as "with the purpose to commit an offense therein." Montana's statute requires knowingly entering unlawfully or knowingly remaining unlawfully.[26] Texas provides that a person who, without "the effective consent of the owner," enters or unlawfully remains in a dwelling or a building (or any portion of the building) with the intent to commit a theft, a felony, or an assault commits a burglary.[27]

The Montana statute was interpreted in a 1989 case, *State v. Christofferson*, in which the defendant gained entry to a house by deceit. He told a student who lived there that the owner of the house, a woman he knew, told him to check on the student and the woman's daughter, who had remained in the home with the student when her mother left town. Apparently the mother did not tell the defendant to go *into* the house, but he was admitted to the house by the student. Later the defendant twice told the student he was leaving, but he did not do so. Instead, he went to the daughter's bedroom and engaged in what Montana calls felony sexual intercourse without consent. The Montana Supreme Court upheld the defendant's convictions for that crime and for burglary, the latter based on the fact that he remained in the home unlawfully and with the purpose of committing an offense.[28]

Not all jurisdictions permit the defendant to be charged with both the crime of burglary and the crime for which the defendant committed the illegal entry, for example, larceny-theft. Maine allows convictions for both, as noted in the Maine statute reproduced in Focus 8.4. Other states have restrictions concerning multiple convictions. Pennsylvania, for example, restricts convictions for both burglary and the offense for which that burglary was committed (or attempted) only if the latter is a felony of the first or second degree.[29]

Finally, in recent years some jurisdictions have enacted new statutes to cover the entry of a dwelling for the purpose of committing a robbery. This new approach to crimes against the person and the habitation, called *home invasion*, was discussed in Chapter 7.

Motor Vehicle Theft

Since motor vehicles did not exist, the common law had no need for a theft statute covering them. States differ in how they define vehicle theft, but in the official crime data of the FBI, theft *from* a vehicle is included under larceny-theft while theft *of* a motor vehicle is a separate category of serious property crime, defined as "the theft or attempted theft of a motor vehicle." This definition includes "automobiles, trucks, buses, motorcycles, motorscooters, snowmobiles, etc." but "excludes the taking of a motor vehicle for temporary use by those persons having lawful access."[30]

An estimated 1.1 million motor vehicles were stolen in the United States in 2007, representing an 8.1 percent decrease from 2006 and a 13.1 percent decrease from 2003. Automobiles accounted for 73.4 percent of those thefts.[31]

In most jurisdictions, motor vehicle theft is covered by general theft statutes and thus does not warrant a separate statute. Others retain specific auto theft stat-

---

FOCUS 8.4   The Maine Burglary Statute

Maine Criminal Code, Title 17-A, Part 2, Chapter 17 (2008): M.R.S., Section 401. Burglary

1. A person is guilty of burglary if:
   The person enters or surreptitiously remains in a structure knowing that that person is not licensed or privileged to do so, with the intent to commit a crime therein . . . or [The statute then discusses the differences among the three grades of crimes, with the most serious being a Class A

crime, which involves burglary while armed with a firearm or knowing that an accomplice is so armed.] . . .

3. A person may be convicted both of burglary and of the crime that the person committed or attempted to commit after entering or remaining in the structure, but . . . [The statute then discusses sentencing provisions for these circumstances.]

Under the Uniform Crime Reports, auto theft includes the theft or attempted theft of a motor vehicle. Many cars can be stolen quite quickly, even without tools, although some may require tools and the work of more than one thief for quick success. (IStockPhoto)

utes, and Maine refers to its special statute as *Burglary of a motor vehicle.* The statute provides the following:

1. A person is guilty of burglary of a motor vehicle if:

   A. The person enters a motor vehicle, knowing that the person is not licensed or privileged to do so, with the intent to commit a crime therein. Violation of this paragraph is a Class D crime; or

   B. The person violates paragraph A, and the person forcibly enters a motor vehicle that is locked. Violation of this paragraph is a Class C crime.[32]

Many states distinguish between *motor vehicle theft* and *joyriding*, the unauthorized use of a motor vehicle without the intent to steal it. For example, Maine's statute, *Unauthorized use of property*, covers acts such as joyriding, unauthorized use of a vehicle in one's possession for repair, and knowing failure to comply with returning a rental car on time under circumstances that would constitute a "gross deviation from the [rental] agreement." A defense to any of these crimes is that the person "reasonably believed that the owner would have consented to the person's conduct had the owner known of it."[33]

Arson

The fourth serious property crime according to official FBI crime data is **arson**, which, as noted in Focus 8.1, is defined as "any willful or malicious burning or attempt to burn, with or without intent to defraud, a dwelling house, public building, motor vehicle or aircraft, or personal property of another person." Some statutes include the burning of one's own property if done with the intent to defraud.

In 1978 arson was first classified by the FBI as a serious property crime. Arson is indeed a serious crime, causing significant property damage and, in some cases, injury and death. But it is difficult to acquire sufficient evidence for arson convictions because much, if not all, of the evidence of the crime may be destroyed by the fire. In 2007, agencies reported 64,332 arsons (a decrease of 6.7 percent from 2006), with arson of structures accounting for 42.9 percent of those fires.[34]

In recent years increasing attention has been given to arson not only because of the high percentage of young people involved but also because of the serious injuries, deaths, and extensive property damage caused by this crime, as illustrated by two massively destructive fires in June 2002, both of which were started by firefighters, as noted in Focus 8.5.

FOCUS 8.5 Arson Viewed Historically

In 1903 the deadliest fire in U.S. history claimed the lives of 575 people at the Iroquois Theater in Chicago. In 1992 survivors of the second-largest fire in U.S. history gathered in Boston to mark the fire's fiftieth anniversary. The Cocoanut Grove nightclub fire, which they escaped on 28 November 1942, killed 491 people.[1] Recognition of the lack of adequate safety precautions, which increased the death toll in both of these fires, led many communities to improve fire codes and their enforcement. Improved fire codes are important, but they cannot always eliminate human tragedies, especially when fires are set deliberately. Several recent examples are noted in this focus.

Coconino National Forest in Arizona, 2007

Van Bateman, 57, was sentenced to two years in federal prison, followed by three years on probation; assessed a $5,000 fine; and ordered to pay $10,390 in restitution to the U.S. Forest Service after he was convicted of arson in the fire in the Coconino National Forest. Bateman had served 34 years as a firefighter.

Colorado Wildfires, June 2002

Wildfires that consumed thousands of acres in central Colorado, 55 miles southwest of Denver, in the summer of 2002 were started by Terry Lynn Barton, 38, who worked for the U.S. Forest Service. These fires, the largest in the state's history, required the efforts of thousands of firefighters for three weeks; consumed 133 homes, one commercial building, and 466 outbuildings; and cost $39.1 million to fight. Barton, the mother of two, was charged with four felony counts and faced up to 65 years in prison if convicted. In December 2002 Barton pleaded guilty to starting the fire and then lying about that fact to federal law enforcement authorities. She was sentenced to six years in prison on federal charges and six on state charges, for a total of 12 years. Due to a technicality, however, she was resentenced. The final arrangement was that the sentences would be served concurrently, and she would then serve 15 years on probation in

Colorado on the state charges. Barton was released from federal prison in June 2008 and had 72 hours to report to Colorado for her probationary term. She was also required to get a job and begin paying back $14.6 million in damages to the U.S. Forest Service and over $30 million in private damages. She was also required to perform community service in one of the counties damaged by the fire for which she was responsible.[2]

Arizona Wildfires, June 2002

The most destructive wildfires in Arizona history also occurred in June 2002, consuming over 450,000 acres and destroying more than 500 homes. A part-time firefighter for the forestry department of the Bureau of Indian Affairs, Leonard Gregg, 29, pled guilty to arson and was sentenced to 10 years in prison and ordered to pay $27 million in restitution to his victims.[3]

San Juan Hotel Fire, December 1986

When three members of Local 901 of the International Brotherhood of Teamsters set fire to the Dupont Plaza Hotel in San Juan, Puerto Rico, all they wanted was a small fire that would put pressure on the hotel's management to come to terms with the union. What they got was a runaway blaze that started in the hotel's ballroom and raced up the elevator shafts, killing 97 people as it roared through the hotel.

The fire moved through the ground level of the hotel so fast that many occupants were not able to reach emergency exits. Rescuers found corpses propped up at the bar. Some of the hotel's guests on higher floors made it to the roof, where they were rescued by helicopter. Others scaled walls or jumped out of windows only to find themselves in the pool area with a locked gate. Some climbed over the fence and barbed wire to reach safety.[4]

The three teamsters were arrested and admitted their involvement in setting the fire. For their involvement in the deadliest fire in North America in 40 years, Hector Escudero Aponte was sentenced to two concurrent 99-year terms; Jose Francisco

---

In response to a series of burnings of predominantly African American churches during his administration, President Bill Clinton signed the Church Arson Prevention Act of 1996, which provides $10 million in private loans to assist in rebuilding churches destroyed by fire, doubles (to 20 years) the maximum sentence for arson of a house of worship, and permits the federal government to become involved in arson cases involving racial hatred.[35]

Common Law Arson

Common law arson, which at times carried the penalty of death by burning, had the following elements:

1. The malicious

2. Burning

3. Of the dwelling

4. Of another

Lopez to 97 years; and Jimenez Rivera to 75 years. The U.S. Supreme Court refused to consider the appeals, but subsequently the trial judge, who had given the defendants harsher sentences than the prosecutor requested, reduced the sentences. An appeal to vacate the sentences was denied in 1993.[5]

Bronx Social Club Fire, March 1990

In March 1990, 87 people were asphyxiated or burned to death as fire raged quickly through the Happy Land Social Club, an illegal social club in the Bronx, New York, that had been ordered closed due to fire code violations. This was the nation's worst fire since the San Juan, Puerto Rico, hotel fire just discussed. Julio Gonzalez, 36, a Cuban immigrant, was charged with 178 counts of murder, arson, and related crimes and was convicted and sentenced to 25 years to life in prison on each of 87 murder counts, the sentences to be served concurrently. Gonzalez is eligible for parole after he serves 25 years. The owner entered a guilty plea to two misdemeanor counts of building code violations and was sentenced to 50 hours of community service and a $150,000 fine.[6]

Terry Lynn Barton, a U.S. Forest Service employee, was charged with four felonies, including lying to law enforcement authorities. She entered a negotiated guilty plea for her role in starting a fire in Colorado that cost over $39 million to fight, consumed 133 homes and hundreds of other buildings, and destroyed thousands of acres. After her initial sentencing, Barton was resentenced due to a technicality. She was released from prison in June 2008 and was required to report to Colorado state officials to begin serving her 15-year probationary term and to make arrangements for getting a job, paying restitution, and performing community service. (Ed Andrieski/AP Images)

1. "Cocoanut Survivors Mark Anniversary," *Tampa Tribune* (29 November 1992), p. 9.
2. "Guilty Plea in Huge Fire in Colorado," *New York Times* (7 December 2002), p. 16; "Barton Enters Prison for Hayman Fire," *Denver Post* (23 March 2003), p. 1B; "Hayman Fire's Culprit to Return: Barton Has 72 Hours to Report for Probation in Colorado," *Denver Post* (3 June 2008), p. 1. The legal issues are discussed in *People v. Barton*, 121 P.3d 224 (Colo. Co.App. 2004), *cert. denied*, 2005 Colo. LEXIS 894 (2005).
3. "Part-Time Firefighter Is Held in Setting of Blaze in Arizona," *New York Times* (1 July 2002), p. 2; "National Briefing Southwest: Arizona: Hearing for Arsonist," *New York Times* (14 December 2002), p. 23; "'Radio' Arsonist to Pay $28 Mil, Serve 10 Years," *Arizona Republic* (9 March 2004), p. 1B.
4. "Anatomy of a Disaster: The Dupont Plaza Hotel Fire," *American Bar Association Journal* 73 (1 August 1987): 100.
5. *United States v. Jimenez-Rivera*, 842 F.2d 545 (1st Cir. 1988), *cert. denied*, 487 U.S. 1223 (1988).
6. "Happy Land Arsonist Sentenced to 25 Years to Life for 87 Deaths," *New York Times* (20 October 1991), p. 8.

Each of these elements requires further examination. The first, a *malicious burning*, meant that the perpetrator must have a criminal intent. Negligence was not sufficient to establish arson, nor was there a felony arson crime analogous to felony murder, which was discussed in Chapter 6. A fire that resulted from the commission of another crime was not arson. Nor did one commit arson by burning one's own dwelling. If in the process of burning his own dwelling, however, the owner created an unreasonable fire hazard for other dwellings—one or more of which burned—the property owner could be charged with arson for the burning of the other's dwelling.

The criminal intent element did not require malice toward the property owner or the property in question. It required either the intent to burn the dwelling, the knowledge that a fire would burn the dwelling, or the setting of a fire without excuse or justification that created an obvious hazard to the dwelling of another.

The requirement of *burning* did not mean that the dwelling had to be burned completely. Earlier cases established that there must be a *burning*, not just a smoking or a maliciously set fire that was put out before any of the dwelling was burned.[36]

The common law arson requirement that the burning be of a *dwelling* was identical to that of common law burglary. The requirement *of another* referred to possession, not ownership. If a landlord burned a dwelling rented to a tenant, the element would be satisfied because the tenant had a legal right to possession of that dwelling at the time of the burning.

Statutory Arson

Although some jurisdictions retain the common law definition of arson, others have expanded the crime to include the burning of many structures other than dwellings and the burning of one's own structures. Some statutes eliminate the requirement of actual burning and permit an arson charge when damage is caused by an explosion that does not result in a fire or when a fire that is started purposely does not burn the structure in question. But it must be shown that the actor had the intent to damage or to destroy that structure. The statutes may also include the burning of trees, especially forests.

The Texas Penal Code illustrates these points. This code defines *arson* as follows:

(a) A person commits an offense if the person starts a fire, regardless of whether the fire continues after ignition, or causes an explosion with intent to destroy or damage:

(1) any vegetation, fence, or structure on open-space land; or

(2) any building, habitation, or vehicle:

(A) knowing that it is within the limits of an incorporated city or town;

(B) knowing that it is insured against damage or destruction;

(C) knowing that it is subject to a mortgage or other security interest;

(D) knowing that it is located on property belonging to another;

(E) knowing that it has located within it property belonging to another; or

(F) when the person is reckless about whether the burning or explosion will endanger the life of some individual or the safety of the property of another.[37]

Vermont has a separate statute for arson causing the death of another, leading to a charge of murder. Note also that this statute goes beyond the common law requirement of the dwelling of another:

A person who wilfully and maliciously burns the building of another, or wilfully and maliciously sets fire to a building owned in whole or in part by himself, by means of which the life of a person is lost, shall be guilty of murder in the first degree.[38]

Some states have individual statutes aimed at specific types of structures. For example, North Carolina has a statute covering the burning of a mobile home, a manufactured-type house, or a recreational trailer home. A person who maliciously burns any of these structures, occupied and serving as the dwelling house of another, may be charged with arson in the first degree.[39]

A second North Carolina statute covers the crime of *fraudulently setting fire to dwelling houses*. The act must be malicious or wanton or done for a fraudulent purpose and may include the dwelling of the perpetrator, who may be guilty of the crime even if he or she does not actually burn the structure. It is sufficient to "aid, counsel or procure the burning of such building." The statute also requires, however, that the actor be "the occupant of any building used as a dwelling house."[40] A third statute prohibits burning or aiding or counseling or procuring the burning of numerous types of buildings (such as an uninhabited house or a stable, office, warehouse, coach house, outhouse, shop, mill, barn, and so on) "used or intended to be used in carrying on any trade or manufacture."[41]

North Carolina also has a statute that covers damage (exclusive of burning or attempting to burn) to houses, churches, fences, and walls.[42] In specifying punishment for arson, North Carolina distinguishes between *first-degree arson* (dwelling occupied at the time) and *second-degree arson* (dwelling unoccupied at the time).[43]

Other states also specify degrees of arson but under varying circumstances. New York has four degrees, ranging from the first degree (arson of a building occupied by another not involved in the crime when the offender knows that the circumstances are such that someone is likely to be in that building) to the fourth degree (reckless arson).[44]

LESS SERIOUS PROPERTY OFFENSES

In addition to requesting law enforcement agencies to collect data on the serious property crimes of larceny-theft, burglary, motor vehicle theft, and arson, the FBI compiles data on less serious property crimes, some of which are discussed in this section. The phrase *less serious* does not mean that these offenses have a lesser economic impact on society or their immediate victims. For example, the first crimes discussed, embezzlement and fraud, may result in greater economic losses per year than larceny-theft and burglary. But for the general public, embezzlement and fraud do not arouse the fear and anger that occur with burglary and larceny-theft.

Embezzlement

Acts that are defined as **embezzlement** in today's statutes were not included in common law larceny-theft because a person already in lawful possession of property could not be charged with larceny-theft. Statutory requirements were necessary to bring under the criminal law the acquisition of another's property by misappropriation or misapplication when the actor already had legal control of the property.

Embezzlement refers to misappropriating or misapplying property or money that was already entrusted to the individual. Embezzlement is a general theft crime that can be committed by many people in various settings. The crime requires **conversion**, which refers to the process of using the property or goods of another for one's own use and without permission. Thus, conversion is a serious interference with the owner's property, not merely a movement of that property. Although some statutes define the property that may be subject to embezzlement in the same way as property subject to larceny-theft, other jurisdictions define the crime more broadly, some even including real property. Some jurisdictions have a separate statute to cover embezzlement by public officials, making the penalty more severe for them than for others.

Some jurisdictions today do not distinguish between larceny-theft and embezzlement. The Virginia Criminal Code contains the following provision:

If any person wrongfully and fraudulently use, dispose of, conceal or embezzle any money, bill, note, check, order, draft, bond, receipt, bill of lading or any other personal property, tangible or intangible, which he shall have received for another or for his employer, principal or bailor, or by virtue of his office, trust, or employment, or which shall have been entrusted or delivered to him by another or by any court, corporation or company, he shall be deemed guilty of embezzlement. Proof of embezzlement shall be sufficient to sustain the charge of larceny.[45]

Fraud

The act of *fraud* refers to falsely representing a fact, either by conduct or by words or writing, in order to induce a person to rely on the misrepresentation and surrender something of value. Fraud has several categories, such as securities fraud, savings and loan fraud, mail fraud, consumer fraud, health care fraud, fraudulent transfer of a motor vehicle (or any other item of value), forgery, and fraud by government officials. Thus, it is difficult to generalize, but one court has articulated the following as the elements of fraud:

1. A representation
2. Its falsity
3. Its materiality
4. The speaker's knowledge of its falsity or ignorance of its truth
5. The speaker's intent that it should be acted upon by the person and in the manner reasonably contemplated
6. The hearer's ignorance of its falsity
7. The hearer's reliance upon its truth
8. The right of the hearer to rely upon it
9. The hearer's consequent and proximate injury or damage[46]

Numerous acts are included within the crime of fraud. Several are discussed in Focus 8.6; others are mentioned here in the text, while still others were discussed in Focus 3.3, which showed the relationship between fraud and conspiracy. Focus 8.6 begins with an overview of the 2007 FBI report on financial crimes. But before looking at specific types of fraud, the discussion focuses on one type of victim: the elderly.

Fraud Against the Elderly

The elderly are often easy targets for fraud scams, willing to "invest" their savings and other assets in order to make the promised "big bucks." Many juris-

In May 2008, the FBI reported the following key findings in its 2007 *Financial Crimes Report to the Public*:

- "As of the end of Fiscal Year (FY) 2007, 529 corporate fraud cases were being pursued by the FBI, several of which involve losses to public investors that individually exceed $1 billion.
- FBI securities and commodities fraud cases increased from 937 in FY 2003 to 1,217 in FY 2007, and resulted in $24 million in recoveries, $1.7 billion in restitution orders, and $202.7 million in fines in FY 2007.
- Through FY 2007, the 2,493 health care fraud cases investigated by the FBI resulted in 839 indictments and 635 convictions of health care fraud criminals.
- The 1,204 pending mortgage fraud cases in FY 2007 resulted in 321 indictments, 206 convictions, $595.9 million in restitution orders, and $21.8 million in recoveries.
- The FBI investigated 548 money laundering cases in FY 2007, resulting in 141 indictments, 112 convictions, $66.9 million in restitution orders, $2.2 million in recoveries, and $11.4 million in fines."[1]

Among the fraud cases that rocked the nation in the previous decade are those of several corporations. In 2002 fraud charges were filed against WorldCom, the second-largest long-distance provider in the United States (through MCI) as well as a major Internet carrier. The charges alleged that WorldCom executives falsely reported earnings by approximately $3.8 billion (later stated to be over $11 billion), representing the largest accounting fraud in U.S. history. The company filed for bankruptcy in July 2002, the largest bankruptcy in U.S. history to date. Subsequently the company emerged from bankruptcy under the name of MCI, Inc. Several former top officials of WorldCom either pleaded guilty or were convicted of various crimes. Bernard J. Ebbers, the founder and chair, was sentenced to 25 years in prison with no chance of release until he serves 85 percent of that term. As a result of WorldCom's bankruptcy, approximately 17,000 employees lost their jobs, along with $600 million in pensions, while shareholders also sustained financial losses.[2]

L. Dennis Kozlowski, former chair and chief executive of Tyco International, and Tyco's former chief financial officer, Mark H. Swartz, were charged with grand larceny, fraud, conspiracy, and falsifying documents. The first trial of these two defendants ended in a mistrial in April 2004. Kozlowski and Swartz were tried a second time in the spring of 2005; both were convicted and sentenced to up to 25 years in prison. They will be eligible for parole after serving eight years and four months. Kozlowski was fined 70 million. Swartz was fined $35 million. The two were ordered to pay a total of $154 million in restitution to their victims.[3]

John J. Rigas, founder and CEO of Adelphia Communications Corporation, along with his son, Timothy Rigas, were found guilty of securities, bank fraud, and conspiracy. The company's former assistant treasurer, Michael C. Mulcahey, was acquitted, while

dictions are paying more attention to such scams. For example, on 20 May 2007, the *New York Times* ran this headline on its lead story: "Bilking the Elderly, with a Corporate Assist." Richard Guthrie, 92, who was duped into giving out his personal identifiers to telephone callers, who then sold the information to other criminals, was featured. Guthrie, like many elderly people, according to an attorney for the Federal Trade Commission, was afraid to ask for help for fear his children would take over his accounts. Also, some elderly do not understand what is happening when they attempt to withdraw money and there are insufficient funds. According to the article, names and personal information are sold for as little at 6.5 cents a name. In this case, the victim was quoted as saying, "I loved getting these calls. . . . Since my wife passed away, I don't have many people to talk with. I didn't even know they were stealing from me until everything was gone."[47]

Mortgage Fraud

With the housing market in a downward tailspin in 2008, it was not surprising that the U.S. Department of Justice (DOJ) and the FBI would investigate mortgage fraud. Operation Malicious Mortgage resulted in charges against 406 defendants in 50 judicial districts between the beginning of March and 18 June 2008. According to the FBI director, "Operation Malicious Mortgage is a concerted, joint law enforcement and prosecutorial effort aimed at disrupting individuals and groups engaged in mortgage fraud." In addition to the DOJ and the FBI, numerous other federal agencies were involved in the efforts to apprehend and prosecute persons engaged in any of three types of mortgage fraud, described as follows:

Lending fraud frequently involves multiple loan transactions in which industry professionals construct mortgage transactions based on gross fraud-the jury deadlocked on the charges against another Rigas son, Michael, 52. Subsequently Michael Rigas entered a guilty plea to charges of making a false entry to an accounting record and faced up to three years in prison. He was sentenced to 10 months of

His first trial resulted in a mistrial, but in his second trial, Dennis Kozlowski was convicted of several charges, including defrauding Tyco International, the company he previously headed as chair and chief executive officer. Kozlowski and his former chief financial officer, Mark H. Swartz, were both sentenced to up to 25 years in prison, fined, and ordered to pay restitution to their victims. (Louis Lanzamo/AP Images)

home confinement, followed by 14 months of court-supervised probation. He was also fined $2,000. John Rigas, 80, was sentenced to 15 years in prison; Timothy Rigas, to 20 years.

Energy giant Enron Corporation, headquartered in Houston, Texas, and listed as the seventh-largest company on the Fortune 500 list, filed for bankruptcy in December 2001. U.S. attorneys secured indictments against numerous former Enron officials, with some pleading guilty in plea negotiations, while others were convicted after trials. The main focus was on Enron's founder and former executive, Kenneth L. Lay, and on Jeffrey K. Skilling, Enron's former chief executive. Both were convicted, but Lay died prior to sentencing, and according to established rules of criminal procedure, his conviction was vacated because he could not appeal it. Skilling was sentenced to 24.3 years in prison, with his trial judge at sentencing stating that the defendant sentenced hundreds if not thousands to lives of poverty through his crimes.[4]

1. Federal Bureau of Investigation Press Release, "FBI Issues Financial Crimes Report," http://www.fbi.gov/pressrel/pressre l08/07fcr_052208.htm, accessed 9 July 2008.
2. "WorldCom Ex-CEO Gets 25 Years in Prison," *Washington Post* (17 July 2005), p. 3.
3. "WorldCom Ex-CEO Gets 25 Years."
4. "Skilling Sentenced to 24 Years," *New York Times* (24 October 2006), p. 1B.

ulent misrepresentations about the borrower's financial status, such as overstating the borrower's income or assets. . . . Foreclosure rescue scams involve criminals who target legitimate homeowners in dire financial circumstances and fraudulently collect fees for foreclosure prevention services or obtain ownership interests in residential properties. Both of these fraudulent mortgage schemes may be furthered by filing bankruptcy petitions that automatically stay foreclosure.[48]

Mail and Wire Fraud

Historically, most frauds were prosecuted in state courts by state prosecutors, but federal statutes are necessary to cover fraud across state lines. The mail fraud statute was passed in 1872 and is the oldest of the federal statutes that cover crimes traditionally considered to be state problems. This statute provides a $1,000 fine

or imprisonment for not more than five years, or both, for anyone convicted of using the post office or any other authorized depository for mail matter for the purpose of defrauding people of their money or other property rights. The penalty may increase to a $1 million fine or 30 years in prison, or both, if the violation involves a financial institution.[49]

The development and use of modern technological devices that transport information across state lines have created an even greater need for federal laws. The wire fraud statute, enacted in 1952, provides the same penalties as the mail fraud statute for persons convicted of using "wire, radio, or television communications in interstate or foreign commerce" for the purpose of fraud.[50]

To commit mail or wire fraud, the actor does not have to succeed. Mail and wire fraud statutes constitute an important tool in the government's efforts to combat white-collar crime, for the statutes are broad and flexible. In 1984 Congress added a section on *bank fraud* to the federal statute. It provides for sanctions against writing checks with insufficient funds as well as crimes associated with the failure of banks and other financial institutions.[51]

A successful mail or wire fraud case requires that the government prove three elements:

1. A scheme or artifice formed with the intent to defraud
2. Using or causing the mails or wire to be used
3. In furtherance of the scheme

The government is not required to show that the scheme was successful or even that victims suffered losses; it has to show only that the defendant had the specific intent to defraud.[52]

To satisfy the *use* requirement, the second element, the defendant does not have to be directly involved in using the mail or wire; nor does the victim have to receive the information through either means. But there must be evidence that either the mail or the wire actually was used and that its use was a reasonably foreseeable result of the defendant's actions.

The final element does not require that the mail or wire be essential to the scheme but requires only that either or both are useful to the defendant or closely related to the scheme, as illustrated by the case of *Schmuck v. United States*, in which the U.S. Supreme Court upheld a defendant's conviction for mail fraud after rolling back odometers. The Court held that for a conviction under this statute, the mails do not have to be an essential element of the crime as long as they are incident to an essential part of the scheme. In *Schmuck* the defendant, a Wisconsin used-car distributor, "purchased used cars, rolled back their odometers, and then sold the automobiles to Wisconsin retail dealers for prices artificially inflated because of the low-mileage readings." The dealers then sold the cars at higher prices to their customers. The resale of each used automobile was completed when the retail dealer submitted a title application form to the Wisconsin Department of Transportation on behalf of the buyer of the car. The title to the car could not be transferred without submission of a Wisconsin title, which was secured through the mails.

Schmuck argued that the mail fraud statute does not apply unless the mail "affirmatively assists the perpetrator in carrying out his fraudulent scheme." The U.S. Supreme Court did not agree and held that a rational jury could find that under the facts of this case, the "title-registration mailings were part of the execution of the fraudulent scheme, a scheme which did not reach fruition until the retail dealers resold the cars and effected transfers of title."[53]

Health Care Fraud

One of the high-priority areas for federal prosecutors in recent years has been health care fraud, which includes defrauding Medicare, Medicaid, and the Department of Veterans Affairs or other government and health care insurers as well as individuals. The focus on this area of crime, however, has shifted since the terrorist acts of 11 September 2001, as the U.S. Department of Justice has reallocated much of its staff to counterterrorism.

Still, health care fraud remains an important issue at both the federal and the state levels. The fraud may be related to double billing, the quality of care provided, billing for unnecessary care, or billing for services that were not provided. Cases are typically brought against health care professionals, hospitals, pharmacies, medical supply companies, nursing homes, and persons associated with any of these. The cases may involve large sums of money and many victims, with the estimated cost of health care fraud nationally between $60 billion and $100 billion each year.[54]

Health care fraud may occur at all levels, but it is easier to commit at the federal level because of the size of the programs and the amount of time and effort required for management to respond. Making price adjustments, for example, can take months of paperwork in the federal system.

Concern with fraud in the area of health care led Congress in 1996 to enact a bill that created a new crime of *health care fraud*, which carries a maximum penalty of 10 years in prison for knowingly defrauding any federal health care benefit program. If a person is injured as a result of the violation, the perpetrator may be sentenced to life in prison. A final provision is that a person who commits theft or embezzlement in connection with health care may be incarcerated for up to 10 years in prison.[55]

A recent health care fraud investigation leading to arrests in Florida illustrates health care prosecutions in this area. In June 2008, the FBI announced the indictment of three brothers and an assistant in Miami for allegedly financing 11 corrupt HIV infusion clinics. The indictment charges the defendants with filing

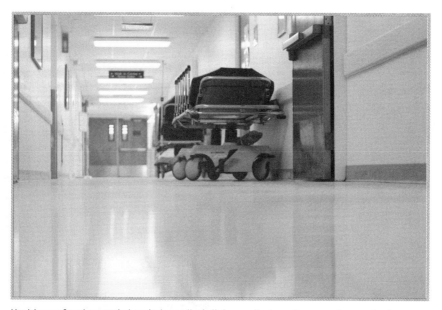

Health care fraud occurs in hospitals, medical clinics, medical supply companies, nursing homes, and pharmacies and is committed by physicians and their assistants, nurses, pharmacists, and others who work in the health care field. The estimated annual cost of health care fraud is between $60 billion and $100 billion. (IStockPhoto)

$110 million with Medicare for services that were not provided. The indictment also charges the defendants with laundering the illegally obtained payments. Carlos, Luis, and Jose Benitez owned the clinics; Thomas McKenzie was a physician's assistant in those clinics. McKenzie was allegedly responsible for training doctors and other health care providers in how to make it "appear that legitimate and appropriate medical services were being provided as well as overseeing the preparation of documents to make it appear that the services were actually rendered and medically necessary." McKenzie, who faces 50 years in prison, pleaded guilty to conspiracy to commit health care fraud and to submitting false Medicare claims. The three brothers, who are fugitives, each face 155 years in prison.[56]

States may also have health fraud statutes. Some are in the criminal code, while others are in public welfare codes. Illinois, for example, has a statute entitled *managed health care fraud* within its chapter on public aid, but the state also has a statute within its criminal code. That statute, entitled *health care benefits fraud*, classifies the crime as a Class A misdemeanor and defines it as follows:

> A person commits health care benefits fraud if he or she with the intent to defraud or deceive any provider, other than a governmental unit or agency, obtains or attempts to obtain health care benefits.[57]

Securities Fraud

The exchange of securities is a highly regulated business in the United States. **Securities** include stocks, bonds, notes, and other documents that are representative of a share in a company or a debt of the company. Of the several federal statutes covering the exchange of securities, two are used most frequently for prosecution of securities violations.

The Securities Act of 1933 requires that securities to be sold to the public must be registered. Complete information must be given concerning the stock offering and the issuer. The Securities Exchange Act of 1934 regulates the operation of over-the-counter trading and the buying and selling of stock. It specifies the information that must be published concerning stocks listed on the national securities exchanges. These statutes and others are administered by the Securities and Exchange Commission (SEC).[58]

The securities statutes prohibit the following:

- ✪ The use of any device, scheme, or artifice to defraud

- ✪ The making of an untrue statement of facts material to the buying and selling of securities

✖ The omission of information that would result in a misleading statement

✖ Acts that operate to defraud or deceive the stock purchaser

Intent is a material element of the crimes under these statutes. In addition, the defendant must use interstate commerce through the mail or other methods, and closely related crimes—such as mail and wire fraud, conspiracy, aiding and abetting, and the making of false statements—may also be prosecuted under these acts. Finally, the object of the transaction in question must be a security as defined by the statutes.

Administrative, civil, and criminal actions and remedies are provided by the securities acts. Initial investigations into possible violations of the statutes (or the rules promulgated by the SEC in accordance with the administrative powers delegated to that agency by Congress) are conducted by the SEC. The U.S. Department of Justice has sole jurisdiction to prosecute criminal violations under these statutes. The FBI estimates that the total annual loss from securities crimes is approximately $40 billion a year.[59] Focus 8.6 contains information concerning the prosecution of securities cases (see again Focus 8.6).

Insider Trading

The most frequent type of securities prosecutions in recent years have been those involving **insider trading**, which occurs when a director, officer, or stockholder who holds more than 10 percent of the stock of a corporation listed on a national exchange buys and sells corporate shares. The SEC requires monthly reports of insider trading. **Insider information** refers to information known (generally by securities officers) before it is made available to the general public. If, contrary to SEC regulations, the insiders do not publicize the information available to them and they trade securities on the basis of that information, they could face criminal charges as well as civil fines and other penalties. The *disclose or abstain rule* exists to make trading more equitable because it is unfair for insiders to make profits based on information that is not available to the public. Such trading violates a fiduciary duty. (A *fiduciary* is one who manages money for another and has special responsibilities and liabilities as a result.)

Prosecutions for insider trading began increasing in 1981, when the SEC initiated a highly publicized campaign to inform stockbrokers, investors, and oth-

Securities and investment fraud includes numerous types of crimes, but the most far-reaching and largest in terms of financial losses is thought to be the fraud committed by New York broker Bernard L. Madoff, arrested in December 2008 in a global scheme that, in Madoff's own assessment, could account for over $50 billion in losses to his victims. Madoff entered a guilty plea in March 2009 and faced up to 150 years in prison. (Daniel Barry/Bloomberg News/Landov)

ers about insider trading and prosecutions for the offense. Congress enacted the Insider Trading Sanctions Act of 1984, which increased the penalties. Among other sanctions, the insider faces civil fines of up to four times the amount of the money earned from insider trading. The maximum criminal fine was increased from $10,000 to $100,000.[60] In 1988 Congress enacted a statute that increased the penalties for insider trading.[61]

The penalties for many corporate crimes, such as insider trading and fraud, were increased by the Sarbanes-Oxley Act (SOX) of 2002. This statute contains new laws concerning **obstruction of justice** (interference with the orderly processes of courts) by destroying documents. It also increases penalties for fraud and conspiracy and requires the chief officers of corporations to certify that financial statements comply with the requirements of the

SEC Act of 1934 and fairly represent the actual financial condition of the companies. Corporate executives who knowingly falsify such certification may be fined up to $5 million and imprisoned for up to 20 years. Penalties for mail and wire fraud were significantly increased. SOX is the first and only federal statute to provide for **whistle-blower claims** (claims that expose a person, group, or business for engaging in illegal acts, such as fraud), thus providing protection for an employee who is fired for reporting financial improprieties of the company. The statute requires the chief executive officer, the chief financial officer, and the auditors to certify the accuracy of the company's financial reports. Under most circumstances, companies are not permitted to extend credit or loans to the company's executive officer or to any director. The company's general counsel is under reporting requirements if he or she suspects any wrongdoing. A conviction for violating any of these requirements can result in a heavy fine, or even a prison sentence. Finally, the SOX directed the U.S. Sentencing Commission (discussed in Chapter 12) to revise the federal sentencing guidelines in accordance with the act and to reconsider the guidelines for all white-collar crimes. In January 2003 the U.S. Sentencing Commission approved an emergency plan that lengthens prison sentences for white-collar crimes. By April 2003 the commission was to have a permanent recommendation concerning the sentences to submit to Congress. That was done, and penalties were increased in 2003.[62] Subsequently the U.S. Supreme Court held that the federal sentencing guidelines are not mandatory, but some federal courts have stated that light sentences, even if the result of plea bargaining, may not be upheld by the courts.[63]

False Pretense

Similar to fraud is the crime of **false pretense**, which refers to obtaining title to property by falsely representing facts to the owner with the intent to defraud. Unlike mail and wire fraud, false pretense requires a successful effort on the part of the perpetrator.

The statutory crime of false pretense was necessary to cover a loophole in the common law crime of larceny-theft. Under the common law a person who obtained title to property by false pretense but did not get possession of that property did not meet the elements of larceny-theft and thus could not be charged with a crime. The English Parliament created the crime of *false pretense* to cover this act, and most U.S. jurisdictions followed that English precedent, although the crime may be called by other names, such as *theft by deception* or *deceptive practices*. For example, New Hampshire has a statute prohibiting *theft by deception*. Although it contains a long description of what is meant by *deception*, the statement of the crime is simple: "A person commits theft if he obtains or exercises control over property of another by deception and with a purpose to deprive him thereof."[64]

The general elements of false pretense are as follows:

1. A false representation of a past or present fact
2. That causes the victim
3. To pass the title of the property
4. To the wrongdoer
5. Who
   (a) knows the representation to be false and
   (b) thereby intends to defraud the victim[65]

Some of these elements need further explanation. The requirement that the statement be false means that the representation must be false at the time the property is obtained; if the representation is false when made but later becomes true, it does not meet the requirement. The false representation must be made about a material fact (one that is essential to the case). It may be communicated orally or in writing.

Traditionally, the false representation had to relate to a past or present but not to a future fact; thus, promises did not count. So, for example, if you walk into my office and tell my secretary that you are the president's son and that you are there to pick up a book for him, which he will pay for the next day, the former but not the latter statement will qualify for this first element. If you are not the president's son, you have misrepresented a present fact; but even if your statement that the president will pay for the book in the future is false, it does not establish this first element of false pretense.

The reason for not including false promises in the crime of false pretense was the concern that the crime would be used against someone who meant to keep a promise but due to changes in circumstances could not live up to the bargain—for example, a person who could not pay a bill and thus became a debtor, but who at the time the financial transaction was made, intended to pay that bill in the future. The current trend is to consider false promises or other false statements of future intentions to meet the requirement for false representations of a fact.

The second, third, and fourth elements of false pretense are that the false representation causes the victim to pass to the wrongdoer the title to the property—that is, the victim's act is done in reliance on the actor's misrepresentation. The title must be passed to the wrongdoer; simple possession is not sufficient in this case, although it would be sufficient for the crime of larceny by trick. Under the common law, the term *property* included tangible personal property and money. The modern trend is to include all items that may be the subject of larceny-theft.

The final element of false pretense is the mental state of the actor. Generally, false pretense statutes require that the misrepresentation must be made knowingly or with the intent to defraud and that this mental element must occur at the time the title is transferred, even if it did not occur at the time the misrepresentation was made.[66]

Forgery and Counterfeiting

Two additional crimes that may be included within a general theft statute or defined separately are **forgery** and **counterfeiting**. *Forgery,* which refers to falsely making or altering, with the intent to defraud, a negotiable and legally enforceable instrument, such as a check, is similar to false pretense in that both require an intent to defraud. They are dissimilar because forgery is complete even when the potential victim is not defrauded of money or property. Thus, one may forge a document but not have the opportunity to pass it on to another.

In most cases forgery is associated with money or securities. There are other crimes related to forgery, such as counterfeiting or uttering, but the trend today is to combine counterfeiting and uttering into one forgery statute. *Counterfeiting* refers to forging, copying, or imitating without authority and with the intent to defraud. The crime involves an offense against property as well as an obstruction of justice. The object of counterfeiting may be coins, paper money, or anything else of value (such as stamps). *Uttering* refers to publishing or passing on a forged or otherwise bad document. The crime of uttering a forged instrument is common. Generally the crime of uttering or passing bad checks is a separate crime, for a person may commit this crime without forging the document. That is, the signature may be genuine, but there are insufficient funds in the account for the check to be good.

Some statutes provide that writing a false or bogus check is a felony. Among these statutes, some require that the check must be more than a specified amount and others require that more than one check must be involved.

Finally, attention should be given to falsifying documents such as letters of recommendation and transcripts, along with plagiarism—dishonest and, in some cases, criminal acts that occur in the workplace and universities. In June 2008 Madonna G. Constantine, a professor of psychology and education at Columbia University, was fired after information surfaced pointing to plagiarism. Yale student Akash Maharaj was accused of lying on his application and forging the transcript he submitted to support it. The fraud was not discovered until a year after he enrolled at Yale, which had given him a $32,000 scholarship, with his total aid package amounting to $47,000. Yale revoked Maharaj's admission. The judge permitted him to plead to first-degree larceny and avoid a jail term, but he is required to pay restitution, and as the judge stated, "This is going to follow you the rest of your life."[67] These and other recent cases draw attention to the problems of cheating in an increasingly competitive world.

Stolen Property: Buying, Receiving, Possessing

Many thieves, particularly professional thieves, do not intend to use the property they steal. They depend on a **fence**, a person who receives stolen property from a thief and in turn disposes of it in a profitable manner. In early common law, the person who received stolen property from the thief could not be convicted of a crime, but the importance of controlling the fence led to statutes making the receipt of stolen property a crime. Generally these statutes are interpreted to mean that, in addition to knowing the property is stolen, the actor must receive the property with the intent to deprive the owner of it.

The crime of receiving stolen property has four elements:

1. Receiving
2. Stolen property
3. Knowing it to be stolen
4. With the intent to deprive the owner of the property

To sustain a conviction for this crime, the prosecution must prove (1) each of these elements and (2) that the knowledge, conduct, and criminal intent concurred in time. The element of receiving may be used or interpreted broadly. For example, Maine defines the crime of *receiving stolen property* as, among other situations, a crime of theft if

> The person receives, retains or disposes of the property of another knowing that it has been stolen, or believing that it has probably been stolen, with the intent to deprive the owner of the property.

The statute states that the word *receives* means "acquiring possession, control or title, or lending on the security of the property." Finally, the word *stolen* means that the property "was obtained or unauthorized control was exercised over it in violation of this chapter."[68]

Some jurisdictions specify types of receivers, such as junk dealers, and provide greater penalties for them than for people who are not usually in the business of receiving stolen property. Some provide greater penalties for larger amounts (grand receiving) as compared to smaller amounts (petit receiving), analogous to penalties for grand and petit theft.

Some states divide criminal possession of stolen property into degrees. Until recently New York had three degrees of stolen property; that was changed to five degrees. Criminal possession of stolen property in the first and second degrees is a felony; in the third, fourth, and fifth degrees, it is a misdemeanor. The value of the stolen property is a critical element. To constitute a first-degree violation, the property value must exceed $1 million, compared to $1,000 for a fourth-degree violation. No value amount is specified for the fifth degree.[69]

Finally, the receipt and possession of stolen property may be covered by a comprehensive theft statute such as that of Texas (see again Focus 8.2). That statute refers to "appropriation of" property, which can include traditional larceny-theft or receiving and possessing.

Malicious Mischief

The malicious destruction or infliction of damage to the property of another constitutes **malicious mischief** or *criminal mischief*. Malicious mischief is similar to larceny-theft in that it involves a crime against the property of another person but dissimilar in that it does not require taking the property away or intending to deprive the owner of possession. Unlike larceny, malicious mischief may target real property. Another difference is that, in some jurisdictions, malicious mischief requires destruction of the property. Malicious mischief is also similar to arson; both involve damage to property. Unlike arson, however, malicious mischief does not require burning.

In modern codes, malicious mischief may be defined broadly. One approach is to consolidate this common law crime with other statutes that relate to destruction of property into a statute entitled "Criminal mischief" or a similar term. This consolidated crime may include damaging or destroying tangible property; causing substantial loss or inconvenience to the owner of the property; and marking, drawing on, or otherwise defacing the property. These and other crimes may be graded by degrees or in terms of the monetary loss caused by the acts in question. The crime may be further classified in terms of whether it was committed intentionally, knowingly, or recklessly. In addition, states may have separate statutes covering graffiti, which includes painting with aerosol paint or using other methods of defacing property without the consent of the owner.[70]

One final approach is illustrated by the Maine Criminal Code, which, in addition to the crime of criminal mischief, specifies one for *aggravated criminal mischief*. The latter includes a damage amount (property exceeding $2,000 in value) as well as any action that "recklessly endangers human life" or the damage or destruction by fire of property that does not fall within the definition of arson.[71]

Trespass

Some jurisdictions provide for punishment of people who trespass but whose actions are not sufficient to sustain convictions for malicious mischief or burglary. This crime involves entering or remaining unlawfully in or on the premises of another (this could include land, houses, offices, garages, boats, or other vehicles), knowing that one is not licensed or privileged to do so, under certain circumstances that may be specified by statute. It does not require the destruction of property (as in malicious mischief) or the intent to commit a crime, which is an element of burglary.

Maine has a statute entitled *Criminal trespass*, which includes entering, or walking on, among other places, any dwelling, any other structure that is locked or barred, places properly posted in accordance with specific statutory requirements, any place in defiance of a lawful order personally communicated by the owner or another authorized person, and entering or remaining "in a cemetery or burial ground at any time between 1/2 hour after sunset and 1/2 hour before sunrise the following day," unless a public ordinance (in the case of a public cemetery) or posting (in the case of a private cemetery) permits visitors during that time.[72]

Copyright Infringement

The common law provided protection for a person's intellectual or artistic works, giving that individual first right to publish or to prevent publication of those works. Today intellectual property is protected through formal statutory provisions, resulting in the issuance of a **copyright**, which is a legal document that gives to the copyright holder the right to copy, reproduce in some other fashion, and sell literary works, books, articles, and other work products of the originator (or, in some cases, such as this text, the publisher) for a limited period of time. Violation of that copyright subjects the offender to civil and criminal penalties. In some cases limited copying is permitted, but in most cases formal permission is required to reproduce works that are protected by a copyright.

The federal copyright statute provides the following statement concerning the subject matter included within copyright protections:

(a) Copyright protection subsists, in accordance with this title, in original works of authorship fixed in any tangible medium of expression, now known or later developed, from which they can be perceived, reproduced, or otherwise communicated, either directly or with the aid of a machine or device. Works of authorship include the following categories:

(1) literary works;

(2) musical works, including any accompanying words;

(3) dramatic works, including any accompanying music;

(4) pantomimes and choreographic works;

(5) pictorial, graphic, and sculptural works;

(6) motion pictures and other audiovisual works;

(7) sound recordings; and

(8) architectural works.[73]

Copyright violations occur frequently, but they are difficult to detect unless committed on a large scale.

Copyright violations are very important to today's world, however, as the dissemination of information through the Internet has become so widespread. Any person who wishes to create a website on a given subject, using copyrighted information, should obtain permission from the copyright owner, just as the print media has been required to do for years. The intellectual property of creative persons must be protected, but at the same time allowances must be made for making information available to the public.

Two less serious property crimes that may involve theft are related to the crime of robbery.

Extortion or Blackmail

Common law robbery, which carried the death penalty, was restricted to threats of *immediate* harm. This left threats of future actions uncovered. Under the common law and in most of the early statutes, **extortion** or **blackmail** was limited to the unlawful taking of money by public officials who did so "by colour of their offices." Congress and many states have extended this definition of extortion to include acts by private individuals. Today *extortion* may be defined as obtaining property from another by wrongful use of actual or threatened force, fear, or violence or the corrupt taking of a fee by a public officer, under color of his or her office, when that fee is not due. *Blackmail* is similar and usually included in extortion statutes, but often this crime is associated with the unlawful demand of money or something else of value by threats to expose some embarrassing or disgraceful allegation or fact about the victim, to accuse that person of a crime, or to do bodily harm to him or her or damage property.

The Maryland criminal statute, entitled *extortion generally*, is illustrative.

A person may not obtain, attempt to obtain, or conspire to obtain money, property, labor, services, or anything of value from another person with the person's consent, if the consent is induced by wrongful use or threatened:

(1) force or violence;

(2) economic injury; or

(3) destruction, concealment, removal, confiscation, or possession of any immigration or government identification document with intent to harm the immigration status of another person.[74]

Extortion statutes may also be part of a general theft statute. Focus 8.2, which contains the Texas consolidated theft statute, mentions extortion as one of the crimes included within the general theft statute (see again Focus 8.2).

COMPUTER CRIMES

During the past two decades computers have played an increasingly important role in our daily lives. In many ways they have made business easier. But when the computer is not functioning properly, many transactions stop, creating frustrating waiting periods and, in some cases, crippling websites, electronic communications, and daily business.

Computers have also made our daily lives more convenient. Money may be obtained from machines as well as from bank tellers, and products may be ordered online. Communications with friends and business associates have become easier through the proliferation of electronic mail. But with these and other conveniences have come problems. Privacy is more likely to be invaded now that extensive personal data are kept in many computer files. Although computers have been used to process valuable data leading to the apprehension of criminals, they have created serious problems and a new field of crime for individuals and businesses to combat.

Computer crime refers to crime committed with the use of a computer. Computer criminals have developed programs that access, scramble, or erase computer files and that aid in theft, as well as the invasion of privacy and stealing of a person's identity. Computer crimes may involve the same kinds of crimes discussed elsewhere in this chapter, as well as those discussed in other chapters, except that a computer is used in the perpetration of the crime. According to a white-collar-crime expert, "Computer crime cases have one commonality: the computer is either the tool or the target of the felon."[75]

Cybercrime refers to the use of the computer to commit a crime through the Internet.

Cybercrime Data

Although the extent of cybercrime is impossible to assess accurately, we do know that it is extensive. In 2006 the FBI released the results of its largest survey on computer crimes, and that is the latest to date. The survey was based on responses from more than 2,000 organizations, both public and private, in four states. Following are some results reported by the FBI:

- ✪ "**Frequency of attacks.** Nearly nine out of 10 organizations experienced computer security incidents in a year's time; 20% of them indicated they had experienced 20 or more attacks.

- ✪ **Types of attacks**. Viruses (83.7%) and spyware (79.5%) headed the list. More than one in five organizations said they experienced port scans and network or data sabotage.

- ✪ **Financial impact.** Over 64% of the respondents incurred a loss. Viruses and worms cost the most, accounting for $12 million of the $32 million in total losses.

- ✪ **Sources of the attacks.** They came from 36 different countries. The U.S. (26.1%) and China (23.9%) were the source of over half of the intrusion attempts, though masking technologies make it difficult to get an accurate reading. . . .

- ✪ **Reporting**. Just 9% said they reported incidents to law enforcement, believing the infractions were not illegal or that there was little law enforcement could or would do."[76]

Cybercrime is also expensive. Computer viruses are expensive to clean, with some estimates for cleaning them running as high as $400 billion a year.[77] In addition to the cost of cleaning, which can take hours and cost between $100 and $300 per computer, is the loss of employee productivity while the computer is cleaned. Additionally, computers may be infected with criminal material by computer hackers, leading to the prosecution of innocent persons as well as the apprehension of guilty ones.

The characteristics of cybercriminals are also changing. A security company, McAfee, stated that no longer are cybercrimes committed primarily by individuals. In place now are cybergangs, and the growth of online banking and commerce "has created its own underworld. . . . Anonymity and global connectivity let crooks engage in digital global versions of extortion, drug-running, pornography and other traditional crimes." According to the McAfee study, law enforcement officials cannot keep pace with the "ever more savvy and better equipped cybercriminals."[78]

Law enforcement officials are focusing on cybercrime. In June 2008 the FBI released numerous examples of convictions or charges for alleged computer crimes, such as the following:

- ✪ Jon Paul Oson was convicted of two counts of intentionally damaging protected computers and sentenced to more than 5 years in prison and ordered to pay $144,358.83 in restitution to one victim organization and $264,979 to another.

- ✪ Lori Drew was indicted on one count of conspiracy and three counts of accessing protected computers without authorization for the purpose of inflicting emotional distress on a 13-year-old girl who later committed suicide. Drew posed as a 15-year-old boy who was romantically interested in the victim but later spurned her and told her, among other things, that the world would be better off without her.

- ✪ Gregory Kopiloff of Seattle, Washington, was convicted of accessing computers to gain information on tax returns, credit reports, bank statutes, and student financial aid applications of 50 people across the United States. By use of file-sharing programs, Kopiloff, who was convicted of accessing a protected computer without authorization to further fraud and aggravated identity theft, was sentenced to 51 months in prison followed by 3 years of supervised release. Kopiloff opened credit cards in the names of his victims and ordered products online, which he had shipped and then sold. The sentencing judge called this crime a "particularly egregious form of identity theft . . . [which involved] invading victims' homes to steal information from their computers."[79]

In April 2008, the FBI reported 2007 data collected by the Internet Crime Complaint Center (IC3) stating that in 2007, 90,000 more complaints of computer crimes were filed than in 2006, representing a $40 million increase in reported losses. In releasing this report, the FBI emphasized that computer crimes are significantly underreported.[80]

Types of Computer Crimes

In addition to viruses and other forms of hacking, *Internet fraud* is a serious crime today. Much of the fraud involves *identity theft*, in which the hacker steals the personal identity (usually by accessing a person's accounts through his or her social security number), as noted in the example of Gregory Kopiloff, mentioned

in the previous section. Identity theft is discussed in more detail later in this chapter.

In addition, persons have been convicted of using computers to distribute sexually explicit material, including child pornography (which is illegal), but detection and successful prosecution of these distributions are difficult because of the widespread use of computer bulletin boards and the lack of legislation dealing explicitly with computer pornography.

However, efforts have been made to control the unwanted receipt of sexually explicit material. Congress enacted the **CAN-SPAM Act of 2003**, a federal antispam law that became effective in January 2004. This act directed the Federal Trade Commission (FTC) to adopt a rule requiring a mark or notice on spam that contains sexually explicit material. Effective 19 May 2004, all such spam must include the warning "SEXUALLY-EXPLICIT" in the subject line. Violation of this requirement may result in civil lawsuits as well as criminal prosecutions that could lead to a prison sentence and fines as high as $250,000 for individuals and $500,000 for organizations.[81]

The computer may also be used to commit violent crimes in that the computer is used to gain access to persons who are then victimized by violence. Consider, for example, the 2002 murder of 14-year-old Nonie Drummond in Fabius, New York. The young woman communicated over the Internet and telephone for nine months with Spencer Lee King, 17. Drummond lived in a rural area and was watched carefully by her grandfather. When he left for an overnight camping trip, Drummond invited King to visit. King later said he was disappointed in the visit (for one, he thought she was 17) and that he "just snapped." King confessed that he stabbed Drummond repeatedly with a kitchen knife; she fought back; he hit her with a stool, a television, and a fan until she died. He then burned the house to destroy the evidence. King was charged with murder. After pleading guilty, he was sentenced to 24 years to life in prison. One news account of this tragedy makes an interesting statement about the role of the Internet in our lives:

> Here in the state's expansive midsection, where the telephone and computer can ease the monotony of rural life, the death of Nonie Dummond is a reminder that the same technology that comforts people can also connect them to danger.[82]

The computer is also used to lure unsuspecting persons into sexual liaisons that do not result in death.

In 2002 James Warren of Hampton Bays, New York, age 42, was convicted of luring a 15-year-old from her home in Massachusetts via an Internet chat room on sadomasochism. He tortured the teen for a week and was convicted of 63 charges, ranging from kidnapping to rape and sodomy, although he was acquitted of the charge of attempted murder. The defense argued that the victim repeatedly lied about her age and that Warren did not know she was underage. The prosecutor argued that he did know, and the jury agreed. Warren and his adult girlfriend picked up the teen at the shopping mall where she worked. They and another male friend engaged in sex with her, choked her with belts and ropes, tied her, whipped her, burned her with a cigarette lighter, and engaged in other violent acts. Warren was sentenced to 150 years and must serve 100 years before he is eligible for parole, which, in effect, means that he has a life sentence without parole.[83]

Controlling Computer Crimes

One of the problems with attempts to control computer crimes is the lack of information about them. One way to avoid becoming a computer crime victim is to be careful about meeting personally with strangers encountered over the Internet. In particular, children and teens should be taught that agreeing to meet in person with strangers with whom they have had Internet contacts may be dangerous, even fatal. It is also crucial to protect one's personal identity information, especially on the Internet. One of the Internet activities listed at the end of this chapter suggests how to do this.

Another way of controlling computer crimes is through legislation. Despite several attempts, Congress did not pass a computer crime statute until 1984. Prior to that time, federal computer crimes were prosecuted under one of about 40 federal statutes. Because these statutes were written for other purposes, many problems arose when they were applied to computer crimes. Examples of statutes were those covering wire and mail fraud, theft and embezzlement, and the transportation of stolen property. The Federal Computer Crime Control Act is part of the general revision of the federal criminal code, known as the Comprehensive Crime Control Act of 1984.[84]

In 2002 the U.S. Congress enacted legislation (as part of the Homeland Security Act, discussed in Chapter 10) to increase the penalties for computer crimes. The Cyber Security Enhancement Act of 2002 also contains provisions for research on cybersecurity. The U.S. Sentencing Commission was directed to study the penalties for computer crimes and to consider a variety of sentencing factors, such as the perpetrator's purpose in committing the crime, whether a government computer was involved in the crime, and whether the offense "was intended to or had the effect of significantly interfering with or disrupting a critical infrastructure." The commission was required to report its recommendations concerning any proposed revision of federal sentencing guidelines to Congress by 1 May 2003.[85] That was done, and the USA Patriot Act (discussed in Chapter 10), among other provisions, amended existing laws concerning computers, increased penalties, and redefined the word *terrorism* to include crimes such as computer hacking and cyberterrorism.[86]

Legislation to control computer crimes has also occurred at the state level. In 1978 Florida and Arizona became the first states to enact computer crime statutes, and most states followed. In 1995 Connecticut became one of the first states to criminalize harassment or stalking by means of a computer. Other jurisdictions have followed, but it is possible that the enactment of statutes designed to prevent computer crimes will not be as effective as some would like to think. First, many establishments might not want the public to know that their employees committed crimes with the company's computers and, thus, may not press charges.

Second, in addition to a lack of reporting or willingness to prosecute and the difficulties of apprehension and prosecution, law enforcement officials may not have the technical expertise to solve computer crimes, and most cases that go to trial are highly technical, costly, and extremely time-consuming.

Third, federal and state computer crime statutes, like all statutes, are subject to interpretation, and we can expect considerable litigation in this area. A challenge to the New Mexico Computer Crimes Act is illustrative of one of the problems.

The New Mexico statute prohibits accessing a computer with an intent to commit fraud. Defendant David Morris Rowell was charged and convicted under the statute based on his making phone calls from Florida to New Mexico in an attempt to get the recipients to send money to help him pay legal expenses for a fictitious lawsuit. He told his victims that after the suit was settled he would send them part of the proceeds. Rowell argued on appeal that using a telephone does not constitute accessing a computer—that is, he was not accessing the telephone company's computers.

The New Mexico Court of Appeals disagreed with Rowell's analysis of the statute, holding that *accessing* simply means *making use of* and that the defendant was making use of telephone company computers for the purpose of committing fraud. Rowell appealed that decision to the New Mexico Supreme Court, which held that the statute was intended to apply only to cases that involved manipulating the computer. In Rowell's case the computer was the "passive conduit through which the defendant's criminal activity passed." In the following brief excerpt the state's supreme court gives its reasons.[87]

STATE v. ROWELL
908 P.2d 1379 (N.M. 1995)

We conclude that the [New Mexico] Computer Crimes Act was intended by the legislature to deter and punish crimes committed, at least in a manner of speaking, against computers, or through the abuse of computer sophistication.

Rowell did not attempt to introduce fraudulent data into a computer, nor did he attempt to steal information from a computer. He used a telephone which, because of modern technology, used computerized switches to perform the work of a telephone network. Application of the Computer Crimes Act in this situation is similar to its application to persons who drive cars with computer "brains" on their way to committing a larceny. . . .

[Rowell's] use of the long-distance telephone network may have resulted in the access of computerized switches, and in fact, access to a computer or a computer network, but access of such components is not the type of conduct the legislature sought to punish by the Act. The computerized components perform the sole function of controlling the switches for the purpose of processing telephone calls. Rowell did not attempt to "program, execute programs on, intercept, instruct, communicate with, store data in, retrieve data from" or otherwise misuse these switches. The switches were designed for a single purpose, and there, they were used only for that purpose. Rowell's use of these computerized switches to place a telephone call, without more, simply is not punishable under the Computer Crimes Act. . . . Therefore, we reverse the Court of Appeals on this issue.

One final issue with regard to computers is that they have made it possible for persons to invade the privacy of individuals in a way not contemplated prior to their use. Computer hackers may commit various crimes against individuals and companies, one of which is to steal identities.

IDENTITY THEFT

Fraud on the Internet is a serious and growing problem. One form that it takes is **identity theft**. This crime involves the stealing of a person's social security number or another personal identifier, such as a bank account number, and using that information to steal from the person.

Identity Theft Data

The far-reaching effects of identity theft were emphasized by a district attorney in New York who, in calling for legislation, argued that this crime is a favorite of terrorists, noting that the investigations of the 11 September 2001 terrorist acts in the United States "disclosed proof that the terrorists repeatedly committed acts of identity theft to advance their destructive goals."[88]

Identity theft is also an issue on the individual personal level, although exact data are not available concerning the number of victims of this crime, said by some to be the fastest growing crime in the world. Focus 8.7 presents data and information collected by the National Crime Victimization Survey (NCVS), along with the definition that organization uses for data collection. The 2005 data presented in that focus were the latest available from the NCVS at the time of this writing, with the BJS reporting that its analysis of 2006 data would be available during the fourth quarter—October through December 2009.

The Federal Trade Commission conducted 4,918 interviews of persons 18 and older in 2006, questioning them about events that occurred in 2005, and published the results in 2007. According to that source, approximately 8.3 million persons in the United States experienced some type of identity theft, with approximately 3.2 million experiencing the misuse of personal credit cards. Approximately 3.3 million found the misuse of accounts other than credit cards, such as bank accounts, while 1.8 million reported victimizations through newly opened accounts or other types of fraud. The median amount taken was $500. Approximately 50 percent of the victims reported no out-of-pocket expenses but

FOCUS 8.7   Identity Theft Victimizations

[The National Crime Victimization Survey (NCVS) presented the following findings from its 2005 survey on identity theft victimizations. Figure 8.2, from the original text, provides a summary of these data.]

"In 2005, 6.4 million households, representing 5.5% of all households in the United States, discovered that at least one member experienced one or more types of identity theft. This is the first full year of data on identity theft available from the National Crime Victimization Survey (NCVS). Questions on identity theft were first added to the NCVS in July 2004.

Unauthorized use of an existing credit card account, the most prevalent type of identity theft, was experienced by about 3 million households. About 1.6 million households experienced theft of existing accounts other than a credit card (such as a banking account) and 1.1 million households discovered misuse of personal information (such as a social security number). An es-timated 790,000 households experienced more than one type of identity theft during the same episode. [Table omitted.]

For the NCVS, the definition of identity theft includes three behaviors:

- unauthorized use or attempted use of existing credit cards
- unauthorized use or attempted use of other existing accounts, such as checking accounts
- misuse of personal information to obtain new accounts or loans, or to commit other crimes.

Three percent of households headed by persons age 65 or older experienced identity theft, a lower percentage than any other age group. Households located in the West were more likely to experience identity theft than households in other regions. Households in urban or suburban areas were more likely than those in rural areas to experience identity theft.

One in 10 households with incomes of $75,000 or higher experienced identity theft, making this income group more vulnerable than households with lower annual incomes. About 7 in 10 households victimized by identity theft reported a financial loss. The average amount was $1,620.

The majority of households that experienced identity theft did not experience any other type of crime measured by the NCVS. Fewer than 1% of households in the U.S. experienced both identity theft and a violent or property crime. These findings represent annual prevalence estimates and were drawn from interviews conducted from January through December 2005 for the NCVS. The interviews were conducted with respondents age 18 or older in each sampled household who knew about discoveries of identity theft of anyone in their household during the previous six months."

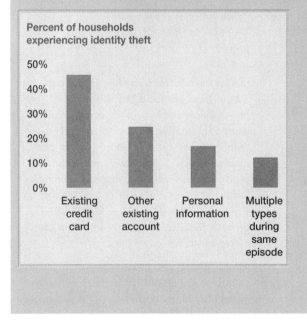

Percent of households experiencing identity theft

Source: Bureau of Justice Statistics Special Report, *Identity Theft, 2005* (November 2007), p. 1, http://www.ojp.usdoj.gov/bjs/pub/pdf/it05.pdf, accessed 16 July 2008.

most spent many hours dealing with the thefts. Thirty-seven percent reported other problems such as harassment by creditors, inability to use credit cards, discontinuation of utilities, and so on.[89]

One final type of identity theft is rather new. In a March 2008 press release, the FBI presented information on *house stealing*. House thieves look for a house to steal, assume the identity of the owners from which they make fake identification records, forge signatures, file fake deeds with the appropriate authorities, sell the house, and keep the profits. The FBI gave the following details of a Los Angeles real estate business owner who pled guilty to defrauding over 100 homeowners and lenders out of approximately $12 million:

> She promised to help struggling homeowners pay their mortgages by refinancing their loans. Instead, she and her partners in crime used stolen identities or "straw buyers" (people who are paid for the illegal use of their personal information) to purchase

The most recent type of identity theft crime is that of house stealing. Thieves steal a homeowner's identity, file false papers, and sell the house, all while the owners are living in the home. (Jetta Productions/The Image Bank/Getty Images)

these homes. They then pocketed the money they borrowed but never made any mortgage payments. In the process, the true owners lost the title to their homes and the banks were out the money they had loaned to fake buyers.[90]

State and Federal Statutes

Most states have identity theft statutes, although they vary significantly in their coverage. An illustrative statute is that of Connecticut, which classifies identity theft as a felony:

(a) A person commits identity theft when such person intentionally obtains personal identifying information of another person without the authorization of such other person and uses that information to obtain or attempt to obtain, money, credit, goods, services, property or medical information in the name of such other person without the consent of such other person.

(b) As used in this section, "personal identifying information" means any name, number or other information that may be used, alone or in conjunction with any other information, to identify a specific individual including, but not limited to, such individual's name, date of birth, mother's maiden name, motor vehicle operator's license number, Social Security number, employee identification number, employer or taxpayer identification number, alien registration number, government passport number, health insurance identification number, demand deposit account number, savings account number, credit card number, debit card number or unique biometric data such as fingerprint, voice print, retina or iris image, or other unique physical representation.[91]

The federal system also has an identity theft statute, which is entitled *Fraud and related activity in connection with identification documents and information.* Under some circumstances, violation of the statute carries a penalty of a fine and imprisonment for not more than 15 years.[92]

The final section of this chapter focuses on a crime that is a property crime, involving car theft, but it is also a violent crime, as it involves confronting the operator of that car—and, in many cases, may result in serious injuries or death.

CARJACKING

The crime is an old one, but it has a new name. Today we speak of **carjacking** when we refer to the theft of a motor vehicle by use of force or the threat of force, especially force involving a deadly weapon. The stealing or attempted stealing of a motor vehicle is classified by the FBI as a property crime, as the discussion earlier in this chapter noted. However, as the discussion of robbery in Chapter 7 emphasized, the stealing from the person with the use of a threat of force or the actual use of force is considered a violent crime. Carjacking obviously has some of the aspects of theft and some of robbery. The escalation of carjackings in recent years, along with their frequent brutality, has led many states and the federal government to enact special statutes to cover the crimes.

Carjacking Data

The FBI does not solicit data on carjacking, and in some jurisdictions it is reported as motor vehicle theft, so data are difficult to obtain, but in July 2004 the Bureau of Justice Statistics (BJS) published the first analysis of national carjacking data, reporting approximately 34,000 carjackings a year for the covered years, 1993–2002, with 45 percent of the attempted carjackings completed. Those data are the latest on a national level from the BJS, but some of the general statements from that report are still relevant in that they give a snapshot of the characteristics of carjacking perpetrators and their victims.

- ⚙ "Men, blacks, and Hispanics were more often carjacking victims than women, whites, and non-Hispanics. . . .

- ⚙ Most carjackings did not result in injury to the victims; most injuries that did occur were minor. However, in 74 percent of the carjackings a weapon was used. . . .

- ⚙ Males committed 93 percent of the crimes, with 3 percent being committed by men and women together.

- ⚙ Most carjackings (63 percent) occurred within five miles of the victim's home. . . .

- ⚙ In 25 percent of the carjackings, the victims' total property was recovered; in 78 percent of the cases, partial or complete recovery occurred."[93]

Some states keep data on carjackings, with New Jersey having done so for 14 years. Following are summary data from that state's latest report, which was for the year 2006. New Jersey's carjacking statute is reprinted in the section following this presentation of data.

- ⚙ "There were 251 carjacking offenses reported to the police; 3 were determined to be unfounded, leaving a total of 248 carjackings, involving 282 victims, including passengers.

- ⚙ Carjackings decreased 7% when comparing 2006 to 2005. . . .

- ⚙ Firearms were involved in 67% (165) of all carjackings. . . .

- ⚙ Nissan . . . was the most frequently carjacked vehicle make, while the most frequently targeted vehicle years were 1997 & 2006 with 10% (24) reported in each vehicle year.

- ⚙ Sixty-three percent (155) of all carjacked vehicles were recovered. . . .

- ⚙ Carjackings occurred in a residential area 67% (165) of the time. The hours of darkness (6:00 p.m. to 6:00 a.m.) accounted for 74% (183) of all carjackings. . . .

- ⚙ The most frequent victim age group was 25–29, which accounted for 25% (70) of the victim total (282). Seventy-three percent (206) of all victims were male. Fifty-five percent (154) of all victims were black. . . .

- ⚙ Of all known offenders (281), 20–24 was the most frequent offender age group and accounted for 41% (114). Ninety-eight percent (274) of all known offenders were male. Eighty-two percent (231) of all known offenders were black.

- ⚙ Juveniles accounted for 39% (14) of the total arrests for carjacking (36), while adults accounted for 61% (22). . . .

- ⚙ No murders were reported in 2006 as the result of carjacking.

- ⚙ Eight percent (19) of all carjackings (248) were cleared by arrest."[94]

State and Federal Statutes

An example of a state carjacking statute is that of New Jersey, which refers to *carjacking* as "a specific type of robbery" that involves "the unlawful taking of a motor vehicle in the course of which the perpetrator":

(1) inflicts bodily injury or uses force upon an occupant or person in possession or control of a motor vehicle;

(2) threatens an occupant or person in control with, or purposely or knowingly puts an occupant or person in control of the motor vehicle in fear of, immediate bodily injury;

(3) commits or threatens immediately to commit any crime of the first or second degree; or

(4) operates or causes said vehicle to be operated with the person who was in possession or control or was an occupant of the motor vehicle at the time of the taking remaining in the vehicle.[95]

The U.S. Congress enacted a federal carjacking statute, which applies only to the theft of a motor vehicle "that has been transported, shipped or received in interstate or foreign commerce" and is taken "from the person or presence of another by force and violence or by intimidation." Attempts are included within this crime.

As part of its 1994 comprehensive crime bill, Congress included an amendment adding the death penalty to the federal carjacking statute when death occurs as a result of the crime. It appeared that the careless wording of that amendment could result in the exclusion from the reach of the statute of all carjackers who did not *intend* to harm their victims. Thus, carjackers who intended to flee if their victims resisted would not be covered by the statute. Presumably Congress could have corrected the error by redrafting the statute, but it did not do so. The issue was decided by the U.S. Supreme Court in 1999. Excerpts from the case are reproduced here to show not only the problem of defining what is included within *carjacking* but also the general issue of what is meant by *intent*. The relevant facts of the case are stated in the opinion.[96]

HOLLOWAY v. UNITED STATES
526 U.S. 1 (1999)

Justice John Paul Stevens delivered the opinion of the Court, joined by Chief Justice William H. Rehnquist and Justices Sandra Day O'Connor, Anthony M. Kennedy, David H.

Souter, Ruth Bader Ginsburg, and Stephen G. Breyer. Justices Antonin Scalia and Clarence Thomas dissented, with Justice Scalia filing a dissenting opinion.

Carjacking "with the intent to cause death or serious bodily harm" is a federal crime. The question presented in this case is whether that phrase requires the Government to prove that the defendant had an unconditional intent to kill or harm in all events, or whether it merely requires proof of an intent to kill or harm if necessary to effect a carjacking. Most of the judges who have considered the question have concluded, as do we, that Congress intended to criminalize the more typical carjacking carried out by means of a deliberate threat of violence, rather than just the rare case in which the defendant has an unconditional intent to use violence regardless of how the driver responds to his threat.

A jury found petitioner guilty on three counts of carjacking, as well as several other offenses related to stealing cars. In each of the carjackings, petitioner and an armed accomplice identified a car that they wanted and followed it until it was parked. The accomplice then approached the driver, produced a gun, and threatened to shoot unless the driver handed over the car keys. The accomplice testified that the plan was to steal the cars without harming the victims, but that he would have used his gun if any of the drivers had given him a "hard time." When one victim hesitated, petitioner punched him in the face but there was no other actual violence.

The District Judge instructed the jury that the Government was required to prove beyond a reasonable doubt that the taking of a motor vehicle was committed with the intent "to cause death or serious bodily harm to the person from whom the car was taken." After explaining that merely using a gun to frighten a victim was not sufficient to prove such intent, he added the following statement over the defendant's objection:

> In some cases, intent is conditional. That is, a defendant may intend to engage in certain conduct only if a certain event occurs.
>
> In this case, the government contends that the defendant intended to cause death or serious bodily harm if the alleged victims had refused to turn over their cars. If you find beyond a reasonable doubt that the defendant had such an intent, the government has satisfied this element of the offense. . . .

The specific issue in this case is what sort of evil motive Congress intended to describe when it used the words "with the intent to cause death or serious bodily harm." . . . More precisely, the question is whether a person who points a gun at a driver, having decided to pull the trigger if the driver does not comply with a demand for the car keys, possesses the intent, at that moment, to seriously harm the driver. In our view, the answer to that question does not depend on whether the driver immediately hands over the keys or what the offender decides to do after he gains control over the car. At the relevant moment, the offender plainly does have the forbidden intent. . . .

The intent requirement . . . is satisfied when the Government proves that at the moment the defendant demanded or took control over the driver's automobile the defendant possessed the intent to seriously harm or kill the driver if necessary to steal the car (or, alternatively, if unnecessary to steal the car).

Carjacking is often combined with kidnapping, discussed in Chapter 7. One of the most unusual cases occurred in the summer of 2002, when Tamara Brooks, 16, and Jacqueline Morris, 17, were abducted at gunpoint from the cars in which they were parked with their respective male friends in an area known as Lover's Lane near Los Angeles. The kidnapper, Roy Ratliff, a convicted sex criminal wanted in connection with an alleged rape, abandoned a car at the site area—a car he had obtained in a violent carjacking the previous October, and, after threatening to kill the two couples (who were in separate cars), bound the men with duct tape, stole one of the cars, and kidnapped the women. Notices were posted on the freeways, using the newly installed Amber Alert system, which led to numerous calls from motorists. The car was tracked down; a police chase ensued; Ratliff was killed, and the two women were rescued.

If Ratliff had not been killed, he would have been subject to trial under the following California statute, entitled "kidnapping in course of carjacking":

(a) Any person who, during the commission of a carjacking and in order to facilitate the commission of the carjacking, kidnaps another person who is not a principal in the commission of the carjacking shall be punished by imprisonment in the state prison for life with the possibility of parole. [The statute then specifies the degree of moving of the victim that must occur to trigger the use of this statute.][97]

SUMMARY

Although the fear of being victimized by violent crimes is greater than that associated with property crimes, property crimes claim the largest number of victims in the United States. It is not easy to separate the two kinds of crimes, for many property crimes—such as robbery, extortion, burglary, arson, and carjacking—may involve personal violence or even death. Nevertheless, for purposes of analysis, crimes are divided into categories. This chapter discussed those crimes generally considered to be crimes against property or crimes that involve both violence against a person and damage to property.

Property rights were extremely important in the common law. The emergence and development of laws to protect property has been closely related to those rights. Some of the restrictions on the elements or requirements for property crimes do not make much sense in modern times. Some of those have changed; others remain. Thus, it is important to understand the common law of property crimes.

One of the most complicated and fascinating of the common law crimes, larceny-theft, illustrates the importance of the common law. Although all the common law elements of this crime are no longer required, some remain. Others are important in interpreting modern statutes. Likewise, the common law division of larceny-theft into grand and petit larceny is retained in some jurisdictions.

Common law larceny-theft required a trespassory taking and a carrying away of the personal property of another with the intent to steal. The requirement of trespassory taking prevented the inclusion of some crimes that evolved over the years. To cover these crimes, judges invented fictions such as constructive possession to refer to the property a master had delivered to his servant to be used for the benefit of the master. If that servant misappropriated the property, his act could be included within common law larceny-theft.

The common law requirement of asportation, or taking away, generally has been replaced with a requirement that the offender exercise unlawful control over property even if it is not carried away, provided he or she does so with the intent and purpose of depriving the owner of that property. Under the common law, the property stolen had to be the personal property of another, meaning tangible personal property. Modern statutes have extended larceny-theft to some types of real property as well as services, admissions to exhibitions, and many other areas.

The common law interpretation of *intent to steal* as requiring an intent to permanently deprive the owner of his property has been retained in some jurisdictions but abolished in others to permit inclusion of crimes such as joyriding. Another way of handling this element, however, has been to create separate offenses for acts such as joyriding.

Burglary is another property offense in which common law definitions and interpretations are important to an understanding of modern statutes. Today the common law requirement of breaking and entering may be met in some statutes by the act of remaining on the property illegally. The breaking requirement may be met by entering illegally. The requirement that the structure be the dwelling of another has been extended to include all dwellings as well as other buildings. The common law required nighttime for burglary; most modern statutes omit that requirement. Today the common law requirement of an intent to commit a felony may include an intent to commit a misdemeanor. Even when modern statutes have abandoned or changed some of the common law elements of burglary, the influence of these older crimes is seen in the differentiation of the crime by degrees. Although it may not be required that the burglar enter a home for the crime to be complete, entering a home may result in a higher degree of burglary and a harsher sentence.

Although larceny-theft includes the theft of parts from motor vehicles, the theft of motor vehicles themselves constitutes a separate category of serious property crimes in the FBI's *Uniform Crime Reports*. The chapter included a brief discussion of motor vehicle theft. The final serious property crime, arson, was discussed in terms of its common law background as well as modern statutory approaches. Some of the most deadly fires caused by arson were discussed.

The second major section of the chapter covered less serious property offenses. These crimes are labeled *less serious* by the FBI, but they may create a significant problem for their immediate victims and for society. For example, embezzlement and fraud-related crimes may involve losses of millions of dollars, compared to far smaller losses from larceny-theft. A number of lesser property crimes were discussed individually. Although the modern trend is toward consolidating theft-type offenses into fewer categories, some jurisdictions retain the common law larceny-theft category,

which excluded such offenses as larceny by trick, fraud, false pretense, forgery, and embezzlement. These jurisdictions have separate statutes for such offenses. Other jurisdictions have abandoned the use of the term *larceny-theft* and refer only to *theft crimes*, which may be subdivided into categories.

The chapter also discussed such property-related crimes as false pretense, forgery and counterfeiting, crimes associated with stolen property, malicious mischief, trespass, copyright infringement, and extortion or blackmail. The chapter contained sections on computer crime, identity theft, and carjacking, all relatively newly recognized crimes that are gaining more attention today and all of which have a significant financial and personal impact.

STUDY QUESTIONS

1. Generally, what is meant by the common law term *larceny-theft*?

2. Distinguish petit larceny from grand larceny under the common law and under the New York statute.

3. Should the amount paid or the market value of a stolen item have any effect on the sentence of a convicted offender? Why or why not?

4. What did the common law mean by (a) a *trespassory taking*, (b) *asportation*, and (c) *with the intent to steal*?

5. What is the difference between actual and constructive possession?

6. How does burglary differ from larceny-theft? What are some of the ways in which modern burglary statutes differ from the common law approach?

7. What are the elements of arson? Why is the crime considered a serious one?

8. What is meant by *larceny by trick*?

9. How does the larceny element of taking apply to shoplifting?

10. How have modern statutes changed the common law definition of *larceny-theft*?

11. Why would embezzlement and fraud not fit in the common law category of larceny-theft?

12. Describe what is meant by *mail* and *wire fraud*. How should these crimes be handled?

13. What is the significance of health care fraud? Give some examples of this category of crimes. Do you have any suggestions for improving our attempts to combat it?

14. Describe the nature and impact of securities fraud.

15. What is meant by *insider trading*? Discuss.

16. Explain what is meant by the following element of false pretense: a false representation of a past or present fact. How do the common law and modern law differ regarding this element?

17. How does forgery differ from false pretense?

18. What is malicious mischief?

19. Define *criminal trespass*.

20. Should we criminalize copyright infringement? How long should a copyright last? Do you agree with the recent U.S. Supreme Court decision regarding this issue?

21. Why are the crimes of extortion and blackmail important?

22. What is computer crime? Discuss the legislative efforts to combat this crime. Can you suggest improvements in the way this crime is handled?

23. What is meant by *cybercrime*?

24. What is identity theft, and how can it be prevented?

25. What is carjacking, and why is it a recently defined crime?

FOR DEBATE

The chapter's discussion of property and related crimes covers numerous acts, some traditional, some relatively new. Of the latter, the crime of identity theft is often featured in the media. Consider the nature and impact of this crime by debating the following two resolutions.

Resolved: Identity theft crimes should be prosecuted as felonies and carry a sentence of 25 years to life.

Resolved: Personal privacy should be less important than solving computer crimes; thus, greater power should be given to law enforcement officials regarding investigations of computer crimes, particularly those involving identity theft.

KEY TERMS

arson, 219	fence, 230
bailee, 211	forgery, 230
bailor, 211	fraud, 209
blackmail, 232	grand larceny, 211
burglary, 215	identity theft, 236
CAN-SPAM Act of 2003, 234	insider information, 228
carjacking, 238	insider trading, 228
computer crime, 233	larceny by trick, 211
constructive possession, 211	larceny-theft, 210
conversion, 223	malicious mischief, 231
copyright, 232	obstruction of justice, 228
counterfeiting, 230	petit larceny, 211
curtilage, 216	property crimes, 209
cybercrime, 233	restraining order, 216
embezzlement, 223	securities, 227
extortion, 232	trespass, 216
false pretense, 229	whistle-blower claims, 229

CASE ANALYSIS

DREW V. STATE
773 So.2d 46 (Fla. 2000)

Case Preview

 This case would, at first glance, seem simple in that the defendant did not deny that he removed tires from a car that he did not own. That constitutes larceny-theft, a crime that he admitted he committed. But, he was also charged with burglary, and he alleged on appeal that he did not commit that crime under the meaning of the Florida statute.

As you read the case, recall the chapter's discussion of the differences between larceny-theft and burglary. Notice in the opinion the attention that the court gives to common law burglary before turning to an analysis of the Florida burglary statute. How do the two differ? All of the court's lengthy analysis of its own precedent cases, along with those of other jurisdictions, has been omitted, but the interested student could turn to the full case to digest that information.

Notice also the references the court makes to the Model Penal Code, discussed earlier in the text. Finally, recall the text's previous discussions of the concepts of vagueness and overbreadth, either one of which can render a statute unconstitutional.

Facts

On July 14, 1997, at approximately 11 p.m., Polk County Sheriff's Deputy James Orgic observed Terrell Curtis Drew and his codefendant, Willie D. Wright, in the vicinity of Mack Lewis Auto Sales. Orgic testified that Drew was carrying a lug wrench at the time and was using it to remove lug nuts from a vehicle. Drew admitted that he took the lug nuts from a brownish-red Chevrolet parked behind the Auto Sales business and that with the assistance of his codefendant, he had removed the missing tires from the car.

Issue

At issue in this case is whether the act of removing hubcaps or tires from a vehicle in and of itself constitutes a burglary.

Holding

Based on the purpose and history of the offense of burglary at common law and our interpretation of the [Florida] burglary statute, we hold that the sole act of removal of hubcaps or tires from a motor vehicle, while clearly constituting an act of criminal larceny, does not constitute a burglary.

Rationale

At common law, burglary was defined as breaking and entering the dwelling house of another at night with the intent to commit a felony therein. The underlying purpose of the crime of burglary was to punish the forcible invasion of a habitation and violation of the heightened expectation of privacy and possessory rights of individuals in structures and conveyances. . . .

In 1962, a definition of burglary was approved by the drafters of the Model Penal Code that closely resembled the common law crime:

1) Burglary Defined. A person is guilty of burglary if he enters a building or occupied structure, or separately secured or occupied portion thereof, with purpose to commit a crime therein, unless the premises are at the time open to the public or the actor is licensed or privileged to enter. . . .

The commentary to this section explains that this definition attempted to restate the original reach of the crime:

The needed reform [of the offense of burglary] should take the direction of narrowing the offense to reflect more appropriately the distinctive situation for which it was originally derived. The offense has thus been limited in the Model [Penal] Code to the invasion of premises under circumstances especially likely to terrorize occupants.

Most of the extensions of the offense that have been added by legislation over the years have been discarded.

Of course, burglary of a conveyance was unknown at common law and is not included as part of the 1962 Model Penal Code definition of burglary as set out above. Rather, burglary of a conveyance is a creature of statute. In Florida, burglary is defined in a way largely consistent with the Model Penal Code but expanded to include conveyances:

Burglary means entering or remaining in a dwelling, a structure, or a conveyance with the intent to commit an offense therein, unless the premises are at a time open to the public or the defendant is licensed or invited to enter or remain.

[Another Florida statute] defines conveyance as "any motor vehicle, ship, vessel, railroad car, trailer, aircraft, or sleeping car." In addition, "'to enter a conveyance' includes taking apart any portion of the conveyance." . . .

[Citing precedent cases, the court emphasized that it had already held that Florida's burglary statute is not unconstitutionally vague or overly broad. The court then cited numerous cases from other jurisdictions before making the following comments.]

In other words, a proper analysis of the offense of burglary must focus both on the act constituting the entry and the intent to commit an offense therein. The language of the burglary statute, as drafted by the Legislature, requires both an entry and the requisite intent to commit a crime within the conveyance. Therefore, it follows that the crime must be one that is capable of being committed within or inside the vehicle. Moreover, it naturally follows that an entry into a vehicle without the requisite intent to commit a separate crime therein is not a burglary. Thus, while the actual penetration into any interior or enclosed area may constitute an entry, including the removal of a portion or part of one of these areas or compartments, an intent to remove an object or commit an unauthorized act therein after the entry has occurred must also be established to satisfy the intent required to commit a crime.

Dissent

The definition of conveyance as outlined in [the] Florida Statutes, provides a meaning also for the term "to enter a conveyance" which includes the taking apart any portion of the conveyance. A portion of the conveyance was in fact taken apart in this case, the tires. . . . Therefore, I would . . . affirm the decision of [the lower court in finding that a burglary occurred].

For Discussion

Based on the reasoning and holding of the Florida Supreme Court, an individual who strips a car of its antenna, hood ornament, hubcaps, tires, and any other outside material would be guilty of larceny but not burglary. Do you think this is consistent with the intent of Florida's burglary statute? Do you agree with the majority opinion that the "enter" language means to enter the vehicle itself and take something from its interior, or do you agree with the dissent's interpretation that "enter" includes taking something from the outside of the car? Could the court's holding apply to a dwelling, boat, motorcycle, or other structure? In the text, there is a discussion of curtilage. Would a theft of items in a curtilage constitute burglary, theft, or both?

INTERNET ACTIVITY

Various government agencies have created websites concerning the problem of identity theft. Review the information provided by the government at the following site. What can you learn about identity theft? http://www.ftc.gov/ (accessed 10 December 2008); click on identity theft.

Check the following site of the Office of Legal Policy of the U.S. Department of Justice and see what you can find out about identity theft: http://www.usdoj.gov/olp/identity_theft.htm (accessed 10 December 2008).

NOTES

1. Federal Bureau of Investigation, *Crime in the United States, Uniform Crime Reports 2007*, http://www.fbi.gov/ucr/cius2007/offenses/property_crime/index.html, accessed 28 November 2008.
2. Federal Bureau of Investigation, *Crime in the United States, Uniform Crime Reports 2007*, http://www.fbi.gov/ucr/cius2007/offenses/property_crime/larceny-theft.html, accessed 28 November 2008.
3. *Rex v. Wheatly*, 97 E.R. 746 (1761).
4. Rollin M. Perkins, *Criminal Law*, 3d ed. (Mineola, N.Y.: Foundation Press, 1982), p. 291.
5. *Hufstetler v. State*, 63 So.2d 730 (Ala.Ct.App. 1953).
6. *The Carrier's Case*, Y.B. 13 Edw. IV, f.9, p.5 (Star Chamber 1473).
7. *People v. Olivo*, 420 N.E.2d 40, 44 (N.Y. 1981), footnotes, cases, and citations omitted.
8. *People v. Meyer*, 17 P. 431 (Cal. 1888).
9. See, for example, NY CLS Penal, Title J, Article 165, Section 165.15 (2008).
10. *People v. Brown*, 38 P. 518, 519 (Cal. 1894).
11. See, for example, Cal Pen Code, Part I, Title 13, Section 499b (2008).
12. NY CLS Penal, Title J, Article 155, Section 155.25 (2008).
13. NY CLS Penal, Title J, Article 155, Section 155.30 *et seq.* (2008).
14. Tex. Penal Code, Title 7, Chapter 31, Section 31.04 *et seq.* (2009).
15. Federal Bureau of Investigation, *Crime in the United States, Uniform Crime Reports 2007*, http://www.fbi.gov/ucr/cius2007/offenses/property_crime/burglary.html, accessed 28 November 2008.
16. *State v. Boon*, 35 N.C. 244, 246 (1852).
17. See *Jones v. State*, 537 P.2d 431 (Okla.Crim.Ct.App. 1975).
18. *State v. McDowell*, 522 N.W.2d 738 (Neb. 1994).
19. See *Walker v. State*, 63 Ala. 49 (1879).
20. *McGraw v. Maryland*, 199 A.2d 229 (Md. 1964), *cert. denied*, 379 U.S. 862 (1964).
21. *People v. Johnson*, 906 P.2d 122 (Colo. 1995).
22. Pa.C.S., Title 18, Chapter 35, Section 3502(a)(b)(2007).
23. Pa.C.S., Title 18, Chapter 35, Section 3501 (2007).
24. Cal Pen Code, Part I, Title 13, Section 459 (2008).
25. NY CLS Penal, Title J, Sections 140.20-140.30 (2008).
26. Mont. Code Anno., Title 45, Chapter 6, Section 45-6-204 (2008).
27. Tex. Penal Code, Title 7, Section 30.02(a)(1)(2)(3) (2009).
28. *State v. Christofferson*, 775 P.2d 690 (Mont. 1989).
29. Pa.C.S., Title 18, Chapter 35, Section 3502(d) (2007).
30. Federal Bureau of Investigation, *Uniform Crime Reports: Crime in the United States 2004* (Washington, D.C.: U.S. Department of Justice, 2005), p. 55.
31. Federal Bureau of Investigation, *Crime in the United States, Uniform Crime Reports 2007*, http://www.fbi.gov/ucr/cius2007/offenses/property_crime/motor_vehicle.html, accessed 28 November 2008.
32. M.R.S., Title 17-A, Part 2, Chapter 17, Section 405 (2008).
33. M.R.S., Title 17-A, Part 2, Chapter 17, Section 360 (2008).
34. Federal Bureau of Investigation, *Crime in the United States, Uniform Crime Reports 2007*, http://www.fbi.gov/ucr/cius2007/offenses/property_crime/arson.html, accessed 28 November 2008.
35. The statute amends U.S. Code, Title 18, Section 247, Damage to Religious Property (2009).
36. See, for example, *State v. Hall*, 93 N.C. 571, 573 (1885).
37. Tex. Penal Code, Title 7, Chapter 28, Section 28.02 (2009).
38. V.S.A., Title 13, Part I, Chapter 11, Section 501 (2009).
39. N.C. Gen. Stat., Chapter 14, Subchapter 04, Article 15, Section 14-58.2 (2008).
40. N.C. Gen. Stat., Chapter 14, Subchapter 04, Article 15, Section 14-65 (2008).
41. N.C. Gen. Stat., Chapter 14, Subchapter 04, Article 15, Section 14-62 (2008).
42. N.C. Gen. Stat., Chapter 14, Subchapter 06, Article 22, Section 14-144 (2008).
43. N.C. Gen. Stat., Chapter 14, Subchapter 04, Article 15, Section 14-58 (2008).
44. NY CLS Penal, Title 1, Article 150, Section 150.05 *et seq.* (2008).
45. Va. Code Ann., Title 18.2, Chapter 5, Article 4, Section 18.2-111 (2008).

46. *Avco Financial Services v. Foreman-Donovan*, 772 P.2d 862, 864 (Mont. 1989).

47. "Bilking the Elderly, with a Corporate Assist," *New York Times* (20 May 2007), p. 1.

48. Federal Bureau of Investigation Press Release, "More Than 400 Defendants Charged for Roles in Mortgage Fraud Schemes as Part of Operation 'Malicious Mortgage,'" (19 June 2008), http://www.fbi.gov/pressrel/pressrel08/mortgagefraud061908.htm, accessed 9 July 2008.

49. See USCS, Title 18, Part I, Chapter 63, Section 1341 (2009).

50. See USCS, Title 18, Part I, Chapter 63, Section 1343 (2009).

51. USCS, Title 18, Part I, Chapter 63, Section 1344 (2009).

52. See USCS, Title 18, Section 1341 *et seq.* (2009).

53. *Schmuck v. United States*, 489 U.S. 705 (1989).

54. Federal Bureau of Investigation, "Health Care Fraud," http://www.fbi.gov/page2/july07/health_care072007.htm, accessed 12 December 2008.

55. See Public Law 104-191, amending U.S. Code, Title 18, Section 1347 (2009). The theft or embezzlement provision amends USCS, Title 18, Section 669 (2009).

56. Federal Bureau of Investigation Press Release, "Three Miami Area Brothers and Physician's Assistant Charged in $110 Million Health Care Fraud Scheme," (11 June 2008), http://miami.fbi.gov/dojpressrel/pressrel08/mm20080611.htm, accessed 9 July 2008.

57. ILCS, Chapter 720, Title III, Part C, Section 5/17-8 (2008).

58. USCS, Title 15, Section 77a *et seq.* (2009).

59. Federal Bureau of Investigation, "Financial Crimes Report to the Public: Fiscal Year 2006," http://www.fbi.gov/publications/financial/fcs_report2006/financial_crime_2006htm, pp. 6–7, accessed 28 February 2008.

60. USCS, Title 15, Section 78c (2009).

61. USCS, Title 15, Section 78o (2009).

62. The Sarbanes-Oxley Act of 2002, Public Law 107-204, is codified, as amended, in various sections of the federal securities statutes in Chapters 15 and 28 of the U.S. Code (2009).

63. See, for example, *United States v. Martin*, 455 F.3d 1227 (11th Cir. 2006; and *United States v. Crisp*, 454 F.3d 1285 (11 Cir. 2006).

64. New Hampshire RSA, Title 62, Chapter 637, Section 637:4 (2008).

65. See Model Penal Code, Section 223.3.

66. See *Clarke v. People*, 171 P. 69 (Colo. 1918).

67. "Columbia Professor in Noose Case Is Fired on Plagiarism Charges," *New York Times* (24 June 2008), p. 13 C; "Man Who Faked Way Into Yale Avoids Jail Time; Gets Three-Year Suspended Sentence, Must Pay Restitution," *Hartford Courant* (6 September 2008), p. 6B.

68. M.R.S., Title 17-A, Part 2, Chapter 15, Section 359 (2008).

69. NY CLS Pen Code, Title J, Article 165, Sections 165.40–165.54 (2008).

70. See, for example, Tex. Penal Code, Section 28.03 *et seq.* (2009).

71. M.R.S., Title 17-A, Part 2, Chapter 33, Section 805 (2008).

72. M.R.S., Title 17-A, Part 2, Chapter 17, Section 402 (2008).

73. USCS, Title 17, Chapter 1, Section 102 (2009).

74. Md. Criminal Law Code Ann., Title 3, Subtitle 7, Section 3-701 (2008).

75. August Bequai, *Computer Crime* (Lexington, Mass.: D. C. Heath, 1978), p. 4.

76. Federal Bureau of Investigation, "Hot Off the Press: New FBI Computer Crime Survey" (18 January 2006), http://www.fbi.gov/page2/jan06/computer_crime_survey011806.htm, accessed 15 July 2008.

77. "Security," *Washington Internet Daily* 6, no. 129 (6 July 2005): 1.

78. "Security."

79. These and other examples are available in the press releases listed by the U.S. Department of Justice, Office of the United States Attorney, Southern District of California, San Diego, California (9 June 2008), http://www.usdoj.gov/criminal/cybercrime/ccnews.html, accessed 15 July 2008.

80. Federal Bureau of Investigation, Press Release, "Reported Dollar Loss from Internet Crimes Reaches All-Time High," (3 April 2008), http://www.fbi.gov/pressrel/pressrel08/ic3_040308.htm, accessed 3 April 2008.

81. "FTC Rule Requires Warning on Sexually Explicit Spam," *Computer & Internet Lawyer* 21, no. 8 (August 2004), p. 26. The CAN-SPAM Act of 2003, Public Law 108–187, is codified at U.S. Code, Chapter 15, Section 7701 (2009).

82. "After Telephone Courtship, a First Date Ends in Death," *New York Times* (17 August 2002), p. 11.

83. "150-Year Sentence in Sex Abuse of Teenager After Internet Meeting," *New York Times* (12 February 2003), p. 7B.

84. Federal Computer Crime Control Act, USCS, Title 18, Section 1030 (2009).

85. Section 225 (b)(2)(B)iii-vii of the Homeland Security Act of 2002, Public Law 107-296 (H.R. 50051) (25 November 2002).

86. The USA Patriot Act is codified as Public Law 107-56 (2006).

87. *State v. Rowell*, 908 P.2d 1379 (N.M. 1995). The statute is codified at N.M. Stat. Ann., Section 30-45-1 *et seq.* (2008).

88. "Brown Seeks Identity Theft Law," *New York Law Journal* (5 June 2002), p. 9.

89. Federal Trade Commission, *2006 Identity Theft Survey Report* (November 2007), http://www.ftc.gov/os/2007/

11/SynovateFinalReportIDTheft2006.pdf, pp. 4, 6, 7, accessed 15 July 08.

90. Federal Bureau of Investigation, "Headline Archives: House Stealing: The Latest Scam on the Block" (25 March 2008), p. 2, http://www.fbi.gov/page2/march08/housestealing_032508.html, accessed 28 March 2008.

91. Conn. Gen. Stat., Title 53a, Chapter 952, Section 53a-129a (2008).

92. USCS, Title 18, Section 1028 (2009).

93. Bureau of Justice Statistics, Crime Data Brief, *Carjacking 1993–2002* (Washington, D.C.: U.S. Department of Justice, Office of Justice Programs, July 2004), pp. 1–2.

94. New Jersey State Police, *New Jersey Carjacking Offense Report* (31 December 2006), p. 3.

95. N.J. Stat., Title 2C, Chapter 15, Section 2C:15-2(a) (2008).

96. *Holloway v. United States*, 526 U.S. 1 (1999), cases and citations omitted. The federal statute is codified at U.S. Code Stats., Title 18, Section 2219 (2009).

97. Cal Pen Code, Part I, Title 8, Chapter 3, Section 209.5 (2008).

CHAPTER 9

Crimes Against Public Order and Public Decency

INTRODUCTION

This chapter covers crimes that are often omitted from criminal law casebooks. Perhaps the primary reason is that in criminal law courses little attention is given to misdemeanors, and many of the crimes in this chapter fall into that category, although statutes may provide that subsequent convictions of these crimes are felonies. Even though by definition misdemeanors are less serious offenses than felonies, some are important because of the frequency with which they occur. In addition, although there are few prosecutions for some of the crimes covered in this chapter, statutes regulating the offenses may infringe on basic constitutional rights. Finally, some of the covered offenses represent areas in which there is no agreement concerning whether the criminal law should be used to regulate the activity.

Although space does not permit an extensive discussion of constitutional law, it is important to keep the subject in mind while reading this chapter. Chapter 1 briefly discussed the relationship of the U.S. Constitution to criminal law and examined the void-for-vagueness and overbreadth doctrines. These doctrines require that statutes must be written so that reasonable people know what they mean, and they must be specific regarding the conduct prohibited. Statutes must not reach beyond conduct that may be prohibited constitutionally and include conduct that is protected by the Constitution. Frequently these issues arise in cases involving free speech. Although the First Amendment (see Appendix A) states that Congress shall pass no law inhibiting free speech, the interpretation has been that some speech and some actions that convey speech may be regulated, although the rules for doing so are strict.

Chapter 1 also introduced another constitutional doctrine important to this chapter—the right of privacy. Unlike free speech and assembly, this right is not articulated specifically within the Constitution or any of its amendments. Rather, according to the U.S. Supreme Court, the right of privacy emanates from several amendments, including the First, Third, Fourth, Fifth, and Ninth (see Appendix A), as discussed in *Griswold v. Connecticut*, which invalidated criminal statutes concerning birth control devices when used by a married woman.[1] That discussion provided a backdrop for this chapter's analysis of some sexual acts that are still defined as criminal in some jurisdictions. However, the statutes criminalizing sex acts between consenting adults in private may be considered unconstitutional as the result of a recent U.S. Supreme Court decision involving gay men. That decision is the focus of this chapter's Case Analysis.

This chapter discusses offenses that go to the heart of a free society, offenses that force us to consider under what circumstances the rights of individuals should prevail over the alleged need to protect society by criminalizing certain acts.

CRIMES AGAINST PUBLIC ORDER

Early common law was concerned with preserving peace and order to the extent that in England most statutes concluded with the phrase "to preserve the peace of the King" or "against the peace of the King." In the United States many early statutes contained the phrase "against the peace and dignity of the state." These phrases emphasized the need to preserve the peace and tranquillity of society. To do that it was thought necessary to criminalize behaviors that might incite people to fight or retaliate in other ways.

All crimes might be considered offenses against the peace of the king or the state, but common law and modern statutes use "offenses against the public peace and order" to refer to those offenses that are punishable primarily because they threaten or invade society's peace and tranquillity.[2]

Breach of the Peace

An act that disturbs the public tranquillity or order may constitute **breach of the peace**, a willfully committed act that disturbs the public tranquillity or order and for which there is no legal justification. Under the common law, breach of the peace covered numerous actions, but the main thrust of the crime was to include acts that otherwise were not defined as criminal but that tended to disturb peace and tranquillity. If otherwise the acts were defined as crimes, generally they were prosecuted as those crimes.

A breach-of-the-peace statute that was held to be constitutional was the subject of appeal in a 1967 Georgia case in which the defendant was convicted of saying, "You son of a bitch, I'll choke you to death." He was prosecuted under a statute that prohibited "opprobrious words or abusive language, tending to cause a breach of the peace." The court held that the words of that phrase "have a definite meaning as to the conduct forbidden, measured by common understanding and practice, and are not unconstitutionally vague, indefinite or uncertain."[3]

In a later case the Georgia disorderly conduct statute was successfully challenged by the facts of the case but not in general. The statute provides as follows:

(a) A person commits the offense of disorderly conduct when such person commits any of the following:

(1) Acts in a violent or tumultuous manner toward another person whereby such person is placed in reasonable fear of the safety of such person's life, limb, or health;

(2) Acts in a violent or tumultuous manner toward another person whereby the property of such person is placed in danger of being damaged or destroyed;

(3) Without provocation, uses to or of another person in such other person's presence, opprobrious or abusive words which by their very utterance tend to incite to an immediate breach of the peace, that is to say, words which as a matter of common knowledge and under ordinary circumstances will, when used to or of another person in such other person's presence, naturally tend to provoke violent resentment, that is, words commonly called "fighting words"; or

(4) Without provocation, uses obscene and vulgar or profane language in the presence of or by telephone to a person under the age of 14 years which threatens an immediate breach of the peace.[4]

In the case of *Delaney v. State*, the defendant stopped his car behind a police vehicle, which had stopped another car; the police officer was writing a citation. The defendant began honking his horn and yelling at the officer, who could not ascertain all of the words, but essentially reported that the man yelled, "What are you doing parked in the middle of the roadway? I want to get home." He honked his horn, exited his vehicle, and began screaming and throwing his hands in the air. He was charged with improper use of a horn, disorderly conduct, and obstruction of a law enforcement officer. He was found guilty of disorderly conduct (with which the horn offense had been merged) but not of obstructing a law enforcement officer. He appealed on the grounds that his words did not constitute a breach of peace. The appellate court agreed, emphasizing that to avoid free speech issues, the fighting words doctrine must be limited. The words must be abusive and opprobrious, words that naturally tend to provoke violent resentment.[5]

The problem in this case was not that the statute was unconstitutional per se, but that the words spoken did not meet the statutory requirements. In the next example, the statute was held to be unconstitutionally vague. A Kentucky statute aimed at breach-of-the-peace behavior provided: "No person shall upbraid, insult or abuse any teacher of the public schools in the presence of the school or in the presence of a pupil of the school."[6] In *Commonwealth v. Ashcraft*, an obviously upset father stormed into his daughter's classroom late one afternoon after most students had gone. In the presence of the remaining children, including his daughter, the father yelled criticisms at the teacher.

In *Ashcraft* the Kentucky Court of Appeals held that the statute was vague and that it infringed on the First Amendment right of communication (see Appendix A). Parents have a right to criticize teachers. The court noted that the statute as worded made it a crime for parents to criticize teachers or coaches at home or at school or elsewhere in the presence of children: "A parent could be prosecuted for insulting a teacher at a dinner table in the presence of his child/student. . . . Likewise, one can be penalized for insulting or abusing a teacher at the school when no students are present."[7]

In *Ashcraft* there was no evidence that the father was violent or becoming violent. The statute, designed to prevent breaches of the peace, was so vague that it was used to go beyond the state's legitimate right to keep peace. It infringed on the father's First Amendment right to criticize his daughter's teacher. Presumably these issues were handled in the subsequent revision of the statute, which now provides as follows:

> Whenever a teacher or school administrator is functioning in his capacity as an employee of a board of education of a public school system, it shall be unlawful for any person to direct speech or conduct toward the teacher or school administrator when such person knows or should know that the speech or conduct will disrupt or interfere with normal school activities or will nullify or undermine the good order and discipline of the school.[8]

Some statutes covering disturbance of the peace are much broader. Consider the following provisions of a California statute, which defines *disturbing the peace* as including:

(1) Any person who unlawfully fights in a public place or challenges another person in a public place to fight.

(2) Any person who maliciously and willfully disturbs another person by loud and unreasonable noise.

(3) Any person who uses offensive words in a public place which are inherently likely to provoke an immediate violent reaction.[9]

How difficult do you think it would be to convict under this statute? Would the requirements of *maliciously* and *willfully* be barriers? Examine the facts of the following North Carolina case, for example, and consider how you would apply a statute like that of California to these facts: A neighbor devised a plan that he thought might deter noise from nearby auto races. After seven years of complaining to no avail, Junior Medlin of Elm City, North Carolina, put 11 security horns on top of his home and blared the high-pitched, sirenlike noises when the races were in full swing. Medlin, who paid about $750 for the horns, said they bounced the sound back onto the track and enabled him to carry on a conversation inside the house in which he had lived for 28 years. Medlin's neighbor, James Richardson, erected a sign with the words "World's Most Annoying Neighbor" and an arrow pointing to Medlin's property. He uncovered the sign when the horns were turned on.[10] Who was disturbing the peace—the persons who operated the race track, Medlin, Richardson, or all of

them? If the California statute were applicable, how would you apply it to these facts?

Fighting Words

A crime similar to breach of the peace is that of **fighting words**, which refers to words that have a tendency to incite violence by the person to whom they are directed. Fighting words are not protected by the First Amendment. They are viewed as words designed to inflict harm rather than to communicate ideas. As such, fighting words are more analogous to a punch in the mouth than to the communication of ideas. They are designed to elicit immediate violent reaction (unprotected speech), not to arouse people to thought and debate (protected speech). In 1942, in *Chaplinsky v. New Hampshire*, the U.S. Supreme Court considered the subject of fighting words and enunciated its position in the following excerpt from the case, which has been frequently criticized in subsequent years but remains good law.[11]

CHAPLINSKY v. NEW HAMPSHIRE
315 U.S. 568 (1942)

Justices Harlan F. Stone, Owen J. Roberts, Hugo L. Black, Stanley F. Reed, Felix Frankfurter, William O. Douglas, Frank Murphy, James F. Byrnes, and Robert H. Jackson; Justice Murphy delivered the Court's opinion.

Appellant, a member of the sect known as Jehovah's Witnesses, was convicted in the municipal court of Rochester, New Hampshire, for [speaking these words to the complainant]. "You are a God damned racketeer" and "a damned Fascist and the whole government of Rochester are Fascists or agents of Fascists." . . . .

    There is no substantial dispute over the facts. Chaplinsky was distributing the literature of his sect on the streets of Rochester on a busy Saturday afternoon. Members of the local citizenry complained to the City Marshall, Bowering, that Chaplinsky was denouncing all religion as a "racket." Bowering told them that Chaplinsky was lawfully engaged, and then warned Chaplinsky that the crowd was getting restless. Some time later, a disturbance occurred. The traffic officer on duty at the busy intersection started with Chaplinsky for the police station, but did not inform him that he was under arrest or that he was going to be arrested. On the way they encountered Marshall Bowering, who had been advised that a riot was under way and was therefore hurrying to the scene. Bowering repeated his earlier warning to Chaplinsky, who then addressed to Bowering the words set forth in the complaint.

Chaplinsky's version of the affair was slightly different. He testified that, when he met Bowering, he asked him to arrest the ones responsible for the disturbance. In reply, Bowering cursed him and told him to come along. Appellant admitted that he said the words charged in the complaint, with the exception of the name of the Deity. . . . .

[I]t is well understood that the right of free speech is not absolute at all times and under all circumstances. There are certain well-defined and narrowly limited classes of speech, the prevention and punishment of which have never been thought to raise any Constitutional problem. These include the lewd and obscene, the profane, the libelous, and the insulting or "fighting" words—those which by their very utterance inflict injury or tend to incite an immediate breach of the peace. It has been well observed that such utterances are no essential part of any exposition of ideas, and are of such slight social value as a step to truth that any benefit that may be derived from them is clearly outweighed by the social interest in public order and public decency. "Resort to epithets or personal abuse is not in any proper sense communication of information or opinion safeguarded by the Constitution, and its punishment as a criminal act would raise no question under that instrument."

We are unable to say that the limited scope of the statute as thus construed contravenes the Constitutional right of free expression. It is a statute narrowly drawn and limited to define and punish specific conduct lying within the domain of state power, the use in a public place of words likely to cause a breach of the peace. . . .

Argument is unnecessary to demonstrate that the appellations "damned racketeer" and "damned Fascist" are epithets likely to provoke the average person to retaliation, and thereby cause a breach of the peace.

In later cases the U.S. Supreme Court retreated somewhat from the presumption in *Chaplinsky* that fighting words incite people to violence. In *Terminiello v. Chicago*, decided in 1949, the Court upheld the trial court's jury instruction that the statute in question "stirs the public to anger, invites dispute, brings about a condition of unrest or creates a disturbance." The Court stated that part of the purpose of speech is to arouse debate and invite dispute. Although in *Terminiello* the statute was held unconstitutional because it was vague and too broad, thereby enabling the U.S. Supreme Court to avoid deciding whether the speech in question was protected by the First Amendment, the case represents a reluctance to broaden the fighting words doctrine.[12]

In *Feiner v. New York*, decided in 1951, the U.S. Supreme Court upheld Irving Feiner's conviction for disorderly conduct when he described President Harry S. Truman as a bum, the Syracuse mayor as a champagne-sipping bum, and the American Legion as a Nazi Gestapo. Feiner urged minorities to "rise up in arms and fight for equal rights." According to the Supreme Court, "[T]hese racial statements stirred up a little excitement. Some of the onlookers made remarks to the police about their inability to handle the crowd and at least one threatened violence if the police did not act. There were others who appeared to be favoring petitioner's arguments."

The Court said Feiner's arrest was not effected as a censor to his speech but rather as an effort to maintain the peace. The Court stated: "It is one thing to say that the police cannot be used as an instrument for the suppression of unpopular views, and another to say that, when as here the speaker passes the bounds of argument or persuasion and undertakes incitement to riot, they are powerless to prevent a breach of the peace."[13]

The line between permissible and impermissible speech is difficult to draw, as illustrated by the U.S. Supreme Court's 1963 decision in *Edwards v. South Carolina*. In *Edwards* the Court refused to hold as fighting words the religious and patriotic songs of demonstrators who were urging the audience to go to segregated lunch counters in protest against segregation. The Court acknowledged that an expansion of the *Feiner* holding could permit authorities to unreasonably suppress the civil rights demonstrations by contending that the audience was becoming restive and potentially dangerous.[14]

In analyzing these earlier cases, we must look carefully at the facts and what might be expected to occur as a result of the alleged fighting words. Police may not suppress words because they (or others) do not agree with those words; something more must be present.

Some insight comes from *Cohen v. California*, decided by the U.S. Supreme Court in 1971. The Court reversed the conviction of Robert Cohen, who in protest of the draft, walked into a Los Angeles courthouse wearing a jacket on which were imprinted the words "Fuck the Draft." The Court concluded that in the context in which this occurred, there was not a substantial invasion of privacy "in an intolerable manner" (people in public must expect to see and hear some words and signs of which they may not approve). The words were not a "direct personal insult" directed specifically at the hearer. Nor were the police, in arresting Cohen (in contrast to the *Feiner* case) attempting "to prevent a speaker from intentionally provoking a given group to a hostile reaction."[15]

The *Cohen* case was cited with approval by a federal circuit court of appeals in a 1997 case, which held that an individual who used the gesture known as "giving the finger" while shouting "fuck you" as he rode in a car past a group of antiabortion picketers was exercising his right to free speech and thus should not have been arrested. According to the court, these actions "were not likely to inflict injury or to incite an immediate breach of the peace." The words were not "fighting words" as the U.S. Supreme Court has interpreted that concept, and, finally, referring to *Cohen*, "the use of the 'f-word' in and of itself is not criminal conduct."[16]

In terms of the future status of the fighting words doctrine, it appears that in reviewing allegations of fighting words, the U.S. Supreme Court will look carefully at the makeup of the audience to whom the words are directed, the results that occur, and the wording of the statute that serves as the basis for the criminal charge. The Supreme Court has not overruled *Chaplinsky*, but it has proceeded with caution in recent cases, holding similar statutes unconstitutional for overbreadth or vagueness rather than reaching the First Amendment free speech issue. In 1974, in *Lewis v. City of New Orleans*, for example, the Court refused to sustain the conviction of a defendant who referred to the police officer as the "goddamn motherfucking police." According to the Court, words that convey or are intended to convey disrespect are not, for that reason alone, fighting words.[17]

A more recent case, decided by the Ohio Supreme Court in 2002, illustrates the changing nature of the fighting words doctrine, along with the crime of solicitation, which was discussed in Chapter 3. In *State v. Thompson*, Ohio's highest court reversed the conviction of an appellant who was found guilty of violating the state's statute prohibiting soliciting sex from a member of the same gender. After he offered to perform a sex act on another jogger, the appellant was charged with violating the statute providing that "no person shall solicit a person of the same sex to engage in sexual activity with the offender, when the offender knows such solicitation is offensive to the other person, or is reck-

less in that regard." In 1979 the Ohio Supreme Court had upheld that statute, stating that the acts prohibited were the equivalent of fighting words. In 2002, however, the court ruled that the statute violated the equal protection clause of the Fourteenth Amendment (see Appendix A) because the state did not prohibit such behavior when the target was a member of the opposite gender.[18]

These and other cases suggest that although the U.S. Supreme Court and lower courts have not rejected the fighting words doctrine, any conviction under it will be examined closely and may be reversed.

Disorderly Conduct, Vagrancy, and Loitering

The common law did not include the crime of **disorderly conduct**, which refers to minor offenses, such as drunkenness or fighting, that disturb the peace or behavior standards of a community or shock the morality of its population. But some acts that were included in the common law breach-of-the-peace crime are typical of acts covered by modern disorderly conduct statutes. Today most jurisdictions have a statute providing for the criminal punishment of certain minor acts, sometimes enumerated, and in many jurisdictions these offenses are called *disorderly conduct*. The statutes vary considerably from one jurisdiction to another, and they may be confused with **vagrancy** statutes (discussed next).

A disorderly conduct statute may specify that being vagrant is an example of the proscribed conduct, or it may refer to people who behave in a disorderly manner. It is important to check the wording and interpretation of the statutes, assess whether they are vague or too broad, and determine whether they are often used along with other statutes.

An example of a disorderly conduct statute, along with two recent and significant but unsuccessful constitutional challenges to that statute, is included in Focus 9.1.

A crime often associated with disorderly conduct, *vagrancy* dates back centuries, focusing on idle persons. The common law crime of vagrancy referred to people who wandered about from place to place without any visible means of support, refusing to work even though able to do so, and living off the charity of others. Early English statutes required able-bodied people to work and made it a crime for them to wander about the country looking for higher wages or avoiding work.

FOCUS 9.1 **Disorderly Conduct Statute Challenged in a 9/11/01 Incident**

An example of a state's efforts to criminalize disorderly conduct is the New York statute entitled *disorderly conduct*, which lists seven circumstances that may constitute the crime when they are committed "with intent to cause public inconvenience, annoyance or alarm, or recklessly creating a risk thereof." The offense is considered a violation, which does not rise even to the level of a misdemeanor. A person engages in disorderly conduct if he (or she) does any of the following:

(1) He engages in fighting or in violent, tumultuous or threatening behavior; or

(2) He makes unreasonable noise; or

(3) In a public place, he uses abusive or obscene language, or makes an obscene gesture; or

(4) Without lawful authority, he disturbs any lawful assembly or meeting of persons; or

(5) He obstructs vehicular or pedestrian traffic; or

(6) He congregates with other persons in a public place and refuses to comply with a lawful order of the police to disperse; or

(7) He creates a hazardous or physically offensive condition by any act which serves no legitimate purpose.[1]

New York also has a statute prohibiting *Inciting to Riot*, which provides as follows:

A person is guilty of inciting to riot when he urges ten or more persons to engage in tumultuous and violent conduct of a kind likely to create public alarm.[2]

These statutes were challenged by a defendant who was charged and convicted after an incident that occurred just a few days after the terrorist attacks in New York City on 11 September 2001. The New York statutes were upheld against the defendant's allegations that he was exercising his free speech rights to express a point of view when he and others praised the terrorist acts that, among other results, destroyed the World Trade Center's twin towers and killed thousands. The defendant had stated that more people should have been killed, while he verbally accosted and threatened a crowd of people in New York City. The court refused the defendant's request to have the charges dismissed, determining that he did not intend his remarks as merely an expression of his point of view but rather intended to incite the crowd to engage in violence.[3]

In a similar case, William Harvey was arrested near the Trade Center ruins on 4 October 2001. Harvey allegedly said that the acts were revenge against Americans for the manner in which they treated Islamic nations. A judge ruled that the time and place of these comments made it reasonable to assume that Harvey knew that public alarm and annoyance would result.[4]

1. NY CLS Penal, Title N, Article 240, Section 240.20 (2008).
2. NY CLS Penal, Title N, Article 240, Section 240.08 (2008).
3. "Post-September 11 Actions Were Intended to Incite Violence, Not to Express Point of View," *New York Law Journal* (29 March 2002), p. 17.
4. "Nation at a Glance," *St. Louis Post-Dispatch* (31 March 2002), p. 8.

Most vagrancy laws are broader than disorderly conduct laws, and many of them have been declared unconstitutional. They have been challenged as permitting police too much discretion, which has led to discrimination against racial and ethnic minorities, the homeless, and others. To illustrate, in 1997 the Massachusetts Supreme Court held that the state's statute making it a crime to wander and beg or to "go about from door to door or in public or private" for the "purpose of begging or to receive alms" without a license to do so was unconstitutional. The court held that begging, even when it does not involve a verbal message, is a form of communication protected by the First Amendment just as organized requests for charitable contributions are constitutional.[19]

Vagrancy and disorderly conduct statutes may be unconstitutional because they are vague or overbroad, an issue discussed in Chapter 1, in which the U.S. Supreme Court case from California, *Kolender v. Lawson*, was analyzed. That case involved an African American who was arrested frequently for disorderly conduct under a statute that prohibited loitering or wandering about without apparent reason or business and refusing to identify oneself when asked to do so by peace officers. The state statute in effect at the time of this case permitted officers to stop individuals and ask for identification "if the surrounding circumstances are such as to indicate to a reasonable man that the public safety demands such identification." The U.S. Supreme Court held that the statute was unconstitutional because it vested too much discretionary power in the police, encouraging "arbitrary enforcement by failing to describe with sufficient particularity what a suspect must do in order to satisfy the statute."[20]

Some modern statutes use the term *loitering* rather than *vagrancy*. Such statutes may be found unconstitutional if they are vague or overbroad; they may be upheld if they are clear. To illustrate, in *Milwaukee v. Nelson*, the Wisconsin Supreme Court upheld a municipal ordinance that makes it an offense to loiter "in a place, at a time, or in a manner not usual for law-abiding individuals under circumstances that warrant alarm for the safety of persons or property in the vicinity."[21] Likewise, the California statute that prohibits, among other situations, loitering "in or about any toilet open to the public for the purpose of engaging in or soliciting any lewd or lascivious or any unlawful act" was upheld against charges of vagueness.[22]

In contrast, a Tampa, Florida, ordinance that prohibited loitering "in a manner and under circumstances manifesting the purpose" to solicit prostitution was declared unconstitutional by the Florida Supreme Court. The decision was 4-3; the majority wrote three opinions, with little agreement on why the ordinance was unconstitutional. Some of the reasons given were that the ordinance was overly broad, vague, too harsh compared to similar Florida statutes, and violative of substantive due process. The ordinance could be interpreted to prohibit known prostitutes from hailing a cab, waving to a friend, or engaging in other protected behavior.[23]

In recent years many cities and states have enacted ordinances or statutes preventing begging as well as camping, sitting, or lying down in some public places. Some of these regulations have been upheld; others have not. A federal district judge in San Francisco ruled that the Berkeley ordinance banning people from sitting on the sidewalks or asking for money in some public areas was unconstitutional. The court issued a preliminary **injunction** against enforcing the ordinance. The judge noted that the city could address problems in ways that do not inhibit free speech and expression—such as prohibiting littering, public drunkenness, blocking public sidewalks, and so on—but that, as written, the ordinance in question violated First Amendment rights. The preliminary injunction was dismissed two years later (in 1997), when the parties stipulated an agreement. After the City of Berkeley repealed the ordinance and was ordered to pay plaintiff's attorney fees, a less restrictive ordinance was enacted.[24]

In a contrasting case, the Ninth Circuit upheld a Seattle ordinance that prohibits sitting or lying on city sidewalks in commercial areas between 7 a.m. and 9 p.m. The ordinance provides that no one may be cited for violations unless first notified by an officer that the behavior is prohibited.[25] Subsequently, that same court reversed the convictions of six homeless people charged under a Los Angeles ordinance stating that "no person shall sit, lie or sleep in or upon any street, sidewalk or public way." The Ninth Circuit referred to this ordinance as "one of the most restrictive municipal laws regulating public spaces in the United States." The appellants had argued that the ordinance resulted in cruel and unusual punishment because they could not find another place to sleep on the nights in question. The LA police chief, William Bratton, stated that his officers were not targeting the homeless but, rather, people who were violating the ordinance. The city had about 9,000–10,000 spaces for the homeless to sleep at night, an insufficient number for the city's 11,000–12,000 homeless persons. The court compared the ordinance as enforced to one that criminalizes the *status* of being a drug addict or an alcoholic and ruled that as long as the city did not have sufficient housing for the appellants, it could not arrest them for sleeping on the streets. In 2007 the city of Los Angeles and the six plaintiffs who challenged the ordinance agreed to a settlement whereby the city would permit sleeping on streets during the night, with some restrictions, until the city built more low-cost housing with services for the homeless.[26]

The California Supreme Court has ruled that an ordinance that bans camping and the storing of personal property in designated public places is not a violation of the constitutional rights of homeless persons. According to the court, the ordinance bans *conduct*, not *status*. It is not too broad, and it complies with the right of police to regulate conduct in public places. The ordinance does not punish people for their status, and it does not restrict travel impermissibly. There is no fundamental constitutional right to camp or to store one's personal belongings in a public place.[27]

In 1999 the U.S. Supreme Court struck down a Chicago antiloitering ordinance that had been used to arrest over 42,000 persons while it was in effect from 1992 until the state court ruled on it in 1995. This ordinance served as a model for many other cities that, like Chicago, were trying to bring gangs under control. The ordinance made it a crime to "remain in any one place with no apparent purpose" in the presence of a gang member if requested by a police officer to leave.[28]

In *Chicago v. Morales*, the U.S. Supreme Court held that the Chicago ordinance was vague. It left too much discretion to the subjective judgment of the police officer. Thus, it made no difference whether a gang member and his father might loiter at the baseball field

Ordinances and statutes aimed at punishing homeless persons for loitering or sleeping on city streets may be held unconstitutional if they are vague or too broad or if they violate any specific constitutional rights, such as the First Amendment right to free speech or assembly. (IStockPhoto)

waiting to rob someone or to "get a glimpse of Sammy Sousa leaving the ball park."[29]

The city tried again, and in 2002 it enacted an ordinance designed to inconvenience gangs by disbursing them frequently to prevent their getting a hold on any area of the city. Three Hispanic men were unsuccessful in their challenge to the constitutionality of this ordinance. The judge who upheld the ordinance stated that *Morales* provided a road map for a constitutional ordinance and "the Chicago framers of the revised ordinance knew how to read the map."[30]

It can be expected that local ordinances and state and federal statutes designed to regulate behavior in public places will continue to be challenged in the courts. But for those determined to free the streets and parks of persons they consider undesirable, an easier way is to ban public intoxication. The next section analyzes that approach, along with other substance-issue offenses.

Alcohol and Drug-Related Offenses

Many offenses related to substance use are covered by criminal statutes. Chapter 11 is devoted to a thorough discussion of drug abuse and drug trafficking, but here we consider several offenses, often categorized as misdemeanors, that are related to the use of alcohol and other drugs.

Public Intoxication and Drug Incapacitation

Chapter 5 examined the issue of whether substance abuse is a disease or an act of free will. That discussion focused on the use of intoxication (by either alcohol or other drugs) as a defense to criminal acts. This chapter examines the practice of criminalizing public substance abuse. Statutes that do so are based on the assumption that substance abusers may disturb public order or public decency and that they may be a threat to themselves or to others. They may also encourage or even entice others to engage in substance abuse. Whether designated as a separate crime or prosecuted as disorderly conduct, vagrancy, or disturbing the peace, the public abuse of alcohol and other drugs is another category of criminal activity that raises significant constitutional law issues.

In *Powell v. Texas*, the U.S. Supreme Court upheld the appellant's conviction based on its conclusion that the appellant's public drunkenness was an *act*, not a *condition*.[31] As long as the Court embraces that position, most public drunkenness statutes will be upheld. These statutes should be distinguished from those that prohibit driving while under the influence of alcohol and other drugs.

Driving Under the Influence (DUI)

It is illegal to operate motor vehicles while under the influence of alcohol or other drugs, although states

---

FOCUS 9.2 **Prohibitions Against Driving While Impaired**

The following is an example of a statute that prohibits driving a motor vehicle while under the influence of alcohol or other drugs.

(1) [Until October 31, 2010] A person, whether licensed or not, shall not operate a vehicle upon a highway or other place open to the general public or generally accessible to motor vehicles, including an area designated for the parking of vehicles, within this state if the person is operating while intoxicated. As used in this section, "operating while intoxicated" means either of the following applies:

(a) The person is under the influence of alcoholic liquor, a controlled substance, or a combination of alcoholic liquor and a controlled substance.

(b) The person has an alcohol content of 0.08 grams or more per 100 milliliters of blood, per 210 liters of breath, or per 67 milliliters of urine, or, beginning October 1, 2013, the person has an alcohol content of 0.10 grams or more per 100 milliliters of blood, per 210 liters of breath, or per 67 milliliters of urine.[1]

1. Michigan Motor Vehicle Code, MCLS, Chapter 257, Section 257.625 (2008).

---

and counties vary with regard to how they define the offenses as well as what those offenses are called. Such terms as *driving under the influence (DUI), operating under the influence of liquor (OUIL), driving while intoxicated (DWI),* and *unlawful blood alcohol level (UBAL)* are examples. Focus 9.2 presents the Michigan statute, which illustrates one way to define offenses related to the operation of motor vehicles while under the influence.

With regard to both public drunkenness and driving under the influence, some jurisdictions now emphasize treatment and rehabilitation. For example, Michigan provides as follows:

> Before imposing sentence for a violation of [the state statute] or a local ordinance substantially corresponding to [the state statute] the court shall order the person to undergo screening and assessment by a person or agency designated by the office of substance abuse services to determine whether the person is likely to benefit from rehabilitative services, including alcohol or drug education and alcohol or drug treatment programs. Except as otherwise provided in this subsection, the court may order the person to participate in and successfully complete 1 or more appropriate rehabilitative programs as part of the sentence. If the person has 1 or more prior convictions, the court shall order the person to participate in and successfully complete 1 or more appropriate rehabilitative programs as part of the sentence. The person shall pay for the costs of the screening, assessment, and rehabilitative services.[32]

It is also illegal for licensees to sell to a person who is obviously intoxicated, which, according to the Arizona Code, "means inebriated to such an extent that a person's physical faculties are substantially impaired and the impairment is shown by significantly uncoordinated physical action or significant physical dysfunction that would have been obvious to a reasonable person."[33]

Alcohol Offenses and Minors

Although some substance-related offenses, such as the possession and sale of specific drugs, are prohibited for all, others are prohibited only for persons under a specified age.

Sale of Alcohol to Minors

The legal drinking age in the United States is 21, and in general, it is illegal to sell, give, or in any other way furnish alcohol to persons under that age. For example, Arizona provides that it is unlawful:

> Except as provided in . . . [other sections of this statute] for a licensee or other person to sell, furnish, dispose of or give, or cause to be sold, furnished, disposed of or given, to a person under the legal drinking age or for a person under the legal drinking age to buy, receive, have in the person's possession or consume spirituous liquor.[34]

Minors in Possession

Some readers of this text will no doubt be familiar with the criminal offense known as *minors in possession,* or MIP. As the Arizona statute prohibiting the illegal sale of alcohol to minors makes clear, it is also illegal for minors to be in possession of alcohol. MIP refers to a broad array of situations, such as being in an automobile in which others have placed alcohol even though the minor did not know that. MIP does not require that the minor drink the alcohol, only that the minor is actually or constructively in possession of the illegal substance. The offense of MIP may also apply to other acts, such as a minor in possession of weapons, although the legal age of majority may be lower in those cases.[35]

Unlawful Assembly, Rout, and Riot

Under the common law, **unlawful assembly**, a misdemeanor, referred to the meeting of three or more persons to disturb the public peace with the intention of participating in a forcible and violent execution of an unlawful enterprise or of a lawful enterprise in an unauthorized manner. Unlawful assembly did not require that individuals carry out their plan, but if they took steps to do so, they committed a **rout**. If they carried out the plan, they committed a **riot**.

Riot and *rout* come from the same word; *rout* is used to communicate that those who have assembled unlawfully are on their way. *Riot* may be defined as "a tumultuous disturbance of the peace by three or more persons assembled and acting with a common intent; either in executing a lawful private enterprise in a violent and turbulent manner, to the terror of the people, or in executing an unlawful enterprise in a violent and turbulent manner."[36]

The English Riot Act of 1714 made it a capital felony for 12 or more persons to continue together for an hour after an official proclamation that people should disperse because of an existing riot. The official command to disperse was known as *reading the riot act*.[37]

Some modern statutes retain the crimes of unlawful assembly and riot; fewer retain rout. California statutes include all three, although the definitions differ somewhat from the common law crimes. For example, California defines *unlawful assembly* as requiring two or more persons, whereas the common law required three or more. Texas requires seven or more and specifies that the act must be done *knowingly*.[38]

Most statutes classify riots as misdemeanors, although some jurisdictions provide that aggravated riots are felonies. Some provide for additional penalties if defendants commit other crimes, such as carrying weapons, during the riots. Some statutes contain related crimes.

Some statutes divide riots into categories according to seriousness, such as by degrees. In New York, for example, "A person is guilty of riot in the second degree when, simultaneously with four or more other

The U.S. Constitution guarantees the right to free assembly, but that does not give individuals a right to unlawful assembly, to disturb the peace, or to riot. Ordinances and statutes designed to curb illegal acts must be carefully written; if they are vague or too broad, they will be declared unconstitutional. (Max Whittaker/ Getty Images)

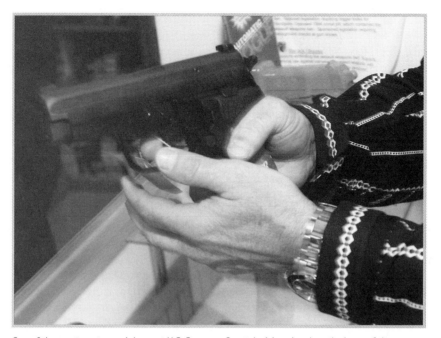

One of the most controversial recent U.S. Supreme Court decisions involves the issue of the meaning of the right to bear arms. In 2008 the Court held that the Washington, D.C., statute regulating hand guns was unconstitutional under the Second Amendment to the U.S. Constitution. The case of District of Columbia v. Heller is excerpted in the text. (Getty Images)

persons, he engages in tumultuous and violent conduct and thereby intentionally or recklessly causes a grave risk of causing public alarm." Riot in the first degree occurs when a person engages in such behavior with 10 or more other people and when someone other than those involved in the riot is injured or when property damage occurs as a result of the riot.[39]

In addition to disruptions caused by riots, they may also be associated with weapons offenses.

Weapons Offenses

Under the common law, because of the danger of breaching the peace if weapons were carried, it was a misdemeanor to "terrify the good people of the land by riding or going armed with dangerous or unusual weapons." The emphasis was on terrifying the king's citizens.[40]

Today most U.S. jurisdictions have statutes regulating the sale, possession, and carrying of weapons, but the statutes differ so much that it is not possible to generalize. Many of the statutes have been tested in the courts. The most restrictive of its time, the Morton Grove (Illinois) ordinance, which bans both the

sale and the ownership of handguns, was upheld by a lower federal court. The U.S. Supreme Court refused to review the case, thus leaving the lower court decision that the ordinance does not violate the federal constitution.[41] The following year, the Illinois Supreme Court held that the Morton Grove ordinance did not violate the Illinois state constitution.[42]

In June 2008, the U.S. Supreme Court struck down a District of Columbia statute, the strictest in the country concerning the banning of handguns. This 5-4 decision recognized a federal *constitutional* right for individuals to own a hand gun, at least under the facts of the case, which are noted in the following excerpt from the case.[43]

DISTRICT OF COLUMBIA v. HELLER

128 S.Ct. 2783 (U.S. 2008)

Justice Antonin Scalia delivered the opinion of the Court, in which Chief Justice John Roberts and Justices Anthony Kennedy, Clarence Thomas, and Samuel Alito joined. Justice John Paul Stevens filed a dissenting opinion, in which

Justices David Souter, Ruth Bader Ginsburg, and Stephen Breyer joined. Justice Breyer filed a dissenting opinion, in which Justices Stevens, Souter, and Ginsburg joined.

We consider whether a District of Columbia prohibition on the possession of usable handguns in the home violates the Second Amendment to the Constitution.

I

The District of Columbia generally prohibits the possession of handguns. It is a crime to carry an unregistered firearm, and the registration of handguns is prohibited. Wholly apart from that prohibition, no person may carry a handgun without a license, but the chief of police may issue licenses for 1-year periods. District of Columbia law also requires residents to keep their lawfully owned firearms, such as registered long guns, "unloaded and dissembled or bound by a trigger lock or similar device" unless they are located in a place of business or are being used for lawful recreational activities. . . .

Respondent Dick Heller is a D.C. special police officer authorized to carry a handgun while on duty at the Federal Judicial Center. He applied for a registration certificate for a handgun that he wished to keep at home, but the District refused. He thereafter filed a lawsuit in the Federal District Court for the District of Columbia seeking, on Second Amendment grounds, to enjoin the city from enforcing the bar on the registration of handguns, the licensing requirement insofar as it prohibits the carrying of a firearm in the home without a license, and the trigger-lock requirement insofar as it prohibits the use of "functional firearms within the home." . . .

II

We turn first to the meaning of the Second Amendment.

A

The Second Amendment provides: "A well regulated Militia, being necessary to the security of a free State, the right of the people to keep and bear Arms, shall not be infringed." In interpreting this text, we are guided by the principle that "[t]he Constitution was written to be understood by the voters; its words and phrases were used in their normal and ordinary as distinguished from technical meaning." Normal meaning may of course include an idiomatic meaning, but it excludes secret or technical meanings that would not have been known to ordinary citizens in the founding generation.

The two sides in this case have set out very different interpretations of the Amendment. Petitioners and today's dissenting Justices believe that it protects only the right to possess and carry a firearm in connection with militia service. Respondent argues that it protects an individual right to possess a firearm unconnected with service in a militia, and to use that arm for traditionally lawful purposes, such as self-defense within the home. . . .

The Second Amendment is naturally divided into two parts: its prefatory clause and its operative clause. The former does not limit the latter grammatically, but rather announces a purpose. . . .

[The Court discussed the two clauses in detail, examining the historical meaning of each phrase before continuing as follows:]

The debate with respect to the right to keep and bear arms, as with other guarantees in the Bill of Rights, was not over whether it was desirable (all agreed that it was) but over whether it needed to be codified in the Constitution. During the 1788 ratification debates, the fear that the federal government would disarm the people in order to impose rule through a standing army or select militia was pervasive in Antifederalist rhetoric. . . .

It is therefore entirely sensible that the Second Amendment's prefatory clause announces the purpose for which the right was codified: to prevent elimination of the militia. The prefatory clause does not suggest that preserving the militia was the only reason Americans valued the ancient right; most undoubtedly thought it even more important for self-defense and hunting. But the threat that the new Federal Government would destroy the citizens' militia by taking away their arms was the reason that right—unlike some other English rights—was codified in a written Constitution. . . .

Our interpretation is confirmed by analogous arms-bearing rights in state constitutions that preceded and immediately followed adoption of the Second Amendment. [The Court discussed these and the commentaries on the Second Amendment before concluding as follows:]

. . . We conclude that nothing in our precedents forecloses our adoption of the original understanding of the Second Amendment. It should be unsurprising that such a significant matter has been for so long judicially unresolved. For most of our history, the Bill of Rights was not thought applicable to the States, and the Federal Government did not significantly regulate the possession of firearms by law-abiding citizens. Other provisions of the Bill of Rights have similarly remained unilluminated for lengthy periods. . . .

It is demonstrably not true that, as JUSTICE STEVENS claims, "for most of our history, the invalidity of Second-Amendment-based objections to firearms regulations has been well settled and uncontroversial." For most of our history the question did not present itself.

III

Like most rights, the right secured by the Second Amendment is not unlimited. . . . [N]othing in our opinion should be taken to cast doubt on longstanding prohibitions on the possession of firearms by felons and the mentally ill, or laws forbidding the carrying of firearms in sensitive places such as schools and government buildings, or laws imposing conditions and qualifications on the commercial sale of arms.

We also recognize another important limitation on the right to keep and carry arms. [A precedent case] said, as we have explained, that the sorts of weapons protected were those "in common use at the time." We think that limitation is fairly supported by the historical tradition of prohibiting the carrying of "dangerous and unusual weapons." . . .

IV

We turn finally to the law at issue here. As we have said, the law totally bans handgun possession in the home. It also requires that any lawful firearm in the home be disassembled or bound by a trigger lock at all times, rendering it inoperable.

. . . [T]he inherent right of self-defense has been central to the Second Amendment right. The handgun ban amounts to a prohibition of an entire class of "arms" that is overwhelmingly chosen by American society for that lawful purpose. The prohibition extends, moreover, to the home, where the need for defense of self, family, and property is most acute. Under any of the standards of scrutiny that we have applied to enumerated constitutional rights, banning from the home "the most preferred firearm in the nation to 'keep' and use for protection of one's home and family," would fail constitutional muster.

Few laws in the history of our Nation have come close to the severe restriction of the District's handgun ban. And some of those few have been struck down. . . .

[T]he American people have considered the handgun to be the quintessential self-defense weapon. There are many reasons that a citizen may prefer a handgun for home defense: It is easier to store in a location that is readily accessible in an emergency; it cannot easily be redirected or wrestled away by an attacker; it is easier to use for those without the upper-body strength to lift and aim a long gun; it can be pointed at a burglar with one hand while the other hand dials the police. Whatever the reason, handguns are the most popular weapon chosen by Americans for self-defense in the home, and a complete prohibition of their use is invalid.

We must also address the District's requirement (as applied to respondent's handgun) that firearms in the home be rendered and kept inoperable at all times. This makes it impossible for citizens to use them for the core lawful purpose of self-defense and is hence unconstitutional. [The Court discussed that issue and the licensing provision, which permits the police chief to issue a one-year license, but that was refused in this case, which involves a special policeman.] . . .

In sum, we hold that the District's ban on handgun possession in the home violates the Second Amendment, as does its prohibition against rendering any lawful firearm in the home operable for the purpose of immediate self-defense. Assuming that Heller is not disqualified from the exercise of Second Amendment rights, the District must permit him to register his handgun and must issue him a license to carry it in the home.

We are aware of the problem of handgun violence in this country, and we take seriously the concerns raised by the many *amici* who believe that prohibition of handgun ownership is a solution. The Constitution leaves the District of Columbia a variety of tools for combating that problem, including some measures regulating handguns. But the enshrinement of constitutional rights necessarily takes certain policy choices off the table. These include the absolute prohibition of handguns held and used for self-defense in the home. Undoubtedly some think that the Second Amendment is outmoded in a society where our standing army is the pride of our Nation, where well-trained police forces provide personal security, and where gun violence is a serious problem. That is perhaps debatable, but what is not debatable is that it is not the role of this Court to pronounce the Second Amendment extinct. . . .

We affirm the judgment of the Court of Appeals.

Justice John Paul Stevens, with whom the other three dissenting justices agreed:

The Second Amendment was adopted to protect the right of the people of each of the several States to maintain a well-regulated militia. It was a response to concerns raised during the ratification of the Constitution that the power of Congress to disarm the state militias and create a national standing army posed an intolerable threat to the sovereignty of the several States. Neither the text of the Amendment nor the arguments advanced by its proponents evidenced the slightest interest in limiting any legislature's authority to regulate private civilian uses of firearms. Specifically, there is no indication that the Framers of the Amendment intended to enshrine the common-law right of self-defense in the Constitution. . . .

The view of the Amendment we took in [a precedent case] that it protects the right to keep and bear arms for certain military purposes, but that it does not curtail the Legislature's power to regulate the nonmilitary use and ownership of weapons—is both the most natural reading of the Amendment's text and the interpretation most faithful to the history of its adoption.

Obstructing a Highway or Public Passage

Public authorities have the right to regulate the flow of traffic and people on public streets, highways, and sidewalks. The issue in this section, however, is whether the police may engage in stops and searches for the purpose of infringing on free speech and expression. Statutes designed to regulate the obstruction of highways or public passages may not be vague or so broad that they grant excessive discretion to those charged with enforcing the statutes.

Most problems arise when authorities attempt to suppress demonstrations they consider unpopular. An example is provided by the classic case of *Cox v. Louisiana*, decided in 1965. Rev. B. Elton Cox was the leader of a group of demonstrators who marched to the courthouse to protest the jailing of their friends, who were arrested for picketing. They were peaceful in their demonstration, did not block the street, and moved to the west side of the street when told to do so by police. But at noon Rev. Cox told the crowd to go to the lunch counters to protest racial discrimination.

The sheriff told Rev. Cox that although his protest to that point had been more or less peaceful, "what you are doing now is a direct violation of the law, a disturbance of the peace, and it has to be broken up immediately." Rev. Cox and the demonstrators did not break up the demonstration; police exploded a tear gas bomb after which the demonstrators dispersed quickly. The next day Rev. Cox was arrested, tried, and convicted. On appeal, the U.S. Supreme Court reversed the breach of peace and the obstruction of a public passage convictions. In the following excerpt, the U.S. Supreme Court addressed its comments to Rev. Cox's conviction for obstructing public passages.[44]

COX v. LOUISIANA
379 U.S. 536 (1965)

 Justices Earl Warren, Hugo L. Black, William O. Douglas, Tom C. Clark, John Marshall Harlan, William J. Brennan Jr., Potter Stewart, Byron R. White, and Arthur J. Goldberg all voted together, with Justice Goldberg writing the opinion for the Court. Justices Black and Clark wrote concurring opinions; Justice White wrote an opinion concurring in part and dissenting in part.

The rights of Free Speech and assembly, while fundamental in our democratic society, still do not mean that everyone with opinions or beliefs to express may address a group at any public place and at any time. The constitutional guarantee of liberty implies the existence of an organized society maintaining public order, without which liberty itself would be lost in the excesses of anarchy. The control of travel on the streets is a clear example of governmental responsibility to insure this necessary order. A restriction in that relation, designed to promote the public convenience in the interest of all, and not susceptible to abuses of discriminatory application, cannot be disregarded by the attempted exercise of some civil right which, in other circumstances, would be entitled to protection. One would not be justified in ignoring the familiar red light because this was thought to be a means of social protest. . . . . A group of demonstrators could not insist upon the right to cordon off a street, or entrance to a public or private building, and allow no one to pass who did not agree to listen to their exhortations. . . . . [The Court noted that authorities have the right to limit demonstrations by time, place, duration, or manner, provided those limitations do not involve unfair discrimination and are uniformly and consistently based on the facts of each case.]

But here it is clear that the practice in Baton Rouge allowing unfettered discretion in local officials in the regulation of the use of the streets for peaceful parades and meetings is an unwarranted abridgment of appellant's freedom of speech and assembly secured to him by the First Amendment, as applied to the States by the Fourteenth Amendment. It follows, therefore, that appellant's conviction for violating the statute as so applied and enforced must be reversed.

Animal Abuse

An act that was usually ignored in the past but that is now being treated as *criminal* is the abuse of animals. Professional journals, law school case books, and law school courses now include this area of law. The issue of animal abuse has arisen in the context of what constitutes acceptable research in contrast to animal cruelty, but there have been recent cases of animal abuse outside the research arena as well. In some jurisdictions animal abuse is treated as a serious crime, especially if the offender has committed other crimes or is convicted of repeated acts of animal abuse. The American Bar Association (ABA) refers to the area of animal law as "one of the fastest-growing—and more emotional—niches" of American law.[45]

In 2007 a shocking and extensive case of animal abuse dominated the papers for months, culminating in the guilty plea of Michael Vick, Atlanta Falcons quarterback. Vick, who protested for weeks that he had not violated the law, entered a plea to the federal crime of conspiracy with regard to dog fighting allegations. Under the federal criminal code, "It shall be unlawful for any person to knowingly sell, buy, possess, train, transport, deliver, or receive any animal for purposes of having the animal participate in an animal fighting venture."[46] Vick was sentenced to 23 months in prison. He was released in May 2009.

In addition to the federal statute, animal abuse statutes exist in all states, with some of the statutes enacted years ago. New York, the first state to enact legislation in this area, passed its first statute in 1828. But according to the ABA, in the "43 states where anti-cruelty laws are felonies, 29 were enacted in the past 10 years."[47] In recent years awareness of the need to enforce the statutes has increased, as has the coverage and penalties of those laws. The Texas statute, reproduced in Focus 9.3, illustrates the extent of the acts that are defined as cruelty to nonlivestock animals in that state. This

---

FOCUS 9.3   Cruelty to Nonlivestock Animals

Tex. Penal Code, Title 9, Chapter 42, Section 42.092 (2009)

(a) In this section:

 (1) "Abandon" includes abandoning an animal in the person's custody without making reasonable arrangements for assumption of custody by another person.

 (2) "Animal" means a domesticated living creature, including any stray or feral cat or dog, and a wild living creature previously captured. The term does not include an uncaptured wild living creature or a livestock animal. [Note that Texas has a separate statute covering the abuse of livestock animals. See Tex. Penal Code, Title 9, Chapter 42, Section 42.09 (2009).]

 (3) "Cruel manner" includes a manner that causes or permits unjustified or unwarranted pain or suffering.

 (4) "Custody" includes responsibility for the health, safety, and welfare of an animal subject to the person's care and control, regardless of ownership of the animal. . . . .

 (7) "Necessary food, water, care, or shelter" includes food, water, care, or shelter provided to the extent required to maintain the animal in a state of good health.

 (8) "Torture" includes any act that causes unjustifiable pain or suffering.

(b) A person commits an offense if the person intentionally, knowingly, or recklessly:

 (1) tortures an animal or in a cruel manner kills or causes serious bodily injury to an animal;

 (2) without the owner's effective consent, kills, administers poison to, or causes serious bodily injury to an animal;

 (3) fails unreasonably to provide necessary food, water, care, or shelter for an animal in the person's custody;

 (4) abandons unreasonably an animal in the person's custody;

 (5) transports or confines an animal in a cruel manner;

 (6) without the owner's effective consent, causes bodily injury to an animal;

 (7) causes one animal to fight with another animal, if either animal is not a dog;

 (8) uses a live animal as a lure in dog race training or in dog coursing on a racetrack; or

 (9) seriously overworks an animal.

[The statute contains specific defenses, such as self-defense and legitimate research purposes.]

The abuse of animals, particularly pets, is prohibited by numerous statutes, and more attention is being given to the prosecution of persons who violate those statutes. Some state statutes also specify how pets should be cared for, with some activists calling for changing our references from animal owners to animal custodians. (IStockPhoto)

statute is a new one, which went into effect in 2007, when the previous statute was changed to focus only on livestock animals. The new law was influenced by the mistrial in the case of James M. Stevenson, when the jury deadlocked on the animal cruelty charges based on his killing a cat because it was killing birds. The statute at the time prohibited killing a cat "belonging to another," and the defense argued that the cat in this case was a feral cat and thus excluded from the reach of the statute. The prosecution presented pictures of food, bedding, and toys under the bridge where the cat lived and argued that the cat was cared for by the toll bridge operator and thus "belonged to another." The jury did not agree.[48]

Texas law also requires that if a child is found to have engaged in conduct falling under animal abuse statutes, "the juvenile court shall order the child to participate in psychological counseling for a period to be determined by the court."[49]

An interesting twist on laws protecting pets is that in 2006, Maine became the first state in the nation to provide for the inclusion of pets in protective orders in domestic violence cases. That state's statutes covering domestic relations and protection from abuse now includes threats to harm pets. Maine officials estimated that in 70 percent of domestic violence cases pets as well as humans are threatened.[50]

Examples of the enforcement of state animal abuse statutes are frequently the topic of widespread publicity both nationally and internationally, as illustrated by a California case in 2000. Andrew Burnett, in a fit of road rage after his car was rear ended in heavy traffic, stormed back to the car that hit his, grabbed Leon, a bichon frisé, and threw the puppy into traffic, where it was struck and killed. Burnett was sentenced to three years in prison, the maximum permitted under California law.[51]

California was back in the news with a 2005 animal abuse case that led to donations totaling $17,700 for a reward for information leading to the apprehension of a man caught on the surveillance camera at a carwash killing ducks by running over them and then exiting his red Acura and killing other ducks with his hands. Ten of the ducks died that night; two were treated for weeks by local vets, but one of the injured ducks died. The crime was not solved, and in September 2007, the reward money was given to several organizations devoted to the care of animals.[52]

In recent years California has toughened the state's legal protection of animals, enacting statutes that crimi-nalize leaving a pet unattended in a car in hot and cold weather or without adequate food, water, and ventilation.[53] And that state was one of the first in the country to establish a limit (three hours) on how long a pet can be tethered while its custodian runs errands (effective 1 January 2007), although the latter restriction is part of the Health and Safety Code, not the Penal Code.[54]

Harassment

One final example of a crime against the public order that has received considerable attention in recent years is that of *harassment*. Some jurisdictions criminalize various harassment techniques, such as insults, challenges, phone calls, or other means of inciting an individual to violence; subjecting another to offensive touching; engaging in alarming conduct; or making repeated communications anonymously or at times or in places that are inconvenient to the recipient.

An example of statutes that prohibit harassment are those of New York, reprinted in part in Focus 9.4. In 1992 the New York legislature added the grades of harassment to the statute and changed the word *he* to *he or she*, thus making it clear that women may be charged with harassment and men may be victims. In more recent years the state made significant changes in its aggravated harassment statutes. In particular, both aggravated harassment in the first degree (not included in Focus 9.4) and aggravated harassment in the second degree now apply to aggravated harassment against persons because of the following additional characteristics:

- Ancestry
- Gender
- Religious practices
- Age
- Disability
- Sexual orientation

The statutes regarding aggravated harassment also now include language qualifying the characteristics, noting that it is the *perception* of the actor concerning those characteristics that is critical. Thus, if the actor perceives the proposed victim to be gay and harasses him or her, it makes no difference that the target is not gay. New York also has a statute covering first-degree aggravated harassment, which is the only one of the harassment acts that constitutes a felony for the first offense.[55]

FOCUS 9.4   The Crime of Harassment: The New York Statutes

NY CLS Penal, Title N, Article 240, Section 240.25 (2008)

Harassment in the First Degree

A person is guilty of harassment in the first degree when he or she intentionally and repeatedly harasses another person by following such person in or about a public place or places or by engaging in a course of conduct or by repeatedly committing acts which places [sic] such person in reasonable fear of physical injury. . . .

NY CLS Penal, Title N, Article 240, Section 240.26 (2008)

Harassment in the Second Degree

A person is guilty of harassment in the second degree when, with intent to harass, annoy or alarm another person:

1. He or she strikes, shoves, kicks or otherwise subjects such other person to physical contact, or attempts or threatens to do the same; or

2. He or she follows a person in or about a public place or places; or

3. He or she engages in a course of conduct or repeatedly commits acts which alarm or seriously annoy such other person and which serve no legitimate purpose.

NY CLS Penal, Title N, Article 240, Section 240.30 (2008)

Aggravated Harassment in the Second Degree

A person is guilty of aggravated harassment in the second degree when, with intent to harass, annoy, threaten or alarm another person, he or she:

1. Either
(a) communicates with a person, anonymously or otherwise, by telephone, or by telegraph, mail or any other form of written communication, in a manner likely to cause annoyance or alarm; or

(b) causes a communication to be initiated by mechanical or electronic means or otherwise with a person, anonymously or otherwise, by telephone or telegraph, mail or any other form of written communication, in a manner likely to cause annoyance or alarm; or

2. Makes a telephone call, whether or not a conversation ensues, with no purpose of legitimate communication; or

3. Strikes, shoves, kicks, or otherwise subjects another person to physical contact, or attempts or threatens to do the same because of a belief or perception regarding such person's race, color, national origin, ancestry, gender, religion, religious practices, age, disability or sexual orientation, regardless of whether the belief or perception is correct; or

4. Commits the crime of harassment in the first degree and has previously been convicted of the crime of harassment in the first degree. . . . within the preceding ten years.

CRIMES AGAINST PUBLIC DECENCY

This section focuses on acts that are not considered serious enough to be major crimes but are offensive enough, at least to some, to be included within the criminal law. The discussion of the purposes of criminal law in Chapter 1 looked briefly at the arguments for and against including crimes against public morality or decency within the criminal law. Certainly the criminal law should encompass forced sexual behavior, but should it also include private, consensual sexual behavior between adults? If so, to what extent should the law cover these behaviors? Should the criminal law prohibit all sexual behavior between unmarried persons? Or should it extend only to acts that involve a person under the age of legal consent? If so, what should be the age of consent?

The problem of what to include and what to exclude from the criminal law probably engenders more debate in the area of moral behavior than in any other area. Historically, many of the behaviors discussed in this section of the chapter were considered within the area of morality or decency and to be governed by the church rather than by the state through its criminal statutes, but early criminal statutes of the American colonies and subsequently the United States were patterned after biblical laws and thus were strict. The Puritans equated sin and crime, and frequently they prosecuted offenders for sex crimes, with some crimes carrying the death penalty. After the American Revolution, however, prosecutions focused on property crimes rather than sex crimes.[56]

Despite the declining number of prosecutions for sex offenses, these offenses remained in the criminal law.

Within the past two decades some jurisdictions have decriminalized some of the behaviors, such as private consensual sexual behavior between unmarried adults. But the debate remains over who should control behavior considered to offend public decency and morality—the church, the state, or neither—and which acts should be included within the criminal law.

Lewdness and Indecency

Words such as *lewd, obscene, lascivious, lecherous,* and *indecent* have been used to describe a variety of behaviors that some people find offensive to the extent that the criminal law is invoked to try to curb them. These words may be used to describe acts such as appearing nude in public or living openly and notoriously with a member of the opposite gender without being married (also called *illicit* or *lewd cohabitation*). Although some may consider these behaviors serious violations of law, generally they are defined as misdemeanors and carry only slight penalties.

Some statutes that prohibit lewdness are brief and general. Pennsylvania, for example, has a statute entitled *open lewdness,* defined as follows: "A person commits a misdemeanor of the third degree if he does any lewd act which he knows is likely to be observed by others who would be affronted or alarmed."[57]

Other statutes prohibiting lewd and lascivious acts mention specific sex acts. These statutes may describe any sex acts between members of the same gender even when they occur in private, or they may refer only to sexual acts considered serious no matter whether they involve the same or opposite genders. They may also refer to sex acts with minors when force is not used. The Idaho Code, for example, prohibits *lewd conduct with minor child under sixteen.* This conduct is described as including but not limited to "genital-genital contact, oral-genital contact, anal-genital contact, oral-anal contact, manual-anal contact, or manual-genital contact, whether between persons of the same or opposite sex," or involving minor children in any of these acts when they are done "with the intent of arousing, appealing to, or gratifying the lust or passions or sexual desires of such person, such minor child, or a third party."[58]

Sodomy

Chapter 7 discussed forced sodomy as a violent crime, but some jurisdictions also define *consensual sodomy* as a crime. The current Idaho statute is illustrative. This statute prohibits "the infamous crimes against nature, committed with mankind or with any animal."[59]

To avoid the problem of vagueness, some jurisdictions have revised their sodomy statutes to include specific behavioral acts. For example, California changed its sodomy statute from one referring to "the infamous crime against nature, committed with mankind or with any animal" to "sexual conduct consisting of contact between the penis of one person and the anus of another person." The current California statute does not define sodomy as a punishable offense unless it is committed under any one of several specified circumstances, such as those involving force, violence, or duress or involves acts committed with an underage person, a mentally incompetent person, or a person known by the actor to be unconscious or asleep.[60]

Other jurisdictions do not use the term *sodomy.* If they criminalize the acts traditionally included within this term, they may do so by using words such as *deviate sexual intercourse* or *deviant sexual acts.*

The debate over the use of the criminal law to attempt to regulate private, consensual sexual behavior between adults escalated after the U.S. Supreme Court decision in *Bowers v. Hardwick.* In that case the Court upheld the Georgia statute prohibiting sodomy, defined as "any sexual act involving the sex organs of one person and the mouth or anus of another." The U.S. Supreme Court held that the statute did not violate the fundamental rights of the two gay males who were involved in the case.[61] In 1998 the Georgia Supreme Court held that the statute on which *Bowers v. Hardwick* was based violated the right to privacy as provided in the Georgia Constitution.[62]

Some jurisdictions in which sodomy has been redefined have enacted a separate statute covering sexual intercourse or sexual contact with same gender persons. Texas, for example, defined the crime of homosexual conduct as engaging "in deviate sexual intercourse with another individual of the same sex."[63] In 2003 the U.S. Supreme Court declared that statute unconstitutional, as noted in this chapter's Case Analysis.

Seduction and Fornication

Seduction and fornication are acts that at one time were criminalized in the United States. Both refer to acts that society has thought to be dangerous to its general welfare.

Although under the common law **seduction** was not a criminal offense, many U.S. jurisdictions criminalize the act by statute. *Seduction* refers to the act by a man who uses solicitation, persuasion, promises, bribes, or other methods to entice a woman to have unlawful sexual intercourse with him. In earlier days seduction was a felony, although some statutes provided that a subsequent marriage between the two parties negated the crime. The modern trend has been to repeal seduction statutes, but those that remain generally categorize the crime as a misdemeanor.

California repealed its seduction statute in 1984, but it is still a criminal act in that state to induce consent to a sexual act by the use of fraud or fear.[64]

Another sex act considered a crime against public morals in some jurisdictions is **fornication**, which comes from *fornix*, a Latin word for *brothel*. Usually the term refers to unlawful sexual intercourse between two unmarried persons of opposite genders. An example is the Idaho statute, which includes "Any unmarried person who shall have sexual intercourse with an unmarried person of the opposite sex."[65]

Some jurisdictions do not limit the act to the opposite sex. In Virginia *fornication* refers to "any person, not being married, who voluntarily shall have sexual intercourse with any other person."[66] In January 2005, the Virginia Supreme Court held that this statute is unconstitutional, applying the rationale of *Lawrence v. Texas*, excerpted in the Case Analysis at the end of this chapter.[67]

Adultery

In some states, fornication also applies to a single person who engages in unlawful sexual intercourse with a person who is married to another person. Other states define the acts of both parties in that situation as **adultery**, which refers to consensual sexual intercourse between a married person and someone other than his or her spouse. Like fornication, adultery was not a common law crime, although it was an ecclesiastical offense. Like most other sex crimes, adultery has various definitions. Some jurisdictions define it as sexual intercourse between two people, one of whom is married to someone else, while others hold only the married party in that relationship to the crime of adultery. In earlier laws, only the married woman was committing adultery; sexual behavior by men with women other than their wives was not considered criminal.

A typical current adultery statute is that of New York, which defines the crime as follows:

> A person is guilty of adultery when he engages in sexual intercourse with another person at a time

when he has a living spouse, or the other person has a living spouse.[68]

Some statutes distinguish between *single adultery*, in which only one party is married, and *double adultery*, in which both parties are married to other persons. Some states, such as Illinois, criminalize adultery only when the act is "open and notorious,"[69] but the current trend is toward decriminalizing adultery or simply not prosecuting the crime although admitting it as evidence in divorce and custody proceedings.

Bigamy

Like adultery, **bigamy** is considered a crime against the family; it may be defined as an individual's knowingly and willingly contracting a marriage when he or she is aware that a prior marriage exists. Some jurisdictions consider the crime one of strict liability; thus, knowledge of a prior marriage is not required.

Bigamy was not a common law crime, although it was an ecclesiastical offense. In 1603 the British Parliament criminalized bigamy, making it a felony punishable by death. Historically bigamy has been criminalized in the United States, although few prosecutions have occurred. Despite that fact, however, most states still criminalize the act. The New York statute is typical of bigamy statutes that designate the offense as a felony: "A person is guilty of bigamy when he contracts or purports to contract a marriage with another person at a time when he has a living spouse, or the other person has a living spouse." Bigamy is a felony; adultery is a misdemeanor.[70]

Prostitution

Historically, **prostitution** has been accepted as inevitable, even essential, and in some societies the practice has been esteemed. Another view is that prostitution is a way of exploiting women and children. In the United States, adult prostitution is illegal in all but some rural counties in Nevada. Child prostitution is illegal in all jurisdictions.

Statutory Provisions

Statutes regulating prostitution vary. So do definitions of the term, although basically *prostitution* refers to indiscriminate sexual intercourse for hire. Some statutes specify women as the offenders, but others also include men or use a neutral term, such as *gender*, in describing who may commit the offense. The criminal offense may include not only the prostitute but also any persons who solicit or promote prostitution or who live off a prostitute's earnings.

Prostitution was not a common law crime in some countries, and it remains legal in many countries, although some acts associated with prostitution, such as **pandering,** may be considered criminal. *Pandering* refers to procuring or securing a person, usually a female, to satisfy the lust of another, usually a male, or catering to the lust of another person. Pandering is also called *pimping*.

Statutory prohibitions of prostitution may be extensive. In New York, for example, where prostitution is defined as engaging or agreeing or offering "to engage in sexual conduct with another person in return for a fee," prostitution is a misdemeanor. Despite an extensive list of acts included under the title "Prostitution Offenses" in the New York Penal Code, authorities report that most of the prostitution-related arrests in New York City are for violations of the crime of *loitering for the purpose of engaging in a prostitution offense.* This section of the New York Penal Code criminalizes the act of remaining in or wandering about public places while repeatedly beckoning to, or repeatedly stopping or attempting to stop people on the sidewalk or in passing vehicles or "who repeatedly interferes with the free passage of other persons, for the purpose of prostitution, or of patronizing a prostitute." The provision has been upheld.[71]

New York's prostitution statute was in the spotlight in 2008 with regard to the state's governor after a wiretap intercepted his plans to meet with a high-class call girl, subsequently identified as Ashley Dupre, in Washington, D.C., on two occasions in 2008. Federal prosecutors investigated but did not charge New York governor Eliot Spitzer (who resigned when the allegations were made public) for possible criminal acts. Several persons associated with the Emperor's Club VIP, the agency through which Spitzer allegedly booked Dupre, entered guilty pleas.

Trafficking

A critical issue regarding prostitution is trafficking in humans, mainly women and children, for the purpose of sex, as noted in Focus 9.5, which presents Congressional findings on this topic. Those findings are part of the Trafficking Victims Protection Reauthorization Act (TVPRA). Among other provisions, that act provides funds to establish programs to keep young girls in school.[72]

Many of the 1.5 million children who run away from home each year are picked up by predators and forced into sex trafficking. It is estimated that the average age of these children is between 11 and 14; some are as young as 9 years old. In most jurisdictions these children may be prosecuted for prostitution, although there is a movement toward treating them as sex victims rather than as sex criminals.[73]

Pornography and Obscenity

This section discusses criminal statutes that are enacted to preserve the public decency and morality of society; the statutes, however, are difficult to enforce, and attempts to do so may violate basic constitutional rights, such as the First Amendment right to free speech (see Appendix A) and the right to privacy. In *Stanley v. Georgia*, the U.S. Supreme Court held that "mere private possession of obscene matter" in one's own home is not a crime, but the Court emphasized the government's right to regulate **obscenity**. The Court had problems defining the term *obscenity*, but in 1973, in *Miller v. California*, the Court articulated three conditions, all of which must be met for information to be considered *obscene*.

1. "The average person, applying contemporary community standards, would find that the work, taken as a whole, appeals to the prurient interest [in sex]; and

2. "the work depicts or describes, in a patently offensive way, sexual conduct specifically defined by the applicable state [or federal] law; and

3. "the work, taken as a whole, lacks serious literary, artistic, political, or scientific value."[74]

Although obscenity is illegal, it is not illegal for adults in the United States to possess pornographic materials. It is, however, illegal to possess materials that depict children in pornography. Congress and many states have enacted statutes aimed solely at child pornography. The Protection of Children Against Sexual Exploitation Act of 1977 (since amended) is illustrative. This statute was based on the following Congressional findings:

1. "Child pornography has developed into a highly organized, multimillion-dollar industry which operates on a nationwide scale;

FOCUS 9.5 Human Trafficking

In its 2000 Trafficking Victims Protection Act (reauthorized in 2005), Congress presented the following findings:

1. "As the 21st century begins, the degrading institution of slavery continues throughout the world. Trafficking in persons is a modern form of slavery, and it is the largest manifestation of slavery today. At least 700,000 persons annually, primarily women and children, are trafficked within or across international borders. Approximately 50,000 women and children are trafficked into the United States each year.

2. Many of these persons are trafficked into the international sex trade, often by force, fraud, or coercion. The sex industry has rapidly expanded over the past several decades. It involves sexual exploitation of persons, predominantly women and girls, involving activities related to prostitution, pornography, sex tourism, and other commercial sexual services. The low status of women in many parts of the world has contributed to a burgeoning of the trafficking industry.

3. Trafficking in persons is not limited to the sex industry. This growing transnational crime also includes forced labor and involves significant violations of labor, public health, and human rights standards worldwide.

4. Traffickers primarily target women and girls, who are disproportionately affected by poverty, the lack of access to education, chronic unemployment, discrimination, and the lack of economic opportunities in countries of origin. Traffickers lure women and girls into their networks through false promises of decent working conditions at relatively good pay as nannies, maids, dancers, factory workers, restaurant workers, sales clerks, or models. Traffickers also buy children from poor families and sell them into prostitution or into various types of forced or bonded labor.

5. Traffickers often transport victims from their home communities to unfamiliar destinations, including foreign countries away from family and friends, religious institutions, and other sources of protection and support, leaving the victims defenseless and vulnerable.

6. Victims are often forced through physical violence to engage in sex acts or perform slavery-like labor. Such force includes rape and other forms of sexual abuse, torture, starvation, imprisonment, threats, psychological abuse, and coercion.

7. Traffickers often make representations to their victims that physical harm may occur to them or others should the victim escape or attempt to escape. Such representations can have the same coercive effects on victims as direct threats to inflict such harm.

8. Trafficking in persons is increasingly perpetrated by organized, sophisticated criminal enterprises. Such trafficking is the fastest growing source of profits for organized criminal enterprises worldwide. Profits from the trafficking industry contribute to the expansion of organized crime in the United States and worldwide. Trafficking in persons is often aided by official corruption in countries of origin, transit, and destination, thereby threatening the rule of law."[1]

The statement also pointed out that many other crimes are involved in the commission of trafficking and that victims are subject to serious health risks, including deadly diseases. Some victims are even brutalized and beaten to death.

1. Trafficking Victims Protection Act, USCS, Title 22, Section 7101, Purposes and Findings (2009).

---

2. "thousands of children including large numbers of runaway and homeless youth are exploited in the production and distribution of pornographic materials; and

3. "the use of children as subjects of pornographic materials is harmful to the physiological, emotional, and mental health of the individual child and to society."[75]

This federal statute is a lengthy one. It imposes liability on parents and guardians as well as on coercers, producers, and distributors of child pornography. The statute was quoted in part in Chapter 2 of this text, in the excerpt from *United States v. X-Citement Video*. Chapter 2 included the case and the statute to illustrate the problems of interpreting statutes. The U.S. Supreme Court upheld the statute against a challenge concerning its intent requirement.[76]

Among other provisions, this federal statute permits the government to seize any property or proceeds obtained, used, or produced during the commission of the criminal acts. The statute defines numerous terms and specifies the types of sexual behavior that are covered, which include conduct that is genital-genital, oral-genital, anal-genital, or oral-anal, whether between persons of the same or opposite genders; bestiality; masturbation; conduct that is sadistic or masochistic; abuse; and lascivious exhibition of the genitals or pubic area of any person.[77]

Federal statutes have been enacted to protect children from becoming the subjects of pornography and from viewing pornography. (IStockPhoto)

The federal statute was amended to include the dissemination of pornographic depictions of children by use of a computer. In 2002 in *Ashcroft v. Free Speech Coalition*, the U.S. Supreme Court held that *virtual child pornography*—that which is created by computer simulations—may be produced, owned, or sold without violating federal statutes. This case considered the constitutionality of the Child Pornography Prevention Act of 1996 (CPPA), which prohibits pornography involving depictions of children even though those children do not exist. The images are created by making adults look like children or by using the computer to make the images. The government argued that such depictions might encourage pedophiles, but the Supreme Court, acknowledging that could be the case, emphasized the importance of the First Amendment right to free speech and held that the mere tendency of speech to encourage unlawful acts is not a sufficient reason for banning it. First Amendment freedoms are most in danger when the government seeks to control thought or to justify its laws for that impermissible end. The right to think is the beginning of freedom, and speech must be protected from the government because speech is the beginning of thought. The U.S. Supreme Court agreed that children should not be exposed to viewing pornography but that "speech within the rights of adults to hear may not be silenced completely in an attempt to shield children from it."[78]

In reaction to this U.S. Supreme Court case, Congress passed and President George W. Bush signed the Prosecutorial Remedies and Other Tools to End the Exploitation of Children Today Act of 2003 (the PROTECT Act). The lengthy statute contains provisions aimed at protecting children from sexual assaults, pornography, kidnapping, and other crimes.[79]

In 2008 the U.S. Supreme Court upheld the constitutionality of the PROTECT Act in the case of *United States v. Williams*. Michael Williams, who used a sexually explicit screen name, posted this message on the Internet: "Dad of toddler has 'good' pics of her an [sic] me for swap of your toddler pics, or live cam." Williams and an undercover agent exchanged nonpornographic pictures, which led to a hyperlink that showed children between approximately 5 and 15 years old engaging in sexually explicit conduct. Officers got a search warrant, searched Williams's home, and found pictures of real children engaging in sexually explicit behavior, some of which were sadomasochistic.[80]

In upholding the constitutionality of the PROTECT Act, the majority of the U.S. Supreme Court, in an opinion written by Justice Antonin Scalia, stated that its First Amendment concerns in the previous statute were eliminated by the fact that the current statute limits the crime to the pandering of child pornography and the requirement that the panderer believes and states that the depictions are of real children or that he or she communicates in a way designed to make others so believe. Justice Scalia concluded as follows:

> Child pornography harms and debases the most defenseless of our citizens. Both the State and Federal Governments have sought to suppress it for many years, only to find it proliferating through the new medium of the Internet. This Court held unconstitutional Congress's previous attempt to meet this new threat, and Congress responded with a carefully crafted attempt to eliminate the First Amendment problems we identified. As far as the provision at issue in this case is concerned, that effort was successful.[81]

Another concern is that children will gain access to pornography through the Internet. Congress has made several attempts to prevent this at the federal level, such as enacting the Communications Decency Act (CDA), which criminalizes making indecent or patently offensive words or pictures available online where children can find them.[82] In 1997 the U.S. Supreme Court held that the CDA was too broad and violated the First Amendment right to free speech. According to the Court, in drafting the CDA, Congress did not choose the least restrictive means of prohibiting the online transmission and display of materials that children may view. As a result, the statute also restricted the right of adults to access materials that they have a constitutional right to view. In short, stated the Court, "the level of discourse reaching a mailbox cannot be limited to that which would be suitable for a sandbox."[83]

In 2003 the U.S. Supreme Court upheld a provision of the Children's Online Protection Act (COPA), which requires libraries to place filters on their computers so that children cannot have access to pornography when they are using library computers. Adults who wish to view pornography may have the filters removed. Failure to comply with the statute results in the loss of federal funds provided to libraries to enhance their Internet access.[84]

Policing the Internet is virtually impossible; apprehending and successfully prosecuting those who violate the U.S. child pornography laws is a challenge. U.S. law enforcement officials cooperate with international officials in this effort, and in 2008, the FBI announced that it had cracked a major child porn ring, leading to the arrest of 22 men in five countries, three continents, and 11 U.S. states. The evidence involved more than 400,000 images and videos.[85]

SUMMARY

This chapter discussed a wide range of offenses, many of which are misdemeanors. But some of those acts are important in that their regulation may and often do infringe on basic constitutional rights. However, it is argued that the offenses threaten public order and decency and therefore should be regulated. The chapter raised the issue of how to balance these different positions.

The first substantive crime discussed, breach of the peace, illustrated the philosophy behind the common law crimes included in this chapter. This crime was designed to cover acts not otherwise criminalized that might disrupt society's peace and tranquillity. Breach of the peace has been retained as a crime by most states, although the definitions vary widely. Like many of the other crimes included in this chapter, breach of the peace statutes may be written vaguely or too broadly, in which case they are unconstitutional.

The preservation of peace and order may be threatened by language as well as by actions. The criminal law attempts to avoid these problems by criminalizing fighting words, a situation that comes dangerously close to violating the First Amendment right to free speech. Considerable litigation has arisen as courts have interpreted the variously worded statutes.

Historically it has not been uncommon for societies to attempt to suppress unpopular views and keep certain types of people out of sight. Statutes covering disorderly conduct, vagrancy, and the public abuse of alcohol and drugs are used for this purpose. Many of these statutes are vague, leaving police with wide discretion in deciding whether or not to make an arrest. In recent years some of these statutes have been declared unconstitutional. Either they criminalize status or condition (in contrast to willful acts) because they are vague, or they are so broad that individuals cannot know in advance whether their behavior is covered. Many disorderly conduct and vagrancy statutes have been declared unconstitutional, but these statutes may be used effectively to control order and will withstand a constitutional challenge if they are properly worded. Other statutes, such as those covering alcohol and drug-related offenses, will be upheld if they are not vague or too broad. These statutes, especially those relating to minors, fall within the regulations permitted the government.

The desire to protect society from physical dangers to people and property that may result from some gatherings has led to statutes encompassing unlawful assembly, rout, and riot. Once again, however, these statutes must be examined carefully to ensure that they do not conflict with the constitutional rights to assemble and to communicate ideas.

Criminal laws that cover weapons offenses are a topic of controversy today. Against the beliefs of many persons that individuals have a right to possess weapons to protect themselves is the argument that society has an interest in protecting the health and welfare of its citizens and should be able to penalize those who carry or possess weapons without authorization. In its 2008 decision concerning handguns, the U.S. Supreme Court handed down a controversial ruling, which was excerpted.

A wide variety of other offenses are thought to threaten the public, including obstructing public highways, engaging in cruelty to animals, and harassment.

Another major category of offenses covered in this chapter included acts that some people think should be criminalized to protect public decency. It is difficult to draft and interpret indecency and lewdness statutes to achieve the desired goal of protecting people from being forced to view sexual behavior they choose to avoid. These statutes risk becoming so broad as to prohibit behavior of which many approve today.

Some of the crimes discussed in this chapter are aimed primarily at preserving the family structure. Seduction (now abolished as a crime in most states), fornication, adultery, and bigamy are examples. Although most states have abolished statutes criminalizing fornication and some have abolished adultery statutes, many have retained statutes prohibiting these acts, although the statutes are rarely enforced.

Prostitution is also viewed by some as an act that threatens the family and degrades adult women. Others disagree and view adult prostitution as private. Particular attention was given to the trafficking of women and children in prostitution.

Pornography and obscenity statutes pose the question of what should be allowed as private behavior and what should be regulated by the criminal law. Over the years courts have disagreed in their interpretation of what is and is not permissible in this area. This chapter noted the passage of federal statutes aimed at the protection of children by prohibiting child pornography and by restricting the access that children may have to the Internet and other sources of materials deemed inappropriate for them to view. Like most of the other topics in the chapter, however, this one also involves

constitutional issues. It is important to remember that these constitutional rights may be regulated by the state or federal government under some circumstances. The critical issue is whether the statutes aimed at protecting the welfare of society violate basic individual constitutional rights. Finally, it is important to ensure that statutes such as those discussed in this chapter, most of which are not enforced rigorously, are not used for the purpose of harassing targeted groups, such as racial and ethnic minorities.

STUDY QUESTIONS

1. Discuss the origin of statutes prohibiting breach of the peace and the circumstances under which these and related statutes may be unconstitutional.

2. Explain the fighting words doctrine.

3. What are the potential constitutional hazards of disorderly conduct and vagrancy statutes? Do we need these statutes? Why or why not? Could they be reworded to avoid constitutional problems? Do we need special laws to protect homeless persons?

4. To what extent should public intoxication and drug incapacitation be regulated by the criminal law? What has the U.S. Supreme Court held concerning this issue?

5. What should the criminal law cover in the way of attempting to regulate the behavior of minors with regard to the use of alcohol? Discuss the implications of current statutes in this area.

6. Is the criminal law the best way to control driving while under the influence? Why or why not?

7. Distinguish between rout and riot. Should both be covered by the criminal law?

8. How would you distinguish rioting from inciting to riot in terms of seriousness? What is unlawful assembly?

9. What type of criminal statutes, if any, should we have concerning carrying weapons? Do you agree with the U.S. Supreme Court's decision in the recent handgun case? Why or why not?

10. How is the right to free speech affected by statutes prohibiting obstructing a highway or other public passage?

11. Although it may be offensive to some people if others are cruel to animals, would the law's deter-

rent effect be greater if these acts were part of the civil law only, giving victims a right to compensation from those who victimize them? What does the criminal law add?

12. List all of the behaviors you think should be covered by criminal harassment statutes.

13. Should lewdness and indecency statutes be abolished?

14. Discuss the U.S. Supreme Court's holding and rationale in *Bowers v. Hardwick*. What were the implications of this decision? Discuss this case in relationship to the 2003 U.S. Supreme court decision (featured in this chapter's Case Analysis) concerning the Texas sodomy statute.

15. Which, if any, of the following behaviors—seduction, fornication, adultery, bigamy—should remain within the criminal law? Which should be removed? Which should be defined more clearly?

16. Evaluate the practice of criminalizing prostitution.

17. Discuss the implications of human sex trafficking.

18. What is obscenity?

19. Should we distinguish between pornography involving adults and that involving children? Discuss the U.S. Supreme Court's position on this subject.

20. Discuss and evaluate statutory attempts to regulate the access young people have to pornography on the Internet.

FOR DEBATE

Many of the crimes discussed in this chapter are classified as misdemeanors or less than the highest category of felonies in jurisdictions in which felonies are graded. Given these classifications, debate the following topic.

Resolved: The law should not be utilized to criminalize acts that are private and do not interfere with or threaten the public directly—acts such as the use of most drugs, private sexual behavior between consenting adults, and owning and possessing handguns.

KEY TERMS

adultery, 267
bigamy, 267
breach of the peace, 249
disorderly conduct, 253
fighting words, 251
fornication, 267
fundamental right, 273
injunction, 255
obscenity, 268
pandering, 268
prostitution, 267
riot, 258
rout, 258
seduction, 266
unlawful assembly, 258
vagrancy, 253

CASE ANALYSIS

LAWRENCE v. TEXAS
539 U.S. 558 (2003)

Case Preview

The case selected for this exercise was a long-awaited one, as the U.S. Supreme Court had decided several key cases in which the Court had upheld the right to privacy regarding sexual behavior between consenting adults in private. The Court, however, had not recognized that right between same gender couples, which was at issue in *Lawrence v. Texas*. The case is a long one and has been carefully edited for this text, but there are a number of concepts that are crucial and are included, despite their length, because the case has implications beyond its facts.

In the case, the U.S. Supreme Court talks about a **fundamental right**, which, in U.S. constitutional law, refers to a right that is named in the U.S. Constitution or implied within that document. It includes such rights as free speech and the right to the free exercise of religion, which are specified, along with the right to privacy, which, as we learned in Chapter 1, emanates from several stated rights. Fundamental rights may be controlled by the government but only if the statutes are narrowly tailored—that is, they do not go beyond the conduct they can limit. When you read the case, look for the discussions of privacy and fundamental rights.

The U.S. Supreme Court rarely overrules a prior case specifically and by name. Note how that issue arises in this case with respect to *Bowers v. Hardwick*, discussed earlier in the chapter. Notice also the Court's references to other cases that considered the right to privacy: *Baird v. Eisenstadt* and *Griswold v. Connecticut*, also discussed earlier, and *Roe v. Wade* (right to privacy and upholding abortion as a fundamental right under specified circumstances).[86]

Justices Anthony M. Kennedy, John Paul Stevens, David H. Souter, Ruth Bader Ginsburg, Sandra Day O'Connor, and Stephen Breyer constituted the majority. Justices Antonin Scalia and Clarence Thomas, along with Chief Justice William H. Rehnquist, dissented. Justice Kennedy delivered the opinion of the Court.

Facts

In Houston, Texas, officers of the Harris County Police Department were dispatched to a private residence in response to a reported weapons disturbance. They entered an apartment where one of the petitioners, John Geddes Lawrence, resided. The right of the police to enter does not seem to have been questioned. The officers observed Lawrence and another man, Tyron Garner, engaging in a sexual act. The two petitioners were arrested, held in custody overnight, and charged and convicted before a Justice of the Peace.

The complaints described their crime as "deviate sexual intercourse, namely anal sex, with a member of the same sex (man)." The applicable state law provides: "A person commits an offense if he engages in deviate sexual intercourse with another individual of the same sex." The statute defines "deviate sexual intercourse" as follows:

(A) any contact between any part of the genitals of one person and the mouth or anus of another person; or
(B) the penetration of the genitals or the anus of another person with an object.

The petitioners . . . challenged the statute as a violation of the Equal Protection Clause of the Fourteenth Amendment [of the U.S. Constitution] and of a like provision of the Texas Constitution. Those contentions were rejected. The petitioners . . . were each fined $200 and assessed court costs of $141.25. . . .

Issues

The question before the Court is the validity of a Texas statute making it a crime for two persons of the same sex to engage in certain intimate sexual conduct. . . .

We granted certiorari to consider three questions:

1. Whether petitioners' criminal convictions under the Texas Homosexual Conduct law which criminalizes sexual intimacy by same-sex couples, but not identical behavior by different-sex couples violates the Fourteenth Amendment guarantee of equal protection of laws?

2. Whether petitioners' criminal convictions for adult consensual sexual intimacy in the home violate their vital interests in liberty and privacy protected by the Due Process Clause of the Fourteenth Amendment?

3. Whether *Bowers v. Hardwick* should be overruled?

Holding

[1. The Texas statute violates the Equal Protection Clause of the Fourteenth Amendment.

2. The liberty and privacy interests protected by the Due Process Clause are violated by the Texas statute.

3. *Bowers v. Hardwick* is overruled.]

Rationale

We conclude the case should be resolved by determining whether the petitioners were free as adults to engage in the private conduct in the exercise of their liberty under the Due Process Clause of the Fourteenth Amendment to the Constitution. For this inquiry we deem it necessary to reconsider the Court's holding in *Bowers*. There are broad statements of the substantive reach of liberty under the Due Process Clause in earlier cases; but the most pertinent beginning point is our decision in *Griswold v. Connecticut*.

In *Griswold* the Court invalidated a state law prohibiting the use of drugs or devices of contraception and counseling or aiding and abetting the use of contraceptives. The Court described the protected interest as a right to privacy and placed emphasis on the marriage relation and the protected space of the marital bedroom.

After *Griswold* it was established that the right to make certain decisions regarding sexual conduct extends beyond the marital relationship. In *Eisenstadt v. Baird*, the Court invalidated a law prohibiting the distribution of contraceptives to unmarried persons. The case was decided under the Equal Protection Clause, but with respect to unmarried persons, the Court went on to state the fundamental proposition that the law impaired the exercise of their personal rights. It quoted from the statement of the Court of Appeals finding the law to be in conflict with fundamental human rights, and it followed with this statement of its own:

It is true that in *Griswold* the right of privacy in question inhered in the marital relationship. . . . If the right of privacy means anything, it is the right of the individual, married or single, to be free from unwarranted governmental intrusion into matters so fundamentally affecting a person as the decision whether to bear or beget a child.

The opinions in *Griswold* and *Eisenstadt* were part of the background for the decision in *Roe v. Wade*. As is well known, the case involved a challenge to the Texas law prohibiting abortions, but the laws of other States were affected as well. . . .

Roe recognized the right of a woman to make certain fundamental decisions affecting her destiny and confirmed once more that the protection of liberty under the Due Process Clause has a substantive dimension of fundamental significance in defining the rights of the person. . . .

The facts in *Bowers* had some similarities to the instant case. . . . One difference between the two cases is that the Georgia statute prohibited the conduct whether or not the participants were of the same sex, while the Texas statute, as we have seen, applies only to participants of the same sex. . . .

[The U.S. Supreme Court discussed the history of sodomy laws and the prosecution of such laws in the United States, noting that] [T]he model sodomy indictments presented in a

19th-century treatise, addressed the predatory acts of an adult man against a minor girl or minor boy. Instead of targeting relations between consenting adults in private, 19th-century sodomy prosecutions typically involved relations between men and minor girls or minor boys, relations between adults involving force, relations between adults implicating disparity in status, or relations between men and animals. . . .

In summary, the historical grounds relied upon in *Bowers* are more complex than the majority opinion and the concurring opinion by Chief Justice Burger indicate. Their historical premises are not without doubt and, at the very least, are overstated.

It must be acknowledged, of course, that the Court in *Bowers* was making the broader point that for centuries there have been powerful voices to condemn homosexual conduct as immoral. The condemnation has been shaped by religious beliefs, conceptions of right and acceptable behavior, and respect for the traditional family. For many persons these are not trivial concerns but profound and deep convictions accepted as ethical and moral principles to which they aspire and which thus determine the course of their lives. These considerations do not answer the question before us, however. The issue is whether the majority may use the power of the State to enforce these views on the whole society through operation of the criminal law. "Our obligation is to define the liberty of all, not to mandate our own moral code." . . .

This emerging recognition should have been apparent when *Bowers* was decided. In 1955 the American Law Institute promulgated the Model Penal Code and made clear that it did not recommend or provide for "criminal penalties for consensual sexual relations conducted in private." It justified its decision on three grounds: (1) The prohibitions undermined respect for the law by penalizing conduct many people engaged in; (2) the statutes regulated private conduct not harmful to others; and (3) the laws were arbitrarily enforced and thus invited the danger of blackmail. In 1961 Illinois changed its laws to conform to the Model Penal Code. Other States soon followed. . . . [The Court discussed changing laws concerning sodomy in other countries.]

In our own constitutional system the deficiencies in *Bowers* became even more apparent in the years following its announcement. The 25 States with laws prohibiting the relevant conduct referenced in the *Bowers* decision are reduced now to 13, of which 4 enforce their laws only against homosexual conduct. In those States where sodomy is still proscribed, whether for same-sex or heterosexual conduct, there is a pattern of nonenforcement with respect to consenting adults acting in private. The State of Texas admitted in 1994 that as of that date it had not prosecuted anyone under those circumstances.

Two principal cases decided after *Bowers* cast its holding into even more doubt. In [one of these cases] the Court reaffirmed the substantive force of the liberty protected by the Due Process Clause. [That] decision again confirmed that our laws and tradition afford constitutional protection to personal decisions relating to marriage, procreation, contraception, family relationships, child rearing, and education. In explaining the respect the Constitution demands for the autonomy of the person in making these choices, we stated as follows:

> These matters, involving the most intimate and personal choices a person may make in a lifetime, choices central to personal dignity and autonomy, are central to the liberty protected by the Fourteenth Amendment. At the heart of liberty is the right to define one's own concept of existence, of meaning, of the universe, and of the mystery of human life. Beliefs about these matters could not define the attributes of personhood were they formed under compulsion of the State. . . .

The central holding of *Bowers* has been brought in question by this case, and it should be addressed. Its continuance as precedent demeans the lives of homosexual persons. The stigma this criminal statute imposes, moreover, is not trivial. The offense, to be sure, is but a class C misdemeanor, a minor offense in the Texas legal system. Still, it remains a criminal offense with all that imports for the dignity of the persons charged. The petitioners will bear on their record the history of their criminal convictions. Just this Term we rejected various challenges to state laws requiring the registration of sex offenders. We are advised that if Texas convicted an adult for private, consensual homosexual conduct under the statute here in question the convicted person would come within the registration requirements.

This underscores the consequential nature of the punishment and the state-sponsored condemnation attendant to the criminal prohibition. Furthermore, the Texas criminal conviction carries with it the other collateral consequences always following a conviction, such as notations on job application forms, to mention but one example. . . .

The doctrine of *stare decisis* is essential to the respect accorded to the judgments of the Court and to the stability of the law. It is not, however, an inexorable command. In [another case] we noted that when a Court is asked to overrule a precedent recognizing a constitutional liberty interest, individual or societal reliance on the existence of that liberty cautions with particular strength against reversing course. The holding in *Bowers*, however, has not induced detrimental reliance comparable to some instances where recognized individual rights are involved. Indeed, there has been no individual or societal reliance on *Bowers* of the sort that could counsel against overturning its holding once there are compelling reasons to do so. *Bowers* itself causes uncertainty, for the precedents before and after its issuance contradict its central holding. . . .

Bowers was not correct when it was decided, and it is not correct today. It ought not to remain binding precedent. It should be and now is overruled.

Dissent by Justice Scalia

. . . Proscriptions against [consensual sodomy] have ancient roots. Sodomy was a criminal offense at common law and was forbidden by the laws of the original 13 States when they ratified the Bill of Rights. In 1868, when the Fourteenth Amendment was ratified, all but 5 of the 37 States in the Union had criminal sodomy laws. In fact, until 1961, all 50 States outlawed sodomy, and today, 24 States and the District of Columbia continue to provide criminal penalties for sodomy performed in private and between consenting adults. Against this background, to claim that a right to engage in such conduct is "deeply rooted in this Nation's history and tradition" or "implicit in the concept of ordered liberty" is, at best, facetious.

It is (as *Bowers* recognized) entirely irrelevant whether the laws in our long national tradition criminalizing homosexual sodomy were "directed at homosexual conduct as a distinct matter." Whether homosexual sodomy was prohibited by a law targeted at same-sex sexual relations or by a more general law prohibiting both homosexual and heterosexual sodomy, the only relevant point is that it was criminalized—which suffices to establish that homosexual sodomy is not a right "deeply rooted in our Nation's history and tradition." The Court today agrees that homosexual sodomy was criminalized and thus does not dispute the facts on which *Bowers* actually relied. . . .

Bowers' conclusion that homosexual sodomy is not a fundamental right "deeply rooted in this Nation's history and tradition" is utterly unassailable. . . .

I turn now to the ground on which the Court squarely rests its holding: the contention that there is no rational basis for the law here under attack. This proposition is so out of accord with our jurisprudence—indeed, with the jurisprudence of any society we know—that it requires little discussion. . . .

Today's opinion is the product of a Court, which is the product of a law-profession culture, that has largely signed on to the so-called homosexual agenda, by which I mean the agenda promoted by some homosexual activists directed at eliminating the moral opprobrium that has traditionally attached to homosexual conduct. I noted in an earlier opinion the fact that the American Association of Law Schools (to which any reputable law school must seek to belong) excludes from membership any school that refuses to ban from its job-interview facilities a law firm (no matter how small) that does not wish to hire as a prospective partner a person who openly engages in homosexual conduct.

One of the most revealing statements in today's opinion is the Court's grim warning that the criminalization of homosexual conduct is "an invitation to subject homosexual per-

sons to discrimination both in the public and in the private spheres." It is clear from this that the Court has taken sides in the culture war, departing from its role of assuring, as neutral observer, that the democratic rules of engagement are observed. Many Americans do not want persons who openly engage in homosexual conduct as partners in their business, as scoutmasters for their children, as teachers in their children's schools, or as boarders in their home. They view this as protecting themselves and their families from a lifestyle that they believe to be immoral and destructive. The Court views it as "discrimination" which it is the function of our judgments to deter. So imbued is the Court with the law profession's anti-anti-homosexual culture, that it is seemingly unaware that the attitudes of that culture are not obviously "mainstream"; that in most States what the Court calls "discrimination" against those who engage in homosexual acts is perfectly legal; that proposals to ban such "discrimination" under Title VII have repeatedly been rejected by Congress, that in some cases such "discrimination" is mandated by federal statute, and that in some cases such "discrimination" is a constitutional right.

Let me be clear that I have nothing against homosexuals, or any other group, promoting their agenda through normal democratic means. Social perceptions of sexual and other morality change over time, and every group has the right to persuade its fellow citizens that its view of such matters is the best. That homosexuals have achieved some success in that enterprise is attested to by the fact that Texas is one of the few remaining States that criminalize private, consensual homosexual acts. But persuading one's fellow citizens is one thing, and imposing one's views in absence of democratic majority will is something else. I would no more require a State to criminalize homosexual acts—or, for that matter, display any moral disapprobation of them—than I would forbid it to do so. What Texas has chosen to do is well within the range of traditional democratic action, and its hand should not be stayed through the invention of a brand-new "constitutional right" by a Court that is impatient of democratic change. It is indeed true that "later generations can see that laws once thought necessary and proper in fact serve only to oppress," and when that happens, later generations can repeal those laws. But it is the premise of our system that those judgments are to be made by the people, and not imposed by a governing caste that knows best. . . .

The matters appropriate for this Court's resolution are only three: Texas's prohibition of sodomy neither infringes a "fundamental right" (which the Court does not dispute), nor is unsupported by a rational relation to what the Constitution considers a legitimate state interest, nor denies the equal protection of the laws. I dissent.

Justice Thomas, Dissenting

I join Justice Scalia's dissenting opinion. I write separately to note that the law before the Court today "is . . . uncommonly silly." If I were a member of the Texas Legislature, I would vote to repeal it. Punishing someone for expressing his sexual preference through noncommercial consensual conduct with another adult does not appear to be a worthy way to expend valuable law enforcement resources. Notwithstanding this, I recognize that as a member of this Court I am not empowered to help petitioners and others similarly situated. My duty, rather, is to "decide cases 'agreeably to the Constitution and laws of the United States.'"

Discussion

What are the major arguments that the U.S. Supreme Court uses to support reversing its decision in *Bowers*? What is the importance of due process and equal protection in this case? How does the Texas statute differ from that of the Georgia statute in effect at the time *Bowers* was decided? Should the existence of laws prohibiting conduct (such as sodomy) be relevant to courts if those statutes are rarely, if ever, enforced? What is the role of the right to privacy in this case? Did Texas have a rational reason for its statute? What was the state protecting? What is the position of the dissent? Do you agree with the majority or the dissent? Give reasons for your answers. If the U.S. Supreme Court reverses *Roe v. Wade* and rules that abortion is not a fundamental right, will that have an impact on the issues in this case?

INTERNET ACTIVITY

The First Amendment is particularly relevant to some of the crimes discussed in Chapter 9. This amendment protects fundamental rights such as the rights to free speech and to assemble peacefully. The U.S. Supreme Court has given *speech* a very broad interpretation that includes various forms of expression. A First Amendment rights issue may become relevant in criminal cases involving fighting, disorderly conduct, offenses against public order, pornography and obscenity, and obstruction of justice. The following websites provide information about the First Amendment (both accessed 20 July 2008): http://www.en.wikipedia.org/wiki/Freedom_of_speech and http://www.aclu.org/freespeech/index.html.

NOTES

1. *Griswold v. Connecticut*, 381 U.S. 479 (1965).
2. For a discussion, see Rollin M. Perkins and Ronald N. Boyce, *Criminal Law*, 3d ed. (Mineola, N.Y.: Foundation Press, 1982), pp. 477–497. That source is the basis of the discussion in this section.
3. *Wilson v. State*, 156 S.E.2d 446, 448 (Ga. 1967), *cert. denied*, 390 U.S. 911 (1968).
4. O.C.G.A., Title 16, Chapter 11, Article 2, Section 16-11-39 (2008).
5. *Delaney v. State*, 599 S.E.2d 333 (Ga. App. 2004).
6. KRS, Title 13, Chapter 161, Section 161.190 (1985).
7. *Commonwealth v. Ashcraft*, 691 S.W.2d 229, 232 (Ky. Ct.App. 1985).
8. KRS, Title 13, Chapter 161, Section 161.190 (2008).
9. Cal Pen Code, Part 1, Title 11, Section 415 (2008).
10. "Neighbor Fights Loud Racetrack with Noisy Horns," *Sun-Sentinel* (Ft. Lauderdale, Fla.) (23 September 1995), p. 4.
11. *Chaplinsky v. New Hampshire*, 315 U.S. 568 (1942), footnotes and citations omitted.
12. *Terminiello v. Chicago*, 337 U.S. 1 (1949).
13. *Feiner v. New York*, 340 U.S. 315, 317, 321 (1951).
14. *Edwards v. South Carolina*, 372 U.S. 229 (1963).
15. *Cohen v. California*, 403 U.S. 15, 20 (1971), *reh'g. denied*, 404 U.S. 876 (1971).
16. *Sandul v. Larion*, 119 F.3d 1250 (6th. Cir. 1997), *cert. dismissed*, 522 U.S. 979 (1997).
17. *Lewis v. City of New Orleans*, 415 U.S. 130, 133 (1974).
18. *State v. Thompson*, 767 N.E.2d 251 (Ohio 2002).
19. *Benefit v. Cambridge*, 679 N.E.2d 184 (Mass. 1997).
20. *Kolender v. Lawson*, 461 U.S. 352, 361 (1983). The statute was Cal Pen Code, Title 11, Section 647(e) (1983). The current statute is similar, with only a few changes. For a similar holding, see *Papachristou v. City of Jacksonville*, 405 U.S. 156 (1972).
21. *Milwaukee v. Nelson*, 439 N.W.2d 562 (Wis. 1989), *cert. denied*, 493 U.S. 858 (1989).
22. *People v. Superior Court (Oswell)*, 758 P.2d 1046 (Cal. 1988). The statute is located at Cal Pen Code, Part I, Title 15, Chapter 2, Section 647(d) (2008).
23. *Wyche v. State*, 619 So.2d 231 (Fla. 1993); and *Holliday v. City of Tampa, Florida*, 619 So.2d 244 (Fla. 1993). The Tampa ordinance is Section 24-61. Florida's loitering statute is codified at Fla. Stat., Title 46, Chapter 856, Section 856.021 (2009). Florida's prostitution and solicitation statute is codified at Fla. Stat., Title 46, Chapter 796, Section 796.07 (2009).
24. "Cities Cannot Outlaw Beggars, Judge Says," *New York Times* (10 May 1995), p. 12. The case is *Berkeley Community Health Project v. City of Berkeley*, 902 F.Supp. 1084 (N.D.Cal. 1995), *dismissed*, 966 F.Supp. 941 (N.D.Cal. 1997).
25. *Roulette v. City of Seattle*, 97 F.3d 300 (9th Cir. 1996).
26. *Jones v. City of L.A.*, 404 F.3d 1118 (9th Cir. 2006), *vacated, remanded, dismissed*, 505 F.3d 1006 (9th Cir. 2007); "Los Angeles to Permit Sleeping on Sidewalks," *New York Times* (11 October 2007), p. 21.
27. *Tobe v. City of Santa Ana, Calif.*, 892 P.2d 1145 (Cal. 1995).
28. Chicago Municipal Code, Section 8-4-015.

29. *Chicago v. Morales*, 527 U.S. 41 (1999).

30. "Anti-Loiter Ordinance: Does It Have a Leg to Stand On?" *South Bend Tribune* (Indiana) (1 April 2002), p. 1C.

31. *Powell v. Texas*, 392 U.S. 514 (1968).

32. Michigan Motor Vehicle Code, MCLS, Chapter 257, Section 257.625b(5) (2008).

33. A.R.S., Title 4, Chapter 3, Article 2, Section 4-311D (2008).

34. A.R.S., Title 4, Chapter 3, Article 2, Section 4-244.9 (2008).

35. See A.R.S., Title 13, Chapter 31, Section 13-3111 (2008).

36. *State v. Abbadini*, 192 A. 550, 551-552 (Del. 1937).

37. Judge Stephen, *A History of the Criminal Law of England* (1883), p. 203.

38. Cal Pen Code, Part 1, Title 11, Section 404 *et seq* (2008); Tex. Penal Code, Title 9, Chapter 42, Section 42.02 (2007).

39. NY CLS Penal, Title N, Article 240, Sections 240.05 and 240.06 (2008).

40. Perkins and Boyce, *Criminal Law*, p. 492.

41. *Quilici v. Village of Morton Grove*, 695 F.2d 261 (7th Cir. 1982), *cert. denied*, 464 U.S. 863 (1983).

42. *Kalodimos v. Village of Morton Grove*, 470 N.E.2d 266 (Ill. 1984).

43. *District of Columbia v. Heller*, 128 S.Ct. 2783 (2008), notes and citations omitted.

44. *Cox v. Louisiana*, 379 U.S. 536 (1965), notes and citations omitted.

45. Terry Carter, "Beast Practices," *American Bar Association Journal* 93 (November 2007): 39.

46. USCS, Chapter 7, Chapter 54, Section 2156(b) (2009).

47. Carter, "Beast Practices," p. 40.

48. "Judge Declares a Mistrial in Texas Cat Killing Case," *New York Times* (17 November 2007), p. 11. The statute is Tex. Penal Code, Title 9, Chapter 42, Section 42.092 (2009). The statute covering abuse of livestock is Section 42.09 (2009).

49. Tex. Fam. Code, Title 3, Chapter 54, Section 54.0407 (2009).

50. M.R.S., Title 19-A, Part 4, Chapter 101, Section 4006 (2008); Arin Greenwood, "Saving Fido: New State Law Allows Pets to Be Included in Protective Orders," *American Bar Association Journal* (4 August 2006), p. 1, http://www.abanet.org/journal/ereport/au4pet.html, accessed 4 August 2006.

51. "Killer of Dog Sought as Outrage Grows," *New York Times* (12 March 2000), p. 21.

52. "Reward in Duck Case to Aid Animals," *San Jose Mercury News* (California) (11 September 2007), n.p.

53. Cal Pen Code, Part I, Title 14, Section 597.7 (2008).

54. See Cal Health & Safety Code, Division 105, Part 6, Chapter 8, Section 122335 (2008).

55. See NY CLS Penal, Title N, Article 240, Section 240.31 (2008).

56. William E. Nelson, "Emerging Notions of Modern Criminal Law in the Revolutionary Era," in *Crime, Law, and Society*, ed. Abraham S. Goldstein and Joseph Goldstein (New York: *Free Press*, 1971), p. 73.

57. Pa.C.S., Title 18, Part II, Article F, Section 5901 (2008).

58. Idaho Code, Title 18, Chapter 15, Section 18-1508 (2008).

59. Idaho Code, Title 18, Chapter 66, Section 18-6605 (2008).

60. Cal Pen Code, Title 9, Chapter 5, Section 286 (2008).

61. *Bowers v. Hardwick*, 478 U.S. 186 (1986); *and overruled by Lawrence v. Texas*, 539 U.S. 558 (2003). The statute is codified at O.C.G.A., Title 16, Chapter 6, Section 16-6-2 (2008).

62. *Powell v. State*, 510 S.E.2d 18 (Ga. 1998).

63. Tex. Penal Code, Title 5, Chapter 21, Section 21.06 (2009).

64. See Cal Pen Code, Part I, Title 9, Chapter 1, Section 268, repealed 1984; and Inducing consent to sexual act by fraud or fear, Section 266c (2008).

65. Idaho Code, Title 18, Chapter 66, Section 18-6603 (2008).

66. Va. Code Ann., Title 18.2, Chapter 8, Article 3, Section 18.2-344 (2008).

67. *Martin v. Ziherl*, 607 S.E.2d 367 (Va. 2005).

68. NY CLS Penal, Part Three, Title O, Article 255, Section 255.17 (2008).

69. See ILCS, Title III, Part B, Article 11, Chapter 720, Section 5/11-7 (2008).

70. NY CLS Penal, Part Three, Title O, Article 255, Section 255.15 (2008). The adultery statute is Section 255.17.

71. *People v. Smith*, 378 N.E.2d 1032 (N.Y. 1978), upholding NY CLS Penal, Title N, Article 240, Section 240.37 (2008).

72. For a discussion of TVPRA, see Takiyah Rayshawn McClain, "An Ounce of Prevention: Improving the Preventative Measures of the Trafficking Victims Protection Act," *Vanderbilt Journal of Transnational Law* 40, no. 2 (1 March 2007): 579 *et seq*.

73. "Help for Victimized Children," *New York Times* (19 July 2008), p. 16.

74. *Miller v. California*, 413 U.S. 15, 24 (1973). See also *Stanley v. Georgia*, 394 U.S. 557 (1969).

75. The Child Protection Act of 1984, USCS, Title 18, Section 2251 *et seq*. (2009).

76. *United States v. X-Citement Video*, 513 U.S. 64 (1994).

77. The federal statute is codified at USCS, Title 18, Section 2251 *et seq*. (2009).

78. *Ashcroft v. Free Speech Coalition*, 535 U.S. 234 (2002).

79. The Prosecutorial Remedies and Other Tools to End the Exploitation of Children Today Act of 2003 (the PROTECT Act), Public Law 108-21 (2006).

80. *United States v. Williams*, 128 S.Ct. 1830 (2008).

81. *United States v. Williams*, 128 S.Ct. 1830 (2008).

82. The Communications Decency Act of 1996, Public Law No. 104-104, Sec. 502, 110 Stat. 56, 133-135, is codified at U.S. Code, Title 47, Section 2236(a) to (h) (2009).

83. *Reno v. American Civil Liberties Union*, 521 U.S. 844 (1997).

84. *United States v. American Library Association*, 539 U.S. 194 (2003).

85. Federal Bureau of Investigation press release, "Major Child Porn Ring Busted and 20 Children Rescued Worldwide," (06 March 2008), http://www.fbi.gov/page2/march08/innocentimages_030608.html, accessed 10 March 2008.

86. *Bowers v. Hardwick*, 478 U.S. 186 (1986); *and overruled by Lawrence v. Texas*, 539 U.S. 558 (2003); *Baird v. Eisenstadt*, 405 U.S. 438 (1972); *Griswold v. Connecticut*, 481 U.S. 479 (1965); and *Roe v. Wade*, 410 U.S. 113 (1973).

Crimes Against the Government and Terrorism

continued

INTRODUCTION

This chapter covers two important areas that are often omitted from criminal law texts despite their importance in today's world: crimes against the government and terrorism. Crimes against the government have been on the criminal law books for years but were infrequently enforced until recently. Acts of terrorism are relatively new in statutory form but in recent years have, unfortunately, been far-reaching in their impact.

At a time in which we are experiencing increasing problems with ethics and morality within the governmental as well as the private sector, it is imperative that students gain some knowledge of major crimes against the administration of government. This chapter examines five types of crime that fall into this category: perjury and related crimes, bribery, official misconduct in office, obstruction of justice, and treason.

Terrorism, the focus of the second major section of this chapter, has been a research interest of criminology and criminal law scholars for years; many colleges and universities offer seminars or regular courses on the topic. It has not, however, generally been a topic covered extensively in undergraduate criminal law texts. Hopefully this will change as a result of the 11 September 2001 terrorist attacks in the United States and subsequently in other parts of the world, which have captured international attention and probably increased the fear that most, if not all, people have of such acts.

In a real sense many crimes are similar to terrorism. Rapists strike fear in the minds of their victims; fear is a crucial element of robbery; assault contains an element of fear; murder may involve torture and fear; domestic violence, especially when it occurs over a period of time, creates fear. Those topics have already been discussed in this text; this chapter fo-cuses specifically on those acts included within discussions of terrorism.

CRIMES AGAINST THE GOVERNMENT

In primitive societies, the acts included in this section were not criminal offenses. Simple societies needed protection from outsiders, but most problems within societies were handled informally. As societies became more complex and developed formal laws and governments, they faced the necessity of dealing with those people who tried to disrupt legal and governmental structures. Additionally, there was the possibility that government and government officials might mistreat citizens.

Crimes committed against the government often target the government's administration, and they are serious. Some of these crimes, such as perjury and bribery, undermine the judicial system. Others, such as the violation of civil rights by law enforcement officials, threaten the rights and security of all citizens. All of the crimes make the administration of government more difficult.

There are many crimes against the government and its administration; this section covers perjury, bribery, official misconduct in office, obstruction of justice, and treason. It is not uncommon to find indictments for more than one of these crimes in the same fact pattern.

Perjury

Under the common law, **perjury** referred only to false statements willfully made under oath in a judicial proceeding. According to a noted English jurist, *perjury* was limited to situations in which "a *lawful* oath is administered, in some *judicial* proceeding, to a person who swears *willfully*, *absolutely* and *falsely*, in a matter material to the issue or point in question." The law considered all other perjuries "unnecessary at least, and therefore [did] not punish the breach of them."[1]

In early common law the punishment for perjury was death. Later the penalty evolved to banishment or cutting out the offender's tongue, forfeiture of goods, and fines and imprisonment. The convicted perjurer was not permitted to give sworn testimony in another judicial proceeding.

Today the elements of perjury vary from jurisdiction to jurisdiction, but the following are generally required:

1. The accused took an oath to tell the truth.
2. The oath was administered by legal authority.
3. The testimony was given during a judicial proceeding (or in a statutory affidavit).
4. The accused testified in that proceeding.
5. The testimony was material to that proceeding.
6. The testimony was false.
7. The testimony was given willingly, with the knowledge that it was false and with the intention that it be believed.

Focus 10.1 contains perjury statutes, along with one on the **subornation of perjury**, also a common law crime, which involved procuring someone to commit perjury. It carried the same penalties as perjury. Although the original common law crimes of perjury and subornation of perjury were limited to statements made under official oath in judicial proceedings, as other kinds of sworn statements gained recognition the English courts developed additional crimes to cover the offenses, but they did not carry the term *perjury*. Many of these false statements were included in the offense of **false swearing**, which included false statements that would have been perjury had they been made during a judicial proceeding.

Today both perjury and subornation of perjury are crimes under the federal code, along with the crime of false declarations before a grand jury or court.[2]

In addition to statutes on perjury, subornation of perjury, and false swearing, many jurisdictions have statutes prohibiting offenses such as unsworn falsification to authorities, false alarms to agencies of public safety, false reports to law enforcement authorities, tampering with witnesses and informants or retaliating against them, tampering with or fabricating physi-

---

FOCUS 10.1 **Perjury and Related Crimes**

Hawaii Penal Code, HRS, Division 5, Title 37, Chapter 710, Part V, Section 710-1060 (2008)

Perjury

(1) A person commits the offense of perjury if in any official proceeding the person makes, under an oath required or authorized by law, a false statement which the person does not believe to be true.

(2) No person shall be convicted under this section unless the court rules that the false statement is a "materially false statement" as defined by [another section]. It is not a defense that the declarant mistakenly believed the false statement to be immaterial.

Virgin Islands Code, V.I.C., Title 14, Chapter 77 (2008)

Section 1541. Perjury Defined

Whoever, in or in connection with, any action, proceeding, hearing or inquiry or on any occasion when an oath may be lawfully administered—

(1) swears or affirms—

(A) that he will truly testify, declare, depose or certify; or

(B) that any testimony, declaration, deposition, certificate, affidavit or other writing subscribed by him is true; and

(2) willfully and knowingly testifies, declares, deposes or certifies falsely or states in his testimony, deposition, affidavit or certificate any matter to be true which he knows to be false—shall be imprisoned not more than 10 years.

Section 1548. Subornation of Perjury

Whoever willfully procures or induces another to commit perjury, shall be imprisoned not more than 10 years.

Section 1549. Perjury Resulting in Conviction of Innocent Person

Whoever, by willful perjury or subornation of perjury, procures the conviction and punishment of any innocent person, is punishable by the same penalty that was inflicted upon such innocent person; but in no case shall the punishment be less than one year imprisonment.

Conn. Gen. Stat., Title 53a, Chapter 952, Part XI, Section 53a-156 (2008)

Perjury: Class D Felony

(a) A person is guilty of perjury if, in any official proceeding, he intentionally, under oath, makes a false statement, swears, affirms or testifies falsely, to a material statement which he does not believe to be true.

cal evidence, tampering with public records or information, and impersonating a public servant.

Bribery

Beginning in antiquity and continuing through early English and American legal writings were the prohibitions against the offense that today is called **bribery**. As a common law misdemeanor, *bribery* was limited to actions concerning judicial officials (a judge or another person performing judicial functions) and applied only to the judicial official who actually took the bribe. Today, *bribery* refers to the offering, giving, receiving, or soliciting of anything of value to influence action by public (or in some jurisdictions, nonpublic) officials, such as public officers and anyone else who performed a public function or duty when the gift involved a corrupt intention to influence the discharging of that duty. By statute in many jurisdictions, bribery has been broadened so that today the offense includes quasi-official and occupational bribery.

Current bribery statutes also define who may be bribed and require as an element of bribery that there be a criminal intent. This is the most important element of the crime, for if it cannot be shown that the giver gave to the official for the purpose of influencing a decision, there is no bribery. If the recipient is the defendant, it must be shown that he or she received the gift with the intent of being influenced in making a decision affecting the one who offered the gift. It is possible, of course, that one party has the requisite criminal intent and the other does not. In that case, only the party with the required intent may be convicted of bribery. The evil motive or intent may be proved by circumstantial evidence. For *official bribery*, a conviction requires that the money (or other items of value) be given to a public official to influence action over which that person has some *official* control.

A common law crime related to bribery was **embracery**, a misdemeanor referring to a corrupt attempt to influence a juror by means of promises, money, persuasions, or similar techniques. Today the crime of bribery may include attempts to influence a juror, although some jurisdictions have a separate statute for jury tampering. For example, Pennsylvania law, under which bribery is a felony, provides for the misdemeanor of *jury tampering*, defined as follows:

> Any person who, having in any manner ascertained the names of persons drawn from the master list of prospective jurors or jury wheel, shall

thereafter discuss with any prospective juror the facts or alleged facts of any particular suit or cause then listed for trial in the court for which the prospective juror has been summoned for jury service, with the intent to influence the juror in his service or in the consideration of the evidence in the matter, commits a misdemeanor of the second degree. The penalty provided in this section shall be in addition to the penalties provided by law for bribery.[3]

Pennsylvania also has a statute prohibiting *aggravated jury tampering*, which is a felony of the first, second, or third degree, depending on the type of case in which it occurs.[4]

Official Misconduct in Office

Any willful, unlawful behavior by public officials in the course of their official duties may constitute the crime of **official misconduct in office**. This may include the failure to act (*nonfeasance*); engaging in a wrongful act that the official has no right to do (*malfeasance*); or improperly performing an act that the official has a right to do (*misfeasance*).

Official misconduct in office has the following elements:

1. The actor must be a public official or one acting in that capacity.
2. The misconduct must occur during the course of that officer's official duties, or **under color of law** (during official duties).
3. The actor must have an evil intent.

To sustain a conviction for official misconduct, it must be shown that the officer's act was accompanied by an evil intent. An act performed because of ignorance or in good faith will not qualify. The act itself must be an unlawful act of corruption or one of depravity, perversion, or taint—that is, an act requiring an evil intent or motive.

The federal criminal statutes provide penalties for persons who meet the following description:

> Whoever, under color of any law, statute, ordinance, regulation, or custom, willfully subjects any person of any State, Territory, Commonwealth, Possession, or District to the deprivation of any rights, privileges, or immunities secured or protected by the Constitution or Laws of the United

FOCUS 10.2   Civil Rights Charges Against Law Enforcement Officials

Allegations of mistreatment by law enforcement officers are difficult to prove, and many are not prosecuted at the local level according to some reports.[1] Those that are tried frequently result in acquittals, illustrated by the first trial of the officers involved in the 1991 beating of Rodney King, an African American suspect. The beating of King by Los Angeles police officers was captured on video by an amateur photographer, but the officers were acquitted at their trial in nearby Simi Valley. These acquittals were followed by three days of intense rioting in Los Angeles, causing the deaths of more than 50 persons and property damage in excess of $1 billion.

Subsequently the officers were tried in *federal* court on charges of violating King's federal civil rights. Two of the officers, Timothy Wind and Theodore Brisno, were acquitted, but Sergeant Stacey Koon and Officer Laurence Powell were convicted. Koon and Powell began serving their two-and-a-half-year prison terms at a minimum security facility in October 1993.

In August 1994 a federal appeals court ordered resentencing because the trial judge failed to follow the federal sentencing guidelines, which could have sent the defendants to prison for 70 to 87 months. In June 1996, the U.S. Supreme Court ruled on the case, giving credence to the discretion of trial judges who sentence under federal sentencing guidelines. The Court approved the trial judge's consideration of the fact that Koon

and Powell had endured a significant burden because of trials in state and federal courts and that they were at risk of abuse by other inmates in prison. It did not approve the trial court's consideration of the low probability that the defendants would commit these or similar offenses again and the adverse effects that the convictions would have on their careers. The Supreme Court did, however, hold that it was appropriate for the lower court to consider King's behavior, which contributed significantly to provoking the defendants' misconduct. The case was sent back for the trial judge to decide whether the sentence was appropriate under the U.S. Supreme Court's interpretation of the federal sentencing guidelines. After reconsidering his initial decisions, the trial judge did not alter the original sentences of Koon and Powell.[2]

Koon and Powell served time in prison, were released for brief stays in halfway houses, and then released unconditionally. Despite what some considered lenient sentences, the case does demonstrate that federal civil rights charges may be successful after (or in lieu of) state charges.

1. "Police Are Rarely Prosecuted Unless Case Is Bulletproof," *Los Angeles Times* (9 December 2005), p. 2B.
2. See *United States v. Koon*, 34 F.3d 1416 (9th Cir. 1994), *aff'd. in part and rev'd. in part, remanded*, 515 U.S. 1190 (1996).

States, or to different punishments, pains, or penalties, on account of such person being an alien, or by reason of his color, or race, than are prescribed for the punishment of citizens, shall be [the statute continues with the penalties].[5]

The violation of civil rights by law enforcement officers has been a matter of increasing national concern, with calls for more prosecutions. Focus 7.3 discussed the police brutality in New York City involving the attack on Abner Louima. Focus 10.2 illustrates the successful use of the federal Civil Rights Act after acquittals on state charges in a case of police violence in Los Angeles.

Obstruction of Justice

In early common law, interference with the orderly processes of the civil and criminal courts was a misdemeanor known as *obstruction of justice*. The crime could take many forms, including tampering with a jury; interfering with an officer who was attempting

to perform official duties; suppressing or refusing to produce evidence; intimidating witnesses; and bribing judges, witnesses, or jurors.

Obstruction of justice and related acts are recognized today by criminal statutes in most jurisdictions. They may be prosecuted as obstruction of justice crimes or as related crimes such as contempt, conspiracy, perjury, embracery, bribery, or extortion. The crime may be committed by judicial and other officials and might constitute official misconduct in office.

Obstruction of justice charges may be brought against businesses or corporations as well as against individuals. Recent examples of the latter are the convictions of Lewis "Scooter" Libby and Martha Stewart. Libby, the top aide to Vice President Dick Cheney, was convicted of obstruction of justice and perjury in the investigation into the leak of the identity of Valerie Plame, who was with the Central Intelligence Administration (CIA). Stewart, who founded the billion-dollar business empire Martha Stewart Omnimedia, was convicted of obstruction of justice for lying to federal authorities with regard to questionable stock sales. Stewart served time in a federal prison; Libby's prison sentence (but not his probation orders and fine) was commuted by President George W. Bush. Finally, all of the crimes discussed thus far in this chapter were at issue in the 2008 charges against the Detroit, Michigan, mayor and his mistress, both of whom are the subject of Focus 10.3.

Treason

The most serious crimes against the administration of government and its people are treason and related offenses. *Treason*, which means attempting to overthrow the government of which one is a citizen or betraying that government to a foreign power, was thought to be such a serious offense that it is the only crime included in the U.S. Constitution. Article III, Section 3, provides:

> Treason against the United States, shall consist only in levying War against them, or in adhering to their Enemies, giving them Aid and Comfort. No Person shall be convicted of Treason unless on the Testimony of two Witnesses to the same overt Act, or on Confession in open Court.

The Constitution gives Congress the power to legislate punishment for treason. The U.S. Criminal Code's chapter entitled "Treason, Sedition, and Subversive Activities" contains numerous sections defining the relevant crimes and their punishments. The punishment for treason against the United States is death or imprisonment for not less than five years and a fine of not less than $10,000. A person convicted of treason under the federal code may not hold any office in the U.S. government.[6] In view of the U.S. Supreme Court's decisions regarding capital punishment (discussed in Chapter 12) the constitutionality of the death penalty for treason may be questioned.

In his *Commentaries on the Laws of England*, noted English jurist William Blackstone stated that implicit in the word *treason* is "betraying, treachery, or breach of faith." Treason referred not only to an act against the king and government but also to situations in which an inferior betrayed a superior. Treason thus included the actions of a wife against her lord or husband and of a servant against his master or mistress, although these offenses were called **petit treason**.[7] For that offense the penalty was drawing and hanging for a male offender, drawing and burning for a female. The word *drawing*

meant to drag the offender by horse to the place of execution. Petit treason did not become part of U.S. legal tradition, although some states, such as California, enacted a petit treason statute but subsequently repealed it, as noted in Focus 10.4, which contains several state statutes concerning treason and treason-related crimes.

Treason has been labeled the worst of all crimes.[8] Because of its seriousness, it is defined carefully and consists of two elements:

1. An allegiance owed to the government (which may be state or federal)
2. An intentional act that violates the offender's allegiance

A person may be convicted of treason only upon a confession in open court or the testimony of two witnesses.

A person who is not a U.S. citizen cannot commit treason against the United States because, by definition, treason requires an allegiance to the government. This allegiance requirement applies even if the person has had U.S. citizenship and either lost or renounced it. The owed allegiance must be breached by an overt act; treasonous thoughts are not sufficient. As the Constitution specifies, the allegiance may be breached by levying war against the country or by aiding and comforting the enemy, which may consist of acts such as providing arms and other supplies for the enemy to use against the United States or delivering deserters and prisoners to the enemy. The criminal intent for treason may be shown by proving that the accused was aware that the actions in question would assist the enemy in its efforts against the United States.

Most states have treason statutes that apply to offenses against the state government. These statutes may not violate the U.S. Constitution's provisions; otherwise, states have discretion in framing their statutes or constitutional provisions regarding treason. Focus 10.4 provides several examples.

Fewer than 50 cases of treason have been prosecuted in the United States, although some cases involving treasonous act have been brought under other statutes. Julius and Ethel Rosenberg, who were accused of providing protected information to the Soviet Union during World War II, were convicted of conspiracy to violate the federal espionage act. **Espionage**, or spying, is defined by the federal code as "gathering, transmitting or losing" national defense information with the

Multiple Charges of Crimes Against the Government: The Case of the Detroit Mayor

The 2008 investigations into the evidence of an alleged adulterous relationship between Detroit, Michigan, mayor Kwame Kilpatrick and his former chief of staff, Christine Beatty, led to multiple charges against both. The case illustrates how multiple crimes may be alleged in charges against one or more persons.

Kilpatrick and Beatty were charged with conspiracy, perjury, obstruction of justice, and official misconduct in office arising from text messages between the two. News media secured those messages and published them, showing that the two public officials allegedly signed a secret agreement to keep the messages confidential. At issue was testimony under oath that both the mayor and his then chief of staff made in 2007 in a civil whistle-blower case involving the removal of Gary Brown, the deputy police chief. Both defendants were charged with lying about that situation (which resulted in an $8.4 million settlement) about their own personal relationship, and about a secret agreement to keep the text messages confidential.[1]

Mayor Kilpatrick assembled a large legal team to represent him in the increasing civil issues as well as the criminal charges against him. He also fought efforts to remove him from office, but in September 2008 he entered guilty pleas involving 120 days in jail, paying $1 million in restitution, and giving up his law license. Kilpatrick will be on probation for five years, during which time he cannot run for public office. In December 2008, Beatty accepted a plea bargain. She was sentenced to 120 days in jail, $100,000 in restitution, and probation for five years, during which time she is not permitted to attend law school.[2]

1. "Judge: Reporters Cannot Be Questioned About Obtaining Kilpatrick Texts," *Detroit News* (18 July 2008), n.p.
2. Mayor Builds Huge Defense Team," *Detroit News* (21 July 2008), p. 6; "More Text Messages to Be Released Today," *Detroit News* (24 October 2008), online edition, n.p.; "Campaign for Detroit Mayor," *Detroit Free Press* (21 November 2008), p. 1; "Worthy: Kilpatrick Broke Deal," *Detroit News* (3 December 2008), p. 1B.

Detroit's former mayor, Kwame Kilpatrick (r), and his former chief of staff and mistress, Christine Beatty (l), pictured here at a news conference, were both charged with conspiracy, perjury, obstruction of justice, and official misconduct in office arising from text messages between the two concerning the removal of the city's deputy police chief. Kilpatrick and Beatty were charged with lying about that situation (which resulted in an $8.4 million settlement), about their own personal relationship, and about a secret agreement to keep their text messages confidential. Both former public officials entered into plea agreements and were each sentenced to 120 days in jail, restitution, and fines. Kilpatrick was required to surrender his bar membership, while Beatty agreed not to attend law classes during her probationary period. (Rebecca Cook/Reuters/Landov)

FOCUS 10.4 Treason and Related Crimes: A Sample of State Statutes

Alabama

**Code of Ala., Title 13A, Chapter 11, Article 1
Section 13A-11-2 (2008)**
13A-11-2. Treason

(a) A person commits the crime of treason if he levies war against the State of Alabama or adheres to its enemies, giving them aid and comfort.

(b) No person shall be convicted of treason unless upon the testimony of two witnesses to the same overt act or upon confession in open court.

Arkansas

A.C.A, Title 5, Chapter 51, Subchapter 2 (2009)
Section 5-51-201. Treason

(a) Treason against the state shall consist only in levying war against the state or adhering to its enemies, giving them aid and comfort.

(b) No person shall be convicted of treason unless on the testimony of two (2) witnesses to the same overt act or his own confession in open court.

California

Cal Pen Code, Part 1, Title 3 (2008)
Section 38. Misprision of treason

Misprision of treason is the knowledge and concealment of treason, without otherwise assenting to or participating in the crime.

Florida

Fla. Stat., Title 46, Chapter 876 (2009)
Section 876.33. Misprision of treason

Whoever having knowledge of the commission of treason conceals the same and does not, as soon as may be, disclose and make known such treason to the Governor or one of the justices of the Supreme Court or a judge of the circuit court, shall be judged guilty of the offense of misprision of treason.

Vermont

Vt. Stat. Ann., Title 13, Part I, Chapter 75, Subchapter 1 (2009)
Section 3403. Misprision of treason

A person owing allegiance to this state, knowing such treason to have been committed, or knowing of the intent of a person to commit such treason, who does not, within fourteen days from the time of having such knowledge, give information thereof to the governor of the state, to one of the justices of the supreme court, a superior or district judge or a justice of the peace, shall be guilty of misprision of treason.

California

Cal Pen Code, Part 1, Title 8, Chapter 1 (2008)
Section 191. Petit treason abolished

The rules of the common law distinguishing the killing of a master by his servant, and of a husband by his wife, as petit treason, are abolished, and these offenses are homicides, punishable in the manner prescribed by this chapter.

Florida

Fla. Stat., Title 46, Section 876 (2009)
Section 876.36. Inciting insurrection

If any person shall incite an insurrection or sedition amongst any portion or class of the population of this state, or shall attempt by writing, speaking, or by any other means to incite such insurrection or sedition, the person so offending shall be guilty of a felony of the second degree.

---

intent or reasonable belief that the information will be used against the United States." The Rosenbergs were executed in 1953.[9] In 1993 the American Bar Association observed the fortieth anniversary of the Rosenbergs' executions with a mock trial during which the Rosenbergs were "acquitted," with the jury ruling that the prosecution's case was shabby.[10]

Several crimes are related to treason. The concealment of the known treason of another, called **misprision of treason**, is punishable under federal and most state statutes, some of which are presented in Focus 10.4. The federal code also includes inciting a rebellion against the United States, seditious conspiracy, advocating the overthrow of the government, willfully interfering with the armed forces, recruiting for service against the United States, and enlistment to serve against the United States.[11]

State statutes also include some offenses similar to treason, though some have been held unconstitutionally broad or vague. In 1931, for example, California's prohibition against displaying a red flag "in any public place . . . as a sign, symbol or emblem of opposition to organized government" was held to be unconstitutional because this prohibition might include "peaceful and orderly opposition to government by legal means and within constitutional limitations."[12]

Another crime related to treason is **sedition**, which is defined in part by the federal criminal code as follows:

> [W]hoever knowingly or willfully advocates, abets, advises, or teaches the duty, necessity, desirability, or propriety of overthrowing or destroying the government of the United States or any state, territory, district or possession thereof, or the government of any political subdivision therein, by force or violence or by the assassination of any officer of any such government; or
>
>   Whoever, with intent to cause the overthrow or destruction of any such government, prints, publishes, edits, issues, circulates, sells, distributes, or publicly displays any written or printed matter advocating, advising, or teaching the duty, necessity, desirability, or propriety of overthrowing or destroying any government in the United States by force or violence or attempts to do so. . . .[13]

Thus, sedition is a communication or agreement aimed at stirring up treason or defaming the government. Focus 10.4 contains Florida's prohibition against the crime of *inciting insurrection.*

This brief look at treason and related crimes sets the stage for a more detailed discussion of terrorism.

TERRORISM

In his May 2001 foreword to a college text on **terrorism**, criminologist Todd R. Clear stated that the "very word *terrorism* holds us at attention. To be terrified is a dreadful experience." Clear emphasized that terror is "an alarming emotion, and to provoke it is to invite alarm." But invoking terror is often not a limited, focused attempt; rather, it is used as a means for social change, and when that occurs, "it invites among us a kind of social alarm, a disturbance of the basic sense of social order."[14]

Although it is not a prerequisite of terrorism, most terrorist acts do involve violence, and most victims are innocent and unsuspecting persons who become the targets of violent attacks that frequently result in death. This was tragically demonstrated on 19 April 1995, when Timothy McVeigh bombed the federal building in Oklahoma City, killing 168 people, including 19 children in a day care center within the building, and injuring hundreds. This was the worst act of

The terrorist attacks in November 2008 in Mumbai, India, the center of that country's financial district, reminded the world of the extreme violence that occurs in many terrorist acts and the randomness of the victims. The attacks on the Taj Mahal Palace and Tower hotel, pictured here, and other targets left over 100 persons dead, including 9 of the 10 gunmen; and almost 300 people injured. Buildings were damaged or destroyed and the city was under siege for three days. (Prashanth Vishwanathan/Bloomberg News/Landov)

terrorism on American soil until the events of 11 September 2001.

The Problem of Definition

There is little agreement on a definition of terrorism, although most people have a concept of what it means. A broad legal definition is found in the American Law Institute's Model Penal Code (MPC), which defines *terrorist threats* as follows:

> A person is guilty of a felony if he threatens to commit any crime of violence with purpose to terrorize

another or to cause evacuation of a building, place of assembly, or facility of public transportation, or otherwise to cause serious public inconvenience, or in reckless disregard of the risk of causing such terror or inconvenience.[15]

Applied to the political arena, terrorism has been defined simply as "motivated violence for political ends."[16] The Task Force on Disorders and Terrorism of the National Advisory Committee on Criminal Justice Standards and Goals (hereafter referred to as The Task Force) defined *terrorism* as "a tactic or technique by means of which a violent act or the threat thereof is used for the prime purpose of creating overwhelming fear for coercive purposes." Terrorism is a political crime, but it may also be a violent personal crime. Terrorist acts are planned in advance, and, to be effective, terrorists must manipulate the community to which the message is addressed. The inculcation of fear is paramount and deliberate; it is the real purpose of the activity, and an audience is important. In this respect, the terror involved in an individual robbery, for example, differs from the fear created by a terrorist. In the latter, the immediate victim is not the important focus; the emphasis is on the larger audience.[17] It is in this respect that terrorism differs significantly from violent personal crimes.

One final definition of terrorism is relevant. Law professor H. H. A. Cooper, a noted international authority on terrorism, published an article in 2001 in which he referred to his definition of terrorism, which he said evolved during his 25-year teaching career. According to Cooper, "Terrorism is the intentional generation of massive fear by human beings for the purpose of securing or maintaining control over other human beings." He continued, "Terrorism is not a struggle for the hearts and minds of the victims nor for their immortal souls. Rather, it is, as Humpty Dumpty would have said, about who is to be master, that is all." It is a "naked struggle for power, who shall wield it, and to what ends." Cooper admitted that the definition of terrorism is "as needful and as illusory as ever." But, he said, as with pornography, "we know it well enough when we see it."[18]

Because there is no consensus on the definition of *terrorism*, it is not possible to recite a particular history of the acts that constitute this crime. Nor is there agreement on the history of terrorism or who are terrorists. For example, consider the discussion in Focus 10.5. Would you consider a person who spends over 20 years as a law-abiding citizen a terrorist because, in her earlier life, she committed acts that could be considered those of a terrorist?

The Federal Criminal Code

Traditional criminal statutes, such as those prohibiting murder, robbery, or conspiracy, may be used to prosecute terrorist acts, but the federal criminal code, as well as individual state criminal codes, contains statutes expressly prohibiting terrorism, along with definitions of the term.

The federal criminal code defines two types of terrorism: international and domestic. Those definitions are as follows:

(1) the term "international terrorism" means activities that—

(A) involve violent acts or acts dangerous to human life that are a violation of the criminal laws of the United States or of any State, or that would be a criminal violation if committed within the jurisdiction of the United States or of any State;

(B) appear to be intended—

(i) to intimidate or coerce a civilian population;

(ii) to influence the policy of a government by intimidation or coercion; or

(iii) to affect the conduct of a government by mass destruction, assassination or kidnapping; and

(C) occur primarily outside the territorial jurisdiction of the United States, or transcend national boundaries in terms of the means by which they are accomplished, the persons they appear intended to intimidate or coerce, or the locale in which their perpetrators operate or seek asylum; . . .

(5) the term "domestic terrorism" means activities that—

(A) involve acts dangerous to human life that are a violation of the criminal laws of the United States or of any State;

(B) appear to be intended—

(i) to intimidate or coerce a civilian population;

(ii) to influence the policy of a government by intimidation or coercion; or

(iii) to affect the conduct of a government by mass destruction, assassination, or kidnapping; and

(C) occur primarily within the territorial jurisdiction of the United States.[19]

Examples of State Terrorism Statutes
In its government code, California defines an "act of terrorism" as "any unlawful harm, attempted harm, or threat to do harm to any state employee, state property, or the person or property of any person on the premises of any state-occupied building or other property leased or owned by the state."[20]

California's penal code contains several provisions relating to terrorist acts. Title 7 is entitled the "California Street Terrorism Enforcement and Prevention Act." These statutes are aimed at preventing the terrorism caused by street gangs. The statute states that, although it is not the intention of the legislature to infringe on the civil rights of anyone in California, the state is under siege with street gangs and all persons in the state are entitled to protection against the terrorist acts of such gangs.[21]

FOCUS 10.5   Who Is a Terrorist?

An article in the *New York Times* magazine in May 2001 was entitled "Was This Soccer Mom a Terrorist?" The article referred to Sara Jane Olson, who was going on trial for crimes she was alleged to have committed 25 years previously when, as Kathleen Soliah, she befriended the Symbionese Liberation Army (SLA), the radical group that kidnapped newspaper heiress Patricia Hearst in 1974. Olson, the wife of a doctor and mother of three daughters, was often identified after her arrest as a "soccer mom" and was portrayed by some as an outstanding mother, wife, and citizen. Her family apparently did not know of Olson's background.[1]

The FBI viewed Olson as a fugitive terrorist. FBI authorities captured her in July 1999 and charged her with conspiring with the SLA to bomb two Los Angeles Police Department vehicles in August 1975. Specifically, Olson, 52 when she was arrested, was accused of placing two pipe bombs under Los Angeles police cars in retaliation for the shoot-out. The bombs did not go off, and some of the targeted police were in the courtroom when bail was set at $1 million for Olson. Also in the Los Angeles courtroom were Olson's husband and three daughters, along with many friends from Minnesota. Olson was released on bail pending her trial. Subsequently, in a surprise move after a plea bargain with prosecutors, she entered guilty pleas, only to declare later in the courthouse hall that she was innocent. Back in the courtroom, she again entered guilty pleas. The judge was concerned, declaring that the "integrity of the criminal justice system is at stake" and that "[a] guilty plea is not a way-station on the way to a press conference."[2]

Olson was initially sentenced to two 10-year-to-life terms, but the judge said it would be up to the state Board of Prison Terms to determine how long she served. The board determined 14 years, then in September 2004 the board reduced that to 13 years but added one year to her 6-year term for the crime discussed next.

On the day that she was sentenced by the judge, Olson was charged with robbery and murder for the death of a bank customer who was killed during a robbery by members of the SLA, including Patricia Hearst, who identified Olson as one of those present at the robbery. Hearst was convicted for her involvement with the SLA's bank robbery while she was being held captive after the SLA kidnapped her. She was granted immunity and was expected to be the major prosecution witness in the trial of Olson and other SLA members, Emily Montague (who fired the shot that killed the victim), her ex-husband William Harris, and Michael Bortin.[3] In July 2002, however, the defendants entered into negotiated pleas of guilty of second-degree murder. In February 2003 all were formally sentenced to prison—Montague, eight years; Harris, seven years; Bortin and Olson, each six years.

The crimes charged against these SLA members illustrate an important point about terrorism: No matter how it is defined, acts that some might consider terrorist may be prosecuted under traditional criminal statutes, such as robbery, murder, and conspiracy.

In March 2008 Olson was released from prison in California but was arrested a week later when authorities realized that they had released her too early. She was released on parole in March 2009.

1. Maryanne Vollers, "Was This Soccer Mom a Terrorist?" *New York Times Magazine* (20 May 2001), p. 38.
2. "70's Radical Reaffirms Guilty Plea," *New York Times* (7 November 2001), p. 14.
3. "Patty Hearst's Credibility Challenged in SLA Case," *San Francisco Chronicle* (3 August 2002), p. 13.

Title 1 of the California Penal Code contains several sections pertaining to weapons of mass destruction and is referred to as the Hertzberg-Alarcon California Prevention of Terrorism Act. The legislative findings cited in this act, enacted in 1999, are as follows:

> The Legislature hereby finds and declares that the threat of terrorism involving weapons of mass destruction, including, but not limited to, chemical, biological, nuclear, or radiological agents, is a significant public safety concern. The Legislature also recognizes that terrorism involving weapons of mass destruction could result in an intentional disaster placing residents of California in great peril. The Legislature also finds it necessary to sanction the possession, manufacture, use, or threatened use of chemical, biological, nuclear, or radiological weapons, as well as the intentional use or threatened use of industrial or commercial chemicals as weapons against persons or animals.[22]

Some jurisdictions do not include in their statutes specific acts defined as terrorism but, rather, define *terrorism* in general terms and then indicate that the commission of specific acts under the listed conditions constitute *terrorism*. For example, Alabama enumerates specific offenses as predicate offenses for an act of terrorism. These offenses constitute subdivision (4) in the following statute from the Alabama Criminal Code's Anti-Terrorism Act of 2002:

> (1) Act of terrorism. An act or acts constituting a specified offense as defined in subdivision (4) for which a person may be convicted in the criminal courts of this state, or an act or acts constituting an offense in any other jurisdiction within or outside the territorial boundaries of the United States which contains all of the essential elements of a specified offense, that is intended to do the following:
>
> a. Intimidate or coerce a civilian population.
>
> b. Influence the policy of a unit of government by intimidation or coercion.
>
> c. Affect the conduct of a unit of government by murder, assassination, or kidnapping.
>
> (2) Material support or resources. Currency or other financial securities, financial services, lodging, training, safehouses, false documentation or identification, communications equipment, facilities, weapons, lethal substances, explosives, personnel, transportation, and other physical assets, except medicine or religious materials.
>
> (3) Renders criminal assistance.
>
> (4) Specified offense. A Class A felony, manslaughter, kidnapping in the second degree, assault in the first or second degree, stalking, intimidating a witness, criminal tampering, or any attempt or conspiracy to commit any of these offenses.[23]

Some state terrorism and terrorism-related statutes are in direct response to the terrorist acts of 9/11. The Vermont Public Safety Act of 2002, for example, in its statement of purpose, attributes that state's need for a counterterrorism statute as being required by the events of 9/11. That section also states that the purpose of the statute is to protect the state's citizens, not to deny them their civil rights and liberties.[24]

One final example of state approaches to terrorism is that of New York. That state's statute defines *terrorism* as follows:

> 1. "Act of terrorism":
>
> (a) for purposes of this article means an act or acts constituting a specified offense as defined in subdivision three of this section for which a person may be convicted in the criminal courts of this state pursuant to article twenty of the criminal procedure law, or an act or acts constituting an offense in any other jurisdiction within or outside the territorial boundaries of the United States which contains all of the essential elements of a specified offense, that is intended to:
>
> (i) intimidate or coerce a civilian population;
>
> (ii) influence the policy of a unit of government by intimidation or coercion; or
>
> (iii) affect the conduct of a unit of government by murder, assassination or kidnapping; or . . .
>
> 3. (a) "Specified offense" for purposes of this article means a class A felony offense [with some exceptions], . . . a violent felony

offense . . . manslaughter in the second degree . . . criminal tampering in the first degree . . . identity theft in the second degree . . . identity theft in the first degree . . . unlawful possession of personal identification information in the second degree . . . unlawful possession of personal identification information in the first degree . . . [and specified degrees of money laundering in support of terrorism].[25]

New York also has other statutes relating to terrorism. Among them are the following:

✪ Hindering prosecution of terrorism in the first degree[26]

✪ Criminal possession of a chemical weapon or biological weapon in the first degree[27]

✪ Criminal use of a chemical weapon or biological weapon in the first degree[28]

✪ Soliciting or providing support for an act of terrorism in the first degree[29]

The Categories of Terrorism

Long before the recent terrorist attacks in the United States and in other countries, attempts were made to categorize terrorism. The Task Force on Disorders and Terrorism, mentioned earlier, which was directed by H. H. A. Cooper, divided terrorism into six categories:

✪ *Civil disorders*: "[A] form of collective violence interfering with the peace, security, and normal functioning of the community."

✪ *Political terrorism*: "[V]iolent criminal behavior designed primarily to generate fear in the community, or a substantial segment of it, for political purposes."

✪ *Nonpolitical terrorism*: Terrorism that is not aimed at political purposes but that exhibits "conscious design to create and maintain a high degree of fear for coercive purposes, but the end is individual or collective gain rather than the achievement of a political objective."

✪ *Quasi-terrorism*: "Those activities incidental to the commission of crimes of violence that are similar in form and method to true terrorism but which nevertheless lack its essential ingredient." It is not the main purpose of the quasi-terrorists "to induce terror in the instant victim," as in the case of true terrorism. Typi-cally, the fleeing felon who takes a hostage is a quasi-terrorist, whose methods are similar to those of the true terrorist but whose purposes are quite different.

✪ *Limited political terrorism*: "[A]cts of terrorism which are committed for ideological or political motives but which are not part of a concerted campaign to capture control of the State." Limited political terrorism differs from real terrorism in the former's lack of a revolutionary approach.

✪ *Official or state terrorism*: Activities carried out by "nations whose rule is based upon fear and oppression that reach terrorist proportions."[30]

Any of these categories of terrorism may consist of acts or threats or both.

Terrorist acts may also be categorized as *classical* or as *modern*. The Task Force discussed several characteristics that distinguish modern terrorism from classical terrorism. First, as the result of our technological vulnerability, the potential for harm is greater today than in the past. This development, which includes improved intercontinental travel and mass communication, has also increased the bargaining power of the modern terrorist. Second, television has carried the activities of terrorists to the entire world, giving modern terrorists more power than classical terrorists. Finally, modern terrorists believe that through violence they can maintain or increase hope for their causes. Some of these points are demonstrated in the discussions of recent terrorist acts on American soil presented in Focus 10.6.

In addition to categorizing terrorism, it is possible to articulate some of the objectives, strategies, and tactics of terrorist acts and of terrorists.

Terrorism Objectives, Strategies, and Tactics

A primary objective of terrorists is to create violence or to instill the fear of violence as well as to destroy the confidence people have in their government.

Terrorist groups have been categorized as *xenofighters*, who fight for foreigners, or *homofighters*, who fight for their own people. Often xenofighters are seeking removal of a foreign power or a change of political boundaries regarding a foreign power. They have such goals as the following:

✪ To attract international attention

✪ To harm the relations of the target country with other nations

FOCUS 10.6   Terrorist Acts in the United States: A Sample

Numerous examples of terrorist attacks on American soil could be cited, along with the many that have occurred in other countries. This focus summarizes only a few, ranging from the most violent, the terrorist acts of 11 September 2001, to the 1963 church bombing that killed four little African American girls. The similarities between those two terrorist acts are noted.

The Terrorist Acts of 9/11

In the largest terrorist acts that have ever occurred on U.S. soil, more than 3,000 people died when carefully coordinated hijacked airplanes were flown into the twin towers of the World Trade Center in New York City—two of the tallest buildings in the world, representing the financial strength of the United States—and the Pentagon in Washington, D.C.—one of the sources of U.S. government and military strength. A fourth hijacked plane, apparently headed for another Washington, D.C., building (perhaps the U.S. Capitol or the White House), crashed in a Pennsylvania field after passengers presumably fought with the hijackers. The death toll would have been much higher, but thousands were able to evacuate the World Trade Center towers before they collapsed.

Immediate reactions to the events of 9/11 were swift and significant. All U.S. airports were closed until 13 September, when planes were once again allowed to fly but with increased security, creating long waits at airport check-ins and security checkpoints and reduced flight schedules.

The Reign of the Unabomber

In April 1996 Theodore "Ted" Kaczynski was arrested in a small cabin in Montana for allegedly committing the crimes attributed to the *Unabomber*. In June he was charged with several Unabomber crimes and moved to Sacramento, California, to await his first trial. Ironically, the man who shunned high technology found that one of the best pieces of evidence against him was the old standard typewriter seized from his cabin. It was alleged that the 35,000-word Unabomber manifesto was written on that typewriter.[1]

The Unabomber terrorized the nation for 17 years, causing 3 deaths and 22 injuries, along with property damage associated with the mailed bombs. Kaczynski was identified after his brother and sister-in-law reported to their attorney that they suspected him, based on their reading of a manifesto, part of which was published by the media. Kaczynski was arrested peacefully at his one-room mountain shack in Montana. Kaczynski is a former University of California–Berkeley math professor, a loner who dropped out of university life and discontinued contacts with his friends and even his family.

Kaczynski was tried in California for the deaths resulting from the bombs mailed from Sacramento. He pleaded not guilty to the charges but subsequently entered into a plea bargain that resulted in a life sentence and thus enabled him to avoid the death penalty. Kaczynski, who was representing himself at the time, appealed, alleging that his plea was not voluntary. The Ninth Circuit Court of Appeals denied his motion for a new trial, and in 2002 the U.S. Supreme Court refused to review the case.[2]

The Oklahoma City Bombing

On 19 April 1995, 168 people were killed when a massive bomb ripped through the Alfred P. Murrah Federal Building in Oklahoma City, Oklahoma. Timothy McVeigh and Terry L. Nichols were charged with the bombing. The defendants were successful in their motions for separate trials and a change of venue. They were tried in Denver, Colorado, on federal charges. McVeigh was convicted of murder and conspiracy and sentenced to death. After one postponement, he was executed in June 2001.

Nichols was convicted of conspiracy and manslaughter (but not of murder) in his federal trial and sentenced to life in prison. He was subsequently tried in Oklahoma on state murder charges. He was convicted but was not sentenced to death.

The third defendant, Michael Fortier, who was accused of having knowledge of the plot to bomb the building but did not notify authorities, pleaded guilty to the following crimes:

- Conspiring to transport stolen firearms
- Transporting stolen firearms
- Making a false statement to the FBI
- **Misprision of felony** (the act of concealing a felony committed by another but without any involvement in that felony that would constitute an accessory before or after the fact)

Fortier was sentenced to 12 years in prison. He appealed and was resentenced to the same term. After serving 85 percent of his sentence, he was released in January 2006. It was reported that he and his family asked U.S. Marshals Service to grant them new identities and protection under the federal witness protection program, known as the Witness Security Program. Fortier's attorney, Michael McGuire, and government prosecutors declined to comment on that speculation.[3]

Terrorist Acts at U.S. Abortion Clinics

Since abortion was legalized in 1973, when the U.S. Supreme Court decided *Roe v. Wade*,[4] some protestors have turned violent, engaging in bombings and shootings at abortion clinics.

continued

Protestors argue that the only way they can prevent a greater harm (death of a fetus) is to protest at abortion clinics by attempting to prevent pregnant women (or doctors) from entering the clinics. The extreme cases involve killing the women or the physicians as they approach the clinics or bombing the clinics and possibly injuring or killing many persons and causing extensive property damage.

During the 1980s approximately 40 bombings occurred at abortion clinics in the United States; in the following decade bombings increased and murders occurred. Court orders were issued and legislation was enacted in states and in the federal system in an effort to curtail violence at abortion clinics.[5]

In May 1994 President Bill Clinton signed a bill that prohibits bombings, arson, and blockades at abortion clinics, along with shootings and threats of violence against doctors, nurses, and other abortion clinic employees. Under the Freedom of Access to Clinic Entrances Act (FACE), blocking access to abortion clinics is a federal crime, with violent offenders facing heavy fines and prison sentences upon conviction.[6]

The 1963 Church Bombing and the 2001, 2002 Trials

The bomb ripped through the basement of the Sixteenth Street Baptist Church in Birmingham, Alabama, on 15 September 1963, killing four African American girls: Addie Mae Collins, Cynthia Wesley, and Carole Robertson, all 14, and Denise McNair, 11. The case ended in May 2002 when a jury of black and white men and women convicted white supremacist Bobby Frank Cherry, 71, of murder. In 2001 the second defendant, Thomas Blanton Jr., was convicted and sentenced to life in prison.

The bombing target was a church that provided space for civil rights meetings, and the criminal acts occurred just days after the city's public schools had been integrated after a long court battle. Both Cherry and Blanton were members of the Ku Klux Klan, a secret organization located primarily in the South and devoted to suppressing the newly acquired rights of African Americans. The Klan was associated with using violence to achieve its objectives. Initial efforts to prosecute those accused in this church bombing case were ended in 1968 after then FBI director J. Edgar Hoover had decided, in 1965, that it would be difficult to get a guilty verdict. Two others involved in the bombing, Herman Cash and Troy Ingram, died before they were prosecuted; a final defendant, Robert Chambliss, was convicted in 1977 and died in prison.

In an analysis of the 1963 bombings and the 2002 trial, one commentator compared the 15 September 1963 terrorist acts with those of 11 September 2001. Both were "unthinkable," and both involved persons who described themselves as "religious warriors fighting off godless modernity and the imperial will of the U.S. government."[7] Both involved innocent victims.

1. "A Circumstantial Case: Low-Tech Typewriter May Help Convict Unabomber Suspect," *American Bar Association Journal* 82 (June 1996): 18.
2. *United States v. Kaczynski*, 239 F.3d 1108 (9th Cir. 2001), *cert. denied*, 535 U.S. 933 (2002).
3. "Key McVeigh Case Witness Seeking U.S. Protection," *Buffalo News* (26 June 2005), p. 13.
4. *Roe v. Wade*, 410 U.S. 113 (1973).
5. See, for example, *Madison v. Women's Health Center*, 512 U.S. 753 (1994).
6. Freedom of Access to Clinic Entrances Act of 1994, USCS, Title 18, Section 248 (2009).
7. "Echoes of 9/11 in Church Bombing Case," *The Record* (Bergen County, N.J.), (29 May 2002), p. L09.

- To cause insecurity and to damage the economy and public order in the target country

- To build feelings of distrust and hostility toward the government among the target country's population

- To cause actual damage to civilians, security forces, and property in the target country[31]

Homofighters must win the support of their compatriots in their fight to discredit their own government; thus, they must adopt policies that do not alienate the citizenry. One approach is the *Robin Hood demand*, in which terrorists use an acceptable cause to justify their unacceptable tactics. The kidnapping of Patricia Hearst in 1974 is an example. The Symbionese Liberation Army (SLA) demanded that Hearst's family distribute free food to the needy.

Some of the strategies and tactics used by homofighters are as follows:

- Undermining internal security, public order, and the economy in order to create distrust of the government's ability to maintain control

- Acquiring popular sympathy and support by positive action

⚙ Generating popular repulsion from extreme counterterrorist repressive measures

⚙ Damaging hated foreign interests

⚙ Harming the international position of the existing regime

⚙ Causing physical damage and harassing persons and institutions that represent the ruling regime[32]

Terrorism Victims

In one sense all of society is victimized by terrorist acts. The action taken against the immediate victim is coercive, designed to impress others. The immediate victims may be involved incidentally, as when they are killed by a randomly placed bomb, or they may be selected with considerable discrimination, as, for example, when a prominent politician is assassinated or a businessperson is kidnapped. Terrorism is characterized by gross indifference toward the victims, which includes their dehumanization and their treatment as mere elements in a deadly power play. All of these characteristics were evident in the terrorist acts of 9/11.

The randomness of victimization by terrorism is illustrated by most of the examples discussed earlier. The ultimate objective of the terrorist, particularly the political terrorist, is the establishment of a bargaining position, so the identity of the victims is unimportant in most cases. Kidnapping and taking hostages are terrorist techniques par excellence for this purpose. The victims are treated largely as objects to be traded for what the terrorist wants: money, release of prisoners, publication of manifestos, escape, and so on. These bargains are extralegal and rest on a recognition of the powers of life and death that the terrorist holds over victims. This aspect raises serious social, political, and humanitarian issues for those who must make these awesome decisions affecting the lives and safety of the victims. For example, the United States, England, and other countries refused to negotiate with Iraqi terrorists who captured their citizens and threatened to behead them if the countries did not follow their demands—to withdraw troops from Iraq, release Iraqi women from English prisons, and so on. The 2004 executions of British citizen Kenneth Bigley, 62, along with Americans Jack Hensley, 48, and Eugene Armstrong, 52, all taken hostage in Iraq, came after pleas from their families to spare their lives. The beheadings were filmed and made public.

Terrorist victimization produces special individual and collective traumas. Many hostages and kidnap victims experience incongruous feelings toward their captors, and the events may constitute a serious challenge to their own value systems. The most striking manifestation of this is the **Stockholm syndrome**, named after an incident that occurred in the Swedish capital in 1973. The *Stockholm syndrome* is an incongruous feeling of empathy toward the hostage takers and a displacement of frustration and aggression on the part of the victims toward authorities. In some terrorist acts, such as those of 9/11, death and destruction occur so rapidly that the Stockholm syndrome concept is not applicable. In others, such as the kidnapping of Patty Hearst, the syndrome applies. Hearst identified with her captors and was subsequently convicted of willingly participating with them in a bank robbery. In 2001 Hearst was pardoned by President Bill Clinton.

Another way in which many individuals are victimized by terrorist attacks is in the creation of fear that leads people to change their lifestyles. This result has occurred among many Americans who were not direct victims of the 9/11 events but who fear additional terrorist acts. Perhaps the fear of flying that led many to cancel flights (or decline to book them) after these events was the greatest manifestation of the fear created by the terrorist acts of that day. All Americans were victimized by the enormous cost to taxpayers of

The United States refuses to negotiate with those who hold her citizens as hostages, and some hostages have been killed. Before the killings the terrorists, such as these in Iraq, shown with their captives, often use the media to publicize the hostage-taking and their intentions of killing that innocent person or, in many cases, persons. (AP IMages)

the increased airport and other types of security instituted after the 9/11 attacks. The initial declines in the stock market and massive layoffs and firings at some companies sent shock waves throughout much of the economy. These and other financial setbacks are, to some extent, associated with the terrorist acts of 9/11.

Victimization as we have known it, however, may be mild compared to the implications of the next topic: weapons of mass destruction.

Weapons of Mass Destruction (WMDs)

Terrorism today is potentially more deadly than in the past, as we now have weapons that have the capacity to destroy not only thousands or millions of people but also entire cities, states, and countries. The seriousness and potential harm from weapons of mass destruction (WMDs), along with the belief that Iraq had WMDs and would use them, led the United States and Great Britain to invade and occupy Iraq in the spring of 2003 despite the lack of support from other countries and the inability of United Nations inspectors to locate such weapons in 2002 and 2003. The war was still in progress as of this writing; no WMDs had been found.

Preparedness to combat WMDs occurs at the national and the state levels in the United States. At the national level, the FBI refers to WMDs as a *serious concern* and states that the agency utilizes "all the tools we use to combat terrorists, spies, and criminals—to counter the threat." The FBI's work falls into four areas. First, the FBI coordinates national efforts, including countermeasures and preparedness, investigative and operations, and intelligence analysis. Second, the FBI works on the local level, with a highly trained WMD coordinator in each of its 56 field offices. Third, the FBI has an outreach and information-sharing program that includes dialogue and work with the private sectors, "such as the chemical and agricultural industries, to increase awareness and sensitivities to potential threats and to facilitate reporting of information with potential intelligence value." Finally, the FBI works with law enforcement agencies, first responders, and health agencies at the local levels to stage mock exercises and coordinate efforts for the agency's fourth focus: preparedness.[33]

The FBI defines a *WMD* as follows:

- "Any explosive or incendiary device [as defined in the federal criminal code]: bomb, grenade, rocket, missile, mine, or other device with a charge of more than four ounces;

- Any weapon designed or intended to cause death or serious bodily injury through the release, dissemination, or impact of toxic or poisonous chemicals or their precursors;

With the emergence of weapons of mass destruction, terrorists can kill millions of people and destroy huge geographical areas in a few moments. (IStockPhoto)

⚙ Any weapon involving a disease organism; or

⚙ Any weapon designed to release radiation or radioactivity at a level dangerous to human life."[34]

The United Nations (UN) also focuses on countering WMDs. The UN's Weapons of Mass Destruction Branch provides support in the areas of nuclear, chemical, and biological weapons, following the developments and trends in all of these areas and participating in "multilateral efforts to strengthen the international norm on disarmament and non-proliferation" of WMDs. In particular, the UN focuses on compliance with the Treaty on the Non-Proliferation of Nuclear Weapons, which became effective on 5 March 1970 and has been signed by 190 international states. The goal of this effort is to "promote cooperation in the peaceful uses of nuclear energy and to further the goal of achieving nuclear disarmament and general and complete disarmament."[35]

Individual states within the United States have also taken legislative action to counter WMDs and other terrorist threats. For example, in its recently enacted antiterrorism statute, Virginia defines a *weapon of terrorism* as:

> any device or material that is designed, intended or used to cause death, bodily injury or serious bodily harm, through the release, dissemination, or impact of (i) poisonous chemicals; (ii) an infectious biological substance; or (iii) release of radiation or radioactivity.[36]

Virginia statutes provide that if a victim dies as the result of a terrorist act, the perpetrator may be charged with capital murder.[37]

The following sections examine two WMDs that have been around for some time—chemical agents and biological agents—before looking at the more recently developed nuclear devices.

Chemical Agents

In his book *The New Terrorism: Fanaticism and the Arms of Mass Destruction*, Walter Laqueur traced the idea of using poisonous gas to destroy the enemy back to the 1870s in England, but it was not actually used until 1915, when the Germans killed 5,000 and injured others by use of this method. Since that time poisonous gas has been used primarily in the Middle East, specifically by Iraq against Iran. Numerous chemical agents available today are not gases but liquids that can be divided and used as droplets. The problem with using these means for terrorist acts today is that they are more difficult to disseminate effectively. They are affected by wind and air; some are not effective in water reservoirs. Laqueur concluded:

> While in laboratory conditions a few milligrams might be sufficient to kill several thousand human beings, experts believe that tons of poison would be needed in the open air or in water because there are always biological activities that diminish the toxicity of the agent.[38]

Despite the dissemination problems, the most devastating effect of chemical agents used for terrorist reasons is the psychological impact the fear of them has on potential victims. According to Laqueur, "Even the authors of books on gas warfare in the 1930s warned that an enemy would launch such an attack mainly because of its devastating psychological impact."[39]

Biological Agents

The potential for **bioterrorism**—the use of biological agents, such as the spread of smallpox—in terrorist threats or attacks also creates fear. The biological agents that are a terrorist threat today are of recent origin, but bioterrorism has a long history, with biological warfare used as far back as the fourteenth century. There is a dispute regarding the use of biological warfare after World War II, but major nations conducted research and built stockpiles of biological weapons.[40]

There has never been a "single successful biological-weapons attack by terrorists," but the concern is that such weapons could become a reality, not just a threat. Interest in biological warfare is keen because it is believed that biological weapons are more cost-effective than other methods of killing or incapacitating people. Some of the advantages of biological over other types of weapons are the following:

⚙ Biological weapons are easier to produce.

⚙ They are less expensive than other weapons.

⚙ They are difficult to detect.

⚙ They cause economic damage (e.g., to crops) as well as injury and death to humans.

⚙ They can be produced in places such as garages, tool rooms, or kitchens.

⚙ They can cause as much fear and panic as other weapons and perhaps even more than chemical agents.[41]

In 2002 U.S. health officials expressed concern that the smallpox virus, the deadly disease against which most have been vaccinated and that we thought had been eradicated, would be unleashed as a terrorist weapon. Plans were being made for a possible widespread bioterrorist attack with this dreaded disease. A statement about preparation for reacting to a bioterrorist attack of smallpox, obtained from the Centers for Disease Control and Prevention, is reproduced in Focus 10.7.

States have also reacted to the possibility of a widespread bioterrorist attack. For example, Virginia has a statute defining *bioterrorism* against crops and animals as a felony. The statute provides as follows:

> Any person who maliciously destroys or devastates agricultural crops or agricultural animals having a value of $2,500 or more through the use of an infectious biological substance with the intent to (i) intimidate the civilian population or (ii) influence the conduct or activities of the government of the United States, a state or locality through intimidation, is guilty of a Class 3 felony.[42]

Nuclear Devices

A third method of biological warfare is the use of nuclear devices. This method constituted a great fear after World War II, which had experienced the use of nuclear bombs dropped by the United States over Hiroshima and Nagasaki after the Japanese bombed Pearl Harbor. Movies and novels about nuclear attacks fueled the fear, but by 1975 these had declined, along with public interest in them. Scientists, however, continued to be preoccupied with the possibility of a nuclear attack, and nations prepared for such. In his brief discussion of the issue, Walter Laqueur concluded as follows:

> Though the danger of a nuclear attack by a hostile country or a terrorist group has figured prominently in the public consciousness and expert commentary, after more than fifty years of books, movies, and war games, the horrible event has not yet come to pass. It is not surprising, then, that there is now a belief among some experts that nuclear terrorism has been an overrated nightmare.[43]

Not everyone agrees with that assessment, however, and the threat of a nuclear attack remains of concern. In April 2008, the U.S. Senate Committee on Homeland Security and Government Affairs considered the impact of a possible nuclear attack near the U.S. White House. The director of the Institute of Health Management and Mass Destruction Defense at the University of Georgia testified before that committee: "I definitely conclude the threat is greater and is increasing every year with the march of technology." The hearing was the third that this committee had conducted in recent months.[44]

Cyberterrorism

Chapter 8 discussed the impact of computers on life in general and on crime in particular. The use of the Internet for terrorist threats, called **cyberterrorism**, is also of concern. Cyberterrorism involves disseminat-

---

FOCUS 10.7   Bioterrorism and the Smallpox Threat

The website for the Centers for Disease Control and Prevention posted the following information about preparation for a bioterrorist attack involving the dissemination of smallpox, a disease that has been virtually eliminated in the United States, for which there is no cure, only prevention through vaccination.

Smallpox is an acute, contagious, and sometimes fatal disease caused by the variola virus (an orthopoxvirus), and marked by fever and a distinctive progressive skin rash. In 1980, the disease was declared eradicated following worldwide vaccination programs. However, in the aftermath of the events of September and October, 2001, the U.S. government is taking precautions to be ready to deal with a bioterrorist attack using smallpox as a weapon. As a result of these efforts: 1) There is a detailed nationwide smallpox preparedness program to protect Americans against smallpox as a biological weapon. This program includes the creation of preparedness teams that are ready to respond to a smallpox attack on the United States. Members of these teams—health care and public health workers—are being vaccinated so that they might safely protect others in the event of a smallpox outbreak. 2) There is enough smallpox vaccine to vaccinate everyone who would need it in the event of an emergency. (Last reviewed 6 February 2007.)

Source: Centers for Disease Control and Prevention, http://www.bt.cdc.gov/agent/smallpox/disease/faq.asp, accessed 26 July 2008.

ing viruses or even destroying an entire information infrastructure. It does not carry the threats of immediate injury, property destruction, or even death that may result from the other methods of mass destruction, but its harmful effects can be far-reaching and frightening. Chapter 8, for example, discussed *identity theft*, which can result in severe economic losses to its victims. Other harmful uses of the computer are:

- Dissemination of information on how to build bombs and other destructive devices

- Information on how to infiltrate or destroy telecommunication networks

- Posting of terrorist propaganda urging action

- Computer viruses

- "Logic bombs, set to detonate at a certain time and destroy or rewrite data"

- "High-energy radio frequency guns that disable electronic targets through high-power radio signals"[45]

Although much of the potentially dangerous information disseminated through computers can also be located in books, the difference is that with the use of the Internet, more information can be dispersed to more people in a much shorter time and with less risk of detection.

THE CONTROL OF TERRORISM

What is the most effective way to respond to terrorism? If the government meets the demands of the terrorists, does that concession raise the specter of creating inconvenient or unreasonable precedents for the handling of future incidents? Ted Robert Gurr, author of *Why Men Rebel*, said, "The most fundamental human response to the use of force is counterforce. Force threatens and angers men. Threatened, they try to defend themselves; angered, they want to retaliate."[46]

After terrorist attacks on U.S. planes, skyjacked in large numbers in the 1970s, increased security measures were implemented in U.S. airports, and skyjacking decreased. But terrorists are adaptable, as demonstrated by their planting of bombs *outside* the secure areas of airports. It was obvious on 9/11 that increased security efforts were not sufficient to prevent terrorist attacks. The 9/11 hijackers boarded airplanes carrying box cutters, which were apparently used to subdue and

murder flight attendants. And even with the increased security that followed those attacks, passengers have boarded planes with knives and guns.

In December 2001 Richard C. Reid boarded a U.S.-bound flight in Paris, France, with explosives in his shoes. He was overpowered (he subsequently pleaded guilty to attempting to blow up the plane and was sentenced to life in prison), but the fact that he got on board is a cause of concern. Even more stringent security measures were put into effect in the aftermath of this and other security breaches since 9/11.

Security has been increased by non-American airlines, too, but in November 2002, a passenger with a switchblade struck a flight attendant on an Israeli passenger jet as it approached landing in Istanbul. The hijacking suspect, Tevfik Fukra, then headed for the cockpit but was restrained by air marshals flying in civilian clothes. Fortunately, there were no injuries among the 168 people on board El Al Flight 581, but once again airline passengers had reason to be concerned about flight security.[47] (For a more detailed discussion of flight rage, see again Focus 5.2)

The National Level

Legislation is a major approach to controlling terrorism at both national and state levels. Some of the legislation is based on the recommendations of a national commission that was appointed after 9/11 to study terrorist acts in the United States.

The 9/11 Commission

After the 9/11 terrorist attacks, the U.S. Congress and President Bush created the National Commission on Terrorist Attacks upon the United States, known as the 9/11 Commission. After interviewing more than 1,200 people in 10 countries, holding 10 days of hearings, and taking testimony from over 160 witnesses, along with reviewing more than 2.5 million pages of documents, the commission presented its 567 pages of findings and recommendations to the Congress, the president, and the public in the summer of 2004. The commission members concluded the following:

> We learned about an enemy who is sophisticated, patient, disciplined, and lethal. The enemy rallies broad support in the Arab and Muslim world by demanding redress of political grievances, but its hostility toward us and our values is limitless. Its purpose is to rid the world of religious and

political pluralism, the plebiscite, and equal rights for women. It makes no distinction between military and civilian targets. *Collateral damage* is not in its lexicon.[48]

The commission made the following five major recommendations for reorganizing the government:

⊙ "unifying strategic intelligence and operational planning against Islamist terrorists across the foreign-domestic divide with a National Counterterrorism Center;

⊙ unifying the intelligence community with a new National Intelligence Director;

⊙ unifying the many participants in the counterterrorism effort and their knowledge in a network-based information-sharing system that transcends traditional governmental boundaries;

⊙ unifying and strengthening congressional oversight to improve quality and accountability;

⊙ and strengthening the FBI and homeland defenders."[49]

The commission issued its report on 22 July 2004, but it was highly controversial,[50] and many questions remain, not only about the 9/11 Commission report but also about the possibility of additional terrorist acts. Public debate centered on how to secure peace and safety in U.S. airports and other places in which large numbers of people gather. The terrorist acts of 9/11 targeted the United States, but the nation's allies were aware that other countries could be next.

Some of the recommendations of the 9/11 Commission, including the national intelligence director, are provided by the Intelligence Reform and Terrorism Prevention Act of 2004, which is discussed later in this chapter.

Legislation at the national level also followed the April 1995 terrorist bombing of the federal building in Oklahoma City, Oklahoma.

The Antiterrorism and Effective Death Penalty Act of 1996

Shortly before the first anniversary of the April 1995 bombing of the federal building in Oklahoma City, the Antiterrorism and Effective Death Penalty Act of 1996 was passed. This act is an extensive piece of legislation. Among other provisions, this statute restricts the le-

gal opportunities for death row and other inmates to appeal their sentences. It makes it more difficult for foreign terrorist groups to raise money in the United States and provides for easier deportation of alien terrorists. It authorizes funds for fighting terrorism in the United States. The statute contains provisions for terrorism victims, such as mandatory restitution, and a provision for victims to have access to closed-circuit television to view a trial that has been moved more than 350 miles from the venue in which they were victimized by a terrorist act.[51]

After the 9/11 terrorist acts, the White House and Congress also enacted measures to make it more difficult for terrorists to operate. One method was to freeze the financial assets of those thought to have aided the terrorist acts of 9/11. The most controversial legislation, however, was the Uniting and Strengthening America by Providing Appropriate Tools Required to Intercept and Obstruct Terrorism Act, known best by its shortened name, the **USA Patriot Act**.

The USA Patriot Act

In the fall of 2001, President George W. Bush signed legislation approved by Congress that would expand the powers of law enforcement to deal with terrorism threats. The USA Patriot Act included, among others, the following general powers:

⊙ Expansion of wiretaps on terrorist suspects' e-mail, use of the Internet, and telephone conversations

⊙ Tighter controls on immigration

⊙ Greater control on money laundering (discussed in Chapter 11)[52]

The extensive USA Patriot Act was enacted so quickly that, according to some critics, there was insufficient debate on its 157 sections. Others took the position that we needed legislation quickly and could not take time for more debate under the extraordinary circumstances of 9/11 and its aftermath.

By spring 2003 the Bush administration proposed even more comprehensive measures for security, while the American Civil Liberties Union (ACLU) and other organizations and individuals proclaimed that such measures would violate civil liberties. One of the main issues with the USA Patriot Act was the provision giving the president the power to designate a person as an **enemy combatant** (a person who is alleged to have been associated with terrorist attacks against the United States) and to hold that individual for questioning without being charged and without counsel. In June 2004, in the case of Yaser Esam Hamdi, the U.S. Supreme Court ruled that an enemy combatant cannot be held indefinitely without due process. That case is the subject of this chapter's Case Analysis.

The enemy combatant provision was also challenged in 2005 by José Padilla, who was born in New York and grew up in Chicago. Padilla had been in U.S. custody since June 2002 without being charged with a crime.

Padilla was arrested at Chicago's O'Hare airport in May 2002 and subsequently held at the military brig in Charleston, South Carolina, as an enemy combatant. In February 2005, a U.S. District judge in Spartanburg, South Carolina, held that within 45 days Padilla must be charged with a crime, released, or this order appealed. The case was reversed by the Fourth Circuit Court of Appeal in September 2005, with that court holding that the detention of Padilla was necessary for national security. In April 2006, in *Padilla v. Hanft*, a divided U.S. Supreme Court refused to review the case.[53]

Justice Ruth Bader Ginsburg wrote an opinion dissenting in the refusal to hear the *Padilla* case. She pointed out that in 2004, when the U.S. Supreme Court first considered Padilla's case, which raised two issues, the Court should have decided both of those issues. Rather, having decided the procedural issue of whether Padilla had petitioned the correct court for his request for a **writ** of ***habeas corpus***, the Court held that it need not decide the second issue, of whether Padilla could be held indefinitely and without counsel. According to Ginsburg, quoting Justice John Paul Stevens's dissent in the 2004 decision, this is an issue of "profound importance to the Nation." In Ginsburg's words, the issue is as follows: "Does the President have authority to imprison indefinitely a United States citizen arrested on United States soil distant from a zone of combat, based on an Executive declaration that the citizen was, at the time of his arrest, an 'enemy combatant?'" Justice Ginsburg argued that the issue was not moot even though Padilla had been transferred to civilian custody the previous January.[54]

On 4 January 2006, the U.S. Supreme Court had granted the request by the Bush administration to transfer Padilla from federal *military* custody in South Carolina to federal *civilian* custody in Florida, where he had been indicted for allegations unrelated to and less serious than those for which the U.S. government had held him as an enemy combatant for over three years. Padilla was moved to a Miami, Florida, jail, where he was held without bail awaiting his trial on charges of providing support to terrorist cells. He was convicted and sentenced to 17 years and 4 months in prison; he could have been sentenced to life.[55]

In a prior case, *Rasul v. Bush*, decided in 2004, the U.S. Supreme Court had ruled that all persons in U.S. custody, even foreign nationals, have some due process rights. They have a right to know why they are being detained, to consult with an attorney, and to have a hearing before a neutral judge. The case was brought by 2 Australian citizens and 12 Kuwaiti citizens who were captured abroad and incarcerated at Gauntanamo Bay, Cuba, along with approximately 640 other foreign nationals who had been captured by U.S. military forces abroad.[56]

Apparently as a reaction to U.S. Supreme Court decisions concerning enemy combatants, Congress passed and President Bush signed the Military Commissions Act of 2006, which granted special military tribunals the sole power to hear the *habeas corpus* petitions of persons designated as enemy combatants, thus removing that power from the jurisdiction of U.S. courts.[57] In 2008 the U.S. Supreme Court considered the constitutionality of this act in two cases involving 37 detainees and combined for hearing and decision. The Court held the act unconstitutional because it stripped U.S. courts of their jurisdiction in *habeas corpus* petitions filed by enemy combatants. As a result of *Boumediene v. Bush*, all persons held by U.S. officials once again have the right to challenge their detention before a neutral judge in U.S. courts. According to Justice Anthony Kennedy, who wrote the opinion for the Court's majority of five justices, the provision of military tribunals to hear *habeas corpus* petitions from those detained at the United States Naval Station at Guantanamo Bay is not an adequate substitute for the procedural protections provided by the U.S. Constitution. Kennedy emphasized, however, that

> It bears repeating that our opinion does not address the content of the law that governs petitioners' detention. That is a matter yet to be determined. We hold that petitioners may invoke the fundamental procedural protections of habeas corpus. The laws and Constitution are designed to survive, and remain in force, in extraordinary

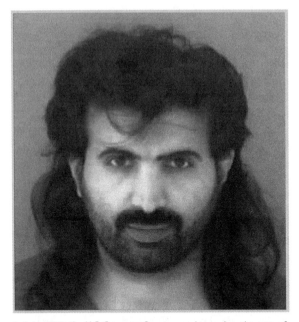

In late 2008, the U.S. Supreme Court agreed to review the case of Ali al-Marri, a former graduate student at Bradley University in Peoria, Illinois. This case raised constitutional issues concerning the designation of al-Marri as an enemy combatant and the degree of due process to which he is entitled with regard to that designation and its implications, especially indefinite confinement. In March 2009 the Court granted the Obama administration's motion to transfer al-Marri to civilian custody, where he was to be tried before a civilian criminal court on charges of terrorist acts, but he subsequently pleaded guilty. (Reuters/Landov)

times. Liberty and security can be reconciled; and in our system they are reconciled within the framework of the law. The Framers decided that habeas corpus, a right of first importance, must be a part of that framework, a part of that law.[58]

In June 2007, in *Al-Marri v. Wright*, a three-judge panel of the Fourth District Court of Appeals held that the government may not hold indefinitely in a military facility a person who entered the United States legally and established connections within the country. The case involved a Bradley University student, Ali al-Marri, a citizen of Qatar, who was arrested in 2001 at his college in Peori, Illinois, and charged with credit card fraud and lying to federal authorities. Prior to al-Marri's trial on those charges, President Bush found him to be a serious threat to the United States and designated him an enemy combatant based on

allegations by the U.S. Department of Justice that al-Marri had attended Osama bin Laden's terrorist training camp in Afghanistan. Al-Marri was detained in military custody in Charleston, South Carolina, for four years. During his first 16 months of detention, he was not permitted any contact with his family or with an attorney. Al-Marri challenged his detention as an enemy combatant. A three-judge panel of the Fourth Circuit Court of Appeals agreed that the detention was unlawful and ordered it ended. Subsequently the full court vacated that decision and agreed that the full court would hear the case. In November 2007 the full court heard the case, and in July 2008, the Fourth Circuit Court of Appeals issued the following ruling *per curiam* (meaning no specific judge authored the opinion). As noted in the citation, the U.S. Supreme Court agreed to review the case.

AL-MARRI v. PUCCIARELLI

534 F. 3d 213 (4th Cir. 2008), cert granted, 129 S.Ct. 680 (2008), motion granted, al-Marri v. Spagone, 2009 U.S. Lexis 888 (U.S. 2009), and vacated, remanded, application granted, al-Marri v. Spagone, 2009 U.S. Lexis 1777 (U.S. 6 March 2009).

 Ali Saleh Kahlah al-Marri filed a petition for a writ of habeas corpus challenging his military detention as an enemy combatant. After the district court denied all relief, al-Marri noted this appeal. A divided panel of this court reversed the judgment of the district court and ordered that al-Marri's military detention cease. Subsequently, this court vacated that judgment and considered the case *en banc [considered by the full court]*.

The parties present two principal issues for our consideration: (1) assuming the Government's allegations about al-Marri are true, whether Congress has empowered the President to detain al-Marri as an enemy combatant; and (2) assuming Congress has empowered the President to detain al-Marri as an enemy combatant provided the Government's allegations against him are true, whether al-Marri has been afforded sufficient process to challenge his designation as an enemy combatant.

We deny the Government's motion to dismiss this case for lack of jurisdiction. The Government relied on section 7 of the Military Commissions Act (MCA) of 2006, which amended the Detainee Treatment Act (DTA) of 2005. After we heard *en banc* argument in this case, the Supreme Court declared section 7 of the MCA unconstitutional. [referring to *Boumediene v. Bush*] The Government now concedes that we have jurisdiction over al-Marri's habeas petition.

Having considered the briefs and arguments of the parties, the *en banc* court now holds: (1) by a 5 to 4 vote [names of judges omitted], that, if the Government's allegations about al-Marri are true, Congress has empowered the President to detain him as an enemy combatant; and (2) by a 5 to 4 vote [names of judges omitted] that, assuming Congress has empowered the President to detain al-Marri as an enemy combatant provided the Government's allegations against him are true, al-Marri has not been afforded sufficient process to challenge his designation as an enemy combatant.

 Accordingly, the judgment of the district court is reversed and remanded for further proceedings consistent with the opinions that follow.

In March 2009, the U.S. Supreme Court reacted to a motion from the Obama administration with regard to this case. The Court's holding and brief opinion is as follows.

The application of the Acting Solicitor General respecting the custody and transfer of petitioner [Ali al-Marri], seeking to release petitioner from military custody and transfer him to the custody of the Attorney General, presented to The Chief Justice and by him referred to the Court is granted. The judgment is vacated and the case is remanded to the United States Court of Appeals for the Fourth Circuit with instructions to dismiss the appeal as moot.[59]

This holding mean that al-Marri would be tried in a U.S. civilian criminal court rather than by a military tribunal. By granting this motion, the Court did not decide the two major issues raised in al-Marri's appeal. Al-Marri was scheduled to appear on 10 March 2009 before a U.S. Magistrate to begin the civilian pretrial processes toward being charged with aiding terrorism as an al-Qaeda sleeper agent. The case became moot, however, when al-Marri pleaded guilty.

One final note on the USA Patriot Act is that it was scheduled to expire in 2005. The Bush administration pushed for it to be extended and threatened to veto a bill from Congress that did not include all sections of the USA Patriot Act. Just days before Christmas 2005, the U.S. Senate voted to extend the USA Patriot Act to 3 February 2006, thus postponing the fight over

the bill, which had already been approved by the U.S. House of Representatives. The act was then extended to 16 March 2006, but prior to that date and after lengthy negotiations, the Congress sent President Bush a bill to renew the USA Patriot Act. That bill, which was signed into law, essentially makes most of the provisions of the original USA Patriot Act permanent, although it does add some judicial oversight to executive authority under the act.[60]

The Department of Homeland Security (DHS)

One of the major federal reactions to 9/11 was the establishment of the **Department of Homeland Security (DHS)**, which is a cabinet-level position, merging 22 agencies into one agency and constituting the most sweeping overhaul in federal government in 50 years.

The National Homeland Security and Combating Terrorism Act of 2002 provides for the establishment of the DHS, which, among other responsibilities, coordinates the federal agencies involved in domestic preparedness and emergency planning. The DHS has direct control over the Federal Emergency Management Agency (FEMA), the U.S. Customs Service, and the U.S. Border Patrol and Coast Guard. In addition, the legislation provided for the creation of a White House Office of Combating Terrorism that is empowered to oversee government-wide antiterrorism policies and coordinate threats, be in charge of a national strategy to combat terrorism, and exercise control over the budget for counterterrorism. Despite the fact that 22 federal agencies were included in this new department established to fight terrorism, the Federal Bureau of Investigation (FBI) and the Central Intelligence Agency (CIA), both key agencies in the fight against terrorism, were not included. The new agency does, however, have its own intelligence-gathering functions. The organization of the top levels of DHS, approved on 20 March 2008, are diagrammed in Focus 10.8.[61]

To travelers, perhaps the most important department reporting to the DHS is the one in charge of security at airports.

The Transportation Security Administration (TSA)

The **Transportation Security Administration (TSA)** was created by the Aviation and Transportation Security Act (ATSA), enacted in November 2001. The agency was created to assume the screening functions

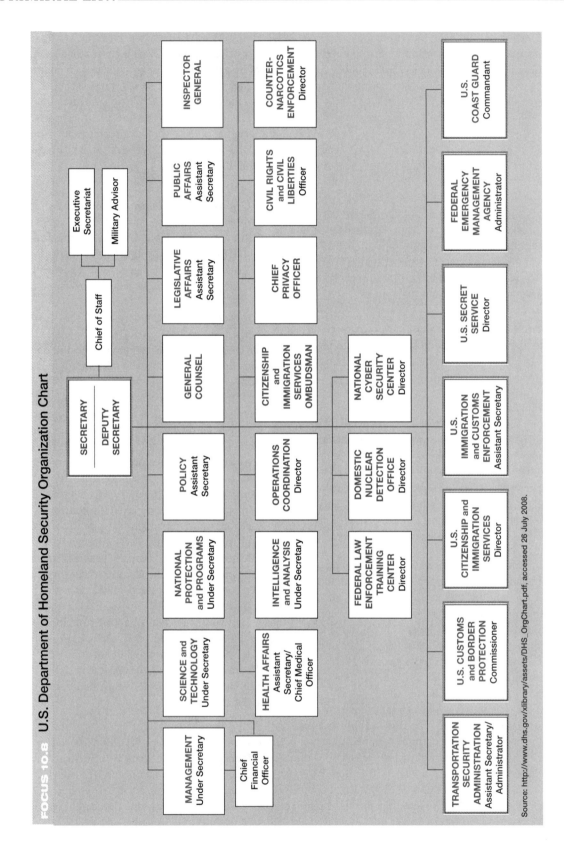

FOCUS 10.8   U.S. Department of Homeland Security Organization Chart

Source: http://www.dhs.gov/xlibrary/assets/DHS_OrgChart.pdf, accessed 26 July 2008.

for all commercial flights, a responsibility that previously had been under the Federal Aviation Administration (FAA), which was restructured by the statute. The TSA originally reported to the U.S. Department of Transportation but became part of the DHS in March 2003. The TSA website defines the agency as follows:

> We are your neighbors, friends and relatives. We are 43,000 security officers, inspectors, directors, air marshals and managers who protect the nation's transportation systems so you and your family can travel safely. We look for bombs at checkpoints in airports, we inspect rail cars, we patrol subways with our law enforcement partners, and we work to make all modes of transportation safe.[62]

Anyone who has traveled recently and encountered security issues may not think of TSA as family or friend, but probably all would agree that enhanced security is necessary.

The Enhanced Border Security and Visa Entry Reform Act of 2002

Another new piece of legislation designed to improve security in the United States is the Enhanced Border Security and Visa Entry Reform Act of 2002, enacted in May of that year. This is an extensive act that has many facets, all of which are designed to provide greater security with regard to the entrance of foreigners into the United States. Some of the provisions are as follows:

- ✪ Requirement that a "comprehensive report assessing the actions that will be necessary" to accomplish stated goals be submitted within 180 days

- ✪ Issuance to aliens of "machine-readable, tamper-resistant visas and other travel and entry documents that use biometric identifiers"

- ✪ By 26 October 2004 installation "at all ports of entry of the United States equipment and software to allow biometric comparison and authentication of all United States visas and other travel and entry documents issued to aliens"

- ✪ Use of "highly accurate" readers and scanners at all ports of entry

- ✪ Requirement of a "terrorist lookout committee to be maintained within each United States mission to a foreign country"

- ✪ Requirement that "all consular officers responsible for adjudicating visa applications, before undertak-

ing to perform consular responsibilities, receive specialized training in the effective screening of visa applicants who pose a potential threat to the safety or security of the United States"[63]

In recent years other changes have been made in security at U.S. borders. The largest agency within DHS (see again the organization chart in Focus 10.8) is the U.S. Customs and Border Protection (CBP). The CBP is charged with "stopping terrorists, terrorist weapons, illegal drugs, aliens, and materials harmful to agriculture from entering at, or between, ports of entry."[64]

DHS estimated that 11 million illegal immigrants were living in the United States in 2006, and in May of that year, President Bush announced that, as a stopgap measure, he was sending National Guard troops to the borders to stop the entry of illegal aliens. Congress passed and President Bush signed the Secure Fence Act of 2006, which, among other provisions, increases the number of border security agents, increases funding for border security, and provides for constructing miles of new fencing along the United States/Mexico borders.[65]

Local and state jurisdictions also enacted legislation to eliminate illegal immigration, courts faced significant increases in immigration appeals, immigration officers handled increased applications for citizenship, politicians debated, and social scientists researched the issue of whether illegal immigrants are more likely than others to commit crimes.[66]

The Public Health Security and Bioterrorism Preparedness Response Act of 2002

In June 2002 Congress passed a bill authorizing $4.6 billion to fund measures to protect the United States from bioterrorist attacks. The Public Health Security and Bioterrorism Preparedness Response Act of 2002 focuses on the improvement of the country's ability to respond quickly and efficiently to bioterrorist attacks. The act funds programs that provide for public health preparedness. It also provides for enhanced controls on biological agents and increases protections for the nation's food, drug, and drinking water supplies. Funds are made available to states, local governments, and other public and private health facilities to assist in the preparation for potential health epidemics.[67]

The Intelligence Reform and Terrorism Prevention Act of 2004

On 17 December 2004, President George W. Bush signed into law the Intelligence Reform and Terrorism Prevention Act of 2004 after which Congress created the Office of National Intelligence. The statute implemented one of the recommendations of the 9/11 Commission—that "the federal government should set standards for the issuance of birth certificates, and sources of identification, such as drivers' licenses." The new law gives the secretary of transportation, in consultation with the director of the DHS, the authority to issue regulations concerning federal standards for issuing such items as drivers' licenses. The act also contains requirements for strengthening the security of social security numbers, including the manner in which they are assigned to newborns. The law prohibits states and their political subdivisions from displaying social security numbers on drivers' licenses, motor vehicle registrations, or any other personal identification documents.[68]

The Intelligence Reform Act also created the position of Director of National Intelligence (DNI), to be nominated by the president and confirmed by the Senate. In signing the act, the President referred to it as the "most dramatic reform of our nation's intelligence capabilities since President Harry S. Truman signed the National Security Act of 1947." Bush continued:

> Under this new law, our vast intelligence enterprise will become more unified, coordinated and effective. It will enable us to better do our duty, which is to protect the American people. . . . The Director will lead a unified intelligence community and will serve as the principal advisor to the President on intelligence matters. The DNI will have the authority to order the collection of new intelligence, to ensure the sharing of information among agencies and to establish common standards for the intelligence community's personnel. It will be the DNI's responsibility to determine the annual budgets for all national intelligence agencies and offices and to direct how these funds are spent. These authorities vested in a single official who reports directly to me will make all our intelligence efforts better coordinated, more efficient, and more effective. . . .
>
> The new law will preserve the existing chain of command and leave all our intelligence agencies, organizations, and offices in their current departments. Our military commanders will continue to have quick access to the intelligence they need to achieve victory on the battlefield. And the law supports our efforts to ensure greater information sharing among federal departments and

agencies, and also with appropriate state and local authorities.[69]

In May 2005, John D. Negroponte, who had served as the U.S. Ambassador to Iraq and, before that, as the U.S. Ambassador to the United Nations, was sworn in as the first DNI. John Michael McConnell succeeded Negroponte under President Bush. In January 2009, President Barack Obama appointed Admiral Dennis C. Blair to the post.

The State Level

Attempts to control terrorism have also been made at the state level. For example, in response to the terrorist events of 9/11, New Jersey enacted the September 11th, 2001 Anti-Terrorism Act. This act was passed without a dissenting vote or an abstention. The legislation has been described as "one of the most sweeping measures passed by a state since the September 11 attacks, being aimed at terrorists, those who aid them and those whose acts play on public fears of terrorism." The law is viewed as a backup if the federal statutes are deemed invalid or federal prosecutors decline to prosecute.[70] Some of the provisions are as follows:

- The law creates a crime of first-degree terrorism.

- The law criminalizes aiding or harboring terrorists, hindering their apprehension or prosecution, and raising money to support their activities.

- The law provides indirectly for faster apprehension of terrorist suspects as the result of the provision above.

- The law provides the death penalty for terrorist acts resulting in death to a victim. It adds killing in the course of committing, fleeing from, or trying to commit a terrorist act to the list of aggravating factors specified by statute for the punishment of death in a capital murder case.

- For cases in which a terrorist act does not cause death, a perpetrator faces a prison term of 30 years without parole to life in prison.

- The law establishes a first-degree offense for developing, possessing, using, or threatening to use biological, chemical, or nuclear devices. A person who has legitimate use for these devices can be punished for a second-degree crime for negligent behavior in allowing access to them by an unauthorized person.

⚛ The No Early Release Act is amended to include within its provisions terrorist acts. That law requires offenders under its umbrella to serve 85 percent of their terms before they are eligible for parole.

⚛ Terrorist acts are not subject to statute of limitation provisions.

⚛ Other provisions of the criminal code, such as aggravated manslaughter, vehicular homicide, producing or possessing chemical weapons, damaging a nuclear plant, carjacking, and disarming a law enforcement officer are considered terrorist acts if they are committed "with the intent to incite an act of terror, terrorize five or more people; influence government policy or conduct; or interfere with public transportation, public communications, public or private buildings or public services."[71]

The statute includes many other changes to the existing criminal code, all of which are designed to deter terrorism threats.

SUMMARY

This chapter began with a look at offenses against the state, exploring a variety of acts against the orderly administration of government, including legislative as well as judicial processes. It began with the common law crimes of perjury and subornation of perjury. These crimes were originally limited to false statements under oath in a judicial proceeding but have been expanded by statutes to cover other proceedings, such as grand jury and congressional hearings. Some jurisdictions accomplish the same purpose by enacting separate statutes, such as false swearing or false declarations before a grand jury, rather than expanding the common law crime of perjury.

The second offense against the administration of government was bribery. In the English common law, bribery was more limited in scope than it is today. Common law bribery referred to offering, receiving, giving, or soliciting anything of value for the purpose of influencing action by public officials. It referred only to the judge who took the bribe. Modern statutes have extended bribery to include the one who makes as well as the one who receives the bribe. Some statutes extend the definition of bribery to include people other than public officials.

In many cases bribery is combined with other crimes, such as official misconduct in office. To be convicted of official misconduct in office, an official must have been acting under color of law.

Another crime that makes administration of justice more difficult is obstructing justice. This crime takes many forms. Some of the more common forms are tampering with a jury to try to influence jurors' votes, suppressing or refusing to produce evidence relevant to a trial, or interfering with an officer while he or she is attempting to perform official duties. It may include bribery, the attempt to bribe, or the conspiracy to bribe a public official.

The chapter then focused on treason, the highest crime against the government. To be convicted of treason against the U.S. government, a defendant must owe an allegiance to the federal government, commit an act that violates that allegiance, and have the required criminal intent. Two witnesses must testify to the crime unless the defendant confesses.

Treason may also be committed against a state. States are free to define this crime within their own statutes as long as they do not violate the U.S. Constitution. Like the federal government, some state constitutions include treason, thereby indicating the seriousness of the offense.

Several crimes related to treason were also discussed. Misprision of treason refers to concealing a known treasoner. Sedition, a crime that was prosecuted more frequently in the early years of the United States, has been limited by court interpretations of the First Amendment right to free speech. But that right does not include the right to communications aimed at stirring up treason or defaming the government.

The chapter then turned to a discussion of terrorism, a relatively new subject for criminal law texts, emphasizing that the 9/11 terrorist attacks on the United States forever changed not only our landscape but also the lives of people all over the world. No longer can we feel safe and secure despite all of the efforts and assurances of politicians and law enforcement officials. And we are paying more attention to ways in which terrorism can be prevented.

In a real sense all violent crimes are crimes of terrorism, but this chapter focused on the acts that are most frequently associated with the word *terrorism* today, noting, however, that it is difficult to define what is included in that word. The chapter looked at various ways of defining *terrorism* before presenting the definition of H. H. A. Cooper, who defined *terrorism* as "the intentional generation of massive fear by human beings for the purpose of securing or maintaining control over other human beings." It is actually a very simple definition—and it distinguishes *terrorism* from other violent crimes by using the term *massive fear*. Rape is a terrorizing experience, but it does not generate massive fear, although a serial rapist at large in one area might do so.

After the discussion of definitional issues, which included state as well as the federal approaches, the chapter looked at categories of terrorism, while Focus 10.6 summarized several examples of recent terrorist acts in the United States. The objectives, strategies, and tactics of terrorists were noted, along with terrorism victims, some of whom even identify with their captors, falling into the Stockholm syndrome pattern.

One major section of this chapter concentrated on weapons of mass destruction. Perhaps this is the aspect of potential terrorism that we most fear: the use of chemical, biological, or nuclear agents or devices to cause widespread injuries and deaths as well as contamination of property. Most of these potential weapons have been threats for a long time, but they seem more real in light of the events of 9/11. The chapter noted the significant impact that cyberterrorism could have on our country and our world. Of the many suggestions for controlling terrorism, U.S. officials and politicians have focused on statutory changes as well as education and preparedness. This discussion began with the federal level, looking first at the 9/11 Commission, followed by the Antiterrorism and Effective Death Penalty Act of 1996. The discussion of the USA Patriot Act included the facts and legal actions to date on issues such as the enemy combatant cases, a discussion that continues in the chapter's Case Analysis.

Several other recently enacted federal laws were discussed, including those that established the Department of Homeland Security and the Transportation Security Administration. The Enhanced Border Security and Visa Entry Reform Act of 2002, the Public Health Security and Bioterrorism Preparedness Response Act of 2002, and the Intelligence Reform and Terrorism Prevention Act of 2004 were also discussed. These (and other) statutory changes illustrate that U.S. legislators are focusing on overall security issues but particularly those problems at the borders, as well as preparing for the use of weapons of mass destruction. The discussion of controlling terrorism closed with a look at one state's approach, that of New Jersey.

STUDY QUESTIONS

1. Distinguish perjury, subornation of perjury, and false swearing.

2. Explain the different types of bribery and how modern bribery statutes differ from the English common law.

3. Discuss the impact of bribery statutes on politics.

4. What is meant by *official misconduct in office*? How does the phrase *under color of law* affect the crime? Discuss examples of the use of the federal statute against government officials.

5. Explain what is meant by obstruction of justice.

6. Explain the elements of treason, and contrast that crime with misprision of treason.

7. What is sedition? What are the First Amendment problems with prosecuting defendants for this crime? Define *espionage*.

8. If you had been the judge, what would have been your sentence for Sara Jane Olson? Do you think she was a terrorist? Do you think she should have been rearrested after she was mistakenly released from prison in 2008?

9. How would you compare the terror created by the Unabomber to that of the fears resulting from 9/11?

10. Explain what happened in the Oklahoma City bombing.

11. What is the rationale used by those who attack abortion clinics and those who appear at them? What should be done to those who engage in violence in that setting?

12. What occurred in the 1963 bombings in Alabama?

13. What are the major objectives of terrorists?

14. What is meant by the *Stockholm syndrome*, and what is your personal assessment of the validity of this concept?

15. List and explain the three major weapons of mass destruction discussed in the chapter.

16. Define *cyberterrorism*, and discuss its implications.

17. What does the Antiterrorism and Effective Death Penalty Act of 1996 have to do with terrorism?

18. What is an *enemy combatant*, and what is the current significance of the concept?

19. What is the USA Patriot Act?

20. What is the function of the Department of Homeland Security (DHS)?

21. What is the function of the Transportation Security Administration (TSA)?

22. Summarize the functions of other federal agencies discussed in this chapter.

23. Analyze the New Jersey approach to controlling terrorism.

FOR DEBATE

This chapter discussed several crimes, many of which create fear in the targeted victims and often also in others. Some of the crimes are more serious than others, but all have potentially enormous impacts on individuals and on the entire society. Attempts to deter any or all of these crimes may infringe on individual liberties. With these issues in mind, debate the following resolutions.

Resolved: Criminal laws covering the following crimes should be enforced more strictly and all should be classified as felonies: disorderly conduct, perjury, bribery, official misconduct in office, and obstruction of justice.

Resolved: Given the significant impact that terrorism and related crimes have on individuals and on society, local, state, and the federal governments should be given extensive powers in their efforts to combat these crimes, even if that means curbing the individual constitutional rights of the accused.

KEY TERMS

CASE ANALYSIS

HAMDI v. RUMSFELD
542 U.S. 507 (2004)

Case Preview

 This case represents the first successful challenge to the USA Patriot Act before the U.S. Supreme Court. It raises the importance of striking a balance between the rights of citizens guaranteed by the U.S. Constitution and the responsibility of the U.S. government to protect its citizens from terrorist acts. As you read the case, try to recall what you have already learned about the right to due process of law, the right to counsel, the right to know why the government is detaining you, and the meaning of *habeas corpus*. But also consider the government's need to protect its people from the kinds of terrorist acts that have occurred in your lifetime.

This case is a lengthy one, with hundreds of citations to and quotations from precedent cases and significant historical and other documents. The presentation here is more lengthy than others in this text to give readers a sense of the complexity of the case and the disagreement among the justices. The case emphasizes the overall importance of due process and the right to counsel for all persons, even those designated as enemy combatants, a term the Obama administration abandoned and then restored.

Justice Sandra Day O'Connor announced the judgment of the Court and delivered an opinion, in which Chief Justice William H. Rehnquist and Justices Anthony Kennedy and Stephen Breyer joined. Justice David H. Souter filed an opinion concurring in part, dissenting in part, and concurring in the judgment, in which Justice Ruth Bader Ginsburg joined. Justice Antonin Scalia filed a dissenting opinion, in which Justice John Paul Stevens joined. Justice Clarence Thomas filed a dissenting opinion.

Facts

On September 11, 2001, the al Qaeda terrorist network used hijacked commercial airliners to attack prominent targets in the United States. Approximately 3,000 people were killed in those attacks. One week later, in response to these "acts of treacherous violence," Congress passed a resolution authorizing the President to "use all necessary and appropriate force against those nations, organizations, or persons he determines planned, authorized, committed, or aided the terrorist attacks" or "harbored such organizations or persons, in order to prevent any future acts of international terrorism against the United States by such nations, organizations or persons." Soon thereafter, the President ordered United States Armed

Forces to Afghanistan, with a mission to subdue al Qaeda and quell the Taliban regime that was known to support it.

This case arises out of the detention of a man whom the Government alleges took up arms with the Taliban during this conflict. His name is Yaser Esam Hamdi. Born an American citizen in Louisiana in 1980, Hamdi moved with his family to Saudi Arabia as a child. By 2001, the parties agree, he resided in Afghanistan. At some point that year, he was seized by members of the Northern Alliance, a coalition of military groups opposed to the Taliban government, and eventually was turned over to the United States military. The Government asserts that it initially detained and interrogated Hamdi in Afghanistan before transferring him to the United States Naval Base in Guantanamo Bay [Cuba] in January 2002. In April 2002, upon learning that Hamdi is an American citizen, authorities transferred him to a naval brig in Norfolk, Virginia, where he remained until a recent transfer to a brig in Charleston, South Carolina. The Government contends that Hamdi is an "enemy combatant," and that this status justifies holding him in the United States indefinitely—without formal charges or proceedings—unless and until it makes the determination that access to counsel or further process is warranted.

In June 2002, Hamdi's father, Esam Fouad Hamdi, filed the present petition for a writ of habeas corpus . . . naming as petitioners his son and himself as next friend. The elder Hamdi alleges in the petition that he has had no contact with his son since the Government took custody of him in 2001, and that the Government has held his son "without access to legal counsel or notice of any charges pending against him." . . .

[The father alleged that his son was in Afghanistan to do relief work, was there only two months prior to 9/11, and that he could not possibly have received military training. The government disputed those allegations and alleged that Hamdi trained with and received weapons training with a Taliban military unit. The government further alleged that] a series of "U. S. military screening team[s]" determined that Hamdi met "the criteria for enemy combatants," and "a subsequent interview of Hamdi has confirmed that he surrendered and gave his firearm to Northern Alliance forces, which supports his classification as an enemy combatant." . . .

Issue

The threshold question before us is whether the Executive has the authority to detain citizens who qualify as "enemy combatants." There is some debate as to the proper scope of this term, and the Government has never provided any court with the full criteria that it uses in classifying individuals as such. It has made clear, however, that, for purposes of this case, the "enemy combatant" that it is seeking to detain is an individual who, it alleges, was "'part of or supporting forces hostile to the United States or coalition partners'" in Afghanistan and who "'engaged in an armed conflict against the United States'" there. We therefore answer only the narrow question

before us: whether the detention of citizens falling within that definition is authorized.

Holding . . .

We hold that although Congress authorized the detention of combatants in the narrow circumstances alleged here, due process demands that a citizen held in the United States as an enemy combatant be given a meaningful opportunity to contest the factual basis for that detention before a neutral decisionmaker.

Rationale

The President [is authorized by law] to use "all necessary and appropriate force" against "nations, organizations, or persons" associated with the September 11, 2001, terrorist attacks. There can be no doubt that individuals who fought against the United States in Afghanistan as part of the Taliban, an organization known to have supported the al Qaeda terrorist network responsible for those attacks, are individuals Congress sought to target in passing the [statute]. We conclude that detention of individuals falling into the limited category we are considering, for the duration of the particular conflict in which they were captured, is so fundamental and accepted an incident to war as to be an exercise of the "necessary and appropriate force" Congress has authorized the President to use.

The capture and detention of lawful combatants and the capture, detention, and trial of unlawful combatants, by "universal agreement and practice," are "important incident[s] of war." The purpose of detention is to prevent captured individuals from returning to the field of battle and taking up arms once again. . . . It is now recognized that 'Captivity is neither a punishment nor an act of vengeance,' but 'merely a temporary detention which is devoid of all penal character.' . . . 'A prisoner of war is no convict; his imprisonment is a simple war measure.'" "The object of capture is to prevent the captured individual from serving the enemy. He is disarmed and from then on must be removed as completely as practicable from the front, treated humanely, and in time exchanged, repatriated, or otherwise released."

There is no bar to this Nation's holding one of its own citizens as an enemy combatant. . . . A citizen, no less than an alien, can be "part of or supporting forces hostile to the United States or coalition partners" and "engaged in an armed conflict against the United States." Such a citizen, if released, would pose the same threat of returning to the front during the ongoing conflict.

In light of these principles, it is of no moment that the [statute] does not use specific language of detention. Because detention to prevent a combatant's return to the battlefield is a fundamental incident of waging war, in permitting the use of "necessary and appropriate force," Congress has clearly and unmistakably authorized detention in the narrow circumstances considered here. Hamdi objects, nevertheless, that

Congress has not authorized the indefinite detention to which he is now subject. . . . We take Hamdi's objection to be not to the lack of certainty regarding the date on which the conflict will end, but to the substantial prospect of perpetual detention. . . .

[The opinion noted that Hamdi argued that he could be held indefinitely and the Court agreed that was not an unreasonable concern.]

Even in cases in which the detention of enemy combatants is legally authorized, there remains the question of what process is constitutionally due to a citizen who disputes his enemy-combatant status. Hamdi argues that he is owed a meaningful and timely hearing and that "extra-judicial detention [that] begins and ends with the submission of an affidavit based on third-hand hearsay" does not comport with the Fifth and Fourteenth Amendments. The Government counters that any more process than was provided below would be both unworkable and "constitutionally intolerable." Our resolution of this dispute requires a careful examination both of the writ of habeas corpus, which Hamdi now seeks to employ as a mechanism of judicial review, and of the Due Process Clause, which informs the procedural contours of that mechanism in this instance.

Though they reach radically different conclusions on the process that ought to attend the present proceeding, the parties begin on common ground. All agree that, absent suspension, the writ of habeas corpus remains available to every individual detained within the United States. Only in the rarest of circumstances has Congress seen fit to suspend the writ. At all other times, it has remained a critical check on the Executive, ensuring that it does not detain individuals except in accordance with law. All agree suspension of the writ has not occurred here. Thus, it is undisputed that Hamdi was properly before an Article III court to challenge his detention. Further, all agree that [the statute section] and its companion provisions provide at least a skeletal outline of the procedures to be afforded a petitioner in federal habeas review. Most notably, [the statute] provides that "the person detained may, under oath, deny any of the facts set forth in the return or allege any other material facts," and [the statute] allows the taking of evidence in habeas proceedings by deposition, affidavit, or interrogatories.

[The Court discussed the nature of habeas petitions and reviewed the arguments of both sides in this case.] . . .

Both of these positions highlight legitimate concerns. And both emphasize the tension that often exists between the autonomy that the Government asserts is necessary in order to pursue effectively a particular goal and the process that a citizen contends he is due before he is deprived of a constitutional right. The ordinary mechanism that we use for balancing such serious competing interests, and for determining the procedures that are necessary to ensure that a citizen is not "deprived of life, liberty, or property, without due process of law," [according to our precedents, is that] the process due in any given instance is determined by weighing "the private interest that will be affected by the official action" against the Government's asserted interest, "including the function involved" and the burdens the Government would face in providing greater process. The [precedent case] . . . contemplates a judicious balancing of these concerns, through an analysis of "the risk of an erroneous deprivation" of the private interest if the process were reduced and the "probable value, if any, of additional or substitute safeguards." We take each of these steps in turn.

It is beyond question that substantial interests lie on both sides of the scale in this case. Hamdi's "private interest . . . affected by the official action," is the most elemental of liberty interests—the interest in being free from physical detention by one's own government.

[This interest is not] . . . offset by the circumstances of war or the accusation of treasonous behavior, for "[i]t is clear that commitment for any purpose constitutes a significant deprivation of liberty that requires due process protection." "Procedural due process rules are meant to protect persons not from the deprivation, but from the mistaken or unjustified deprivation of life, liberty, or property." Indeed, . . . the risk of erroneous deprivation of a citizen's liberty in the absence of sufficient process here is very real. Moreover, as critical as the Government's interest may be in detaining those who actually pose an immediate threat to the national security of the United States during ongoing international conflict, history and common sense teach us that an unchecked system of detention carries the potential to become a means for oppression and abuse of others who do not present that sort of threat. Because we live in a society in which "[m]ere public intolerance or animosity cannot constitutionally justify the deprivation of a person's physical liberty," our starting point for the analysis is unaltered by the allegations surrounding the particular detainee or the organizations with which he is alleged to have associated. We reaffirm today the fundamental nature of a citizen's right to be free from involuntary confinement by his own government without due process of law, and we weigh the opposing governmental interests against the curtailment of liberty that such confinement entails.

On the other side of the scale are the weighty and sensitive governmental interests in ensuring that those who have in fact fought with the enemy during a war do not return to battle against the United States. . . . [T]he law of war and the realities of combat may render such detentions both necessary and appropriate, and our due process analysis need not blink at those realities. Without doubt, our Constitution recognizes that core strategic matters of warmaking belong in the hands of those who are best positioned and most politically accountable for making them.

The Government also argues at some length that its interests in reducing the process available to alleged enemy combatants are heightened by the practical difficulties that would accompany a system of trial-like process. In its view, military officers who are engaged in the serious work of waging battle would be unnecessarily and dangerously distracted by litigation half a world away, and discovery into military operations would both intrude on the sensitive secrets of national defense and result in a futile search for evidence buried under the rubble of war. To the extent that these burdens are triggered by heightened procedures, they are properly taken into account in our due process analysis.

Striking the proper constitutional balance here is of great importance to the Nation during this period of ongoing combat. But it is equally vital that our calculus not give short shrift to the values that this country holds dear or to the privilege that is American citizenship. It is during our most challenging and uncertain moments that our Nation's commitment to due process is most severely tested; and it is in those times that we must preserve our commitment at home to the principles for which we fight abroad. . . .

We therefore hold that a citizen-detainee seeking to challenge his classification as an enemy combatant must receive notice of the factual basis for his classification, and a fair opportunity to rebut the Government's factual assertions before a neutral decisionmaker. . . .

At the same time, the exigencies of the circumstances may demand that, aside from these core elements, enemy combatant proceedings may be tailored to alleviate their uncommon potential to burden the Executive at a time of ongoing military conflict. Hearsay, for example, may need to be accepted as the most reliable available evidence from the Government in such a proceeding. Likewise, the Constitution would not be offended by a presumption in favor of the Government's evidence, so long as that presumption remained a rebuttable one and fair opportunity for rebuttal were provided. Thus, once the Government puts forth credible evidence that the habeas petitioner meets the enemy-combatant criteria, the onus could shift to the petitioner to rebut that evidence with more persuasive evidence that he falls outside the criteria. A burden-shifting scheme of this sort would meet the goal of ensuring that the errant tourist, embedded journalist, or local aid worker has a chance to prove military error while giving due regard to the Executive once it has put forth meaningful support for its conclusion that the detainee is in fact an enemy combatant. . . .

We think it unlikely that this basic process will have the dire impact on the central functions of warmaking that the Government forecasts. The parties agree that initial captures on the battlefield need not receive the process we have discussed here; that process is due only when the determination is made to continue to hold those who have been seized. . . .

In sum, while the full protections that accompany challenges to detentions in other settings may prove unworkable and inappropriate in the enemy-combatant setting, the threats to military operations posed by a basic system of independent review are not so weighty as to trump a citizen's core rights to challenge meaningfully the Government's case and to be heard by an impartial adjudicator.

[The opinion discussed the separation of powers issue.]

. . . We have long since made it clear that a state of war is not a blank check for the President when it comes to the rights of the Nation's citizens. Whatever power the United States Constitution envisions for the Executive in its exchanges with other nations or with enemy organizations in times of conflict, it most assuredly envisions a role for all three branches when individual liberties are at stake. Likewise, we have made clear that, unless Congress acts to suspend it, the Great Writ of habeas corpus allows the Judicial Branch to play a necessary role in maintaining this delicate balance of governance, serving as an important judicial check on the Executive's discretion in the realm of detentions. Thus, while we do not question that our due process assessment must pay keen attention to the particular burdens faced by the Executive in the context of military action, it would turn our system of checks and balances on its head to suggest that a citizen could not make his way to court with a challenge to the factual basis for his detention by his government, simply because the Executive opposes making available such a challenge. Absent suspension of the writ by Congress, a citizen detained as an enemy combatant is entitled to this process. . . .

Aside from unspecified "screening" processes and military interrogations in which the Government suggests Hamdi could have contested his classification, Hamdi has received no process. An interrogation by one's captor, however effective an intelligence-gathering tool, hardly constitutes a constitutionally adequate factfinding before a neutral decisionmaker. . . . Plainly, the "process" Hamdi has received is not that to which he is entitled under the Due Process Clause. . . .

Hamdi asks us to hold that the Fourth Circuit also erred by denying him immediate access to counsel upon his detention and by disposing of the case without permitting him to meet with an attorney. Since our grant of *certiorari* in this case, Hamdi has been appointed counsel, with whom he has met for consultation purposes on several occasions, and with whom he is now being granted unmonitored meetings. He unquestionably has the right to access to counsel in connection with the proceedings on remand. No further consideration of this issue is necessary at this stage of the case.

The judgment of the United States Court of Appeals for the Fourth Circuit is vacated, and the case is remanded for further proceedings.

It is so ordered.

Justice Scalia, with whom Justice Stevens joins, dissenting

. . . This case brings into conflict the competing demands of national security and our citizens' constitutional right to personal liberty. Although I share the Court's evident unease as it seeks to reconcile the two, I do not agree with its resolution.

Where the Government accuses a citizen of waging war against it, our constitutional tradition has been to prosecute him in federal court for treason or some other crime. Where the exigencies of war prevent that, the Constitution's Suspension Clause allows Congress to relax the usual protections temporarily. Absent suspension, however, the Executive's assertion of military exigency has not been thought sufficient to permit detention without charge. No one contends that the congressional Authorization for Use of Military Force, on which the Government relies to justify its actions here, is an implementation of the Suspension Clause. Accordingly, I would reverse the decision below. . . .

The allegations here, of course, are no ordinary accusations of criminal activity. Yaser Esam Hamdi has been imprisoned because the Government believes he participated in the waging of war against the United States. The relevant question, then, is whether there is a different, special procedure for imprisonment of a citizen accused of wrongdoing by aiding the enemy in wartime. . . .

[The opinion discussed the history of treason statutes.]

The Founders well understood the difficult tradeoff between safety and freedom. . . .

The Founders warned us about the risk, and equipped us with a Constitution designed to deal with it.

Many think it not only inevitable but entirely proper that liberty give way to security in times of national crisis. . . . Whatever the general merits of the view that war silences law or modulates its voice, that view has no place in the interpretation and application of a Constitution designed precisely to confront war and, in a manner that accords with democratic principles, to accommodate it. Because the Court has proceeded to meet the current emergency in a manner the Constitution does not envision, I respectfully dissent.

Justice Thomas, dissenting

The Executive Branch, acting pursuant to the powers vested in the President by the Constitution and with explicit congressional approval, has determined that Yaser Hamdi is an enemy combatant and should be detained. This detention falls squarely within the Federal Government's war powers, and we lack the expertise and capacity to second-guess that decision. As such, petitioners' habeas challenge should fail, and there is no reason to remand the case. The plurality reaches a contrary conclusion by failing adequately to consider basic principles of the constitutional structure as it relates to national security and foreign affairs and by using the balancing scheme of [a precedent case]. I do not think that the Federal Government's war powers can be balanced away by this Court.

Arguably, Congress could provide for additional procedural protections, but until it does, we have no right to insist upon them. But even if I were to agree with the general approach the plurality takes, I could not accept the particulars. The plurality utterly fails to account for the Government's compelling interests and for our own institutional inability to weigh competing concerns correctly. I respectfully dissent.

For Discussion

Which version of the facts do you think are true—that of the government or that of the petitioner? Do you agree with the Court in its decision? Or do you think the dissent has the better point of view? Does your view of the arguments and their resolution in this case change when you consider that the government never did charge Hamdi with a crime?

Review the material on treason discussed earlier in the chapter. Do you think Hamdi should have been charged with treason? If Hamdi was such a dangerous person, why do you think the government released him after this decision rather than charge him with a crime and try him?

INTERNET ACTIVITY

The USA Patriot Act is a set of laws passed to give federal agencies new tools to fight terrorism. Critics claim the Act allows the government to invade the privacy of all Americans. Visit the following websites to examine both sides of the argument: http://www.lifeandliberty.gov/ and http://www.aclu.org/safe-free/patriot/index.html (both accessed 25 November 2008). Can you find out anything about national security letters in either of these sites? What are the implications of such letters?

Go to the following website of the Centers for Disease Control (CDC) and watch the video entitled "A New Era of Preparedness," which concerns health: http://www.bt.cdc.gov/cdc (accessed 25 November 2008).

NOTES

1. William Blackstone, *Commentaries on the Laws of England*, vol. 4 (Birmingham, Ala.: Special edition, privately printed for The Legal Classics Library, 1983), p. 137, emphasis in the original.
2. See, for example, USCS, Title 18, Sections 1621–1623 (2009).
3. Pa.C.S., Title 42, Part V, Chapter 45, Section 4583 (2008). The bribery statute is codified at Pa.C.S., Title 18, Part II, Article E, Chapter 47, Section 4701 (2008).
4. Pa.C.S., Title 42, Part V, Chapter 45, Section 4583.1 (2008).
5. USCS, Title 18, Section 242 (2009).
6. The federal treason statute is codified at USCS, Title 18, Section 2381 (2009).

7. Blackstone, *Commentaries on the Laws of England*, vol. 4, p. 75.

8. See *Hanauer v. Doane*, 79 U.S. 341, 347 (1870).

9. *Rosenberg v. United States*, 346 U.S. 273 (1952). The federal espionage act is codified at USCS, Title 18, Section 793 *et seq.* (2009).

10. "A Different Verdict," *Houston Chronicle* (11 August 1993), p. 2.

11. USCS, Title 18, Section 2383 *et seq.* (2009).

12. *Stromberg v. California*, 283 U.S. 359 (1931).

13. USCS, Title 18, Section 2385 (2009).

14. Todd R. Clear, "Foreword," in Jonathan R. White, *Terrorism: An Introduction*, 3d ed. (Belmont, Calif.: Wadsworth Thompson Learning, 2001), p. xi.

15. American Law Institute, Model Penal Code, Section 211.3.

16. Brian Crozier, *Terroristic Activity, International Terrorism, Part 4: Hearings Before the Subcommittee to Investigate the Administration of the Internal Security Laws of the Senate Committee on the Judiciary*, 94th Cong., 1st Sess. 180 (1975); quoted in H. H. A. Cooper, "Terrorism: New Dimensions of Violent Criminality," *Cumberland Law Review* 9 (1978): 370.

17. National Advisory Committee on Criminal Justice Standards and Goals, *Disorders and Terrorism* (Washington, D.C.: U.S. Government Printing Office, 1976), p. 3.

18. H. H. A. Cooper, "Terrorism: The Problem of Definition Revisited," *American Behavioral Scientist* 44 (February 2001): 881–893; quotations are on pp. 883, 890, 891, 892. For one of his earlier publications on the definition of terrorism, see Cooper, "What Is a Terrorist? A Psychological Perspective," *Legal Medical Quarterly* 1, no. 1 (1977): 16–32.

19. USCS, Title 18, Part I, Chapter 113B, Section 2331 (2009).

20. Cal Gov Code, Title 2, Chapter 6.5, Section 8549.2 (2008).

21. Cal Pen Code, Title 7, Chapter 11, Section 186.21 (2008).

22. Cal Pen Code, Title 1, Chapter 3, Article 4.6, Section 11416 (2008).

23. Code of Ala., Title 13A, Chapter 10, Article 7, Section 13A–10-151 (2008).

24. V.S.A., Title 13, Part 1, Chapter 76, Section 3501 (2009).

25. NY CLS Penal, Part Four, Title Y-1, Article 490, Section 490.05 (2008).

26. NY CLS Penal, Part Four, Title Y-1, Article 490, Section 490.35 (2008).

27. NY CLS Penal, Part Four, Title Y-1, Article 490, Section 490.45 (2008).

28. NY CLS Penal, Part Four, Title Y-1, Article 490, Section 490.55 (2008).

29. NY CLS Penal, Part Four, Title Y-1, Article 490, Section 490.15 (2008).

30. National Advisory Committee, *Disorders and Terrorism*, pp. 3–7.

31. Ariel Merari, "A Classification of Terrorist Groups," *Terrorism* 1, no. 2 (1978): 332–347.

32. Merari, "Classification," p. 339.

33. Federal Bureau of Investigation, "Weapons of Mass Destruction," http://www.fbi.gov/hq/nsb/wmd/wmd_home.htm, accessed 25 July 2008.

34. Federal Bureau of Investigation, Weapons of Mass Destruction: What Is a Weapon of Mass Destruction?" http://www.fbi.gov/hq/nsb/wmd/wmd_definition.htm, accessed 24 October 2008.

35. United Nations, Peace and Security Through Disarmament, "Weapons of Mass Destruction Branch of the UN Office for Disarmament Affairs," http://disarmament.un.org/WMD/, accessed 25 July 2008.

36. Va. Code Ann., Title 18.2, Chapter 4, Article 2.2, Sections 18.2-46.4 and 18.2-46.5 (2008).

37. Va. Code Ann., Title 18.2, Chapter 4, Article 2.2, Section 18.2-31(13) (2008).

38. Walter Laqueur, *The New Terrorism: Fanaticism and the Arms of Mass Destruction* (New York: Oxford, 1999), pp. 49–60; quotation is on p. 60.

39. Laqueur, *New Terrorism*, pp. 60-61.

40. Laqueur, *New Terrorism*, p. 62.

41. Laqueur, *New Terrorism*, p. 65.

42. Va. Code Ann., Title 18.2, Chapter 4, Article 2.2, Section 18.2-46.7 (2008).

43. Laqueur, *New Terrorism*, pp. 70–74; quotation is on p. 73.

44. "Risk of Nuclear Attack on Rise," *Washington Post* (16 April 2008), http://www.washingtonpost.com, accessed 26 July 2008.

45. Laqueur, *New Terrorism*, pp. 74–75.

46. Ted Robert Gurr, *Why Men Rebel* (Princeton, N.J.: Princeton University Press, 1970), p. 232; quoted in Robert G. Bell, "The U.S. Response to Terrorism Against International Civil Aviation," in *Contemporary Terrorism: Selected Readings*, ed. John D. Elliott and Leslie K. Gibson (Gaithersburg, Md.: International Association of Chiefs of Police, 1978), p. 191. For a detailed discussion of the attempts by the United States to deter terrorism, see Richard M. Pious, *The War on Terrorism* (Los Angeles, Calif.: Roxbury Publishing Company, 2006).

47. "Attempted Hijacking Foiled Aboard an Israeli Airliner," *New York Times* (18 November 2002), p. 8.

48. The Commission was established by Public Law 107-306 (27 November 2002). The report is entitled *The 9/11 Commission Report: Final Report of the National Commission on Terrorist Attacks upon the United States*, Authorized Edition (New York: Norton, 2004), p. xvi.

49. *9/11 Commission Report*, pp. 399–400. The Intelligence

Reform and Terrorism Prevention Act of 2004 is codified as Public Law 108-458 (2006).

50. See, for example, the following: "9/11 Commission's Staff Ignored Military's Early Identification of Chief Hijacker," *New York Times* (11 August 2005), p. 14; "Former 9/11 Commissioners Say U.S. Is Not Safe," *CNN Lou Dobbs Tonight* (5 December 2005).

51. Antiterrorism and Effective Death Penalty Act of 1996, 104th Cong., 2d Session, No. 104-518 (1996), codified at USCS, Title 18, Section 2254 (2009).

52. The USA Patriot Act, revised and codified, USCS, Title 42, Section 5332 *et seq.* (2009).

53. *Padilla v. Hanft*, 389 F.Supp. 2d 678 (D.S.C. 2005), *rev'd.*, 423 F.3d 386 (4th Cir. 2005), *and cert. denied*, 547 U.S. 1062 (2006).

54. *Padilla v. Hanft*, 547 U.S. 1062 (2006), Justice Ruth Bader Ginsburg dissenting. The case to which Justice Ginsburg referred is *Rumsfeld v. Padilla*, 542 U.S. 426 (2004).

55. "Justices Let U.S. Transfer Padilla to Civilian Custody," *New York Times* (5 January 2005), p. 21.

56. *Rasul v. Bush*, 542 U.S. 466 (2004).

57. Military Commissions Act of 2006, Public Law 109-366, 120 Stat. 2600, USCS, Title 28, Section 2241(e) (2009).

58. *Boumediene v.Bush*, 128 S.Ct. 2229 (2008).

59. *Al-Marri v. Pucciarelli*, 534 F.3d 213 (4th Cir. 2008), *cert. granted, Al-Marri v. Pucciarelli*, 129 St. Ct. 680 (2008), *mot. granted, Al-Marri v. Spagone*, 2009 U.S. Lexis 888 (U.S. 2009), *and vacated, remanded, application granted, al-Marri v. Spagone*, 2009 U.S. Lexis 1777 (6 March 2009).

60. The revision Reauthorization Act of 2005, Public Law No. 109-177, 120 is referred to as the USA Patriot Improvement and Reauthorization Act of 2005, Public law No. 109-177, 120 Stat. 192 (9 March 2006). The USA

Patriot Act, revised and codified, is located at USCS, Title 42, Section 5332 *et seq.* (2009).

61. The Homeland Security Act of 2002 is codified as Public Law 107-296 (25 November 2006).

62. Transportation Security Administration, http://www.tsa.gov/who_we_are/index.shtm, accessed 25 July 2008.

63. Enhanced Border Security and Visa Entry Reform Act of 2002, USCS, Title 8, Section 1701 *et seq.* (2009).

64. Brian A. Reaves, Bureau of Justice Statistics Bulletin, *Federal Law Enforcement Officers*, 2004 (July 2006), http://www.ojp.usdoj.gov/bjs/pub/pdf/fle04.pdf, accessed 25 July 2008.

65. Secure Fence Act of 2006, Public Law 109-367 (2006).

66. See, for example, Laura J. Hickman and Marika J. Suttorp, "Are Deportable Aliens a Unique Threat to Public Safety? Comparing the Recidivism of Deportable and Non-deportable Aliens," *Crime and Public Policy* 7, no. 2 (February 2008): 59–92.

67. Public Health Security and Bioterrorism Preparedness Response Act of 2002, Public Law 107-188 (2006), codified at USCS, Title 42, Section 201 (2009).

68. Intelligence Reform and Terrorism Prevention Act of 2004, Public Law 108-458 (2004), 118 Stat. 3638 (2009).

69. The White House, "President Signs Intelligence Reform and Terrorism Prevention Act," http://www.whitehouse.gov/news/releases/2004/12/20041217-1.html, accessed 25 July 2007.

70. "Sweeping Criminal Law Puts State at Front Line of the War on Terror," *New Jersey Law Journal* (28 June 2002), n.p.

71. September 11th, 2001 Anti-Terrorism Act is codified at N.J. Stat., Title 2C, Subtitle 2, Part 5, Chapter 38, Section 2C:38-1 (2008).

CHAPTER 11

Drug Abuse and Drug Trafficking

INTRODUCTION

As emphasized throughout this text, crime is widely recognized as a serious problem in the United States, but there is little agreement over how to cope with it. From time to time the federal, state, and local governments, along with law enforcement agencies, focus on one or more target areas of criminality. Tougher legislation is enacted; longer sentences are imposed; treatment programs are eliminated; punishment is the key. Today the focus of many law enforcement agencies has shifted to terrorism, discussed in Chapter 10. But in the very recent past drug abuse and drug trafficking have been primary targets of legislation and law enforcement, and the lingering effects of that focus are reflected in current punitive policies.

This chapter begins with a look at the definitional problems associated with drugs and drug abuse before focusing on issues regarding the prohibition and regulation of alcohol. The chapter then turns to a discussion of controlled substances, looking at the crimes of possession of drugs and of drug paraphernalia, followed by an analysis of the manufacture, prescription, and sale of drugs.

The nature and extent of drug abuse are noted before the discussion turns to an analysis of the impact of drug abuse. In particular it explores the relationship between drug abuse and crime in general and then focuses on club drugs, alcohol, and campus crime. Federal and state laws are examined before the topic of education about club drugs is covered. The discussion of the impact of drug abuse closes with an analysis of fetal abuse.

The economic cost of drug abuse is overviewed before the chapter considers the impact of drug abuse on criminal justice systems. All aspects of criminal justice systems are impacted by drug abuse; this chapter considers three areas: courts, law enforcement officials, and prison and jail overcrowding.

The second major focus of the chapter is drug trafficking. The dynamics of this major area of criminal activity are discussed, followed by a look at federal and state statutes covering the crime of money laundering, which is utilized by many drug dealers to conceal their illegal funds.

The chapter then turns to an analysis of some of the approaches that federal and state governments have taken to control drug abuse and drug trafficking. This discussion begins with the federal level, examining the U.S. war on drugs and looking at recent White House drug policies. The discussion then notes the fact that some states enacted long and mandatory sentences for drug possession, looking in particular at New York's Rockefeller laws. The recent turn toward treatment rather than punishment of drug offenders in a few jurisdictions is noted, with particular attention given to drug courts. Finally, the efforts of a few states to legalize the production, sale, and possession of marijuana for medicinal purposes are highlighted, along with the legal implications of these attempts.

DRUG ABUSE

Chapter 1 mentioned the use of the criminal law to control behavior, such as *mala prohibita* crimes, acts that some people consider none of the law's business. Chapter 9 elaborated on the controversial practice of using the criminal law to attempt to control morality, such as sexual behavior between consenting adults in private. The personal use of some drugs, such as marijuana, is another area in which many people believe the criminal law either should not be employed or should be less punitive. But the fact is, U.S. criminal laws define some drug use as well as drug trafficking as illegal, and the problems associated with these areas of criminal activity are sufficient to warrant a chapter on the subject. First, however, we must look at definitional issues.

THE PROBLEM OF DEFINITION

The first issue is what is meant by the word **drug**. The term can be defined in many ways, ranging from moral to medical. This is a criminal law text, however, and the term *drug*, like other terms, is defined legally. In that regard, *Black's Law Dictionary* defines *drug* as follows:

> An article intended for use in the diagnosis, cure, mitigation, treatment, or prevention of disease in man or other animals and any article other than food intended to affect the structure or any function of the body of man or other animals.[1]

This definition is a positive rather than a negative one—that is, it presumes there is nothing wrong with drugs. Drugs are used for medical reasons. It is the *abuse* of drugs that is at issue where the law is concerned, but defining **drug abuse** is also difficult. Turning again to *Black's*, an accepted source of legal definitions, we find *drug abuse* defined as a "state of chronic or periodic intoxication detrimental to the individual and to society, produced by the repeated consumption of a drug, natural or synthetic."[2]

The *Random House Dictionary* takes a different perspective in defining *drug abuse* as (1) "an addiction to drugs" or (2) "substance abuse involving drugs."[3] That definition is, however, too broad for our purposes. When we discuss *drug abuse* in this chapter, we are referring to the illegal use of drugs even if the user in question is not addicted to drugs, but we also consider the legal use of some drugs that can be harmful or even fatal under some circumstances (such as alcohol consumed by an adult pregnant woman).

One other approach to the definition of *drug abuse* should also be considered. The American Social Health Association defines *drug abuse* as "the use of mood modifying chemicals outside of medical supervision, and in a manner which is harmful to the person and the community."[4] That definition is rather broad, but it does capture the essence of what we are concerned with in this chapter: harmful behaviors involving drugs. The first focus is on alcohol.

ALCOHOL PROHIBITION AND REGULATION

There is general agreement that alcohol is a drug and that it is the most frequently used of all drugs. *Alcohol* is "a liquid obtained by fermentation of carbohydrates by yeast or by distillation."[5] Alcohol comes in many forms, and it is even considered medicinal by some authorities, who suggest limiting consumption to two drinks per day for men and one for women. However, when used to excess, alcohol, a depressant, may lead to various mental and physical health issues. Nevertheless, in most U.S. jurisdictions, it is legal for adults to possess and to consume alcoholic beverages, although this has not always been the case.

The Eighteenth Amendment to the U.S. Constitution, which was ratified by the states in 1919 (to become effective one year later) prohibited the "manufacture, sale, or transportation of intoxicating liquors" within the country, along with the importation or exportation of alcohol. The prohibitions of this amendment were widely ignored, and in 1933, the states ratified the Twenty-first Amendment, which repealed prohibition.

Alcohol is, however, still regulated today. It may not be sold in some areas; it may not be sold or given to persons considered to be underage, usually 21; it may not be consumed under some circumstances (e.g., within so many feet of a place that has a license to sell). The regulations are not always criminal; in fact, many of the regulations concerning alcoholic beverages appear in a special code section, such as *alcohol beverage control law*, rather than in the state's criminal code. For example, New York has a statute within its alcohol beverage control law section entitled *Unlawful Possession of an Alcoholic Beverage with the Intent to Consume by Persons Under the Age of Twenty-one Years*. A person who violates this statute may be required to appear before a court, fined up to $50, ordered to perform community service of up to 30 hours, and required to complete an alcohol awareness program. This particular statute, however, does not give arrest powers to law enforcement authorities. New York's statute, like some other jurisdictions, includes statutory exceptions; for example, it excludes minors who are attending a licensed or registered course that requires alcohol tasting, along with minors whose parents or guardians give them an alcoholic beverage.[6]

The statutes regulating the possession of alcohol by minors, (called *minors in possession*, or MIP) and the methods by which minors obtain alcohol also include such acts as providing false identification to minors or, if a minor, using false identification for the purpose of buying alcoholic beverages. Statutes and ordinances also govern which institutions may serve alcohol and under what circumstances. They provide penalties for persons who drive under the influence (DUI) of alcohol or other drugs or who drive with an open container of an alcoholic beverage in the vehicle.

For regulations pertaining to alcoholic beverages that are contained in a section of law other than the criminal code, statutes may provide that under specified circumstances, violation of these regulations could lead to criminal charges, even felonies. Thus, a DUI might be categorized as a traffic violation or offense for the first occurrence, but as a crime for repeat offenses or for an offense that results in the death of another. The latter could also be classified as vehicular or DUI manslaughter, discussed in Chapter 6.

Jurisdictions also regulate drugs other than alcohol.

Controlled Substances

The federal government and the various states have the power to regulate the possession as well as the sale, distribution, and classification of **controlled substances**, which refers to any drug that the statute in question has designated as such. The best known of the controlled substances statutes is that of the federal government, the Controlled Substances Act (CSA), which establishes five categories of controlled substances. These categories are listed and explained in the portion of the statute that is reproduced in Focus 11.1. References are made to this Focus where pertinent throughout the chapter. States are free to devise their own controlled substances statutes as long as they do not conflict with the federal statute.

The discussion of controlled substances begins with the issue of *possession*.

Possession of Controlled Substances
The possession of controlled substances may be actual or constructive. *Actual possession* means that a person has physical control over the drug in question. *Constructive possession* occurs when a person who may not have actual possession has the power to possess. For example, New York has a statute covering *criminal possession of a controlled substance; presumption*. That statute, with a few exceptions, permits a presumption that all persons in an automobile (other than a public omnibus) are presumed to know about the existence of a controlled substance.[7]

Statutes prohibiting the possession of controlled substances may be categorized as felonies or misdemeanors, and they vary widely in terms of which category they use and the extent of the fines or other sanctions imposed. For example, consider marijuana, which is the most frequently used illicit drug. The National Organization for the Reform of Marijuana Laws (NORML) website contains a map of the United States (click on state laws); you can click on your state and find its penalties for conviction for the possession of marijuana.[8]

Focus 11.2 contains the definitions of some of the most common controlled substances.

Possession of Drug Paraphernalia
Criminal laws against possession are not limited to the possession of a controlled substance. They also prohibit the possession of **drug paraphernalia**, which refers to any item, product, or material that could be used to violate the controlled substance statutes of that particular jurisdiction. The statute may require that the accused be in possession of the items *with the intent* to violate a statute designed to regulate controlled substances.[9]

Statutes, such as that of New Jersey, may also specify that it is illegal to "own, possess, keep or store . . . any implement or paraphernalia for the manufacture, sale, distribution, bottling, rectifying, blending, treating, fortifying, mixing, processing, warehousing or transportation of alcoholic beverages with intent to use the same" in any one of several illegal ways.[10] The Iowa statute specifically includes as a felony the act of using drug paraphernalia to transmit HIV, providing that a person commits *criminal transmission of human immunodeficiency virus* if:

the person, knowing that the person's human immunodeficiency virus status is positive, does any of the following:

    a. Engages in intimate contact with another person.

    b. Transfers, donates, or provides the person's blood, tissue, semen, organs, or other potentially infectious bodily fluids for transfusion, transplantation, insemination, or other administration to another person.

    c. Dispenses, delivers, exchanges, sells, or in any other way transfers to another person any nonsterile intravenous or intramuscular drug paraphernalia previously used by the person infected with the human immunodeficiency virus.[11]

Statutes may also divide the possession or use of drug paraphernalia into degrees of seriousness, may have separate sections to cover minors, and may specify trafficking in drug paraphernalia.

The Manufacture, Prescription, and Sale of Drugs
Governments may permit the manufacture, prescription, and sale of alcohol and other drugs. Thus,

---

FOCUS 11.1   Schedule of Drugs in the U.S. Federal System

[The U.S. Congress has categorized drugs into five groups, ranging from the most serious (Schedule 1) to the least serious. Included in this focus is the statute defining those five groups. Following this portion of the statute is a very long list of drugs by category. That list is not reproduced because of its length and the fact that this chapter does not consider most of those drugs, but the statute stating the characteristics of each schedule number is reproduced.]

Schedules of Controlled Substances, USCS, Title 21, Section 812 (2009)

(a) Establishment. There are established five schedules of controlled substances, to be known as schedules I, II, III, IV, and V. Such schedules shall initially consist of the substances listed in this section. The schedules established by this section shall be updated and republished on a semiannual basis during the two-year period beginning one year after the date of enactment of this title [enacted October 27, 1970] and shall be updated and republished on an annual basis thereafter.

(b) Placement on schedules; findings required. Except where control is required by United States obligations under an international treaty, convention, or protocol, in effect on the effective date of this part, and except in the case of an immediate precursor, a drug or other substance may not be placed in any schedule unless the findings required for such schedule are made with respect to such drug or other substance. The findings required for each of the schedules are as follows:

(I) SCHEDULE I.
  (A) The drug or other substance has a high potential for abuse.
  (B) The drug or other substance has no currently accepted medical use in treatment in the United States.
  (C) There is a lack of accepted safety for use of the drug or other substance under medical supervision.

(2) SCHEDULE II.
  (A) The drug or other substance has a high potential for abuse.
  (B) the drug or other substance has a currently accepted medical use in treatment in the United States or a currently accepted medical use with severe restrictions.
  (C) Abuse of the drug or other substances may lead to severe psychological or physical dependence.

(3) SCHEDULE III.
  (A) The drug or other substance has a potential for abuse less than the drugs or other substances in schedules I and II.
  (B) The drug or other substance has a currently accepted medical use in treatment in the United States.
  (C) Abuse of the drug or other substance may lead to moderate or low physical dependence or high psychological dependence.

(4) SCHEDULE IV.
  (A) The drug or other substance has a low potential for abuse relative to the drugs or other substances in schedule III.
  (B) The drug or other substance has a currently accepted medical use in treatment in the United States.
  (C) Abuse of the drug or other substance may lead to limited physical dependence or psychological dependence relative to the drugs or other substances in schedule III.

(5) SCHEDULE V.
  (A) The drug or other substance has a low potential for abuse relative to the drugs or other substances in schedule IV.
  (B) The drug or other substance has a currently accepted medical use in treatment in the United States.
  (C) Abuse of the drug or other substance may lead to limited physical dependence or psychological dependence relative to the drugs or other substances in schedule IV.

---

licensed manufacturers are permitted to manufacture drugs, pharmacists and others are permitted to sell drugs, and licensed medical persons are permitted to prescribe drugs. Persons under the care of those licensed medical personnel may possess controlled substances without fear of criminal sanctions provided they comply with the statutes pertaining to those drugs.

Governmental restrictions concerning alcohol and other drugs may govern the locations and conditions under which they may be manufactured; how they are packaged and shipped; who may legally transport and accept them; the hours of sales; the ages of those permitted to sell, possess, or consume drugs; the size of containers in which drugs may be packaged; the circumstances under which alcoholic beverages may

---

FOCUS 11.2 **Controlled Substances: A Sample of Definitions and Facts**

Cocaine

"A white crystaline narcotic alkaloid extracted from coca leaves. Used as a local anesthetic. A controlled substance as included in narcotic laws."[1]

Heroin

"Narcotic drug which is a derivative of opium and whose technical name is diacetyl-morphine. It is classified as a Class A substance for criminal purposes and the penalty for its possession is severe."[2]

Marijuana

"An annual herb, cannabis sativa, having angular rough stem and deeply lobed leaves. . . .

Marijuana is also commonly referred to as 'pot,' 'grass,' 'tea,' 'weed,' or 'Mary Jane'; and in cigarette form as a 'joint' or 'reefer.'"[3]

Club Drugs

"In recent years, certain drugs have emerged and become popular among teens and young adults at dance clubs and 'raves.' These drugs, collectively termed 'club drugs,' include MDMA/Ecstasy (methylenedioxymethamphetamine), Rohypnol (flunitrazepam), GHB (gamma hydroxybutyrate), and ketamine (ketamine hydrochloride).

MDMA is a synthetic, psychoactive drug chemically similar to the stimulant methamphetamine and the hallucinogen mescaline.

The tasteless and odorless depressants Rohypnol and GHB are often used in the commission of sexual assaults due to their ability to sedate and intoxicate unsuspecting victims. Rohypnol, a sedative/tranquilizer, is legally available for prescription in over 50 countries outside the U.S. and is widely available in Mexico, Colombia, and Europe. . . .

GHB, available in an odorless, colorless liquid form or as a white powder material, is taken orally, and is frequently combined with alcohol. In addition to being used to incapacitate individuals for the commission of sexual assault/rape, GHB is also sometimes used by body builders for its alleged anabolic effects.

The abuse of ketamine, a tranquilizer most often used on animals, became popular in the 1980s, when it was realized that large doses cause reactions similar to those associated with the use of PCP, such as dream-like states and hallucinations. The liquid form of ketamine can be injected, consumed in drinks, or added to smokable materials. The powder form can also be added to drinks, smoked, or dissolved and then injected. In some cases, ketamine is being injected intramuscularly."[4]

1. *Black's Law Dictionary*, Special Deluxe fifth edition (St. Paul, Minn.: West Publishing Co., 1979), p. 233.
2. *Black's Law Dictionary*, p. 564.
3. *Black's Law Dictionary*, p. 871.
4. Office of National Drug Control Policy, *Drug Facts*, http://www.whitehousedrugpolicy.gov/drugfact/club/club_drug_ff.html#healtheffects, accessed 25 November 2008.

---

be given away or sold; the prohibition of the sale of alcohol to intoxicated persons; and many other requirements. Specifically with regard to controlled substances, governments may regulate the following:

⊕ Which substances are included within the controlled substances act

⊕ Transportation

⊕ Possession of drug paraphernalia

⊕ Licensing

⊕ Sales by manufacturers and others (such as pharmacies)

⊕ Disposal of drugs

⊕ Record keeping

⊕ Drug prescriptions

⊕ Labeling of drugs

⊕ Drug testing of products and of individuals

⊕ Counterfeit drugs

Governments may also designate persons (such as medical personnel and pharmacists) who are exempt from these restrictions; even then, laws regulate the conditions under which those persons may possess, prescribe, or sell controlled substances. Likewise, individuals are permitted to possess controlled substances when those are prescribed by licensed persons, but persons who obtain prescription drugs illegally may be charged with a crime such as *illegal possession of a prescribed controlled substance*.

Those who violate criminal law statutes regulating the manufacture and sale of controlled substances may also be charged with **drug trafficking**, which is one of

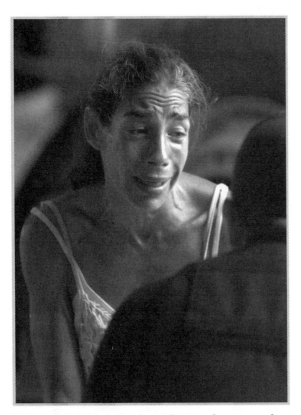

The use of alcohol and other drugs takes many forms, some of which are illegal for all, others just for minors. Drugs may be abused even when legal, and substance abuse is a serious issue in the United States and throughout the world, causing health problems; impacting relationships, especially those within the abuser's immediate environment; and costing social agencies and governments billions for control and treatment efforts. This woman tells her story after being arrested for trying to buy illegal drugs from an undercover police officer during a sting operation in Camden, New Jersey. (Newscom)

the most widespread criminal problems in the world. *Drug trafficking* refers to the illegal sale of or dealing in controlled substances. Statutes covering drug trafficking may be simple, stating that, for example, a person is guilty of the criminal sale of a controlled substance if he or she knowingly and unlawfully sells a narcotic drug. But, such a phrase usually will be followed by a long list of conditions. It may specify the types of drug, and there are many; it may specify the amount of the drug that is required for the offense in question; and so on. Often these statutes are written in terms of degrees and may involve the sale of drug paraphernalia as well as of the actual drugs. Other crimes, such as aiding and abetting, attempt crimes, and conspiracy, may also be applicable. The illegal sale of drugs may

be committed by small-time offenders, and they are most frequently the ones who are apprehended and prosecuted, but it is the large-scale traffickers, who are often connected to organized crime, that governments target.

The Nature and Extent of Drug Abuse

Data on the nature and extent of drug abuse are difficult to acquire, but the major source is the Substance Abuse and Mental Health Services Administration (SAMHSA) of the U.S. Department of Health and Human Services. SAMHSA reports data from its annual survey on the abuse and illegal use of alcohol, other drugs, and tobacco among nonstitutionalized populations ages 12 and over. In its latest report on illicit drug use (based on 2007 data) SAMHSA reported the following:

- "In 2007, an estimated 19.9 million Americans aged 12 or older were current (past month) illicit drug users, meaning they had used an illicit drug during the month prior to the survey interview. This estimate represents 8.0 percent of the population aged 12 years old or older.

- Illicit drugs include marijuana/hashish, cocaine (including crack), heroin, hallucinogens, inhalants, or prescription-type psychotherapeutics used nonmedically.

- The rate of current illicit drug use among persons aged 12 or older in 2007 (8.0 percent) was similar to the rate in 2006 (8.3 percent).

- Marijuana was the most commonly used illicit drug (14.4 million past month users). . . .

- Hallucinogens were used in the past month by 1.0 million persons (0.4 percent) aged 12 or older in 2007, including 503,000 (0.2 percent) who had used Ecstasy. These estimates were similar to the corresponding estimates for 2006.

- There were 6.9 million (2.8 percent) persons aged 12 or older who used prescription-type psychotherapeutic drugs nonmedically in the past month. Of these, 5.2 million used pain relievers, the same as the number in 2006. . . .

- Among youths aged 12 to 17, the current illicit drug use rate remained stable from 2006 (9.8 percent) to 2007 (9.5 percent). Between 2002 and 2007, youth rates declined significantly for illicit drugs in general (from 11.6 to 9.5 percent) and for marijuana, cocaine, hallucinogens, LSD, Ecstasy, prescription-type drugs used nonmedically, pain relievers, stimulants, methamphetamine, and the use of illicit drugs other than marijuana.

⊙ The rate of current marijuana use among youths aged 12 to 17 declined from 8.2 percent in 2002 to 6.7 percent in 2007. . . .

⊙ Among young adults aged 18 to 25, there were decreases from 2006 to 2007 in the rate of current use of several drugs. . . .

⊙ From 2002 to 2007, there was an increase among young adults aged 18 to 25 in the rate of current use of prescription pain relievers, from 4.1 to 4.6 percent. . . .

⊙ Among persons aged 12 or older who used pain relievers nonmedically in the past 12 months, 56.5 percent reported that the source of the drug the most recent time they used was from a friend or relative for free. Another 18.1 percent reported they got the drug from just one doctor. Only 4.1 percent got the pain relievers from a drug dealer or other stranger, and 0.5 percent reported buying the drug on the Internet. . . .

⊙ In 2007, there were 9.9 million persons aged 12 or older who reported driving under the influence of illicit drugs during the past year. This corresponds to 4.0 percent of the population aged 12 or older, similar to the rate in 2006 (4.2 percent), but lower than the rate in 2002 (4.7 percent)."[12]

Not all who abuse drugs are arrested, but most drug abuse arrests, 82.5 percent in 2007, were for the *possession* of illegal drugs, not for their sale or manufacture. Among possession arrests, by far the greatest percentage, 42.1 percent, was for marijuana.[13]

One type of drug abuse for which we have inadequate data is the abuse of prescription drugs. Persons engaging in this type of drug abuse are often referred to treatment centers, not to criminal justice agencies. As noted earlier, the most common source for these drugs is a friend or family member who secured the drugs legally.

The Impact of Drug Abuse

Drug abuse has harmful effects on users, their families and friends, and society. Of the many harmful effects of drug abuse, this section discusses the impact of drugs on crime in general, on college and university students, and on the unborn.

Drugs and Crime

One of the stated reasons for criminalizing the use of drugs is that substance abuse is associated with criminal acts. Table 11.1 contains a summary of the relationship between crime and the use of drugs. Further, government data reveal that adult respondents who use marijuana or cocaine are much more likely to be involved in illegal acts than those who do not use these drugs.[14]

Some drug users commit property crimes in order to finance their drug habits; others may engage in violent crimes. The use of drugs per se may not *cause* these crimes, but the association between drug use and crime must be given serious attention. In that light, the Bureau of Justice Statistics (BJS) reported the following data about drugs and crime:

⊙ About one in four convicted property and drug offenders committed their crimes to pay for their drugs, and the numbers have increased over the years.

⊙ Of persons on probation, almost one-half of the mentally ill and 46 percent of the others stated that they were using alcohol or other drugs at the time of their offenses.

⊙ Among incarcerated offenders, 32 percent of state inmates and 26 percent of federal inmates said they were using drugs when they committed the offenses for which they were currently incarcerated. Among those convicted of drug offenses, 44 percent were on drugs at the time of the offense, as were 39 percent of property offenders.

⊙ Inmates who report that they were abused earlier in life are more likely than nonabused offenders to have been using drugs at the time of their offense; this is particularly the case among abused women (46 percent) as compared with nonabused women (32 percent). Among offenders who are parents, 32 percent of women and 19 percent of men committed their crimes to get drugs or money for drugs.

⊙ Drug use was particularly high among jail inmates. "Seventy-six percent of jail inmates who had a mental health problem were dependent on or abused alcohol or drugs, compared to 53 percent of inmates without a mental health problem."

⊙ Alcohol and drug use was high among persons involved in domestic violence altercations.[15]

TABLE 11.1   Drugs and Crime: A Summary of Their Relationship

Drugs/Crime Relationship	Definition	Examples
Drug-defined offenses	Violations of laws prohibiting or regulating the possession, use, distribution, or manufacture of illegal drugs.	Drug possession or use. Marijuana cultivation. Methamphetamine production. Cocaine, heroin, or marijuan sales.
Drug-related offenses	Offenses to which a drug's pharmacologic effects contribute; offenses motivated by the user's need for money to support continued use; and offenses connected to drug distribution itself.	Violent behavior resulting from drug effects. Stealing to get money to buy drugs. Violence against rival drug dealers.
Drug-using lifestyle	A lifestyle in which the likelihood and frequency of involvement in illegal activity are increased because drug users may not participate in the legitimate economy and are exposed to situations that encourage crime.	A life orientation with an emphasis on short-term goals supported by illegal activities. Opportunities to offend resulting from contacts with offenders and illegal markets. Criminal skills learned from other offenders.

Source: Office of National Drug Control Policy, *Drug-Related Crime* (Washington, D.C.: U.S. Government Printing Office, March 2000), p. 1.

There is also evidence that substance abuse among teens is associated with juvenile and criminal acts. While noting that substance abuse does not *cause* delinquency, the Office of National Drug Control Policy reports that abuse has been *linked* to delinquency.[16] And officials with the Drug Enforcement Administration (DEA) have noted a relationship between drug trafficking and terrorism.[17]

Another area in which drugs are linked to criminal activity is in gangs. The police chief in Los Angeles, a city referred to as the U.S. gang capital, concluded that gangs are the "emerging monster of crime in America" and the greatest terrorist threat to the country. The police chief of Chicago, which is second to Los Angeles in gang activity, stated that gangs were killing more people than organized crime in his city.[18]

Finally, the combination of gangs and drugs is impacting our nation's schools, with research showing a high correlation between the presence of gangs and drugs (and guns) in schools.[19]

Drug abuse is also an issue among college and university students.

Club Drugs, Alcohol, and Campus Crime
The abuse of alcohol and club drugs on college and university campuses is widely recognized. The National Institute on Alcohol Abuse and Alcoholism (NIAAA) posts on its website information about the risks of drinking by college and university students between the ages of 18 and 24. Based on its review of relevant research, the organization reported the following information among other data concerning college students.

- Each year, over 1,700 die; more than 599,000 are injured; and over 696,000 are assaulted in alcohol-related incidents.

- Over 97,000 sexual abuse or date rape victims are involved in alcohol-related situations.

- Approximately 25 percent have academic difficulties related to drinking.

- Approximately 11 percent engage in vandalism.

- Thirty-one percent abuse alcohol and 6 percent are alcohol dependent.[20]

The abuse of alcohol on college and university campuses may involve *binge drinking*, which is defined, along with relevant facts on the problem, in Focus 11.3. As that focus reveals, over 40 percent of college and university students are binge drinkers.

College

Highlights of a new report on alcohol use by U.S. college students, ages 18 to 24:

Alcohol-related incidents per year

■ Deaths: 1,400

■ Injuries: 500,000

■ Assaults: 600,000 students assaulted by student who had been drinking

■ Sexual assaults: 70,000 victims of alcohol-related sexual assault or date rape

■ Sex: 100,000 said they were too drunk to know if they had consented to having sex

■ Driving: 2.1 million drove under the influence of alcohol

© 2002 KRT
Source: U.S. National Institute on Alcohol Abuse and Alcoholism,
KRT Photo Service   Graphic: Judy Treible, Lee Hulteng

The abuse of alcohol and other drugs is a major concern on college and university campuses and is linked with crimes such as date rape and other violent crimes. (Newscom)

A psychiatric report notes that the abuse of alcohol and other drugs may be among the "most prevalent mental health problems among young adults today. . . . Young adults are among the heaviest drinkers in the United States, and college students drink more heavily than their non-college attending peers." The study noted that college students are particularly at risk for mental health and behavior problems, not only with alcohol but also with tobacco and the use of illicit drugs.[21]

One of the results on college campuses, when alcohol and other drugs are involved, is that date rape may occur. Recall that Chapter 7 emphasized that date rape is real rape, a violent act, not just an individual problem for the victim. Focus 11.4 contains information on the physical and psychological effects of Ecstasy, a drug that is associated with date rape. A second club drug, GHB (gamma hydroxybutyrate), is even more closely associated with date rape. In fact, GHB is often called the *date rape drug* because it is odorless and colorless and, when slipped into a drink, can cause the victim to lose consciousness within 20 minutes and usually have no memory of the acts that occurred subsequently. The impact of GHB has led to legislation against it.

Federal Laws and Club Drugs

Focus 11.4 mentions a statute governing Ecstasy. Other statutes regulating club drugs are also in effect. In 2000 President Bill Clinton signed into law a bill that toughened the penalties for possessing and distributing GHB. This law places GHB in the category of drugs

---

FOCUS 11.3   Substance Abuse and the College Campus

The National Council on Alcoholism and Drug Dependence reports on its website the following information on binge drinking on college and university campuses.[1]

- "Binge drinking is defined as consuming five or more drinks in a row at one sitting for boys and four or more in a row for girls.
- 43% of college students say they are binge drinkers and 21% say they binge frequently.
- Fraternity and sorority members drink more and drink more frequently than their peers and accept as normal high levels of alcohol consumption and associated problems.
- As many as 360,000 of the nation's 12 million undergraduates will ultimately die from alcohol-related causes. This is more than the total number who will be awarded advanced degrees.
- Students who binge drink are more likely to damage property, have trouble with authorities, miss classes, have hangovers, and experience injuries than those who do not.
- College students drink an estimated 4 billion cans of beer each year. And the total amount of alcohol consumed by them annually is 430 million gallons, which is enough for each college and university in the United States to fill an Olympic-size pool.
- Each year, college students spend $5.5 billion on alcohol (mostly beer). This is more than they spend on books, soda, coffee, juice and milk combined. On a typical campus, the average amount a student spends annually on alcohol is $466.
- 80% of students who live on college campuses but who do not binge drink report that they have experienced at least one second-hand effect of binge drinking, such as being the victim of an assault or an unwanted sexual advance, having property vandalized, or having sleep or study interrupted.
- Binge drinking in high school, especially among men, is strongly predictive of binge drinking in college."

1. National Council on Alcoholism and Drug Dependence (NCADD), "Binge Drinking," citations omitted, http://www.ncadd.org/facts/fyibinge.html, retrieved 25 November 2008.

FOCUS 11.4 Ecstasy, the Club Drug

Ecstasy (also referred to as MDMA)[1] is a synthetic drug that was used by some doctors to facilitate psychotherapy; however, in 1988 the U.S. Congress designated the drug as a Schedule I (see again Focus 11.1) substance under the federal substance control laws. In recent years Ecstasy, also referred to as a *club drug*, has been used primarily at all-night dance parties (called *raves*), but it has recently moved to such venues as private homes and shopping malls as well as high schools and college dorms. The drug, which is usually taken orally in pill form, produces a psychedelic effect that can last for several hours. The drug is also a stimulant.

Ecstasy may produce psychological effects such as confusion, depression, anxiety, sleeplessness, drug craving, and paranoia. The drugs may also produce physical reactions, such as muscle tension, involuntary teeth clenching, nausea, blurred vision, faintness, tremors, rapid eye movement, and sweating or chills. Persons who use Ecstasy at raves are at a higher risk of the side effects that may occur when the drug is used in hot, crowded situations, combined with the long hours of dancing users have the capability of doing. These side effects are possible: dehydration, hyperthermia, heart, and kidney failure. Death may also occur. The drug may also cause damage to the parts of the brain that are associated with thought and memory.

The effects of using Ecstasy may linger for a long time. Repeated use of the drug may cause long-term neuropsychiatric problems and major physical health problems. Some of the side effects of the drug, such as problems with sleep or mood, anxiety disturbances, and even memory deterioration,

"may persist for up to two years after the user ceases taking the drug."[2]

Another point about the harmful effects of Ecstasy should be noted. Men who use the drug in combination with Viagra to enhance their sexual abilities may face a greater risk of stroke and heart attack. This combined use is also associated with a higher risk of contracting diseases, such as HIV.[3]

The Ecstasy Anti-Proliferation Act of 2000 instructed the U.S. Sentencing Commission to recommend increased penalties for trafficking in MDMA. The new penalties, which became effective 1 November 2001, increased by 300 percent the penalty for trafficking 800 MDMA pills from 15 months to 5 years. The penalty for selling 8,000 MDMA pills was increased nearly 20 percent, from 41 months to 10 years.[4]

1. Unless otherwise noted, the information in this focus is summarized or quoted from Office of National Drug Control Policy, Drug Policy Information Clearinghouse, *Fact Sheet*: *MDMA (Ecstasy)*, February 2004), http://www.streetdrugs.org/pdf/MDMA2004.pdf, accessed 25 November 2008.
2. "Chronic Ecstasy Use May Promote Long-Term Neuropsychiatric Damage," *Alcoholism & Drug Abuse Weekly* 14, no. 30 (5 August 2002): 6.
3. "Men Combining Viagra, Illicit Drugs, to Heighten Sexual Experience," *Alcoholism & Drug Abuse Weekly* 13, no. 33 (3 September 2001): 8.
4. The Ecstasy Anti-Proliferation Act of 2000 is codified as Section 3664 of Pub. Law 106-310 (2006).

---

that receive the highest regulation by the federal Controlled Substances Act, Schedule I (see again Focus 11.1), and provides for a prison term of up to 20 years for anyone convicted of manufacturing, distributing, or possessing GHB.[22]

In the summer of 2002, bills designed to crack down on Ecstasy and other club drugs were introduced into both the U.S. House and the Senate. These bills, referred to as the Reducing Americans' Vulnerability to Ecstasy (RAVE) Act of 2002, were passed and signed into law by President George W. Bush in 2003 and constitute an amendment to the controlled substances provision of the Comprehensive Drug Abuse and Prevention Act of 1970. RAVE cracks down on persons who put teenagers at risk of using Ecstasy or other club drugs by prohibiting renting, leasing, or profiting from any place in which the drugs are used. RAVE provides both civil and criminal penalties.[23]

State Laws and Club Drugs

Over 20 states have also enacted legislation to regulate club drugs. The Vermont statute is illustrative. In 2001 Vermont enacted a statute entitled *Ecstasy*, which is divided into two categories of drug offenses: (1) possession and (2) selling or dispensing. Each of these categories is subdivided, with penalties increasing as the amount of the involved drug increases.[24]

Education and Club Drugs

Other actions, such as educational efforts, have been taken to decrease the use of club drugs. For example, Arizona enacted a statute providing that instruction on the harmful effects of club drugs on the human system, along with instruction on the laws concerning these drugs, may be offered in elementary and high schools, emphasizing grades 4–9. Instruction on the effects of the enumerated drugs on the human fetus may be included in grades 6–12. Guidelines are established, and the statute provides that the instruction may be included in existing courses. School districts may request technical assistance from the department of education.[25]

Fetal Abuse

Another area of concern related to the use of alcohol and other drugs is **fetal abuse**, leading some states to change their murder statutes to include killing a fetus. For example, California now defines *murder* as "the unlawful killing of a human being, or a fetus, with malice aforethought."[26] This change in the common law view that murder applied only to persons already born has resulted in convictions for murder for those who kill the fetus of a pregnant woman. The issue here, however, is whether substance abuse by a pregnant woman, when it causes birth defects or the death of the fetus, should form the basis for a criminal charge against the mother.

Some jurisdictions have considered prosecuting pregnant women who abuse drugs, but most of these cases have not resulted in convictions. A few examples illustrate. In Illinois a grand jury refused to indict a young mother whose infant died shortly after birth and whose death was linked to the mother's use of cocaine. The prosecutor's earlier announcement of his intention to bring charges brought serious criticism on the grounds that such action might deter pregnant drug users from seeking prenatal care. The practice was objected to on the privacy issue as well. One attorney questioned, "If the state can create prenatal patrols for cocaine use, then where would they draw the line?"[27]

The Florida Supreme Court held that the state's statute prohibiting delivering drugs to minors is not applicable to the case of a woman who ingested illegal drugs while pregnant and gave birth to a drug-addicted baby.[28]

The Connecticut Supreme Court ruled that a pregnant woman's cocaine injections shortly before she gave birth did not constitute child neglect in the case of her child, who was born suffering from cocaine withdrawal. The court held that the statute did not cover a pregnant woman's prenatal conduct.[29]

Different results occurred in South Carolina, which has the toughest laws on drug use during pregnancy and is the only state in which a woman can be charged with murder for using drugs while pregnant. Regina McKnight, 24, was convicted of homicide by child abuse and sentenced to 12 years in prison after she smoked crack cocaine during her pregnancy and gave

birth to a stillborn fetus. In 2003 the South Carolina Supreme Court upheld the conviction. The U.S. Supreme Court refused to review the case. McKnight petitioned the trial court for post-conviction relief on the grounds that she had ineffective assistance of counsel. Her motion was denied by that court, but in 2008, the South Carolina Supreme Court reversed that decision.[30]

Prior to the McKnight case another South Carolina woman, Brenda Kay Peppers, was charged with child abuse after her stillborn baby was found to have cocaine in its bloodstream. Peppers accepted a plea bargain under which she was placed on probation for two years, but she appealed the case to the state supreme court, which vacated her conviction and sentence on technical grounds, thus not reaching other issues.[31]

The U.S. Supreme Court has ruled that pregnant women suspected of drug abuse may not be tested for drugs without their permission if the purpose of the test is to alert police to their substance abuse.[32]

The Economic Cost of Drug Abuse

The economic cost of drug abuse to individuals and to society is impossible to measure accurately, but there are many facets, the cost of which may be estimated. The 2009 National Drug Control Strategy budget summary included a request for a 3.4 percent increase (of $459 million) over the 2008 federal budget, which was $13.7 billion. That budget, however, only includes the money allocated for federal government drug programs and law enforcement.[33] The Office of National Drug Control Policy's most recent publication (2004) estimated that in 2002 all costs for illegal drugs amounted to approximately $180.9 billion. That figure includes the loss of productivity (71.2 percent of the total cost), health costs (8.7 percent), and other (20.1 percent), which includes costs related to drug crimes, such as the expenditures of criminal justice systems and the cost to victims. It also includes a modest amount for the administration of the social welfare system. State and federal correctional systems, including the cost of incarceration, are the largest of the detailed costs, at $14.2 billion.[34]

The Impact of Drugs on Criminal Justice Systems

Every aspect of criminal justice systems is impacted by drug abuse and efforts to control it. Courts are

Many civil courts have long waits for trials, due in large part to the number of criminal cases involving substance abuse offenses. Such crimes negatively impact all phases of the judicial system. (IStockPhoto)

crowded, creating a backlog of cases in the civil division as the courts try to process cases in the criminal division. More defense lawyers, prosecutors, judges, and court staff are needed, along with courtrooms and other facilities as well as law enforcement officers and support personnel.

Drug trafficking also results in corruption of personnel, violence, enormous expense, and a crushing blow to all elements of criminal justice systems.

Impact on the Courts

A significant number of cases before U.S. appellate courts, including the U.S. Supreme Court, involve drug-related issues. Many of these are procedural issues and thus not included within a criminal law text, but the point is that they take time and resources and most deal with legal issues concerning efforts to enforce drug laws. For example, in 2002 the U.S. Supreme Court ruled that it is legal for public housing authorities to evict tenants who have guests or family members who possess illegal drugs, and this is true even if the leaseholder did not know about the drugs. The case of *Oakland Housing Authority et al. v. Rucker et al.* involved four elderly residents of public housing units in Oakland, California. The grandsons, who were living with two of the residents, were apprehended smoking marijuana in the parking lot. One

resident had a caregiver who was frequently found with cocaine in the apartment, and a final resident had a mentally challenged daughter who was found with illegal drugs (cocaine) three blocks from the housing development. The Oakland Housing Authority began eviction proceedings against the four tenants, who sued. The U.S. Supreme Court noted that the language of the congressional statute in question is plain and that Congress had enacted that statute after expressing concern that drug dealers were "increasingly imposing a reign of terror on public and other federally assisted low-income housing residents." The Supreme Court continued with these comments, quoting from the federal statute:

> With drugs leading to "murders, muggings, and other forms of violence against tenants" and to the "deterioration of the physical environment that requires substantial governmental expenditures," it was reasonable for Congress to permit no-fault evictions in order to "provide public and other federally assisted low-income housing that is decent, safe, and free from illegal drugs."[35]

A second example of a recent U.S. Supreme Court decision involving drugs is that of *Kyllo v. United States*, in which the Supreme Court considered whether police use of thermal imaging devices to detect the illegal growing of marijuana in a home constituted an unreasonable search and seizure. The case involved Danny Kyllo, who was suspected of growing marijuana in his home with the use of high-intensity lights. Kyllo's home was part of a triplex in Florence, Oregon. The police scanned the triplex with a thermal imager, noting in the process that one wall over the garage of Kyllo's home was hotter than the other areas of the complex. Based on that information, tips from informants, and Kyllo's electric bill, the police obtained a search warrant, searched the premises, and found more than 100 marijuana plants. Kyllo entered a conditional guilty plea and petitioned the court to exclude the evidence, arguing that the search was a violation of his constitutional rights. The Ninth Circuit ruled against Kyllo, stating that the imaging device did not reveal any intimate details of the petitioner's life inside his home. The U.S. Supreme Court, in a 5-4 decision, reversed, with Justice Antonin Scalia, writing for the majority, stating that this type of search strikes "at the very core of the Fourth Amendment," which protects the freedom "to retreat into [one's] own home and there be free from unreasonable governmental intrusion." Justice John Paul Stevens

wrote in his dissent that this was not a search and was a reasonable action on the part of the police.[36]

In sheer numbers, the drug cases coming before courts are staggering. Figure 11.1 graphs the drug arrests by age, from 1970 to 2006, separated by adults and juveniles. Figure 11.2 graphs the state prison population by offense type from 1980 to 2006. Although violent crimes far exceed drug crimes, note the increase in inmates confined for drug offenses.

Influence over Law Enforcement Officials
Illegal drugs also have a negative impact on law enforcement officials, who face a serious problem—fighting illegal drugs with inadequate resources while drug offenders tempt them. In 1997 in Chicago, 124 narcotics cases were

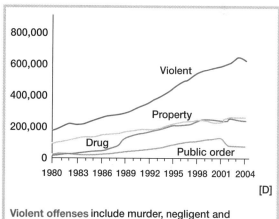

FIGURE 11.2 State Prison Population by Offense Type 1980–2004
Source: Bureau of Justice Statistics, Office of Justice Programs, http://www.ojp.usdoj.gov/bjs/glance/corrtyp.htm, last revised 5 December 2008, accessed 10 December 2008.

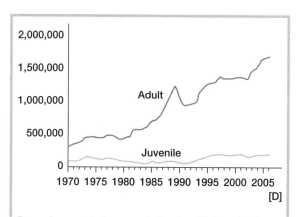

FIGURE 11.1 Drug Arrests by Age. 1970–2006
Source: Bureau of Justice Statistics, Office of Justice Programs, last revised 25 January 2008, http://www.ojp.usdoj.gov/bjs/glance/drug.htm, accessed 25 November 2008.

dismissed because the primary witness for the prosecution in each case was one of the police officers apprehended the previous year for extorting and robbing undercover officers who were posing as drug dealers.[37]

Other types of corrupt acts by law enforcement officers are as follows:

⭐ Selling information about upcoming police raids, agents, and police information

⭐ Accepting bribes to tamper with evidence or committing perjury in order to protect an illegal drug dealer

⭐ Stealing drugs from police property rooms or laboratories for personal use or sale

⭐ Stealing drugs or money for personal use from sellers and users without arresting them

⭐ Extorting money or property from drug dealers in exchange for failure to arrest them or seize their drugs[38]

Prison and Jail Overcrowding

Many U.S. penal facilities are overcrowded. A 2008 press release from the U.S. Department of Justice revealed that at the end of 2007, federal prisons were operating at 136 percent of capacity or higher. "State and federal correctional authorities had jurisdiction or legal authority over nearly 1.6 million prisoners, an increases of 1.8 percent since yearend 2006." According to the Bureau of Justice Statistics publication on which that statement was based, between 2006 and 2007, the total number of state and federal prisoners increased by 1.8 percent (3.4 percent in the federal system and 1.5 percent in state systems). Male inmates increased by 1.8 percent, female inmates by 1.7 percent. Much of the increase in inmates in recent years has resulted in part because of the number of drug offenders sentenced to serve time or awaiting trial for drug abuse offenses. For example, in the federal system, drug offenders accounted for 26 percent of the increase in federal inmates between 2000 and 2006, constituting 53 percent of all federal inmates in 2006. Between 2006 and 2007 the number of federal inmates whose most serious offense was drugs increased by 1.8 percent. Of the 179,204 federal inmates incarcerated at the end of 2007, 95,446 were convicted of drug offenses, far ahead of the next category of offenders, those convicted of public-order offenses (including immigration, weapons, and other related offenses), a total of 56,273.[39]

DRUG TRAFFICKING

One of the most widespread criminal problems in the world is *drug trafficking*. This section considers the dy-

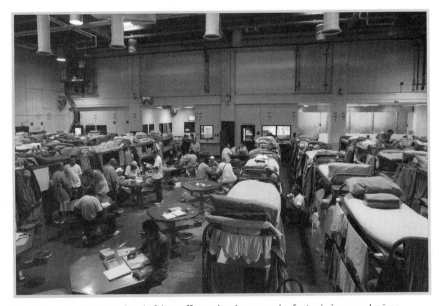

The influx of inmates convicted of drug offenses has been a major factor in increased prison populations to the extent that many prisons are seriously overcrowded. In this picture, inmates are housed in a converted gymnasium in California's Mule Creek State Prison. (Getty Images)

namics of drug trafficking and the methods of hiding the illegal profits.

The Dynamics of Drug Trafficking

Although some illegal drugs are produced in the United States, significant quantities are smuggled into the country. Illegal drugs are difficult to detect for a number of reasons. They may be hidden in many ways. Drugs are brought into the country by couriers, who have been found with drugs surgically implanted under the skin of their thighs, stuffed in teddy bears, sewn into undergarments, secreted in shoes, or contained in swallowed balloons. Drugs have been shipped inside concrete fencing posts, in packages with bananas or other fruits on top, inside fake bottles or boxes, in plastic packets within fruit, in fruit and asparagus cans, inside dead fish, and by many other means. Drugs may be airdropped from planes. They have been hidden in secret fuel tanks of cabin cruisers and in van compartments that could only be opened electronically. Suitcases filled with drugs have been found hidden behind interior panels within commercial airplanes, sewn into the interior roof of a station wagon driven by a family pretending to be on vacation, and buried under eight tons of onions in a truck.[40] Further problems arise because of the many points of entry by air, sea, and land and because of the millions of people who cross U.S. borders daily, many of them illegally.

Some drugs are smuggled into the United States (or any other country) in small amounts, which are valuable because of the high price they command. Drugs are also smuggled in large shipments and then divided and sold to dealers. The purity of the drugs may be diluted. There may be several stages in the processes of receiving, distributing, and selling drugs, and the transactions may cover a large geographic area, be highly organized, and involve many people.

Violence is common in drug trafficking. It is used to reduce or eliminate competition, expand markets, and intimidate anyone who interferes with the trafficking. That includes witnesses, law enforcement officers, and others. Drug informers and anyone who cheats, steals from, or lies to a drug dealer may be killed. Another important characteristic of illegal drug trafficking is that, although a few drug dealers make millions, most are not wealthy. Many of the lower-level dealers are drug addicts whose habits consume their profits, and these persons may spend extensive time in jails or prisons.

Money Laundering

An important problem faced by drug traffickers is concealing their illegal earnings. They do this primarily through **money laundering**, which is a process of concealing the existence, source, and disposition of money secured from illegal sources. The term is derived from the reference criminals make to "dirty" money that is "laundered clean" so that it can be used openly. Large amounts of cash are difficult to handle and may be easily stolen. But, the money must be placed somewhere, preferably in a place that will earn even more money. Thus, large sums of money obtained by selling illegal drugs are channeled through legitimate sources to make it appear that the money has been obtained legally. The money-laundering transaction might be as simple as sending the cash to a foreign bank account or as complex as taking over a bank. More complicated money-laundering schemes may involve multiple transactions and financial institutions in several countries.[41]

Federal Statutes

In the past, not all money laundering was illegal, and even today, many money-laundering transactions are legal if they involve money secured from legal sources or activities. The alleged acts in the federal system were formerly prosecuted under the Bank Secrecy Act, which required banks to report any domestic transaction of more than $10,000. In 1986 Congress enacted legislation making money laundering a crime. The Money Laundering Control Act of 1986 imposes criminal penalties on anyone who knowingly uses proceeds from unlawful activities to conduct a financial transaction (1) to conceal the nature or ownership of the proceeds or (2) to avoid transaction reporting requirements. Both criminal and civil penalties are provided. The statute has been amended in subsequent years.[42]

Other federal statutes have been enacted for the purpose of expanding the authority of bank regulators to combat money laundering. In April 1996 the Suspicious Activity Reporting (SAR) requirements went into effect. These regulations apply to transactions above $5,000. Bank officials are required to report depositors whom they suspect of depositing money from illegal activities or money that does not appear to be from a lawful purpose or legitimate business or when the bank officials do not know of any reasonable explanation for the transaction. These provisions are vague, leaving the possibility that bankers may either overlook illegal transactions and risk being fined or report transactions that are legal and risk losing business.[43]

Prosecution of money-laundering cases is assisted by the Money Laundering Prosecution Improvement Act of 1988, which enables financial institutions to require additional information from persons who purchase checks, traveler's checks, or money orders for $3,000 or more. It authorizes the secretary of the Treasury to target some types of institutions or geographic areas for additional reporting requirements.[44]

The money-laundering statute is complicated and has been challenged. In 1994 the U.S. Supreme Court held that the *willfulness* requirement of the statute requires the government to prove that the defendant "acted with the knowledge that the structuring he or she undertook was unlawful, not simply that the defendant's purpose was to circumvent a bank's reporting obligation."[45]

Since the 9/11 terrorist attacks, money-laundering statutes have been strengthened. The USA Patriot Act, discussed earlier, tightens the Bank Secrecy Act and the Anti-Money Laundering Act and requires banks to develop new programs and guidelines for knowing their customers well. It imposes significant new anti-money-laundering requirements, especially on money that may have been used to finance terrorist acts against the United States. The U.S. Treasury Department has the authority to interpret the USA Patriot Act, and it is expected that the interpretations will be broad. The act applies to "all financial institutions," and that probably will include many programs and fund managers not previously covered by anti-money-laundering-statutes. The USA Patriot Act requires bankers and other professionals to monitor monies that may be laundered and used for terrorist acts.

In addition, the USA Patriot Act includes within its reach "persons involved in real estate closings and settlements." That includes lawyers, who are objecting, complaining that in its efforts to control money laundering and fight terrorism, the federal government is interfering with the important and long recognized **attorney client privilege**, which prohibits attorneys from revealing to others information told to them by their clients. Attorneys argue that the privilege would be violated if they have to disclose financial information about their clients without their permission.

State Statutes

Many states also have money-laundering statutes. The Texas statute is an example:

(a) A person commits an offense [of money laundering] if the person knowingly;

(1) acquires or maintains an interest in, receives, conceals, possesses, transfers, or transports the proceeds of criminal activity;

(2) conducts, supervises, or facilitates a transaction involving the proceeds of criminal activity; or

(3) invests, expends, or receives, or offers to invest, expend, or receive, the proceeds of criminal activity or funds that the person believes are the proceeds of criminal activity.[46]

The Tennessee money-laundering statute specifies that the intent requirement for the crime does not mean that the individual must know that the laundered money came from a specific criminal activity "so long as the defendant knew that the property or proceeds were derived from some form of criminal activity."[47]

THE CONTROL OF DRUG ABUSE AND DRUG TRAFFICKING

In recent years, efforts to control drug abuse and drug trafficking in the United States have focused primarily on long and mandatory prison sentences. For example, several sections of the Violent Crime Control and Law Enforcement Act of 1994 involved enhanced penalties for drug offenses, including drug trafficking in prisons.[48]

Long sentences for drug offenses must be considered in terms of their total impact on criminal justice systems. It is very costly to investigate and prosecute drug trafficking cases because of the sophisticated techniques required for intelligence gathering. Trials are long and complicated. In addition, drug traffickers are known to intimidate or even kill witnesses. Potential danger to witnesses requires the federal government to protect some of them through its **Witness Protection Program**. This program is sponsored by the U.S. Marshals and provides a new identity and a new location for persons who aid the government in dangerous high-profile prosecutions. This is a very expensive process, and not everyone wishes to give up family and friends and assume a new identity. Expensive rewards are used to entice witnesses to give information that will lead to the indictment and arrest of high-level drug traffickers. Nevertheless, despite the impact of long and mandatory sentences on all aspects of criminal justice systems, they remain the primary approach in the drug control strategy.

The Federal Level

The major attempt to control drug trafficking is at the federal level, and the overall approach of the federal government's efforts to control drugs is generally referred to as the *war on drugs.*

The U.S. War on Drugs: A Brief History

The war on drugs that was begun in the early 1970s during the administration of President Richard M. Nixon was continued by President Ronald Reagan and his administration. In June 1982 President Reagan appointed a 19-member special group of government agency heads and instructed them to report back to him with suggestions on how to fight drug abuse. Four years later the President signed the Anti-Drug Abuse Act of 1986, which increased penalties for federal drug-related offenses and provided funding for alcohol and drug abuse treatment, prevention, and rehabilitation programs. This legislation has withstood some constitutional challenges.[49]

As another part of the war on drugs, Congress passed the Anti-Drug Abuse Act of 1988, which directs the president to examine the extent and nature of the drug problem and to propose policies for dealing with it. The Office of National Drug Control Policy (ONDCP) was established within the executive office of the president, with the director appointed by the president and confirmed by the Senate. In September 1989 President George H. W. Bush issued his National Drug Control Strategy, in which he called for a "larger and more flexible information base in order to help us refine and target our counterdrug efforts." In January 1990, the ONDCP director (also known as the *drug czar*), William J. Bennett, released an updated version of the president's drug control strategy, with this comment: "Prevention and treatment, however successful, require the support of drug enforcement activities that lead to the arrest of drug traffickers, that stop drugs

from being smuggled into the country, and that keep dealers off the streets."[50]

This drug control strategy contained provisions for federal grants to state and local agencies for law enforcement purposes, along with numerous provisions for attempts at drug enforcement. It was praised strongly by some and criticized bitterly by others, but no significant effects were seen in the fight against illegal drugs. In an effort at greater control over drug violations, Congress increased penalties for drug offenses, including drug trafficking in prisons, in its comprehensive crime act, the Violent Crime Control and Law Enforcement Act of 1994.[51]

Other changes occurred in the 1990s, beginning with the resignation of Bennett. He was followed by Robert Martinez, who was succeeded by President Bill Clinton's appointee, Lee P. Brown, former New York City police commissioner. Brown resigned in December 1995 amid criticism that Clinton's efforts at drug control were insignificant. There was also speculation that Congressional cuts of the drug czar's budget fueled Brown's resignation.

In 1996, after appointing General Barry McCaffrey as the drug policy chief, President Clinton announced one of his new drug strategies. He called for encouraging young people to reject drugs, strengthening efforts to prevent drug use and to provide drug treatment, and intensifying efforts to stop the supply of illegal drugs in the United States and in other countries. McCaffrey noted that the plan would not change the drug situation overnight but should be viewed as a long-term plan. Critics called the policy a recycled one and emphasized that Clinton did little to combat drugs during his first three years in office.[52] Criticisms of Clinton's drug policies intensified during the 1996 presidential campaign and even after his success in winning another term.

Not only Clinton's drug plans were criticized, however. The entire war on drugs has been severely questioned. Critics argue that the war denies to some sick people the drugs needed for treatment, noting that drugs such as marijuana and heroin are helpful in the treatment of cancer pain, nausea due to radiation and chemotherapy, and glaucoma (an eye disease that results in the loss of vision and can cause blindness). The legalization of marijuana for medicinal purposes is discussed later in this chapter. But with regard to the war on drugs, an internationally acclaimed drug policy expert, Arnold S. Trebach, stated in 1988 that, although drug policies victimize millions, they bring little benefit to anyone. According to Trebach, "We do not now have, and never had, the capability to manage a successful war on any drug."[53]

Social scientists have also been critical of the war on drugs. Three sociologists traced what they described as the failure of the war on drugs back to the efforts of Harry Anslinger, director of the Federal Bureau of Narcotics (FBN) from 1930 until his retirement (which, they alleged, was forced) in 1962. During that period, according to these scholars, Anslinger used measures to discredit, humiliate, and harass Alfred Lindesmith, a sociologist and researcher who argued for approximately four decades that drug addicts should be treated, not punished. One of Anslinger's methods was to discredit a Canadian film, *Drug Addict*, that was developed for the training of police and drug counselors. The film embraced the following themes, also supported by Lindesmith:

1. that addicts and traffickers are recruited from all races and classes;

2. that high-level drug traffickers are white;

3. that law enforcement only targets low-level dealers;

4. that addiction is a sickness;

5. that addiction to legal and illegal drugs are essentially the same;

6. that cocaine is not necessarily addictive; and

7. that law enforcement control of drugs is in the final analysis impossible.[54]

The sociologists concluded that "in hindsight [the film] appeared to be the last and best chance to create a rational and humane policy on narcotics." Anslinger and his colleagues at the FBN, however, convinced Congress "to stiffen drug penalties and thus set the nation on a course that has led to its current failed policy."[55]

The war on drugs remains controversial, with former president George W. Bush claiming progress and others challenging that conclusion. In a recent scholarly presentation, criminologist Matthew Robinson took issue with the Bush claims. Robinson entitled his presentation "Drug War Lies 2007: Still More Shenanigans from the Office of National Drug Control Policy." Robinson's presentation consisted of an in-depth examination and critique of the national drug policy. According to Robinson, the administration's claim that the policy is "both balanced and effective" was questionable. "In fact, the drug war under President Bush is not balanced . . . nor has it been particularly effective." Robinson concluded that most of the money in the proposed 2008 drug war budget was "intended for 'fighting' the drug war, not for those efforts that are most cost-effective and efficacious—preventing drug use and drug abuse, and for healing drug abusers through treatment."[56]

Following an analysis of the proposed spending on the war, Robinson concluded that the policy left out "almost all data on drug policy costs" and was simply "more of the same from ONDCP—a dishonest, incomplete report that is ill-suited to assist in a truthful assessment of the nation's drug control efforts." Robinson noted that there was some good news in the drug war and that was highlighted in the report, but it "continues to produce a flawed assessment of the nation's drug war."[57]

The war on drugs is also very expensive, costing billions of dollars. Illegal drugs are still readily available, drug addiction remains a serious problem, and the association between drug abuse and violent and property crimes is reportedly strong. Further, illegal drug trafficking associated with organized crime in general and drug gangs in particular continues to be a cause of concern both inside and outside U.S. prisons.

Another issue that should be considered in the war on drugs is whether the government's approach has a differential impact on persons of color and the poor. Three scholars who analyzed National Institute of Justice (NIJ) publications concerning drug control concluded that the war on drugs perpetuates the image of the poor and minorities as a "criminal class." The scholars concluded that "minorities and the poor are affected disproportionately by drug control campaigns, which lead to their overrepresentation in arrests, prosecutions, convictions, and incarcerations." They alleged that the studied reports "not only ignore the scholarly literature on race, class, and drugs but also fail to include research by other government agencies . . . that document such biases in drug control." The scholars proposed that this is a form of government propaganda—"the distortion of information for the purpose of influencing social action."[58]

Other areas of racial discrimination with regard to the drug war have been suggested. The Sentencing Project, a nonprofit research and advocacy group located in Washington, D.C., that promotes a greater reliance on sentencing alternatives, argued that the differences between the sentences for crack and powder cocaine negatively impact minorities, especially blacks. The Sentencing Project noted that supporters of the 100-to-1 sentencing ratio, which provided harsher penalties for crack (used primarily by blacks) than for powder cocaine (used primarily by whites), argue that crack cocaine is more dangerous and that those who use it are more violent than the users of powder cocaine. The Project argued, however, that the effects of the two drugs are essentially the same.[59] The issue of sentencing differentials is discussed in greater detail in Chapter 12.

In addition to differential penalties, blacks have argued that they are more often targeted for drug prosecutions. In 1996, in *United States v. Armstrong*, the U.S. Supreme Court faced the issue but ruled that a defendant who alleges racial bias regarding prosecutorial discretion must show that similarly situated persons of other races were not prosecuted. This case involved crack cocaine, and the Supreme Court held that the appellants did not show actual racial bias in the prosecutions for that crime.[60]

Recent White House Drug Policies

In January 2001 George W. Bush became president of the United States. In May of that year President Bush nominated John P. Walters as drug czar. In February 2002 President Bush announced his long-term goal of cutting drug abuse by 25 percent in five years through prevention, treatment, and law enforcement efforts. Describing drug abuse as an individual tragedy and a national crisis, Bush called for families, religious groups, and communities to do their part to achieve the goal of drug abuse reduction, stating, "Drugs rob men and women and children of their dignity and their character. Illegal drugs are the enemies of ambition and hope."[61]

Also in February 2002, President Bush released a national drug-control strategy that called for treatment as well as punishment for drug offenders. Bush stated his desire to "provide addicts with effective and compassionate drug treatment . . . and [to] be compassionate to those addicted to drugs." Bush expressed his belief that drug prevention begins at home and that we should target "people like pregnant moms, the homeless, people with HIV/AIDS, and teenagers."[62] In February 2005 President Bush declared that his drug control treatment strategy had exceeded its goal of a 10 percent reduction in youth drug use during two years. Citing data from the Monitoring the Future Study,

Bush emphasized that drug use had fallen by 11 percent during the first two years of his drug control plan and by 17 percent in three years.[63]

On 11 December 2008, the day this chapter was finalized, the White House released information claiming "significant success reducing drug availability and use." Citing the most recent data from the Monitoring the Future study, President Bush and his drug czar John Walters emphasized that the overall drug use among the students sampled (eighth-, tenth-, and twelfth-graders nationwide) had declined 25 percent since 2001 and that in 2008 there were 1 million fewer drug users in the sample than in 2001. In particular, the press release stated the following declines between 2001 and 2008:

- "25% reduction in marijuana use;

- 50% reduction in methamphetamine use;

- 50% reduction in Ecstasy use; and

- 33% reduction in steroid use."[64]

In early May 2009, President Barack Obama's choice for national drug czar, R. Gil Kerlikowske, Seattle, Washington's police chief, was confirmed and announced that he would focus the U.S. drug policy on reducing the demand for illegal drugs. It was expected that Obama's administration would change many of the Bush policies, including raiding marijuana growing facilities in California, where the use of the drug (and thus its production) is permitted for medicinal reasons.

The State Level

Although many drug offenses are handled at the federal level, state and local control is also important. Jurisdictions vary significantly in the offenses included as well as in the sentences that may be (and in some cases *must* be) imposed. But for years New York has had the harshest drug laws; that state serves as the focal point in this discussion.

Rockefeller and Other Harsh Laws

Statutes that went into effect in 1973 in New York increased the penalties for drug possession and the sale of drugs. Called the Rockefeller laws, after Governor Nelson Rockefeller (a popular governor who believed in the deterrence nature of stiff laws), these statutes were passed with two purposes in mind: (1) to frighten drug users and drug dealers into quitting and (2) to curb drug-related crimes. A report published in 1977 concluded that neither goal had been met. The study by the bar association and a drug abuse council concluded that "it is implausible that social problems as basic as these [that cause drug use and sales] can be effectively solved by the criminal law."[65]

This study of the effects of tough drug laws in New York also revealed a significant increase in court congestion, increased costs of all criminal justice court-related matters, and overcrowding of jails and prisons. Crimes related to drug use did not go down; rather, some crimes (such as theft, robbery, and burglary)—often associated with heroin users—increased faster in New York than in some neighboring states.[66]

Some New York offenders were sentenced to long terms for convictions involving the possession of small amounts of narcotics. For example, Martha Carmona was sentenced to six years to life in prison after pleading guilty to possession of an ounce of a substance containing cocaine. Roberta Fowler was convicted of selling 0.00455 ounce of a substance containing cocaine to an undercover agent for $20. She was sentenced to serve four years to life in prison. After the U.S. Supreme Court refused to review Carmona's case, New York governor Hugh Carey commuted the life sentences of these and two other offenders.[67]

New York judges openly criticized the stiff Rockefeller laws. In imposing a mandatory minimum sentence of 15 years to life on a defendant convicted of possessing 4 ounces of a controlled substance, a trial judge said, "I am obliged to enforce the law, however stupid and irrational and barbarous it be." Another judge noted that the long mandatory sentences provided in the Rockefeller laws discouraged defendants from exercising their constitutional right to a trial, for if they were convicted, the sentence had to be imposed. Many would plead guilty to a lesser offense (some even if they were not guilty) to avoid taking the risk of the longer term.[68]

New York made some changes in its drug laws. For example, the New York Marijuana Reform Act of 1977 defined possession of 25 grams or less of marijuana as *unlawful* rather than *criminal*. The act is classified as a *violation*, which is a noncriminal offense. It is punishable only by a fine not to exceed $100. The fine may increase with subsequent convictions within a specified time period. However, the statute was not applied retroactively to reduce charges against those already convicted under the harsher laws. Possessing more than 25 grams (along with possession in a public place when the marijuana is burning or open to public view) is a crime, classified as a Class B misdemeanor.[69]

In 2001 and 2002 attempts were again made to ease the Rockefeller laws. Governor George E. Pataki supported these attempts, and reform of drug sentencing laws was a major issue in the fall 2002 governor's race. Tom Golisano, who lost his bid for the governorship, called for the repeal of the laws, which, at that time, resulted in an annual expenditure of over $700 million to incarcerate drug offenders sentenced under the Rockefeller laws.[70]

Limited changes have been made in New York's harsh drug laws, but in the summer of 2008, one editorial proclaimed, "The Rockefeller Drug Laws Still Need Fixing."[71] Specifically, it was argued that the legislature should return some sentencing discretion to judges and remove the long mandatory sentences. According to one group that monitors New York prison conditions, in 2008 it was costing the state over $500 million a year to incarcerate its drug offenders, 4 out of 10 of whom were convicted for possession, not selling drugs. Many of those persons are drug addicts who might benefit from treatment rather than incarceration, but under the harsh mandatory sentencing policies, that is not possible.[72] It was predicted that in the 2009 legislative session the state would revise the strict Rockefeller laws but that Governor David A. Patterson would not support as significant a change as some had hoped.

Other states also have long mandatory minimum sentences for drug offenses, and although these sentences may have been designed to incarcerate the hard-core traffickers for years, that has not been the result. An analysis of the 58,000 drug convictions won by local prosecutors in the Houston, Texas, area revealed that 77 percent involved defendants who had less than a gram of a drug in their possession. Of these "small-time offenders," 35,000 were sent to jail or prison. According to the local paper, "The numbers suggest that these men and women are collateral damage in the war on drugs, arrested because they were easy targets rather than objects of a grand strategy."[73]

Such results have been confirmed on a national basis by the Sentencing Project, which states on its current website that over one-half of inmates serving prison time for drug offenses have no history of "high-level" drug acts (importing drugs and distributing them to dealers) and no history of violence. Furthermore, three-fourths of all inmates serving time for drug offenses are persons of color.[74]

Some states have reduced penalties for drug offenses; some have done so in favor of treatment of drug offenders, as we will see later in the chapter. In 2002, Michigan made significant changes in its drug laws, as the following quotation from a newswire indicates:

Public Acts 676, 666, and 670 of 2002 eliminate most of the state's Draconian mandatory minimum sentences for drug offenses. Judges can now use sentencing guidelines to impose sentences based on a range of factors in each case, rather than solely drug weight, and lifetime probation for the lowest-level offenders has been replaced with a five-year probationary period. Earlier parole is now possible for some prisoners, at the discretion of the parole board.[75]

With a slow move toward state removals or lessening of mandatory minimum drug sentences, especially long ones for minor, nonviolent offenders, we are seeing a cautious move toward treatment rather than punishment of minor drug offenders with substance abuse issues.

Substance Abuse and Treatment

The treatment approach is illustrated by the following Idaho statute:

It is the policy of this state that alcoholics, intoxicated persons or drug addicts may not be subjected to criminal prosecution or incarceration solely because of their consumption of alcoholic beverages or addiction to drugs but rather should be afforded treatment in order that they may lead normal lives as productive members of society.[76]

The statute continues with the declaration that the government should utilize state and federal resources to facilitate research of and treatment for alcoholism and drug addiction.

The boldest example of a return to treatment of drug offenders is that of California. California's Proposition 36, providing for treatment for first and second minor drug offenders, took effect in 2001. The provisions do not apply to persons who sell or manufacture drugs, but they do apply to minor drug offenders who violate their parole. Funds provided for treatment may not be used for drug testing, and once an offender has completed his or her treatment program, the conviction is dismissed. The California statute, *Possession of Controlled Sub-*

stances; Probation; Exceptions, in part, is as follows, with the italicized words added by a 2006 amendment:

(a) Notwithstanding any other provision of law, and except as provided in subdivision (b), any person convicted of a nonviolent drug possession offense shall receive probation. As a condition of probation the court shall require participation in and completion of an appropriate drug treatment program. The court may also impose, as a condition of probation, participation in vocational training, family counseling, literacy training and/or community service. A court may not impose incarceration as an additional condition of probation. Aside from the limitations imposed in this subdivision, the trial court is not otherwise limited in the type of probation conditions it may impose. Probation shall be imposed by suspending the imposition of sentence. *No person shall be denied the opportunity to benefit from the provisions of the Substance Abuse and Crime Prevention Act of 2000 based solely upon evidence of a co-occurring psychiatric or developmental disorder. To the greatest extent possible, any person who is convicted of, and placed on probation pursuant to this section for a nonviolent drug possession offense shall be monitored by the court through the use of a dedicated court calendar and the incorporation of a collaborative court model of oversight that includes close collaboration with treatment providers and probation, drug testing commensurate with treatment needs, and supervision of progress through review hearings.*

In addition to any fine assessed under other provisions of the law, the trial judge may require any person convicted of a nonviolent drug possession offense who is reasonably able to do so to contribute to the cost of his or her own placement in a drug treatment program. [The statute then specifies the types of offenders who are excluded from this statute.][77]

Another move toward treatment of substance abusers is the nationwide implementation of drug courts.

Drug Courts

Drug courts, which are based on a diversion and treatment approach to substance abusers, were begun in 1989 in Miami, Florida. Drug courts constitute an alternative to traditional prosecution in criminal courts, and most nonviolent defendants arrested on drug possession charges are funneled into these courts where they exist. The *drug court* has been described as follows: "Supervised by a sitting judge, a drug court is an intensive, community-based treatment, rehabilitation, and supervision program for drug defendants."[78]

It is suggested that a model drug court program should include the following:

- "Incorporating drug testing into case processing

- Creating a non-adversarial relationship between the defendant and the court

- Identifying defendants in need of treatment and referring them to treatment as soon as possible after arrest

- Providing access to a continuum of treatment and rehabilitation services

- Monitoring abstinence through frequent, mandatory drug testing

- Establishing a coordinated strategy to govern drug court responses to participants' compliance

- Maintaining judicial interaction with each drug court participant

- Monitoring and evaluating program goals and gauging their effectiveness

- Continuing interdisciplinary education to promote effective drug court planning, implementation, and operations

- Forging partnerships among drug courts, public agencies, and community-based organizations to generate local support and enhance drug court effectiveness"[79]

In the 1994 federal criminal code revision, Congress included a provision for drug courts.[80] By 2001 drug courts were in operation in all states, the District of Columbia, Puerto Rico, Guam, and two federal districts.[81] The 2008 presidential report on drug control strategy cited a California study concluding that drug courts cost an average of $3,000 per participant but save that state approximately $11,000 per participant.[82] The 2009 presidential report included a request for $27.9 million over the 2008 level for the Adult, Juvenile, and Family Drug Courts program awards grants for treatment of offenders within the federal system.[83]

Drug courts vary in size, type, and function. Some focus on offenders convicted of driving while under the influence of alcohol and are referred to as *DWI/Drug courts*, with an emphasis on deterring drunk driving.

Some drug courts focus on reintegrating children into their families after they have been removed because of their parents' drug abuse. Others focus on rehabilitative programs and services for substance abusers. Even though they vary, in general, drug courts have the same goals: to reduce drug abuse and crime and to rehabilitate the drug abusers.

This renewed emphasis on treatment, both at the state and the national level, especially of substance abusers, is enhanced by the changes in the way some people today view marijuana—at least for medicinal purposes.

LEGALIZING MARIJUANA FOR MEDICINAL PURPOSES

Many people agree that some aspects of substance abuse should be included in the criminal law. The production and sale of dangerous narcotics are examples. There is not much agreement, however, on the criminalization of the possession of small amounts of drugs such as marijuana, the use of which is considered by many people to be a private matter. Others say the drug is dangerous and should not be legalized under any circumstances.

It is also argued that prosecution for marijuana possession is not an effective use of the criminal law. In 1995 federal judge Richard Posner, appointed by President Ronald Reagan and considered to be one of the "most brilliant judges in the country," called for legalizing marijuana. According to Judge Posner,

> It is nonsense that we should be devoting so many law enforcement resources to marijuana. . . . I am skeptical that a society that is so tolerant of alcohol and cigarettes should come down so hard on marijuana use and send people to prison for life without parole.[84]

The chapter has already noted some changes in the criminal laws encompassing the possession of marijuana. In addition, 13 states—including California—have legalized the use of marijuana for some medicinal purposes.[85]

In 1996 California voters passed Proposition 215, which legalized the use of marijuana by seriously ill persons, with a physician's prescription. It is argued that patients suffering from AIDS, glaucoma, cancer, and other illnesses can benefit from the use of marijuana and that for some patients no other pain reliever is effective. In reaction to Proposition 215, the Oakland Cannabis Buyers' Cooperative was organized to provide for the distribution of marijuana to such patients. But, as we have already noted, in the federal system marijuana is a Schedule I drug; thus, there are no legal reasons for its sale or use other than research approved by the federal government. Subsequently, the district court enjoined the cooperative (told it to stop distributing), but the group refused and was held in contempt of court. The Ninth Circuit Court of Appeals ruled that the defense of necessity applies in such cases. Thus, a medical need would constitute a defense to prosecution of the federal controlled substances statute.

In 2001 the U.S. Supreme Court reversed the Ninth Circuit and held that no necessity defense exists. According to the Supreme Court, when Congress enacted the federal Controlled Substances Act, it allowed only one exception to the use of marijuana: It is permitted for government-approved research projects. The avoidance of an exception for medical necessity, ruled a unanimous Supreme Court, means that Congress did not intend that exception. The issue was not resolved, however. Government prosecutors did not want to pursue violators in criminal courts because the penalties for drug violations are so severe. They petitioned the court in California to issue an injunction prohibiting providing marijuana for medical reasons. The court issued first a temporary and then a permanent injunction.[86]

The injunction permitted the government to process any violators (i.e., those who grow, sell, or use marijuana for medicinal purposes) through the civil courts and thus avoid the potential of a harsh prison term as is required by the federal statute. The Obama administration announced in the spring of 2009 that it would prosecute the medicinal use of marijuana only if the practice violated state and federal laws.

In 2005, by a 6-3 vote, the U.S. Supreme Court ruled that under the Commerce Clause of the U.S. Constitution, Congress has the authority to enact legislation to regulate the growth and sale of drugs even by persons who use marijuana for medicinal reasons. That case is the subject of the Case Analysis at the end of this chapter.[87]

SUMMARY

Drug abuse and drug trafficking are serious problems throughout the world, and this chapter explored many of the issues associated with these problems. It began with an exploration of the difficulties of defining such terms as *drugs* and *drug abuse*, taking the legal position rather than moral or philosophical ones, as the chapter focused on the impact of laws enacted for the purpose of regulating drug offenses. Alcohol is a primary drug of abuse; the history of its prohibition and the current efforts to regulate it were noted before the discussion turned to an overview of controlled substances and drug paraphernalia. Attention was also given to statutes that regulate the manufacture, prescription, and sale of drugs.

The nature and extent of drug abuse was introduced to set the stage for a discussion of the impact of drug abuse. Although we do not know the precise relationship between drugs and crime, and it is reasonable to assume that in some cases drug abuse does not involve criminal activity, it is also reasonable to assume that drug abuse and crime are associated. In particular we looked at the relationship between the illegal use of drugs and crime in general as well as at issues on college and university campuses. With regard to the latter, the use of club drugs was noted, followed by an examination of federal and state laws concerning such drugs. The importance of education regarding the use of club drugs was emphasized.

The chapter examined the relationship between drug abuse and fetal abuse and noted some of the legal developments in this area before concentrating on the economic cost of drug abuse.

Drug abuse impacts every area of criminal justice systems. Courts are crowded with the trials of persons accused of drug violations, creating backlogs among civil trials, which must wait for the criminal trials. Appeals from drug convictions and sentences, often involving procedural issues, are increasing, resulting in additional burdens on the courts. Law enforcement officers face daily temptations from drug abusers, especially those who traffic in drugs; most officers refuse to become involved, but a few succumb. A final area of impact of drug abuse discussed in this chapter is the overcrowding of jails and prisons, a problem caused primarily because of the influx of offenders convicted of violating drug laws who were sentenced under harsh mandatory drug laws.

Drug abuse is serious, but drug trafficking is an even more critical issue, leading to violence and the corruption of many legitimate businesses. The chapter explored some of the dynamics of drug trafficking before turning to an analysis of how drug trafficking offenders hide their illegal money. Money laundering has become an important target of prosecutions in recent years, and state as well as federal attempts to control it were noted.

It is, however, the *control* of drug abuse and drug trafficking that is a major focus today. This discussion began with the efforts at the federal level, analyzing the U.S. war on drugs historically and looking closely at the recent White House proposals for a drug control strategy. Likewise, the efforts of states to control drug trafficking and illegal possession were noted, especially the harsh sentencing laws that are part of the New York drug control efforts.

Recently, a return to drug treatment efforts has evolved. Some are realizing that long prison sentences have not reduced the drug problem but have created other problems for social institutions. The current emphasis in some jurisdictions on treatment rather than punishment of substance abusers, at least at some levels, was discussed. Special attention was given to the developments in California, which now provides treatment rather than punishment for nonviolent first and second drug offenders. The treatment approach is often combined with the use of drug courts (rather than the usual adult criminal courts) for processing drug offenders. The successes and problems of this approach were analyzed.

The final section of the chapter looked at recent efforts to legalize the use of marijuana for medicinal purposes, an effort that has led to a battle between states (especially California) and the federal government. The U.S. Supreme Court ruled that the fact that California voters passed an initiative permitting the restricted use of marijuana for medicinal purposes does not provide a defense against prosecution for violating the federal statutes prohibiting such use.

The war on drugs will continue at the federal level; states will continue to explore ways to combat drugs at their levels; drug education will be a priority. The success of any of these measures, however, is not so obvious. Reducing drug abuse and drug trafficking will take enormous work on the part of local and state governments as well as the federal government, but it will also take a massive effort on the part of private institutions as well as the family. Those efforts have been hindered to some extent by harsh sentencing policies, which are explored more thoroughly in the next chapter.

STUDY QUESTIONS

1. Define the terms *drug* and *drug abuse*, and give reasons for your definitions.

2. Discuss the history of alcohol prohibition and regulation.

3. What types of crimes are most often associated with drug abuse?

4. Distinguish between actual and constructive possession of drugs, and analyze the criminalization of the possession of small amounts of marijuana.

5. What is meant by *drug paraphernalia*, and what types of statutes control possession of it?

6. How may the government regulate the manufacture, prescription, and sale of drugs?

7. Discuss the nature and extent of drug abuse.

8. What is the relationship between drug use and crime?

9. What are the facts and issues surrounding the use of alcohol and other drugs on college and university campuses?

10. What is Ecstasy, and why is this drug dangerous? What changes have been made in legislation concerning this drug?

11. What is meant by *club drugs*, and what can be done to negate their impact on young people? Discuss efforts at the national and the state levels to control the dissemination and use of club drugs.

12. What efforts have been made to educate young people about the harmful effects of club drugs?

13. Define *fetal abuse*, and explain how is it related to drug abuse.

14. What effect does drug abuse have on courts?

15. What effect does drug abuse have on law enforcement?

16. What is the relationship between drug convictions and jail and prison overcrowding?

17. What is meant by *drug trafficking*, and what is its impact?

18. Define *money laundering*, and discuss the relationship of this process to drug trafficking. Briefly review statutory changes and proposed changes regarding money laundering.

19. What do you think is the best method for controlling drug abuse and drug trafficking?

20. Assess the success or failure of the U.S. war on drugs, and make recommendations for the future.

21. Discuss the recent White House approaches to a drug control strategy.

22. What are the arguments that the war on drugs discriminates against minorities?

23. Based on your reading of the material in this chapter, what do you think we should do about state and federal drug laws?

24. What should be the role of treatment in the war against drugs? Are we making any progress in this area?

25. Evaluate the use of drug courts.

26. Should the use of marijuana be permitted for medicinal purposes? For any other reasons? Why or why not? What are the recent legal developments regarding these issues?

FOR DEBATE

The use of marijuana for medicinal purposes is permitted by statute in California and several other states, but federal prosecutors have succeeded in nullifying those statutes, in effect, by obtaining an injunction in California, along with a U.S. Supreme Court ruling concerning the use of marijuana for medicinal purposes. In view of these developments, debate the following resolution; in your debate consider the implications of your position on other social and/or legal issues.

Resolved: The use of marijuana for medicinal purposes should be legalized.

KEY TERMS

attorney client privilege, 332

controlled substances, 319

declaratory relief, 341

drug, 317

drug abuse, 318

drug paraphanalia, 319

drug trafficking, 321

fetal abuse, 327

medical necessity doctrine, 341

money laundering, 331

Witness Protection Program, 332

CASE ANALYSIS

GONZALES v. RAICH

545 U.S. 1 (2005)

Case Preview

In *Gonzales v. Raich*, the Ninth Circuit Court of Appeals ruled that, under the state's Compassionate Use Act of 1996, Californians may grow and use marijuana for medicinal reasons and that the court would not reconsider its decision upholding that statute. In 2005 the U.S. Supreme Court, by a 6-3 vote, reversed the Ninth Circuit and ruled that, under the Commerce Clause of the U.S. Constitution, the U.S. Congress has the right to regulate the sale and use of marijuana.

Recall that earlier in the chapter we discussed the U.S. Congress's categorization of drugs, noting that marijuana is a Schedule I drug, meaning that it cannot be used or prescribed for any purpose (except approved government research). As you read the following case, consider carefully whether you think the U.S. Supreme Court's opinion or the dissent's views are a reasonable interpretation of the Commerce Clause.

Some terms used in this case that we have not defined before are as follows:

Declaratory relief. An order from the court stating the rights of the parties who petition the court for a decision regarding those rights.

Medical necessity doctrine. Refers to a legal doctrine that permits a defendant to argue that an otherwise criminal act was taken for the purposes of meeting a medical necessity. If the defendant can prove an acceptable medical reason for committing the act, the defense may serve as a complete defense, thereby relieving the defendant of criminal culpability.

In reading the case, it will be helpful to keep in mind the California Compassionate Use Act of 1996, which is as follows:

(1) The people of the State of California hereby find and declare that the purposes of the Compassionate Use Act of 1996 are as follows:

(A) To ensure that seriously ill Californians have the right to obtain and use marijuana for medical purposes where that medical use is deemed appropriate and has been recommended by a physician who has determined that the person's health would benefit from the use of marijuana in the treatment of cancer, anorexia, AIDS, chronic pain, spasticity, glaucoma, arthritis, migraine, or any other illness for which marijuana provides relief.

(B) To ensure that patients and their primary caregivers who obtain and use marijuana for medical purposes upon the recommendation of a physician are not subject to criminal prosecution or sanction.

(C) To encourage the federal and state governments to implement a plan to provide for the safe and affordable distribution of marijuana to all patients in medical need of marijuana.[88]

The decision in the case was 6–3, with Justices John Paul Stevens, Anthony Kennedy, David H. Souter, Ruth Bader Ginsburg, and Stephen Breyer joining in the Court's opinion and Justice Antonin Scalia writing a concurring opinion. Justice Sandra Day O'Connor filed a dissenting opinion, in which Chief Justice William H. Rehnquist and Justice Clarence Thomas joined in part. Justice Thomas filed a dissenting opinion.

Justice Stevens delivered the opinion of the Court.

California is one of at least nine States that authorize the use of marijuana for medicinal purposes. . . .

Facts

California has been a pioneer in the regulation of marijuana. In 1913, California was one of the first States to prohibit the sale and possession of marijuana, and at the end of the century, California became the first State to authorize limited use of the drug for medicinal purposes. In 1996, California voters passed Proposition 215, now codified as the Compassionate Use Act of 1996. The proposition was designed to ensure that "seriously ill" residents of the State have access to marijuana for medical purposes, and to encourage Federal and State Governments to take steps towards ensuring the safe and affordable distribution of the drug to patients in need. The Act creates an exemption from criminal prosecution for physicians, as well as for patients and primary caregivers who possess or cultivate marijuana for medicinal purposes with the recommendation or approval of a physician. A "primary caregiver" is a person who has consistently assumed responsibility for the housing, health, or safety of the patient. . . .

Respondents Angel Raich and Diane Monson are California residents who suffer from a variety of serious medical conditions and have sought to avail themselves of medical marijuana pursuant to the terms of the Compassionate Use Act. They are being treated by licensed, board-certified family practitioners, who have concluded, after prescribing a host of conventional medicines to treat respondents' conditions and to alleviate their associated symptoms, that marijuana is the only drug available that provides effective treatment. Both women have been using marijuana as a medication for several years pursuant to their doctors' recommendation, and both rely heavily on cannabis to function on a daily basis. Indeed, Raich's physician believes that forgoing cannabis treatments would certainly cause Raich excruciating pain and could very well prove fatal.

Respondent Monson cultivates her own marijuana, and ingests the drug in a variety of ways including smoking and using a vaporizer. Respondent Raich, by contrast, is unable to cultivate her own, and thus relies on two caregivers, litigating as "John Does," to provide her with locally grown marijuana at no charge. These caregivers also process the cannabis into hashish or keif, and Raich herself processes some of the marijuana into oils, balms, and foods for consumption.

On August 15, 2002, county deputy sheriffs and agents from the federal Drug Enforcement Administration (DEA) came to Monson's home. After a thorough investigation, the county officials concluded that her use of marijuana was entirely lawful as a matter of California law. Nevertheless, after a 3-hour standoff, the federal agents seized and destroyed all six of her cannabis plants.

Respondents thereafter brought this action against the Attorney General of the United States and the head of the DEA seeking injunctive and declaratory relief prohibiting the enforcement of the federal Controlled Substances Act (CSA), to the extent it prevents them from possessing, obtaining, or manufacturing cannabis for their personal medical use. In their complaint and supporting affidavits, Raich and Monson described the severity of their afflictions, their repeatedly futile attempts to obtain relief with conventional medications, and the opinions of their doctors concerning their need to use marijuana. Respondents claimed that enforcing the CSA against them would violate the Commerce Clause, the Due Process Clause of the Fifth Amendment, the Ninth and Tenth Amendments of the Constitution, and the doctrine of medical necessity.

The District Court denied respondents' motion for a preliminary injunction. . . . A divided panel of the Court of Appeals for the Ninth Circuit reversed and ordered the District Court to enter a preliminary injunction. . . . The obvious importance of the case prompted our grant of certiorari.

Issue

The question presented in this case is whether the power vested in Congress by Article I, Section 8, of the Constitution "to make all Laws which shall be necessary and proper for carrying into Execution" its authority to "regulate Commerce with foreign Nations, and among the several States" includes the power to prohibit the local cultivation and use of marijuana in compliance with California law. . . .

The case is made difficult by respondents' strong arguments that they will suffer irreparable harm because, despite a congressional finding to the contrary, marijuana does have valid therapeutic purposes. The question before us, however, is not whether it is wise to enforce the statute in these circumstances; rather, it is whether Congress' power to regulate interstate markets for medicinal substances encompasses the portions of those markets that are supplied with drugs produced and consumed locally.

Holding

Well-settled law controls our answer. The CSA is a valid exercise of federal power, even as applied to the troubling facts of this case. We accordingly vacate the judgment of the Court of Appeals [and hold that Congress has the power to prohibit the local cultivation and use of marijuana for medical purposes].

Rationale

Shortly after taking office in 1969, President Nixon declared a national "war on drugs." As the first campaign of that war, Congress set out to enact legislation that would consolidate various drug laws on the books into a comprehensive statute, provide meaningful regulation over legitimate sources of drugs to prevent diversion into illegal channels, and strengthen law enforcement tools against the traffic in illicit drugs. That effort culminated in the passage of the Comprehensive Drug Abuse Prevention and Control Act of 1970.

This was not, however, Congress' first attempt to regulate the national market in drugs. Rather, as early as 1906 Congress enacted federal legislation imposing labeling regulations on medications and prohibiting the manufacture or shipment of any adulterated or misbranded drug traveling in interstate commerce. Aside from these labeling restrictions, most domestic drug regulations prior to 1970 generally came in the guise of revenue laws, with the Department of the Treasury serving as the Federal Government's primary enforcer. For example, the primary drug control law, before being repealed by the passage of the CSA, was the Harrison Narcotics Act of 1914. The Harrison Act sought to exert control over the possession and sale of narcotics, specifically cocaine and opiates, by requiring producers, distributors, and purchasers to register with the Federal Government, by assessing taxes against parties so registered, and by regulating the issuance of prescriptions.

Marijuana itself was not significantly regulated by the Federal Government until 1937 when accounts of marijuana's addictive qualities and physiological effects, paired with dissatisfaction with enforcement efforts at state and local levels, prompted Congress to pass the Marihuana Tax Act. Like the Harrison Act, the Marihuana Tax Act did not outlaw the possession or sale of marijuana outright. Rather, it imposed registration and reporting requirements for all individuals importing, producing, selling, or dealing in marijuana, and required the payment of annual taxes in addition to transfer taxes whenever the drug changed hands. Moreover, doctors wishing to prescribe marijuana for medical purposes were required to comply with rather burdensome administrative requirements. Noncompliance exposed traffickers to severe federal penalties, whereas compliance would often subject them to prosecution under state law. Thus, while the Marihuana Tax Act did not declare the drug illegal per se, the onerous administrative requirements, the prohibitively expensive taxes, and the risks attendant on compliance practically curtailed the marijuana trade.

Then in 1970, after declaration of the national "war on drugs," federal drug policy underwent a significant transformation. A number of noteworthy events precipitated this policy shift. . . .

In enacting the CSA, Congress classified marijuana as a Schedule I drug. . . . By classifying marijuana as a Sched-

ule I drug, as opposed to listing it on a lesser schedule, the manufacture, distribution, or possession of marijuana became a criminal offense, with the sole exception being use of the drug as part of a Food and Drug Administration pre-approved research study. . . .

Congress can regulate purely intrastate activity that is not itself "commercial," in that it is not produced for sale, if it concludes that failure to regulate that class of activity would undercut the regulation of the interstate market in that commodity. . . . [Respondents] are cultivating, for home consumption, a fungible commodity for which there is an established, albeit illegal, interstate market. . . .

[A] primary purpose of the CSA is to control the supply and demand of controlled substances in both lawful and unlawful drug markets. . . . Congress had a rational basis for concluding that leaving home-consumed marijuana outside federal control would [like precedent cases] affect price and market conditions. . . .

One need not have a degree in economics to understand why a nationwide exemption for the vast quantity of marijuana (or other drugs) locally cultivated for personal use (which presumably would include use by friends, neighbors, and family members) may have a substantial impact on the interstate market for this extraordinarily popular substance. . . .

Respondents . . . contend that their activities were not "an essential part of a larger regulatory scheme" because they had been "isolated by the State of California, and [are] policed by the State of California," and thus remain "entirely separated from the market." The dissenters fall prey to similar reasoning. The notion that California law has surgically excised a discrete activity that is hermetically sealed off from the larger interstate marijuana market is a dubious proposition, and, more importantly, one that Congress could have rationally rejected.

Indeed, that the California exemptions will have a significant impact on both the supply and demand sides of the market for marijuana is not just "plausible," . . . it is readily apparent. The exemption for physicians provides them with an economic incentive to grant their patients permission to use the drug. In contrast to most prescriptions for legal drugs, which limit the dosage and duration of the usage, under California law the doctor's permission to recommend marijuana use is open-ended. The authority to grant permission whenever the doctor determines that a patient is afflicted with "any other illness for which marijuana provides relief," is broad enough to allow even the most scrupulous doctor to conclude that some recreational uses would be therapeutic. And our cases have taught us that there are some unscrupulous physicians who overprescribe when it is sufficiently profitable to do so.

The exemption for cultivation by patients and caregivers can only increase the supply of marijuana in the California market. The likelihood that all such production will promptly terminate when patients recover or will precisely match the patients' medical needs during their convalescence seems remote; whereas the danger that excesses will satisfy some of the admittedly enormous demand for recreational use seems obvious. Moreover, that the national and international narcotics trade has thrived in the face of vigorous criminal enforcement efforts suggests that no small number of unscrupulous people will make use of the California exemptions to serve their commercial ends whenever it is feasible to do so. . . . Congress could have rationally concluded that the aggregate impact on the national market of all the transactions exempted from federal supervision is unquestionably substantial. . . . [The Court explained that Congress is free to change the CSA and permit the medical use of marijuana.] . . . [U]nder the present state of the law, however, the judgment of the Court of Appeals must be vacated. The case is remanded for further proceedings consistent with this opinion.

It is so ordered.

Justice O'Connor, with whom Chief Justice Rehnquist and Justice Thomas join as to all but Part III, dissenting

. . . One of federalism's chief virtues, of course, is that it promotes innovation by allowing for the possibility that "a single courageous State may, if its citizens choose, serve as a laboratory; and try novel social and economic experiments without risk to the rest of the country."

This case exemplifies the role of States as laboratories. The States' core police powers have always included authority to define criminal law and to protect the health, safety, and welfare of their citizens. Exercising those powers, California (by ballot initiative and then by legislative codification) has come to its own conclusion about the difficult and sensitive question of whether marijuana should be available to relieve severe pain and suffering. Today the Court sanctions an application of the federal Controlled Substances Act that extinguishes that experiment, without any proof that the personal cultivation, possession, and use of marijuana for medicinal purposes, if economic activity in the first place, has a substantial effect on interstate commerce and is therefore an appropriate subject of federal regulation. In so doing, the Court announces a rule that gives Congress a perverse incentive to legislate broadly pursuant to the Commerce Clause—nestling questionable assertions of its authority into comprehensive regulatory schemes—rather than with precision. That rule and the result it produces in this case are irreconcilable with our decisions in [precedent cases]. . . .

California, like other States, has drawn on its reserved powers to distinguish the regulation of medicinal marijuana. To ascertain whether Congress' encroachment is constitutionally justified in this case, then, I would focus here on the personal cultivation, possession, and use of marijuana for medicinal purposes.

Having thus defined the relevant conduct, we must determine whether, under our precedents, the conduct is economic and, in the aggregate, substantially affects interstate commerce. Even if intrastate cultivation and possession of marijuana for one's own medicinal use can properly be characterized as economic, and I question whether it can, it has not been shown that such activity substantially affects interstate commerce. Similarly, it is neither self-evident nor demonstrated that regulating such activity is necessary to the interstate drug control scheme.

The Court's definition of economic activity is breathtaking. It defines as economic any activity involving the production, distribution, and consumption of commodities. And it appears to reason that when an interstate market for a commodity exists, regulating the intrastate manufacture or possession of that commodity is constitutional either because that intrastate activity is itself economic, or because regulating it is a rational part of regulating its market. Putting to one side the problem endemic to the Court's opinion—the shift in focus from the activity at issue in this case to the entirety of what the CSA regulates, the Court's definition of economic activity for purposes of Commerce Clause jurisprudence threatens to sweep all of productive human activity into federal regulatory reach. . . .

In [precedent cases], we suggested that economic activity usually relates directly to commercial activity. The homegrown cultivation and personal possession and use of marijuana for medicinal purposes has no apparent commercial character. Everyone agrees that the marijuana at issue in this case was never in the stream of commerce, and neither were the supplies for growing it. (Marijuana is highly unusual among the substances subject to the CSA in that it can be cultivated without any materials that have traveled in interstate commerce.) [A precedent case] makes clear that possession is not itself commercial activity. And respondents have not come into possession by means of any commercial transaction; they have simply grown, in their own homes, marijuana for their own use, without acquiring, buying, selling, or bartering a thing of value. . . .

Even assuming that economic activity is at issue in this case, the Government has made no showing in fact that the possession and use of homegrown marijuana for medical purposes, in California or elsewhere, has a substantial effect on interstate commerce. Similarly, the Government has not shown that regulating such activity is necessary to an interstate regulatory scheme. . . .

There is simply no evidence that homegrown medicinal marijuana users constitute, in the aggregate, a sizable enough class to have a discernable, let alone substantial, impact on the national illicit drug market—or otherwise to threaten the CSA regime. . . . Because here California, like other States, has carved out a limited class of activity for distinct regulation, the inadequacy of the CSA's findings is especially glaring. The California Compassionate Use Act exempts from other state drug laws patients and their caregivers who possess or cultivate marijuana for the personal medical purposes of the patient upon the written or oral recommendation of a physician to treat a list of serious medical conditions. The Act specifies that it should not be construed to supersede legislation prohibiting persons from engaging in acts dangerous to others, or to condone the diversion of marijuana for nonmedical purposes. To promote the Act's operation and to facilitate law enforcement, California recently enacted an identification card system for qualified patients. We generally assume States enforce their laws and have no reason to think otherwise here.

The Government has not overcome empirical doubt that the number of Californians engaged in personal cultivation, possession, and use of medical marijuana, or the amount of marijuana they produce, is enough to threaten the federal regime. Nor has it shown that Compassionate Use Act marijuana users have been or are realistically likely to be responsible for the drug's seeping into the market in a significant way. The Government does cite one estimate that there were over 100,000 Compassionate Use Act users in California in 2004, but does not explain, in terms of proportions, what their presence means for the national illicit drug market. . . . The Court also offers some arguments about the effect of the Compassionate Use Act on the national market. It says that the California statute might be vulnerable to exploitation by unscrupulous physicians, that Compassionate Use Act patients may overproduce, and that the history of the narcotics trade shows the difficulty of cordoning off any drug use from the rest of the market. These arguments are plausible; if borne out in fact they could justify prosecuting Compassionate Use Act patients under the federal CSA. But, without substantiation, they add little to the CSA's conclusory statements about diversion, essentiality, and market effect. . . .

Relying on Congress' abstract assertions, the Court has endorsed making it a federal crime to grow small amounts of marijuana in one's own home for one's own medicinal use. This overreaching stifles an express choice by some States, concerned for the lives and liberties of their people, to regulate medical marijuana differently. If I were a California citizen, I would not have voted for the medical marijuana ballot initiative; if I were a California legislator I would not have supported the Compassionate Use Act. But whatever the wisdom of California's experiment with medical marijuana, the federalism principles that have driven our Commerce Clause cases require that room for experiment be protected in this case. For these reasons I dissent.

Justice Thomas, dissenting

Respondents Diane Monson and Angel Raich use marijuana that has never been bought or sold, that has never crossed state lines, and that has had no demonstrable effect on the national market for marijuana. If Congress can regulate this under the Commerce Clause, then it can regulate virtually anything—and the Federal Government is no longer one of limited and enumerated powers.

Respondents' local cultivation and consumption of marijuana is not "Commerce . . . . among the several States." . . .

[T]he Commerce Clause empowers Congress to regulate the buying and selling of goods and services trafficked across state lines. . . .

Even the majority does not argue that respondents' conduct is itself "Commerce among the several States." Monson and Raich neither buy nor sell the marijuana that they consume. They cultivate their cannabis entirely in the State of California—it never crosses state lines, much less as part of a commercial transaction. . . .

California's Compassionate Use Act sets respondents' conduct apart from other intrastate producers and users of marijuana. The Act channels marijuana use to "seriously ill Californians," and prohibits "the diversion of marijuana for nonmedical purposes." California strictly controls the cultivation and possession of marijuana for medical purposes. To be eligible for its program, California requires that a patient have an illness that cannabis can relieve, such as cancer, AIDS, or arthritis, and that he obtain a physician's recommendation or approval. Qualified patients must provide personal and medical information to obtain medical identification cards, and there is a statewide registry of cardholders. Moreover, the Medical Board of California has issued guidelines for physicians' cannabis recommendations, and it sanctions physicians who do not comply with the guidelines.

This class of intrastate users is therefore distinguishable from others. . . . The scant evidence that exists suggests that few people—the vast majority of whom are aged 40 or older—register to use medical marijuana. In part because of the low incidence of medical marijuana use, many law enforcement officials report that the introduction of medical marijuana laws has not affected their law enforcement efforts. . . .

In sum, neither in enacting the CSA nor in defending its application to respondents has the Government offered any obvious reason why banning medical marijuana use is necessary to stem the tide of interstate drug trafficking. Congress' goal of curtailing the interstate drug trade would not plainly be thwarted if it could not apply the CSA to patients like Monson and Raich. . . .

This Court has carefully avoided stripping Congress of its ability to regulate interstate commerce, but it has casually allowed the Federal Government to strip States of their ability to regulate intrastate commerce—not to mention a host of local activities, like mere drug possession, that are not commercial.

One searches the Court's opinion in vain for any hint of what aspect of American life is reserved to the States. Yet this

Court knows that "'the Constitution created a Federal Government of limited powers.'" . . .

The majority prevents States like California from devising drug policies that they have concluded provide much-needed respite to the seriously ill. . . . Our federalist system, properly understood, allows California and a growing number of other States to decide for themselves how to safeguard the health and welfare of their citizens. I would affirm the judgment of the Court of Appeals. I respectfully dissent.

For Discussion

The opinions in this case are very lengthy and have been severely cut for this text. But the selections do cover the history of the federal government's reaction to the manufacture, sale, and use of marijuana. Summarize that history, and discuss whether, in light of that history, you think states should be able to legalize the use of marijuana for medicinal purposes. Does the Commerce Clause of the U.S. Constitution alter your opinion? Do you think the criminal regulation of drugs should be left to the states, with the federal government's control remaining only in the tax arena?

What is the difference between permitting physicians to prescribe marijuana for medicinal use and permitting them to prescribe other drugs?

What is the rationale for allowing states to experiment with, for example, drug control, to serve as laboratories for determining the best way to control the negative impact of drugs? Analyze the controversy between the Court's opinion and those of the dissents over the issue of whether the California provision for the use of marijuana for medicinal purposes is an economic activity that legitimately falls under the umbrella of the federal government's constitutional right to regulate interstate commerce. Or, in your analysis, does the Court's decision really rest on other reasons?

This case concerns the rights of the states versus those of the federal government. Analyze this issue, and comment on Justice Thomas's conclusion that if the federal government can regulate the growth and sale of marijuana for medicinal reasons in California, it can "regulate virtually anything."

Subsequent Events

The *Raich* case was sent back to the lower federal court, and in March 2007, a panel of that court held that although it sympathized with Angel McClary Raich, she had not presented uncontroverted evidence that she needed marijuana to survive and thus did not have legal grounds to be exempted from the federal law. Raich, 41, who has an inoperable brain tumor, along with other medical problems, argued that she used marijuana because it kept her alive. Specifically, she testified that it was the only drug that relieved her pain and stimulated her appetite. The panel

stated that it "recognizes the use of marijuana for medical purposes is gaining traction." However, it "has not yet reached the point where a conclusion can be drawn that the right to use medical marijuana is 'fundamental.'"[89]

In 2008 another California plaintiff, Gary Ross, lost his legal battle to use marijuana for medicinal purposes when the California Supreme Court upheld Ross's employer's right to terminate his employment for such use.[90]

INTERNET ACTIVITY

The chapter notes that efforts have been made to reform drug laws and that 13 states have legalized the use of marijuana for medicinal purposes. Consult the website of The National Organization for the Reform of Marijuana Laws (NORML), http://norml.org/index.cfm?Group_ID-5541 (accessed 12 May 2009) and answer the following questions:

1. What are the 13 states, and how do their laws differ?

2. How is marijuana used for medical reasons, and for which diseases?

3. What does research show with regard to the use of marijuana for medicinal reasons?

One might consider NORML to have a biased view toward the use of marijuana. Search the Internet and see whether you can locate organizations, agencies, and other sources that produce information that would challenge the information published on NORML's website.

NOTES

1. *Black's Law Dictionary*, special delux 5th ed. (St. Paul, Minn.: West Publishing, 1979), p. 446.
2. *Black's Law Dictionary*, p. 446.
3. Random House *Compact Unabridged Dictionary*, special 2d ed. (New York: Random House, 1996), p. 600.
4. Quoted in Howard Abadinsky, *Drug Abuse: An Introduction* (Chicago: Nelson-Hall, 1989), p. 2.
5. *Street Drugs: A Drug Identification Guide* (Plymouth, Minn.: Publishers Group, 2004), p. 76.
6. NY CLS Al Bev, Article 5, Section 65-c (2008).
7. NY CLS Penal, Title M, 220.25 (2008).
8. The National Organization for the Reform of Marijuana Laws (NORML), http://www.norml.org, accessed 11 March 2009.
9. See, for example, the Iowa statute, Iowa Code, Title IV, Subtitle 1, Chapter 124, Division IV, Section 124.414 (2008), Drug Paraphernalia.

10. See N.J. Stat., Title 33, Chapter 1, Section 33:1–50 (2008), Manufacture, sale, possession, etc., in violation of chapter; misdemeanor.

11. Iowa Code, Title XVI, Subtitle 1, Chapter 709C, Section 709C.1 (2008).

12. Department of Health and Human Services, Substance Abuse and Mental Health Services Administration, Office of Applied Studies, *Results from the 2007 National Survey on Drug Use and Health: National Findings* (September 2008), http://www.oas.samhsa.gov/nsduh/2k7nsduh/2k7 Results.pdf, accessed 28 July 2008, pp. 1–6.

13. Federal Bureau of Investigation, *Crime in the United States, Uniform Crime Reports 2007* (24 September 2008), http://www.fbi.gov/ucr/cius2007/arrests/index .html, accessed 25 November 2008.

14. Fact Sheet: *Drug-Related Crime* (Rockville, Md.: Drug Policy Information Clearing House, National Criminal Justice Reference Service, March 2000), p. 1.

15. Bureau of Justice Statistics, U.S. Department of Justice, *Drug Use and Crime*, http://www.ojp.usdoj.gov/bjs/dcf/ duc.htm, pp 1–13, accessed 11 March 2009.

16. Office of National Drug Control Policy, *Juveniles and Drugs*, p. 3, www.whitehousedrugpolicy.gov/drugfact/ juveniles/index.html, retrieved 15 August 2005.

17. Karen P. Tandy, Administrator, Drug Enforcement Administration, statement before the House Appropriations subcommittee on Commerce, Justice, State and the Judiciary (24 March 2004).

18. "Rise in Killings Spurs New Steps to Fight Gangs," *New York Times* (17 January 2004), p. 1; "Bratton Shuffles LAPD Brass: Department to Focus on 'Top 10 Percent,'" *Daily News of Los Angeles* (18 November 2003), p. 3N.

19. James C. Howell and James P. Lynch, *Youth Gangs in Schools* (Washington, D.C.: U.S. Department of Justice, Office of Justice Programs, Office of Juvenile Justice and Delinquency Prevention, August 2000), p. 1.

20. National Institute of Alcohol Abuse and Alcoholism (NIAAA)," A Snapshot of Annual High-Risk College Drinking," www.collegedrinkingprevention.gov/, last reviewed 11 July 07, accessed 25 November 2008.

21. "Social Developmental Overview of Heavy Episodic or Binge Drinking Among U.S. College Students," *Psychiatric Times*, Special report: Addition (1 February 2004), p. 57.

22. The Controlled Substances Act is codified at USCS, Title 18, Section 812 (2009).

23. Comprehensive Drug Abuse and Prevention Act of 1970, USCS, Title 21, Sections 801–966 (2009).

24. V.S.A., Title 18, Part V, Chapter 84, Section 4235a (2007).

25. A.R.S., Title 15, Chapter 7, Article 1, Section 15-712 (2008).

26. Cal Pen Code, Part I, Title 8, Chapter 1, Section 187(a)(b)(2008).

27. "Here Come the Pregnancy Police," Time (22 May 1989), p. 104.

28. *Johnson v. State*, 602 So.2d 1288 (Fla. 1992).

29. *In re Valerie D.*, 613 A.2d 748 (Conn. 1992).

30. "Woman Is Convicted of Killing Her Fetus by Smoking Cocaine," *New York Times* (18 May 2001), p. 12; *State v. McKnight*, 576 S.E.2d 168 (S.C. 2003), *cert. denied*, 540 U.S. 819 (2003), *and post-conviction relief granted, McKnight v. State*, 661 S.E.2d 343 (2008).

31. *State v. Peppers*, 552 S.E.2d 288 (S.C. 2001).

32. *Ferguson v. Charleston*, 532 U.S. 67 (2001).

33. The White House, *National Drug Congrol Strategy: FY 2009 Budget Summary* (February 2008), http:// www.whitehousedrugpolicy.gov/publications/policy/ 09budget.pdf, accessed 25 November 2008.

34. Executive Office of the President, Office of National Drug Control Policy, *The Economic Costs of Drug Abuse in the United States 1992-2002* (December 2004), pp. vi–xi, http://www.whitehousedrugpolicy.gov/publications/ economic_costs.pdf, accessed 1 August 2008.

35. *Oakland Housing Authority et al. v. Rucker et al.*, 535 U.S. 125 (2002).

36. *Kyllo v. United States*, 533 U.S. 27 (2001).

37. "Drug Cases Are Upended by the Police in Chicago," *New York Times* (27 December 1997), p. 6.

38. Bureau of Justice Statistics, *Drugs, Crime, and the Criminal Justice System* (Washington, D.C.: U.S. Department of Justice, December 1992), referring to a study by David L. Carter, "Drug-Related Corruption of Police Officers: A Contemporary Typology," *Journal of Criminal Justice* 18 (1990): 88.

39. William J. Sabol, Heather Couture, and Paige M. Harrison, Bureau of Justice Statistics Bulletin, *Prisoners in 2006* (Washington, D.C.: U.S. Department of Justice, Office of Justice Programs, December 2007), pp. 5–6, 9; Heather C. West and William J. Sabol, Department of Justice, Bureau of Justice Statistics, *Prisoners in 2007* (December 2008), p. 1; http://ojp.usdoj/gov/bjs/pub/po7.pdf, accessed 11 March 2009; Department of Justice Press release (11 December 2008), http://ojp.usdoj/gov/bjs/pub/ press/p07ppuspr.htm, accessed 11 March 2009.

40. Bureau of Justice Statistics, *Drugs, Crime and the Criminal Justice System*, pp. 44–45.

41. Bureau of Justice Statistics, *Drugs*, p. 62.

42. USCS, Title 18, Sections 1956–1957 (2009).

43. "Suspicious Activity; Reporting Rules Rely on Bank's Good Judgement," *New York Law Journal* (4 April 1996), p. 5. See also Public Law 91-508 (2006).

44. USCS, Title 31, Sections 5325–5326 (2009).

45. *Ratzlaf v. United States*, 510 U.S. 135 (1994).

46. Tex. Penal Code, Title 7, Chapter 34, Section 34.02 (2009).

47. Tenn. Code Ann., Title 39, Chapter 14, Part 9, Section 39-14-906 (2008).

48. Violent Crime Control and Law Enforcement Act of 1994, Public Law 103-222 (13 September 1994). See Title IX, Drug Control.

49. Anti-Drug Abuse Act of 1986, Section 1 et seq., 100 Stat. 3207; USCS, Title 21, Section 801 (2009). See *United States v. Jackson*, 863 F.2d 1168 (4th Cir. 1989).

50. Quoted in "New Drug Strategy Continues Expansion of Justice System," *Criminal Justice Newsletter* 21 (1 February 1990): 5.

51. Violent Crime Control and Law Enforcement Act of 1994, Public Law 103-222 (2006). See Title IX, Drug Control.

52. "Clinton Unveils Policy to Fight Illicit Narcotics," *Los Angeles Times* (30 April 1996), p. 1.

53. News release from Macmillan Publishing Company concerning the book by Arnold S. Trebach, *The Great Drug War* (New York: Macmillan, 1988).

54. John F. Galliher et al., "*Lindesmith v. Anslinger*: An Early Government Victory in the Failed War on Drugs," *Journal of Criminal Law & Criminology* 88 (Winter 1988): 661-682; quotation is on pp. 670–671.

55. Galliher et al., "*Lindesmith v. Anslinger*," p. 681.

56. Matthew Robinson, "Drug War Lies 2007: Still More Shenanigans from the Office of National Drug Control Policy." Presented to the annual meeting of the Southern Criminal Justice Association, Savannah, Georgia (September 2007), pp. 1, 3.

57. Robinson, "Drug War Lies," p. 13.

58. Michael Welch et al., "Decontextualizing the War on Drugs: A Content Analysis of NIJ Publications and Their Neglect of Race and Class," *Justice Quarterly* 15 (December 1998): 719–742; quotations are on p. 734.

59. "Crack Cocaine Sentencing Policy: Unjustified and Unreasonable," The Sentencing Project, www.sentencing project.org, retrieved 19 August 2005.

60. *United States v. Armstrong*, 517 U.S. 456 (1996).

61. News releases (13 February 2002).

62. "Drug Strategy Must Address Needs of Different Populations," *Alcoholism & Drug Abuse Weekly* 14, no. 9 (4 March 2002): 5.

63. "The President's National Drug Control Strategy," Office of National Drug Control Policy, February 2005, p. 1, www.whitehousedrugpolicy.gov/publications/policy/ndcs05/intro.html, retrieved 15 August 2005.

64. "Recession in Illegal Drug Market Signaled by Falling Youth Use," Press Release, Office of National Drug Control Policy, http://www.whitehousedrugpolicy.gov/news/press08/121108.html, accessed 11 December 2008.

65. National Institute of Law Enforcement and Criminal Justice, *The Nation's Toughest Drug Law: Evaluating the New York Experience: Final Report of the Joint Committee on New York Drug Law Evaluation* (Washington, D.C.: U.S. Government Printing Office, 1977). The statutes are codified at NY CLS Penal Code, Section 220.00 et seq. (2008).

66. Association of the Bar of the City of New York, *News Release* (21 June 1977).

67. See *Carmona v. Ward*, 436 F.Supp. 1153 (S.D.N.Y. 1977), rev'd., 576 F.2d 405 (2d Cir. 1978), *cert. denied*, 439 U.S. 1091 (1979).

68. "Many New York Judges Oppose Strict Drug Laws, Report Says," *Criminal Justice Newsletter* 31, no. 23 (24 December 2001): 4.

69. NY CLS Penal, Part Three, Title M, Article 221, Sections 221.05 and 221.10 (2008).

70. "The Race for Governor: The Drug Laws: Golisano to Take to Airwaves to Condemn Rockefeller Laws," *New York Times* (14 October 2002), p. 4B.

71. "Trying to Slide out of Town," *New York Times* (7 June 2008), p. 16.

72. "Thirty-Five Years of Rockefeller 'Justice,'" *New York Times* (27 May 2008), p. 22.

73. "War on Drugs Nets Small-Time Offenders," *Houston Chronicle* (15 December 2002), p. 1.

74. The Sentencing Project, http://www.sentencingproject.org, accessed 1 August 2008.

75. "Mandatory Minimum Drug Sentences Toppled in Michigan," *U.S. Newswire* (27 December 2002), n.p.

76. Idaho Code, Title 39, Chapter 3, Section 39-301 (2008).

77. The California Statute for First and Second-Time Drug Offenders, as amended, Calif. Penal Code, Part 2, Title 8, Chapter 1, Section 1210.1 (2008).

78. Office of National Drug Control Policy, *Drug Treatment in the Criminal Justice System* (Washington, D.C.: U.S. Department of Justice, March 2001), p. 4.

79. National Criminal Justice Reference Service, "Drug Courts," http://www.ncjrs.gov/spotlight/drug_courts/Summary.html, accessed 26 November 2008.

80. The enactment statute for drug courts may be found in Sections 50001-50002 of the Violent Crime Control and Law Enforcement Act of 1994, Public Law 103-322 (2009).

81. Office of National Drug Control Policy, *Drug Treatment in the Criminal Justice System*, p. 4.

82. The President's National Drug Control Strategy 2008 Annual Report (1 March 2008), pp. 29 and 31, http://www.whitehousedrugpolicy.gov/publications/policy/ndcs08/2008ndcs.pdf, accessed 2 August 2008.

83. The President's National Drug Control Strategy 2009 Annual Report, *Executive Summary* (January 2008), p. 4, http://www.whitehousedrugpolicy.gov/publications/policy/09budget/exec_summ.pdf, accessed 26 November 2008.

84. "Legalize Marijuana, Prominent Jurist Says," *USA Today* (14 September 1995), p. 2.

85. "In Florida, an Initiative Intended to End Bias Is Killed," *New York Times* (6 November 2008), p. 20.

86. *United States v. Oakland Cannabis Buyers' Cooperative*, 532 U.S. 483 (2001), *injunction granted sub nom.*, 2002 U.S. Dist. LEXIS 10660 (N.D.Cal. 2002).

87. *Gonzales v. Raich*, 545 U.S. 1 (2005).

88. Compassionate Use Act of 1996, Cal. Health & Safety Code, Section 11362.5 (2008).

89. *Gonzales v. Raich*, 545 U.S. 1 (2005), *on remand, Raich v. Gonzales*, 500 F.3d 850 (9th Cir. Cal. 2007).

90. *Ross v. Ragingwire Telcommunications, Inc.*, 174 P.3d 200 (Cal. 2008).

CHAPTER 12

Sentencing and the Criminal Law

INTRODUCTION

The first chapter of this text contained a brief discussion of the historical reasons for punishment, noting that rehabilitation lost its position of prominence during the latter part of the twentieth century (although there are some signs of increasing interest in this philosophy today). In its place are retribution (or just deserts), deterrence, and incapacitation. All of these philosophies of sentencing or punishment have had a place of importance at some period in history. Their respective positions change as social, economic, and political conditions change. The philosophy in vogue at any given time is reflected in the nature and types of sentences that society uses for convicted offenders.

In recent years we have seen some significant changes in sentencing philosophies. Considerable attention has been given to criminal justice reform but especially to sentencing. In many jurisdictions the emphasis on punishment rather than rehabilitation, along with the concern that sentencing should be more uniform, has led to significant changes in the type and nature of punishment, with punishment now a stated goal. However, as already noted, some states, such as California, have refocused attention on rehabilitation and treatment rather than punishment in the area of drug offenses.

Focus 12.1 contains part of the Washington penal code, which states several purposes of punishment. Note in particular that although Washington enacted that statement of purpose in 1981, the last purpose, to reduce reoffending, was added in 1999.

Many procedures and issues regarding sentencing could be discussed, but space and the purpose of an undergraduate text impose some limitations. Thus, this chapter focuses on several of the more recent trends in sentencing and sentencing reform as well as some of the legal issues posed by these measures. But first, the chapter contains an overview of how sentences are determined.

DETERMINING SENTENCES

A **sentence** is the judgment pronounced formally by a trial court and imposed on a defendant who pleads guilty or who is found guilty after a trial. The type and length of the sentence may be determined in one of several ways: legislatively, judicially, or administratively.

Sentence Models

Most sentencing involves a combination of the legislative, judicial, and administrative models; for analytical purposes, each must be defined.

In the *legislative model*, the type and length of sentence for each crime are determined by the legislature and codified into the criminal law. In the purest form of this model, no discretion is permitted in sentencing. For example, upon conviction of first-degree burglary, a defendant must be sentenced to 10 years in the state prison. That term cannot be reduced administratively by prison officials or by parole boards. Such a sentence established by the legislature is called a **determinate sentence**, in contrast to an **indeterminate sentence**, in which the legislature either does not set a term, leaves the decision to judicial discretion, or sets minimum and maximum terms and permits judges to set the actual sentence in each case.

In the *judicial model*, judges are the final determiners of sentences; that is, no administrative releases are permitted.

In reality the pure forms of legislative and judicial sentencing rarely occur. Even during the push for determinate sentencing, most states left some discretionary sentencing power with judges. Some retained at least part of the administrative model, in which parole boards may grant early releases or prison administrators may reduce time served by granting **good-time credits** to inmates who do not violate prison rules.

FOCUS 12.1 Legislative Statements of the Purpose of Sentencing

Until recently many jurisdictions did not include the purpose of sentencing in their statutes, and those that did often reflected only a punishment purpose. Some states have moved toward a rehabilitation philosophy in recent years. For example, California's treatment approach to minor drug offenders has been noted. Additionally, in recent years, that state changed the name of its department of corrections to include the words *and rehabilitation*.

In 1981 Washington enacted a comprehensive revision of its criminal code, the Sentencing Reform Act of 1981, in which the legislature for the first time stated the purpose of sentencing. Specifically, the legislature made six declarations in the first section of the sentencing act. In 1999 the state added the seventh statement.

The purpose of this chapter is to make the criminal justice system accountable to the public by developing a system for the sentencing of felony offenders which structures, but does not eliminate, discretionary decisions affecting sentences designed to:

(1) Ensure that the punishment for a criminal offense is proportionate to the seriousness of the offense and the offender's criminal history;
(2) Promote respect for the law by providing punishment which is just;
(3) Be commensurate with the punishment imposed on others committing similar offenses;
(4) Protect the public;
(5) Offer the offender an opportunity to improve him or herself;
(6) Make frugal use of the state's resources; and
(7) Reduce the risk of reoffending by offenders in the community.[1]

1. Rev. Code Wash., Title 9, Chapter 9.94A, Section 9.94A.010 (2008).

The *administrative model* was prominent during the period in which the philosophy of rehabilitation was popular. Rehabilitation is based on the philosophy that offenders should be sent to prison for an indeterminate period and receive treatment. When they are rehabilitated, they should be released. Allegations of abuse of the rehabilitation approach, along with a belief that the philosophy could not work anyway, led to a deemphasis on it.

Some states specify sentences for each type of offense, such as a certain number of years for second-degree murder. Others classify all misdemeanors and all felonies and specify sentences (or sentence ranges) for each category. The Texas statutes, which follow the latter pattern, are reasonably short and are reprinted in full in Focus 12.2. As is obvious from those statutes, Texas classifies misdemeanors as Class A, B, or C and felonies as capital, first degree, second degree, third degree, and state jail felony.

In any of these sentencing models, the power to determine the length of sentences may be altered by other factors. Power may be given to the governor (or the president, in the case of federal crimes) to reduce a sentence, to commute a life sentence to a term of years, or to commute a death sentence to life, a process called *clemency*. The governor (or president) may also have the power to grant a **pardon**, an act of grace that exempts the offender from punishment (or further punishment if some time has already been served). Some legislatures have given governors the authority to order the release of inmates when prisons reach their court-imposed maximum populations. This permits the system to incarcerate new (and presumably more dangerous) inmates.

Presumptive Sentencing

In **presumptive sentencing** the legislature specifies the normal sentence for each crime, and judges are permitted to deviate only under specified types of circumstances or by giving written reasons or both. Presumptive sentencing may be contrasted with indeterminate sentencing, which is not necessarily based on any guidelines, conditions, or presumptions and thus gives broader discretion to the sentencing judge, who is not required to justify his or her decision by providing written reasons.

In its 1976 report, the Twentieth Century Task Force on Criminal Sentencing recommended presumptive sentencing based on a detailed study of sentencing. Presumptive sentencing is based on the assumption that "a finding of guilty of committing a crime would predictably incur a particular sentence unless specific mitigating or aggravating factors are established." Presumptive sentencing enables the legislature to "retain the power to make those broad policy decisions that

FOCUS 12.2 Statutory Penalties in the Texas Criminal System

Texas Penal Code, Title 3, Chapter 12 (2009)

Subchapter B. Ordinary Misdemeanor Punishments

Section 12.21. Class A misdemeanor

An individual adjudged guilty of a Class A misdemeanor shall be punished by:

(1) a fine not to exceed $4,000;
(2) confinement in jail for a term not to exceed one year; or
(3) both such fine and confinement.

Section 12.22. Class B misdemeanor

An individual adjudged guilty of a Class B misdemeanor shall be punished by:

(1) a fine not to exceed $2,000;
(2) confinement in jail for a term not to exceed 180 days; or
(3) both such fine and confinement.

Section 12.23. Class C misdemeanor

An individual adjudged guilty of a Class C misdemeanor shall be punished by a fine not to exceed $500.

Texas Penal Code, Title 3, Chapter 12 (2009)

Subchapter C. Ordinary Felony Punishments

Section 12.31. Capital felony

(a) An individual adjudged guilty of a capital felony in a case in which the state seeks the death penalty shall be punished by imprisonment in the institutional division for life or by death. An individual adjudged guilty of a capital felony in a case in which the state does not seek the death penalty shall be punished by imprisonment in the institutional division for life without parole.

(b) In a capital felony trial in which the state seeks the death penalty, prospective jurors shall be informed that a sentence of life imprisonment or death is mandatory on conviction of a capital felony. In a capital felony trial in which the state does not seek the death penalty, prospective jurors shall be informed that the state is not seeking the death penalty and that a sentence of life imprisonment without parole is mandatory on conviction of the capital felony.

Section 12.32. First degree felony punishment

(a) An individual adjudged guilty of a felony of the first degree shall be punished by imprisonment in the institutional division for life or for any term of not more than 99 years or less than 5 years.

(b) In addition to imprisonment, an individual adjudged guilty of a felony of the first degree may be punished by a fine not to exceed $10,000.

Section 12.33. Second degree felony punishment

(a) An individual adjudged guilty of a felony of the second degree shall be punished by imprisonment in the institutional division for any term of not more than 20 years or less than 2 years.

(b) In addition to imprisonment, an individual adjudged guilty of a felony of the second degree may be punished by a fine not to exceed $10,000.

Section 12.34. Third degree felony punishment

(a) An individual adjudged guilty of a felony of the third degree shall be punished by imprisonment in the institutional division for any term of not more than 10 years or less than 2 years.

(b) In addition to imprisonment, an individual adjudged guilty of a felony of the third degree may be punished by a fine not to exceed $10,000.

Section 12.35. State jail felony punishment

(a) Except as provided by Subsection (c), an individual adjudged guilty of a state jail felony shall be punished by confinement in a state jail for any term of not more than 2 years or less than 180 days.

(b) In addition to confinement, an individual adjudged guilty of a state jail felony may be punished by a fine not to exceed $10,000.

(c) An individual adjudged guilty of a state jail felony shall be punished for a third degree felony if it is shown on the trial of the offense that:

(1) a deadly weapon as defined by Section 1.07 was used or exhibited during the commission of the offense or during immediate flight following the commission of the offense, and that the individual used or exhibited the deadly weapon or was a party to the offense and knew that a deadly weapon would be used or exhibited; or

(2) the individual has previously been finally convicted of any felony [enumerated in either of two specific sections of the state's code of criminal procedure].

can be wisely and justly made about crime and do not involve the particulars of specific crimes and criminals." At the same time, it allows the sentencing judge "some degree of guided discretion to consider and weigh those pertinent factors that cannot be wisely evaluated in the absence of the particular crime and criminal."[1]

Two points should be considered in presumptive sentencing. First, judicial discretion is not abolished, and, second, "the proper mechanism for establishing the presumptive sentence guidelines, after full public hearing and careful consideration of what *might* be done in sentencing, is a sentencing commission."[2]

Sentencing Guidelines

Presumptive sentencing may be accomplished through the use of a sentencing commission that establishes **sentencing guidelines**. These guidelines may be viewed as a way to control judicial discretion without abolishing it and as a means of correcting the disparity that can result from individualized sentencing. Basically, this is what happens. A judge has an offender to sentence. Without any sentencing guidelines, the judge may consider the individual's background, the nature of the offense, or other variables. When sentencing guidelines are used, the difference is that the relevance of the variables considered may have been researched and quantified. In addition, the judge has a benchmark of an appropriate penalty in each case. The judge may decide it is reasonable to deviate from the guidelines; in that situation, reasons should be given.

Guidelines need not be based on previous sentences. They may be developed on the basis of any reasons deemed appropriate. Some states have experimented with appointing advisory committees, usually consisting of judges, to develop voluntary sentencing guidelines. States may also have sentencing guidelines established by the legislature while providing for appellate judicial review of the application of those guidelines. Judicial review would be available to the prosecution as well as to the defense. This approach is illustrated by recent reforms at both the state and the federal levels. Reforms differ from state to state, and any attempt to summarize them might be confusing to the beginning student. Washington offers an example of a state that has developed sentencing guidelines. The discussion of these guidelines in the next section is followed by an analysis of the federal sentencing guidelines and reactions to them.

State Sentencing Guidelines

The Washington state sentencing guidelines illustrate state approaches. After much controversy and a five-year study, the Washington state legislature enacted its Sentencing Reform Act of 1981, described by one scholar as "the most comprehensive—and in many respects the most thoughtful—sentencing reform measure enacted in the United States in the last half-century."[3]

The Washington legislature rejected the underlying assumptions of the indeterminate sentencing approach, which permits tailoring sentences to the individual needs of a particular defendant. But the legislature recognized that it is impossible (and undesirable) to attempt to eliminate all judicial discretion. (See again Focus 12.l, where the purpose of the 1981 Washington sentencing reform is reprinted in part.)

The result in Washington was legislative formulation of presumptive sentences that retain considerable judicial discretion but are within the framework of legislative standards. The judge's sentencing decision is final (and in that sense, the sentence is a determinate, not an indeterminate, one), but if it deviates from the legislative standards, reasons must be given for the deviation, and the decision is subject to judicial review.[4]

A judge may sentence outside the range appropriate for a particular defendant, thereby departing from the sentencing guidelines, if **mitigating circumstances** or **aggravating circumstances** exist. *Mitigating circumstances* are those that do not justify or excuse a crime but that, because of justice and fairness, make the crime less reprehensible. They may be used to reduce a crime to a lesser offense, such as from murder to manslaughter. *Aggravating circumstances* are those that are above or beyond the elements required for the crime but that make the crime more serious. They may be used with reference to many crimes, but both aggravating and mitigating circumstances must be considered before capital punishment may be imposed.

Under specified conditions, the exceptional sentence would be subject to judicial review. The Washington statute enumerates some circumstances that may be considered by judges imposing an exceptional sentence, although the list, reproduced in part in Focus 12.3, is not meant to be exhaustive.

Federal Sentencing Guidelines

The federal sentencing guidelines were authorized by the Sentencing Reform Act of 1984, a part of the federal criminal code revision that was passed after years of dis-

FOCUS 12.3 Aggravating and Mitigating Circumstances in Sentencing

[The Washington Sentencing Reform Act of 1981 provides that judges may impose sentences outside the sentencing guidelines after considering aggravating or mitigating circumstances such as provided by statute. Some of the illustrations are as follows:]

(1) Mitigating Circumstances . . .

   (a) To a significant degree, the victim was an initiator, willing participant, aggressor, or provoker of the incident.

   (b) Before detection, the defendant compensated, or made a good faith effort to compensate, the victim of the criminal conduct for any damage or injury sustained.

   (c) The defendant committed the crime under duress, coercion, threat, or compulsion insufficient to constitute a complete defense but which significantly affected his or her conduct.

   (d) The defendant, with no apparent predisposition to do so, was induced by others to participate in the crime.

   (e) The defendant's capacity to appreciate the wrongfulness of his conduct or to conform his or her conduct to the requirements of the law was significantly impaired. Voluntary use of drugs or alcohol is excluded.

   (f) The offense was principally accomplished by another person and the defendant manifested extreme caution or sincere concern for the safety or well-being of the victim.

   (g) The operation of the multiple offense policy of [another code section] results in a presumptive sentence that is clearly excessive in light of the purpose of this chapter, as expressed in [another code section].

   (h) The defendant or the defendant's children suffered a continuing pattern of physical or sexual abuse by the victim of the offense and the offense is a response to that abuse.

(2) Aggravating Circumstances—Considered and Imposed by the Court . . .

(3) Aggravating Circumstances—Considered by a Jury—Imposed by the Court . . .

   (a) The defendant's conduct during the commission of the current offense manifested deliberate cruelty to the victim.

   (b) The defendant knew or should have known that the victim of the current offense was particularly vulnerable or incapable of resistance.

   (c) The current offense was a violent offense, and the defendant knew that the victim of the current offense was pregnant.

   (d) The current offense was a major economic offense or series of offenses, so identified by a consideration of any of the following factors:

     (i) The current offense involved multiple victims or multiple incidents per victim;

     (ii) The current offense involved attempted or actual monetary loss substantially greater than typical for the offense;

     (iii) The current offense involved a high degree of sophistication or planning or occurred over a lengthy period of time; or

     (iv) The defendant used his or her position of trust, confidence, or fiduciary responsibility to facilitate the commission of the current offense.

   (e) The current offense was a major violation of the Uniform Controlled Substances Act (VUCSA), related to trafficking in controlled substances, which was more onerous than the typical offense of its statutory definition. The presence of ANY of the following may identify a current offense as a major VUCSA violation: [the statute then lists eight factors relating to drugs].[1]

1. Rev. Code Wash., Title 9, Chapter 9.94A, Section 9.94A.535 (2008), citations omitted.

cussion and multiple drafts.[5] One of the most important provisions was the establishment of the U.S. Sentencing Commission to develop sentencing guidelines.

The federal sentencing commission consists of seven voting and two nonvoting, ex officio members. The commission was required by law to submit its initial guidelines by 13 April 1987, which it did. Those guidelines were to become law unless Congress enacted another law prior to 1 November 1987. Congress did not do so. The commission is a permanent agency. It may submit amendments to the sentencing guidelines each year between the beginning of a regular congressional session and May 1. Those amendments become effective unless Congress passes a law to the contrary prior to November of the year in which the commission makes the proposals.

Theoretically, the federal sentencing guidelines eliminate the unfairness and uncertainty of the indeterminate sentence by abolishing parole and limiting early release by reducing the effect of good-time credits. Fairness is allegedly achieved by numbers, with offenses grouped by categories (e.g., offenses involving persons and offenses involving property). A basic-offense point value is assigned, and, in making that assignment, the sentencing judge is to look at the total circumstances involved when the offense was committed.

The commission recognized that it might be impossible to achieve two of the goals established by Congress: uniformity and proportionality. To achieve *uniformity*, Congress intended for the sentencing structure to result in a narrowing of the wide disparity in sentences received by defendants committing the same offenses in different federal jurisdictions. *Proportionality* means that the sentence imposed should be commensurate with the severity of the offense; an armed robbery is more serious than an unarmed robbery.

The U.S. Supreme Court upheld the constitutionality of the federal sentencing guidelines in its 1989 decision in *Mistretta v. United States*.[6] Reactions to the federal sentencing guidelines continued to vary, however, with some federal judges upholding the guidelines and others striking at least portions of them. Some federal judges and attorneys called for the abolition of the guidelines.[7]

In 2003, the American Bar Association (ABA) appointed the Kennedy Commission to study federal sentencing guidelines. The Kennedy Commission, named after U.S. Supreme Court Associate Justice Anthony M. Kennedy, who challenged lawyers to pay more attention to sentencing and specifically called for more judicial discretion in criminal sentencing, issued numerous resolutions, which were adopted by the ABA's House of Delegates in 2004.[8]

Litigation Concerning Sentencing Guidelines

Numerous issues have been raised concerning state and federal sentencing guidelines. The most significant U.S. Supreme Court decisions are noted.

In *Blakely v. Washington* in 2004,[9] the Court held that some aspects of the Washington (state) sentence structure are unconstitutional. Ralph Blakely Jr. had entered a guilty plea to kidnapping his estranged wife, Yolanda. Blakely bound Yolanda with duct tape, forced her into a wooden box by threatening her with a knife, placed the box in his truck, and drove to a friend's house in Montana. The couple's son was in a car following the truck. Blakely's purpose in committing this crime was to pressure Yolanda to abandon her plans to divorce him.

Blakely was charged with first-degree kidnapping, which had a statutory maximum sentence of 10 years in prison. Under a plea deal with the prosecutor, Blakely was permitted to plead to a lesser charge, for which the sentencing guidelines recommended a maximum sentence of 53 months. The sentencing judge, stating 32 findings of fact on which he based his decision that Blakely acted with deliberate cruelty, added 37 months to the recommended maximum of 53 months. The U.S. Supreme Court held that, in sentencing, defendants have a right to have a jury determine *all* facts that might lead to sentence enhancement.

In reversing Blakely's sentence, the majority of the U.S. Supreme Court justices said they were adhering to their controversial 2000 precedent case of *United States v. Apprendi*. Charles C. Apprendi was accused of firing shots into the home of African American neighbors and stating that he did not want them living there (Apprendi subsequently denied making that statement). Apprendi pleaded guilty to two counts of second-degree possession of a firearm for an unlawful purpose and one count of third-degree unlawful possession of a bomb. The judge found that the defendant acted with the intent required by the hate crime statute, which provides sentence enhancement for a crime if it can be shown that the defendant acted with bias; the judge then enhanced Apprendi's penalty in accordance with that statute. The U.S. Supreme Court held that any fact (other than a prior conviction) that can be used to enhance a sentence must be submitted to the jury and found to be true beyond a reasonable doubt.[10]

In 2005 the U.S. Supreme Court decided two cases involving issues left unanswered by *Blakely*: (1) whether, if a trial judge alone conducts fact-finding at the sentencing hearing, that violates the defendant's Sixth Amendment rights and (2) whether the federal sentencing guidelines are still viable.

The first case, *United States v. Booker*, involved Freddie J. Booker, who was convicted of being in possession of and distributing crack cocaine. When Booker was arrested, the police seized 92.5 grams of the illegal drug. Under the federal sentencing guidelines, that amount of illegal drugs, added to Booker's 23 prior convictions, would result in a prison sentence of a little less than 22 years. At the sentencing hearing, the judge added 20 more ounces of cocaine because Booker had told detectives that he sold that amount in the months prior to his arrest. The judge also concluded that Booker committed perjury at the trial and thus added an obstruction of justice conviction. These additional factors enabled the judge to sentence Booker to 30 years. The circuit court of appeals reversed.[11]

The second case, *United States v. Fanfan*, involved Ducan Fanfan, who was convicted in Maine in 2003 of conspiring to distribute at least 500 grams of *powder* cocaine. At the sentencing hearing, the prosecution offered evidence that Fanfan also dealt in *crack* cocaine, which carried a significantly longer penalty than offenses associated with powder cocaine. The federal sentencing judge initially gave Fanfan a 16-year sentence, but, on the basis of *Blakely*, which was decided four days prior to Fanfan's sentence hearing, the judge reduced that sentence to 6-and-a-half years, basing that sentence on the amount of drugs considered by the jury in its fact-finding.[12]

Booker and *Fanfan* were decided in January 2005. The U.S. Supreme Court released 124 pages, consisting of two separate 5-4 majority opinions. The opinion written by Justice John Paul Stevens states that the Sixth Amendment guarantee of a right to trial by jury is violated when a sentence is based on facts determined only by a judge. The second opinion, written by Justice Stephen G. Breyer, reduces the federal sentencing guidelines to an advisory role. According to Breyer, "The district courts, while not bound to apply the guidelines, must consult those guidelines and take them into account when sentencing." But, Breyer noted that Congress could act when he said, "The ball now lies in Congress' court. The national legislature is equipped to devise and install, long-term, the sentencing system compatible with the Constitution, that Congress judges best for the federal system of justice. . . . Ours is not the last word."[13]

But Congress did not act, and during its 2006–2007 term, with federal courts disagreeing on how to resolve the issues left by these cases, the U.S. Supreme Court heard two cases that involved some of the unanswered questions. The first case, *Rita v. United States*, concerned the issue of whether a sentence in the federal guidelines is *presumed* to be reasonable, which would effectively limit or eliminate an appeal should that sentence be imposed. The issue arose in the case of Victor Rita, who was convicted of offenses related to providing false testimony before a grand jury. The defendant argued before the trial court that the guidelines were unreasonable in his case and that he should be given a lighter sentence due to his health, his fear of being

abused in prison, and his distinguished military service. The U.S. Supreme Court upheld the lower court's ruling that the imposed sentence was reasonable because it was within the federal sentencing guidelines. Thus, a decision that falls within the federal sentencing guidelines is reasonable.[14]

The second case, *Claiborne v. United States*, concerned the requirements of a federal judge who imposes a sentence that is significantly shorter than that of the sentencing guidelines. In *Claiborne*, prosecutors challenged a 15-month prison sentence imposed on a defendant who was convicted of possession with intent to distribute crack cocaine. The federal sentencing guidelines provide for a three-year minimum sentence for this offense. Unfortunately, the 23-year-old defendant in this case was murdered shortly before the Court's decision was announced, and the Court vacated the case.[15]

The U.S. Supreme Court continued its analysis of federal sentencing guidelines by deciding two key cases on 10 December 2007. Both appellants were drug offenders. In *Gall v. United States*, the Supreme Court upheld the trial court's decision to put the defendant, Brian Michael Gall, on probation for 36 months rather than sentence him to prison after he entered a guilty plea to conspiracy to distribute MDMA (also referred to as *Ecstasy*), which is a class C felony and carries a prison term within the guidelines, with the length of that term depending on the facts of the case. The defendant made a motion for a downward departure from the federal sentencing guidelines, and, based on his limited prior criminal record, age, cooperation with the government, remorse, post-offense rehabilitation (he was a college student), and several other reasons, the judge decided on probation rather than prison.[16]

The facts of the second case and the sentencing issues are explained in the following excerpt from that case.[17]

KIMBROUGH v. UNITED STATES
128 S.Ct. 558 (2007)

Justice Ruth Bader Ginsburg delivered the opinion of the Court, in which Chief Justice John Roberts and Justices John Paul Stevens, Antonin E. Scalia, Anthony M. Kennedy, David H. Souter, and Stephen G. Breyer, joined. Justice Scalia filed a concurring opinion. Justices Clarence Thomas and Samuel Alito filed dissenting opinions.

This Court's remedial opinion in *United States v. Booker* instructed district courts to read the United States Sentencing Guidelines as "effectively advisory." In accord with [the federal statute], the Guidelines, formerly mandatory, now serve as one factor among several courts must consider in determining an appropriate sentence. *Booker* further instructed that "reasonableness" is the standard controlling appellate review of the sentences district courts impose. . . .

The question here presented is whether, as the Court of Appeals held in this case, "a sentence . . . outside the guidelines range is per se unreasonable when it is based on a disagreement with the sentencing disparity for crack and powder cocaine offenses." We hold that, under *Booker*, the cocaine Guidelines, like all other Guidelines, are advisory only, and that the Court of Appeals erred in holding the crack/powder disparity effectively mandatory. A district judge must include the Guidelines range in the array of factors warranting consideration. The judge may determine, however, that, in the particular case, a within-Guidelines sentence is "greater than necessary" to serve the objectives of sentencing. In making that determination, the judge may consider the disparity between the Guidelines' treatment of crack and powder cocaine offenses.

In September 2004, petitioner Derrick Kimbrough was indicted in the United States District Court for the Eastern District of Virginia and charged with four offenses: conspiracy to distribute crack and powder cocaine; possession with intent to distribute more than 50 grams of crack cocaine; possession with intent to distribute powder cocaine; and possession of a firearm in furtherance of a drug-trafficking offense. Kimbrough pleaded guilty to all four charges.

Under the relevant statutes, Kimbrough's plea subjected him to an aggregate sentence of 15 years to life in prison. . . . [The Court discussed the details of the application of the guidelines to this case and the much longer sentence that would have been involved. The Court continued.]

A sentence in this range, in the District Court's judgment, would have been "greater than necessary" to accomplish the purposes of sentencing set forth in [the applicable statute]. As required by [the statute], the court took into account the "nature and circumstances" of the offense and Kimbrough's "history and characteristics." The court also commented that the case exemplified the "disproportionate and unjust effect that crack cocaine guidelines have in sentencing." In this regard, the court contrasted Kimbrough's Guidelines range of 228 to 270 months with the range that would have applied had he been accountable for an equivalent amount of powder cocaine: 97 to 106 months, inclusive of the 5-year manda-

tory minimum for the firearm charge. Concluding that the statutory minimum sentence was "clearly long enough" to accomplish the objectives listed in [the statute], the court sentenced Kimbrough to 15 years, or 180 months, in prison plus 5 years of supervised release. . . .

[The Court discussed the similarities between the two types of cocaine and noted the dissimilarity in sentencing for violating the statutes for powder and crack cocaine. The Court also discussed the history of the legislation and the development of the federal sentencing commission and its mission, its reasons for the differential sentencing, and its efforts to change that differential in recent years. The Court discussed the impact of *Booker* on sentencing guidelines and concluded.] . . .

While rendering the Sentencing Guidelines advisory, we have nevertheless preserved a key role for the Sentencing Commission. As explained in [other cases], district courts must treat the Guidelines as the "starting point and the initial benchmark." Congress established the Commission to formulate and constantly refine national sentencing standards. Carrying out its charge, the Commission fills an important institutional role: It has the capacity courts lack to "base its determinations on empirical data and national experience, guided by a professional staff with appropriate expertise."

We have accordingly recognized that, in the ordinary case, the Commission's recommendation of a sentencing range will "reflect a rough approximation of sentences that might achieve [the statute's] objectives." The sentencing judge, on the other hand, has "greater familiarity with . . . the individual case and the individual defendant before him than the Commission or the appeals court." He is therefore "in a superior position to find facts and judge their import in each particular case. In light of these discrete institutional strengths, a district court's decision to vary from the advisory Guidelines may attract greatest respect when the sentencing judge finds a particular case "outside the 'heartland' to which the Commission intends individual Guidelines to apply." On the other hand, while the Guidelines are no longer binding, closer review may be in order when the sentencing judge varies from the Guidelines based solely on the judge's view that the Guidelines range "fails properly to reflect [statutory] considerations."

The U.S. Supreme Court has also recently decided cases concerning state sentencing laws. In January 2007, the Court decided a case involving California's criminal sentencing law. In *Cunningham v. California*, the appellant had been convicted of the continuous sexual abuse of a child. Under California law, this offense is punishable by a lower term sentence of 6 years, a middle term of 12 years, or an upper term of 16 years. California law required the trial court to impose the middle term unless there was evidence of mitigating or aggravating circumstances. The trial judge had imposed the upper term of 16 years after finding, by a preponderance of the evidence, six aggravating circumstances. The U.S. Supreme Court reversed, holding that the aggravating circumstances must be determined by a jury, which is required to find facts by the higher evidence standard of beyond a reasonable doubt. According to the majority opinion, "Factfinding to elevate a sentence from 12 to 16 years, our decisions make plain, falls within the province of the jury."[18]

In March 2005, the U.S. Supreme Court decided *Shepard v. United States*. This case reexamined the role of judges in sentencing. In the *Apprendi* case, the Court had ruled that any fact, other than a prior conviction, that is used in sentence enhancement must be determined by a jury. *Shepard* involved a defendant who had previously entered guilty pleas to four burglaries, but the necessary details of those crimes were not contained in the plea agreement. The appeals court had ruled that the trial court should have inquired into police reports to determine whether any of those prior felonies met the requirements of the federal statute under which Reginald Shepard was convicted. That statute, the Armed Career Criminal Act (ACCA), provides for enhanced penalties for offenders who have been convicted of specified prior violent felonies. Burglary counts as a violent felony only if it occurred in a building or enclosed space, such as a house; burglarizing a car or boat does not count. The federal district court ruled that the prosecutor did not present sufficient evidence that the prior burglaries qualified Shepard (who entered a guilty plea to being a felon in possession of a firearm) for the 15-year mandatory minimum sentence under the federal statute. The judge imposed a sentence of three years. The appellate court reversed and, in effect, ordered the lower court to impose the 15-year mandatory minimum sentence.[19]

The U.S. Supreme Court, by a 5-3 vote (Chief Justice William H. Rehnquist did not participate in the case), reversed the decision of the appellate court. Justice David H. Souter, who wrote the majority opinion, stated that *Apprendi* and other recent precedent cases limit trial judges to official court documents when they investigate the nature of prior felonies for purposes of sentence enhancement. Thus, in Shepard's case, the

trial judge should not have gone beyond the official transcript of the plea bargaining process to determine whether Shepard's prior burglaries met the requirements for sentence enhancement under the ACCA.[20]

Critique of Sentencing Guidelines

Both state and federal sentencing guidelines have been criticized for numerous reasons, but the brunt of the criticism has been leveled at the federal system. These critiques are still relevant, for as the *Booker* case indicates, the guidelines are still in effect; they are just not mandatory. Of course, given the lack of teeth in the guidelines, it could reasonably be argued that the critiques we discuss will be even more critical. For example, if **sentence disparity** existed under the mandatory guidelines, we could expect it to be even more extensive under guidelines that are only advisory. Part

Despite legislative attempts to decrease the discretion of judges at the sentencing stage, some jurisdictions still permit wide judicial decision making in sentencing. (Jacom Stephens/IStockPhoto)

of the problem, however, is to determine what is meant by *sentence disparity*. Generally, the term is used to describe the variations and inequities that result when defendants convicted of the same crime receive different sentences, but it may also refer to varying legislative sentences among the states. The federal sentencing guidelines could do nothing about sentence disparity in that regard.

In addition to the criticisms aimed specifically at the U.S. Sentencing Commission and the federal guidelines are problems created by both the state and the federal guidelines. Not all agree on these problems, but one conclusion is clear: In most cases sentencing guidelines have resulted in longer sentences being served. In his testimony before the U.S. Sentencing Commission on 17 November 2004, Christopher A. Wray, an assistant attorney general in the U.S. Department of Justice, stated that from 1992 to 2002, "[T]he average time served in prison for a drug offense increased by 31% from 32.7 months to 42.9 months." Wray also noted that since the federal sentencing guidelines were fully implemented in 1989, "disparity in sentencing between African Americans and whites has increased." Specifically, from 1994 to 2002, time served by African Americans increased more (29.1 compared to 57.2 months) than time served by whites (29.1 compared to 37.2 months). Wray attributed this discrepancy primarily to the 100-to-1 ratio of crack compared to powder cocaine sentences, which was discussed in Chapter 11 and for which updates are provided later in this chapter.

Attempts to eliminate or reduce judicial sentencing discretion at the state level have also occurred. The Washington Sentencing Reform Act is an example. This statute highlights some additional issues involved in structured sentencing. Although the Washington statute is more structured than its predecessor, it is still open to interpretation. Refer back to Focus 12.3, and consider carefully some of the words and phrases used in describing mitigating and aggravating circumstances. How are they to be interpreted? The answer is by the decision of the sentencing judge. In addition, judges have wide discretion when sentencing within the ranges of the legislative guidelines.

Discretion goes beyond the judge. Most of the sentencing reforms will have little or no effect on prosecutorial discretion. Prosecutors may refuse to prosecute a particular case or may control the nature and number of charges that will be filed. Prosecutors also have wide discretion in plea bargaining with defendants, and, as noted earlier, they may use that ability to avoid mandatory minimum sentences for offenders who cooperate with them. In addition, juries have considerable discretion. If they think a determinate sentence that would be imposed after a guilty verdict is unreasonable, they may refuse to convict.

Another problem is that most reforms using sentencing guidelines provide that they apply only to prison or jail terms, with wide discretion permitted in the imposition of alternative sentences, leaving open the possibility of disparity.

Other results may also occur. When sentencing reform results in longer sentences, it intensifies the already overcrowded conditions of most prisons. Furthermore, mathematical approaches to sentencing give the appearance of being precise and more scientific than other methods, but arbitrariness and discrimination may creep into the system when guidelines contain ambiguous words that must be interpreted in the context of a specific case.

Sentencing guidelines may be so complicated that judges, prosecutors, and defense attorneys do not understand the system or must spend considerable time learning it. Although sentencing reform in some manner has occurred in most jurisdictions and in the federal system, the systems vary, which means that sentence disparity may continue when the various jurisdictions are compared.

Finally, as long as the time served by an inmate may be reduced by good-time credits or by a parole board (or some other administrative agency) acting on those or other factors, disparity may result.

The solution to this problem in some jurisdictions has been to abolish **parole** as a form of early release. *Parole* refers to the early release of an inmate from incarceration. The inmate is permitted to return to the community but is frequently required to wear an electronic monitor. Conditions are imposed on the parolee, such as not being permitted to leave the county, drive, associate with certain persons, drink alcoholic beverages, or use other drugs. Violation of a parole condition can result in being returned to prison.

Abolition of parole removes one method that has been used to alleviate prison overcrowding or to reduce the harshness of sentences in particular cases. Parole as early release was abolished by the federal system and several states, although some states, such as Florida, which had abolished parole in 1983, reinstated it because of severe prison overcrowding. In other states a system similar to parole but using another name has emerged, thus reintroducing administrative release, which can lead to the very abuses that were intended to be eliminated with the abolition of parole boards.

RECENT SENTENCING REFORM MEASURES

Reforms other than sentence guidelines have been implemented both at the state and the federal levels. Two of the most significant changes are discussed here: three strikes and you're out and truth in sentencing.

Three Strikes and You're Out Legislation

Three strikes and you're out legislation is a recent movement of an old philosophy that embodies enhanced penalties for repeat offenders. Generally this modern version provides for long mandatory or life sentences for persons who are convicted of a third offense, which usually must be a felony. Some jurisdictions state that the felony must be serious, violent, or one of a specified number of felonies. Others state only that it must be a felony.

The current enhanced sentencing movement may be traced to California's statute enacted in 1994. That statute provides for the mandatory sentence for persons convicted of a third felony, which may be any felony, although the first two must be serious or violent ones. Harsher penalties are also mandated for second felony convictions.[21] In 1996, however, the state supreme court interpreted the statute as retaining more judicial discretion than many had anticipated. According to that court, the legislation did not eliminate traditional judicial discretion to disregard a prior conviction in assessing punishment in a case. The statute allows prosecutors but not judges that discretion. The court, in a unanimous ruling in *People v. Superior Court*, held that it would be unconstitutional to interpret the statute as precluding judges from disregarding a prior conviction if they believed that action was necessary "in the furtherance of justice."[22]

In 1998 the California Supreme Court elaborated on the meaning of that phrase as an avenue for striking a previous felony to avoid a three strikes sentence. It requires courts to consider

> whether, in light of the nature and circumstances of his present felonies and prior serious and/or violent felony convictions, and the particulars of his background, character, and prospects, the de-

fendant may be deemed outside the scheme's spirit, in whole or in part, and hence should be treated as though he had presently not committed one or more felonies and/or had not previously been convicted of one or more serious and/or violent felonies.[23]

In January 1999, the U.S. Supreme Court refused to review a case appealed by a California defendant who was sentenced to 25 years to life under the state's statute after he was convicted of stealing a $20 bottle of vitamins. Although the Supreme Court refused to review the case, *Riggs v. California*, in a written opinion, Justices Stevens, Souter, and Ginsburg raised serious questions about the legality of such long sentences and suggested that other defendants should challenge them.[24]

In 1999 the California Supreme Court recognized an expansion of a trial judge's power to disregard a defendant's prior felony convictions when considering sentencing under three strikes legislation. Jerry Garcia, who had five prior serious felonies, was convicted of two burglaries. The trial judge considered Garcia's prior felonies in sentencing for one but not both of the burglary convictions. Garcia's sentence of 31 years is long, but not as long as it could have been had the prior felonies been applied to both of his current convictions. The sentencing decision was upheld by the state supreme court.[25]

In April 2002, the U.S. Supreme Court agreed to consider three strikes legislation when it granted *certiorari* in two California cases. Those cases are discussed in Focus 12.4. These cases could have had a significant impact on California's criminal justice system. California has the most severe three strikes legislative package, as a third strike in that state may be a nonviolent offense, such as shoplifting. Of the 7,000 inmates who were serving life under California's three strikes legislation at the time of the U.S. Supreme Court decision, 331 were in prison because their third strike was for petty theft. The third strike for 603 additional inmates was for drug possession. If the U.S. Supreme Court had ruled all or part of the California statute unconstitutional, hundreds of cases could have required resentencing, and reductions of those sentences would have had an impact on all phases of the system.[26]

A study of the results of California's three strikes legislation conducted by the Sentencing Project, a nonprofit research and advocacy group, concluded that California was targeting nonviolent criminals, who

FOCUS 12.4   The U.S. Supreme Court Upholds Three Strikes Laws

The two California three strikes cases that the U.S. Supreme Court decided during its 2002-2003 term are those of Gary A. Ewing and Leandro Andrade. Both cases challenged the constitutionality of the state's three strikes legislation. The specific legal issue was whether cruel and unusual punishment had been imposed on either (or both) with the sentences in their respective cases. Both were sentenced under state law, and to reverse those sentences, the U.S. Supreme Court had to find the violation of a federal constitutional right, such as the Eighth Amendment prohibition against cruel and unusual punishment.

Ewing was sentenced to 25 years to life in prison for a third strike involving the theft of golf clubs totaling $1,200. Ewing's previous strikes were for burglary and robbery. Andrade's third strike was for stealing $153.54 worth of children's videotapes from two KMart stores, for which he received two sentences of 25 years to life. His first strike was for burglarizing three homes, but because the videotapes were stolen from two stores, the trial judge counted those thefts as two strikes, thus giving Andrade three strikes for purposes of sentencing. Both Andrade and Ewing were sentenced for what California calls "petty theft with a prior," with the priors permitting the courts to treat the current misdemeanors as felonies. The sentence for petty theft without a prior in California is six months or less in jail. Andrade will be eligible for parole in 50 years, Ewing in 25. One of the prosecutors described Andrade as "a hopeless heroin addict" and concluded, "There comes a point at which the state has a right to say, 'Enough is enough.'"[1]

During the oral arguments before the U.S. Supreme Court, Justice Antonin Scalia stated that Ewing "is precisely the kind of person you want to get off the streets. . . . He's going to do it again." Chief Justice William H. Rehnquist asked Mr. Ewing's attorney, "Why can't California decide that enough is enough, that someone with a long string like that simply deserves to be put away?"

The *Ewing* and *Andrade* cases were decided in March 2003, with a bitterly divided U.S. Supreme Court ruling 5-4 that the sentences did not violate the Eighth Amendment prohibition against cruel and unusual punishment. Justice Sandra Day O'Connor, writing for the majority in the *Ewing* case, emphasized that the California legislature had a right to enact three strikes penalties in order to protect the public from criminals already convicted of at least one serious violent crime, noting that precedent cases have established that "States have a valid interest in deterring and segregating habitual criminals." O'Connor reviewed the history of three strikes legislation in California, noting a study reporting that 67 percent of former inmates were charged with a new "serious" crime within one year of release from state prisons. She concluded, "Ewing's sentence is justified by the State's public-safety interest in incapacitating and deterring recidivist felons, and amply supported by his own long, serious criminal record."[2]

Justice David H. Souter wrote the dissenting opinion in the *Andrade* case. In discussing the issue of proportionality, Justice Souter concluded, "If Andrade's sentence is not grossly disproportionate, the principle has no meaning."[3]

1. "California's 3-Strikes Law Tested Again," *New York Times* (6 November 2002), p. 19.
2. *Ewing v. California*, 538 U.S. 11 (2003).
3. *Lockyer v. Andrade*, 538 U.S. 63 (2003)

accounted for 58 percent of the sentences under this legislation. Under the state's companion two strikes legislation, 69 percent of those sentenced were convicted of nonviolent crimes. California had sentenced more than 50,000 persons under its three strikes law since it was approved in 1994. This number was far in excess of other states. The report emphasized that most criminals peak early in life and thus do not need long periods of incarceration. Further, such long sentences increase the state's costs for medical and other types of care for offenders. Finally, the researchers found no evidence that the three strikes legislation was responsible for the crime reduction in California, pointing out that crime decreased across the country, including in states such as New York and Massachusetts, which did not have three strikes legislation.[27]

Another study, conducted by Franklin Zimring and other noted social scientists who looked into the results of the California three strikes legislation, agreed with the conclusion concerning crime reduction. Zimring and his colleagues emphasized that the California legislation gives "awesome and unreviewable" discretion to prosecutors. In addition, the legislation has added so many inmates to California's prison populations that between 2009 and 2014 tens of thousands of them will become "a permanent residue in the California correctional system."[28]

In the 2004 election, 53 percent of Californians rejected Proposition 66, which, among other provisions, would have resulted in the release of many nonviolent offenders from the budget-strapped state penal system. Proposition 66 would also have required that the third strike be a violent or serious felony in order to trigger a life sentence. Early polls showed that a majority of voters were in favor of Proposition 66, but the governor, Arnold Schwarzenegger, pushed an extensive and aggressive advertising campaign to defeat the measure. It is expected that efforts to reduce the prison population will continue, however, as the state, like many others, battled fiscal issues.

Truth in Sentencing Legislation

The second major recent development in sentencing is **truth in sentencing**, which means that actual time served by offenders should be closer to the time allocated for their sentences. Many jurisdictions are establishing 85 percent as their goal, meaning that offenders must serve 85 percent of their prison sentences before they are eligible for early release.

The federal government offers incentives to encourage states to establish truth in sentencing practices. The federal Violent Offender Incarceration and Truth in Sentencing Incentive Grants Act provides money to states for prison construction and operation, but requires that violent offenders serve 85 percent of their time for the state to be eligible. Most states have enacted such legislation, and prison populations have soared, in large part as a result of inmates' serving longer portions of their sentences.[29]

One example of a recently enacted truth in sentencing law is that of Illinois, which requires defendants convicted of first-degree murder or terrorism to serve all of their sentences. All other violent offenders must serve at least 85 percent of their sentences. Specifically, the statute requires the Department of Corrections to prescribe the rules and regulations for the early release of inmates. For offenses committed on or after 19 June 1998 the following applies:

(i) that a prisoner who is serving a term of imprisonment for first degree murder or for the offense of terrorism shall receive no good conduct credit and shall serve the entire sentence imposed by the court;

(ii) that a prisoner serving a sentence for attempt to commit first degree murder, solicitation of murder, solicitation of murder for hire, intentional homicide of an unborn child, predatory criminal sexual assault of a child, aggravated criminal sexual assault, criminal sexual assault, aggravated

kidnaping, aggravated battery with a firearm, heinous battery, being an armed habitual criminal [added in 2005], aggravated battery of a senior citizen, or aggravated battery of a child shall receive no more than 4.5 days of good conduct credit for each month of his or her sentence of imprisonment. . . .

(4.6) The rules and regulations on early release shall also provide that a prisoner who has been convicted of a sex offense as defined in Section 2 of the Sex Offender Registration Act shall receive no good conduct credit unless he or she either has successfully completed or is participating in sex offender treatment as defined by the Sex Offender Management Board. However, prisoners who are waiting to receive such treatment, but who are unable to do so due solely to the lack of resources on the part of the Department, may, at the Director's sole discretion, be awarded good conduct credit at such rate as the Director shall determine.[30]

The statute continues with provisions concerning other violent crimes and then states that for all crimes not enumerated, the inmate may receive one day of good-conduct credit for each day served.

Although space limitations of this text do not permit a discussion of all types of sentences, the chapter does take a close look at capital punishment, as that punishment sets the stage for the subsequent discussion of the constitutional issues of sentencing.

CAPITAL PUNISHMENT

Capital punishment is an important area of criminal law, but over the years of this text the demand for inclusion of it in the text has wavered. Today the subject is in vogue or in style, and as a result **capital punishment** is receiving more coverage in academic as well as in other circles.

Capital punishment may be considered the most severe of all sentences the government imposes. The U.S. Supreme Court has interpreted the Constitution as placing restrictions on this punishment, but in 1972, in *Furman v. Georgia*, the Court held that capital punishment is not per se unconstitutional although it was found to be so in that case. Capital punishment in Georgia at that time was imposed in an arbitrary, capricious, and discriminatory manner, but the Supreme Court left open the possibility that other statutes could be drafted to survive constitutional scrutiny.[31]

In 1976, in *Gregg v. Georgia*, the U.S. Supreme Court upheld the constitutionality of the new Georgia statute, which required a consideration of aggravating and mitigating circumstances before imposition of the death penalty. That same year the Supreme Court had invalidated a statute that provided for the *mandatory* imposition of capital punishment.[32] In the intervening years, the U.S. Supreme Court has decided numerous capital punishment cases, some of which are discussed later in this chapter.

Death row data have fluctuated in recent years. The number of persons on death row increased from 334 in 1972, when *Furman* was decided, to 3,726 on 1 January 2001, although the figure dropped to 3,581 by the end of 2001. As of 1 July 2008, there were 3,307 inmates on death row. Of those inmates, 45 percent were white, 42 percent were African American, 11 percent were Hispanic, and 2 percent were other. Since 1976, when executions were resumed after *Furman*, 1,158 executions had occurred as of 17 April 2009, with 42 of those occurring in 2007, and 37 in 2008, and 22 in 2009. Since 1976, 130 inmates were removed from death row as the result of subsequent investigations (many involving DNA evidence) proving their innocence, and released from death row.[33] Figure 12.1

graphs the number of executions by year between 1976 and 17 April 2009.

In August 2005, U.S. Supreme Court justice John Paul Stevens, in an address before the annual meeting of the American Bar Association, deviated from his prepared remarks (and from the fact that U.S. Supreme Court justices normally do not speak out on public issues) and blasted the death penalty. Justice Stevens, in referring to the exonerated death row inmates as examples of wrongful convictions, called the U.S. death penalty systems deeply flawed.[34]

The major constitutional issues to the death penalty are considered in the following section, along with other sentencing issues, but first we look at one other relevant issue concerning capital punishment, that of cost. The Death Penalty Information Center (DIPC) provides on its website the following information:

- ✪ "The California death penalty system costs taxpayers $114 million per year beyond the costs of keeping convicts locked up for life. Taxpayers have paid more than $250 million for each of the state's executions.

- ✪ In Kansas, the costs of capital cases are 70% more expensive than comparable non-capital cases, including the costs of incarceration.

- ✪ In Indiana, the total costs of the death penalty exceed the complete costs of life without parole sentences by about 38%, assuming that 20% of death sentences are overturned and reduced to life.

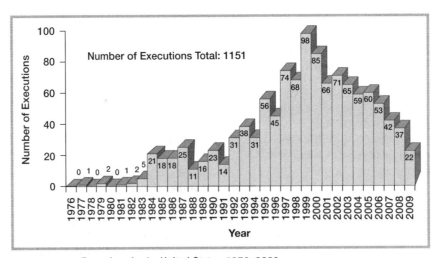

Figure 12.1 Executions in the United States, 1976–2009
Source: Death Penalty Information Center, 17 April 2009, http://www.deathpenaltyinfo.org/FactSheet.pdf, accessed 12 May 2009.

- The most comprehensive study in the country found that the death penalty costs North Carolina $2.16 million per execution *over* the costs of sentencing murderers to life imprisonment. The majority of those costs occur at the trial level.

- Enforcing the death penalty costs Florida $51 million a year above what it would cost to punish all first-degree murderers with life in prison without parole. . . .

- In Texas, a death penalty case costs an average of $2.3 million, about three times the cost of imprisoning someone in a single cell at the highest security level for 40 years."[35]

CONSTITUTIONAL ISSUES IN SENTENCING

Appellate courts are hesitant to interfere with legislative or judicial sentencing powers, but they do hear and decide sentences on appeal if it appears that those sentences violate defendants' constitutional rights. The U.S. Supreme Court hears cases that are alleged to have violated *federal* constitutional rights, such as the constitutional issues raised by sentence guidelines, discussed earlier in this chapter. Other constitutional issues are discussed in this section.

A crucial issue with regard to all of the constitutional issues and especially with those relating to the death penalty is that defendants are entitled to adequate representation of counsel. The Justice for All Act of 2004, which contains the Innocence Protection Act, was designed to improve the quality of legal representation for state death row inmates as well as to provide greater access to DNA testing for those inmates who challenge their death sentences.[36]

Execution of the Mentally Challenged

In 1986, in *Ford v. Wainwright*, the U.S. Supreme Court held that it is cruel and unusual punishment to execute the insane or "someone who is unaware of the punishment they are about to suffer and why they are to suffer it."[37] But subsequently, in *Penry v. Lynaugh*, the Supreme Court held that a mildly retarded person could be executed. John Paul Penry, who was on death row in Texas, has an IQ of a seven-year-old. He was found competent to stand trial, and his insanity defense was rejected by the jury, "which reflected their conclusion that Penry knew that his conduct was wrong and was

The death sentence of John Paul Penry, who was convicted of rape and murder while he was on parole for another rape, was reversed three times, twice by the U.S. Supreme Court and once by the highest court of criminal appeals in Texas. Penry, who has the IQ of a 7-year-old, confessed to the crime for which he was originally given the death sentence. Penry was resentenced, this time to three life sentences. (AP Images)

capable of conforming his conduct to the requirements of the law." The U.S. Supreme Court stated:

> In light of the diverse capacities and life experiences of mentally retarded persons, it cannot be said on the record before us today that all mentally retarded people, by definition, can never act with the level of culpability associated with the death penalty.[38]

Penry came within three hours of execution on 16 November 2000 but was granted a stay. In June 2001 the U.S. Supreme Court reversed his death sentence and sent the case back for resentencing. However, this decision was based on narrow procedural grounds and did not reach the issue of whether it is constitutional to execute mentally retarded persons.[39] Penry was again sentenced to death, but in October 2005 the Texas Court of

Criminal Appeals reversed that sentence.[40] In April 2008 a Texas news report stated that the previous February, the prosecution and the defense agreed to commute Penry's death sentence to three life sentences and that Penry would stipulate that he is not mentally retarded.[41]

In a 6-3 decision in June 2002, the U.S. Supreme Court, stating that a national consensus rejects the execution of mentally retarded offenders, held that it is unconstitutional to do so. The case involved a Virginia offender, Daryl R. Atkins, with an IQ of 59, who was sentenced to be executed for committing murder and robbery when he was 18 years old. The Court left it to the states to determine the meaning of mentally retarded and provided little guidance for them in doing so.[42]

In March 2003, Texas executed James Colburn, who had been diagnosed as paranoid schizophrenic since he was 14. Colburn had made approximately 15 suicide attempts, claiming that voices in his head told him to take his own life. But there was also evidence that Colburn knew what was happening to him, understood the criminal justice process, and even apologized to the victim's family before he was executed.[43]

In May 2004, Texas executed another mentally ill inmate. Kelsey Patterson, 50, who was diagnosed as schizophrenic, was executed after the state's governor refused to approve a rare plea from the state pardons board, which had ruled 5-1 to recommend clemency or a stay of execution. Patterson was under a death sentence for killing two persons in 1992. During his trial, Patterson was frequently removed from the courtroom because he was shouting claims that his behavior was being controlled by remote devices and implants.[44]

During its 2006–2007 term, the U.S. Supreme Court, in *Panetti v. Quarterman*, ruled by a 5-4 vote that a mentally ill murderer who did not have a rational understanding of why the state planned to execute him could not be executed. A brief excerpt explains the majority's position.[45]

PANETTI v. QUARTERMAN
127 S.Ct. 2842 (2007)

Justice Anthony M. Kennedy delivered the opinion of the Court, joined by Justices John Paul Stevens, David H. Souter, Ruth Bader Ginsburg, and Stephen G. Bryer. Justice Clarence Thomas filed a dissenting opinion, in which Chief Justice John Roberts and Justices Antonin E. Scalia and Samuel Alito joined.

We . . . find no support in [a precedent case] . . . for the proposition that a prisoner is automatically foreclosed from demonstrating incompetency once a court has found he can identify the stated reason for his execution. A prisoner's awareness of the State's rationale for an execution is not the same as a rational understanding of it. [Precedent] does not foreclose inquiry into the latter.

This is not to deny the fact that a concept like rational understanding is difficult to define. And we must not ignore the concern that some prisoners, whose cases are not implicated by this decision, will fail to understand why they are to be punished on account of reasons other than those stemming from a severe mental illness. The mental state requisite for competence to suffer capital punishment neither presumes nor requires a person who would be considered "normal," or even "rational," in a layperson's understanding of those terms. Someone who is condemned to death for an atrocious murder may be so callous as to be unrepentant; so self-centered and devoid of compassion as to lack all sense of guilt; so adept in transferring blame to others as to be considered, at least in the colloquial sense, to be out of touch with reality. Those states of mind, even if extreme compared to the criminal population at large, are not what petitioner contends lie at the threshold of a competence inquiry. The beginning of doubt about competence in a case like petitioner's is not a misanthropic personality or an amoral character. It is a psychotic disorder.

Petitioner's submission is that he suffers from a severe, documented mental illness that is the source of gross delusions preventing him from comprehending the meaning and purpose of the punishment to which he has been sentenced. This argument, we hold, should have been considered.

Right to a Trial by Jury

As already noted, the U.S. Supreme Court has dealt with the issue of whether a judge or a jury may determine sentencing issues. Specifically, in *United States v. Apprendi*, the Court held that the due process clause of the U.S. Constitution (see Appendix A) requires that any fact (other than a prior conviction) used to enhance a sentence must be submitted to a jury and found to be true beyond a reasonable doubt.[46]

Two years later, in *Ring v. Arizona*, the U.S. Supreme Court extended *Apprendi*. The Arizona statute provided that after the finding of guilt by the jury in a first-degree murder case, the judge must conduct a separate sentencing hearing to consider the existence of the statute's enumerated circumstances for the

The U.S. Supreme Court has held that the right to trial by a jury includes the right to have the jury involved in sentencing, including an unanimous decision in death penalty cases. In December 2008, a jury deadlocked 6-3 on whether capital punishment should be imposed on Brian Nichols, who, while a defendant in the Fulton County courthouse in Atlanta, Georgia, killed Judge Rowland Barnes, his court reporter, and a sheriff's deputy. Nichols escaped the courthouse and killed a federal agent before he was convinced by a hostage to turn himself in to authorities. Nichols was sentenced to 485 years in prison plus four life sentences without parole and an additional seven life sentences that provide for parole after 30 years of incarceration. In this photo, honor guards march past the pictures of the victims who were killed at the Fulton County Courthouse in March 2005. (Tami Chappell/Reuters/Landov)

purpose of determining the offender's sentence. The statute specified that this hearing "shall be conducted before the court alone," with the court determining the facts at issue in that hearing. The judge was to sentence the offender to death if there was a finding of at least one aggravating circumstance and "no mitigating circumstances sufficiently substantial to call for leniency." Because the defendant in *Ring* was involved in a felony murder rather than a premeditated murder charge, he could have been sentenced to death only if it was found that he was the triggerman. The judge did not make that finding but did find two aggravating circumstances and only one nonstatutory mitigating factor, which, the judge ruled, was not sufficient to support leniency. He sentenced Ring to death. The U.S. Supreme Court reversed. Under Arizona law, Ring could not have been sentenced to death based only on the jury's finding of facts, as the jurors were not permitted to consider aggravating and mitigating circumstances. The U.S. Supreme Court held that the aggravating factor must be determined by the jury, not the judge. Otherwise, the accused is denied his Sixth Amendment (see Appendix A) right to a trial by jury.[47] In 2004, the U.S. Supreme Court held that *Ring* does not apply retroactively to cases that were already final on direct review before *Ring* was decided.[48]

In June 2002, the U.S. Supreme Court decided *Harris v. United States*, in which the justices showed their willingness to limit *Apprendi*. William J. Harris, a North Carolina pawnbroker, was charged with illegal drug trafficking when he sold four ounces of marijuana to federal undercover officers. Harris admitted that he distributed the drug to friends. He carried a gun during that transaction, a crime that carries a sentence of five years to life. The trial judge, finding that Harris "brandished" the gun, sentenced the defendant to the mandatory minimum sentence for that offense: seven years in prison. By a 5-4 vote, the U.S. Supreme Court upheld that sentence, thus refusing to extend *Apprendi* to mandatory minimum sentences by requiring that the additional fact on which that sentence was based must be determined by a jury rather than by a judge.[49]

As noted earlier, in 2005 in *Shepard v. United States*, the U.S. Supreme Court held that *Apprendi* and other recent precedent cases limit trial judges to official court documents when they investigate the nature of prior felonies for purposes of sentence enhancement. Thus, in Shepard's case, the trial judge should not have gone beyond the official transcript of the plea bargaining process to determine whether Shepard's prior burglaries met the requirements for sentence enhancement under the Armed Career Criminal Act (ACCA).[50]

Another issue with regard to sentencing and a defendant's right to a trial by jury involves jury selection. In 2003, the U.S. Supreme Court considered the issue of racial bias in jury selection in the case of death row inmate Thomas Miller-El, an African American. At Miller-El's jury selection, the prosecution eliminated 10 of the 11 African Americans in the jury pool. The prosecution argued that its actions did not constitute bias but, rather, represented the prejudice of those potential jurors, who stated that they would be hesitant to impose the death penalty. Miller-El presented evidence of racial bias in jury selection in the Texas county in which he was tried. His request to have the jury struck was denied. He was convicted and sentenced to death. His appeal was rejected by the federal Fifth Circuit. He appealed to the U.S. Supreme Court, which heard the case and sent it back with instructions that Miller-El was entitled to present evidence to the Fifth Circuit. The U.S. Supreme Court chastised that court and urged the judges to rethink their "dismissive and strained interpretation of the proof in the case and to give more serious consideration to the significant evidence pointing to unconstitutional discrimination against black jurors during the jury selection process."[51]

The Fifth Circuit did not follow the U.S. Supreme Court's instructions and quoted extensively from that Court's dissenting justice, Clarence Thomas. Miller-el again appealed to the U.S. Supreme Court, which in June 2005, by a vote of 6-3, ruled in his favor. Justice David H. Souter, who wrote the opinion for the Court, discussed the various tactics (which he called "trickery") used by the prosecution to avoid selecting African Americans for Miller-El's jury. One tactic was to ask different questions of African Americans, as compared to whites, in an attempt to make it appear that they were disqualified because they opposed the death penalty, a position described by Justice Souter as one that "reeks of afterthought." Justice Clarence Thomas, the only African American on the U.S. Supreme Court,

dissented, stating that he found the prosecution's explanation "eminently reasonable."[52]

On remand, the Fifth Circuit held that Miller-El did not prove that the state had committed error. The U.S. Supreme Court again reversed and remanded. In July 2005 the Fifth Circuit remanded the case to the district court, instructing that court to enter an order:

> (1) granting the petition for writ of habeas corpus; (2) setting aside Petitioner's conviction and sentence for capital murder; (3) order the release of Petitioner from custody unless the State grants Petitioner a new trial within 120 days from the date of the entry of the district court's order; and (4) entering final judgment for Petitioner.[53]

Miller-El accepted a plea offer of life in prison.

Equal Protection

The sentencing process may not violate a defendant's right to equal protection under the law. The issue arises in many cases, particularly with regard to race and gender. First, it is necessary to understand that by requiring equal protection in sentencing, the Constitution does not require that *all* defendants be treated identically. The U.S. Supreme Court has held, "The belief no longer prevails that every offense in a like legal category calls for an identical punishment without regard to the past life and habits of a particular offender."[54] Equal protection in sentencing means that, when there are differences, the bases for sentencing must be factors other than, for example, race or gender. Particular attention is given to race.

Allegations of equal protection violations in sentencing minorities, particularly when capital punishment is involved and the defendant is African American, have been made, as we saw in the discussion of jury selection in the *Miller-El* case. The issue of race was also faced by the U.S. Supreme Court in 1987 in *McCleskey v. Kemp*, which involved an African American defendant sentenced to death in Georgia for murdering a white police officer. Warren McCleskey argued unsuccessfully that a statistical study by University of Iowa law professor David C. Baldus supported his argument that he had been discriminated against because of his race *and* the race of his victim. The U.S. Supreme Court rejected this claim and concluded as follows:

> At most, the Baldus study indicates a discrepancy that appears to correlate with race. Apparent dis-

parities in sentencing are an inevitable part of our criminal justice system. . . . [W]e hold that the Baldus study does not demonstrate a constitutionally significant risk of racial bias affecting the Georgia capital-sentencing process.[55]

McCleskey was executed in 1991 after 13 years on death row.

Law professor Michael Tonry reported the results of his analyses of race and sentencing in a publication in which he concluded that racial disparities had "steadily gotten worse since 1980." Tonry was referring to the 100-to-1 ratio of sentence length for crack cocaine possession compared to violating laws regarding cocaine powder, initially discussed in Chapter 11. Crack cocaine use is more common among African Americans, while the use of cocaine powder (which is more expensive) is more characteristic of whites.[56] The issue, however, is whether the differential in sentences for these two drugs constitutes racial discrimination.

In 1996, in *United States v. Armstrong* (mentioned in Chapter 11), the U.S. Supreme Court held that selective prosecutions in cases involving crack cocaine do not alone support a claim of racial discrimination. The Court ruled that the African American men in Los Angeles who appealed their convictions did not meet the burden of proving unfair racial discrimination. Data show that African Americans account for 88.3 percent of federal crack convictions and only 27.4 percent of cocaine powder convictions (of which 32 percent involve whites and 39.3 percent, Hispanics). The U.S. Sentencing Commission had proposed to replace the 100-to-1 sentencing ratio mentioned earlier, but Congress refused to approve the recommendation, and in 1995 President Clinton signed a bill that retained the differential.[57]

In March 2008, former President Clinton said that he wished he had worked harder to change the 100-1 differential, adding that he was "prepared to spend a significant portion of whatever life I've got left on the earth trying to fix this because I think it's a cancer."[58] Clinton's remarks came after some changes had been made, although some argue that the changes are not sufficient. In May 2007, the U.S. Sentencing Commission again recommended to Congress that the sentences for crack cocaine be lowered. Congress did not reject those recommendations and, as provided by law, they became effective 1 November 2007. Under the new guidelines, the average sentence will be reduced from 10 years and 1 month to 8 years and 10 months.

In December 2007, the Sentencing Commission made the new guidelines retroactive, effective 3 March 2008, permitting inmates to petition to have their sentences lowered. The impact of this change was emphasized by the ABA, although the organization underscored the need for more extensive changes in the statute.

> The amendments could make more than 3,000 crack offenders eligible for release by the end of the year, although sentence reductions must be approved by a federal judge after offenders have completed their mandatory minimum sentences. More than 19,000 people now in prison on drug charges could be affected by the amendments over the next few decades.[59]

The Sentencing Project has repeatedly emphasized the need to reduce racial disparity within criminal justice systems. A 2007 publication by the organization focused on disparities in state sentencing, noting the following data concerning race and incarceration and emphasizing that on any given day, one out of every eight black males in their twenties is in prison:

- ✪ "African Americans are incarcerated at nearly six (5.6) times the rate of whites;

- ✪ Hispanics are incarcerated at nearly double (1.8) the rate of whites;

- ✪ States exhibit substantial variation in the ratio of black-to-white incarceration, ranging from a high of 13.6-to-1 in Iowa to a low of 1.9-to-1 in Hawaii;

- ✪ States with the highest black-to-white ratio are disproportionately located in the Northeast and Midwest. . . . This geographic concentration is true as well for the Hispanic-to-white ratio."[60]

Proportionality

The Eighth Amendment prohibition against cruel and unusual punishment (see Appendix A) has been interpreted to mean that a sentence must be proportionate to the offense for which it is imposed. Proportionality may involve the type or the length of punishment. This issue arises most often with respect to the death penalty. The major case is *Coker v. Georgia*, in which the U.S. Supreme Court held that the death penalty is disproportionate for the crime of raping, but not killing, an adult female.[61]

Coker was decided in 1977, and it was not until 2008 that the U.S. Supreme Court held that capital punishment for the rape but not murder of a child also violates the rule of proportionality and thus constitutes cruel and unusual punishment. That case, *Kennedy v. Louisiana*, is hotly debated and deserves attention here.[62] The following excerpt explains part of the Court's reasoning.

KENNEDY v. LOUISIANA

128 S.Ct. 2641 (2008)

 Justice Anthony M. Kennedy delivered the opinion of the Court, in which Justices John Paul Stevens, David H. Souter, Ruth Bader Ginsburg, and Stephen G. Breyer joined. Justice Samuel Alito filed a dissenting opinion, in which Chief Justice John Roberts and Justices Antonin E. Scalia and Clarence Thomas joined.

Patrick Kennedy, the petitioner here, seeks to set aside his death sentence under the Eighth Amendment. He was charged by the respondent, the State of Louisiana, with the aggravated rape of his then-8-year-old stepdaughter. After a jury trial petitioner was convicted and sentenced to death under a state statute authorizing capital punishment for the rape of a child under 12 years of age. This case presents the question whether the Constitution bars respondent from imposing the death penalty for the rape of a child where the crime did not result, and was not intended to result, in death of the victim. We hold the Eighth Amendment prohibits the death penalty for this offense. The Louisiana statute is unconstitutional.

Petitioner's crime was one that cannot be recounted in these pages in a way sufficient to capture in full the hurt and horror inflicted on his victim or to convey the revulsion society, and the jury that represents it, sought to express by sentencing petitioner to death. At 9:18 a.m. on March 2, 1998, petitioner called 911 to report that his stepdaughter, referred to here as L. H., had been raped. He told the 911 operator that L. H. had been in the garage while he readied his son for school. Upon hearing loud screaming, petitioner said, he ran outside and found L. H. in the side yard. Two neighborhood boys, petitioner told the operator, had dragged L. H. from the garage to the yard, pushed her down, and raped her. Petitioner claimed he saw one of the boys riding away on a blue 10-speed bicycle. When police arrived at petitioner's home between 9:20 and 9:30 a.m., they found L. H. on her bed, wearing a T-shirt and wrapped in a bloody blanket. She was bleeding profusely from the vaginal area. Petitioner told police he had carried her from the yard to the bathtub and then to the bed. Consistent with this explanation, police found a thin line of blood drops in the garage on the way to the house and then up the stairs. Once in the bedroom, petitioner had used a basin of water and a cloth to wipe blood from the victim. This later prevented medical personnel from collecting a reliable DNA sample.

L. H. was transported to the Children's Hospital. An expert in pediatric forensic medicine testified that L. H.'s injuries were the most severe he had seen from a sexual assault in his four years of practice. A laceration to the left wall of the vagina had separated her cervix from the back of her vagina, causing her rectum to protrude into the vaginal structure. Her entire perineum was torn from the posterior fourchette to the anus. The injuries required emergency surgery.

At the scene of the crime, at the hospital, and in the first weeks that followed, both L. H. and petitioner maintained in their accounts to investigators that L. H. had been raped by two neighborhood boys. One of L. H.'s doctors testified at trial that L. H. told all hospital personnel the same version of the rape, although she reportedly told one family member that petitioner raped her. L. H. was interviewed several days after the rape by a psychologist. The interview was videotaped, lasted three hours over two days, and was introduced into evidence at trial. On the tape one can see that L. H. had difficulty discussing the subject of the rape. She spoke haltingly and with long pauses and frequent movement. . . .

[The investigators found physical evidence that led them to question the allegations that two boys raped the victim.] Eight days after the crime, and despite L. H.'s insistence that petitioner was not the offender, petitioner was arrested for the rape. . . .

About a month after petitioner's arrest L. H. was removed from the custody of her mother, who had maintained until that point that petitioner was not involved in the rape. On June 22, 1998, L. H. was returned home and told her mother for the first time that petitioner had raped her. . . . The State charged petitioner with aggravated rape of a child and sought the death penalty [under relevant Louisiana statute, which has since been amended.]

The trial began in August 2003. . . .

The jury unanimously determined that petitioner should be sentenced to death. The Supreme Court of Louisiana affirmed. . . . The court acknowledged that petitioner would be the first person executed for committing child rape since [the Louisiana statute] was amended in 1995 and that Louisiana is in the minority of jurisdictions that authorize the death penalty for the crime of child rape. . . .

On this reasoning the Supreme Court of Louisiana rejected petitioner's argument that the death penalty for the rape of a child under 12 years is disproportionate and upheld the constitutionality of the statute. . . .

We granted certiorari. . . .

[The] Eighth Amendment's protection against excessive or cruel and unusual punishments flows from the basic "precept of justice that punishment for [a] crime should be graduated and proportioned to [the] offense." Whether this requirement has been fulfilled is determined not by the standards that prevailed when the Eighth Amendment was adopted in 1791 but by the norms that "currently prevail." The Amendment "draw[s] its meaning from the evolving standards of decency that mark the progress of a maturing society." This is because "[t]he standard of extreme cruelty is not merely descriptive, but necessarily embodies a moral judgment. The standard itself remains the same, but its applicability must change as the basic mores of society change."

Evolving standards of decency must embrace and express respect for the dignity of the person, and the punishment of criminals must conform to that rule. As we shall discuss, punishment is justified under one or more of three principal rationales: rehabilitation, deterrence, and retribution. It is the last of these, retribution, that most often can contradict the law's own ends. This is of particular concern when the Court interprets the meaning of the Eighth Amendment in capital cases. When the law punishes by death, it risks its own sudden descent into brutality, transgressing the constitutional commitment to decency and restraint.

For these reasons we have explained that capital punishment must "be limited to those offenders who commit 'a narrow category of the most serious crimes' and whose extreme culpability makes them 'the most deserving of execution.'" Though the death penalty is not invariably unconstitutional, the Court insists upon confining the instances in which the punishment can be imposed.

Applying this principle, we held in *Roper* and *Atkins* that the execution of juveniles and mentally retarded persons are punishments violative of the Eighth Amendment because the offender had a diminished personal responsibility for the crime. The Court further has held that the death penalty can be disproportionate to the crime itself where the crime did not result, or was not intended to result, in death of the victim. In *Coker,* for instance, the Court held it would be unconstitutional to execute an offender who had raped an adult woman. . . . [The Court discussed other cases in which it did or did not find the imposed punishment to be proportionate to the crime.]

In these cases the Court has been guided by "objective indicia of society's standards, as expressed in legislative enactments and state practice with respect to executions." . . . The inquiry does not end there, however. Consensus is not dispositive. Whether the death penalty is disproportionate to the crime committed depends as well upon the standards elaborated by controlling precedents and by the Court's own understanding and interpretation of the Eighth Amendment's text, history, meaning, and purpose.

Based both on consensus and our own independent judgment, our holding is that a death sentence for one who raped but did not kill a child, and who did not intend to assist another in killing the child, is unconstitutional under the Eighth and Fourteenth Amendments.

[The Court discussed the history of the death penalty for the crime of rape and other crimes. The Court noted that . . .] 44 States have not made child rape a capital offense. As for federal law, Congress in the Federal Death Penalty Act of 1994 expanded the number of federal crimes for which the death penalty is a permissible sentence, including certain nonhomicide offenses; but it did not do the same for child rape or abuse. . . .

The evidence of a national consensus with respect to the death penalty for child rapists, as with respect to juveniles, mentally retarded offenders, and vicarious felony murderers, shows divided opinion but, on balance, an opinion against it. . . .

At least one difference between this case and our Eighth Amendment proportionality precedents must be addressed. Respondent and its *amici* [those who submit "friends of the Court" briefs in the case] suggest that some States have an "erroneous understanding of this Court's Eighth Amendment jurisprudence." They submit that the general propositions set out in *Coker,* contrasting murder and rape, have been interpreted in too expansive a way, leading some state legislatures to conclude that *Coker* applies to child rape when in fact its reasoning does not, or ought not, apply to that specific crime. . . .

[In] . . . *Coker* . . . [t]he distinction between adult and child rape was not merely rhetorical; it was central to the Court's reasoning. The opinion does not speak to the constitutionality of the death penalty for child rape, an issue not then before the Court. . . . [The Court reviewed state decisions.]

We conclude on the basis of this review that there is no clear indication that state legislatures have misinterpreted *Coker* to hold that the death penalty for child rape is unconstitutional. The small number of States that have enacted this penalty, then, is relevant to determining whether there is a consensus against capital punishment for this crime. [The Court then looked at the six states in which child rape was a capital offense.] . . .

After reviewing the authorities informed by contemporary norms, including the history of the death penalty for this and other nonhomicide crimes, current state statutes and new enactments, and the number of executions since 1964, we conclude there is a national consensus against capital punishment for the crime of child rape. . . .

We turn, then, to the resolution of the question before us, which is informed by our precedents and our own understanding of the Constitution and the rights it secures.

It must be acknowledged that there are moral grounds to question a rule barring capital punishment for a crime against an individual that did not result in death. These facts illustrate the point. Here the victim's fright, the sense of betrayal, and the nature of her injuries caused more prolonged physical and mental suffering than, say, a sudden killing by an unseen assassin. The attack was not just on her but on her childhood. For this reason, we should be most reluctant to rely upon the language of the plurality in *Coker*, which posited that, for the victim of rape, "life may not be nearly so happy as it was" but it is not beyond repair. Rape has a permanent psychological, emotional, and sometimes physical impact on the child. We cannot dismiss the years of long anguish that must be endured by the victim of child rape.

It does not follow, though, that capital punishment is a proportionate penalty for the crime. The constitutional prohibition against excessive or cruel and unusual punishments mandates that the State's power to punish "be exercised within the limits of civilized standards." Evolving standards of decency that mark the progress of a maturing society counsel us to be most hesitant before interpreting the Eighth Amendment to allow the extension of the death penalty, a hesitation that has special force where no life was taken in the commission of the crime. It is an established principle that decency, in its essence, presumes respect for the individual and thus moderation or restraint in the application of capital punishment.

To date the Court has sought to define and implement this principle, for the most part, in cases involving capital murder. One approach has been to insist upon general rules that ensure consistency in determining who receives a death sentence. . . .

The tension between general rules and case-specific circumstances has produced results not all together satisfactory. This has led some Members of the Court to say we should cease efforts to resolve the tension and simply allow legislatures, prosecutors, courts, and juries greater latitude. For others the failure to limit these same imprecisions by stricter enforcement of narrowing rules has raised doubts concerning the constitutionality of capital punishment itself.

Our response to this case law, which is still in search of a unifying principle, has been to insist upon confining the instances in which capital punishment may be imposed. Our concern here is limited to crimes against individual persons. We do not address, for example, crimes defining and punishing treason, espionage, terrorism, and drug kingpin activity, which are offenses against the State. As it relates to crimes against individuals, though, the death penalty should not be expanded to instances where the victim's life was not taken. . . .

Consistent with evolving standards of decency and the teachings of our precedents we conclude that, in determining whether the death penalty is excessive, there is a distinction between intentional first-degree murder on the one hand and nonhomicide crimes against individual persons, even including child rape, on the other. The latter crimes may be devastating in their harm, as here, but "in terms of moral depravity and of the injury to the person and to the public," they cannot be compared to murder in their "severity and irrevocability."

In reaching our conclusion we find significant the number of executions that would be allowed under respondent's approach. The crime of child rape, considering its reported incidents, occurs more often than first-degree murder. Approximately 5,702 incidents of vaginal, anal, or oral rape of a child under the age of 12 were reported nationwide in 2005; this is almost twice the total incidents of intentional murder for victims of all ages (3,405) reported during the same period. Although we have no reliable statistics on convictions for child rape, we can surmise that, each year, there are hundreds, or more, of these convictions just in jurisdictions that permit capital punishment. As a result of existing rules, only 2.2% of convicted first-degree murderers are sentenced to death. But under respondent's approach, the 36 States that permit the death penalty could sentence to death all persons convicted of raping a child less than 12 years of age. This could not be reconciled with our evolving standards of decency and the necessity to constrain the use of the death penalty.

It might be said that narrowing aggravators could be used in this context, as with murder offenses, to ensure the death penalty's restrained application. We find it difficult to identify standards that would guide the decisionmaker so the penalty is reserved for the most severe cases of child rape and yet not imposed in an arbitrary way. Even were we to forbid, say, the execution of first-time child rapists, or require as an aggravating factor a finding that the perpetrator's instant rape offense involved multiple victims, the jury still must balance, in its discretion, those aggravating factors against mitigating circumstances. In this context, which involves a crime that in many cases will overwhelm a decent person's judgment, we have no confidence that the imposition of the death penalty would not be so arbitrary as to be "freakis[h]." We cannot sanction this result when the harm to the victim, though grave, cannot be quantified in the same way as death of the victim. . . .

Our concerns are all the more pronounced where, as here, the death penalty for this crime has been most infrequent. We have developed a foundational jurisprudence in the case of capital murder to guide the States and juries in imposing the death penalty. . . . Evolving standards of decency are difficult to reconcile with a regime that seeks to expand the death penalty to an area where standards to confine its use are indefinite and obscure.

Our decision is consistent with the justifications offered for the death penalty. . . .

[The Court discussed the punishment goals of deterrence and rehabilitation with regard to the death penalty in child rape cases and then considered the harm that rape does to a child victim.]

It is not at all evident that the child rape victim's hurt is lessened when the law permits the death of the perpetrator. Capital cases require a long-term commitment by those who testify for the prosecution, especially when guilt and sentencing determinations are in multiple proceedings. In cases like this the key testimony is not just from the family but from the victim herself. During formative years of her adolescence, made all the more daunting for having to come to terms with the brutality of her experience, L. H. was required to discuss the case at length with law enforcement personnel. In a public trial she was required to recount once more all the details of the crime to a jury as the State pursued the death of her stepfather. And in the end the State made L. H. a central figure in its decision to seek the death penalty, telling the jury in closing statements: "[L. H.] is asking you, asking you to set up a time and place when he dies."

Society's desire to inflict the death penalty for child rape by enlisting the child victim to assist it over the course of years in asking for capital punishment forces a moral choice on the child, who is not of mature age to make that choice. The way the death penalty here involves the child victim in its enforcement can compromise a decent legal system; and this is but a subset of fundamental difficulties capital punishment can cause in the administration and enforcement of laws proscribing child rape.

There are, moreover, serious systemic concerns in prosecuting the crime of child rape that are relevant to the constitutionality of making it a capital offense. The problem of unreliable, induced, and even imagined child testimony means there is a "special risk of wrongful execution" in some child rape cases. This undermines, at least to some degree, the meaningful contribution of the death penalty to legitimate goals of punishment. Studies conclude that children are highly susceptible to suggestive questioning techniques like repetition, guided imagery, and selective reinforcement.

Similar criticisms pertain to other cases involving child witnesses; but child rape cases present heightened concerns because the central narrative and account of the crime often comes from the child herself. She and the accused are, in most instances, the only ones present when the crime was committed. And the question in a capital case is not just the fact of the crime, including, say, proof of rape as distinct from abuse short of rape, but details bearing upon brutality in its commission. These matters are subject to fabrication or exaggeration, or both. Although capital punishment does bring retribution, and the legislature here has chosen to use it for this end, its judgment must be weighed, in deciding the constitutional question, against the special risks of unreliable testimony with respect to this crime.

With respect to deterrence, if the death penalty adds to the risk of non-reporting, that, too, diminishes the penalty's objectives. Underreporting is a common problem with respect to child sexual abuse. Although we know little about what differentiates those who report from those who do not report, one of the most commonly cited reasons for nondisclosure is fear of negative consequences for the perpetrator, a concern that has special force where the abuser is a family member. The experience of the *amici* who work with child victims indicates that, when the punishment is death, both the victim and the victim's family members may be more likely to shield the perpetrator from discovery, thus increasing underreporting. As a result, punishment by death may not result in more deterrence or more effective enforcement.

In addition, by in effect making the punishment for child rape and murder equivalent, a State that punishes child rape by death may remove a strong incentive for the rapist not to kill the victim. Assuming the offender behaves in a rational way, as one must to justify the penalty on grounds of deterrence, the penalty in some respects gives less protection, not more, to the victim, who is often the sole witness to the crime. It might be argued that, even if the death penalty results in a marginal increase in the incentive to kill, this is counterbalanced by a marginally increased deterrent to commit the crime at all. Whatever balance the legislature strikes, however, uncertainty on the point makes the argument for the penalty less compelling than for homicide crimes.

Each of these propositions, standing alone, might not establish the unconstitutionality of the death penalty for the crime of child rape. Taken in sum, however, they demonstrate the serious negative consequences of making child rape a capital offense. These considerations lead us to conclude, in our independent judgment, that the death penalty is not a proportional punishment for the rape of a child. . . .

The rule of evolving standards of decency with specific marks on the way to full progress and mature judgment means that resort to the penalty must be reserved for the worst of crimes and limited in its instances of application. In most cases justice is not better served by terminating the life of the perpetrator rather than confining him and preserving the possibility that he and the system will find ways to allow him to understand the enormity of his offense. Difficulties in administering the penalty to ensure against its arbitrary and capricious application require adherence to a rule reserving its use, at this stage of evolving standards and in cases of crimes against individuals, for crimes that take the life of the victim.

The judgment of the Supreme Court of Louisiana upholding the capital sentence is reversed. This case is remanded for further proceedings not inconsistent with this opinion.

Dissent by Justice Alito

In light of the points discussed above, I believe that the "objective indicia" of our society's "evolving standards of decency" can be fairly summarized as follows. Neither Congress nor juries have done anything that can plausibly be interpreted as evidencing the "national consensus" that the Court perceives. State legislatures, for more than 30 years, have operated under the ominous shadow of the *Coker* dicta and thus have not been free to express their own understanding of our society's standards of decency. And in the months following our grant of certiorari in this case, state legislatures have had an additional reason to pause. Yet despite the inhibiting legal atmosphere that has prevailed since 1977, six States have recently enacted new, targeted child-rape laws.

I do not suggest that six new state laws necessarily establish a "national consensus" or even that they are sure evidence of an ineluctable trend. In terms of the Court's

metaphor of moral evolution, these enactments might have turned out to be an evolutionary dead end. But they might also have been the beginning of a strong new evolutionary line. We will never know, because the Court today snuffs out the line in its incipient stage. . . .

A major theme of the Court's opinion is that permitting the death penalty in child-rape cases is not in the best interests of the victims of these crimes and society at large. In this vein, the Court suggests that it is more painful for child-rape victims to testify when the prosecution is seeking the death penalty. The Court also argues that "a State that punishes child rape by death may remove a strong incentive for the rapist not to kill the victim," and may discourage the reporting of child rape.

These policy arguments, whatever their merits, are simply not pertinent to the question whether the death penalty is "cruel and unusual" punishment. The Eighth Amendment protects the right of an accused. It does not authorize this Court to strike down federal or state criminal laws on the ground that they are not in the best interests of crime victims or the broader society. The Court's policy arguments concern matters that legislators should—and presumably do—take into account in deciding whether to enact a capital child-rape statute, but these arguments are irrelevant to the question that is before us in this case. . . .

The Court also contends that laws permitting the death penalty for the rape of a child create serious procedural problems. . . .

[The opinion refutes these arguments at length and then discusses methods for ensuring the reliability of evidence in child rape cases.] . . .

The Court's final—and, it appears, principal—justification for its holding is that murder, the only crime for which defendants have been executed since this Court's 1976 death penalty decisions, is unique in its moral depravity and in the severity of the injury that it inflicts on the victim and the public. But the Court makes little attempt to defend these conclusions. . . .

The deep problems that afflict child-rape victims often become society's problems as well. Commentators have noted correlations between childhood sexual abuse and later problems such as substance abuse, dangerous sexual behaviors or dysfunction, inability to relate to others on an interpersonal level, and psychiatric illness. Victims of child rape are nearly 5 times more likely than nonvictims to be arrested for sex crimes and nearly 30 times more likely to be arrested for prostitution.

The harm that is caused to the victims and to society at large by the worst child rapists is grave. It is the judgment of the Louisiana lawmakers and those in an increasing number of other States that these harms justify the death penalty. The Court provides no cogent explanation why this legislative judgment should be overridden. Conclusory references to "decency," "moderation," "restraint," "full progress," and "moral judgment" are not enough.

In summary, the Court holds that the Eighth Amendment categorically rules out the death penalty in even the most extreme cases of child rape even though: (1) This holding is not supported by the original meaning of the Eighth Amendment; (2) neither *Coker* nor any other prior precedent commands this result; (3) there are no reliable "objective indicia" of a "national consensus" in support of the Court's position; (4) sustaining the constitutionality of the state law before us would not "extend" or "expand" the death penalty; (5) this Court has previously rejected the proposition that the Eighth Amendment is a one-way ratchet that prohibits legislatures from adopting new capital punishment statutes to meet new problems; (6) the worst child rapists exhibit the epitome of moral depravity; and (7) child rape inflicts grievous injury on victims and on society in general.

The party attacking the constitutionality of a state statute bears the "heavy burden" of establishing that the law is unconstitutional. That burden has not been discharged here, and I would therefore affirm the decision of the Louisiana Supreme Court.

The proportionality issue also arises with respect to sentence length. Although most appellate courts defer to trial judges on this issue, some sentencing decisions are reversed on appeal. For example, a lower federal court reversed the sentence of a defendant who received a 10-year sentence (the maximum allowed by law) for conviction of illegal drug possession. When arrested, the defendant possessed only half of his daily dosage of drugs, a clear indication, said the court, that he was not intending to sell the drugs. Although possession was illegal, the court said the sentence was disproportionate in that it was

> at least twice as long as the *maximum* federal sentence for such major felonies as extortion, blackmail, perjury, assault with a dangerous weapon or by beating, arson (not endangering a human life), threatening the life of the president, and selling a man into slavery. It is severe both in its length and in its callous disregard for appellant's obvious need for treatment.[63]

A contrary conclusion was reached on appeal in a New York case, which illustrates the reluctance of courts to interfere with legislatively established minimum

and maximum sentences. The state court had struck down sentences on the proportionality issue involving sentencing under the state's 1973 Rockefeller laws (discussed in Chapter 11), which provide mandatory indeterminate sentences of a number of years to life for specified drug convictions. The court held that a maximum sentence of life in these cases violated the Eighth Amendment ban against cruel and unusual punishment (see Appendix A). The Second Circuit reversed the lower court, and the U.S. Supreme Court refused to hear the case, thus allowing the sentence to remain.[64]

The proportionality issue also arises in habitual offender or recidivism statutes (see again Focus 12.4 and the corresponding text discussion of three strikes statutes), which provide for an increased penalty once a defendant has been convicted of multiple offenses. The U.S. Supreme Court had decided several cases involving sentence length leading up to the three strikes legislation.[65] In one of those cases the Court stated objective criteria on which such decisions are to be based:

> In sum, a court's proportionality analysis under the Eighth Amendment should be guided by objective criteria, including (i) the gravity of the offense and the harshness of the penalty; (ii) the sentences imposed on other criminals in the same jurisdiction; and (iii) the sentences imposed for commission of the same crime in other jurisdictions.[66]

Cruel and Unusual Punishment

The basis for reversing most sentences is the Eighth Amendment's prohibition against the infliction of cruel and unusual punishment (see Appendix A), but the definition of that concept is not clear. We have seen that a sentence may constitute cruel and unusual punishment because it is too long in proportion to the offense, because the type of sentence is excessive when compared to the nature of the offense, or because it involves racial or other discrimination. Some types of sentence or probation conditions may also constitute cruel and unusual punishment.

In addition, the U.S. Supreme Court has recently looked at two crucial areas of claims of cruel and unusual punishment: the execution of juveniles and the use of lethal injection as a method of execution.

The Execution of Juveniles

In 1988, in *Thompson v. Oklahoma*, the U.S. Supreme Court held that imposing capital punishment on a

The U.S. Supreme Court has ruled that the execution of a person who committed a capital crime as a juvenile constitutes cruel and unusual punishment and is thus a violation of the U.S. Constitution. (IStockPhoto)

person who was 15 at the time the murder was committed constitutes cruel and unusual punishment, thus overturning the sentence of William Wayne Thompson. Thompson was convicted of the brutal murder of his brother-in-law. The victim was shot twice; his throat, chest, and abdomen were slashed; and he had multiple bruises and a broken leg. The body was then chained to a concrete block and thrown into a river.[67]

Three other men over the age of 18 were convicted and sentenced to death for this murder. The U.S. Supreme Court's opinion in the *Thompson* case did not answer the question of where the line is to be drawn in deciding whether capital punishment is cruel and unusual in light of a defendant's age.

In October 2002 the U.S. Supreme Court refused to reconsider whether it is constitutional to execute persons who were 16 or 17 when they committed capital offenses. Justice David H. Souter wrote a dissenting opinion for himself and three colleagues, stating that executing juvenile offenders is "a relic of the past that is inconsistent with evolving standards of decency in a civilized society." The dissenters proclaimed, "We should put an end to this shameful practice." The Supreme Court refused to decide the issue in the case of *Stanford v. Parker*, which involved a defendant who was 17 when he murdered his cousin.[68]

In 1985 the Supreme Court had upheld the death sentence of a defendant who was 18 at the time he committed his atrocious capital crime.[69] This chapter's Case Analysis provides an opportunity to analyze a 2005 decision by the U.S. Supreme Court on the issue of whether juveniles may be executed.

Methods of Execution

Another aspect of the cruel and unusual punishment prohibition concerns the methods of execution. Westley Allan Dodd, an admitted child molester, was convicted of murder and executed by hanging in Washington in 1993. Dodd admitted that he molested children, an act he enjoyed and engaged in frequently. "I liked molesting children and did what I had to do to avoid jail so I could continue molesting." After hearing some of the details in court, "hardened reporters who covered the case sought counseling to help them handle what they had heard." A therapist who treated the offender said that he "ought to fry." The Washington constitution prohibits cruel punishment (in contrast to the U.S. Constitution, which prohibits cruel *and unusual* punishment), and the American Civil Liberties Union argued unsuccessfully in this case that hanging is a cruel punishment.[70]

A federal court has held that hanging is not a cruel and unusual punishment in violation of the federal

Constitution,[71] but it has also held that hanging might constitute cruel and unusual punishment if a person is so large (409 pounds) that hanging might result in decapitation. On appeal, the latter case, *Rupe v. Wood*, was affirmed on an evidence issue that is not relevant to this discussion and vacated on the issue of the constitutionality of hanging. That issue was ruled moot (no longer an issue) in light of the state's new statute, which reversed the presumption. The previous statute presumed that the condemned person would be hanged unless he or she chose lethal injection. The convicted man was not willing to choose and challenged the constitutionality of the presumption. This challenge, if successful, would have led to his death by hanging. The new statute presumes that death will be by lethal injection unless the condemned chooses hanging.[72]

Likewise, in California, which until recently provided capital punishment only by use of the gas chamber, the statute was changed to provide the alternative of lethal injection, with the choice that of the condemned person. The previous statute provided that if the condemned person refused to choose, execution would be in the gas chamber. That presumption was changed by a subsequent statute after a federal court ruled that death by means of gas constitutes cruel and unusual punishment. Thus, today the default method in California, as in Washington, is lethal injection.[73]

The issue of whether electrocution is constitutional was raised in several Florida cases, and the state's supreme court ruled in favor of the method.[74] During its 1999–2000 term the U.S. Supreme Court agreed to review a Florida case on the issue. Prior to the scheduled oral arguments, however, the case was dismissed as moot after the Florida legislature changed the state's statute to permit condemned inmates to choose between lethal injection and electrocution.[75]

Most states that have capital punishment statutes use lethal injection or at least a choice that permits that method. On 16 April 2008, the U.S. Supreme Court upheld the constitutionality of this method against arguments that it could constitute cruel and unusual punishment as administered in Kentucky. The case, *Baze v. Rees*, was brought by two inmates who raised the issue of whether there is a sufficient probability that proper procedures for administering lethal injection would not be followed in Kentucky, resulting in sufficient pain to constitute cruel and unusual punishment when the death sentence is carried out by lethal injection. According to Chief Justice John Roberts, who wrote the majority opinion for the Court's 7-2 decision, the petitioners had not sustained their burden of proving "that the risk of pain from maladministration of a concededly humane lethal injection protocol, and the failure to adopt untried and untested alternatives, constitute cruel and unusual punishment." There is some risk of pain in any method of execution, maintained Roberts, and "the Constitution does not demand the avoidance of all risk of pain in carrying out executions." In his concurring opinion, Justice Clarence Thomas stated that an execution method "violates the Eighth Amendment only it if is deliberately designed to inflict pain."[76]

The dissent in *Baze* emphasized that the first of three drugs administered during Kentucky's lethal injection is for the purpose of sedating the inmate, and if that drug is not administered properly, the next two drugs will cause excrutiating pain. Thus, the case should be returned to Kentucky to consider whether the failure to include specific safeguards utilized by other states "poses an untoward, readily avoidable risk of inflicting severe and unnecessary pain."[77] Executions had been on hold since 25 September 2007; after the *Baze* decision they were resumed.

MEGAN'S LAWS

This final topic in the chapter does not involve sentencing per se, but it is related to one philosophy of why we sentence offenders: to keep them from engaging in additional crimes. Protection of society is a primary goal of punishment, and since 1994, when seven-year-old Megan Kanka was murdered by her New Jersey neighbor, Jesse Timmendequas, a released sex offender, all states, the District of Columbia, and the federal system have enacted **Megan's laws**, which require that released sex offenders register when they move into a community. Some jurisdictions require that the community be notified, either by the sex offender or by law enforcement authorities.

Megan Kanka was enticed into the neighbor's home with a promise of a puppy. Timmendequas, who lived in that home, along with two other sex offenders, was on parole after serving time for convictions of previous sex offenses against young girls. Megan's parents did not know about the sex offender backgrounds of Timmendequas and his housemates. Megan was murdered on 29 July 1994, and by 31 October 1994 New

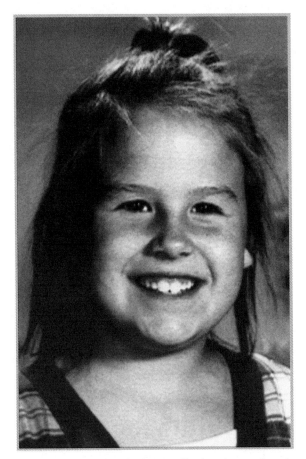

Megan's laws, which require that sex offenders who are released from custody must register after they move back in to the community, are named for Megan Kanka. Megan was raped and murdered by a sex offender who lived across the street from her family home and enticed her into his home with the promise of a puppy. (AP Images)

Jersey had enacted its Sexual Offender Registration Act. It was followed quickly in other jurisdictions.

There have been numerous challenges to Megan's laws, and during its 2002–2003 term the U.S. Supreme Court decided two cases, one from Connecticut and one from Alaska. The Alaska case raised the issue of whether the state's sex offender registration law violates the *ex post facto* prohibition of the U.S. Constitution (for a discussion, see again Chapter 1), while the Connecticut case raised a due process issue. These cases are discussed in Focus 12.5.

The fact that the U.S. Supreme Court decided these two cases and upheld Megan's laws does not mean that all issues are resolved, so it is important to consider some of those issues, especially the practical ones. First is the issue of whether the laws are effective. Megan's laws are based on the presumption that if people know who the sex offenders are and where they live, society will be protected from sexual abuse. This is not necessarily the case. First, in many cases the sexual abuser is a family member or friend, and even when those persons are apprehended, they are rarely prosecuted successfully, if at all. Second, law enforcement officials do not always have accurate information for posting. Third, sufficient personnel and resources for handling notification are not available in all jurisdictions. Fourth, sex offender notification will not solve the problem of notification in other communities to which sex offenders may travel to commit their crimes. Finally, not all in the community will get the notification. Some jurisdictions require that persons who want the information must access it on the Internet or go to the police station or sheriff's office. Even when door-to-door notification is required, not everyone will "get the message."

It is possible that some violent acts may be avoided if sex offenders are registered and the community knows where they are living. Consider, for example, the case of Jessica Lunsford. In 2004 the nation's attention was captured by the abduction and subsequent sexual attack and murder of this little Florida girl, age 9, who was taken from the home she shared with her father and her grandparents. A sex offender who had failed to register, John E. Couey, 46, was convicted of these crimes and sentenced to death. Jessica's father, along with others, pushed for stronger federal legislation on sex offender registration. One of those, the Jessica Lundsford Act, increases sentences for convicted sex offenders and tightens reporting and monitoring requirements in sex offender cases.[78] Yet, in this case a sex offender registration requirement could not have saved the victim because the offender violated that statute and did not register.

Human rights organizations have also raised issues about the required registration of sex offenders. Human Rights Watch, based in New York, issued a 146-page report in 2007, *No Easy Answers: Sex Offender Laws in the United States*. The two-year investigation included over 200 interviews with victims and their families, law enforcement officers, and others. The report concluded that despite the worthwhile goal of protecting children from sexual predators, the current laws were poorly crafted and ill-conceived. They are based on the crimes that precipitated them and do not address the fact that few children are sexually abused

---

FOCUS 12.5 **The Constitutionality of Megan's Laws**

During its 2002–2003 term the U.S. Supreme Court considered two versions of Megan's laws, having accepted appeals from Alaska and Connecticut. As the text notes, Megan's laws exist in all 50 states and in the federal system. The versions vary, and the Supreme Court's decision may not affect all of them, but it can be expected that the Court's ruling will go beyond the boundaries of these two states.

The issue in the Alaska case was whether the statute violated the *ex post facto* clause of the U.S. Constitution in that it requires registration of sex offenders who committed their crimes before the statute was enacted. The Ninth Circuit found that it violated that clause by imposing what amounts to additional punishment on the offender by requiring registration. The court invalidated the statute. The Alaska law was challenged by two men, each of whom was convicted of sexually molesting his daughter. Each man was released from prison in 1990 after serving eight years in prison. Each argued that the statute was punitive in that it imposed on him a penalty that was not part of the law until 1994, after his crime was committed. Most states, like Alaska, have applied their sex offender registration statutes retroactively, and some of these statutes have been held constitutional by state or lower federal appellate courts.

The issue in the Connecticut case was whether the due process clause of the U.S. Constitution was violated in that the statute does not provide a hearing to determine whether offenders required to register are in fact currently dangerous to society. Connecticut provides for publishing the names of sex offenders even though there has been no attempt to distinguish between those who are dangerous and those who may not be. In October 2001 the U.S. Court of Appeals for the Second Circuit ruled that individual offenders are entitled to a hearing to determine whether "they are particularly likely to be currently dangerous before being labeled as such." The court issued an injunction, banning the publication of these names, although the offenders are still required to register with the state's Department of Public Safety. Approximately one-half of the states have statutes similar to that of Connecticut and require no hearing.

The Connecticut appeal was supported by 23 other states and the Bush administration, which was concerned that if the high court ruled against Connecticut it would jeopardize a new federal statute, the Campus Sex Crimes Prevention Act, that went into effect in October 2002. This act requires states to notify communities when sex offenders enroll in or are employed by colleges and universities. There is no requirement of a hearing to determine whether a particular individual offender is a public risk.

The federal government was represented in both cases by the U.S. solicitor general, Theodore B. Olson, who argued that high rates of recidivism on the part of sex offenders justify the notification measures. Said Olson, "People are asking their government, please allow us to know." Justice Anthony Kennedy asked Olson whether it would be appropriate for states to require sex offenders to display a special notice on their car license plates. Olson responded that would be quite different, to which Justice Kennedy said, "I don't think it's very different."[1]

In March 2003 the U.S. Supreme Court rejected challenges to the Connecticut and Alaska Megan's laws. In a 6-3 ruling, the Court held that Alaska may apply its laws to persons who were convicted before the law was enacted—that is, the law does not constitute a violation of the prohibition against *ex post facto* laws. That prohibition bars punishment, but the registration requirement does not constitute punishment, ruled the Court. Rather, the purpose of Megan's laws is to protect the public.[2] The Court also ruled, by a unanimous vote, that the Connecticut statute, which requires Internet registry, is not unconstitutional because it does not require a prior hearing on the issue of whether the offender is dangerous.[3]

1. Quoted in "Court Looks at Sex Offenders' Lists," *New York Times* (14 November 2002), p. 22.
2. *Smith v. Doe*, 538 U.S. 84 (2003).
3. *Connecticut Department of Public Safety v. Doe*, 538 U.S. 1 (2003).

---

and murdered by sexual predators. Rather, most of the abused children were victims of family members, family friends, or acquaintances. Further, the assumption that most sex offenders reoffend is not founded in research; three out of every four do not reoffend. The report noted that in many states, juveniles who are convicted of sex offenses are subject to registration as sex offenders for life. But, in many cases, their acts "while frowned upon, do not suggest a danger to the community, including consensual sex, 'playing doctor,'

and exposing themselves." Indeed, requiring all sex offenders to register for life may make it impossible for law enforcement to deal with the most serious offenders, those we really do want to keep off the streets.[79]

Recent Legislative Action

Legislative attempts to control the opportunities for sexual predators to entice children have focused on the Internet. On 13 October 2008, a bill entitled Keeping the Internet Devoid of Sexual Predators Act of 2008, or the shortened version, the KIDS Act of 2008, was passed by the Senate. The House had passed the bill the previous year. The law requires registered sex offenders to register their e-mail and instant messenger addresses with the National Sex Offender Registry. The Department of Justice is required to make the information available to sites that can use it to block these predators from preying on children. The law provides that it is a crime for Internet users to misrepresent their ages for the purpose of luring children into sexual conduct. It amends the federal criminal code to impose a fine and/or prison term of up to 10 years for failure to comply with the informational provisions of the act and up to 20 years for age misrepresentation as provided by the act. After bills concerning this act were introduced in January 2007, ten states (Arizona, Colorado, Connecticut, Florida, Illinois, Kansas, Kentucky, Louisiana, Mississippi, and Virginia) passed similar legislation, and other states were considering such legislation.[80]

Civil Commitment Procedures

Since registration requirements for released sex offenders may not be effective, some states require civil commitment of these offenders. In 1997, in *Kansas v. Hendricks*, the U.S. Supreme Court upheld the Kansas civil commitment statute in the case of Leroy Hendricks, who was convicted in 1984 of indecent liberties with two 13-year-old boys. After serving most of his 10-year sentence, Hendricks was scheduled for release from prison, but a jury determined that he was a sexual predator, and the judge found that he had a mental abnormality. He was involuntarily confined indefinitely under the Kansas Sexually Violent Predator Act, which defines a *sexually violent predator* as "any person who has been convicted of or charged with a sexually violent offense and who suffers from a mental abnormality or personality disorder which makes the person likely to engage in the predatory acts of sexual violence." In a 5-4 decision, the U.S. Supreme Court upheld the civil commitment on the grounds that Hendricks was to be treated not punished.[81]

Hendricks remains in a Kansas prison where, in his 70s, he spends most of his time in a wheelchair or leaning on a cane because of various medical problems, including a stroke. By 2007, 20 states had civil commitment procedures in place for sex offenders who are released from prison, and approximately 2,700 such offenders were being held at that time. One newspaper pointed out that Hendricks, who at that time had been in so-called treatment for 13 years, was costing the state $185,000 per year, eight times the cost of keeping an inmate in prison in Kansas.[82]

Megan's laws requiring the registration of sex offenders, along with laws requiring civil commitment of such offenders once they complete their prison sentences, can be expected to continue to generate debate and controversy, especially until the U.S. Supreme Court answers all the issues surrounding these relatively new statutes.

SUMMARY

This text began with an examination of the purposes of criminal law, a discussion that included an overview of punishment philosophies. The philosophy that dominates at any given time is reflected in sentencing practices. Thus, with the trend toward retribution and deterrence came a movement away from the indeterminate sentencing structure. In recent years, however, there has been some movement back toward rehabilitation and treatment.

Allegations of legislative and judicial sentence disparity and judicial leniency resulted in public pressure to exert controls over sentencing judges and to influence legislative changes in sentence lengths. This chapter examined sentence types and sentencing guidelines. The essence of the federal mandate and subsequent proposed guidelines has been to decrease sentencing discretion and to abolish parole release over a period of time. Although mitigating and aggravating circumstances of a crime and characteristics of an offender may be considered in sentencing, the U.S. Sentencing Commission developed statistical data and tables designed to minimize the disparity that results when any or several individualized factors are considered. It is an attempt to avoid the harshness of a system that sentences every offender of a particular crime to the same sentence. But it is also an attempt to eliminate extreme disparity that may result in a less structured system. The federal guidelines and the Sentencing Commission remain controversial. The U.S. Supreme Court initially upheld the constitutionality of the commission's mandate, but in 2005 the Court ruled that the guidelines are just that—they are advisory, not mandatory.

The chapter included a discussion of the recent attempts by federal and state jurisdictions to increase the penalties of multiple offenders. The resulting "three strikes and you're out" legislation was analyzed in the context of its practical and legal implications, emphasizing the U.S. Supreme Court's rulings upholding these statutes. Attempts to increase the amount of time served by enacting truth in sentencing legislation were noted.

The current focus on capital punishment warrants its return to criminal law texts. The chapter discussed the recent data and trends in this punishment. Legal issues regarding capital punishment were noted in the discussion on the constitutional issues in sentencing. That section began with the changes in the U.S. Supreme Court's analysis of the execution of the mentally challenged. Issues concerning the assessment of facts submitted at the sentencing stage were summarized, with the roles of the judge and the jury analyzed in the context of the most recent U.S. Supreme Court decisions. Constitutional issues surrounding sentencing on the basis of race were probed. Proportionality and cruel and unusual punishment issues were discussed, with the primary emphasis on their application to capital punishment. The most recent U.S. Supreme Court decisions were analyzed. Particular attention was given to the constitutional issues regarding executing juveniles and the use of lethal injection for capital punishment.

The final section of the chapter was devoted to a look at Megan's laws. These laws vary in their provisions, but all require the registration of sex offenders once they return to the community from confinement. The assumption is that if others who live in the community can find out the location of sex offenders, they can keep their children secure from them, and this will reduce the opportunities those predators have to repeat their crimes. The constitutional issues raised with these statutes culminated in the recent U.S. Supreme Court's analysis of the Connecticut and the Alaska statutes. Recent legislative changes regarding sex offender registration were noted, including the passage of the KIDS Act of 2008, along with the use of civil commitment procedures of sex offenders after they complete their prison terms.

The chapter's Case Analysis features the 2005 U.S. Supreme Court's decision concerning the execution of juveniles, one of the more controversial issues to come before the Court in recent years.

This completes our analysis of criminal law, a subject of great complexity and extreme importance. This discussion provided only an overview of the subject; criminal law varies among jurisdictions, and in some cases that variance is significant. It is possible to gain only an introduction to the general issues, problems, and trends in such a vast, rapidly changing field. Many issues related to these discussions are left to a text in criminal procedure; some are primarily criminological in nature, whereas others relate to the correctional system. All are interrelated and important to a comprehensive understanding of U.S. criminal justice systems.

STUDY QUESTIONS

1. Explain how punishment philosophies relate to sentencing.

2. Explain the differences in these sentencing models: legislative, judicial, and administrative. Relate your answer to specific sentencing reforms discussed in this chapter.

3. What is presumptive sentencing? Give examples.

4. If sentencing guidelines are used, should they be based on a jurisdiction's previous sentencing practices or on ideal sentencing practices? If the latter, how would you propose to draft the guidelines? How much discretion would you allow? Discuss in relationship to the federal system.

5. Washington state legislators claim that their 1981 sentencing code revision represents a move from indeterminate to determinate sentencing. Analyze this claim.

6. Describe the U.S. Sentencing Commission, its purpose, and its problems. What are some of the constitutional issues with regard to its sentencing guidelines? Analyze the recent U.S. Supreme Court decisions concerning these guidelines.

7. Define and discuss the implications of three strikes and you're out and truth in sentencing legislation.

8. What are some of the results of sentencing reform?

9. Discuss the current status and recent data concerning capital punishment. Do you think capital punishment should be abolished?

10. What is the status of executing the mentally challenged?

11. Analyze the recent U.S. Supreme Court decisions concerning sentencing issues and the right to a trial by jury.

12. Outline the constitutional issues concerning race and sentencing.

13. What is meant by *proportionality* in sentencing? What has the U.S. Supreme Court held about this concept? Discuss in relationship to capital punishment for rape but not murder of the victim.

14. List and explain cases that challenge the Eighth Amendment's prohibition against cruel and unusual punishment.

15. Discuss recent developments regarding the constitutionality of various methods of capital punishment.

16. What is the legal status of executing juveniles in the United States?

17. What is meant by *Megan's laws*? Assess the importance, the validity, and the constitutionality of such laws.

18. What is the purpose of the civil commitment of sex offenders after they complete their prison terms? Is this practice constitutional? Is it reasonable?

FOR DEBATE

The issue of capital punishment has become one of national importance in the last few years, with some states declaring a moratorium on its use. The extreme nature of this penalty requires that it be imposed only in rare cases. The U.S. Supreme Court has ruled that capital punishment is unconstitutional under some circumstances. With that in mind, debate the following issue.

Resolved: Capital punishment should be abolished in the United States because it constitutes cruel and unusual punishment and this violates the Eighth Amendment of the U.S. Constitution.

KEY TERMS

CASE ANALYSIS

ROPER V. SIMMONS
543 U.S. 551 (2005)

Case Preview

The case analysis for this last chapter in the book is from one of the most significant recent opinions of the U.S. Supreme Court. In 2005 the Court held that juveniles may not be executed. The opinions in *Roper v. Simmons*[83] are very long; they have been cut significantly for this text. The interested student may want to read the entire opinions.

As the Court notes, prior to this decision, most states prohibited the execution of a person who committed a crime when he or she was under the age of 18, and no foreign countries officially permitted the practice. Consider the relevance of this information to the decision. The opinions also discuss the constitutional requirement of proportionality for punishments.

Justice Anthony M. Kennedy delivered the opinion of the Court, in which Justices John Paul Stevens, David H. Souter, Ruth Bader Ginsburg, and Stephen G. Breyer joined. Justice Stevens filed a concurring opinion, in which Justice Ginsburg joined. Justice Sandra Day O'Connor filed a dissenting opinion. Justice Antonin Scalia filed a dissenting opinion, in which Chief Justice William H. Rehnquist and Justice Clarence Thomas joined.

Facts

At the age of 17, when he was still a junior in high school, Christopher Simmons, the respondent here, committed murder. About nine months later, after he had turned 18, he was tried and sentenced to death. There is little doubt that Simmons was the instigator of the crime. Before its commission Simmons said he wanted to murder someone. In chilling, callous terms he talked about his plan, discussing it for the most part with two friends, Charles Benjamin and John Tessmer, then aged 15 and 16 respectively. Simmons proposed to commit burglary and murder by breaking and entering, tying up a victim, and throwing the victim off a bridge. Simmons assured his friends they could "get away with it" because they were minors.

The three met at about 2 a.m. on the night of the murder, but Tessmer left before the other two set out. (The State later charged Tessmer with conspiracy, but dropped the charge in exchange for his testimony against Simmons.) Simmons and Benjamin entered the home of the victim, Shirley Crook, after reaching through an open window and unlocking the back door. Simmons turned on a hallway light. Awakened, Mrs. Crook called out, "Who's there?" In response Simmons entered Mrs. Crook's bedroom, where he recognized her from a previous car accident involving them both. Simmons later admitted this confirmed his resolve to murder her.

Using duct tape to cover her eyes and mouth and bind her hands, the two perpetrators put Mrs. Crook in her minivan and drove to a state park. They reinforced the bindings, covered her head with a towel, and walked her to a railroad trestle spanning the Meramec River. There they tied her hands and feet together with electrical wire, wrapped her whole face in duct tape and threw her from the bridge, drowning her in the waters below.

By the afternoon of September 9, Steven Crook had returned home from an overnight trip, found his bedroom in disarray, and reported his wife missing. On the same afternoon fishermen recovered the victim's body from the river. Simmons, meanwhile, was bragging about the killing, telling friends he had killed a woman "because the bitch seen my face."

The next day, after receiving information of Simmons' involvement, police arrested him at his high school and took him to the police station in Fenton, Missouri. They read him his Miranda rights. Simmons waived his right to an attorney and agreed to answer questions. After less than two hours of interrogation, Simmons confessed to the murder and agreed to perform a videotaped reenactment at the crime scene.

The State charged Simmons with burglary, kidnaping, stealing, and murder in the first degree. As Simmons was 17 at the time of the crime, he was outside the criminal jurisdiction of Missouri's juvenile court system. He was tried as an adult. At trial the State introduced Simmons' confession and the videotaped reenactment of the crime, along with testimony that Simmons discussed the crime in advance and bragged about it later. The defense called no witnesses in the guilt phase. The jury having returned a verdict of murder, the trial proceeded to the penalty phase.

The State sought the death penalty. As aggravating factors, the State submitted that the murder was committed for the purpose of receiving money; was committed for the purpose of avoiding, interfering with, or preventing lawful arrest of the defendant; and involved depravity of mind and was outrageously and wantonly vile, horrible, and inhuman. The State called Shirley Crook's husband, daughter, and two sisters, who presented moving evidence of the devastation her death had brought to their lives.

In mitigation Simmons' attorneys first called an officer of the Missouri juvenile justice system, who testified that Simmons had no prior convictions and that no previous charges had been filed against him. Simmons' mother, father, two younger half brothers, a neighbor, and a friend took the stand to tell the jurors of the close relationships they had formed with Simmons and to plead for mercy on his behalf. Simmons' mother, in particular, testified to the responsibility Simmons demonstrated in taking care of his two younger half brothers and of his grandmother and to his capacity to show love for them.

During closing arguments, both the prosecutor and defense counsel addressed Simmons' age, which the trial judge had instructed the jurors they could consider as a mitigating factor. . . .

The jury recommended the death penalty after finding the State had proved each of the three aggravating factors submitted to it. Accepting the jury's recommendation, the trial judge imposed the death penalty.

Simmons obtained new counsel, who moved in the trial court to set aside the conviction and sentence. One argument was that Simmons had received ineffective assistance [of counsel] at trial. . . .

Part of the submission [of evidence] was that Simmons was "very immature," "very impulsive," and "very susceptible to being manipulated or influenced." The experts testified about Simmons' background including a difficult home environment and dramatic changes in behavior, accompanied by poor school performance in adolescence. Simmons was absent from home for long periods, spending time using alcohol and drugs with other teenagers or young adults. The contention by Simmons' postconviction counsel was that these matters should have been established in the sentencing proceeding. . . .

[The Court reviewed the decisions below and confirmed the state court's decision.] . . .

Issue

This case requires us to address, for the second time in a decade and a half, whether it is permissible under the Eighth and Fourteenth Amendments to the Constitution of the United States to execute a juvenile offender who was older than 15 but younger than 18 when he committed a capital crime. In *Stanford v. Kentucky*, a divided Court rejected the proposition that the Constitution bars capital punishment for juvenile offenders in this age group. We reconsider the question. . . .

Holding

The Eighth and Fourteenth Amendments forbid imposition of the death penalty on offenders who were under the age of 18 when their crimes were committed. The judgment of the Missouri Supreme Court setting aside the sentence of death imposed upon Christopher Simmons is affirmed.

Rationale

As the Court explained in *Atkins* [*Atkins v. Virginia*, discussed earlier in this chapter], the Eighth Amendment guarantees individuals the right not to be subjected to excessive sanctions. . . . By protecting even those convicted of heinous crimes, the Eighth Amendment reaffirms the duty of the government to respect the dignity of all persons.

The prohibition against "cruel and unusual punishment," like other expansive language in the Constitution, must be interpreted according to its text, by considering history, tradition, and precedent, and with due regard for its purpose and function in the constitutional design. To implement this framework we have established the propriety and affirmed the necessity of referring to "the evolving standards of decency that mark the progress of a maturing society" to determine which punishments are so disproportionate as to be cruel and unusual. . . .

[The opinion discussed the history of cases involving the execution of persons for crimes committed when they were juveniles. It then reviewed the Court's recent decision in *Atkins*, which banned the execution of the mentally retarded. The Court noted that between the *Atkins* decision and the Court's earlier decision upholding the practice at issue in the case, a significant number of states had banned the execution of the mentally retarded. The Court announced its decision in this case and continued with its reasons.]

Because the death penalty is the most severe punishment, the Eighth Amendment applies to it with special force. Capital punishment must be limited to those offenders who commit "a narrow category of the most serious crimes" and whose extreme culpability makes them "the most deserving of execution." This principle is implemented throughout the capital sentencing process. States must give narrow and precise definition to the aggravating factors that can result in a capital sentence. In any capital case a defendant has wide latitude to raise as a mitigating factor "any aspect of [his or her] character or record and any of the circumstances of the offense that the defendant proffers [offers] as a basis for a sentence less than death." There are a number of crimes that beyond question are severe in absolute terms, yet the death penalty may not be imposed for their commission. The death penalty may not be imposed on certain classes of offenders, such as juveniles under 16, the insane, and the mentally retarded, no matter how heinous the crime. These rules vindicate the underlying principle that the death penalty is reserved for a narrow category of crimes and offenders.

Three general differences between juveniles under 18 and adults demonstrate that juvenile offenders cannot with reliability be classified among the worst offenders. First, . . . "[a] lack of maturity and an underdeveloped sense of responsibility are found in youth more often than in adults and are more understandable among the young. These qualities often result in impetuous and ill-considered actions and decisions." It has been noted that "adolescents are overrepresented statistically in virtually every category of reckless behavior." In recognition of the comparative immaturity and irresponsibility of juveniles, almost every State prohibits those under 18 years of age from voting, serving on juries, or marrying without parental consent.

The second area of difference is that juveniles are more vulnerable or susceptible to negative influences and outside pressures, including peer pressure. This is explained in part by the prevailing circumstance that juveniles have less control,

or less experience with control, over their own environment.

The third broad difference is that the character of a juvenile is not as well formed as that of an adult. The personality traits of juveniles are more transitory, less fixed.

These differences render suspect any conclusion that a juvenile falls among the worst offenders. . . .

In *Thompson* a plurality of the Court recognized the import of these characteristics with respect to juveniles under 16, and relied on them to hold that the Eighth Amendment prohibited the imposition of the death penalty on juveniles below that age. We conclude the same reasoning applies to all juvenile offenders under 18. . . .

The differences between juvenile and adult offenders are too marked and well understood to risk allowing a youthful person to receive the death penalty despite insufficient culpability. An unacceptable likelihood exists that the brutality or cold-blooded nature of any particular crime would overpower mitigating arguments based on youth as a matter of course, even where the juvenile offender's objective immaturity, vulnerability, and lack of true depravity should require a sentence less severe than death. In some cases a defendant's youth may even be counted against him. In this very case, as we noted above, the prosecutor argued Simmons' youth was aggravating rather than mitigating. While this sort of overreaching could be corrected by a particular rule to ensure that the mitigating force of youth is not overlooked, that would not address our larger concerns.

It is difficult even for expert psychologists to differentiate between the juvenile offender whose crime reflects unfortunate yet transient immaturity, and the rare juvenile offender whose crime reflects irreparable corruption. . . . If trained psychiatrists with the advantage of clinical testing and observation refrain, despite diagnostic expertise, from assessing any juvenile under 18 as having antisocial personality disorder, we conclude that States should refrain from asking jurors to issue a far graver condemnation—that a juvenile offender merits the death penalty. When a juvenile offender commits a heinous crime, the State can exact forfeiture of some of the most basic liberties, but the State cannot extinguish his life and his potential to attain a mature understanding of his own humanity. . . .

The age of 18 is the point where society draws the line for many purposes between childhood and adulthood. It is, we conclude, the age at which the line for death eligibility ought to rest. . . . Our determination that the death penalty is disproportionate punishment for offenders under 18 finds confirmation in the stark reality that the United States is the only country in the world that continues to give official sanction to the juvenile death penalty. . . .

[The court reviewed the decline of the use of the death penalty for juveniles in other countries.]

In sum, it is fair to say that the United States now stands alone in a world that has turned its face against the juvenile death penalty. . . .

The opinion of the world community, while not controlling our outcome, does provide respected and significant confirmation for our own conclusions.

Over time, from one generation to the next, the Constitution has come to earn the high respect and even . . . the veneration of the American people. . . . It does not lessen our fidelity to the Constitution or our pride in its origins to acknowledge that the express affirmation of certain fundamental rights by other nations and peoples simply underscores the centrality of those same rights within our own heritage of freedom.

Justice Stevens, with whom Justice Ginsburg joins, concurring

Perhaps even more important than our specific holding today is our reaffirmation of the basic principle that informs the Court's interpretation of the Eighth Amendment. If the meaning of that Amendment had been frozen when it was originally drafted, it would impose no impediment to the execution of 7-year-old children today. The evolving standards of decency that have driven our construction of this critically important part of the Bill of Rights foreclose any such reading of the Amendment. In the best tradition of the common law, the pace of that evolution is a matter for continuing debate; but that our understanding of the Constitution does change from time to time has been settled since John Marshall breathed life into its text. If great lawyers of his day—Alexander Hamilton, for example—were sitting with us today, I would expect them to join Justice Kennedy's opinion for the Court. In all events, I do so without hesitation.

Justice O'Connor, dissenting

The Court's decision today establishes a categorical rule forbidding the execution of any offender for any crime committed before his 18th birthday, no matter how deliberate, wanton, or cruel the offense. Neither the objective evidence of contemporary societal values, nor the Court's moral proportionality analysis, nor the two in tandem suffice to justify this ruling. Although the Court finds support for its decision in the fact that a majority of the States now disallow capital punishment of 17-year-old offenders, it refrains from asserting that its holding is compelled by a genuine national consensus. Indeed, the evidence before us fails to demonstrate conclusively that any such consensus has emerged in the brief period since we upheld the constitutionality of this practice in . . . [1989].

Instead, the rule decreed by the Court rests, ultimately, on its independent moral judgment that death is a disproportionately severe punishment for any 17-year-old offender. I do not subscribe to this judgment. Adolescents as a class are undoubtedly less mature, and therefore less culpable for their misconduct, than adults. But the Court has adduced no evidence impeaching the seemingly reasonable conclusion reached by many state

legislatures: that at least some 17-year-old murderers are sufficiently mature to deserve the death penalty in an appropriate case. Nor has it been shown that capital sentencing juries are incapable of accurately assessing a youthful defendant's maturity or of giving due weight to the mitigating characteristics associated with youth. . . .

It is beyond cavil that juveniles as a class are generally less mature, less responsible, and less fully formed than adults, and that these differences bear on juveniles' comparative moral culpability. But even accepting this premise, the Court's proportionality argument fails to support its categorical rule.

First, the Court adduces no evidence whatsoever in support of its sweeping conclusion that it is only in "rare" cases, if ever, that 17-year-old murderers are sufficiently mature and act with sufficient depravity to warrant the death penalty. The fact that juveniles are generally less culpable for their misconduct than adults does not necessarily mean that a 17-year-old murderer cannot be sufficiently culpable to merit the death penalty. At most, the Court's argument suggests that the average 17-year-old murderer is not as culpable as the average adult murderer. But an especially depraved juvenile offender may nevertheless be just as culpable as many adult offenders considered bad enough to deserve the death penalty. Similarly, the fact that the availability of the death penalty may be less likely to deter a juvenile from committing a capital crime does not imply that this threat cannot effectively deter some 17-year-olds from such an act. . . .

Christopher Simmons' murder of Shirley Crook was premeditated, wanton, and cruel in the extreme. . . . Whatever can be said about the comparative moral culpability of 17-year-olds as a general matter, Simmons' actions unquestionably reflect "'a consciousness materially more "depraved" than that of' . . . the average murderer." And Simmons' prediction that he could murder with impunity because he had not yet turned 18—though inaccurate—suggests that he did take into account the perceived risk of punishment in deciding whether to commit the crime. . . .

The Court's proportionality argument suffers from a second and closely related defect: It fails to establish that the differences in maturity between 17-year-olds and young "adults" are both universal enough and significant enough to justify a bright-line prophylactic rule against capital punishment of the former. The Court's analysis is premised on differences in the aggregate between juveniles and adults, which frequently do not hold true when comparing individuals. Although it may be that many 17-year-old murderers lack sufficient maturity to deserve the death penalty, some juvenile murderers may be quite mature. Chronological age is not an unfailing measure of psychological development, and common experience suggests that many 17-year-olds are more mature than the average young "adult." In short, the class of offenders exempted from capital punishment by today's decision is too broad and too diverse to warrant a categorical prohibition. . . .

For purposes of proportionality analysis, 17-year-olds as a class are qualitatively and materially different from the mentally retarded. "Mentally retarded" offenders . . . are defined by precisely the characteristics which render death an excessive punishment. A mentally retarded person is, "by definition," one whose cognitive and behavioral capacities have been proven to fall below a certain minimum. [T]he mentally retarded are not merely less blameworthy for their misconduct or less likely to be deterred by the death penalty than others. Rather, a mentally retarded offender is one whose demonstrated impairments make it so highly unlikely that he is culpable enough to deserve the death penalty or that he could have been deterred by the threat of death, that execution is not a defensible punishment. There is no such inherent or accurate fit between an offender's chronological age and the personal limitations which the Court believes make capital punishment excessive for 17-year-old murderers. Moreover, it defies common sense to suggest that 17-year-olds as a class are somehow equivalent to mentally retarded persons with regard to culpability or susceptibility to deterrence. Seventeen-year-olds may, on average, be less mature than adults, but that lesser maturity simply cannot be equated with the major, lifelong impairments suffered by the mentally retarded. . . .

Reasonable minds can differ as to the minimum age at which commission of a serious crime should expose the defendant to the death penalty, if at all. Many jurisdictions have abolished capital punishment altogether, while many others have determined that even the most heinous crime, if committed before the age of 18, should not be punishable by death. Indeed, were my office that of a legislator, rather than a judge, then I, too, would be inclined to support legislation setting a minimum age of 18 in this context. But a significant number of States, including Missouri, have decided to make the death penalty potentially available for 17-year-old capital murderers such as respondent. Without a clearer showing that a genuine national consensus forbids the execution of such offenders, this Court should not substitute its own "inevitably subjective judgment" on how best to resolve this difficult moral question for the judgments of the Nation's democratically elected legislatures. I respectfully dissent.

Justice Scalia, with whom Chief Justice Rehnquist and Justice Thomas join, dissenting

. . . The Court . . . proclaims itself sole arbiter of our Nation's moral standards—and in the course of discharging that awesome responsibility purports to take guidance from the views of foreign courts and legislatures. Because I do not believe that the meaning of our Eighth Amendment any more than the meaning of other provisions of our Constitution, should be determined by the subjective views of five Members of this Court and like-minded foreigners, I dissent.

For Discussion

Clearly the justices of the U.S. Supreme Court had strong reactions to the issue in this case, raising a number of interesting questions for students, some of whom may be juveniles.

Compare the opinions of those justices who voted to ban execution of juveniles with the opinions of those who dissented. Outline the basic issues and consider which you think are most accurate. Do you think Simmons can be rehabilitated? Would you have dropped the charges against the third defendant? If so, why? If not, why not? Should juvenile defendants be permitted to waive their right to counsel without having counsel to assist them in making that decision?

Compare what you believe to be the mitigating and aggravating factors in this case. Should the opinions of the victims carry great weight?

Recall the case of *Atkins v. Virginia*, discussed earlier in the chapter, and compare the reasons raised in that case with those in this case.

This is the last chapter in the text. Take the opportunity to review what you have learned and to reconsider, for example, Chapter 1's discussion of the reasons for punishment. Compare that discussion to the facts of this case in discussing whether you think the U.S. Supreme Court or the dissents were correct in their respective presentations. Consider the meaning of cruel and unusual punishment as it relates to the facts of this case.

INTERNET ACTIVITY

The text noted that the Justice for All Act of 2004, which contains the Innocence Protection Act, was designed to improve the quality of legal representation for state death row inmates as well as to provide greater access to DNA testing for those inmates who challenge their death sentences. To find out more about the admission of DNA evidence into trials, access the website of the National Commission on the Future of DNA Evidence, which was established by the attorney general, http://www.ojp.usdoj.gov/nij/topics/forensics/dna/commission/welcom.htm (accessed 12 March 2009).

1. What was the commission's mission?

2. What issues did it address?

Check the website of the DNA Initiative, http://www.dna.gov/info/(accessed 3 March 2009).

1. What are its goals?

2. What is the significance in postconviction exoneration of the innocent?

3. Is federal funding available for social scientists who wish to research exoneration of the innocent?

NOTES

1. Twentieth Century Task Force on Criminal Sentencing, *Fair and Certain Punishment*, with a background paper by Alan M. Dershowitz (New York: McGraw-Hill, 1976), pp. 19–20.

2. Richard Singer, "In Favor of 'Presumptive Sentences' Set by a Sentencing Commission," *Crime & Delinquency* 24 (October 1978): 402, 421, emphasis in the original.

3. David Boerner, *Sentencing in Washington: A Legal Analysis of the Sentencing Reform Act of 1981* (Seattle: Butterworth Legal Publishers, 1985), p. 1–1.

4. See, for example, RCWA, Title 9, Section 9.94A.535 (2008).

5. The Sentencing Reform Act was passed as part of the Comprehensive Crime Control Act of 1984, Public Law 98-473, 98 Stat. 1837, 1976 (1984), and is codified with its subsequent amendments in USCS, Title 18, Sections 3551 *et seq.* (2009), and USCS, Title 28, Sections 991–998 (2009).

6. *Mistretta v. United States*, 488 U.S. 361 (1989).

7. "Chorus of Judicial Critics Assail Sentencing Guides," *New York Times* (17 April 1992), p. 2.

8. "American Bar Assn. Delegates Pass Resolution Against Mandatory Minimum Sentencing Laws," *Minnesota Lawyer* (16 August 2004), n.p.

9. *Blakely v. Washington*, 542 U.S. 296 (2004).

10. *United States v. Apprendi*, 530 U.S. 466 (2000).

11. *United States v. Booker*, 543 U.S. 220 (2005).

12. *United States v. Fanfan*, 543 U.S. 220 (2005).

13. *United States v. Booker*, 543 U.S. 220 (2005); *United States v. Fanfan*, 543 U.S. 220 (2005).

14. *Rita v. United States*, 551 U.S. 338 (2007).

15. *Claiborne v. United States*, 551 U.S. 87 (2007).

16. *Gall v. United States*, 128 S.Ct. 586 (2007).

17. *Kimbrough v. United States*, 128 S.Ct. 558 (2007), cases and citations omitted.

18. *Cunningham v. California*, 549 U.S. 270 (2007). The relevant California statutes are Cal Pen Code, Part 1, Title 9, Chapter 5, Sections 288.5(a) and Part 2, Title 7, Chapter 4,5, Article 1, Section 1170(b)(2008).

19. *Shepard v. United States*, 544 U.S. 13 (2005).

20. *Shepard v. United States*, 544 U.S. 13 (2005).

21. See Cal Pen Code, Part 1, Title 16, Section 667(e)(2) (2008).

22. *People v. Superior Court*, 917 P.2d 628 (Cal.Sup. 1996), *modified and reh'g. denied*, 1996 Cal. LEXIS 4445 (1996).

23. *People v. Williams*, 948 P.2d 429 (Ca. 1988), *modified, reh'g. denied*, 1998 Cal. LEXIS 1151 (1998).

24. *Riggs v. California*, 525 U.S. 1114 (1999), *denying cert. on a pro se motion.*

25. *People v. Garcia*, 976 P.2d 831 (Ca. 1999).

26. "Ruling on 3-Strikes Laws Could Heavily Impact Corrections," *Corrections Professional* 7, no. 15 (19 April 2002): n.p.

27. *Aging Behind Bars: "Three Strikes" Seven Years Later*, http://www.sentencingproject.org, accessed 6 August 2008.

28. Franklin Zimring et al., *Three Strikes and You're Out in California* (New York: Oxford University Press, 2001), cited in *Criminal Justice Newsletter* 31, no. 12 (25 May 2001): 10.

29. Violent Offender Incarceration and Truth in Sentencing Incentive Grants, USCS, Title 42, Section 13701 *et seq.* (2009).

30. ILCS, Chapter 730, Article 6, Section 5/3-6-3 (2) (i) (ii) and (4.6) (2009).

31. *Furman v. Georgia*, 408 U.S. 238 (1972).

32. See *Gregg v. Georgia*, 428 U.S. 153 (1976); and *Woodson v. North Carolina*, 428 U.S. 280 (1976).

33. "Facts About the Death Penalty," Death Penalty Information Center, http://www.deathpenaltyinfo.org/Fact Sheet.pdf, accessed 12 May 2009.

34. Margaret Graham Tebo, "Stevens Blasts Death Penalty Mistakes," *ABA Journal Report*, pp. 1–4, http://www.abanet.org/journal/ereport/au12stevens.html, accessed 12 August 2005.

35. Death Penalty Information Center, "Facts About the Death Penalty," p. 4, citations omitted.

36. Justice for All Act of 2004, Pub. Law 109-405 (2009).

37. *Ford v. Wainwright*, 477 U.S. 399 (1986).

38. *Penry v. Lynaugh*, 492 U.S. 302 (1989).

39. *Penry v. Johnson*, 532 U.S. 782 (2001).

40. *Penry v. State*, 2005 Tex. Crim. App. LEXIS 1620 (Tex. Crim.App. 5 October 2005).

41. "Switching Sides on Justice," *Dallas Morning News* (20 April 2008), p. 8.

42. *Atkins v. Virginia*, 536 U.S. 304 (2002).

43. "A Mentally Ill Killer Is Executed in Texas," *New York Times* (27 March 2003), p. 12.

44. "National Briefing Southwest: Texas: Schizophrenic Is Executed," *New York Times* (19 May 2004), p. 21.

45. *Panetti v. Quarterman*, 128 S.Ct. 2842 (2007).

46. *United States v. Apprendi*, 530 U.S. 466 (2000).

47. *Ring v. Arizona*, 534 U.S. 1103 (2002).

48. *Schriro v. Summerlin*, 542 U.S. 348 (2004).

49. *Harris v. United States*, 536 U.S. 545 (2002).

50. *Shepard v. United States*, 544 U.S. 13 (2005).

51. *Miller-El v. Cockrell*, 537 U.S. 322 (2003).

52. *Miller-El v. Cockrell*, 545 U.S. 2317 (2005).

53. *Miller-El v. Cockrell*, 537 U.S. 322 (2003), *on remand, Miller-El v. Johnson*, 330 F.3d 690 (5th Cir. 2003), *subsequent appeal, Miller-El v. Dretke*, 361 F. 3d 849 (5th Cir. 2004), *rev'd., remanded sub nom.*, 545 U.S. 231 (2005), *and on remand, remanded*, 2005 U.S. App. LEXIS 15206 (5th Cir. 2005), abrogated as stated in *Davis v. Fisk Electric Co.*, 268 S.W. 3d 508 (Tex. 2008).

54. *Williams v. New York*, 337 U.S. 241, 247 (1949).

55. *McCleskey v. Kemp*, 481 U.S. 279 (1987).

56. Michael Tonry, "Racial Politics, Racial Disparities, and the War on Crime," *Crime & Delinquency* 40 (October

1994): 475, 483–488. See also Tonry, *Malign Neglect: Race, Crime, and Punishment in America* (New York: Oxford University Press, 1994).

57. "Congress Asked to Lower Crack Penalties," *American Bar Association Journal* 81 (July 1995): 30. See also Public Law 104-38 (1995) and *United States v. Armstrong*, 517 U.S. 456 (1996).

58. "Bill Clinton Admits 'Regret' on Crack Cocaine Sentencing," (3 March 2008), quoted on the website of The Sentencing Project, http://www.sentencingproject.org, accessed 9 March 2008.

59. "In Need of a Fix: ABA Urges Elimination of Disparity in Federal Sentences for Cocaine Violations," *American Bar Association Journal* 94 (May 2008): 66. See also United States Sentencing Commission, *Report to Congress: Cocaine and Federal Sentencing Policy* (May 2007), p. 73. Inmates may petition to have their sentences lowered under USCS, Title 18, Section 3582(c)(2) (2009).

60. Marc Mauer and Ryan S. King, *Uneven Justice: State Rates of Incarceration by Race and Ethnicity*, The Sentencing Project (July 2007), p. 3, http://www.sentencingproject.org, accessed 6 August 2008.

61. *Coker v. Georgia*, 433 U.S. 584 (1977).

62. *Kennedy v. Louisiana*, 128 S.Ct. 2641 (2008), cases and citations omitted.

63. *Watson v. United States*, 439 F.2d 442, 473 (D.C.Cir. 1970).

64. *Carmona v. Ward*, 436 F.Supp. 1153 (S.D.N.Y. 1977), *rev'd.*, 576 F.2d 405 (2d Cir. 1978), *cert. denied*, 439 U.S. 1091 (1979).

65. See, for example, the following: *Rummel v. Estelle*, 445 U.S. 263 (1980) and *Solem v. Helm*, 463 U.S. 277 (1983), *superseded by statute as stated in In re Petition of Lauer*, 788 F.2d 135 (8th Cir. 1985).

66. *Solem v. Helm*, 463 U.S. 277 (1983), *superseded by statute as stated in In re Petition of Lauer*, 788 F.2d 135 (8th Cir. 1985).

67. *Thompson v. Oklahoma*, 487 U.S. 815 (1988).

68. *Stanford v. Parker*, 266 F.3d 442 (6th Cir. 2001), *cert. denied*, 537 U.S. 831 (2002).

69. *Baldwin v. Alabama*, 472 U.S. 372 (1985).

70. "Child Sex Killer Is Executed in First U.S. Hanging Since 1965," *Miami Herald* (6 January 1993), p. 6.

71. *Campbell v. Wood*, 18 F.3d 729 (9th Cir. 1994).

72. *Rupe v. Wood*, 863 F.Supp. 1307 (W.D.Wash. 1994), *aff'd. in part and vacated in part*, 93 F.3d 1434 (9th Cir. 1996), *cert. denied*, 519 U.S. 1142 (1996). The statute is RCWA, Title 10, Chapter 10.95, Section 10.95.180 (1) (2008).

73. See *Fierro v. Gomez*, 865 F.Supp. 1387 (N.D.Cal. 1994). *aff'd.*, 77 F.3d 301 (9th Cir. 1996), *vacated, remanded*, 519 U.S. 918 (1996), *on remand, remanded, Fierro v. Terhune*, 147 F.3d 1158 (9th Cir. 1998).

74. *Provenzano v. Moore*, 744 So.2d 413 (Fla. 1999), *cert. denied*, 528 U.S. 1182 (2000).

75. *Bryan v. Moore*, 528 U.S. 960 (1999), *cert. dismissed*, 528 U.S. 1133 (2000).

76. *Baze v. Rees*, 128 S.Ct. 1520 (2008). The statute is KRS 431.220 (2007).

77. *Baze v. Rees*, 128 S.Ct. 1520 (2008), Justice Ginsburg dissenting.

78. "More and More States Pass Laws to Strengthen Sex Crime Penalties," *Criminal Justice Newsletter* (1 March 2007), p. 3. The Florida statute, the Jessica Lunsford Act, is codified at Fla. Stat., Title 47, Chapter 948, Section 948.30 (2008).

79. Human Rights Watch, *No Easy Answers: Sex Offender Laws in the United States*" (11 September 2007), http://www.hrw.org/, accessed 9 December 2008.

80. "Rep. Pomeroy Testifies on His Bill to Keep Kids Safe from Sex Offenders on Internet," *US Fed News* (17 October 2007), n.p. The law is entitled Keeping the Internet Devoid of Sexual Predators of the KIDS Act of 2008, which is codified at P.L. 110-400 (2008).

81. Sexually Violent Predator Act, Kan. Stats. Ann., Section 59-29a01 *et seq.* (2006). The case is *Kansas v. Hendricks*, 521 U.S. 346 (1997).

82. "Doubts Rise as States Hold Sex Offenders After Prison," *New York Times* (4 March 2007), p. 1; "Wrong Turn on Sex Offenders," *New York Times* (13 March 2007), p. 18.

83. *Roper v. Simmons*, 543 U.S. 551 (2005), citations and footnotes omitted.

APPENDIX A

Selections from the Constitution of the United States

[In the following selections from the Constitution, spelling, capitalization, and punctuation conform to the text of the engrossed parchment.]

We the People of the United States, in Order to form a more perfect Union, establish Justice, insure domestic Tranquility, provide for the common defence, promote the general Welfare, and secure the Blessings of Liberty to ourselves and our Posterity, do ordain and establish this Constitution for the United States of America.

ARTICLE I.

SECTION. 1. All legislative Powers herein granted shall be vested in a Congress of the United States, which shall consist of a Senate and House of Representatives. . . .

SECTION. 8. The Congress shall have Power To . . . regulate Commerce with foreign Nations, and among the several States, and with the Indian Tribes; . . .

[9] To constitute Tribunals inferior to the supreme Court; . . .

[18] To make all Laws which shall be necessary and proper for carrying into Execution the foregoing Powers, and all other Powers vested by this Constitution in the Government of the United States, or in any Department or Officer thereof.

SECTION. 9 . . . .

[2] The Privilege of the Writ of Habeas Corpus shall not be suspended, unless when in Cases of Rebellion or Invasion the public Safety may require it.

[3] No Bill of Attainder or ex post facto Law shall be passed. . . .

ARTICLE II.

SECTION. 1. [1] The executive Power shall be vested in a President of the United States of America. . . .

SECTION. 2. [1] The President shall be Commander in Chief of the Army and Navy of the United States, and of the Militia of the several States, when called into the actual Service of the United States; . . .

[2] He shall have Power, by and with the Advice and Consent of the Senate, to make Treaties, provided two thirds of the Senators present concur; and he shall nominate, and by and with the Advice and Consent of the Senate, shall appoint Ambassadors, other public Ministers and Consuls, Judges of the supreme Court, and all other Officers of the United States, whose Appointments are not herein otherwise provided for, and which shall be established by Law: but the Congress may by Law vest the Appointment of such inferior Officers, as they think proper, in the President alone, in the Courts of Law, or in the Heads of Departments. . . .

SECTION. 4. The President, Vice President and all civil Officers of the United States, shall be removed from Office on Impeachment for, and Conviction of, Treason, Bribery, or other high Crimes and Misdemeanors.

ARTICLE III.

SECTION. 1. The judicial Power of the United States, shall be vested in one supreme Court, and in such inferior Courts as the Congress may from time to time ordain and establish. The Judges, both of the supreme and inferior Courts, shall hold their Offices during good Behaviour, and shall, at stated Times, receive for their Services a Compensation, which shall not be diminished during their Continuance in Office.

SECTION. 2. [1] The judicial Power shall extend to all Cases, in Law and Equity, arising under this Constitution, the Laws of the United States, and Treaties made, or which shall be made, under their Authority;—to all Cases affecting Ambassadors, other public Ministers and Consuls;—to all Cases of admiralty and maritime Jurisdiction;—to Controversies to which the United States shall be a Party;—to Controversies between two or more States;—between a State and Citizens of another State;—between Citizens of different States;—between Citizens of the same State claiming Lands under Grants of different States, and between a State, or the Citizens thereof, and foreign States, Citizens or Subjects.

[2] In all Cases affecting Ambassadors, other public Ministers and Consuls, and those in which a State shall be Party, the supreme Court shall have original Jurisdiction. In all the other Cases before mentioned, the supreme Court shall have appellate Jurisdiction, both as to Law and Fact, with such Exceptions, and under such Regulations as the Congress shall make.

[3] The Trial of all Crimes, except in Cases of Impeachment, shall be by Jury; and such Trial shall be held in the State where the said Crimes shall have been committed; but when not committed within any State, the Trial shall be at such Place or Places as the Congress may by Law have directed.

SECTION. 3. [1] Treason against the United States, shall consist only in levying War against them, or in adhering to their Enemies, giving them Aid and Comfort. No Person shall be convicted of Treason unless on the Testimony of two Witnesses to the same overt Act, or on Confession in open Court.

[2] The Congress shall have Power to declare the Punishment of Treason, but no Attainder of Treason shall work Corruption of Blood, or Forfeiture except during the Life of the Person attainted.

ARTICLE IV.

SECTION. 1. Full Faith and Credit shall be given in each State to the public Acts, Records, and judicial Proceedings of every other State. . . .

SECTION. 4. The United States shall guarantee to every State in this Union a Republican Form of Government,

and shall protect each of them against Invasion; and on Application of the Legislature, or of the Executive (when the Legislature cannot be convened), against domestic Violence. . . .

ARTICLE VI.

. . . [2] This Constitution, and the Laws of the United States which shall be made in Pursuance thereof; and all Treaties made, or which shall be made, under the Authority of the United States, shall be the supreme Law of the Land; and the Judges in every State shall be bound thereby, any Thing in the Constitution or Laws of any State to the Contrary notwithstanding. . . .

AMENDMENT I [1791]

Congress shall make no law respecting an establishment of religion, or prohibiting the free exercise thereof; or abridging the freedom of speech, or of the press; or the right of the people peaceably to assemble, and to petition the Government for a redress of grievances.

AMENDMENT II [1791]

A well regulated Militia, being necessary to the security of a free State, the right of the people to keep and bear Arms, shall not be infringed.

AMENDMENT III [1791]

No Soldier shall, in time of peace be quartered in any house, without the consent of the Owner, nor in time of war, but in a manner to be prescribed by law.

AMENDMENT IV [1791]

The right of the people to be secure in their persons, houses, papers, and effects, against unreasonable searches and seizures, shall not be violated, and no Warrants shall issue, but upon probable cause, supported by Oath or affirmation, and particularly describing the place to be searched, and the persons or things to be seized.

AMENDMENT V [1791]

No person shall be held to answer for a capital, or otherwise infamous crime, unless on a presentment or indictment of a Grand Jury, except in cases arising in the land or naval forces, or in the Militia, when in actual service in time of War or public danger; nor shall any person be subject for the same offence to be twice put in jeopardy of life or limb; nor shall be compelled in any criminal case to be a witness against himself, nor be deprived of life, liberty, or property, without due process of law; nor shall private property be taken for public use, without just compensation.

AMENDMENT VI [1791]

In all criminal prosecutions, the accused shall enjoy the right to a speedy and public trial, by an impartial jury of the State and district wherein the crime shall have been committed, which district shall have been previously ascertained by law, and to be informed of the nature and cause of the accusation; to be confronted with the witnesses against him; to have compulsory process for obtaining witnesses in his favor, and to have the Assistance of Counsel for his defence.

AMENDMENT VII [1791]

In Suits at common law, where the value in controversy shall exceed twenty dollars, the right of trial by jury shall be preserved, and no fact tried by a jury, shall be otherwise re-examined in any Court of the United States, than according to the rules of the common law.

AMENDMENT VIII [1791]

Excessive bail shall not be required, nor excessive fines imposed, nor cruel and unusual punishments inflicted.

AMENDMENT IX [1791]

The enumeration in the Constitution, of certain rights, shall not be construed to deny or disparage others retained by the people.

AMENDMENT X [1791]

The powers not delegated to the United States by the Constitution, nor prohibited by it to the States, are reserved to the States respectively, or to the people.

AMENDMENT XI [1798]

The Judicial power of the United States shall not be construed to extend to any suit in law or equity, commenced or prosecuted against one of the United States by Citizens of another State, or by Citizens or Subjects of any Foreign State. . . .

AMENDMENT XIV [1868]

SECTION. 1. All persons born or naturalized in the United States, and subject to the jurisdiction thereof, are citizens of the United States and of the State wherein they reside. No State shall make or enforce any law which shall abridge the privileges or immunities of citizens of the United States; nor shall any State deprive any person of life, liberty, or property, without due process of law; nor deny to any person within its jurisdiction the equal protection of the laws. . . .

SECTION. 5. The Congress shall have power to enforce, by appropriate legislation, the provisions of this article. . . .

AMENDMENT XVIII [1919]

SECTION. 1. After one year from the ratification of this article the manufacture, sale, or transportation of intoxicating liquors within, the importation thereof into, or the exportation thereof from the United States and all territory subject to the jurisdiction thereof for beverage purposes is hereby prohibited.

SECTION. 2. The Congress and the several States shall have concurrent power to enforce this article by appropriate legislation.

SECTION. 3. This article shall be inoperative unless it shall have been ratified as an amendment to the Constitution by the legislatures of the several States, as provided in the Constitution, within seven years from the date of the submission hereof to the States by the Congress. . . .

AMENDMENT XXI [1933]

SECTION. 1. The eighteenth article of amendment to the Constitution of the United States is hereby repealed.

SECTION. 2. The transportation or importation into any State, Territory, or possession of the United States for delivery or use therein of intoxicating liquors, in violation of the laws thereof, is hereby prohibited. . . .

APPENDIX B

How to Read a Court Citation

McKinney v. Anderson, 959 F.2d 853 (9th Cir. 1992), *aff'd., remanded, sub nom., Helling v. McKinney*, 509 U.S. 25 (1993), *on remand, remanded*, 5 F.3d 365 (9th Cir. 1993).

ORIGINAL CITATION

[*McKinney v. Anderson*][1] [959][2] [F.2d][3] [853][4] [9th Cir.][5] [1992][6].

1. Name of case
2. Volume number of reporter in which case is published
3. Name of reporter; see Abbreviations for Commonly Used Reporters.
4. Page in the reporter where the decision begins
5. Court deciding the case
6. Year decided

ADDITIONAL CASE HISTORY

[*aff'd., remanded, sub nom.*][7] [*Helling v. McKinney*][8] [509][9] [U.S.][10] [25][11] [1993][12] [on remand, remanded] [13] [5][14] [F.3d][15] [365][16] [9th Cir. 1993][17]

7. *Affirmed and remanded, sub nom.* (affirmed and sent back for further proceedings) under a different name
8. The name under which the case was affirmed and remanded
9. Volume number of the reporter in which case is published

10. Abbreviated name of reporter
11. Page number on which the opinion begins
12. The year the U.S. Supreme Court decided the case. The name of the Court is not included as it is understood that the *U.S. Reports* contain only cases decided by the U.S. Supreme Court.
13. Additional history—the case on remand
14. Volume number of reporter in which the remanded case is published
15. Abbreviated name of reporter
16. Page number on which the decision begins
17. Court that heard the remanded case and year it was decided

ABBREVIATIONS FOR COMMONLY USED REPORTERS FOR COURT CASES

Decisions of the U.S. Supreme Court

S.Ct.: Supreme Court Reporter
U.S.: United States Reports

Decisions from Other Courts: A Selected List

A., A.2d: Atlantic Reporter, Atlantic Reporter Second Series

Cal.Rptr: California Reporter

F.2d: Federal Reporter Second Series; F.3d, Third Series

F.Supp: Federal Supplement

N.Y.S.2d: New York Supplement Second Series

N.W., N.W.2d: North Western Reporter, North Western Reporter Second Series

N.E., N.E.2d: North Eastern Reporter, North Eastern ReporterSecond Series

P., P.2d: Pacific Reporter, Pacific Reporter Second Series

S.E., S.E.2d: South Eastern Reporter, South Eastern Reporter Second Series

DEFINITIONS

Aff'd. Affirmed; the appellate court agrees with the decision of the lower court.

Aff'd. sub nom. Affirmed under a different name; the case at the appellate level has a different name from that of the trial court level.

Aff'd. per curiam. Affirmed by the court. The opinion is attributed to the entire court rather than designated as written by one of the judges or justices; a decision affirmed but no written opinion is issued.

Cert. denied. *Certiorari* denied; the U.S. Supreme Court refused to hear and decide the case. Other courts may refuse cases also, and frequently that is referred to as *review denied*.

Concurring opinion. An opinion agreeing with the court's decision but giving more explanation or offering different reasons.

Dissenting opinion. An opinion disagreeing with the reasoning and result of the majority opinion.

Reh'g. denied. Rehearing denied; the court refused to rehear a case.

Remanded. The appellate court sent a case back to the lower court for further action, often with instructions.

Rev'd. Reversed, overthrown, set aside, made void. The appellate court reversed the decision of the lower court.

Rev'd. and remanded. Reversed and remanded; the appellate court reverses the decision and sends the case back for further action.

Vacated. Abandoned, set aside, made void. The appellate court set aside the decision of the lower court.

Glossary

A

Accessory after the fact. One who—knowing that a felony has been committed—receives, relieves, comforts, or assists the alleged felon to hinder apprehension and conviction.

Accessory before the fact. One who incites, orders, commands, or abets a crime but is not present when the crime is committed.

Accomplice. A person who knowingly and voluntarily participates in the responsibility for a criminal act even though he or she may not participate in the actual crime. Such a person assumes criminal culpability in terms of his or her degree of participation in the criminal act.

Acquired immune deficiency syndrome (AIDS). A disease first discovered in 1979 and for which no cure is available. The virus (the human immunodeficiency virus, or HIV) that causes AIDS is spread through the exchange of bodily fluids, which occurs most frequently during sexual contact. The virus may also be contracted in other ways, such as through blood transfusions and the use of contaminated needles.

Actus reus. An act that, if combined with other elements of a crime, may lead to the arrest, trial, and conviction of the accused.

Administrative law. Rules and regulations made, through proper procedures, by agencies to which power has been delegated by a state legislature or, in the federal system, by the U.S. Congress. Administrative agencies also investigate and decide cases concerning potential violations of their rules.

Adultery. Consensual sexual intercourse between a married person and someone other than his or her spouse. Some statutes provide that the sex act constitutes adultery by both parties even if only one is married to someone else. Others limit the crime to the married party.

Adversary system. The Anglo-American system for settling disputes in court. It assumes the defendant is innocent until proven guilty. Prosecuting attorneys, representing the state, and defense attorneys, representing the defendant, try to convince a judge or jury of their version of the case. *See also* **Inquisitorial system**.

Affirmative defense. The introduction by the defense of new facts which, if true, constitute a complete or partial defense to the crime charged. *See also* **Defense**.

Aggravated assault. An assault committed with particular outrage or atrocity or involving a dangerous weapon; may also involve an assault with the intention of committing another crime.

Aggravating circumstances. Circumstances that are above or beyond those required for the crime but that make the crime more serious; may be used with reference to many crimes, but the concept is particularly critical in capital punishment cases, where it is required. *See also* **Mitigating circumstances**.

Aid and abet. The act of assisting or facilitating the commission of a crime.

Appeal. A step in a judicial proceeding, petitioning a higher court to review a lower court's decision.

Appellant. The party in a lawsuit who appeals the court's decision to a higher court, arguing that the lower court made a mistake that prejudiced the appellant, who now deserves a reversal of the conviction (or a change in the sentence if that is the issue). The party against whom this appeal is filed is called the **Appellee**.

Appellee. *See* **Appellant**.

Arson. Any willful or malicious burning or attempt to burn, with or without an intent to defraud, a dwelling house, public building, motor vehicle or aircraft, or the personal property of another person. Some statutes include the burning of one's own property with the intent to defraud.

Asportation. The act of moving things or people from one place to another.

Assault. Technically, an assault is a threat to commit a **battery**, but often the term is used to refer to a battery, which is the unauthorized, harmful touching of another. If the unauthorized threat or touching results in serious bodily harm or death, the crime may be considered aggravated assault, which may involve the use of a weapon.

Attempt. In criminal law, an act involving two basic elements: a step toward the commission of a crime and a specific intent to commit that crime.

Attendant circumstances. Facts surrounding a crime, which are considered to be a part of that crime, and which must be proved along with the elements of the crime.

Attorney client privilege. The doctrine that prohibits attorneys from revealing to others information told to them by their clients. The privilege belongs with the clients; so they can, if they choose to do so, release their attorneys from this confidential relationship.

Automatism. A defense for a defendant who has proof that he or she was unconscious or semiconscious when the crime was committed. Epilepsy, a concussion, or an emotional trauma are examples of conditions that may be used for this defense.

B

Baby Moses laws. Laws protecting mothers and fathers who abandon their newborn and unwanted babies in ways that will ensure the health and safety of those infants. Generally, these laws permit parents to leave the infants in safe places and avoid prosecution.

Bailee. A person to whom goods are entrusted by a **bailor**.

Bailor. A person who entrusts goods to another party, known as the **bailee**.

Battered person syndrome. A syndrome arising from a cycle of abuse by a special person, often a parent or a spouse, that leads the battered person to perceive that violence against the offender is the only way to end the abuse. In some cases the battered person murders the batterer, and in some jurisdictions evidence of the battered person syndrome constitutes a defense to that murder.

Battery. *See* **Assault**.

Beyond a reasonable doubt. The standard of proof in criminal cases; refers to evidence that is fully satisfactory, entirely convincing, and true to a moral certainty.

Bigamy. Knowingly and willingly contracting a marriage when one is aware that another marriage is undissolved. Some jurisdictions consider the crime one of strict liability; thus, *knowledge* of an existing marriage is not required.

Bill of attainder. An act by the legislature that condemns a person even though a judicial trial has not occurred. A bill of attainder is forbidden by the U.S. Constitution.

Bioterrorism. The use of biological agents, such as the spread of smallpox, in terrorist threats.

Blackmail. Similar to **extortion**, this crime is usually associated with the unlawful demand for money or something else of value by threats to expose some embarrassing or disgraceful allegation or fact about the target, to accuse that person of a crime, or to do bodily harm to him or her or damage that person's property.

Breach of the peace. A willfully committed act that disturbs the public tranquillity or order and for which there is no legal justification.

Bribery. The offering, giving, receiving, or soliciting of anything of value to influence action by public (or in some jurisdictions, nonpublic) officials.

Burden of proof. In a legal case, the duty of proving a disputed fact. For example, in a criminal case the state has the burden of proving the defendant guilty **beyond a reasonable doubt**.

Burglary. Under the common law, breaking and entering any type of enclosed structure without consent and with the intent to commit a felony therein. Most modern statutes are not as restrictive, and many do not require an actual breaking.

C

CAN-SPAM Act of 2004. A federal statute containing, among other provisions, measures for the elimination of unwanted spam on computers and directing the Federal Trade Commission (FTC) to adopt a rule requiring a warning on spam that is sexually explicit. The FTC did that, and the provision carries civil and criminal penalties, with the latter including a possible prison sentence and a stiff fine.

Capital punishment. The imposition of the death penalty on an offender who has been convicted of a capital crime.

Carjacking. Auto theft by force or threat of force.

Case law. Judicial decisions, which are legally binding court interpretations of written statutes and previous court decisions or rules made by courts in the absence of written statutes or other sources of law.

Causation. A relationship between two phenomena in which the occurrence of the former brings about changes in the latter. Causation is the element of a crime that requires the existence of a causal relationship between the offender's conduct and the particular harmful consequences, such as damage to property or the injury or death of a person.

Child abuse. The physical or psychological abuse of a child by parents, other relatives, acquaintances, or strangers. Statutes criminalizing child abuse may, and often do, include child pornography.

Circumstantial evidence. Direct evidence—such as eyewitness testimony—of facts other than those for which proof is needed but from which deductions or inferences may be drawn concerning the facts in dispute.

Civil law. In contrast to criminal law, civil law pertains to rules that are concerned with private or civil rights. The wronged person seeks compensation rather than criminal punishment through state prosecution.

Clemency. Mercy, kindness, leniency; a term used to describe the actions of a governor or president when he or she commutes a sentence—for example, from death to life—or grants a **pardon**.

Codified. Reducing customs, unwritten laws, and rules to written statutes.

Common law. Contrasted to written law, common law consists of legally binding rules derived from judicial decisions, customs, and traditions. Broadly defined, it refers to the legal system that began in England and was followed in the United States.

Complicity. A term used to describe the actions of persons who are considered legally responsible for a crime although they did not participate in the act itself. *See also* **Accomplice**.

Computer crime. Crime committed by use of the computer. Computer criminals have developed programs that access, scramble, or erase computer files and that aid in theft, such as the stealing of a person's identity, as well as the invasion of privacy.

Condonation. The forgiving of a criminal act by a victim. Usually condonation is not a defense, but in some cases a victim of a nonserious crime may negotiate a settlement with the defendant, after which the court may drop the criminal charge.

Conspiracy. Agreeing with another to join together for the purpose of committing an unlawful act, or agreeing to use unlawful means to commit an act that would otherwise be lawful. The unlawful act does not have to be committed; the crime of conspiracy involves the *agreement* to engage in the unlawful act.

Constructive possession. A legal doctrine referring to the condition of having the power to control an item, along with having the intent to do so.

Controlled substances. Refers to any drug that a given statute characterizes as such. The best known of U.S. controlled substances statutes is that of the federal government, the Controlled Substances Act (CSA), which establishes five categories of controlled substances, ranging from the most serious drugs to the least serious, and stating the legal position of each category.

Conversion. The process of using the property or goods of another for one's own use and without permission.

Copyright. A legal document that gives to the copyright holder the right to copy, reproduce in some other fashion, and sell literary works, books, articles, and other work products of the originator (or, in some cases, such as this text, the publisher) for a limited period of time.

Corpus delicti. Literally "the body of the crime"; the body or other evidence that generally must be produced to prove that a crime has occurred.

Corroborating evidence. Additional data to support the charge of a crime, especially in rape and other cases in which there were no witnesses to the alleged act.

Counterfeiting. Forging, copying, or imitating without authority and with the intent to defraud. The crime involves an offense against property as well as an **obstruction of justice**. The object of counterfeiting may be coins, paper money, or anything else of value (such as stamps).

Crime. An act or omission that violates criminal case or statutory law and is punishable by law.

Crime rate. The number of crimes per 100,000 in the population.

Crimes known to the police. All serious offenses that have been reported to the police and for which the police have sufficient evidence to believe that those crimes were actually committed.

Criminal law. The statutes that define behavior considered to be a threat to the well-being of society. The accused must be prosecuted by the government.

Cruel and unusual punishment. Punishment that is prohibited by the Eighth Amendment of the U.S. Constitution. Examples are torture, excessively long sentences, and the death penalty for rape without homicide. State constitutions may also prohibit cruel and (or) unusual punishment.

Culpability. Being guilty or at fault. There are four criteria that may be used to determine culpability: intention, knowledge, negligence, and recklessness. Different crimes may require different kinds of culpability to prove guilt.

Curtilage. The enclosed ground and buildings immediately surrounding a dwelling place or house; may also include grounds that are not enclosed but that are considered part of the area.

Cybercrime. Computer crime that involves the Internet.

Cyberstalking. Stalking someone by use of the Internet. *See also* **Stalking**.

Cyberterrorism. The use of the Internet to commit terrorist acts.

D

Date rape. Forced sexual acts that occur during a social occasion. The alleged victim may have agreed to some intimacy but not to the activities defined in that jurisdiction as constituting the elements of rape.

Deadly force. Force that is likely to cause serious bodily injury or death.

Declaratory relief. An order from a court stating the rights of the parties who petition the court for a decision regarding those rights.

Defense. A legal response by the defendant. It may consist only of a denial of the factual allegations of the prosecution. A defense that offers new factual allegations in an effort to negate the charges is an **affirmative defense**.

Defense attorney. The attorney for the defendant in a legal proceeding.

Department of Homeland Security (DHS). A federal cabinet-level position created after the 9/11 terrorist attacks; the agency combined 22 previous agencies into one organization, which coordinates the federal agencies involved in domestic preparedness, all of the federal agencies that are involved in activities for domestic preparedness, and agencies that coordinate plans for natural and person-made crises and emergency planning.

Determinate sentence. *See* **Sentence.**

Deterrence. A punishment philosophy that assumes that behavior may be controlled and criminal behavior prevented by the threat of punishment. *General deterrence* strives to discourage criminality by other people by intimidating them with the punishment of an offender. *Specific deterrence* prevents additional crimes by an offender by punishing that offender.

Discretion. Decisions based on one's judgment rather than legal rules. In criminal justice systems discretion can result in inconsistency but also in actions suitable for individual circumstances.

Disorderly conduct. Minor offenses, such as drunkenness or fighting, that disturb the peace or behavior standards of a community or shock the morality of its population.

Domestic violence. Causing physical or other types of harm or even death to members of the family, including children, parents, spouses, siblings, grandparents, and step-relatives; the concept may be extended to include nonrelatives with whom one has an intimate relationship.

Double jeopardy. A doctrine established by the federal constitution and providing that once a defendant has been tried and acquitted of a crime, he or she may not be tried again for the same crime.

Drug. A substance used to alter the body or mind of a living being. Drugs may be prescribed by doctors for medical treatment; some are available without prescriptions. Drugs may also be used for illegal purposes. In either case, drugs may be harmful or fatal.

Drug abuse. The chronic or periodic misuse of alcohol or other drugs. Drug abuse is considered detrimental to society as well as to the individual abuser. Drug abuse may occur even if the substance has been prescribed by the individual's physician.

Drug paraphanalia. Any item, product, or material that could be used to violate the controlled substance statutes of a particular jurisdiction.

Drug trafficking. Trading in illegal drugs.

Dual court system. System that characterizes U.S. court systems, consisting of a federal system and 50 state systems, which pass and enforce their own laws, along with municipal systems that make and enforce their own ordinances.

Due process. Constitutional principle that a person's life, liberty, or property cannot be deprived without lawful procedures. The courts interpret what due process requires in specific fact patterns.

Duress. In criminal law, a condition in which an individual is coerced or induced by the wrongful act of another to commit a criminal act. May be used as a defense.

Durham rule. A test of insanity (also known as the *product rule*) that states that "an accused is not criminally responsible if his unlawful act was the product of mental disease or mental defect."

E

Elder abuse. Violent and other types of abuse of elderly persons, including such acts as fraud, assault and battery, withholding food stamps or other economic benefits, theft of savings and Social Security checks, threats to send the person to a nursing home, and so on. The perpetrators are often family members, but an increasing number of crimes against the elderly are committed by strangers.

Elements of a crime. All aspects of a criminal act that must be proved beyond a reasonable doubt by the prosecution to substantiate a conviction. This includes the concurrence of an act and a criminal state of mind that produces a harmful result. It may also include **attendant circumstances**.

Embezzlement. Misappropriation or misapplication of money or property entrusted to one's care, custody, or control.

Embracery. A common law misdemeanor meaning a corrupt attempt to influence a juror by means of promises, money, or other persuasions. Today many jurisdictions include this offense under a separate title such as "corrupt influencing of jurors" or include it within the crime of obstructing justice.

Enemy combatant. A person who is alleged to have been associated with the 9/11 terrorist attacks against the United States. Congress authorized the president to order such persons held for questioning even though they were not charged with a crime or provided access to attorneys. The U.S. Supreme Court has ruled that some due process rights must be made available to enemy combatants.

Enterprise liability. The process of holding an entire business enterprise legally liable for an event.

Entrapment. The defense that a defendant was induced by a government agent to commit a crime that the defendant would not have been inclined to commit without such inducement.

Equal protection. The constitutional principle guaranteeing that U.S. legal systems shall not deny to any person or class of persons the same treatment as other persons or classes of persons in the same or similar situations. Of particular significance are the circumstances of race, ethnicity, religion, gender, and sexual orientation.

Espionage. Spying; that is, gathering, transmitting, or losing information about the national defense, with the expectation or knowledge that such information will be used against the country or to the advantage of a foreign country (or state).

Euthanasia. A term applied to the act of killing someone, often at that person's request, because of a terminal illness, considerable pain, or a debilitating handicap.

Excusable homicide. A killing that is accidental or is the result of self-defense or other circumstances that the law permits.

Expert testimony. Opinion evidence given at a trial by a person who possesses technical knowledge or skill that is both relevant to the case and not possessed by the average person.

Ex post facto law. A law that provides punishment for an act that was not defined as a crime when the act was committed or that increases the penalty for a crime committed prior to the enactment of the statute.

Extortion. Obtaining property from another by wrongful use of actual or threatened force, fear, or violence, or the corrupt taking of a fee by a public officer, under color of his or her office, when that fee is not due. *See also* **Blackmail**.

F

Facilitation. Making it easier for another to commit a crime.

Factual impossibility. In the law, a defense that is possible only when there are circumstances, unknown to the actor, that prevent the commission of an offense, such as an attempt crime.

False imprisonment. The unlawful and knowing restraint of a person against his or her wishes so as to deny freedom. *See also* **Kidnapping**.

False pretense. Representation of some fact or circumstance that is not true and that is meant to mislead the other party.

False swearing. Untrue statements willfully and knowingly made under oath or equivalent affirmation inside or outside a judicial proceeding. *See also* **Perjury**.

Felony. A serious offense such as murder, armed robbery, or rape. Punishments for felonies range from one year's imprisonment to death.

Felony murder. An unlawful killing of a person that occurs while attempting to commit or while committing another felony, such as robbery, rape, or arson.

Fence. A person who receives stolen property from a thief and in turn disposes of it in a profitable manner.

Fetal abuse. Abusing a fetus. In some jurisdictions any resulting injury may lead to legal culpability; in some states, killing a fetus may result in a murder charge.

Fetal alcohol syndrome. Refers to a cluster of abnormalities that a fetus may have due to the fact that its mother consumed alcohol during her pregnancy. The effects include growth deficiencies, facial abnormalities, and mental retardation.

Fighting words. Words that tend to incite violence by the person to whom they are directed. Fighting words are more like a slap on the face than a communication of ideas. They are not protected by the First Amendment right to free speech.

Fleeing felon. A person trying to avoid arrest after committing a felony.

Forcible rape. *See* **Rape**.

Forfeiture. The process of taking from an accused items (such as money, a boat, or a car) thought to be associated with illegal acts, such as drug trafficking. The property may be taken by the government and held until the case is decided; upon a conviction it may be retained by the government and sold or disposed of in some other way.

Forgery. Falsely making or altering, with the intent to defraud, a negotiable and legally enforceable instrument, such as a check.

Fornication. Unlawful sexual intercourse between two unmarried persons.

Fraud. Falsely representing a fact, either by conduct or by words or writing, in order to induce a person to rely on the misrepresentation and surrender something of value.

Fundamental right. In U.S. constitutional law, a right that is named in the U.S. Constitution or implied within that document. It includes such rights as free speech and the right to free exercise of religion. Fundamental rights may be controlled by the government but only if the government has a compelling reason and the statutes are narrowly tailored—that is, they do not go beyond the conduct they can limit.

G

Good-time credits. Credits that allow the reduction of a prison term because of an inmate's good behavior during incarceration.

Grand larceny. *See* **Petit larceny**.

Guilty but mentally ill. An alternative to the insanity defense; permits finding that defendants were mentally ill but not insane at the time they committed the crimes charged. They are guilty, and they may be punished, but generally the jurisdictions that have this concept require that these defendants must receive psychiatric treatment while they are confined, often in a psychiatric facility rather than a prison.

H

Habeas corpus. Literally means "you have the body." This Latin term is given to a variety of petitions filed by parties asking the court to order some action, such as to determine the legality of the custody and confinement of the inmate who files the petition.

Hate crime. A crime associated with evidence of prejudice based on any or all of the following, depending on the jurisdiction's approach: race, religion, disability, gender, national origin, sexual orientation, or ethnicity.

Home-invasion robbery. Robbery that occurs when a person enters a dwelling for the purpose of committing a robbery and engages in a robbery of the occupant.

Homicide. An inclusive term that refers to all cases in which human beings—by their own acts, omissions, or procurement—kill other human beings. Homicide may be criminal (murder, manslaughter, or negligent homicide) or noncriminal (committed with justification or excuse).

I

Identity theft. The stealing of an individual's social security number or other important information about his or her identity and using that information to commit crimes, such as removing funds from the victim's bank account.

Incapacitation. A punishment theory and a sentencing goal, generally implemented by incarcerating offenders to prevent them from committing any other crimes. In earlier times incapacitation involved such measures as removing the hands of thieves or castrating rapists.

Incest. Sexual relations between members of the immediate family who are too close in legal relationships to marry, such as between siblings, a parent and child, or a grandparent and grandchild.

Inchoate crimes. Crimes that are imperfect or uncompleted and that may lead to other crimes. For example, an attempt to commit rape may lead to rape, but even if it does not, the attempt is a crime.

Indeterminate sentence. *See* **Sentence**.

Infanticide. The killing of an infant at or soon after its birth.

Inference. A concept permitting the drawing of a conclusion based on other facts or logic presented in a case. The jury may use its reason and common sense to infer, for example, that based on certain evidence, a crime was committed by the defendant.

Injunction. A prohibitive remedy issued by a court and ordering someone or an agency to do something or stop doing something; based on a request by a party who petitions the court for the relief. There are several kinds of injunctions, including those that are preliminary (until a further hearing), partial, temporary, or permanent.

Inquisitorial system. A system in which the accused is presumed guilty and must prove his or her innocence.

Insanity. A state of mind that negates a defendant's responsibility for his or her actions.

Insider information. Information known (generally by securities officers) before it is made available to the general public.

Insider trading. Securities trading by a director, officer, or stockholder who holds more than 10 percent of the stock of a corporation listed on a national exchange and buys and sells corporate shares. The SEC requires monthly reports of insider trading.

Intent. State of mind referring to the willful commission of an act or the omission of an act that a person has a legal duty to perform. *See also* **Mens rea**.

Intervening act. An act that occurs after an alleged criminal act and the resulting injury; may be considered the legal cause, or at least a contributing cause, of the injury.

Intimate personal violence (IPV). Violence toward a current or former spouse but could also include romantic friends of either gender (often referred to as *courtship violence*).

Intoxication. The condition that exists when a person consumes alcohol or other drugs to the extent that his or her mental or physical abilities are significantly affected.

Involuntary manslaughter. *See* **Manslaughter**.

Involuntary intoxication. Intoxication without choice or will, such as that which occurs when someone slips drugs into the food or drink of an unsuspecting person. *See also* **Voluntary intoxication**.

Irresistible impulse test. A test for insanity providing that an accused cannot be found guilty for a criminal act if he or she is unable to control the actions leading to a crime even though the accused may have known the act was wrong.

J

Judicial review. The process that occurs when appellate courts review and interpret the acts that occur in the lower courts. Those issues on review may be upheld, altered, reversed, or remanded. In some cases, appellate courts may also review acts that occur within the legislative and executive branches of government.

Jurisdiction. The lawful exercise of authority, and the geographic area (or subject matter) in which authority may be exercised. For instance, city police have legal authority only within the city limits. Courts may only hear cases for which they have jurisdiction (such as civil or criminal cases, misdemeanor or felony cases, probate, or drug case, and so on).

Jury nullification. The power of juries to ignore the evidence and acquit even in the face of strong evidence supporting a conviction.

Justifiable homicide. A killing that is intentional but carries no evil intent and is permitted by law, such as one involving capital punishment or a killing by a law enforcement officer in the line of duty when attempting to prevent a felony.

K

Kidnapping. Restricting the freedom of a victim against his or her will and removing the victim from one place to another. Kidnapping is **false imprisonment** with aggravating circumstances, such as ransom, torture, extortion, prostitution, or pornography.

L

Larceny by trick. Deceptively obtaining possession of goods from a victim who surrenders possession voluntarily and without knowledge of the deceit involved.

Larceny-theft. The unlawful taking, carrying, leading, or riding away of property from the possession of another with the intent to steal. Larceny may be categorized as **petit larceny**, or **grand larceny**, depending on the value of the stolen property.

Legal duty. A duty imposed by statutory or case law or through an explicit or implied contract.

Legal impossibility. Defense providing that even if the defendant's intentions, for example, to commit an attempt crime, were fully performed or set in motion, a crime would not have been committed.

Lesser included offense. A crime less serious than the one with which a defendant is being charged.

M

Mala in se. Acts that are considered by most people to be morally wrong in themselves, such as rape, murder, or robbery.

Mala prohibita. Acts that are considered to be wrong because they are prohibited by legislation, although they may not be recognized by most people as morally wrong.

Malice aforethought. A required element of murder, providing that the killing be predetermined and intentional and without legal justification or excuse. *See also* **Premeditation**.

Malicious mischief. The malicious infliction of damage to or the destruction of the property of another.

Manslaughter. An unlawful killing without malice. **Voluntary manslaughter** is a killing that would be murder except that it was committed in the heat of passion for which there is a reasonable explanation or excuse. **Involuntary manslaughter** is a killing that is committed recklessly but unintentionally, as when one is under the influence of alcohol or other drugs. **Negligent manslaughter** is a killing that is not lawful or justified and involves no malice—only negligence.

Marital rape. Forced sexual intercourse (or other specific sex acts, such as sodomy) with a spouse. The act is not recognized as a crime in all jurisdictions.

Mayhem. At common law, an offense that rendered the victim unable to fight, such as by dismemberment. Today the crime does not carry military significance and may include an act that permanently disfigures the victim as well as one that dismembers. In some jurisdictions, this crime is within assault and battery statutes.

Medical necessity doctrine. A legal doctrine that permits a defendant to argue that an otherwise criminal act was taken for the purpose of meeting a medical necessity. If the defendant can prove an acceptable medical reason for committing the act in question, the defense may serve as a complete defense, thereby relieving the defendant of criminal culpability.

Megan's laws. Laws requiring designated sex offenders to register with law enforcement authorities in the community in which they live. Some jurisdictions require the offenders to notify neighbors as well. Sex offenders may also be required to notify federal officials. Finally, they may be restricted from living within specified distances of schools, playgrounds, or other places in which children can be expected to congregate.

Mercy killings. *See* **Euthanasia**.

Mens rea. The guilty intent or evil mind required for criminal culpability.

Misdemeanor. A crime that is less serious than a felony and that is punishable by a fine, probation, a short jail term, or by other means.

Misprision of felony. The act of concealing a felony committed by another but without any involvement in that felony that would constitute an accessory before or after the fact.

Misprision of treason. The concealment from proper officials of the known treason of another but without sufficient involvement to constitute the elements of a **principal** in the crime.

Mistake. A defense arguing that a defendant would not have committed a criminal act if he or she had possessed accurate knowledge of the law or the facts.

Mistrial. A trial declared invalid for a variety of reasons, such as the inability of a jury to reach a verdict, the death of a juror or counsel, or improper behavior by a juror or others involved in the trial.

Mitigating circumstances. Circumstances that do not justify or excuse a crime but that, because of justice and fairness, make the crime less reprehensible; may be used to reduce a crime to a lesser offense, such as to reduce murder to manslaughter. Mitigating circumstances must be considered before the death penalty is imposed. *See also* **Aggravating circumstances**.

M'Naghten rule. Also known as the *right-versus-wrong* insanity test, the rule states that an accused cannot be considered guilty of a criminal act if, as a result of a defect of reason caused by a disease of the mind, the accused did not know the nature and quality of the act or did not know that the act was wrong.

Model Penal Code. The American Law Institute's systemized statement of criminal law; its provisions are suggested as models for state criminal law revisions.

Money laundering. Hiding the existence, illegal use of, or illegal source of income and making that income appear legal by disguising it.

Motive. In criminal law, the reason for a defendant's actions.

Murder. The unlawful and unjustified killing of another human being (or a fetus in some jurisdictions) with malice aforethought. Types of murder include the intent to kill, the intent to do great bodily harm, an act done in willful disregard of the strong likelihood that death or great injury would result, or a killing committed during the commission of another felony.

N

National Incident Based Reporting System (NIBRS). A method of collecting crime data that views crimes as involving numerous elements. Twenty-two crimes are categorized in this system.

Necessity. Condition in which an act, though criminal in other circumstances, may not be considered criminal because of the compelling force of the present circumstances.

Negligence. An act that a reasonable person would not do, or would not fail to do under similar circumstances. It does not require a criminal intent.

Negligent manslaughter. *See* **Manslaughter**.

O

Obscenity. Written or visual material that is not protected by the First Amendment of the U.S. Constitution because of its offensive, clear description or depiction of sexual acts; because of its lack of any political, literary, scientific, or artistic value; and because of its tendency to arouse improper sexual reactions in the average person.

Obstruction of justice. Interference with the orderly processes of civil and criminal courts, such as refusing to produce evidence, intimidating witnesses, and bribing judges. The crime may be committed by judicial and other officials and might constitute **official misconduct in office**.

Official misconduct in office. Any willful, unlawful behavior by public officials in the course of their official duties. The misconduct may be a failure to act, a wrongful act, or the improperly performed act that the official has a right to do.

P

Pandering. Procuring or securing a person, usually a female, to satisfy the lust of another, usually a male; catering to the lust of another person; also called *pimping*.

Pardon. An act by a state governor or the president of the United States that exempts an individual from punishment for a crime for which he or she was convicted and that removes the legal consequences of that conviction. Pardons may be absolute or conditional; may be individual or granted to a group or class of offenders; and may be full or partial, in which case the pardon remits only part of the punishment or removes some, but not all, of the legal consequences resulting from conviction.

Parole. The process that describes the release of an offender prior to the completion of his or her sentence. The decision may be made by a parole board or, in some states, by the governor. In many jurisdictions parolees must be supervised by a parole officer.

Per curiam. By the whole court; referring to an opinion attributed to the entire court rather than being written by a named judge or justice.

Perjury. False statements made willfully and knowingly under oath in a judicial proceeding. **Subornation of perjury** is the offense of procuring someone to commit perjury. *See also* **False swearing**.

Personal property. Technically, in the law, *property* refers to anything that belongs exclusively to an individual. It is divided into two types: personal and real. *Personal property* refers to property that can be moved, in contrast to *real property*, which cannot be moved.

Petit larceny. *Petit* literally means *small. Petit larceny*, in contrast to **grand larceny**, refers to the stealing of smaller amounts. Generally the statutes will specify the amount of money that must be stolen to move a theft from a charge of petit to one of grand larceny.

Petit treason. Under English common law, the killing of a husband by his wife, the lord or master by his servant, or other acts of betrayal by a subordinate against a superordinate but not including killing the king. *See also* **Treason**.

Pinkerton rule. A rule stating that a co-conspirator may be held accountable for the acts of fellow conspirators even though the requirements of liability for the acts of accomplices are not met.

Postpartum depression (PPD) syndrome. A disorder that some women experience after giving birth.

Posttraumatic stress disorder (PTSD). A disorder in which stress is experienced by people who have suffered severe trauma, such as war trauma, rape, or abuse. Symptoms include nightmares, feelings of guilt, disorientation, and reliving the traumatic event(s). It is argued that victims of this disorder should not be held accountable for their criminal acts because they cannot control their behavior.

Premeditation. The act of planning, deliberating, designing, or thinking out in advance an intention to kill another person. *See also* **Malice aforethought**.

Premenstrual syndrome (PMS). The physiological changes (e.g., depression, irritability, and temporary psychosis) that occur in some woman before menstruation; some courts permit the introduction of evidence on this syndrome as a defense.

Preponderance of the evidence. Evidence showing that, on the whole, it supports the fact in question. This burden of proof in a civil case is less than the criminal standard of **beyond a reasonable doubt**.

Presumption. In law, a required assumption (such as the presumption of innocence); may be conclusive or rebuttable depending on the law.

Presumptive sentencing. A sentencing model in which the legislature specifies the normal sentence for each crime, and judges are permitted to deviate only under specified types of circumstances, or by giving written reasons, or both.

Principal. Under common law, the person who committed the crime, in contrast to the **accessory after the fact** or **accessory before the fact**, who assisted in the crime or who encouraged another to commit a crime. Most modern statutes do not make this distinction. Both are treated as principals, and accessories may be convicted even if the principal has not been convicted.

Principal in the first degree. The one who perpetrates the crime either through his or her own acts or by the use of inanimate objects or innocent people.

Principal in the second degree. The one who incites or abets the commission of the crime and is present actually or constructively.

Procedural law. The body of law that provides the legal methods and procedures by which **substantive law** is to be enforced.

Property crimes. Crimes that are directed toward property rather than toward the person. The four serious property crimes as categorized by the FBI are burglary, larceny-theft, motor vehicle theft, and arson.

Prosecutor or prosecuting attorney. A government official whose duty is to initiate and maintain criminal proceedings on behalf of the government against persons accused of committing crimes.

Prostitution. Indiscriminate sexual intercourse for hire. Some statutes specify women as the offenders, but others also include men. The criminal offense may include not only the prostitute but also any persons who solicit or promote the business of prostitution or who live off the prostitute's earnings.

R

Racketeer Influenced and Corrupt Organizations Act. *See* **RICO**.

Racketeering. The process of engaging in a racket (such as **extortion** or **conspiracy**) to obtain an illegal goal by means of threats.

Rape. Historically defined as unlawful vaginal intercourse with a woman who was not the offender's wife. More recently, some rape statutes have been rewritten to include spouses and male victims, as well as **rape by instrumentation** (penetration of any body opening—or specified body openings—such as the anus or the vagina by a foreign object, including but not limited to, the penis.) *See also* **Date rape, Marital rape, Statutory rape**.

Rape by instrumentation. *See* **Rape**.

Rape shield statute. Statute that prohibits the introduction into a rape trial of any information concerning the past sexual experiences of the alleged victim. An exception might be the alleged victim's sexual history with the defendant, providing that information is relevant to an understanding of whether the alleged victim consented to sex in the case at issue.

Rape trauma syndrome (RTS). Stress that occurs after forced sex; now considered a **posttraumatic stress disorder (PTSD)**. Evidence of the syndrome is permitted in an increasing number of courts.

Rebuttable presumption. A presumption that may be refuted by evidence.

Recidivism. Further violations of the law by released suspects or inmates, or noncriminal violations of conditions by probationers and parolees.

Rehabilitation. Punishment philosophy that attempts to reform the offender through education, work, or other appropriate treatment modalities.

Restraining order. A judicial order forbidding a specific person to do something, as for example, contact or go within a certain distance of another person, such as a spouse, estranged spouse, former spouse, or any other named person.

Retribution. The philosophy that offenders should receive the punishment they deserve in light of the crimes they committed.

Revenge. Historically, an act performed by a victim to punish an offender. Today public retaliation through criminal justice systems has replaced private revenge, which was previously permitted of alleged victims.

RICO. The Racketeer Influenced and Corrupt Organizations Act, which Congress passed in 1970 to combat organized crime, but which has also been applied beyond that area of criminal activity.

Riot. *See* **Unlawful assembly**.

Robbery. The taking or attempting to take anything of value from the possession or immediate presence of a person without that person's will and accomplished by force or threat of force or violence or by putting the victim in fear. *See also* **Home-invasion robbery**.

Rout. *See* **Unlawful assembly**.

S

Sanction. A penalty or punishment that is imposed on a convicted person in order to enforce the law.

Securities. Stocks, bonds, notes, and other documents that are representative of shares in or debts of a company.

Sedition. A communication or agreement aimed at stirring up **treason** or at defaming the government.

Seduction. Traditionally, the act by a man who uses solicitation, persuasion, promises, bribes, or other methods to entice a woman to have unlawful sexual intercourse with him. Most seduction laws have been repealed, but those that remain generally categorize the crime of seduction as a misdemeanor.

Sentence. A judgment pronounced by the court (trial judge) and imposed on a defendant who pleads guilty or who is found guilty after a trial. A **determinate sentence** is one in which the legislature has set the type and length of sentence for each crime, leaving the judge little or no discretion. An **indeterminate sentence** leaves the sentence decision up to judges or sets a minimum and maximum term and permits the judge to set the exact sentence in each case.

Sentence disparity. A term used to describe the variations and inequities that result when defendants convicted of the same crime receive varying sentences; may also refer to varying legislative sentences from state to state.

Sentencing guidelines. Guidelines established by legislatures, judges, or others (such as sentencing commissions) to be followed by judges in assessing sentences. Some divergence is allowed but usually must be accompanied by a statement of reasons.

Sexual abuse. Sexual mistreatment of children and or adults; may include involving children in the production or viewing of pornography.

Sodomy. Generally interpreted as an act involving anal or oral sex with another person of the same or opposite sex or with an animal.

Solicitation. The asking, inciting, ordering, urgently requesting, or enticing of another person to commit a crime.

Stalking. Defined in the National Violence Against Women Survey as "a course of conduct directed at a specific person that involves repeated visual or physical proximity, nonconsensual communication, or verbal, written or implied threats, or a combination thereof, that would cause a reasonable person fear." The term *repeated* means two or more times. State statutes may vary from this definition. *See also* **Cyberstalking**.

Stare decisis. Literally, "let the decision stand." *Stare decisis* means that although the law must be flexible and change with the times, it must also be stable and predictable, and courts are reluctant to make changes.

Statutory law. Law that originates with the legislature in a written enactment.

Statutory rape. Sexual intercourse (or, in some jurisdictions, other sexual acts as well) with an underage person even though that person consented. An underage person is deemed by the law to be incapable of giving legal consent to sexual acts.

Stockholm syndrome. An incongruous feeling of empathy by hostages toward the hostage takers and a displacement of frustration and aggression on the part of the victims against authorities.

Strict liability. A legal concept that holds defendants responsible for wrongful acts even when they are not guilty of negligence, fault, or bad faith. This concept is often used in **tort** law to hold an employer liable for the acts of their employees.

Subornation of perjury. *See* **Perjury.**

Substantial capacity test. Provides that persons cannot be held accountable for criminal acts if they have a mental disease or defect that is a substantial factor in their inability either to appreciate the fact that the acts are wrong or to conform their conduct to the law. The concept is used in the Model Penal Code definition of insanity.

Substantial factor. One that a reasonable person might conclude was sufficient to support the resulting damage to property or personal injury or death.

Substantive law. Law that defines the elements of crimes and the punishments legally available for those acts. *See also* **Procedural law**.

T

Terrorism. Violent acts or threats of violence to create fear, alarm, dread, or coercion, usually against governments.

Three strikes and you're out. Legislation enacted in recent years and designed to impose long sentences on persons who are convicted of a third serious crime. Some jurisdictions, such as California, extend the concept to conviction for the second serious crime.

Tort. Literally, a wrong; refers to the area of law that may lead to civil liability for negligent acts (such as automobile accidents or medical malpractice); intentional acts (such as assault, battery, libel, or slander); products liability (such as making and selling defective products or failing to warn when a warning would be reasonable); and strict liability (such as statutory rape). Some actions, such as trespassing on real property, assault and battery, and rape, constitute crimes as well as torts.

Transportation Security Administration (TSA). Agency created by the Aviation and Transportation Security Act (ATSA) enacted in November 2001. The agency was created to assume the screening functions for all commercial flights, a responsibility that previously had been under the Federal Aviation Administration (FAA), which was restructured by the statute. Originally reporting to the U.S. Department of Transportation, the TSA became part of the **Department of Homeland Security (DHS)** in March 2003.

Treason. At attempt to overthrow the government of which one is a member, or a betrayal of that government to a foreign power. Treason was thought to be such a serious offense that it was included within the U.S. Constitution, the only crime specified in that document. Under English common law the betrayal or killing of the sovereign or king was referred to as *high treason*. *See also* **petit treason**.

Trespass. The entering or remaining unlawfully in or on the premises (including land, boats, or other vehicles) of another under certain circumstances as specified by statute.

Trespasser. One who commits a **trespass**.

Truth in sentencing. A concept requiring that actual time served by offenders is close to the time allocated for the sentence. Many jurisdictions are establishing 85 percent as their goal, meaning that offenders may not be released for any reason until they have served 85 percent of their sentences.

U

Under color of law. A term referring to a public official's assigned duties. For a person to be convicted of **official misconduct in office**, the person must be a public official or one acting in that capacity. The misconduct must occur during the course of that person's official duties.

Uniform Crime Reports (UCR). Official crime data, which is collected, compiled, and published annually by the Federal Bureau of Investigation (FBI). The data are based on **crimes known to the police—**crimes that are reported to or observed by the police and that the police have reason to believe were committed. The report also publishes arrest data.

Unlawful assembly. The meeting of three or more persons to disturb the public peace with the intention of participating in a forcible and violent execution of an unlawful enterprise or of a lawful enterprise in an unauthorized manner. To constitute unlawful assembly, the group need not carry out its purpose; but if it takes steps to do so, it commits a **rout**. If it actually carries out the plan, it commits a **riot**.

USA Patriot Act. A law (the Uniting and Strengthening America by Providing Appropriate Tools Required to Intercept and Obstruct Terrorism Act of 2001), enacted after the 11 September 2001 terrorist attacks on the United States (and subsequently amended). The statute is designed to provide tools for combating terrorism and other issues.

V

Vagrancy. Under common law, an act or condition of wandering about from place to place without any visible means of support, refusing to work even though able to do so, and living off the charity of others. Many statutory vagrancy laws have been declared unconstitutional because of their vagueness and tendency to discriminate against racial and ethnic minorities and the poor.

Vicarious liability. The placing of legal liability on one person (or corporation) for the action of another. An example would be to hold the owner of a bar responsible for an employee who sold liquor to an underage or an intoxicated person who then drove a car and killed another person.

Violent crime. A crime defined by the FBI's *UCR* as a serious crime against a person. The four serious violent crimes in the *UCR* are murder and nonnegligent manslaughter, robbery, forcible rape, and aggravated assault.

Voluntary intoxication. Intoxication brought on by the free will of the individual. *See also* **Involuntary intoxication**.

Voluntary manslaughter. *See* **Manslaughter**.

W

Wharton rule. A rule stating that two people engaging in crimes such as adultery, bigamy, and incest or other acts that require more than one person for their commission may not be prosecuted for conspiracy to commit those crimes. A third party must be involved for a conspiracy to exist. Some jurisdictions reject this rule.

Whistle-blower claims. Claims that expose a person, group, or business for engaging in illegal acts, such as fraud. Statutes have been enacted to provide protection for employees (or others) who are fired (or otherwise disciplined) for filing whistle-blower claims, such as reporting financial improprieties of the company.

Witness Protection Program. A program sponsored by the U.S. Marshals; it provides a new identity and a new location for persons who aid the government in dangerous high-profile prosecutions or who, for other reasons, would be at risk in society without such protection.

Writ. An order from a court mandating that specified action be taken or giving someone the authority to take the action requested.

Y

Year-and-a-day rule. Common law rule requiring that for a murder charge, death of the victim must occur within one year and one day from the time the alleged crime was committed. Today many jurisdictions have abandoned that rule, although they may still impose some restrictions, such as three years and a day.

Case Index

409

Name Index

General Index

415